George Ronald Bahá'í Studies Series

A Most Noble Pattern

Photocopy of the first page of the oldest extant manuscript of the Qayyúm al-Asma' bearing the beginning of the Surat al-Mulk which was revealed to Mullá Husayn Bushrú'í on the evening of 5 Jumádá al-Awwal 1260 AH corresponding to 22 May 1844 CE, the date on which, according to the Persian Bayán, the new era is deemed to have begun. The scribe is one Muhammad ibn Karbalá'í Sháh Karam and the colophon gives the date of 28 Jumádá al-Awwal 1261 corresponding to 3 June 1845 as the date of transcription.

The vertical mark running from the top of the page to about the 11th line of the manuscript is said to be damage caused by the sword of a religious official to whom Mullá Husayn himself had presented the book on behalf of the Báb. The original is in the International Bahá'í Archives in Haifa.

George Ronald Bahá'í Studies Series

A MOST NOBLE PATTERN

Collected Essays on the Writings of the Báb,
'Alí Muhammad Shírází
(1819–1850)

edited by

Todd Lawson
and
Omid Ghaemmaghami

George Ronald
Oxford

George Ronald, *Publisher*
Oxford
www.grbooks.com

© Todd Lawson and Omid Ghaemmaghami 2012
Reprinted 2023
All Rights Reserved

*A catalogue record for this book is available
from the British Library*

ISBN 978–0–85398–556–3

*The translations of the sacred writings included in these various essays
are provisional in character
and their content the responsibility of those rendering them.*

Cover design by Steiner Graphics

Contents

Introduction by Todd Lawson	ix
Acknowledgements	xvii
1 A General Introduction to the Qayyúm al-Asmá' *Muhammad Afnan (translated by Omid Ghaemmaghami)*	1
2 The Commentary on the Sura of Joseph *Nosratollah Mohammadhosseini*	6
3 *Khutbat al-iftikhár* *Introduced and translated by Khazeh Fananapazir*	28
4 Colours in the Writings of the Báb *Vahid Rafati (translated by Omid Ghaemmaghami)*	33
5 A Grammar of the Divine: Solecisms in the Arabic Writings of the Báb and His Thoughts on Arabic Grammar *William F. McCants*	52
6 Secrets Concealed by Secrets: *Taqiyya* as Arcanization in the Autobibliographies of the Báb *J. Vahid Brown*	88
7 The Súrat adh-Dhikr of the Qayyúm al-Asmá' (chapter 108): A Provisional Translation and Commentary *Moojan Momen*	105
8 The Súrat al-'Abd of the Qayyúm al-Asmá' (Chapter 109): A Provisional Translation and Commentary *Todd Lawson*	116
9 The *Khutba al-Jidda* (The Literary Sermon at Jeddah) of the Báb *Stephen Lambden*	146
10 Muhammad Shah Qájár in Four Early Writings of the Báb *Sholeh A. Quinn*	160

11 A Youth of Medium Height: The Báb's Encounter with the Hidden Imam
  in *Tafsír Súrat al-Kawthar*
  Omid Ghaemmaghami 175

12 Phenomenology of Occultation and Prayer in the Báb's
  Sahífiy-i Ja'faríyyih
  Nader Saiedi 196

13 The Báb's *Panj Sha'n* (Five Modes)
  John Walbridge 217

14 Undermining the Foundations of Orthodoxy: Some Notes on the Báb's
  Sharia (Sacred Law)
  Armin Eschraghi 223

15 Concealment and Burial of the Báb
  Translated and annotated by Peter Terry 248

16 Collusion and Re-creation: Dogen and the Báb as Interpreters of Scripture
  Gary Fuhrman 282

Biographical Notes 289

His heart lies not of what it saw
(Qur'an 53:11)

*This book is dedicated to
the cause, vision and reality of peace*

Introduction

The title of this book may call to mind, especially among older readers, an early translation of Bahá'u'lláh's Long Healing Prayer where the rather interesting and perhaps somewhat opaque divine name 'Most Noble Pattern' was read as one in a long litany of divine names and attributes invoked in this especially powerful prayer. The Arabic original is *rasm al-akram* (lit: 'trace, depiction, picture or model of the Most Noble (God)') and it appeared as follows:

> I invoke Thee, O Most High Mention, O Most Ancient Name, O Thou Most Noble Pattern! Thou the Sufficing, Thou the Healing, Thou the Abiding, O Thou Abiding One![1]

In this interesting choice the translators Ali Kuli Khan and Marzieh Gail may have been influenced by the Rodwell translation of the Qur'an[2] – a translation admired by Shoghi Effendi – of an epithet found in verse 21 of the Sura of the Confederates (33):

> A noble pattern had ye in God's Apostle, for all who hope in God, and in the latter day, and oft remember God!

The Arabic of this Quranic 'noble pattern' is *uswatun hasanatun* not *rasm al-akram* (which, by the way, does not occur in the Qur'an). However, such an apparent linguistic discrepancy is no cause for alarm. In this case it is actually quite a happy development because it causes us to consider dimensions of prophethood and revelation common to both Islam and the Bahá'í Faith. *Uswatun hasanatun* is also frequently translated as 'good example'. As such it points to the role of the prophet or bearer of revelation as a model of behaviour. This model or paradigm of behaviour is also evoked in the familiar term *sunna*, which means wont, path or way. The word *rasm* summons up a completely different but also intimately related semantic field. It denotes the act of making a mark, or writing. In this combination it may be literally translated as 'the clear indication and emblem [of God] the most Noble'. Ali Kuli Khan and Marzieh Gail demonstrated their deep knowledge by choosing the word 'pattern' – a more complex notion than 'mark' or 'sign' or perhaps even 'example', because the signs and indications of God are on the one hand quite simple in that they all come from the same source but on the other quite complex since they are all related or connected to each other, even if these connections and relations are not immediately visible or readable. These signs and indications thus describe a noble or holy pattern, even if we are unable to perceive it directly. And the most noble aspect or feature of this pattern is the Manifestation. The 'confluence' of *rasm* and *uswah* in the English word 'pattern' and the confluence of *al-akram* and *hasana* in the English word 'noble' is also instructive because it brings together in one epithet the two sources of authority which meld into one in the lives of these Manifestations: the authority of the prophetic self and the authority of the revelation. Nothing could suit more perfectly the subject of the present book. With this epithet – Most Noble Pattern – we are introduced to the rich, eternal and infinite world of divine revelation and the sacred imagination. It is especially apt as a title for a book about one whose life and work, or more accurately, ministry (since 'life and work' might imply some false dichotomy) was characterized by an unshakeable faith, knowledge and vision that, again, from one point of view is simple, yet from another exquisitely complex. All things are deeply interconnected and involved with each other, and true religion fosters universal peace built upon this perceived real kinship. This in turn leads to the unfoldment of true civilization, and the time for waiting for this visionary truth is at an end and will be forever.

To understand – or rather to begin to understand – the far-reaching implications and the cultural (historical, religious, social) resonances and profound historical reverberations of such a revolutionary idea we are offering this book. It is a collection of essays and scholarly articles by some of today's leading experts on the subject: Sayyid 'Alí Muhammad Shirazi, known to history, by admirers and detractors alike, as the Báb. This last name is an Arabic word and it means 'gate' or 'door'. While our subject is known by a wide variety of other honorifics and doxological epithets (*al-nuqtat al-úlá*, the Primal Point; *qurratu'l-'ayn*, Solace of the Eye; *dhikr Alláh al-akbar*, the Most Great Remembrance of God; *kalimat Alláh al-kubrá*, the Most Compelling Word of God, to name only a few), it is a deceptively simple 'the Báb' which has come to be most commonly used to describe or refer to him. Why is this? In its first meaning it connotes the office of representative of the Hidden Imam. However, studies of the word have demonstrated that in fact the term was most often used for the link between man and God. This is its meaning with regard to the vertical or spiritual dimension. In the Báb's writings it is clear that there is another dimension to be taken into consideration, namely the horizontal, or what we are fond of calling the historical. Viewed from this angle, the Báb's writings indicate that he is to be seen as the gate to the future, specifically as a harbinger of the appearance of He Whom God will make manifest. Bahá'ís are confident that this latter person appeared as Bahá'u'lláh, the founder of the Bahá'í Faith. The horizontal or historical dimension proceeds in two directions, however. The future is one, the past is the other. It is in this way that the word represents a door or gate that opens onto two historical vistas, suggesting that the proper perception and understanding of one is dependent upon the other.

By giving particular importance to the spiritual heroes of the past, the Báb wishes to assert once again the seamless unity of time and history. Of course, the heroes to whom he refers and whom he venerates most often are those who had already been sanctified and honoured by the Islamic tradition. A prophet, as the Qur'an says, addresses his community in their own language (Q 14:4). The Báb is most interested in such figures as embodiments or personifications of timeless spiritual values and ideas. His discourse, then, is richly laden with what experts in biblical studies have long referred to as 'typological figuration'. Typology is at work, for example, when Jesus is referred to in the New Testament as the Lamb of God. Thus he is automatically – again seamlessly – regarded as the fulfilment or reappearance of a figure introduced in the Hebrew Bible, or Old Testament. In fact, the generous deployment of typological figuration may be one of the chief means by which both the Báb, in numerous of his writings, and Bahá'u'lláh, especially in the Book of Certitude, affirm the organic unity of history and time and thereby assert unflinchingly the unity of humanity.

The interested reader is warmly encouraged to keep the question of the meaning of the term 'the Báb' alive while reading the several essays in this book, for it is a question that becomes more interesting as one ponders it and responses to it seem to become more productive and fruitful the more it is posed. For the moment, it is important and helpful to recall that the Báb spoke to an audience that was culturally conditioned by religion and history to be in a constant state of messianic expectation. The technical term for this in Arabic is *intizár* from the Arabic root N-Z-R: 'to watch and wait'. In this context, the waiting and watching is specifically for the return of the Hidden Imam, the Twelfth Imam of the Ithná 'Asharí Shi'i Islam which has, from the early 16th century through the time of the Báb and until today, represented the religious ethos if not the majority of Persia/Iran. In the key of messianic expectation, and as an isolated but perhaps instructive example of the rich expressive power of Arabic, the language in which the Báb revealed his earliest major works, the Hidden Imam is thus also known as the Awaited or Longed for Imam (*al-imám al-muntazár*). In the special piety of Shi'ism, then, waiting has a special and important spiritual worth. In a sense, all waiting is merely a shadow of that true and glorious waiting which is destined to culminate in the appearance (*zuhúr*) or return (*raj'a*) of the Hidden Imam. In the same way, and as a by-product of the distinctive history of Shi'ism when compared with Sunni Islam, sadness, *huzn*, acquired a special religious or spiritual worth because of the tragedy of Karbala and the martyrdom of Husayn. In this connection, also, martyrdom and its attendant sufferings and deprivations – especially thirst – have also acquired powerful meaning in the intricate tapestry of Shi'i religious thought. Such details as these, and many more to be found explicated in the following pages, together with the critical and analytical treatment so characteristic of the best in scholarly inquiry and scientific method, are featured, studied and analysed because they make up the specific language in which the Báb expressed his Revelation. Their critical study, together with the various texts in which they figure prominently, constitute a direct and sincere response to the lucid advice of the beloved Guardian of the Bahá'í Faith (*valí amri'lláh*), Shoghi Effendi Rabbani, who in instructing the Bahá'ís, heirs to the revelatory vision of the Báb, on the way to best share this vision with the world at large, offered the following:

> They must strive to obtain, from sources that are authoritative and unbiased, a sound knowledge of the history and tenets of Islám – the source and background of their Faith – and approach reverently and with a mind purged from pre-conceived ideas the study of the Qur'án which, apart from the sacred scriptures of the Bábí and Bahá'í Revelations, constitutes the only Book which can be regarded as an absolutely authenticated Repository of the Word of God. They must devote special

attention to the investigation of those institutions and circumstances that are directly connected with the origin and birth of their Faith, with the station claimed by its Forerunner, and with the laws revealed by its Author (Shoghi Effendi 1953, p. 226).

So it is as a study of 'the station claimed by its Forerunner' that this book was conceived. And, it will not be irrelevant to dwell here briefly on the unique and characteristic spirit which is seen to animate these words of Shoghi Effendi, especially today as Islam acquires more and more prominence in current events, a prominence which is frequently quite negative. The Guardian's clear-eyed, compassionate advice leads the reader to ponder the abiding and profoundly spiritual relationship the Bahá'í Faith sees for itself with Islam, despite the repeated attempts of some who esteem themselves Muslims to diminish or even annihilate the Bahá'í community and religion. Here in this succinct statement the teachings of both the Báb and Bahá'u'lláh on the unity of humanity, religion, history and God may be thought distilled in both spirit and form.

It is usual for revolutions to negate or deform the past, despite the best efforts of their founding heroes. We do not find in the literature of other young movements such certainty that its life and destiny depend upon a courageous, analytical understanding and indeed unapologetic celebration of its immediate past and cultural matrix. A similar conviction is found expressed again in the following words of Shoghi Effendi, this time from his Foreword to his own interpretation of the century of the history of the Bahá'í Faith, composed during the difficult years of World War II and presented, in 1944, to the worldwide Bahá'í community as a gift and guide to their own identity and action for the present and future:

> I shall seek to represent and correlate, in however cursory a manner, those momentous happenings which have insensibly, relentlessly, and under the very eyes of successive generations, perverse, indifferent or hostile, *transformed a heterodox and seemingly negligible offshoot of the Shaykhí school of the Ithná-'Asharíyyih sect of Shi'ah Islám into a world religion* whose unnumbered followers are organically and indissolubly united . . . whose adherents are recruited from the diversified races and chief religions of mankind . . . (Shoghi Effendi 1995, p. xii, emphasis added).

In these two passages the Guardian not only demonstrates and affirms the Bahá'í dedication to the inherent oneness and unity of all religions, he also demonstrates a prescient if not clairvoyant knowledge of the importance of what in time would become one of the major guiding principles in the scientific study of religion and culture. The axiom or principle is that all established religions may be seen to have begun as heresy, challenging the status quo, attracting the persecution and ignominy of the 'host' society, eventually, sometimes slowly, sometimes more rapidly, to evolve into a social and religious entity with its own characteristic institutions, practices and social rhythms. The great paradox being that the 'previous' religion or social system remains alive, preserved, honoured and celebrated even as it is apparently superseded. Not in any way a cultural palimpsest but more a child – if sometimes seen as prodigal by anxious parents to whom filial piety, love and respect are nonetheless due.

Such a cultural dynamic or civilizational dialectic is not frequently discerned or articulated, but its study and contemplation and elaboration merit the most serious attention, promising to illumine and inspire thoughtful souls in our world of difficult competing ideologies, religions, political parties and economic forces. Again: all are profoundly and intricately connected, both in time and space and, more to the point, in a way that transcends these problematic, sometimes obfuscating if not totally arbitrary, categories.

The 'pattern' referred to in the title chosen for this collection of essays has a variety of interlocking and mutually enhancing meanings and resonances: in the primary and foundational sense it refers to the way a Manifestation of God, such as Muhammad, also has the function of being an example of behaviour and comportment for his followers and his community. The usual word for this in Islam is *sunna*, a word which means path or method. According to the Qur'an, the community of the Manifestation may also be seen as such an example:

> Indeed, you have in Abraham and in those who were with him an excellent example . . . in them you certainly have a beautiful example (Q 60:4–5).

Here, it is the community's insistence upon the oneness of God and its refusal to worship the sun and the moon and the stars – 'things that set' – which is being called out by the Qur'an as a necessary and essential object of emulation.

Another way in which the word 'pattern' is understood here is as characterizing the interrelatedness and integrity of the revelation in its entirety, with regard to specific teachings, values, factual information, style and form. In all cases, as we know, each of the Manifestations of God known to history has transmitted a revelation following upon a profoundly moving, sometimes even disturbing, spiritual experience or encounter. Thus the pattern repeats itself through time and history and also carries within it a distinct and separate pattern which renders it sensible and understandable to otherwise unrelated communities and audiences widely separated by geography, language, cultural presuppositions and tastes: a pattern within a pattern.

Finally, pattern may also refer to the inherent aesthetic beauty, as is indicated by the Quranic word *hasana*, of the relationship between God, Manifestation and community, on the one hand, and the beauty of the expression of this relationship in the revelation or vision communicated, whether moral, spiritual, historical, scientific or aesthetic.

It is certainly no accident that this notion of beauty, highly valued by Islamic intellectual and spiritual culture, became a direct focus in both the Revelation of the Báb and later in the Revelation of Bahá'u'lláh. The apocalyptic event that marks the beginning of the Báb's mission, the composition of the unprecedented Qayyúm al-Asmá', is a case in point. From one perspective, the problem and nature of beauty may be thought the central theme of the Quranic sura, Joseph (Q 12), that is the object of this commentary. Chiefly symbolized by Joseph's physical beauty, it is moral and spiritual beauty that is soon brought into focus. The story of this beauty and its relationship to love, separation, knowledge, obedience, reunion and even history itself provides the special spiritual energy of the sura and had made the Quranic narrative a favourite of the entire tradition, despite the fact that some early dissenting (and, we might add, unimaginative) voices insisted that because of these otherwise compelling literary and thematic characteristics, the Sura of Joseph clearly was not truly part of the Qur'an.

The mind of the Báb, the following essays will indicate, was profoundly wedded to the reality of the invisible realm. His writings – a vast and still unplumbed sea of scriptural commentary, prayers, laws and ordinances and responses to specific questions – are cast in the language of their first audience. Understanding the audience is therefore the first task for those who would wish to read intelligently this unique and vibrant *oeuvre*. Such a language, given its cultural and religious specificity, may rightly be regarded a code – another way of understanding the Arabic word *rasm*, perhaps suggested by its phonic companion *ramz*, 'mystery'), a code sometimes more transparent, sometimes less. It is composed of the lexical and terminological legacy of the entire Arabic and Persian Islamic learned tradition: Qur'an, hadith, scriptural commentary (*tafsír*), law (*fiqh*), grammar, theology (*'ilm al-kalám*), philosophy (*falsafa*), mysticism (*'irfán, tasawwuf*), *adab* (belles-lettres), moralia (*akhláq*), poetry, physical sciences, geography and history. This is not to say that the conclusions or hypotheses of all of these various sciences and disciplines are subscribed to but, rather, their vocabulary is employed in the process of articulating the Báb's simultaneously eternal and new (*badí'*) message. Thus the variety of approaches, themes and subject matter the following essays present is both unavoidable and well suited to the central subject and ultimately reflects an important truth about the monumental 'literary' activity of its author.

We are especially fortunate to have two contributions from Dr Muhammad Afnan: one from his pen and one through his voice (which is posted on the George Ronald website[3]). The initiated will know from this name that he is a descendant of the family of the Báb and thus his contributions provide a living link to the central subject of our book. It is thus with abiding gratitude that we are now able to listen to parts of the Báb's Revelation as chanted by one who has not only a deep genealogical connection with these texts but also an unparalleled knowledge of their scope, profundity and range, from every aspect. The following contributions by scholars from a variety of backgrounds afford insight and understanding for both the revelational compositions of the Báb and some of the key texts that may be seen to be reinterpreted and transformed through this vision. Rather than attempt a summary or characterization of each of these essays, it remains now only for me to express my sincere gratitude to all of these scholars for their cooperation, care, acumen, diligence and patience. This volume is, indeed, one of a kind. By no means should it be mistaken for anything approaching an exhaustive treatment. It is not likely, given the nature and vastness of the writings of the Báb, that such a thing will be accomplished, either in the near future or by more distant generations of scholars. However, as the above words of Shoghi Effendi make clear, it is a duty of the present to study the past in order that we may perceive more fully the nobility of the pattern and the meaning that it has for us today.

Todd Lawson
4 February 2011
Montreal

Bibliography

Bahá'í Prayers: A Selection of Prayers revealed by Bahá'u'lláh, the Báb and 'Abdu'l-Bahá. Wilmette, IL: Bahá'í Publishing Trust, 2002.

Shoghi Effendi. *God Passes By*. Wilmette, IL: Bahá'í Publishing Trust, rev. ed. 1995.

— *Guidance for Today and Tomorrow*. London: Bahá'í Publishing Trust, 1953.

Notes

1. This translation was, as far as I know, never officially published. It was circulated in typewritten and mimeographed form. The copy at hand indicates that the translators completed the Long Healing Prayer in 1945. (Cf. the more recent translation of this prayer in *Bahá'í Prayers* 2002, pp. 102–10. The passage under discussion is found on page 107 and reads: I call on Thee O Greatest Remembrance, O Noblest Name, O Most Ancient Way!)
2. The Rodwell translation, based on the Fluegel edition of the Qur'an text, was first published in 1861 but gained wide popularity in the edition prepared by G. Margoliouth for the Everyman series in 1909.
3. To be found with information about this book on George Ronald's website: www.grbooks.com.

Acknowledgements

A publication such as this presents a number of technical problems, whether from the point of view of scholarship or from the point of view of publishing. We would like to thank a number of people for their otherwise invisible yet essential contributions, technical assistance, encouragement and general support over the years. These are Omid Afnan, Hooper Dunbar, Franklin Lewis, Wendi Momen, Golgasht Mossafa'i, Seosamh Watson and Burhan Zahra'i.

1

A General Introduction to the Qayyúm al-Asmá'

Muhammad Afnan

(Translated by Omid Ghaemmaghami)

This is our Book proclaiming the truth unto you.[1]

In his Book, which he hath entitled Qayyúmu'l-Asmá' – the first, the greatest and mightiest of all books . . . (Bahá'u'lláh 1989, p. 231).

The following is a short article by Dr Muhammad Afnan introducing the Báb's seminal commentary on the Sura of Joseph. The original article, *Kulliyát-i muqaddamátí darbárih-yi kitáb-i Qayyúm al-Asmá'*, was published in the sixth volume of *Safínih-yi 'Irfán* (vol. 6, pp. 24–7).

Names and appellations of the Qayyúm al-Asmá'

The Qayyúm al-Asmá' is known by various names:

1) Commentary on the Sura of Joseph, the twelfth sura of the Qur'an.

2) Commentary on 'the most beautiful of stories' (Q 12:3). In the Qur'an the story of Joseph is described as 'the most beautiful of stories' (*ahsan al-qasas*). The term *qasas* (narrative or stories) in the Qur'an refers to stories that serve to remind humanity about the history and shared experiences of those who lived in the past. The Sura of the Narrative (al-Qasas, sura 28) is an example of this inasmuch as the greater part of this sura is stories about the prophet Moses.

3) Qayyúm al-Asmá' (the one who sustains the divine names): The names 'Peerless' (*fard*), 'Ever-Living' (*hayy*), 'Self-Subsisting' (*qayyúm*), 'Authority' (*hukm*), 'Divine Justice' (*'adl*) and 'Holy' (*quddús*) are specific to the Supreme Manifestation of the Primal Will and are found repeatedly throughout the writings of the Báb. On one hand, the name Qayyúm al-Asmá' describes God's self-sufficiency above any need of his creatures. On the other, it speaks to his sovereignty and the fact that his knowledge encompasses all existence. In this particular case, since the words 'Qayyúm' and 'Yúsuf' have the same numerical

value in the abjad system, by dint of esoteric interpretation, the title 'Qayyúm al-Asmá" is an allusion to the divine reality of the Primal Point. This name has been revealed by the Báb and refers to both the Manifestation of God present at the moment of its revelation (i.e. the Báb) as well as the Manifestation promised to appear after him (i.e. Bahá'u'lláh).

Time of its revelation

The revelation of the Qayyúm al-Asmá' began on the eve of the Báb's declaration. According to an unambiguous statement found in one of the Báb's tablets, this work was revealed within 40 days in Shiraz:

> This lowly one completed the commentary on the Sura of Joseph in 40 days during which I wrote some of it each day. Whenever I wish to write something, the spirit of God assists me. Such is the case with the *sahífa* that I have sent – which I wrote in 24 hours . . . (Mázandarání 1944, vol. 3, p. 285).

Throughout his writings the Báb adduces the speed at which he reveals verses of revelation as a proof of his station. His words in the above tablet are one such example. We can thus be certain that by '40 days' is meant 40 consecutive, uninterrupted days (*rúzhá-yi mutaválí*). The conventions and style of Persian prose confirm this because in Persian when time is mentioned the convention is to speak of successive days. If something contrary to this were intended, i.e. non-consecutive days, it would need to be directly and explicitly stated.

The background to the revelation of the Qayyúm al-Asmá'

According to *Nabíl's Narrative*, the commentary on 'the most beautiful of stories' was revealed in response to an ardent wish harboured by Mullá Husayn (Nabíl 1970, p. 59). The point to remember, however, is that Mullá Husayn was merely the instrument of God's grace. The revelation of this work was preordained by God and, in reality, the Qayyúm al-Asmá' is addressed to each and every human being in the world.

Structure and organization

The Qayyúm al-Asmá' consists of 111 suras. Each sura reveals the esoteric interpretation of one of the verses of the Sura of Joseph. Every sura has a name and commonly consists of 42 verses. Just as the place of revelation is mentioned in each sura of the Qur'an, the place of revelation of each sura has also been mentioned in the Qayyúm al-Asmá'. The term used in every sura – 'Shirazi' – confirms that they were revealed in Shiraz. The similarities between the Qayyúm al-Asmá' and the Qur'an are many. Among the elements they share in common are 1) the manner in which both have been organized into suras and verses with features (e.g. length) that complement one another, and 2) the fact that each sura begins with a group of disconnected letters. Moreover, in the Qayyúm al-Asmá', as in the Qur'an, the terms '*qur'án*' (the recitation) and *furqán* (the criterion)² are used in the text to refer to itself.

The mode of revelation

The works of the Báb are written in five different modes. The Qayyúm al-Asmá' has been revealed in the mode of verses (*áyát*).

Language and style

The Qayyúm al-Asmá' was revealed entirely in Arabic. Its verses are filled with revelatory allusions, spiritual metaphors and intimations wrapped in intimations which generally refer to the Qur'an, the Traditions of the Prophet and the Imams, and different subjects relating to the stories and history of the prophets in general and the prophet Joseph and his brothers in particular. The verses of the Sura of Joseph have been interpreted esoterically (*tafsír-i ta'wílí*).³ Throughout the work Muhammad ibn al-Hasan, the Hidden Twelfth Imam, has uninterrupted connection with the Báb and is in reality one with him.

The purpose of the Qayyúm al-Asmá's revelation

1) On the face of it, the Qayyúm al-Asmá' is an esoteric interpretation of the Qur'an and the principles of Islam. It seeks to unravel the intrinsic structures of both.

2) Inwardly, however, the Qayyúm al-Asmá' speaks of a secret Cause and prepares the believers for the declaration of a supreme Manifestation of God at the appointed time. The Qayyúm al-Asmá' also implicitly announces the coming of the next Manifestation.

Themes and teachings

The themes and teachings found in the Qayyúm al-Asmá' include the oneness of the Manifestations of God; the proclamation of world unity and the advent of the promised day; renewal of spiritual, ethical and confessional teachings; the renewal of the laws of the Qur'an and purifying the Qur'an from the opposing views and beliefs of different sects.

Some of the names of the Báb in the Qayyúm al-Asmá'

Some of the names of the Báb mentioned in the Qayyúm al-Asmá' include the Gate of God, the Most Great Remembrance of God, the Light of God, the Most Great Name 'Alí, the Arabian Youth (*al-fatá al-'arabí*), the Youth (*al-ghulám*),⁴ the Fruit of the Heart and the Solace of the Eyes.⁵

The divine message of the Qayyúm al-Asmá'

The message of the Qayyúm al-Asmá' has two main aspects. First it renews Islam by fulfilling the promises and prophecies found in the Qur'an and the Islamic Traditions. At a theoretical level, within the text of the Qayyúm al-Asmá' the title Qur'an is applied to the work itself while the Muhammadan reality is identified as the Báb. At a more practical level, the Qayyúm al-Asmá' reveals anew the Islamic laws and religious precepts. Second, the Qayyúm al-Asmá' declares symbolically that the Báb is the Promised One of the Qur'an while at the same time it conceals this declaration through use of titles such as the Gate, the Solace of the Eyes, etc.

The relationship of the Qayyúm al-Asmá' to the Mother Book of the Bábí dispensation, the Bayán

There are many similarities between the Qayyúm al-Asmá' and the Bayán, including the mode and method of revelation, their explanation of both the generalities and the details of spiritual knowledge, and their exposition of the laws and principles of religion.

Bibliography

Bahá'u'lláh. *Kitáb-i-Íqán*. Wilmette, IL: Bahá'í Publishing Trust, 1989.

Encylopaedia of Islam [EI2]. Leiden and London: Brill. 2nd ed. 1960.

Mázandarání. *Táríkh-i Zuhúr al-Haqq*, vol. 3. Tehran: n.p., 1944.

Nabíl-i-A'zam. *The Dawn-Breakers: Nabíl's Narrative of the Early Days of the Bahá'í Revelation*. Wilmette, IL: Bahá'í Publishing Trust, 1970.

Paret, R. 'Furkan'. *Encyclopedia of Islam*, 2nd ed., vol. 2.

Safínih-yi 'Irfán, vol. 6. Darmstadt, Germany: Mu'assasih-yi 'Asr-i Jadíd, 160 BE/2003), pp. 24–7.

Notes

1. Qayyúm al-Asmá', Súrat al-'Arsh (16), Súrat al-Tablígh (30), Súrat al-'Izz (31), Súrat al-Mu'minín (111). The numbers refer to the order in which the sura appears in the Qayyúm al-Asmá'. See also Q 45:29.
2. This term is used in the Qur'an as a soteriological expression (e.g. Q 8:29) and in connection with the revelation of divine verses (e.g. Q 2:53; 3:4). See Paret, 'Furkan', *EI2*, pp. 949–50.
3. Qayyúm al-Asmá', Súrat al-'Arsh (95):

   Verily, this Book is interpretation upon esoteric interpretation (*tafsír 'alá al-ta'wíl*) from God, the All-Wise. Verily, He is God, Mighty, Ancient. None knows its esoteric interpretation (*ta'wilahu*) save God and whosoever We have willed [to know] the truth. Ask therefore its esoteric interpretation from the Remembrance. Verily, of a truth, in a handful of dust God has taught him the complete knowledge of the Book through the power of truth.

   This verse shows that the Qayyúm al-Asmá' is a Quranic commentary revealed by

the All-Wise to elucidate the Qur'an's esoteric interpretation. With the exception of God and those he has chosen, no one else knows its esoteric interpretation or inner meaning. Therefore he has ordained that its esoteric interpretation should be sought from the Remembrance, by which is meant the Báb, inasmuch as God has taught him the knowledge of the divine Book (i.e. the Qur'an). *Tafsír* means expounding the content of Quranic verses in a way that conforms to their literal meaning. However by *ta'wíl* is meant elucidating or bringing out the hidden spiritual meaning of the verses which the literal meaning of the words do not convey (i.e. returning to the original meaning or source of the verses). Only the Manifestations of God have the authority to reveal this esoteric interpretation. No one else, not even the religious scholars or ulama have been granted permission to give the esoteric interpretation. The above verse from the Qayyúm al-Asmá' is reminiscent of the seventh verse of the Qur'an's Sura of the Family of 'Imrán: 'And none knows its esoteric interpretation (*ta'wílahu*) except God and those who are firmly grounded in knowledge' (Q 3:7). The Báb has stated that by 'those who are firmly grounded in knowledge' is meant the 12 Shi'i Imams from the family of the Prophet Muhammad.
4. This term has been used in the Qur'an, *inter alia*, as a reference to Joseph (Q 12:19).
5. This locution is derived from a similar locution found in the Qur'an (Q 25:74). According to a Tradition ascribed to the sixth Shi'i Imam, Ja'far al-Sádiq, this verse in the Qur'an was revealed about the Holy Family (i.e. the Prophet, Fatima and the 12 Imams).

2

The Commentary on the Sura of Joseph

Nosratollah Mohammadhosseini

Introduction

The Qayyúm al-Asmá' is the Báb's commentary on the Quranic Sura of Joseph (sura 12). Written in Arabic during 40 days within the first two months after his declaration, the book is structurally similar to the Qur'an. Like the Qur'an it is divided into suras and verses. The Quranic Sura of Joseph consists of 111 verses, so the Qayyúm al-Asmá' has been divided into 111 chapters (suras). Each chapter has a name and consists of 42 verses. Each sura of the Qayyúm al-Asmá' begins with the Quranic phrase 'In the Name of God, the Merciful, the Compassionate'. At the beginning of every sura are disconnected letters, as found at the beginning of some of the suras of the Qur'an. Although there is some similarity between the content of the Qayyúm al-Asmá' and that of the Qur'an, as we will see later in this essay, the former provides new terminology, fresh materials and original, subtle points that cannot be found in the Qur'an.

A careful study of the writings of the Báb makes it clear that his main objective was to elucidate the truths and mysteries of previous scriptures, especially the Qur'an, to prepare humankind for the advent of the Remnant of God (*Baqiyyat Alláh*) or Him Whom God shall make manifest (*Man Yuzhiruhu Alláh*). The Báb called all his writings 'Bayán'[1] because the Qur'an says that its interpretation or exposition (*bayán*) will be given on the Day of Resurrection (Q 75:19). The Báb, who identified his Revelation as the Day of Resurrection, interpreted the Qur'an and explicated its truths. According to the Báb, the main purpose of this interpretation was to create a unity of conviction among the followers of past religions, especially the Twelver Shi'as, and to prepare them for the advent of the Remnant of God or Him Whom God shall make manifest, the Promised One of the Bábí dispensation.

The Báb has divided his writings into five *sha'ns* (categories, modes or forms): 1) *áyát* (verses); 2) *munáját* (prayers); 3) *khutab* (homilies); 4) *kalimát-i 'ilmiyyih* (scientific words); 5) *tafásír* (commentaries).[2] *Áyát* is the divine address to humanity, demonstrating the sovereignty of God. The texts that contain the teachings and precepts of the Báb, such as the Persian Bayán, are in this mode.[3] The Báb's prayers comprise the *munáját* mode. The *khutab* mode includes explanations of the transcendence of divinity and the glorification of the stations of the Báb and the Promised One of his dispensation. *Kalimát-i 'ilmiyyih* consists of the polemical works of the Báb such as the Seven Proofs (*Dalá'il-i-Sab'ih*), the Treatise on Proving [Muhammad's] Specific Prophethood (al-*Risála fi Ithbát al-Nubuwwa al-Khássa*) and the philosophical and mystical works such as the tablet to Muhammad Sa'íd of Zavárih. The *tafsír* mode consists of the Báb's commentaries on the suras and the verses of the Qur'an and the Islamic traditions. Using these classifications of the writings of the Báb, the Qayyúm al-Asmá' epitomizes the *tafsír* mode, although it can be also be included in category of *áyát* because it provides new precepts for the Bábí dispensation.

Manuscripts of the Qayyúm al-Asmá'

The Qayyúm al-Asmá' was written by the Báb himself. Unfortunately, the copy in his handwriting is not extant. The oldest existing manuscript, and perhaps the most reliable, is in the handwriting of Muhammad Mahdí b. Karbalá'í Sháh Karam, dated 1261 AH (1845 CE). This manuscript is kept at the Bahá'í World Centre. In preparing this essay the present writer has used this manuscript and two others: 1) a copy of the Iran National Bahá'í Archives (INBA), vol. 3, 132 BE/1975 CE (indications show that this copy was given to one of the governors of Khurásán by Mullá Husayn Bushrú'í; 2) a copy in the handwriting of Diyá' al-Dín Nabíl-i-Akbar, dated 1956 CE.[4]

The time of the revelation of the Qayyúm al-Asmá'

Súrat al-Mulk, the first chapter of the Qayyúm al-Asmá', was written by the Báb in the presence of Mullá Husayn Bushrú'í (the first to believe in the Báb) on the eve of 23 May 1844 (5 Jumádá al-Úlá 1260 AH) on the second floor of the house of the Báb situated in Shamshírgarhá alley in the Bázár-i-Murgh quarter of Shiraz. In one of his tablets the Báb states that he completed the whole of the Qayyúm al-Asmá' in 40 days.[5] Since, according to the Báb, for the first 40 days after his declaration his only follower was Mullá Husayn[6] and the Báb refers to other believers in the Qayyúm al-Asmá', the book must have been completed some days after the 40-day period. In chapter 92 of the Qayyúm al-Asmá' the Báb refers to the arrival in Shiraz of a few people from Karbala, including the youth of Qazvin (most likely Mullá Muhammad 'Alí Qazvíní), and their acceptance of the new Cause. However, the Qayyúm al-Asmá' had been finished before the departure of Mullá 'Alí Bastámí (one of the Letters of the Living) for Iraq because he took the whole text with him. Bastámí arrived in Iraq in early August 1844,[7] after a journey of more than a month. Thus the Qayyúm al-Asmá' was probably completed in the early days of July 1844. Therefore when the Báb says in chapter 41 of the Qayyúm al-Asmá' that God revealed the book to him on the Night of Power/Destiny (*Laylat al-Qadr*), he does not mean literally the same night mentioned in the Qur'an (believed to be either the 19th, 21st or 23rd of the month of Ramadán) because he himself mentions in the *Khutbatu'l-Jiddih* that he left Bushihr for the Hijaz on 19 Ramadan. By the Night of Power/Destiny he means a blessed night because the Qur'an, according to its own text, was revealed on the Night of Power/Destiny.

The Qayyúm al-Asmá' as the Qur'an of the Báb

From the earliest days of its circulation, the Qayyúm al-Asmá' became known as the Qur'an or *Furqán* (Criterion; Q 25:1) of the Báb. The main reason for this was that the Báb himself had referred to it as his Qur'an or *Furqán*.

At the beginning of the third chapter of the Qayyúm al-Asmá' the Báb mentions three times that the Qur'an has been revealed to his heart. In the seventh chapter he states that God has revealed this *Furqán* to the Remembrance (*dhikr*, i.e. the Báb) to show that he is the bearer of glad-tidings (*bashíran*) and a warner (*nadhíran*). A similar statement is found in chapter 26.

Official Iranian court historians at the time of the Báb have also called the Qayyúm al-Asmá', along with some of his other writings, his Qur'an or *Furqán*.[8]

Individuals and groups addressed in the Qayyúm al-Asmá'

The Qayyúm al-Asmá' is addressed to the whole of humankind. In numerous places the Báb addresses the people of the East and the West and invites them to accept the new Cause.[9] In the first chapter he addresses the people of the earth saying that whoever obeys the Remembrance of God (Dhikr Alláh, i.e. the Báb) and his book (the Qayyúm al-Asmá') has obeyed God and his messengers and in the next world will become a denizen of paradise. In chapter 68 he addresses the people of the earth, saying that the Remembrance of God has come to them with the greatest proof. In a separate address to the peoples of the West in chapter 46, the Báb invites them to accept his Faith and issue forth from their cities to aid the Cause of God.

In the first and the sixty-third chapters the Báb addresses the concourse of kings and sons of kings and invites them to arise for the propagation and promotion of his Cause. He urges Muhammad Shah, the king of Iran, to accept his Faith and arise for its victory. The Báb also addresses Hájj Mírzá Áqásí, the Grand Vizier of Iran, and commands him to abdicate his authority. Further, the Báb sent special tablets to a great number of the prominent Shi'i clergy in Iran and Iraq during His six year mission and invited them to embrace His Cause.[10] He sent several tablets to Muhammad Shah, the royal princes and Hájj Mírzá Áqásí, the prime minister, and to the governors of the Arab states as well as one to Sultan 'Abd al-Majíd, the Ottoman emperor.[11]

In chapters 2, 3, 23 and 48 of the Qayyúm al-Asmá' the Báb calls upon the followers of all past religions to follow him and his Cause, which confirms all the past holy scriptures. He warns them not to turn away from him, saying that should they disobey, they deserve hell fire. In chapter 2 he addresses the whole body of the world's religious leaders, instructing them to embrace the new Faith, to be righteous and not to issue any verdicts based on their speculative presumptions. In chapter 40 the Báb addresses the Shi'i clergy and warns them of the consequence of not accepting his Cause.

The Báb also addresses some of the prominent Shi'i leaders by name. In chapter 27 he invites Shaykh Hasan Ál al-'Usfúr to embrace the new Faith and assist its victory. Shaykh Hasan did not accept the new Cause. In the same chapter the Báb tells Mullá 'Abd al-Kháliq Yazdí, a prominent Shi'i and Shaykhi cleric of the time, that although he did not recognize the sublime station of the Báb when they met in Shiraz, he should not be afraid to embrace and promote the new Cause now. The Báb foretells 'Abd al-Kháliq's imminent acceptance of his Cause.[12]

The Báb invited the outstanding Shi'i scholar Sayyid Ja'far Kashfí (whose son Sayyid Yahyá later joined the new Faith in Shiraz) to accept the new Cause. Kashfí did not reject the Báb's message and when his son met him in Burújird, he gathered that his father was unwilling to repudiate the truth of the new Cause but would prefer to be left alone to pursue his own path.[13]

In chapter 29 of the Qayyúm al-Asmá' the Báb addresses the residents of the province of Fars, saying it is a great honour for them that God has chosen him from among their number and warns them not to turn away from him.

In chapter 28 (Súrat al-Qarába) the Báb addresses the immediate members of his family, wondering why they have not already recognized his high station from his angel-like morality, dignity and divine behaviour. He proclaims that he is the promised Proof (*Hujja*) of God. He states that if they accept his new Cause, God will forgive their past sins, grant them double reward and send them to Paradise. In the same chapter, he praises the sublime station of Fatima Bagum, his mother, saying that she should recognize her own station and appreciate her long association with him, designating her the Mother of the Believers (*Umm al-Mu'minín*). In the hundredth chapter, he beseeches God to grant her faith in the new Cause.

The Báb's wife, Khadíjih Bagum, is told in chapter 28 that if she accepts his Cause, she will not be like ordinary women. He urges her to realize her sublime station and the honour of her association with him. He comforts and consoles her over the death of their son, Ahmad, who is now in Paradise.

In the same chapter the Báb states his own name, 'Alí Muhammad; his mother's name, Fatima; and his father's name, Muhammad Ridá. He implores God in chapter 109 to grant forgiveness to the soul of his father and to grant him salvatiom. In chapters 92 and 110 he calls Mullá Husayn the Bábu'l-Báb (the Gate of the Gate), the first to believe in him.[14]

On numerous occasions in the Qayyúm al-Asmá' the Báb addresses himself as the Gate (*al-Báb*), the Gate of God (*Báb Alláh*), the Greatest Gate (*al-Báb al-A'zam*', the Remembrance (*al-Dhikr*), the Greatest Remembrance of God (*Dhikr Alláh al-A'zam*), the Solace of the Eyes (*Qurrat al-'Ayn*) and the Honourable/Noble/Cherished One (*al-'Azíz*). In chapter 85 he says that he is the descendant of the Prophet Muhammad while in chapter 79 he asserts that his lineage can be traced to Husayn, the third Shi'i Imam. In chapters 19 and 84 the Báb intimates that he has been aware of his great station since childhood. He alludes to his own nobility in chapter 4 and in chapter 56 he speaks of his knowledge and his moderate nature. In chapter 109 he gives a clear depiction of his physical features and remarks on his personal dignity, saying, 'This is a youth of fair complexion, black-eyed, with fine eyebrows, beautiful arms and shoulders whose dignity is like that of the prophets of old.'

Some of the major themes of the Qayyúm al-Asmá'

The meaning of the term 'al-Qayyúm' in Arabic is 'the self-existent' or 'the self-subsisting'. It is one of the names or attributes of God. In the writings of the Báb,

'Qayyúm', in the generic sense, is a title referring to the Manifestations of God, including the Báb himself. But in the specific sense it alludes to the Promised One of the Bábí dispensation, the Remnant of God.[15] 'Qayyúm' is numerically equal to 156, as is the name 'Yúsuf' (Joseph). In one of his tablets the Báb refers to this point saying that by 'Yúsuf' is meant the Qá'im (the Báb himself). He then states that it was for this reason that he interpreted the Quranic Sura of Joseph.[16] The Qayyúm al-Asmá' is the interpretation of the Sura of Joseph.

The story of the life of Joseph in the Quranic Sura of Yúsuf has been called the best/most beautiful of stories (*ahsan al-qasas*) and thus the Báb designated the Qayyúm al-Asmá' *Ahsan al-Qasas* (see QA 43). In chapters 41, 43 and 86 he calls the Qayyúm al-Asmá' the Greatest Book (*al-Kitáb al-Akbar*). In chapter 107 he calls it *al-Tafsír al-Akbar* and in chapter 109 *al-Ta'wíl al-A'zam*, both meaning the Greatest Interpretation. The Báb has also designated the Qayyúm al-Asmá' the Book of Husayn (*Kitáb al-Husayniyya*). As explained below, by Husayn here is meant the return of Imam Husayn (the Promised One of the Bábí dispensation).[17]

The Quranic Sura of Joseph has been interpreted by both Shi'i and Sunni interpreters as part of their general interpretation of the whole Qur'an while others have written separate monographs.[18]

The seventh verse of this Quranic sura states that there are some important signs for those who ask questions (*áyátun li'l-sá'ilín*) in the story of the life of Joseph and his brothers. This point has also been emphasized in verses 109 and 110 of the Sura of Joseph. For this reason Sayyid Kázim Rashtí, the Shaykhi leader, told his students that the Promised Qá'im would provide them with a new and wondrous interpretation of the Sura of Joseph. Based on this statement, on the first night of the Báb's declaration, Bushrú'í asked the Báb to provide him with the interpretation of the Sura of Joseph. The Qayyúm al-Asmá' was written by the Báb as a response to his request.

According to the Sura of Joseph, one day Joseph said to Jacob, his father, 'I saw (in my vision) eleven stars and the sun and the moon; I saw them prostrate themselves before me.' His father said to him: 'Relate not thy vision to thy brothers . . . Thus will thy Lord choose thee and teach thee the interpretations of stories (and events) and perfect His favour to thee.' Because Joseph was deeply loved by his father, out of jealousy his half-brothers took him from their home and threw him into a well. When they returned home they told their father that a wolf had devoured Joseph. It happened that members of a caravan found Joseph in the well and his brothers sold him to them for a paltry price. The members of the caravan then sold Joseph to an Egyptian, who took him to his home.

As Joseph grew up, his beauty increasingly astonished everyone. Zulaykhá, the wife of the Egyptian, fell in love with Joseph but he refused her advances. She then accused Joseph of betrayal and he was sent to jail. The story of Joseph and Zulaykhá spread and the women of the city mocked her for attempting to seduce her slave. Zulaykhá invited some of the women to her home and showed Joseph to them. His beauty was so bewitching and astonishing that the women cut their hands with their knives as they ate.

While Joseph was in prison he realized that he could interpret visions and dreams. It happened that the king of Egypt had a dream which no one was able to interpret. Joseph was summoned to the royal court to interpret the dream. The king had dreamed that seven fat cows were devoured by seven lean ones. He also saw seven green ears of corn and seven withered. Joseph explained that Egypt would experience seven years of greenness and abundance followed by seven years of dryness and famine. Joseph told them that they should save the greater part of their harvest for the years of famine. These events came to pass and the king gave Joseph the highest position in the country.

During the famine, Joseph's brothers came to Egypt to obtain wheat and other goods for their homeland. Joseph recognized them but they did not recognize him. Eventually Joseph introduced himself to them and they and their father prostrated themselves before him. Thus was Joseph's vision fulfilled: the sun and the moon and eleven stars prostrated themselves before him.

In the Qayyúm al-Asmá' the Báb interprets the events in the story of Joseph. By Joseph, he says, is meant the promised Qá'im (the Báb himself) and the promised Remnant of God. By Jacob is meant Muhammad, the Messenger of God, or his descendants who are the Báb's forefathers. Verse 5 of the Sura of Joseph, in which Jacob gives advice to Joseph – 'relate not thy vision to thy brothers' – indicates that the Báb should not reveal the whole truth to the people and should be patient with them. Verse 6, which says 'Thus will thy Lord choose thee and teach thee the interpretation of stories (and events)', means that God has chosen the Báb as the recipient of his Revelation.

According to the Báb in chapters 30 and 44 of the Qayyúm al-Asmá', by Zulaykhá is meant a person or the people who will turn away from the Báb. The women of the city are the people who are not aware of the truth of the divine beauty bestowed upon the Báb (chapters 30, 31 and 33). In chapter 5 of the Qayyúm al-Asmá' the Báb says that by Ya'qúb (Jacob) is meant 'Alí and by Yúsuf (Joseph) is meant Husayn. There are several indications in the Qayyúm al-Asmá' that by Husayn the Báb means himself or the promised Remnant of God. But in chapter 36 the Báb says by Husayn is meant Jacob because the Báb, the divine Joseph, is a descendant of Husayn.

In chapter 5 the Báb says that by the prostration of the sun, the moon and the stars before Joseph is meant the prostration of Muhammad, his daughter Fatima and the Imams (descendants and successors of Muhammad). By Joseph's brothers is meant the people who have not already recognized the sublime station of the Báb and he is trying to introduce himself to them. In chapter 20 the Báb warns the people, especially the Shaykhis (*mala' al-anwár*), not to sell him for a paltry price. In chapter 48 the Báb interprets the seven years of abundance as his own Revelation and the advent of the Promised One of the Bábí dispensation and the years of dryness and famine to the people who will turn away from him. In chapter 57, after the Báb calls himself the divine Joseph, he says that by the power of Joseph in Egypt is meant his own power to convey the Revelation of God.

For Bahá'ís, the similarity of the life of Joseph with the life of the Báb and the promised Remnant of God, Bahá'u'lláh, is quite interesting. Both the Báb and Bahá'u'lláh were subject to the jealousy of their 'brothers'; in the case of the Báb, the jealousy of the members of the Shaykhi community and in the case of Bahá'u'lláh, the jealousy and betrayal of his half-brother Mírzá Yahyá. Both the

Báb and Bahá'u'lláh suffered banishment and imprisonment. Both found their sublime station in 'the divine Egypt' (*Misr al-Ahadiyyih*) as a Manifestation of God. The Báb in his writings, including the Persian Bayán (4:4) and the Seven Proofs (p. 49), quotes an Islamic tradition which says that the life of the Promised One of Islam is similar to the life of the Prophet Joseph – Joseph is mentioned as a prophet in the Qur'an (see Q 6:84 and 40:34). Some Muslim interpreters of the Qur'an and authors[19] believe that Joseph was an independent Messenger of God. The Báb too refers to Joseph as a prophet[20] in chapter 11 of the Qayyúm al-Asmá' and in the tablet to Hájj Mírzá Áqásí. Writing about the Qayyúm al-Asmá' in one of his tablets, the Báb says: 'Know thou that the numerical value of Yúsuf (Joseph) is 156 and this is the same as the numerical value of Qayyúm. By Joseph or Qayyúm is meant the Qá'im of the house of Muhammad, peace be upon him . . . For this reason [the Qá'im] interpreted the book of his name [i.e. the book of Qayyúm] at the beginning of his Revelation.'

As mentioned above, in numerous places in the Qayyúm al-Asmá' the Báb identifies himself and the Remnant of God as Yúsuf (Joseph). For example, he calls himself and the Promised One Yúsuf al-Báb (the Joseph of the Gate; chapter 19); Yúsuf al-'Alí (the Joseph of 'Alí or the Exalted Joseph; chapter 21); Yúsuf al-Haqq (the Joseph of Truth/God; chapter 22); Yúsuf al-Akbar (the Greatest Joseph; chapter 83); and Yúsuf al-Ahadiyyih (the Joseph of Divine Oneness; chapter 90).[21]

The Báb refers to the wondrousness of the content of the Qayyúm al-Asmá' in numerous places in the text and uses the term *badí'* (wondrous/new) when referring to his new Cause, new verses, new knowledge and new ordinances in the Qayyúm al-Asmá'.[22] He also claims that no one has been able to bring a book like the Qayyúm al-Asmá'.[23] Considering the later writings of the Báb, the real wondrousness of the Qayyúm al-Asmá' is in its revolutionary style of creating the new concepts and terminology and providing a new exegesis of the past holy scriptures, especially the Qur'an. We can say that the content of the Qayyúm al-Asmá' is the whole Faith of the Báb in embryonic form. The essence of what the Báb explains in his later writings can be found in the Qayyúm al-Asmá'.

The concepts of *bábiyyat* and *dhikriyyat* in the Qayyúm al-Asmá'

The Qayyúm al-Asmá', being the first major work of the Báb, shows, in a sense, the outwardly different aspects of its nature. In chapter 56 the Báb calls himself 'the gate of your expected Imam' (*báb imámikum al-muntazar*). In chapter 29 he designates himself 'the Gate of the Remnant of God' (*báb Baqiyyat Alláh*). In chapter 9 he says: 'I am the servant of God and I have been given clear tokens by your Imam, the expected Remnant of God.' Even in the first chapter he says that God has decreed that the Qayyúm al-Asmá' come from Muhammad son of Hasan to interpret the best of stories (i.e. the story of Joseph). As explained below, by the Remnant of God, found in numerous places in the Qayyúm al-Asmá', is meant the Promised One of the Bábí dispensation. Although Muhammad son of Hasan had no historical existence,[24] the Báb refers to him as a symbol of the expectation of the Shi'is.

In the Book of Justice (*Sahífih-yi-'Adliyyih*) the Báb states the revelation that he received emanated from a dream in which he drank a few drops of blood from the lacerated head of the Imam Husayn (p. 14). In the same book the Báb explicitly states that the revelation came from the world beyond (p. 10). This clearly demonstrates that the Báb worked within the belief system of the people around him. He claims to be the recipient of the Revelation of God in scores of places in the Qayyúm al-Asmá', which indicates that he himself is a Manifestation of God and not merely the Imam, successor or deputy of a Manifestation.

Explaining why he tolerated the belief system in which he found himself, the Báb says in the Seven Proofs:

> Consider the manifold favours vouchsafed by the Promised One, and the effusions of His bounty which have pervaded the concourse of the followers of Islam to enable them to attain unto salvation. Indeed observe how He Who representeth the origin of creation, He Who is the Exponent of the verse, 'I, in very truth, am God', identified Himself as the Gate [Báb] for the advent of the promised Qá'im, a descendant of Muhammad, and in His first Book enjoined the observance of the laws of the Qur'án, so that the people might not be seized with perturbation by reason of a new Book and a new Revelation and might regard His Faith as similar to their own, perchance they would not turn away from the Truth and ignore the thing for which they had been called into being.[25]

Nearly identical statements of the Báb are found in the Qayyúm al-Asmá'. In chapter 47 we read: 'O Solace of the Eyes [i.e. the Báb]! If thou disclosest what thou knowest and proclaim it to the believers, they will abandon thee . . . have mercy upon them since they are unable to recognize your real station, just as an ant is not able to comprehend the unity of God.'

In chapter 28 the Báb asserts that the mystery of his Revelation is so abstruse and perplexing that no person except he who has absolutely turned to God and his might can unravel it. Statements closely resembling this are found in several other places in the Qayyúm al-Asmá'.[26]

The Báb states in the Qayyúm al-Asmá' (for instance in chapters 5 and 74) that the veil obscuring his station will soon be removed. This prediction was fulfilled three years later when the Báb explicitly revealed his station in numerous writings, including the Persian Bayán, where he says that 'the Sun of Truth [the Manifestation of God, namely the Báb himself] will be shining under the title of "Gatehood" (*Bábiyyat*) until the advent of Him Whom God shall make manifest'.[27]

In his writings, including the Persian Bayán (6:7 and 13 and 8:18), the Báb explains the question of '*taqábul-i-maráyá*' (mirrors facing each other). He says that the Manifestation of God is the mirror of divinity reflecting the existence of God. The successor of the Manifestation of God (in Shi'i terminology, the Imam) reflects the existence of the Manifestation of God and the station of *Bábiyyat* reflects the existence of the Imam. Therefore, based on *taqábul-i-maráyá*, the station of *Bábiyyat* reflects divinity.[28] As the Báb says, 'The last one [i.e. *Bábiyyat*] in truth, reflects the first one [i.e. divinity].'[29]

In the Qayyúm al-Asmá' (for example, in chapters 44 and 68) the Báb explains that these names and titles should not prevent people from recognizing the truth of the Manifestations of God. In the Persian Bayán (4:1) he explains the same point. In several places in the Qayyúm al-Asmá'[30] the Báb refers to himself as the Gate of God (Báb Alláh). It is quite clear that wherever he refers to himself as the Gate of the expected Imam (Muhammad son of Hasan), he is reflecting the belief system of the people around him (the Shi'is)[31] because Muhammad son of Hasan al-'Askari is the symbol of the Promised One of Islam and by making this statement the Báb is claiming that he is that Promised One. In the Qayyúm al-Asmá' the Báb also refers to himself as *Dhikr* (Remembrance). In the Qur'an the term *dhikr* (41:41) is the title of the book itself and of Muhammad (65:10–11). But according to interpreters of the Qur'an, by the term *dhikr* mentioned in verse 105 of the Sura of the Prophets (sura 21) is meant the Promised One of Islam.[32] In numerous places in the Qayyúm al-Asmá' the Báb calls himself Dhikr (Remembrance),[33] al-Dhikr al-Akbar (the Greatest Remembrance),[34] Dhikr Alláh al-Akbar (the Greatest Remembrance of God),[35] and Dhikr Alláh al-A'zam (the Mightiest Remembrance of God).[36] In chapter 62 of the Qayyúm al-Asmá' the Báb says: 'O peoples of the Earth, certainly the Remembrance has come to you in an interval between the advent of the Messengers of God.' Chapter 61 says that God has addressed the Báb as such: 'We have sent to you the divine revelation as we had sent our clear tokens to Muhammad and the Messengers (*al-Rusul*) before him.' On more than 130 occasions the Báb has been addressed as 'Qurrat al-'Ayn' (the Solace of the Eyes) in the Qayyúm al-Asmá'. In the Qur'an, Moses, an independent Messenger of God, has been designated 'Qurrat al-'Ayn',[37] indicating that the Báb claimed the same station.

Based on the discussion above, it can be said that the Báb claimed to be the promised Qá'im and the Dawning Place of the Revelation of God. There are at least two major reasons why the Báb suggested on a few occasions that he was merely the gate to the expected Imam (Qá'im). First, he wanted to fit in with the opinion of the Shi'i Muslims around him, people who believed in atrocious superstitions about the person of the promised Qá'im. It was not possible for the Báb to disclose the mystery of his Revelation all at once to such people. Those who study the Shi'i traditions about the signs of the advent of the promised Qá'im will immediately agree with and applaud the Báb for his handling of this situation (extrinsic contextuality). Second, by the 'gatehood (*bábiyyat*) of the Báb' is in fact meant the gatehood to the city of the Promised One of the Bábí dispensation. As the Báb himself testifies in the Qayyúm al-Asmá' (chapter 86), he is the Gate of Bá' (i.e. Bahá'u'lláh). We will discuss this matter below in more detail. However, the Báb calls all his writings 'Bayán' and says that the Bayán can be understood by referring to both his early writings and the later ones. The Báb says that his early writings are based on Quranic concepts and gradually develop into Bayánic ones. And, as it is more developed, the purpose of God is more explicit in the Bayán. A general look at the Báb's writings, and particularly the connection between the early and the later writings (intrinsic contextuality), will demonstrate the veracity of the claim of the Báb about his station. The Báb himself explained the meaning of his statements in the Qayyúm al-Asmá' in his later writings. In the Qayyúm al-Asmá' itself (chapter three) he says: 'Ask the real meanings (*ta'wíl*) of the Qayyúm al-Asmá' from the Remembrance [i.e. the Báb himself].' Since the Báb explicitly claimed the station of prophethood in the Persian Bayán, the Seven Proofs and his later writings, then what the Báb says in the Qayyúm al-Asmá' about the divine revelation he received refers precisely to his station as an independent Messenger of God.

The station of the Báb in the Qayyúm al-Asmá'

Our discussion so far about the concepts of *bábiyyat* and *dhikriyyat* in the Qayyúm al-Asmá' and about what the Báb says in that book about his divine revelation establishes that he had always claimed the station of prophethood in his writings. Other proofs confirm this notion:

1) In the Qayyúm al-Asmá' (chapter 54) the Báb explains how earlier holy scriptures, including the Torah, Gospel and the Qur'an, have prophesied his advent. He refers to this point in several other chapters as well.[38]

2) In the Qayyúm al-Asmá' the Báb calls his Faith 'a new Cause', 'the Wondrous Cause' (*al-Amr al-Badí'*)[39] and 'the Wondrous Truth' (*al-Haqq al-Badí'*)[40] and his writings 'the new or wondrous verses' (*al-áyát al-badí'a*).[41]

3) In numerous places in the Qayyúm al-Asmá' the Báb explicitly calls[42] or identifies his advent with the appearance of the Day of Resurrection.[43]

4) It was based on the statements of the Báb in the Qayyúm al-Asmá' referring explicitly or implicitly to his station of prophethood that the Islamic clergy issued the verdicts that condemned him to death as an impostor and a heretical claimant. After Mullá 'Alí Bastámí took the book of the Qayyúm al-Asmá' to Iraq and distributed it among both believers and non-believers, he was arrested by the government authorities and imprisoned. Later he was put on trial by the Sunni and Shi'i clergy gathered in Baghdad. They charged both the author of the Qayyúm al-Asmá' and his followers, including Mullá 'Alí Bastámí, with heresy and infidelity (*kufr*). The text of the original verdicts can be found in the Bahá'í World Centre.

The text is in two sections. The first section consists of a question asking what should be done with an impostor who claims he is the recipient of divine revelation after Muhammad. The clergy also quote several statements of the Báb from the Qayyúm al-Asmá' which indicate that he does, in fact, claim to be the recipient of divine revelation. In the second section are the charges of heresy and infidelity made by the clergy against the author of the Qayyúm al-Asmá' and his followers, who deserve the punishment of death. An example is the verdict of Shaykh Ahmad al-Sanandají (d. 1300/1882–3): 'By the Mighty Qur'an! That which this accursed man has brought is heresy in the [true] religion, and abrogation of what the Lord of the Messengers has brought to the effect that he is the Messenger of God and the Seal of the Prophets. And so belief in him is *kufr* (unbelief) and there is no doubt about this.'[44] It is interesting that the clergy focused only on the claim of the Báb to be the recipient of divine revelation.

We should remember that the Qayyúm al-Asmá' and other writings of the Báb caused his opponents to say that he claimed the same station as the recipient of the Qur'an. Hajj Muhammad Karím Khán Kirmání, one of the bitterest enemies of the

Báb, wrote that the Báb 'has claimed that he is the Greatest Gate (*al-Báb al-A'zam*) and the Most Exalted Remembrance (*al-Dhikr al-Ajall al-A'lá*) and the recipient of a new Qur'an . . . and he made his Qur'an like the Qur'an of Muhammad . . . and distributed it among the people and enacted new laws in it . . .'[45] Mírzá Muhammad Taqí Khán Káshání (Sipihr), the Qajar official historian, wrote that the Báb said to his followers that he was the Promised One of Islam and that next year he would proclaim his new Cause in Mecca.[46] In his *Haqá'iq al-Akhbár*, Mírzá Muhammad Ja'far Khán Haqá'iq-Nigár, the other Qajar official historian, wrote about the Báb: 'He never stopped claiming the station of messengerhood (*risálat*) during his lifetime.'[47]

5) Although the Qayyúm al-Asmá' is based on tolerance and wisdom, the Báb repeated and confirmed several ordinances of the Qur'an and enacted and decreed new laws (obligations and prohibitions).

The promised *Baqiyyat Alláh*

The locution *Baqiyyat Alláh* (the Remnant of God), which can be found in the Qur'an (11:86), means a good action or the first and divine reward for a good action. Shi'i interpreters of the Qur'an have given this title to the Promised One of Islam.[48] This designation is the title of the Promised One of the Bábí dispensation in the Báb's early writings including the Qayyúm al-Asmá'. As discussed earlier, although the Báb calls himself the Remembrance in the Qayyúm al-Asmá', this title is also a designation given to the expected *Baqiyyat Alláh*, the Promised One of the Bábí dispensation. Chapter 16 says: 'By the permission of God we give you the glad-tiding of the advent of the Greatest Remembrance (*al-Dhikr al-Akbar*).' In chapter 29 the Báb says about himself that 'he is not but a servant (*'abd*) of God and the gate (*báb*) of the Remnant of God) . . .' In chapter 108 he invites the people to his own Cause and to the Cause of the expected Remnant of God. He then writes about the two 'dawning-places' (*mashriqayn*) of the Sun of Truth. In chapter 28 we read the divine address to the Báb himself which says that he should not disclose all the facts about his Cause because the people are not able to grasp its mysteries. He then emphasizes that the Báb will return again after the expiration of this dispensation. Finally, the address emphasizes again that the Báb should disclose the mystery of his Cause only to the extent of the eye of a needle. By the 'return of his advent' he definitely means the advent of the Promised One of the Bábí dispensation. The Báb also talks about his return in chapters 35 and 95 of the Qayyúm al-Asmá'. This point (the return of the Báb) has been more explicitly and fully explained in his later writings. In several places in the Persian Bayán (for example 2:19; 4:6, 7; and 7:2) the Báb says that 'Him Whom God shall make manifest' (*Man Yuzhiruh Alláh*, namely the *Baqiyyat Alláh* mentioned in the Qayyúm al-Asmá') will be his return.[49] Based on these statements we can infer that by phrases such as *al-núrayn fí al-sirrayn* (the two lights in the two mysteries), *al-haykalayn* (the two temples) and *al-sirájayn fí al-zujájayn* (the two lamps in the two glasses) mentioned in chapter 54 of the Qayyúm al-Asmá' is meant two consecutive revelations, the Báb's and that of his return. However, the might of the advent of the Promised One of the

Bábí dispensation was so splendorous in the estimation of the Báb that he desired to sacrifice his life for him. In chapter 58 of the Qayyúm al-Asmá' the Báb, addressing the Promised One, says:

> O Thou Remnant of God! I have sacrificed myself wholly for Thee; I have accepted curses for Thy sake, and have yearned for naught but martyrdom in the path of Thy love. Sufficient witness unto me is God, the exalted, the protector, the Ancient of Days.[50]

Speaking about his station in chapter 109 of the Qayyúm al-Asmá', the Báb calls himself 'the point abiding over the gate of the two *alifs*' (*al-nuqta al-wáqifa 'alá báb al-alifayn*) and 'the speaker (mouthpiece) of God in two cycles' (*al-muntiq 'an Alláh fí al-kawrayn*). In considering the later writings of the Báb, especially the Persian Bayán, it becomes clear that the Báb explains how he is the Point (the Messenger of God) at the interval between the advent of Muhammad and the Promised One of the Bábí dispensation ('Him Whom God shall make manifest'), between the cycle of Adam and the new cycle.[51] As discussed above, by Joseph in the Qayyúm al-Asmá' is meant both the Báb and the expected Remnant of God. The title of Husayn is also given to both of them.[52] Interestingly, although the Báb explains in numerous places in the Qayyúm al-Asmá' that he is the recipient of the Revelation of God, in 'The Book of Justice' (*Sahífih-yi-'Adliyyih*, p. 14) he says that Husayn is the source of his inspiration. Considering the later writings of the Báb, especially the Persian Bayán, it becomes clear that by Husayn, who is also called Yúsuf (Joseph) in several chapters of the Qayyúm al-Asmá', is meant the Promised One of the Bábí dispensation. For example, in the Persian Bayán (3:3) the Báb says: 'The Bayán and all that is therein revolves around Him Whom God shall make manifest . . . the prolongation of the gaze of the Bayán is only towards the advent of the Remnant of God.' Finally, we accept that the Qayyúm al-Asmá' is the Book of Husayn (*Kitáb al-Husayniyya*) because the whole text speaks of the near advent of the Remnant of God. In the later writings of the Báb, 'the Remnant of God' (*Baqiyyat Alláh*) changes to the title 'Him Whom God shall make manifest' (*Man Yuzhiruh Alláh*). Writing of 'Him Whom God shall make manifest' in the Persian Bayán (3:13), the Báb says: 'The Bayán is, from beginning to end, the repository of all of his attributes . . .'[53] It is to the covenant of this Promised One that the Báb alludes in chapter 38 of the Qayyúm al-Asmá': 'God, in his Greatest Day (*Yawmihi al-Akbar*), will enter into a strong covenant with the people.' In the same chapter he says: 'Be watchful for the Greatest Day of God (*Yawm Alláh al-Akbar*).' This Greatest Day is the day of the advent of Yúsuf (Joseph) as the Qayyúm, for whom the Qayyúm al-Asmá' is titled. The Báb was the Qá'im while the Promised One of the Bábí dispensation would be the Qayyúm. In the Persian Bayán (5:8) the Báb says:

> And know thou of a certainty that every letter revealed in the Bayán is solely intended to evoke submission unto Him Whom God will make manifest, for it is he who hath revealed the Bayán prior to His own manifestation.[54]

According to the Báb, this glorification of the station of the Promised One of the Bábí dispensation is due to the Promised One's infinite greatness. In comparison to his own advent, the Báb glorifies the advent of the Promised One as 'a Revelation more potent, immeasurably [infinitely] more potent, than the one which hath preceded it' (Persian Bayán 9:4). As discussed above, perhaps the connection between the Promised One mentioned in the Qayyúm al-Asmá' and the name of Husayn is one of the reasons why in the *Sahífat al-Radawiyya*, one of the early writings of the Báb, he has called the Qayyúm al-Asmá' the *Kitáb al-Husayniyya* (the Book of Husayn). The Báb refers to the return of Husayn in chapter 47 of the Qayyúm al-Asmá'. If we accept that the Báb was the Promised Qá'im of the Twelver Shi'a then we should accept that by the return of Husayn is meant the advent of the Promised One of the Bábí dispensation. In his writings, the Báb is the Qá'im, while the Remnant of God is the Qayyúm. In his Arabic Bayán (6:15) the Báb calls upon the believers to consider the differences between the Qá'im and the Qayyúm. In a tablet to Shaykh 'Alí 'Azím, the Báb refers to the year nine, saying that 'Azím should wait until that year and at that he should say, 'Blessed is God, who is the best fashioner'. Then the Báb refers to the advent of Husayn after his own Revelation.[55] It is clear that by using the name of Husayn in this statement, the Báb is alluding to the promised Remnant of God.

In the Arabic Bayán (6:15) the Báb addresses the believers, saying that they will attain unto all the good (*kull-i-khayr*) in the year nine. By 'all the good' is meant the Promised One of the Bábí dispensation, as the Báb's own writings attest. When in his Persian Bayán (4:6) the Báb refers to the Promised One, he says that if one recognizes the station of the Promised One he has seen 'all the good' (*kull-i-khayr*). If a person turns away from the Promised One, he has deprived himself of 'all the good'. The same is also expressed elsewhere in the Persian Bayán (3:8). In a tablet to 'Azím the Báb calls the promised Husayn 'the Fruit' (*Thamara*). The term *thamara*, in the sense of 'the fruit of the Cause of the Báb', i.e. 'Him Whom God shall make manifest', has been mentioned by the Báb in the Persian Bayán (4:10, 14).

In the Qayyúm al-Asmá' the word *bahá'* (glory) and its derivatives allude to the title of the Promised One. In chapter 76 the Báb calls himself 'the entrance to the river of *bahá*''. In chapter 29 he states that he is the offspring of *bahá'* while in chapter 47 he says that the Greatest Name will elevate his own name. According to the writings of the Báb, *bahá'* is the Greatest Name. In the Persian Bayán (3:14) the Báb says: 'All the *bahá'* of the Bayán is Him Whom God shall make manifest.' In chapter 86 of the Qayyúm al-Asmá' he says that he is the *báb al-bá'* (the gate of the letter *bá'*). By the letter *bá'* is meant *bahá'*. This is an Islamic expression mentioned in a hadith ascribed to the sixth Shi'i Imam, Ja'far al-Sádiq.[56] In the Persian Bayán (5:3) the name of the first month of the Bábí calendar is *Bahá'*, and the Báb states: 'It is called *Bahá'*, because the *bahá'* of all the months is included in it and God hath set it apart for Him Whom God shall make manifest.' In the same book (5:4) the name Bahá'u'lláh is listed first among the best names,[57] while in 3:16 the Báb explicitly mentions the advent of Bahá'u'lláh and his order: 'Well is it with him who fixeth his gaze upon the Order of Bahá'u'lláh, and rendereth thanks unto his Lord. For He will assuredly be made manifest.'[58] Speaking of the resurrection of the

Bábí dispensation in the Arabic Bayán (2:7), the Báb alludes to the rise of the Sun of Bahá' (*Shams al-Bahá'*). In a tablet published in the compilation *Panj Sha'n* (p. 172ff.) which was submitted to the Promised One, the Báb utilizes several derivatives of the word *bahá'*, demonstrating that the title *bahá'* refers to the expected Promised One. In another tablet in *Panj Sha'n* (p. 61), after warning 'the people of the Báb' (i.e. the Bábís) lest they neglect the advent of the Promised One, the Báb calls the Promised One 'the Possessor of Seven Letters' (*Dhát Hurúf al-Sab'a*) and Bahá'u'lláh. We should note that in Arabic Bahá'u'lláh's given name. Husayn-'Alí, consists of seven letters. In chapter 3 of the Qayyúm al-Asmá', after claiming his own advent to be the advent of Yahyá (John the Baptist), the Báb says that he is the Gate of the Hidden *Bá'* (*al-Bá' al-Mastúr*). Finally, in the Book of Names (*Kitáb al-Asmá'*), in the chapter entitled 'The Name of God, the Bearer of Glad-Tidings' (*Ismu'lláh al-Bashír*), the Báb identifies himself as a herald to the Joseph of Bahá' (*Yúsuf al-Bahá'*), namely the Promised One.

Towards a unity of conviction

Perhaps it is not an exaggeration to say that one of the main objectives of the Báb in writing the Qayyúm al-Asmá' was to create a sort of unity of religious conviction among the followers of the religions, especially Muslims and more specifically the Shi'a. In chapter 109 the Báb says that he has saved the people of the earth from the conjectures of the clergy and has caused them to attain the valley of unity.[59] In chapter 46 the Báb invites the people to enter into brotherhood and consider equality. In chapter 94 he also talks about the huge discrepancies and disagreements within belief systems and their lack of unity. A year after writing the Qayyúm al-Asmá', the Báb's conviction about the need for religious unity was explicitly mentioned in his Book of Justice (*Sahífih-yi-'Adliyyih*). After stating that differences among the Muslims have reached their summit, he explains that the purpose of his Revelation is unity and to remove all these discrepancies. To create this unity and to prepare the people for the advent of the Remnant of God who, as discussed earlier, is the return of Husayn and whose time is, as the Báb explains in the Treatise on Proving [Muhammad's] Specific Prophethood, 'the day of coming together/understanding/ unity and [the day of] love' (*yawm al-ijtimá' wa-l-mahabba*). The Báb at first tried to fit in with the beliefs of the people around him. Thus he outwardly accepted and quoted various Islamic laws in the Qayyúm al-Asmá'. In chapters 45, 48 and 104 the Báb says that his Cause is the same as Islam and that he will promote the Islamic teachings and commandments, whereas in actuality he enacted new laws in the Qayyúm al-Asmá'. This demonstrates that his outward acceptance of Islam was based on his intention to fit in with people, especially the Shi'a. As the Báb testifies in the Qayyúm al-Asmá' (chapter 39), in this way he was able to examine the hearts of the people. It is quite evident that owing to the fanaticism of the Shi'i Muslims, it was not possible for the Báb to disclose the reality of his Cause to them in the early days following his declaration. This is something he alluded to even in the Qayyúm al-Asmá'. In chapter 14, after explaining the thirteenth verse of the Quranic Sura of Yúsuf, in which Jacob tells his sons that he is afraid to let them take Joseph with them because the wolf might devour him, the Báb says: 'If there was no fear [from the fanatic people of the time], the reality of his Cause would be discussed openly like the sun at midday.'

In several places in the Qayyúm al-Asmá' the Báb adopts the laws and ordinances of the Qur'an, especially those concerning holy war (*jihád*), homicide, *hajj* (pilgrimage), *zaká* (alms-giving),[60] *ribá* (usury), inheritance and marriage. At first glance it seems that the Báb has confirmed all these Quranic laws and ordinances but further investigation indicates that he is attempting to abolish or modify those regulations in the Qayyúm al-Asmá' and in his later writings. The law of holy war has been quoted from the Qur'an in several places in the Qayyúm al-Asmá'.[61] The main reason for the Báb mentioning this law was that people, especially the Shi'a, were expecting the advent of a Promised One who would wield the sword against the forces of darkness and oppression in the world. They believed that the Qá'im would fight with the enemies of Islam, defeat them and promote the Cause of God. In Islamic Traditions (especially the Twelver Shi'i ones) it is said that the Promised One will proclaim his Cause from Mecca and Karbala and will try to conquer the world. Thus a few months after his declaration the Báb travelled to Mecca to outwardly fulfil this expectation. In his early writings, including the Qayyúm al-Asmá' (chapter 47), the Báb instructs his followers to go to Karbala and wait there for his arrival. Later, he explained to the believers that God had changed his decree (*badá'*) so they did not have to gather in Karbala.[62] All these indications demonstrate that the Báb was trying to accommodate the expectations of the people. As mentioned earlier, in the Qayyúm al-Asmá' the Báb alludes to the reasons for this accommodation. However, although the Báb speaks about holy war in the Qayyúm al-Asmá', there are indications that he is not willing for the believers to wage jihad at all. In chapter 71 he says that the Remembrance (i.e. the Báb) who has appeared is kind to the believers and forbearing (*halím*) towards the unbelievers (*mushrikín*). In chapter 96 he says that whenever the Remembrance does not permit the believers to wage jihad, it is prohibited to do so. As we know, the Báb never gave permission to the believers to wage holy war. In chapter 100 he says that martyrdom in the path of his Cause is the real jihad and urges the believers to be killed rather to kill. He says that the most foolish people are those who read these verses and do not reflect upon their real meaning. In several places in the Qayyúm al-Asmá' (including chapters 97, 98, 100, 101 and 102) the Báb emphatically warns the believers not to wage holy war without his permission, a permission he never gave.[63] Not only did the Báb not give permission to the believers to wage holy war, he did not even permit them to enter the homes of other people without their consent (chapter 29). In his writings he explains that the path for the guidance of non-believers is one of love and compassion. It is not permitted for the believers to cause sadness to non-believers.

From these teachings of the Báb we can begin to understand the philosophy of Bábí law. In Islam, the early suras of the Qur'an instructed the Muslims to be tolerant towards non-Muslims[64] but some verses in later suras instructed them to deal harshly with non-believers.[65] In contrast, the earlier writings of the Báb give the appearance of a harsh message but gradually it becomes evident that the essence of the Báb's religion is tolerance and forbearance towards non-believers. In the second year after his declaration, the Báb said in the Book of Justice (*Sahífih-*

yi-'Adliyyih) that 'it is incumbent upon all the believers to deal with people with the utmost love' (p. 32). In the same book he says, 'How great is the tolerance of the true believer in this world with the whole of mankind . . . the status of a true believer can be likened to the station of God who, on his own throne of bounty, shows the greatest compassion towards all the people of the world' (p. 37). The word 'compassion' (*rahmániyyat*) unravels the mystery and essence of the Cause of the Báb. From one perspective, the Báb teaches that non-believers have none of the rights given to the believers because they have not accepted the station and authority of the Manifestation of God for this age. Thus 'Abdu'l-Bahá says that the Bábí Faith teaches the annihilation of the non-believers and their literature and holy places.[66] However, according to the Báb, insofar as God is 'the Most Compassionate' (*al-Rahmán*), his mercy and grace encompass all and so the believers must show mercy and grace (*rahmániyyat*) to all, even non-believers. The Báb instructs the believers to promote his Faith only through reasoning and producing the proofs of its truth.[67] In the Arabic Bayán (10:6) he says that God has prohibited the inflicting of harm of any sort on another person, even a slight blow to his shoulder. He goes on to say that the believers are not permitted to discuss the truth of his Faith other than by adducing proofs and evidences with the utmost modesty and courtesy. As mentioned above, the Báb does not permit any believer to enter the house of another person without his or her permission (Qayyúm al-Asmá', ch. 29). In light of this, how is it that some assert that the Báb has instructed his followers to fight and kill non-believers? Not only has the Báb prohibited the act of homicide but he has also prohibited the issuing of a death sentence by anyone under any circumstances (Persian Bayán 4:5). In the Seven Proofs (*Dalá'il-i-Sab'ih*; p. 68) the Báb says that he has taught the people of the Bayán never to cause sadness to anyone. In the Persian Bayán (5:19) he says,

> There is no paradise, in the estimation of the believers in the Divine Unity, more exalted than to obey God's commandments, and there is no fire in the eyes of those who have known God and His signs, fiercer than to transgress His laws and to oppress another soul, even to the extent of a mustard seed.[68]

In another verse in the Persian Bayán (6:16) the Báb says:

> God hath, at all times and under all conditions, been wholly independent of His creatures. He hath cherished and will ever cherish the desire that all men may attain His gardens of Paradise with utmost love, that no one should sadden another, not even for a moment, and that all should dwell within His cradle of protection and security . . .[69]

Regarding the assertion that in the Bayán the Báb has ordered the burning of all past holy scriptures, the fact is there is no such law in either the Persian or the Arabic Bayán. On the contrary, the Báb emphatically warns the believers not to even tear a book (Arabic Bayán 9:13). By the destruction of books mentioned in the Persian Bayán (6: 6) is meant their annulment (*naskh*). In this section of the Persian Bayán the Báb used the words *mahw* and *raf'*, which mean both annulment and abrogation.[70] The destruction of the holy places of earlier religions also means, according to the text of the Persian Bayán (4:12), the annulment of the duty to make pilgrimage to them. The Báb states that the essence of the honour attached to a holy place is that that place is the horizon of the Cause of God and wherever the Cause of God appears that place is a holy shrine. He thus refers to the sacredness of the Bábí holy places and says they are the holy shrines that his believers should visit.

Conclusion

The Báb's main purpose in writing the Qayyúm al-Asmá' was to explain his own station and to prepare the people, particularly the Shi'i Muslims, for the advent of the Remnant of God for whom he was a herald. Since the first believer in the Báb and most of the early believers were Shaykhis who were expecting the advent of the Qá'im in the near future, the Báb used Shaykhi terminology to explain many subtle points about his station as the promised Qá'im and the Gate of the Remnant of God.

The reasons why the Báb chose the story of Joseph to interpret are quite clear. The Islamic hadith state that the promised Qá'im will resemble the prophet Joseph. The story of Joseph's life was almost identical to that of all the prophets: they were all subject to the perfidy of their brothers in religion, were thrown into the well of jealousy and were sold for a paltry price; many were imprisoned, some were killed; but in the end their Cause was victorious.

Chapter 53 of the Qayyúm al-Asmá' addresses both the Báb and Remnant of God, saying: 'Be patient, O Solace of the Eyes! Indeed God has assured your exaltation on Earth.'

The Qayyúm al-Asmá' revolutionized aspects of Islamic thought. For example, in the first chapter the book's explanations are called 'the Pure Islam' or 'the True Path of God' while in the second chapter the Báb says that whoever accepts the divinity of the Qayyúm al-Asmá' has accepted the divinity of the past holy scriptures. He prohibited the waging of holy war without his permission, a permission he never gave. In his later writings the Báb urged his followers to associate with people with the utmost love and accord. Calling himself the Dawning-Place of the Revelation of God in numerous places, he disputes the claim of Muslims that Muhammad is the last divine emissary.

The question of the progressive nature of revelation outlined in the Qayyúm al-Asmá' is explained in more detail and more explicitly in the Báb's later writings. For example, in his Seven Proofs (pp. 2–3) he says that since there is no beginning or end to divine creation, progressive revelation is an absolute reality. Just as God has created and will create human beings, so he will send the Messengers and the holy scriptures to them. In the Persian Bayán (2:15) he explains that God continually creates new institutions, new systems and new ordinances, since the requirements and exigencies of each age are different. In the same book (6:16) he says:

> The Lord of the universe hath never raised up a prophet nor hath He sent down a Book unless He hath established His covenant with all men, calling for their acceptance of the next Revelation and of the next Book; inasmuch as the outpourings of His bounty are ceaseless and without limit.[71]

He also says in the Persian Bayán (4:12) that

> The process of the rise and setting of the Sun of Truth will thus indefinitely continue – a process that hath had no beginning and will have no end.[72]

The Báb referred to progressive revelation in numerous places in the Persian Bayán and other later writings. The subject of the unity of the Manifestations of God has been also mentioned in the Qayyúm al-Asmá'. In chapter 55, addressing the whole of mankind, the Báb says that whoever wishes to look at the countenance of past Messengers of God such as Adam, Noah, Abraham, Moses and Jesus should look at him and that his advent is the same as the advent or return of the past Messengers of God.

The subject of 'return' is explained in detail in the Báb's later writings. From those statements it becomes clear that the Báb is the return of the attributes of earlier divine Prophets, thus demonstrating his belief in the unity of the Messengers of God, a subject he refers to in several verses of the Persian Bayán and in his other writings.[73] In the Persian Bayán (4:12) he says that 'the Revelation of God may be likened to the sun. No matter how innumerable its risings, there is but one sun, and upon it depends the life of all things.'[74]

In the Qayyúm al-Asmá' the Báb interprets the signs of the appearance of the Day of Resurrection to be the signs of his own advent. This new interpretation of Resurrection is a revolution in Islamic thought and, in general, in the field of eschatology. However, it seems that the interpretation of the Quranic Sura of Joseph was a pretext for the Báb's explanation of numerous subtle points related to his Cause. He outwardly tolerated the contemporary belief system of the Shi'a but at the same time, with wisdom, prudence and precaution, he implicitly – and occasionally explicitly – disclosed the subtleties of his teachings to the hearts and minds of the people. Just as the brothers of Joseph did not recognize him in Egypt and Joseph had to introduce himself to them, most of the Báb's contemporaries did not recognize his true station and he gradually introduced himself to them in the land of 'divine Egypt' (*misr al-Ahadiyyih*). The Báb attempted to create a unity of conviction about religious concepts among the followers of the past religions, especially Muslims, and prepared them for the advent of the Remnant of God – 'Him Whom God shall make manifest' – whose time of appearance is 'the day of coming together/understanding/unity and [the day of] love' (*yawm al-ijtimá' wa-l-mahabba*).

Bibliography

'Abdu'l-Bahá. *Makátíb-i-'Abdu'l-Bahá*. Cairo: Matba'ah-yi Kurdistán al-'Ilmiyyah, 1330 AH /1912 CE.

Afnan, Muhammad and William S. Hatcher. 'Western Islamic Scholarship and Bahá'í Origins'. *Religion*, vol. 15 (1985), pp. 29–51.

The Báb (Sayyid 'Alí Muhammad-i-Shírází). *Bayán-i-'Arabí*. Tehran: n.p., n.d.

— *Bayán-i-Farsí*. Tehran: n.p., n.d.

— *Dalá'il-i-Sab'ih*. Tehran: n.p., n.d.

— *Panj Sha'n*. Tehran, n.p., n.d.

— *Qayyúm al-Asmá'*. Manuscript, in the handwriting of Muhammad Mahdí b. Karbalá'í Sháh Karam, 1261 AH/1845 CE.

— *Risálih-yi-Furú'-i-'Adliyyih* (manuscript) INBA collection, pp. 81–120.

— *Risálih-yi-Sulúk* (personal manuscript).

— *Sahífih-yi-'Adliyyih*. Tehran: n.p., n.d.

— *Selections from the Writings of the Báb*. Trans. Habib Taherzadeh with the assistance of a Committee at the Bahá'í World Centre. Haifa: Bahá'í World Centre, 1976.

Bahá'u'lláh. *Kitáb-i-Badí'*. Tihran: n.p., n.d.

— *Kitáb-i-Íqán*. Wilmette, IL: Bahá'í Publishing Trust, 1989.

— *Tablets of Bahá'u'lláh Revealed after the Kitáb-i-Aqdas*. Trans. Habib Taherzadeh with the assistance of a Committee at the Bahá'í World Centre. Wilmette, IL: Bahá'í Publishing Trust, 1988.

Haqá'iq-Nigár, Mírzá Muhammad Ja'far Khán-i-Khúrmújí. *Haqá'iq al-Akhbár*, vol. 1. Tihran: Government Printing Co., 1284 AH/1867 CE.

Iqbal, Abbas. *Khándán-i-Nawbakhtí*. Tihran: Kitábkhánah-yi Tahúrí, 1932.

Iranian National Bahá'í Archives (INBA).

al-Káshání, Muhsin Fayd. *al-Sáfí*. 5 vols. Tehran: Maktab-i Sadr, 1416 AH/1995 CE.

Kirmani, Muhammad Karim Khan. *Irshád al-'Awámm*. 4 vols. Bombay: n.p., 1268 AH /1851 CE.

Lawson, B. Todd. 'Fatima's Religious Authority in an Early Work by the Báb', in ed. L. Walbridge, *The Most Learned of the Shi'a: The Institution of the Marja' Taqlid*. Oxford: Oxford University Press, 2001, pp. 94–127.

— 'Interpretation as Revelation: The Qur'án Commentary of the Báb'. *The Journal of Bahá'í Studies*, vol. 2, no. 4, 1990, pp. 17–43.

— 'Interpretation as Revelation: The Qur'án Commentary of Sayyid 'Alí Muhammad Shírází, the Báb', in ed. A. Rippin, *Approaches to the History of the Interpretation of the Qur'an*. Oxford: Oxford University Press, 1988, pp. 223–53.

— *The Qur'án Commentary of Sayyid 'Alí Muhammad, the Báb*. Unpublished Ph.D. diss., McGill University, 1987.

MacEoin, Denis. *The Sources for Early Bábí Doctrine and History: A Survey*. Leiden: Brill, 1992.

Mázandarání, Asad Alláh Fádil. *Asrár al-Áthár*, 5 vols. Tehran: Bahá'í Publishing Trust, 124–9 BE/1968–73 CE.

— *Táríkh-i-Zuhúr al-Haqq*, vol. 3. Tehran: n.p. c. 1941.

Mohammadhosseini, Nosratollah. *The Báb (Hazrat-i-Báb)*. Dundas, ON: Institute for Bahá'í Studies in Persian, 1995.

— *Táhirih (Hazrat-i-Táhirih)*. Dundas, ON: Association for Bahá'í Studies in Persian, 2000.

— *Yúsuf-i-Bahá*. Dundas, ON: Persian Institute for Bahá'í Studies, 1991.

Momen, Moojan. 'The Trial of Mullá 'Alí Bastámí: A combined Sunní-Shí'í fatwá against the Báb'. *Iran*, vol. 20 (1982), pp. 113–43.

Nabíl-i-A'zam. *The Dawn-Breakers: Nabíl's Narrative of the Early Days of the Bahá'í Revelation*. Wilmette, IL: Bahá'í Publishing Trust, 1970.

Rafati, Vahid. *The Development of Shaykhí Thought in Shí'í Islam*. Unpublished Ph.D. diss., University of California, Los Angeles, 1979.

Rashti, Sayyid Kazim. *Sharh al-Qasída*. Tabriz: n.p., n.d..

Saiedi, Nader. *Gate of the Heart: Understanding the Writings of the Báb*. Waterloo, ON: Association for Bahá'í Studies and Wilfrid Laurier University Press, 2008.

Shoghi Effendi. *God Passes By*. Wilmette, IL: Bahá'í Publishing Trust, rev. ed. 1995.

Sipihr, Mírzá Muhammad Taqí, Lisán al-Mulk. ed. M.B. Bihbúdí, *Násikh al-Tavárikh: Qájáríyyah*, 4 vols. Tehran: Islámiyyah, 1385 AH/1966 CE.

Notes

1. See the Báb, *Bayán-i-Fársí* 3:17.
2. The Báb has provided other classifications of his writings which are similar to these but have slight differences. See Mohammadhosseini 1995, pp. 723–6.
3. *Áyát* (signs/verses) is also a generic title for the whole body of the Báb's writings.
4. For more information about the oldest manuscripts of the Qayyúm al-Asmá' see MacEoin 1992, pp. 195–6.
5. Mázandaráni *c*. 1941, p. 285.
6. The Báb, *Bayán-i-Fársí* 8:15.
7. Momen 1982, p. 116.
8. Mohammadhosseini 1991, p. 21.
9. For example in chapters 2, 16, 17, 26, 28, 29, 30, 37, 38, 47, 51, 60, 63, 77, 82, 91, 92 and 96.
10. See Bahá'u'lláh 1989, p. 229; and Bahá'u'lláh, *Kitáb-i-Badí'*, p. 146.
11. For information on the content of these tablets see Mohammadhosseini 1995, pp. 762–4, 826–45 and 954–5.
12. A few months after the declaration of the Báb, Mullá 'Abdu'l-Kháliq embraced his Cause but three years later his faith became shaky and he withdrew from the Bábí community. He died in 1268 AH/1851–2 CE.
13. See Nabíl-i-A'zam 1970, p. 177; Mohammadhosseini 1995, pp. 226, 258, 261–2, 286, 746; and Mohammadhosseini 1991, pp. 30–1.
14. During his six-year mission the Báb wrote hundreds of verses praising the sublime station of the Bábu'l-Báb. In the Persian Bayán (*Bayán-i-Fársí* 6:7) the Báb calls him 'the Essence of all Existence' (*Jawhar-i-Kull-i-Vujúd*).
15. In one of his tablets Bahá'u'lláh states: 'Indeed the Qayyúm has come to you just as the Qá'im [the Báb] had prophesied his appearance' (Mázandaráni 1968–73, vol. 4, p. 531).
16. Mázandaráni *c*. 1941, pp. 223–4.
17. The Qayyúm al-Asmá' has been mentioned by the Báb in his *Bayán-i Fársí* (7:1). Sometimes Bahá'u'lláh has called this book the 'Qayyúm-i Kutub' (*Kitáb-i-Badí'*, p. 224).
18. Abú Hámid-i Ghazálí (d. 1111 CE) is among the Muslim scholars who have written commentaries specifically on the Sura of Joseph.
19. Mullá Fath Alláh al-Káshání (d. *c*. 997 AH/1588–9 CE) mentions their names in his *Manhaj al-Sádiqín*.

20. Bahá'u'lláh is of the same opinion. See Bahá'u'lláh 1989, pp. 212–13.
21. Similar titles are found in chapters 7, 8, 20, 30, 57, 59 and 83 of the Qayyúm al-Asmá'.
22. See, for example, chapters 3, 6 ,18, 20, 23, 25, 26, 32, 41, 48, 49, 50, 53, 59, 61, 63, 65, 87 and 92.
23. See chapters 3, 40, 46, 52, 58, 63, 66, 68, 73 and 95.
24. See Iqbal 1932, pp. 162–6; and Mohammadhosseini 1995, pp. 970–6.
25. The Báb 1976, p. 119.
26. See for example chapters 36, 53, 68, 72 and 88.
27. The Báb, *Bayán-i-Fársí* 4:6.
28. Most of the prominent Bábí scholars also have referred to the subject of *taqábul-i-maráyá*. For example, Táhirih, the Bábí heroine, has explained this matter in one of her epistles. See Mohammadhosseini 2000, p. 404.
29. The Báb, *Bayán-i-Fársí* 6:13.
30. See for example chapters, 3,13, 24, 30, 50, 67 and 77.
31. For more information on this subject see Mohammadhosseini 1991, pp. 44–6.
32. See Káshání 1995, vol. 3, p. 357.
33. See chapters 1, 4, 7, 19, 27, 28, 29, 41, 60, 61, 67, 70, 81, 83, 84, 94 and 100.
34. See chapters 15, 16, 27, 28, 32 and 90.
35. See chapters 39 and 109.
36. See chapters 25, 47, 48 and 96.
37. See Q 28:9. We should remember that in the Shi'i world the title 'Qurratu'l-'Ayn' was also given to Fatima, 'Alí and other Imams. See Káshání 1995, vol. 4, pp. 26–7. See also Lawson 2001, 102–5.
38. See for example chapters 5, 24, 38, 53, 90, 110 and 111.
39. See for example chapters 8, 20 and 87.
40. See for example chapters 3, 24, 25 and 32.
41. See for example chapters 41, 48, 53, 61, 65 and 92.
42. See for example chapters 7, 74, 76, 79 and 93.
43. See for example chapters 1, 24, 25, 36, 47, 67, 75 and 78.
44. Momen 1982, p. 134. For the full account of the trial of Mullá 'Alí Bastámí and the verdict of the Sunni and Shi'i clergy see Momen 1982.
45. Kirmani 1851, vol. 2, p. 82.
46. Sipihr 1965, p. 427.
47. Haqá'iq-Nigár 1867. Chapter related to the events of the year 1265 AH.
48. See for example Káshání 1995, vol. 2, p. 468.
49. Bahá'u'lláh stated that he was the return of the Báb. See for example Bahá'u'lláh, Kitáb-i-Badí', p. 83; and Bahá'u'lláh 1988, p. 183.
50. Translated by Shoghi Effendi in Bahá'u'lláh 1989, p. 231.
51. Shoghi Effendi, the Guardian of the Bahá'í Faith, calls these two cycles the 'Prophetic Cycle' and 'the Cycle of Fulfilment' (Shoghi Effendi 1995, pp. 54–5, 57).
52. See for example chapters 6, 7, 11, 21 and 103.
53. For this reason Shoghi Effendi, speaking about the content of the Persian Bayán, says that this book 'should be regarded primarily as an eulogy of the Promised One, rather than a code of laws and ordinances designed to be a permanent guide to future generations' (Shoghi Effendi 1995, p. 25).
54. The Báb 1976, p. 104.
55. The Báb, *Panj Sha'n*, pp. 255–6.
56. See Ahsá'í, *Majmu'at al-Rasá'il* and Rashtí, *Sharh al-Qasída*.
57. In the Persian Bayán the title Bahá'u'lláh has two meanings: specific and generic. In the specific sense, by Bahá'u'lláh is meant the Promised One of the Bábí dispensation. Bahá'u'lláh in the generic sense is the title of an independent Manifestation of God in every age (see, for example, *Bayán-i-Fársí* 3:15).

58. Shoghi Effendi, *God Passes By*, p. 25. Based on these statements of the Báb, by the title 'the People of Bahá' (*Ahl al-Bahá'*) in chapter 57 of the Qayyúm al-Asmá' is meant the followers of the Promised One of the Bayán, while the title *al-thamara al-maqsúd* (the intended fruit) is the designation of the Promised One himself. Recall that in the Qayyúm al-Asmá' (chapter 13) the Báb calls his followers 'the People of the Báb' (*Ahl al-Báb*).
59. See also chapters 66 and 74.
60. *Zaká* is a form of alms tax, which imposes the obligation to give a fixed portion of certain categories of income to aid the poor.
61. The Báb also alluded to this law in *Risálih-yi-Furú'-i-'Adliyyih* and *Bayán-i Fársí*.
62. For more information about the gathering in Karbala and the reasons for its cancellation, see Mohammadhosseini 1995, pp. 238–46.
63. For more information about the concept of jihad in the Báb's writings, see Afnan and Hatcher 1985, pp. 29–51; Mohammadhosseini 1995, pp. 426–30; and Mohammadhosseini 1991, pp. 79–86.
64. See for example Q 2:256 and 16:125.
65. See for example Q 4:5 and 48: 29.
66. 'Abdu'l-Bahá 1912, vol. 2, p. 266.
67. The Báb, *Panj Sha'n*, p. 437.
68. The Báb 1976, p. 79.
69. ibid. p. 86.
70. For more information about the meaning of the words *raf'* and *irtifá'* as annulment and abrogation, see the *Bayán-i-Fársí* 6:7 and 8:3, 7; and Saiedi 2008, pp. 208, 254, 274 and 277.
71. The Báb 1976, p. 87.
72. ibid. p. 106.
73. See the Báb, *Bayán-i-Fársí* 3:13 and 4:15; *Dalá'il-i-Sab'ih*, p. 2; *Risálih-yi-Sulúk*, p. 486; *Panj Sha'n*, pp. 31, 42, 58, 63–4, 210, 320, 396, 443.
74. ibid. p. 105.

3

Khutbat al-iftikhár

Introduced and translated by Khazeh Fananapazir

Introduction

This is a translation of the Sermon of Glorification (*khutbat al-iftikhár*) attributed to 'Alí ibn Abí Tálib (d. 661 CE), the first Shi'i Imam.[1]

'Alí delivered the sermons of *tutunjíya*, *núráníya* and *iftikhár* in the language of the world of command (*'álam-i-amr*), all attributing the workings of the Will of God – his Primal Will – in the world of creation. Bahá'u'lláh, the author of the Bahá'í Revelation, says that this world is sanctified above plurality:

> Similar statements have been made by 'Alí. Sayings such as this, which indicate the essential unity of those Exponents of Oneness, have also emanated from the Channels of God's immortal utterance, and the Treasuries of the gems of divine knowledge, and have been recorded in the scriptures. These Countenances are the recipients of the Divine Command, and the day-springs of His Revelation. This Revelation is exalted above the veils of plurality and the exigencies of number. Thus He saith: 'Our Cause is but one.' Inasmuch as the Cause is one and the same, the Exponents thereof also must needs be one and the same. Likewise, the Imáms of the Muhammadan Faith, those lamps of certitude, have said: 'Muhammad is our first, Muhammad our last, Muhammad our all' (Bahá'u'lláh 1989, p. 153).

This illustrious sermon is another luminous example of this mighty theme.

Translation

The Sermon of *Iftikhár* by Imam 'Alí, as narrated by Asbagh, the son of Nubáta

The Imam 'Alí said:

> I am the brother of the Messenger of God and heir to his knowledge, the treasury of his wisdom and possessor of his divine mystery. There is not one letter revealed by God, in any of his Books, that does not allude to me. He hath invested me with a fuller measure of all that hath been and all that is to be[2] up to the day of Resurrection (*yawm al qiyáma*). To me hath been vouchsafed the genealogies and

relations between people. And to me hath been given a thousand keys with each key opening a thousand doors.³ The knowledge of the destinies of all things hath been granted unto me. All these gifts shall continue to flow through the successors that come after me. Night and day will not come to pass until God inherits the earth and all who are on it. Verily, he is the best of inheritors.⁴

Unto me hath been vouchsafed the Path,⁵ the Balance,⁶ the Banner and the *kawthar*.⁷ I am the one who shall face the children of Adam on the day of Resurrection. I will bring them to account and establish them in their dwellings. I am the punishment [meted unto] the denizens of Hell inasmuch as these are the bounties of God unto me. And should anyone deny that I shall return to the earth after the Return⁸ or deny that I shall come back after the *raj'a*,⁹ or should anyone reject the truth that I shall appear again, even as I have done from the beginning that hath no beginning unto the end that hath no end, he, verily, hath denied the truth of all of us. And verily I say unto you, he who denies any one of us hath denied God.¹⁰ I am the Lord of supplication. I am the Master of prayer. I am the Lord of retribution and I am the Master of the signs that lead aright. I am the Lord of the wondrous signs. I am cognisant of the divine mysteries of all creation. I am the one who brought the iron unto men.¹¹ I am forever new and forever preexistent. I am the one who bestowed on the angels their ranks and grades. I am the one, who, in the beginning that hath no beginning, pledged an everlasting covenant with the spirits. I am the one who proclaimed unto them [these words] through a self-subsisting cause from time immemorial even to the present day: 'Am I not your Lord?'¹² I am the Word of God speaking amongst his creation. I am the one who exacts a covenant from all created things during prayer. I am the succour of orphans and widows. I am the gate of the city of knowledge¹³ and the refuge (*kahf*)¹⁴ of patience and forbearance. I am the upraised support of God. I am the bearer of the banner of divine praise, the Lord of infinite bounty and of infinite grace. Were I to tell you all that I am, you would doubtless disbelieve me for I am also the slayer of oppressors, the treasure of divine favours in this world and in the world to come. I am the Master of the believers,¹⁵ and the guide of those who are rightly guided. I am the companion of the right hand.¹⁶ I am certitude. I am the Imam of the righteous.¹⁷ I am the first to acknowledge faith. I am the impregnable Cord of God.¹⁸ I am the one who will fill the world with justice – with this my sword – even as it hath been full of oppression.¹⁹ I am the companion of Gabriel and the one who bears allegiance to Michael. I am the tree of guidance and the essence of righteousness. I will gather all of creation to God through [utterance of] the Word that gathers together all created things. I give life unto humanity and I am he who brings together all the divine commands. I am the possessor of the Luminous Sword²⁰ and the Crimson Camel.²¹

I am the gate of certitude, the Commander of the Faithful, the companion of Khidr. I am the one who shall conquer Syria. I am the Lord of Damascus.²² I vanquish the weak. I am the Master of time. I am the greatest *siddíq* (*al-siddíq al-akbar*).²³ I am the greatest *fárúq* (*al-fárúq al-a'zam*).²⁴ I am the one who speaks revelation. I am the Master of all celestial bodies. Through a command of my Lord, I ordain their orbit. God hath vouchsafed unto me their knowledge. With me are the saffron and crimson coloured flags. I am the hidden one, eagerly awaiting the command of the Most Great.

I am the All-Bountiful, the All-Bounteous. I withhold as I wish. None can describe Me except Myself. I shall protect the faith of my Lord. I am the protector of my Cousin. I was present when his sacred remains were shrouded. I am the friend of the Merciful (*walí al-rahmán*). I am the companion of Khidr[25] and Aaron. I am the friend of Moses and Joshua, the son of Nún. I am the Lord of Paradise. I am he who hath caused the rain to fall and the earth to quake and the sun and moon to be eclipsed. I am the object of the creation of multitudes and it is I who shall slay those who do not believe. Verily, I am the Imam of the righteous. I am the Frequented Fane,[26] the Upraised Canopy,[27] the Ocean that hath been caused to swell.[28] I am the Holy of Holies, the pillar that supports humanity. I am the possessor of the Greatest Cause. Is there anyone capable of speaking about me? Had I not heard the Word of God and the utterance of the Messenger of God – may the blessings of God and his salutations be upon him – I would have struck you with my sword and slain all of you one after another.

I am the month of Ramadán[29] and the night of Power.[30] I am the Mother Book.[31] I am the decisive judgement.[32] I am the Sura of Praise.[33] I am the Lord of Prayer, whether at home or when travelling. Nay, we are the Prayer and the Fast and the nights and the days and the months and the years. I am the Lord of the Resurrection and Judgement, the one who can remove the yoke that lies heavy on the people of Muhammad. I am the gate of prostration. I am [his] worshipper and the one created [by him]. I am both the witness and the one witnessed to. I am the possessor of the green sarsenet.[34] I am he whose name is mentioned in the heavens and the earth. I was the travelling companion of the Messenger of God through the heavens. I possess the Book and the sacred Arc.[35] I am the one who befriended Seth, the son of Adam.[36] I am the companion of Moses and Iram. All metaphors and analogies pertain unto me. Who indeed is there to compare with me? I am the heaven-sent rain that causeth each blade of green to grow, the Lord of this nether realm who brings forth the rains when all have lost their hope in its downpour. I am he who summoneth the mighty lightning and causeth the ocean to rise and swell, the one who speaketh to the sun and causeth the stunning trumpet to blast forth. I am the refuge of all that have obeyed God, and verily, God is my Lord and there is no other God but him. For falsehood offers illusions but truth giveth thee everlasting sovereignty.

I shall soon depart from amongst you but be watchful and aware. Be on your guard against the tests and tribulations caused by the Umayyads and their worldly powers. And after they pass away, the kingdom will revert to the 'Abbásids, who will bring both sorrow and happiness to mankind. And they shall build a city called al-Zawrá',[37] which shall be between the Tigris and the Euphrates. Woe betide men in those latter days, for amongst them will rise the oppressors among my people who shall build palaces for themselves and courts and tabernacles. For they shall seek supremacy through intrigue and impiety. Two score and two kings shall rule among the children of the 'Abbásids, after whose reign shall come to pass the Most Great Tribulation on the surface of the earth. Then shall the True Qá'im rise up once more. Then shall I show my face amongst men, and it shall be as luminous as the face of the moon amid the other stars.

But note well the ten signs associated with my coming: first, the inversion of banners on the alleys of Kúfa; the shutting down of mosques; the suspension of pilgrimage; an eclipse in the lands of Khurásán; the gathering of constellations; the appearance of comets in the sky; chaos; confusion; massacre; and pillage. Many other signs shall there be too, surpassing all these signs, among which is the sign of wonderment. But when all these signs have passed away, then, verily, shall our Qá'im himself arise in truth.

O people, sanctify the Lord your God from all similitudes, for every reference to him fails, and whosoever tries to limit the Creator by description or comparison hath verily disbelieved in the Speaking Book (*al-kitáb al-nátiq*).[38]

Then he said: How great the blessedness of those who love me and who sacrifice their life in my path and who are exiled because of me! They truly are the repositories of God's knowledge and they shall not be put to fear on the Day of the Great Terror.

I am the Light of God who can never be extinguished. I am the Mystery of God that cannot be concealed.

Bibliography

Bahá'u'lláh. *Kitáb-i-Íqán*. Wilmette, IL: Bahá'í Publishing Trust, 1989.

al-Bursí, Háfiz Rajab. *Masháriq anwár al-yaqín fí haqá'iq asrár amír al-mu'minín*. Beirut: Mu'assasat al-A'lamí lil-Matbú'át, 1412/1992, pp. 164–6.

Kitáb fadl al-'ilm (The Book on the Virtues of Knowledge) in al-Kulayní's *al-Káfí*. Tehran: Dár al-Kutub al-Islámíya.

al-Majlisí, Muhammad Báqir. *Bihár al-anwár*, vol. 101. Beirut: Dár Ihyá' al-Turáth al-'Arabí, 1403/1983.

al-Túsí, al-Shaykh Muhammad b. al-Hasan (Shaykh al-Tá'ifa). *al-Amálí*. Qum: Dár al-Thaqáfa, p. 626.

Notes

1. The original text is found in *Masháriq anwár al-yaqín fí haqá'iq asrár amír al-mu'minín*, compiled by Háfiz Rajab al-Bursí, pp. 164–6.
2. Cf. Opening sentence of the Kitáb-i-Aqdas: 'In the Name of Him Who is the Supreme Ruler of over all that hath been and all that is to be.' See also *Kitáb fadl al-'ilm* (The Book on the Virtues of Knowledge) in al-Kulayní's *al-Káfí*. The name of one of the chapters of this book is 'The Imams – peace be upon them – know the knowledge of all that has been and all that is to be and nothing is hidden from them' (ed.).
3. Cf. Hadith ascribed to 'Alí stating that one thousand keys have been entrusted to him, with each key opening a thousand doors and each door leading to a million covenants (*'ahd*). This hadith is cited as early as al-Túsí (Shaykh al-Tá'ifa) (d. 1067 CE) in his *al-Amálí* (ed.).
4. Q 21:89 (ed.).
5. Q 1:6; 20:135; 23:74; 36:66; 37:118; 38:22 (ed.).
6. Q 55:7–9 (ed.).
7. Q 108:1 (ed.).
8. This is a reference to the name 'Alí-Muhammad (i.e. the name of the Báb).
9. This is a reference to the sacred name Husayn-'Alí, the name of Bahá'u'lláh, and in particular, his declaration to be the return (*raj'a*) of the Imam Husayn.
10. Cf. Tradition attributed to the sixth Shi'i Imam, Ja'far al-Sádiq and cited by al-Majlisí in *Bihár al-anwár*, vol. 101, pp. 261–2 (no. 1) (ed.).
11. Cf. Q 18:96; 34:1; 57:25 (ed.).
12. Q 7:172 (ed.).

13. Derived from the second part of the famous prophetic hadith, mentioned in both Shi'i (e.g. Shaykh al-Sadúq's *al-Amálí*) and Sunni (e.g. Ibn Kathír's *Táríkh*) sources: 'I am the city of [all] knowledge and 'Alí is its gate' (ed.).
14. Cf. Q 18:9–11, 16–17, 25 (ed.).
15. This is an epithet of 'Alí, given to him by the Prophet and mentioned in a number of Traditions cited as early as al-Kulayní in his *al-Káfí*, vol. 1, p. 294 (ed.).
16. Cf. 37:28. See also Q 57:26: 'the companions of the right hand (*asháb al-yamín*)', describing the people of Paradise (ed.).
17. Cf. Tradition mentioned in Muhammad bin al-Hasan al-Qummí's (d. *c.* 7th cent. AH i.e. two centuries prior to al-Bursí) *al-'Aqd al-nadíd wa al-durr al-faríd* (a book that includes Traditions about the excellent virtues of the Prophet and the holy family) on the authority of Imam al-Ridá', who narrates that these words were spoken in a famous sermon delivered by Imam 'Alí in Kúfa. The name of the sermon is *al-gharrá'* (the noble woman). The sermon does not appear to have been recorded in *Nahj al-balágha*. *Al-muttaqín* are mentioned numerous times in the Qur'an (ed.).
18. The Cord of God (*habl Alláh*) is a Quranic locution (see Q 3:103) and has been interpreted by Shi'i and Sunni (e.g. al-Tha'labí) exegetes to be a reference to the *ahl al-bayt*. Cf. the previous sermon in the *mashárig*, p. 163 (ed.).
19. These are the words of an important and oft-cited prophetic Tradition appearing in various forms in both Sunni and Sh'i hadith collections (ed.).
20. 'Alláma al-Majlisí mentions *sáhib al-qadáb al-'ajíb* as one of the epithets of the Prophet. See al-Majlisí 1983, vol. 16, p. 106. Others mention that *al-qadíb* was the iron sword used by the Prophet in battle. (ed.)
21. Oblique reference to the Thamúd, their prophet Sálih and the She-Camel so often referred to in the Qur'an (see e.g. 11:61–5) (KF). Or perhaps a reference again to the camel that the Prophet is believed to have ridden, according to numerous Traditions (ed.).
22. *al-faihá'* is an epithet of Damascus and is a reference to the Umayyads who had established their capital there (ed.).
23. This is almost certainly a stab at the first Sunni caliph, Abú Bakr, who was known by the epithet *al-siddíq* (the righteous) (ed.).
24. This again is in all likelihood a stab at the second Sunni caliph, 'Umar ibn al-Khattáb, who was known by the epithet *al-fárúq* (the one who distinguishes truth from falsehood) (ed.).
25. In Islamic tradition, Khidr was a servant of God who had been taught special knowledge and was sent to be a companion and teacher to Moses (see Q 18:65–82). Khidr may not be a reference to a person but, rather, to the inspirational Source.
26. Q 52:4 (ed.).
27. Q 52:5 (ed.).
28. Q 52:6 (ed.)
29. Q 2:185 (ed.)
30. Q 97:1–3.
31. Q 3:7; 13:39; 43:4 (ed.).
32. Q 38:20 (ed.).
33. i.e. the Súrat al-Fátiha, the first sura of the Qur'an (ed.).
34. According to the Qur'an, this is a garment worn by the denizens of Paradise. See Q 76:21; 18:31; 44:53 (ed.).
35. Cf. Q 53:9 (ed.).
36. Seth is named in Genesis as the son of Adam. See Gen. 4:25–5:8. Here, however, the reference to the Companion (*sáhib*) implies that he is the Eternal.
37. Reference to Baghdad.
38. See al-Majlisí 1983, vol. 39, p. 3.

4

Colours in the Writings of the Báb[1]
Vahid Rafati

(Translated by Omid Ghaemmaghami)

Introduction

This article looks at the ways in which colours have been treated in the writings of the Báb. Considering the overwhelming number of tablets and works available, it is goes without saying that the present writer was unable to consult every text. What follows is based on what has been gathered from the most well-known works of the Báb. In an effort to become familiar with the context in which colours have been employed in his writings, we will first briefly consider the treatment of colours in Islamic texts, in particular the Qur'an. Following a cursory study of the topic as presented in Shaykhi texts and the more famous writings of the Báb, we will conclude with a study of the subject in the more well-known writings of the Báb.

Colours mentioned in the Qur'an

The earliest Islamic text in which different colours have been mentioned and discussed is the Qur'an. In this book reference has been made to five different colours: red, green, white, black and yellow. In the 27th verse of Súrat al-Fátir it has been revealed: 'Do you not see how God has sent down water from the sky? With it, We drew forth fruits of varying colours and created white and red streaks in the mountains – (streaks of) varying colours, some intensely black' (Q 35:27).[2] According to this verse, God sent rain down from the sky which caused a variety of fruit of different hues to appear. He also created numerous paths of varying colours – white, red and black. It has been mentioned in the Qur'an that the inhabitants of Paradise shall recline on green-coloured cushions and shall be dressed in green-coloured silk garments: 'Reclining on green cushions and exquisite multicoloured carpets' (Q 55:76); and 'Upon them will be fine green silk and gold embroidery and they will wear bracelets of silver. Their Lord will give them to drink a most pure beverage' (Q 76:21). The same images may also be found in the 31st verse of the 18th sura, Súrat al-Kahf.

On the basis of these verses it can be inferred that in Islam the colour green is the colour of Paradise and is preferred over all other colours. Moreover, as reaching

Paradise is the hope and ardent wish of every believer and since life in Paradise is eternal, the colour green denotes both hopefulness and eternality.

In the Qur'an the colour black stands opposite the colour white. It refers to the infidels (*ahl-i kufr*) who oppose the true believers (*ahl-i ímán*). As the Súrat al-'Imrán states: 'A Day on which (some) faces will turn white and (other) faces will turn black' (Q 3:106). The Muslim exegetes believe that by the faces turning white is meant inner happiness and joy. Likewise, by the faces turning black is meant the sadness that overwhelms a human being. In Persian the expression 'proud of having performed a good deed' (lit. 'to have one's face turn white' or 'to emerge from the water with a white complexion') refers to the sincerity and purity of a person who has been placed in the crucible of tests, whereby he has freed himself from the dross of hate and envy and then emerged from the field of tests pure and sanctified from earthly defilements – a purity which is symbolized as whiteness. The same explanation may be found in the Súrat al-Zumar, where one reads that the faces of those who have lied about God will turn black on the Day of Resurrection (Q 39:60).

In the same manner, the blackening of the face, as a corollary of indignation and rage, has also been alluded to in the Qur'an. For example, the 58th verse of the Súrat al-Nahl states that when Arab men received news that their wives had given birth to a girl, their faces darkened from the intensity of anger (Q 16:58). Therefore in the Qur'an the colour black is a signifier of anger and consternation.

In the Qur'an, the colour white is a sign of faith and belief in God. As such, it stands opposite to black, which is a sign of unbelief and apostasy.

According to the verses of the Qur'an – Súrat Ál-'Imrán – the faces of those who become infidels turn black. They will face a grievous chastisement. In contrast, the faces of those who become believers will be white and they will forever dwell in the light of divine mercy (Q 3:105–7). On the basis of these two verses black is a signifier of punishment and pain, while white is a signifier of grace and joy.

One reads in the Súrat Yúsuf that the eyes of Jacob turned white as a result of his separation from Joseph (Q 12:84). The opinion of the exegetes regarding this verse is that the eyes turning white signifies their having become filled with tears. However, on the basis of this verse the colour white can also be understood as a symbol of 'patience' and 'expectation'. Similarly, in Persian, the expression 'my eyes turned white from gazing at the door' is used when an individual, overwhelmed with grief and worry, sits at home with his eyes glued to the door, in the expectation of someone arriving.

The most famous Quranic phrase that mentions the colour white is 'the white hand' found in the story of Moses' encounter with Pharaoh. This phrase is also found in the Persian language and in works of Persian literature. According to this story, when Moses threw his rod, it transformed into a snake, plain for all to see. Then when he drew out his hand, it was white (see Súrat al-A'ráf, Q 7:108; Súrat Ta Ha, Q 20:22; Súrat al-Shu'ará', Q 26:33; Súrat al-Naml, Q 27:12; Súrat al-Qisas, Q 28:32).

It has been observed in the esoteric commentaries of the Qur'an that the white hand alludes to the evident and manifest proofs that Moses possessed when he came face to face with Pharaoh. Furthermore, white is a symbol of the clarity and intensity of the proofs and evidences of the truthfulness of Moses before the unbelief and waywardness of the Pharaohs.

On the basis of the verses of the Qur'an, the white hand can be said to signify the miracle of Moses. Figuratively, it is a sign of the manifestation of power and dexterity and, likewise, success in completing difficult and arduous tasks.

Furthermore, in the Qur'an white is an attribute of the water of Paradise. This is the water that brims over the springs and whose taste is delectable to its drinkers (see Súrat al-Sáfát, Q 37:46).

The Qur'an also mentions a yellow wind which is the cause of the destruction of trees and the drying up of farm lands. This is the wind that produces the season of autumn (see Súrat al-Rúm, Q 30:51). We observe the same connotation in the 21st verse of the 39th sura, Súrat al-Zumar and the 20th verse of the 57th sura, Súrat al-Hadíd. In these verses we read that God sends rain down from the sky, which causes the springs to billow up with water and the fields to become verdant and green. He then turns the fields yellow. Finally he causes them to become dry. From these verses one can deduce that the colour yellow is a symbol of annihilation and decay and, furthermore, of falling and descent.

In addition to the above verses that mention different colours, there is a reference in the Qur'an's Súrat al-Baqara (Q 2:138) to 'the colour of God': '[We submit to] the colour of God, for who is better than God in colouring? Indeed, we are His worshippers.' In Rághib's *Mufradát*, under the entry for the word 'colour (*sibgh*)', he states:

> Colour (*Sibgh*): The verbal noun (*masdar*) is *al-sabgh* as in 'I coloured' (*sabaghtu*). Other verbal nouns are the aforementioned *al-sibgh* and *al-subúgh*. God's utterance [in the Qur'an], 'the colour of God', alludes to the intellect which God, the Most Exalted, has caused to appear in the human being. The intellect innately distinguishes man from all other animals. Moreover, when a child was born to the Christians, after the seventh day, they immersed him in the water as a form of baptism, claiming that this was a type of colouring. And so, God, the Most Exalted, has mentioned [in the Qur'an 'the colour of God'] and added, 'for who is better than God in colouring?' Elsewhere in the Qur'an, God has said, '... and seasoning for those who eat' [Súrat al-Mu'minín, Q 23:20], that is to say, in order to enhance the taste of their food by adding condiments. This meaning is employed in their saying, 'I have dipped [it] in vinegar' (*asbaghtu bil-khall*) (Al-Rághib al-Isfahání, '*Mu'jam mufradát alfáz al-Qur'an'*, 1972, p. 282).

In their glosses of this verse some of the exegetes of the Qur'an understood the words 'the colour of God' to mean ablutions or divine ritual purification. They interpreted the word 'colour' (*sibgha*) as 'immersion under water or ceremonial cleansing'. They said that this verse refers to the baptism that was common among Christians. Christians believe that as a result of baptism the person who has been baptized formally becomes a Christian and is accounted as one of the faithful. Based on this verse, Muslims believe that faith in God is in and of itself the cause of purification and cleansing, the result of which is the recreation, second birth or faith-birth of an individual. The corollary of the new creation that comes into being as a result of purification is acceptance of the Truth and love for every living person. Therefore by 'colour of God' is meant faith in God and in his religion, or in other words, purity from all manner of impurity and corruption and a return to the essential nature and composition according to which God has created humankind. A similar understanding is found in the Bahá'í writings. For example, in one of the pericopes of the Hidden Words, Bahá'u'lláh states:

> O Children of Vainglory! For a fleeting sovereignty ye have abandoned My imperishable dominion, and have adorned yourselves with the gay livery of the world and made of it your boast. By My beauty! All will I gather beneath the one-coloured covering of the dust and efface all these diverse colours save them that choose My own, and that is purging from every colour (Bahá'u'lláh 1920, p. 395; Bahá'u'lláh 1990, Persian no. 74).

Furthermore, in the Lawh-i Salmán, Bahá'u'lláh, when asked about the meaning of Rumi's couplet, 'Because colourlessness became the captive of colour, Moses waged war on Moses', responded:

> Blessed are they who refuse to become captive to the colours of the world and all that has been created therein and have [instead] attained unto the colour of God, which is to say, they have reached the colour of Truth in this wondrous Dispensation. This station is one of being sanctified from all the varying colours of the world. Save those who have renounced the world, all others are powerless to comprehend this colour. This day, the people of Bahá, who travel on the Ark of Eternity and are wayfarers in the City of Grandeur, recognize each other. Other than these companions, no one else is capable of grasping [this colour] and even if [others] were to comprehend [it], it would be to the same degree in which the blind are capable of apprehending the sun. O Salmán! Say unto men: 'Approach the shores of the everlasting Ocean, so that you may purge yourselves of all colours, attain the Court of the Most Holy, the Most Pure, and [gaze on] the Most Great Beauty.' O Salmán! The different colours of the world have withheld the people from [approaching] the holy shores of the All-Glorious. Consider, for example, the well-known person [i.e. Mírzá Yahyá] who has risen up in conflict [against Me]. I swear by the Day-Star that shines above the horizon of divine mysteries that night and day he circled about Me. At the dawn of every day, as I lay on my bed, he stood before [Me] at its head. The verses of God were shared with him and every day and night he arose to serve Me. When the Cause [of the Báb?] was proclaimed and his name was mentioned, the colour of that name and a love for leadership seized him in such a way that he remained deprived of the holy shores of the Unity of God. By the One in whose Hand is My soul, the like of this person [and his] love of leadership and position has never been seen. By the One who causes all things to proclaim the praise of His own Self! If all the people of the world sought to measure the envy and enmity harboured by him, they would one and all find themselves incapable [of performing such a task]. We implore God to purify his heart, to cause him to return unto Him and to graciously assist him to recognize God, the Powerful, the Exalted, the Mighty.
>
> O Salmán! Behold the Cause of God! One word appears from the Tongue of the Manifestation of the One God and that word was inherently one and has appeared

from one source. But after the dawning of the sun of [that] word from the horizon of the mouth of God over [His] servants, to each soul it manifests itself according to that which he is capable of grasping. For example, in one person [it manifests itself as] denial, to another it is recognition. Likewise, to one person it may be love, to another enmity and the like. Later, this lover and this hater engage in conflict and battle. Colour has stained them both, inasmuch as they were friends and united before the advent of the word but after the dawning of the sun of the word, the true believer was adorned with the colour of God, whilst he who disbelieved, with the colour of self and desire. The dawning of this same divine word has manifested itself in the soul of the true believer with the colour of acceptance and in the soul of the one who disbelieved with the colour of denial. This despite the fact that the essence of the light was immensely above all colours. Behold the sun. Consider how it sheds its light unto mirrors and glasses with (the same) one effulgence and yet in every glass, as is evident and as all have seen, it appears in accordance with the colour of that glass.

Briefly, colour and hue have been made the cause of conflict between the disbeliever and the believer but there is a vast difference between these two colours. One has appeared with the colour of God and the other with the colour of selfish desire. The colour of the true believer and the true seeker has always been the colour of the All-Merciful, whereas the colour of the disbeliever and the hypocrite, the colour of Satan. The former has been the cause and motive for the purification of souls from whatever colour that is not of God. The latter has been the source of the defilement of souls with the various colours of self and passion. The former confers everlasting life, the latter never-ending death. The former guides them who have renounced the world to the river of everlasting life; the latter causes them who are veiled to eat of the infernal tree of evanescence. From the former the fragrance of the All-Merciful continues to waft; from the latter the stenches of Satan . . . (Bahá'u'lláh 1920, pp. 148–51).

It can be deduced from the utterances found in the Lawh-i Salmán that colours consist of all of those things that prevent one from discovering the light of truth or 'the colour of God'. Similar to yellow and red – which are symbols of worldly pursuits – it is possible for colours to become ostentatious and manifest themselves as fame and love for rank and station or as evil passions and corrupt desires. It is in this sense that the Ancient Beauty has said of Hájí Nasír,[3] 'The various, evanescent colours (of the world) did not deter him from (turning to) the Dayspring of the Light of God' (Bahá'u'lláh 1976, p. 210).

Our discussion began with a consideration of the ways in which colours have been employed in the Qur'an, a discussion which led us to the Quranic verse that mentions 'the colour of God'. It must be noted here that despite the limitations of using colours to present the mystical and philosophical thoughts of the Qur'an, in the field of Islamic gnosis, and in particular in the literature produced by the Sufis and, furthermore, in Islamic culture and art, various colours serve to express different meanings. Colours have taken on a far wider range of meanings and connotations than is found in the Qur'an. Each of the colours that have been mentioned in Islamic texts has its own special significance. This significance is either a result of the effect that each colour has on human beings or is the consequence of the spiritual connection that exists between colours and the manner of daily living and the experiences of human beings throughout a lifetime. These two factors cause each colour to acquire its own meaning and connotation and to represent specific conditions, feelings and meanings. By being aware and cognisant of the fact that each colour gives voice to different kinds of thoughts and intellectual and emotional understandings, the matter of appreciating the meanings of colours takes on special significance. What must never be lost sight of is that the meaning of colours varies among different cultures and among diverse peoples. However, in an effort to obtain a general understanding of colours, we present an explanation of the most well-known connotations associated with each colour.

White

In the writings of the Muslim mystics white has been juxtaposed with black and signifies existence. White, moreover, has been described as the station of the Primal Will, the First Intellect, the Primal Point, the Foremost Mystery or that which emanates before all things else from the blackness of the Unseen. In his *Kitáb al-Ta'rifát* (the Book of Definitions), under the entry 'white', Sharíf Jurjání writes:

> White is the First Intellect for it is the centre of the highest heaven and the first [object] which was separated from the blackness of the Unseen. It is the greatest among the lights of His celestial sphere. That is why white has been praised – in order that its whiteness may stand in exact opposite of the blackness of the Unseen and be clearly distinguished by its contrariness and opposition – and because [white] is the first created being, it prefers its existence over its nonexistence. Existence is white and nonexistence is black. Some mystics have said that poverty is white and that all things nonexistent become evident and intelligible in whiteness and all existing things become nonexistent in blackness. By poverty is meant utmost poverty (al-Jurjání 1978, p. 50).

In a tablet revealed in 'Akká and addressed to the Bahá'ís of Khurásán, Bahá'u'lláh, in explaining the source of the primary movement, writes:

> The essence of this movement from the effulgence of the Primal Point – which has been characterized in one sense as the Foremost Mystery, the Primary Ornament and the White Pearl – is manifest and unmistakable. Through him, the fire of Oneness is blazed from the blessed tree[4] (Bahá'u'lláh 1920, p. 268).

In reality, white is an all-pervading light or, rather, the colour of an all-pervading light. Light, which appears essentially to be white, emanates from the sun and is a sign of unity. Colour derives meaning from white light and is capable of manifesting itself. However, in complete blackness, no colour is capable of disclosing itself. Blackness is a symbol for evanescence and is, moreover, the mystery of existence. Owing to its power and brilliance, the light of the sun is impossible to be seen directly and is thus a veil for seeing it itself. Inasmuch as all things are understood with their opposites, one must understand the light of the sun by means of comprehending darkness or view it at a time when the different colours have been separated from one another.

White is a sign of light and, likewise, implies victory, innocence, purity and joy. Moreover, white is a sign of divine power. Since light is diffused everywhere and has ascendancy over blackness, the colour white has been interpreted as divine might. Furthermore, white is 'the world of angels and the habitation of the denizens of the Kingdom on High, about which it has been said,

> Unto God, the Most Exalted, belongs a white land. The procession of the sun on (this land) is thirty times in thirty days, (days) which are just like the days of this world. (It is) filled with creatures who are not aware that anyone on earth has transgressed against God and who do not know that God, the Most Exalted, created Adam and Iblís' (Sajjádí 1975–6, p. 108).

Black

Black is the colour of sorrow and anguish and stands opposite white, the colour of joy and happiness. Since it signifies the nonexistence of the light of colour, the meanings of black are usually the antithesis of white. Blackness is the colour of those forces that oppose and stand in war against light and whiteness. Likewise, it is a symbol of impurity, sin and mourning. Its mystical meanings are associated with annihilation. In similar fashion, black denotes power, calm and abiding tranquillity. According to this understanding, it signifies the motion and agitation that are the products of light.

Green

The colour green is the colour of Paradise, the colour of spring, the colour of eternity, freshness, life and hope. The significance of the colour green and its meanings are very close to the colour blue and at times they are used interchangeably. The colour green is a sign of growth and progress and is also considered a symbol of jealousy.

Red

In the estimation of the mystics, red is the best of colours. It is said that if it were possible to see God, one would see him adorned in a red vesture because red is the colour of the beloved. It is a colour closely connected to the sun and to love. In contrast, the colour yellow is the colour of the disappointed lover.

More than any other colour, red is the generator of movement and emotions in man's being. This colour signifies burning love, heat, energy, fire and emblazonment. The negative connotations associated with this colour include oppression, anger and sin. According to Jurjání's *Ta'rífát*, in Islamic mysticism the colour red and red rubies signify 'the universal soul[5] that has mixed its light with the darkness of attachments of the flesh, contrary to the separated intellect which is considered to be a white pearl' (al-Jurjání 1978, p. 279).

Yellow

After white, yellow is the brightest of colours and is at times employed in place of the former or serves as its proxy. Yellow is a symbol of gold. Just as yellow is the brightest colour, gold is likewise the most valuable metal. Yellow is a sign of the divine love that causes the mind of man to become luminous. Furthermore, yellow signifies vileness, treachery, disloyalty, deceit and deception.

Blue

Blue is the symbol of truth, understanding, divine everlastingness and the eternality of man. In contrast to white, which is the symbol of the very essence of truth, blue refers to that truth which human beings are capable of realizing and which has shed its splendour on humankind. Furthermore, blue is a symbol for love. However, it is less intense and devouring than the burning love symbolized by the colour red. The positive connotations of blue are stability and loyalty, whereas in its negative usages it may symbolize sorrow and gloominess.

These are the general meanings and connotations of colours but it must be kept in mind that these meanings are not presented in a fixed and definite manner. The deductions that can be made from each colour and the various meanings which have been allocated to each are manifold and numerous. One point that must be mentioned is that in the Islamic mystical and philosophical texts four essential colours – red, yellow, green and blue – serve as symbols of the various temperaments, elements, seasons and winds. For example, the colour red is a symbol for the element of fire. Simultaneously, it represents heat, one of the four temperaments. Similarly, red denotes dryness in contrast to humidity. Of the four seasons of the year, red is an indicator of spring. Furthermore, of the four stages of life – i.e. childhood, youth, maturity and old age – red is a symbol for childhood. In the following table the relationships of the four essential colours with the temperaments, elements, seasons, etc. has been specified:

Red	Fire	Hot	Dry	Morning	Spring	Childhood
Yellow	Air	Hot	Humid	Noon	Summer	Youth
Green	Water	Cold	Humid	Evening	Autumn	Maturity
Blue	Earth	Cold	Dry	Night	Winter	Old Age

Now that a summary of the meanings of colours in the Qur'an and Islamic thought has been provided, we are ready to consider the understandings of colours in the more well-known Shaykhi texts and the more famous works of the Báb. Then we will be able to study the topics in the Bahá'í sacred writings.

Colours in the Shaykhi writings

With respect to the meanings of colours in the Shaykhi texts, it must be remembered that in the numerous works written by Shaykh Ahmad Ahsá'í and Sayyid Kázim Rashtí, the meanings and understandings of various colours have been explained in detail. It is clear that a study of the mystical and philosophical meanings of colours in Shaykhi sources, which is in and of itself a vast and extensive topic, requires independent information which is outside the scope of the present article. However, for the purpose of presenting a short account of Shaykh Ahmad's most important views, we will look at what he has written in *Sharh al-Fawá'id*. From there we will consider Sayyid Kázim Rashtí's ideas as presented in his well-known work *Sharh Qasída*.

It bears noting that *Sharh al-Fawá'id* is considered one of the most important works of Shaykh Ahmad.[6] This book was written to explicate and elucidate the themes included in a separate work also written by him and entitled *al-Fawá'id*. The abstruse and cryptic subject matter of this work raised a number of questions in the minds of Shaykh Ahmad's students – questions that were posed to him. As a result, in 1233/1817–18, Shaykh Ahmad wrote *Sharh al-Fawá'id* with the intention of explaining and elucidating the topics he discussed in *al-Fawá'id*. *Sharh al-Fawá'id* is, in reality, a summary and extract of the philosophical and theological beliefs of Shaykh Ahmad. It was published in 1274/1857–8 and includes 18 lessons or *fawá'id* (sing. *fá'ida*).

In the fourth lesson (al-Ahsá'í 1857–8, pp. 61–3) Shaykh Ahmad undertakes a discussion of the four pillars of activity, which he has termed the pillars of the Primal Will, the Divine Purpose, Predestination and Decree. These four pillars are synonymous with four colours, the four pillars of the Throne, the four temperaments and the four archangels. Simultaneously, each of the pillars of activity is associated with one of the four degrees of the realization of matter, i.e. existence, identity, laws and expiration. A summary of this explanation is provided in the following table:

Colours	Pillars of the Throne	Angels	Four Circumstances	Temperaments	Pillars of Activity	Degrees of the Realization of Matter
White	Upper Right	Michael	Sustenance	Cold and Humid	Primal Will	Existence
Yellow	Lower Right	Isráfil	Life	Hot and Humid	Divine Purpose	Identity
Green	Upper Left	'Izrá'íl	Death	Cold and Dry	Predestination	Laws
Red	Lower Left	Gabriel	Creation	Hot and Dry	Decree	Expiration

Sustenance, life, death and creation, which are listed in the fourth column of this table, are derived from the following verse of the Qur'an: 'It is God Who has created you and provided you with sustenance. And it is He who will cause you to die and then grant you a new life'[7] (Súrat al-Rúm, Q 30:40).

Continuing his expositions in *Sharh al-Fawá'id*, in explaining the connection between colours and the stations of the Primal Will, Divine Purpose, Predestination and Decree, Shaykh Ahmad states:

> The light that shone resplendent from the Primal Will was white with the utmost simplicity. This light is a simple sign and thus it is plain. Simplicity requires the colour white . . . The light that emanated from the Divine Purpose was yellow because the Primal Will was white when it emanated from it. The Divine Purpose, which is the reaffirmation of the Primal Will, was stronger in seeking and desiring, while also requiring more heat than the Primal Will. The Divine Purpose was related to the Primal Will which, before its relation to the Divine Purpose, was white. The Divine Purpose projected its heat on that whiteness whose nature, as we have said, is cold and humid. Thus it was yellow in order to change its coldness into heat . . . But the light that emanates from Predestination is green because laws and organizations spring from Predestination. These laws and organizations are numerous. Plurality is black in the same way that simplicity is white . . . The light that emanates from Decree is red because it is composed of the yellow light that emanates from Divine Purpose and from the whiteness of the light that emanates from the Primal Will. It is composed of these two lights with the heat of the preordained ordinance of Decree (al-Ahsá'í 1857, pp. 62–3).

While taking into consideration the 30th verse of the *Súrat al-Rúm*, in a different work, the *Sharh al-Ziyára*, Shaykh Ahmad states that 'the Throne' consists of four pillars. Furthermore, he associates a colour with each pillar and correlates each colour with one of the four attributes of God. He states:

> The Throne consists of four pillars because it is broken up into these four. The All-Merciful established Himself on the red pillar with the attributes of creation and therefrom created all things. He established Himself on the yellow pillar with the attributes of life and therefrom He lent life to all things. The All-Merciful established Himself on the white pillar with the attributes of sustenance and therefrom He provided all things with the means of subsistence. And He established Himself on the green pillar with the attributes of death and therefrom He caused all things to perish (al-Ahsá'í 1850–1, s.v. *'wa ma'dan al-rahma'*).

What has been cited in the works of Shaykh Ahmad Ahsá'í with regard to colours is more or less also reflected in the writings of Sayyid Kázim Rashtí. In his famous work *Sharh Qasída*, Sayyid Kázim explains an important Tradition ascribed to Imam Ja'far al-Sádiq. This Tradition clarifies the relationship between colours and the four pillars of the Throne. The text of this Tradition is as follows:

> It was said to al-Sádiq Ja'far b. Muhammad, 'Why is the Ka'ba quadrangular with four pillars?' He said, 'Because it is face to face with the Frequented Fane,[8] which is quadrangular.' It was said to him: 'Why is the Throne quadrangular?' He said, 'Because it is face to face with the words that Islam has been built on. These are: "Glory be to God", "Praise be to God", "There is no god but the One God" and

"God is Most Great".' The questioner then became silent (al-Rashtí, 1855–6, p. 266).

From this Tradition one may derive the basis for the use of the number four as it relates to the four temperaments, the four colours and the four elements. Similarly, there are four words which comprise the principles of the Islamic affirmation of Divine Unity (*tawhíd*). Since they have desired to promote the principle of the affirmation of the oneness of God in all the worlds, in each world, they believed in four foundational principles; for instance, in the world of nature, in the four essential elements: water, air, earth and fire; in the world of colours, in four colours: white, yellow, green and red; in the world of the heart, in the four pillars: the upper right, the lower right, the upper left and the lower left; and so forth. In *Sharh Qasída*, after citing the above mentioned Tradition, Sayyid Kázim states that having heard the words of the Imam – that since Islam is founded on four principles, the Ka'ba likewise possesses four pillars – the questioner became silent and did not pose any other questions. Sayyid Kázim then continues by saying that if a questioner asks why it is that Islam is founded on four principles, we will respond that these principles are in lieu of the four worlds, i.e. the intellects, the spirits, the souls and the bodies. In other words, the world of intellects is the manifestation of the act of affirming the glory of God (saying glorified be God – *subhán Alláh*), within which there is no mention of the images and limits of the insistent self. The world of spirits is the manifestation of the act of affirming the praise of God (saying praise be to God – *al-hamd li-lláh*). It is the origin of distinguishing all things and their appearance in different forms and images. The world of souls is the manifestation of the act of affirming that there is no god but God (saying there is no god but God – *lá ilah illá Alláh*). In this world, after achieving distinction and individuality, things abandon their egos and lose their arrogance, becoming evidences of the verse: 'So turn in repentance to your Creator and kill your own selves. That will be better for you in the eyes of your Creator' (Súrat al-Baqara, Q 2:54). Finally, the world of corporeal bodies is the manifestation of the act of affirming the greatness of God (saying God is most great – *Alláh akbar*) because, according to Sayyid Kázim, 'Pride and arrogance are among the stations of physical bodies, whilst grandeur is the manifestation of God, glorified is He, in this world' (al-Rashtí, 1855–6, p. 267).

Sayyid Kázim, moreover, continues:

> The four words were in lieu of the four worlds inasmuch as when God, glorified and exalted is He, called the Prophet into being as [His] friend, he fell in a swoon at the feet of the Throne of God and knelt there in prostration for a thousand years. He then regained consciousness. God, glorified and exalted is He, called out to him: 'You are the lover! You are the beloved! You are the heart's desire! You are one who desires! I have created you for the sake of my own self and I have created the world for your sake.' [The Prophet] then bowed down in worship before God, thanking Him. Whilst prostrating, He repeated for a thousand years: 'Glorified be God! Glorified be God!' A white light shone forth from the [Prophet's] glorification of God. It illumined the universe and shed its radiance over all created things. Thereupon, [the Prophet] said: 'Praise be to God.' He continued repeating these words for a thousand years. A bright yellow light shone forth from this remembrance (*al-dhikr*).

It illumined the world with its light. The universe shined brilliantly with this light. Thereupon [the Prophet], may the blessings of God and His salutations be upon him, repeated: 'There is no god but God' for a thousand years. A green light shone forth from this blessed remembrance. It illumined the universe with its light and every living being was filled with it. All things visible and invisible were aglow by its light. Thereupon [the Prophet] repeated, 'God is most great!' for a thousand years. A red light shone forth from this noble remembrance and illumined the universe. All created things were ablaze by its light. Through these four radiant lights and these four sets of words, all created beings were divided, scattered, multiplied, divided [again], separated and brought together in the form that we [presently] observe. The Messenger of God, may the blessings of God and His salutations be upon him, spoke these words in accordance with the four temperaments, each of which is active in its own nature. Through the element of fire the mention of 'God is most great' has been made. Through the element of air the mention of 'Praise be to God' has been made. Through the element of water the mention of 'Glorified be God' has been made. Through the element of earth, the mention of 'There is no god but God' has been made. We have called attention to the feature of structural correspondence in all this (*wa-qad dhakarná wajh al-munásaba fí dhálik*). The elements were four in number. This is due to the fact that when the act of fashioning is associated with that which is fashioned, it results in these temperaments. On the one hand, the action manifests the fire. On the other hand, that which has been fashioned and acted upon manifests the earth. On the one hand, the relationship of the action and the act of fashioning with that which is fashioned manifests air. On the other hand, the relationship of that which has been fashioned and that which has been acted upon with the act of fashioning and action manifests water. By these four [temperaments], the pillars [of the Throne] are erected, the constitution of man is perfected, time and place turn [and change]. By them commands are realized and ages and epochs come to pass. By them the black-eyed maidens (*al-húr*) and [their] palaces are perfected. Indeed, all affairs find their end result in God. It is he who confers divine confirmations. He it is who guides [whomsoever he wills] to the Straight Path (al-Rashtí, 1855–6, p. 267).

Sayyid Kázim's contemplations are summarized in the following table:

Water	White	Intellectuals	Glorified be God!	To affirm (tasbíh)
Air	Yellow	Spirits	Praise be to God!	To affirm (tahmíd)
Earth	Green	Souls	There is no god but God!	To affirm (tahlíl)
Fire	Red	Bodies	God is Most Great!	To affirm (takbír)

Colours in the writings of the Báb

In the writings of the Báb the references to colours are both multifarious and without precedent (*badí'*). Understanding the full scope of their meanings is quite difficult given the complexity of themes, the multitude of texts, the different meanings and tones, and the variety of topics. Since the Báb has drawn attention, in a variety of ways, to an assortment of colours and concepts in his copious books and tablets, here we will content ourselves with undertaking a brief study of the relevant themes in his most important works, such as the Persian Bayán, Tafsír al-Há', Sahífih-yi usúl va furú', Tafsír bismilláh al-rahmán al-rahím and Tafsír súrat wal-'asr. The goal will be to achieve a preliminary introduction to these themes as presented in his writings.

In the Persian Bayán a colour has been designated for each of the four elements that form the existence of man. In the tenth báb of the third váhid of the Persian Bayán, the Báb has written:

> Assume that all are mirrors and the (Primal) Point is the Day-Star of the heavens: If a white mirror is placed before it, the sign of men's hearts is reflected therein; if yellow, the sign of spirits; if green, the sign of souls; if red, the sign of corporeal bodies . . .' (the Báb, Bayán-i Fársí, p. 88).

Similarly, in the 18th báb of the fourth váhid of the Bayán, the Báb states:

> . . . and every year, nineteen souls must take possession, each their own share, of the divine grace and render thanks to their Beloved [for it]. [Wearing] the silk that has been commanded them in the Arabic [Bayán?], they must [seat themselves] on lofty, exquisite and colourful thrones: the first pillar of which shall be white; the second yellow, the third green and the fourth red. They must consume the most cherished and most excellent things, which are a source of honour for the visitors and for themselves, by means of one water. In the eyes of the people of Truth, there has ever been and will continue to be in each of [these acts] an endless number of the symbols of the innermost subtleties . . . ' (the Báb, Bayán-i Fársí, p. 147).

Furthermore, in the fifth báb of the eight váhid, he states:

> It has been decreed that from the Day of the Revelation that is to come until the Day of the next Manifestation (*amr shudih kih dar yawm-i zuhúr tá zuhúr-i dígar*), every soul that is able must collect three diamonds, four yellow garnets, six emeralds and six rubies, [all of which] must in his view be similar [in value] to the first unit. If he is able, let him place these in the shadow of the property of the first váhid. Otherwise, on the Day of the Revelation of Him whom God shall make manifest, at His command they shall be bestowed on His Letters of the Living . . . It behoves those who bring forth proofs of Divine Unity to consider [God's] essence [and] attributes, deeds, acts of worship, creation, the sustenance provided by God, death, life, the glorification of God, the praise of God, the act of affirming His oneness, the utterance of the words 'God is Most Great', fire, air, water, earth, the heart, the

spirit, the soul, the body and the white, yellow, green and red lights [that are found] in the shadows of the letters [in the words], 'In the Name of God, the Inaccessible, the Most Holy' (the Báb, Bayán-i Fársí, p. 285).

What has been mentioned by the Báb in the passage above is presented in the following table:

White	Essence	Creation	Affirming the Glory of God	Fire	Heart	In the Name of	Diamonds
Yellow	Attributes	Sustenance	Affirming the Praise God	Air	Spirit	God	Yellow Garnets
Green	Deeds	Death	Affirming the Unity of God	Water	Soul	The Inaccessible	Emeralds
Red	Worship	Life	Affirming the Greatness of God	Earth	Body	The Most High	Rubies

In the pericopes of the writings of the Báb that elucidate the question of 'the Throne' and provide meanings for it, the divine Throne is described as having four pillars. According to his writings, each of these pillars signifies both one of the names of God and a colour. Furthermore, each pillar denotes one of the various stages of the existent world. A summary of these passages is provided in the following table:

Pillars of the Throne Stage	Name of God	Colour	Stage
The First Pillar	The Superabundant	White	Contingent
The Second Pillar	The Living	Yellow	Actual
The Third Pillar	The Quickener	Green	Potential
The Fourth Pillar	The Killer	Red	Souls and Horizons

In yet another passage, found in Tafsír al-há' (INBA 6010, pp. 231–83), the Báb has divided the seven stages of existence – Primal Will, Divine Purpose, Predestination, Decree, Permission, Term and Book – into two groups. The first group consists of the three stages of the Primal Will, Divine Purpose and Predestination. The Primal Will has been characterized as creating, the Divine Purpose as fashioning and Predestination as devising. The second group consists of the four remaining stages: Decree, Permission, Term and Book. Each of these stages is associated with one of the four elements, colours and causes. A summary is provided in the following table:

The Seven Stages					
Primal Will	Creating				
Divine Purpose	Fashioning				
Predestination	Devising				
Decree	Fire	White	The Primary Cause	Affirming the Glory of God	Life (Creation)
Permission	Air	Yellow	The Material Cause	Affirming the Praise God	Sustenance
Term	Water	Green	The Formal Cause	Declaring there is no god but God	Death
Book	Earth	Red	The Ultimate Cause	Affirming the Greatness of God	Life

The elucidation of these themes in the Báb's Sahífih-yi usúl va furú' (Book of the Principles and Branches (of Religion) shed further light on the subject. In this work, the Báb states:

> Inasmuch as God, the Ancient of Days, has created humankind for the purpose of recognizing His effulgent omnipotence, and has [likewise] ordained reward and punishment as the cause of the same, from nothingness He has called into being the Primal Will – a Will that is ineffable and transcendent – for the sake of His own self. Thereafter, He created all things for the sake of [the Primal Will]. The creation of something which the letters of the Primal Will have entered into is not possible save [in accordance with] the seven stages of existence (*imkán*). A smaller number [of stages] would not be possible. The seven stages are the Primal Will, the Divine Purpose, Predestination, Decree, Permission, Term and Book. The first remembrance of something that is independent of the mention of its subsistence is the existence of the Primal Will. When it becomes dependent, the existence of subsistence is the Divine Purpose. The remembrance of both of these together (i.e. Primal Will and Divine Purpose) is Predestination and the manifestation of these three is the stage of Decree. In this station, it is incumbent upon all created things (*kull mumkinát*) to bear witness to the preexistence of God, glorified is He, the Most Exalted, because there is no beginning after the Decree. The injunctions of Permission, Term and Book after [His] behest (*imdá'*) are firmly established but the truth of fashioning and the mystery of devising *are* the very existence of [all] seven [stages] in the visible and invisible worlds (Mázandárání 1966, vol. 1, pp. 99–100).[9]

In studying the meanings of colours in the writings of the Báb, one must also refer to the commentary revealed by him in interpretation of the verse 'In the Name of God, the Compassionate, the Merciful' (Q 1:1).[10] In this commentary, based on a Tradition narrated by Imam Ja'far al-Sádiq,[11] the Báb draws attention to the four stations of the divine Manifestation in the world of creation. These have been characterized as the four kinds of 'mystery': 1) mystery itself, 2) the mystery of mystery, 3) the mystery hidden in mystery and 4) the mystery masked in mystery.

He has associated each of these four stations with a colour and a letter (The Báb, *Tafsír bismilláh al-rahmán al-rahím*, p. 297). A summary of these points is provided in the following table:

Mystery	Primal Will	Point	Blessed Tree	White	Muhammadan Reality
The Mystery of Mystery	Divine Purpose	Hidden Alif	Burning Bush (the Tree on Mount Sinai)	Yellow	The All-Pervading Guardianship of 'Alí (peace be upon him)
The Mystery Hidden in Mystery	Predestination	Circular Káf	Goodly Tree	Green	Imam Hasan
The Mystery Masked in Mystery	Decree (attested and substantiated)	Bá'	Tree of Benediction	Red	Imam Husayn

In another section of the same commentary, the Báb cites the following Tradition ascribed to the Commander of the Faithful (i.e. Imam 'Alí) regarding Predestination: 'Predestination is a mystery of God and a sanctuary of God that has been hoisted [and concealed] in the veil of God, bearing within itself all things created by God . . .' The Báb then states that the ocean of Divine Predestination has neither beginning nor end. In describing this ocean, he continues:

> It has islands [surrounded] by water that melts and freezes. There are shrines on the islands, the domes of which are made from different and colourful gems of different hues, endless [in number]. God has prescribed the width of each dome. He has fashioned everything that exists between one dome and the next dome – all that may exist between the dawning-place of the Beginning to the setting-place of the End (The Báb, *Tafsír bismilláh al-rahmán al-rahím*, p. 318).

Following this discussion the Báb mentions four domed shrines, within each of which dwell a group of angels engaged in the praise and glorification of God. He affirms that by means of these angels God has granted that which is the right (*haqq*) of every deserving person, just as the Qur'an states: 'It is God who hast created you and provided you with sustenance. And it is He who will cause you to die and then grant you a new life' (Súrat al-Rúm, Q 30:40). After citing this verse, the Báb associates the bestowal of sustenance, life and death with each of the four angels, in the following manner:

> All that exists in creation are among the inhabitants of the white domed shrine; sustenance is among the inhabitants of the yellow shrine, life is among the inhabitants of the green shrine, and death is among the inhabitants of the red shrine. Such is the decree of the Almighty, the All-Wise (The Báb, *Tafsír bismilláh al-rahmán al-rahím*, p. 319).

Angels of the Highest Heaven	They glorify God	White Dome	Creation
Celestial Angels	They praise God	Yellow Dome	Sustenance
Angels Hidden Beyond the Veil	They affirm that there is no god but God	Green Dome	Life
Archangels	They affirm the greatness of God	Red Dome	Death

Amongst the other important works of the Báb that include insights into the meaning of colours is the Tafsír (or Súrat) wal-'Asr.[12] This commentary was revealed in Isfahan in honour of the Imam Jum'a of that city, Sayyid Muhammad Sulán al-'Ulamá' Isfahani. In the Qur'an, Súrat wal-'Asr is composed of 72 letters. In his commentary on this sura, the Báb has offered an interpretation for each of these 72 letters. He explained and expounded on the contents of the sura. In his interpretation of the 15th letter (the letter *nún*), the Báb states:

> The fifteenth letter is the letter *nún* [which represents] the light of the colour white from which every white thing received its colour in [its] potential stage. Thereafter, [one finds] the colour yellow from which everything turns yellow in [its] potential stage. Then, [one finds] the colour green from which everything in the heavens and the earth is made green in accordance with the desire of God, the All-Merciful and is revealed in the Qur'an [lit. the Criterion]. And then [one finds] the colour red from which all things in the mystery of [their] potential stage are made red (The Báb, *Tafsír wal-'Asr*, p. 24).

In His commentary on the 26th letter (the letter *lám*), the Báb draws attention to the four pillars of the Throne. He states that the colour of the first pillar is white, the second pillar yellow, the third pillar green and the fourth pillar red (The Báb, *Tafsír wal-'Asr*, p. 27). Later, in his commentary on the 29th letter (the letter *nún*), he alludes to four lights and relates each light to one of the divine attributes (The Báb, *Tafsír wal-'Asr*, p. 29). These themes may be summarized in the following manner:

Worlds	Attributes	Lights	Colours	Pillars of the Throne
Contingent (*imkán*)	Glorification	Light of Creation	White	First Pillar
Potential (*a'yán*)	Praise	Light of Origination	Yellow	Second Pillar
The Heavens and the Earth	Uttering the words, 'There is no god but God'	Light of Formation	Green	Third Pillar
The Mystery of the Contingent World in the Potential world	Uttering the words, 'God is most great'	Light of Glory	Red	Fourth Pillar

With this brief introduction to the role of colours in the writings of the Báb we can begin to understand the way in which the unity of the world and humanity is conceptualized and taught by him. On the one hand, the discourse derives from the long and rich history of Islamic thought; on the other, his own teachings are obvious departures from that tradition.

Bibliography

Al-Ahsá'í, Shaykh Ahmad. *Sharh al-Fawá'id*. Tabriz: 1274 AH/1857–8.

— *Sharh al-Ziyára*. Tehran: 1267 AH/1850–1.

The Báb. *Bayán-i Fársí*. n.l.: n.p., n.d.

— *Tafsír bismilláh al-rahmán al-rahím*. In INBA (Iranian National Bahá'í Archives) 6014.

— *Tafsír al-há'*. In INBA 6010.

— *Tafsír wal-'Asr*. In INBA 4005.

Bahá'u'lláh. *al-Kalimát al-Maknúna* (*The Hidden Words*). Rio de Janeiro: Editora Baha'i [sic]-Brasil, 152 BE/1995.

— *Majmu'ih-yi alváh-i mubárakih*. Cairo: Sa'ádat, 1920.

— *Majmu'ih-yi alváh mubárakih-yi hadrat-i Bahá'u'lláh 'aksbardárí shudih az rúyi khatt-i 'Alí-Ashraf Láhíjání* ('Andalíb). Tehran: Mu'assasih-yi Millí-i Matbú'át-i Amrí, 132 BE/1976.

Faydí, Muhammad 'Alí. *La'áli'-i Dirakhshán*. Tehran: Mu'assasih-yi Millí-yi Matbú'át-i Amrí, 123 BE/1967.

Hamid, Idris Samawi. *The Metaphysics and Cosmology of Process According to Shaykh Ahmad al-Ahsa'i: Critical Edition, Translation, and Analysis of Observations in Wisdom*. Unpublished Ph.D. diss. State University of New York at Buffalo, 1998.

Iranian National Bahá'í Archives (INBA).

Al-Jurjání, al-Sharíf. *Kitáb al-ta'rífát*. Beirut: Maktabat Lubnán, 1978.

Lawson, B. Todd. *The Qur'an Commentary of Sayyid 'Alí Muhammad, the Báb*. Unpublished Ph.D. diss., McGill University, 1987.

Mázandárání, Fádil. *Amr va Khalq*. Tehran: Mu'assasih-yi Millí-i Matbú'át-i Amrí, 122 BE/1966.

Al-Rághib al-Isfahání. *Mu'jam mufradát alfáz al-Qur'an*. Beirut: Dar al-Kitáb al-'Arabí, 1972.

Al-Rashtí, Sayyid Kázim. *Sharh Qasída*. Tabriz: n.p., 1272 AH/1855–6.

Sajjádí, Sayyid Ja'far. *Farhang-i lughát va istiláhát va ta'bírát-i 'irfání*. 2nd ed. Tehran: Tuhúrí, 1354 AH/1975–6.

Notes

1. This is a translation of the first half of Vahid Rafati's short book '*Alván dar Áthár-i Bahá'í*' (Dundas, Ontario: Persian Institute for Bahá'í Studies, 144 BE/1988). The translation covers pages 5 to 32 of the original, with accompanying endnotes. A translation of the second part of the book is forthcoming by Farshid Kazemi and Omid Ghaemmaghami.
2. This and other verses from the Qur'an have been translated by consulting previous translations.

3. For biographical information on him, see Faydí 1997, pp. 141–3.
4. On 'the blessed Tree', see Q 24:35.
5. Cf. the psyche of Plotinus.
6. This important work has been discussed by Henry Corbin in his magisterial *En Islam iranien* (q.v. index (vol. iv)): Ahmad Ahsa'i (Shaykh), les *Fawá'id*. See also the interesting and useful recent study by Idris Samawi Hamid, *The Metaphysics and Cosmology of Process According to Shaykh Ahmad al-Ahsa'i: Critical Edition, Translation, and Analysis of Observations in Wisdom* (ed.).
7. Although creation comes before daily sustenance in this verse, in his *Sharh al-Fawá'id*, Shaykh Ahmad has given precedence to daily sustenance over life. However, as will soon be demonstrated, the same order that one finds in this Quranic verse has been preserved in the writings of the Báb.
8. See Qur'an 52:4. In Islamic mystical thought, the Frequented Fane (*al-bayt al-ma'múr*) refers to a house that serves as a mosque for the angels. It is situated in the fourth heaven and faces the Ka'ba in Mecca.
9. In his earlier Tafsír súrat al-baqara the Báb quotes, among several others, this well-known hadith from the sixth Imam, Ja'far al-Sádiq: 'Nothing exists in the earth or in heaven except through these seven stages: Will, Purpose, Destiny, Decree, Permission, Book, and Fate. Whoever imagines that he can do without any one of these has committed unbelief.' Translated in Lawson, *The Qur'an Commentary of Sayyid 'Ali Muhammad, the Bab*, p. 148 (ed.).
10. Also found at the heading of every other sura of the Qur'an with the exception of the ninth, Súrat al-Tawba. The Báb's commentary on this verse, Tafsír bismilláh al-rahmán al-rahím, is 372 pages in length and can be found in INBA 6014.
11. This hadith has been cited by Shaykh Ahmad al-Ahsá'í in his book *Sharh al-Fawá'id* under the heading of the third *fá'ida*, as follows: 'Truly, our Cause is the Truth and the Truth of the Truth. It is the exoteric and the esoteric of the exoteric and the esoteric of the esoteric. It is the secret and the secret of the secret, a secret that is enveloped in the secret, and a secret that is veiled (*muqanna'*) in the secret. [A different] narration [of this hadith] has "a secret that is shrouded (*mujallal*) in the secret". The meaning of *mujallal* and *muqanna'* is one and the same' (al-Ahsá'í 1857–8, p. 42).
12. The Báb's commentary on the Qur'an's Súrat wal-'Asr, Tafsír wal-'Asr, can be found in INBA 4005. It was transcribed (in the month of Mashíyyat 132 BE/1976 CE) using a manuscript available in the library of Cambridge University.

5

A Grammar of the Divine:
Solecisms in the Arabic Writings of the Báb and
His Thoughts on Arabic Grammar

William F. McCants

The Báb's Muslim detractors have frequently criticized his Arabic grammar and, consequently, it has been a major subject of Bahá'í apologetics.[1] Despite the amount of ink that has been spilled over the subject, there has been no systematic study of the nature of the Báb's violations of the norms of Arabic grammar or what he thought about the subject. I have written the following survey of the Báb's Arabic prose and prepared a semi-critical edition of his Risála fí al-nahw wa al-sarf (A Treatise on Grammar) as a first step towards filling these lacunae.

The Báb's Arabic prose: Setting up the debate

Muslims who are critical of the Báb's Arabic rightly assert that he makes elementary grammatical errors. They adduce this as proof that he did not know the language and use it to impugn his revelatory claims (see below). Some Bahá'ís counter that he did not make errors but was writing according to a new grammar.[2] I would like to begin this survey by offering an observation that invalidates both positions: the Báb often wrote very conventional, standard Arabic prose. Once this is acknowledged, it brings up a more interesting question: If the Báb could write in standard Arabic, why did he frequently not do so?

Before answering this question I want to say a few words about why such a fuss is made over the Báb's Arabic grammar since people in the West who speak English may not appreciate the linguistic importance of the subject to those translating the Báb's Arabic into English or the religious significance of the subject for Muslims. The Arabic language relies on syntax (word order) and case endings to convey meaning. English speakers are very familiar with syntax; without it, the English language falls apart. For example, try to make sense of the following sentence in which the word order has been jumbled up: 'intention ordered to speaker's order some human language the certain to need idea by intention minds be conventions in have of' ('Human minds need language to be ordered by certain conventions in order to have some idea of the speaker's intention.'). However, English speakers are not that familiar with case endings or endings attached to non-verbal elements in the sentence that indicate their grammatical function. We have a few remnants of this; for example, the difference between 'who' and 'whom'. 'Who' is the subject of a sentence and 'whom' is the direct object or the object of a preposition. Even this distinction is fading fast, driving English teachers insane. Case endings are of such little importance in English that if you say 'who' for 'whom' people will understand what you are talking about. For example, which of these sounds better to your ear: 'Whom did you see last night?' or 'Who did you see last night?' The first is grammatically correct and the second is not but the second sounds better because that is how we speak in everyday language. So while there are a few remnants of case endings in English, by and large we can do without them.

Not so in some other languages. For example, German would collapse without case endings. This makes it really difficult for foreigners to learn but it also means that the language offers a lot of flexibility in terms of syntax; the subject can precede the verb or vice versa and the direct object can pop up almost anywhere. However, people proficient in the language would never be confused because the case ending attached to a word would indicate its grammatical function. The same goes for Arabic. If you put the wrong case ending on a word, it can render the sentence nonsensical.

The Báb's writings are full of incorrect case endings, which sometimes render a sentence unintelligible or difficult to understand. They are also full of other irregularities, particularly incorrect noun-adjective agreement and incorrect genitive constructions. These last two irregularities do not significantly affect the meaning of the sentence but do suggest that the author did not have a grasp of the basics of Arabic grammar. So why are there so many grammatical errors in the Arabic writings of the Báb?

It's the scribes' fault

At the time when the Báb was writing, the use of the printing press was not very widespread in Iran.[3] Therefore his writings were 'published' the old-fashioned way: people copied them by hand. Of course, copying something by hand is a lot more error-prone than using a printing press or making a photocopy. The scribe's eyes could inadvertently skip a line or misread a word when making a copy of the original manuscript, whether written by the Báb or his amanuensis. Now imagine that a different scribe makes a copy of this copy. He is prone to the same errors, as well as passing on any of the errors that the original copyist made. If he is unscrupulous (or perhaps unthinking), he might change a word or phrase to make it sound better. If he is really misbehaving, he will change the whole sense of a word, phrase or more to suit his own agenda. In this world of hand-copied manuscripts, it is easy to imagine that grammatical errors would be introduced into manuscripts of the Báb's writings.

This certainly happened (see the introduction to the Báb's Risála below) and the Báb himself complained of it.[4] But it does not explain all the grammatical errors in the Báb's writings. First, we can collect all the later manuscripts of a work, compare them and, with some precision, discern which errors were introduced by copyists and which were the Báb's own doing. One of the most well-attested and best-preserved of the Báb's works, the Qayyúm al-Asmá', has many grammatical errors.[5] Possibly the most frequent of these is that adjectives do not agree in gender with the nouns they modify. This is a very basic rule in Arabic, as it is in some European languages (Spanish, for instance). In sura 39, for example, the Báb writes *al-kalima al-'azím*, which is incorrect. However, it is also important to note that he does not consistently break this basic Arabic rule; for example, in sura 28 he writes the phrase properly as *al-kalima al-'azíma*. I will return to this point later.

In addition to the errors in manuscript copies of the Báb's writings, we have several texts in the Báb's own handwriting that contain grammatical errors. For example, in a letter to Mullá 'Abd al-Kháliq Yazdí, a Shaykhi leader who became a Bábí, the Báb writes the phrase *fí kitáb muhkam wa áyát mutqan*. The adjective following *áyát* should be *mutqana* (or, for a more Quranic flavour, *mutqanát*), to agree with the feminine gender of the preceding noun, *áyát*.[6] Of course, in this example the Báb may have been exercising poetic licence by writing *mutqan* rather than *mutqana* in order to rhyme with the adjective *muhkam*; but recognizing that he used poetic licence (see below) does not invalidate the larger point that he is sometimes solely responsible for the solecisms that appear in his writings.

In summary, it is very likely that a number of grammatical errors in the Báb's writings were introduced by later scribes. But since these errors are also found in well-attested manuscripts of his writings and works written in his own hand, the question still stands: Why are there so many grammatical errors in the Arabic writings of the Báb?

He was uneducated

This is the most obvious answer. The Báb was a Persian merchant with little formal education, so it is no surprise that his Arabic prose is full of errors. Some of his errors, like the last one mentioned, even exhibit the influence of his native Persian on his Arabic prose, indicating that he did not have command of the foreign language. Western academics studying the Báb would not make much of this, but Shi'i Muslims do. This is because they expect that someone speaking the literal words of God to have good grammar. If the words imputed to God (or an Arab imam) are not eloquent, then they obviously cannot be from him, since he would not speak like an imbecile. Of course, there is the contentious issue of what constitutes 'eloquent' but most Muslims would maintain that God's words must at least conform to the very basic grammatical rules; otherwise, God would be speaking gibberish. And why would God speak gibberish if he wants people to know and obey his Will (you cannot know his Will if his words do not make sense)?

I think it is perfectly reasonable to believe that the Báb did not have a good command of Arabic because he was uneducated, although I am not interested in drawing any theological conclusions from that. Certainly, if God so desires, he can speak through uneducated merchants as well as refined nobles and literati. However, this position is untenable because there are examples of the Báb's prose written in very standard Arabic. For example, in his private letters to Shaykh Salmán and his uncle Khál-i Akbar, written in his own hand, there are no obvious errors in syntax or declension (copies of the letters are reproduced in Afnan 2000, pp. 91–8). There are two irregularities in morphology – *al-nabawiyyún* instead of *al-nabiyyún* (see ibid. pp. 94, 98) and *takhtír* instead of *takhtár* (see ibid. pp. 92, 94) – but in other writings he uses the correct form of these words; besides, they do not impinge a great deal on the meaning of the passages.

In addition to many examples of standard Arabic written by the Báb, there are also instances of him quoting grammatical rules, so he was certainly familiar with the basics of the language. In a letter to a certain 'Isfahání' he quotes the rules on case endings in a statement attributed to 'Alí: 'Every subject is nominative, every object of a verbal clause is accusative, and every second term of a genitive construct is genitive' (cited in Rafati, '*Nigáhí*', *Khúshih-há*, vol. 1, p. 66.). All of this demonstrates that the Báb knew the basic rules of Arabic and often wrote according to these rules. Therefore, if the Báb could write in standard Arabic, why did he often not do so?

He wanted to create a new grammar of Arabic

This is a position that is often put forward by some Bahá'ís and it arises from statements like this from the Báb:

> Should someone criticize my use of vocalization or textual readings or Arabic grammar, I would reject their criticism. For such (grammatical) rules are based on the verses, not vice versa. It cannot be doubted that he has rejected for himself all such rules and the learning that is based on them. Indeed, in the eyes of thinking people, no proof is greater than being ignorant of such rules, when ignorance is combined with the ability to reveal such words and verses as these. This is because the fruit of these sciences is (real) understanding of God's Book, although it is quite unnecessary for the Tree on which the Book of God in person has alighted to have the slightest knowledge of them (the Báb, Persian Bayán 2:1 [provisional translation by Denis MacEoin].

The basic argument goes that the Báb only ostensibly violated the norms of Arabic grammar. What he was actually doing was adhering to new rules of Arabic grammar. Therefore he was not breaking the rules of the language because he was playing by his own rules, which should now be the new standard of the language, much like the Qur'an was the standard for the Arabic language. Proponents of this position go so far as to argue that if we systematically study and collect the grammatical irregularities of the Báb, we can discern this new grammar and spell it out explicitly.

Like the preceding position, this argument ignores the fact that the Báb often wrote in standard Arabic and was conversant with basic grammatical rules. So what is to be the standard: when he violates a rule or when he adheres to it? Moreover, this position also fails to note that the Báb was not consistent in the ways in which he violated Arabic grammar (see the example above for his inconsistent rendering of *al-kalima al-'azím*). If he were consistent, then people could certainly create a new grammar of the Arabic language based on his systematic violations of grammatical rules, which would then become the new norm. However, his lack of consistency makes this impossible. Therefore, if the aim of the Báb were to create a new grammar of Arabic, he failed miserably. If, however, that was not his aim, then why did he frequently violate the rules of Arabic grammar?

Having outlined some of the standard answers to this question, I will now offer some of my own. Unlike the foregoing answers, I believe the following theories are plausible in light of the data, though at this stage in our study of the Báb's writings it is impossible to rule one out in favour of another. Like any good theory, each accounts for the same set of data and there is no contradictory evidence so far available that would invalidate them. To summarize, here is the data:

1) The Báb frequently violates the rules of Arabic grammar.
2) Many of these violations are elementary mistakes.
3) These violations are not consistent.
4) The Báb often wrote in standard Arabic.

With all this in mind, here are several theories that can explain this data.

Revelation as extemporaneous poetic performance

The Báb prided himself on his ability to write or dictate his letters and treatises very rapidly and without forethought. He frequently cites this ability to write *bil-fitra* – extemporaneously or according to the promptings of one's innate nature – as a proof of his mission (he is unlearned but can say learned things without forethought; see, for example, his al-Sahífa al-dhahabiyya) and as a way to deny any claims when put to the question ('I don't claim to be a Báb of the Hidden Imam – my pen may have said that but I'm just writing according to my *fitra*.').[7] Perhaps when the Báb was in the throes of his revelatory experiences he did not pay much attention to the niceties of grammar since he was writing or dictating so rapidly. This kind of ecstatic writing is similar to extemporaneous spoken-word poetry in which the poet does away with grammar for the sake of rhythm, rhyme and conveying raw emotion unencumbered by the normal rules of language. The poet has some feeling or thought and she expresses it as forcefully and lyrically as possible, sometimes bending the language, either consciously or unconsciously, to serve her message and using rhythm and rhyme to heighten the listening experience and, consequently, the impact of the message.[8] The Báb may have gone through a similar process during his revelatory experiences (see the *mutqan* discussion above for one example).

Grammatical errors as mimicry of the Qur'an

On the other hand, the Báb's violation of grammatical rules, particularly rules governing case endings, is reminiscent of similar irregularities that occur in the Qur'an.[9] For Muhammad, there was no fixed grammatical standard by which to abide; rather, the Qur'an was the first extended work in Arabic and it became a model for the development of the language. However, when grammarians applied their rules to the Qur'an, the text was not always agreeable. Therefore they went to some lengths to try to explain why a word that had the correct case in several instances was suddenly improperly declined in a similar grammatical position, rather than accept that Muhammad might not have always been consistent.

Even though Muhammad was fairly consistent, his few inconsistencies are excusable since no standard existed at that time. The Báb, on the other hand, was certainly aware of the rules of grammar that had been the standard for over a thousand years. In the letter to 'Isfahání' mentioned above, he demonstrates a knowledge of the basic rules for Arabic case endings. Despite this, the Báb frequently violates them. But, as pointed out above, so does Muhammad, although with less frequency. Therefore perhaps the Báb deliberately violated some of the rules of Arabic grammar to further enhance the Quranic flavour of his *áyát* or 'verses'. Indeed, *áyát* is the Báb's name for a mode of writing that was purposefully patterned on the Qur'an and he defends his solecisms by referring to similar solecisms in the Qur'an:

> And now regarding some of the passages in which words have been altered or have flowed in contradiction to the grammatical rules of the people of veils: It is so that people will be certain that the author of these passages did not come to them by borrowing verses and scholarly knowledge. Rather, by the light of God his breast was dilated with the divine sciences. The ruling on altering [words] (Q 10:64) was rescinded by a new mode [of writing] and the prohibition on contradicting grammar was rescinded by a divine grammar. Thus innumerable words like those in the Book of God have been revealed. For example, the Lord of the world revealed a masculine pronoun for a word that is feminine when He says, 'word [f.] from him is his [m.] name, the Messiah.' (Q 3:45). And He, glorified and lofty, has revealed a feminine adjective in the phrase 'one [f.] of the calamities' in 'Verily, it is one [f.] of the calamities as a warning [m.] to humans' (Q 74:36-7). He has given permission for a divine grammar for anyone who wants it – for those among you who want to advance, meaning through the divine grammar, or lag behind, meaning through the grammar of the people, since they are an evil and ignorant folk. Moreover, He revealed these words contrary to the grammar of all people of knowledge: 'Verily, they are two magicians.' (Q 20:63)[10] On account of this, every person of certitude realizes that the basis of creating verbal expressions is the decree of God, not the invention of those who are not of the people of the Bayán. In like manner, as the worlds develop, words and their declension also develop. Close is the day on which it will be recognized that the verses of God are to be recited contrary to the technical grammar and declension current among the people.[11]

Similarly, he chastises Mírzá Bábá (d. 1869),[12] the leader of the Dhahabiyya Sufi order, for criticizing his grammar:

> O one gazing upon the effulgences of the heaven of paradise. Do not belittle my cause for the power behind the effulgences encompasses it. Despite your attempt to write two lines at the end of your letter – one of which was simply a verse from

the Qur'an and the other jumbled and ineloquent – only two letters of it are truly eloquent and even that word is not [written] according to innate nature (*al-fitra*) alone. Verily, the solecisms in speech and the lack of cohesion you mention are due to the ignorance of the people, just as the eloquent among the Arabs said previously that *al-qistás*, *al-tannúr* and *al-sijjíl*[13] are foreign words, that some words are stories of the ancients, and that what is between the verse 'And heaven – He raised it up and set the balance' (Q 55:7) are not outwardly congruous. Verily, they were revealed contrary to Arabic grammar, like his saying 'A word from him is his name, the Messiah' (Q 3:45); 'Verily, it is one of the calamities' (Q 74:36–7); and 'Verily, they are two magicians' (Q 20:63). They all disbelieved in God on account of what they said because the balance is what God revealed in the Qur'an, not the idle fancy of the transgressors today. Verily, today the Persian ulama certainly have no innate eloquence like the Arabs. When they say the things they say, there is nothing wondrous in their speech. The difference is that they now believe in the verses and those who mocked the verses in the early days of Islam disbelieved in them.[14]

These explanations notwithstanding, the Báb does not confine his solecisms to works that he classifies as 'verses'. Therefore, although he may have broken grammatical rules to enhance the Quranic flavour of his 'verses', he nonetheless carried this practice into his other modes of writing.

Violations of grammar as subversion and touchstone

One final explanation for the Báb's violations of Arabic grammar is that he was subverting the accepted standards and markers of learning. As in any literate culture, the first indicator of true learning is the mastery of the conventions of language. In the Báb's cultural milieu, this meant a command of Arabic, the language of the Qur'an. If someone could not articulate themselves well or foundered on the rudiments of the language, then what insight could he possibly have into deeper subjects?

Like so many other aspects of his religion, perhaps the Báb deliberately violated the norms of grammar in order to put off people who could not see past the surface of words and appreciate the deeper significance of his message. Contemporary poets and authors thrive on this subversion of expectations and assumptions and are happy to have critics characterize their work as unconventional gobbledygook while those who 'get it' savour the significance that has eluded the guardians of literary tradition. Indeed, unlike much of the pre-modern period, violating conventions is often heralded today as a mark of genius, not ignorance. It is also a way to thumb your nose at the guardians of tradition, as if to say, 'I have violated your conventions so that you will see that I have little regard for them. The persnickety pedants will obsess over these things and only those who are worthy, those who can see past the violations of linguistic norms, will appreciate what I am saying.' Perhaps the Báb had something of this in mind when he violated the very elementary rules of the Arabic language.

From the foregoing readers might conclude that the study of Arabic grammar is an unnecessary prelude to a study of the Báb's writings. This is not the case. As pointed out above, much of the Báb's Arabic prose is quite standard and could only be understood by someone versed in the norms of grammar. An understanding of even the Báb's grammatical irregularities requires a firm foundation in Arabic grammar; otherwise, the reader might be misled by an improper case ending and put something in the mouth of the Báb that he did not intend. Further, a basic knowledge of Arabic grammar is necessary to understand the Báb's neologisms (a subject that is beyond the scope of this essay). Finally, much of the Báb's metaphysical terminology is derived from Shaykh Ahmad, who developed many of his metaphysical ideas by contemplating the operations of Arabic grammar (see below).

Having argued that the Báb was quite capable of writing standard Arabic and knew the rudiments of Arabic grammar, I posed a new question and offered several possible solutions. However, these solutions are not conclusive because the pool of data is currently so small. One method of inquiry that might yield data that will give more weight to one theory over another is to determine the frequency of grammatical violations in the Arabic writings of the Báb. I have already pointed out that there are no egregious errors in his letters to several individuals, two of which are addressed to his uncle, but that there are a large number in the Qayyúm al-Asmá'. Is the mode of writing related to the frequency of errors? I have suggested that errors are found not only in his mode of 'verses' but also in other modes, so perhaps the mimicry of the Qur'an theory is not a satisfying explanation. Further, does the frequency go up or down depending on his audience? If the errors are more frequent in works addressed to men of learning, perhaps this would lend credence to the subversion theory. Finally, are most of the errors committed in the interest of rhythm and sound? This would give more support to the performance theory. Perhaps it is a mixture of all three, as the Báb himself weaves together innate eloquence, subversion and mimicry in his arguments for scriptural authenticity. No matter the ultimate conclusion, we can confidently say at this point that the Báb was neither ignorant of the rules of Arabic grammar nor seeking to create them anew.

Introduction to the Báb's Risála fí al-nahw wa al-sarf (A Treatise on Grammar)

Now that we have some sense of the nature of the Báb's violations of Arabic grammar, we are ready to explore what he thought about the subject. To this end I have made a semi-critical edition of the Báb's Risála fí al-nahw wa al-sarf (A Treatise on Grammar). Even though the Báb gave the treatise this title, he does so ironically since he says very little about the discipline and characterizes it as second-order knowledge compared to contemplation of the rules governing God's interaction with His creation. However, when describing the latter the Báb uses the terminology of the former. Sometimes he does so jokingly, making puns out of words that have both a metaphysical and grammatical meaning in order to drive home his point that study of subjects like the declension of a noun (*i'ráb al-ism*) pale in comparison to contemplation of the appearance of the Name (*i'ráb al-ism*). At other times the use of words with these dual meanings is meant to highlight the fundamentally linguistic nature of God's interaction with the world.

The English word 'grammar' neatly conveys the various shades of meaning that are implicit in the Báb's discussion of the subject. On one level grammar is a system of rules that govern the formation of words (morphology) and their arrangement into units of meaning (syntax). On another a 'grammar' is the basic principles of any branch of knowledge. In this sense we can talk about a grammar of music or a grammar of geography. Although in this treatise the Báb does talk about grammar in the first sense of the word, he is primarily interested in the second sense: namely, the principles governing God's interaction with the world. Therefore the Báb delineates what might be called a grammar of the divine.

As I hope to show, the Báb's delineation of a grammar of the divine draws heavily on Shaykh Ahmad's theories on the linguistic nature of the operation of God's Will in the world. Therefore a proper treatment of our text would compare the works of the two men on this subject. However, not enough is known about Shaykh Ahmad's metaphysical grammar to comment intelligently on the Báb's discussion and almost nothing of the Báb's voluminous writings have been published and exist only in manuscripts that are not available for research.[15] Thus my semi-critical edition of his treatise on grammar meets this final need and offers a translation and gloss of the text to serve as a building block for future studies of the Báb's ideas on the linguistic nature of divine self-disclosure.

The purpose of creating a critical edition is to produce a version of a text that most closely resembles what the author wrote. Of course, if an autograph (a copy of the text in the author's own hand) can be found, then the job of the editor is fairly straightforward: just reproduce the text. However, there may be several copies of the same text written by the author and the editor would have to determine which one represents the final form of the text as the author intended it. While it is useful to compare it with earlier autographs, the base text (the text that is deemed to be most reliable and is reproduced in the critical edition) should reflect the author's final work on the subject.[16]

Given the current resources of the modern Bahá'í community and its general lack of enthusiasm for the creation of critical editions, researchers are not likely to have access to autograph manuscripts, either for viewing in a safe, archival environment or in colour reproduction. Therefore they must rely on manuscript copies by various scribes. Here too the task is daunting since many of these manuscripts are also inaccessible. Those that are accessible are usually in private hands and are photocopies of photocopies, *ad infinitum*. Further, unless the scribe dates his transcription, researchers have no tools available to aid them in guessing the approximate age of the text, such as the nature of the manuscript paper, types of inks and analyses of scribal handwriting. Dating is crucial in the preparation of a critical edition since the goal of the editor is to reproduce the original version of the text, which is most likely the earliest one (unless the author made changes, as detailed above). Based on dating and family resemblances between manuscripts (i.e. certain groups of manuscripts share common scribal errors), one could then determine the genealogical relationship among the various manuscript traditions and work back to the original text as written by the author.

Owing to this lack of resources, most prospective editors of Bábí and Bahá'í texts must be satisfied for the time being with the prefix of 'semi' to their critical editions and adopt a rather primitive procedure. Theoretically, the editor must gather as many manuscript copies as possible and then, after reading each of them thoroughly, designate the oldest manuscript as the base text. The general assumption is that there will be fewer lacunae and scribal errors in a manuscript that was transcribed soon after the original was written. Variants between this text and later manuscripts will then be recorded in the notes, and commentary on the text and explanation of obscure terms are confined to the introduction and translation.[17]

In practice, one of the secondary manuscripts that was transcribed at a later date might better preserve a particular passage than one found in the manuscript designated as the base text. A judicious editor should use the better-preserved passage in the main text of the critical edition and note that the base text contains something different. The measure of a successful critical edition is not its faithfulness to a single manuscript. Rather, the reader should be able to look at the critical edition and the accompanying apparatus and recreate every single manuscript that has been consulted in the preparation of the text (Carter 1995, pp. 570–1). In preparing the critical edition of the Báb's Risála, I have primarily reproduced the oldest manuscript (see below) but I have used variants from a later manuscript if a word in the older manuscript is an obvious error. All the variants are found in the notes. As for the one or two cases of lacunae where a portion is obviously missing from the older manuscript but is preserved in the later one, I have filled the gap in the critical edition with the passage from the later text and enclosed it in brackets.

Finally, a special word of caution for editors of works by the Báb. Morphological or syntactical errors in early manuscripts may not necessarily be the result of scribal errors. As we saw above, the Báb's Arabic grammar was often unconventional, particularly when he wrote in what he called the 'mode of verses' (*sha'n-i áyát*), and ostensible scribal errors could be by the Báb himself. Of course, scribal errors do frequently occur and can confuse an otherwise clear statement by the Báb.[18] Conversely, later scribes could have knowingly or unknowingly corrected grammatical errors in the original text written by the Báb. To be cautious, grammatical errors found in the earliest manuscripts of a work should be preserved in the main text and noted in the critical apparatus along with later variants. This principle is obviously in tension with that enunciated in the preceding paragraph, so editors will have to be very careful about which variant reading is put in the main text of the critical edition. It is sometimes a personal judgement based on long exposure to the Báb's style and therefore somewhat subjective. However, as long as every variant is noted in the critical apparatus, editors need not worry unduly about preserving an early scribal error in the main text.

In preparing the text of the Báb's Treatise on Grammar I have consulted two badly reproduced photocopies of photocopies of INBMC volume 67 and INBA 4011C. Since INBA 4011 is the earlier manuscript, I have taken it as my base text.[19] In the notes the two manuscripts are designated as follows:

INBA 4011, pp. 167–71.
INBMC 67, pp. 121–5.

Both texts are written in *naskh* script, although the handwriting differs. The manuscript in INBMC 67 is composed of 62 lines of text with 16 lines per full page and roughly 14 words per line, while INBA 4011 comprises 87 lines of text with 19 lines per full page and roughly nine words per line. INBMC 67 has some variants in the margins, with one of them designated *nuskha badal*, which means that the scribe was noting a variant in another manuscript at his disposal. All marginal notes by the scribes have been recorded in the endnotes, whether they pertain to variant readings and corrections to the text or to commentary on the text (as occurs once in INBA 4011). Neither text is vocalized, although INBA 4011 does have *tashdíd*. In the edited version I have vocalized the text when necessary and provided the *tashdíd* (differences from INBA 4011 are recorded in the endnotes). However, I have tried to keep vocalization to a minimum and foregone punctuation so as not to prejudice future translators towards any particular reading. I have also stayed away from capitalizing many terms in the English translation for the same reason.

Although I have been unable to date precisely the Risála using information in a colophon or textual clues, it is definitely an early work of the Báb. First, it is found in INBA 4011, which largely contains texts that he composed between 1844 and 1846.[20] Further, Mázandarání states that it was written during his pilgrimage, around the same time that he wrote *al-Sahífa bayn al-haramayn* (Mázandarání 1941, vol. 3, p. 288). Finally, the Báb himself notes in the Kitáb al-fihrist that one of the questions (*al-masá'il*) that he answered concerned grammar ('*fí al-nahw wa al-sarf*').[21] Since the Kitáb al-fihrist is dated Jumádá II 1261 (21 June 1845) (MacEoin 1992, p. 50), the Báb must have written the Risála fí al-nahw wa al-sarf[22] during the first year of his ministry, probably after he left for his *hajj*.

While we know that the Báb composed this treatise very early in his ministry, we do not know who the recipient was. The Báb does address the recipient as *mu'tamad al-quwá* ('one dependable in strength') but this is not necessarily an allusion to someone's name (it is a paraphrase of Q 53:5). Given the gender of the address, the recipient was probably a male. Based on the content of the treatise and the time period in which it was written, the recipient was probably also a Shaykhi.

As I claimed in the opening paragraph, the title of the treatise is somewhat misleading since it purports to discuss grammar (*al-nahw wa al-sarf*).[23] Therefore anyone seeking a text in which the Báb discusses the finer points of grammar or explains some of the more peculiar elements of his syntax, morphology and style will be disappointed. Generally, the Báb did not write about the mechanics of his Arabic, unlike a later claimant to divine revelation, Bahá'u'lláh.[24] Further, the Báb composed this treatise before members of the Shi'i clerical establishment began to criticize his Arabic prose, so we would not expect to see a rebuttal of their criticisms in this text.[25] The Báb does signal, however, his view of Arabic grammar as a hindrance to his revelatory creativity by way of allegory. Near the beginning of the text, he equates syntax (*al-nahw*) with Adam and morphology (*al-sarf*) with Eve. The ubiquitous speaker (the Báb switches between the third and first person) gives them a place in Paradise but warns them to not approach the tree of origination (*shajarat al-bad'*). As in the biblical story, they disobey and are cast out of Paradise. The main lesson seems to be that Arabic grammar is an important part of revelation but it can be discarded if it encroaches upon the expression of divine truth. In a similar vein, the Báb counsels the recipient of his treatise to accustom the children of believers to his Arabic style from an early age. The recipient should do this by writing down the Báb's scripture for them in beautiful handwriting in order that they will know, upon reaching the age of maturity, that the Báb is transcendent (*tanzíh*) above the limitations of exposition (*hadd al-bayán*).

As previously discussed, this is not to say that the Arabic writings of the Báb can be understood without studying Arabic grammar. We have already surveyed some of these reasons why this is so above, so we need not detail them here. Suffice it to say that even though the Báb felt free to violate the norms of Arabic grammar, he relies upon the reader's understanding of those norms and the mechanics of grammar to decipher his prose and his metaphysical terminology.

As for the latter, the Báb in this text divides the operation of God's Will in the created world into three components: Act (*fi'l*),[26] Name (*ism*) and Letter (*harf*). This mirrors the division of Arabic words into their three components: verb (*fi'l*), noun (*ism*) and particle (*harf*). The reader should be aware that my translation of these grammatical terms is somewhat misleading, since there is not a one-to-one correspondence between them and the English equivalents I have given them. The category of *ism*, which is translated by English students of Arabic grammar as 'noun', includes things that English grammarians would not classify as nouns, such as adjectives (*al-safát*). Further, the category of *harf*, which is translated as 'particle', also includes words that would not be classified as particles in English grammar, like *fi* (the preposition 'in') and *wa* (the conjunction 'and'). As with English prepositions and conjunctions, the *hurúf* (pl. of *harf*) are the glue that connects the verbal and non-verbal elements of the sentence together.

At the end of his treatise the Báb uses these three grammatical categories to describe the three basic components of all existence: Act, Name and Letter. Or, as he puts it, three of the four basic 'letters' of the 'word' that God originated and from which all other created things are ultimately derived. For example, the Báb dwells on the movement (*haraka*) and stillness (*sukún*) of the Act (*fi'l*), both terms used in grammar to describe which letters of a verb (*fi'l*) or noun are vocalized (*mutaharrik*) with a diacritical mark (*haraka*) or not vocalized (*sákin*) with a *sukún* (a mark indicating that a consonant is not followed by a short vowel). The Báb also designates some of the subsets of his metaphysical category of Name (*ism*) with terms like *sifa* (quality) that also fall under the category of noun (*ism*) in Arabic grammar (a *sifa* is an adjective). Finally, the Báb writes of the component of Letters (*hurúf*) and describes them in terms that could be used to describe the function of particles (*hurúf*) in Arabic grammar.

In order to avoid a translation that is totally unwieldy (somewhat difficult given the technical nature of the subject matter), I have moved back and forth between rendering the Báb's terminology in its metaphysical and grammatical meanings depending on the context. To ensure that readers are able to recognize the Báb's wordplay, I put the Arabic terms in parentheses followed by notes explaining the grammatical and philosophical denotations of these terms. By this I hope to highlight a grammatical aspect of the Báb's cosmology that has hitherto gone unnoticed in discussions of his metaphysical terminology and in translations of his writings.

In the Name of God, the Merciful, the Compassionate

Praise be to God Who is manifested to (*tajallá 'alá*) humankind (*al-insán*)[27] by means of the separated point[28] starting its motion (*al-nuqta al-munfasila al-mutaharrika*)[29] from the dawning-place of exposition (*al-bayán*)![30] Praise be to God who undertook through His generosity that which He consummated[31] for humankind by means of the joined[32] point coming to rest (*al-nuqta al-muttasila al-musakkina*)[33] in the setting-place of exposition! (This transpires) until the two bodies of water[34] are joined at the point of meeting[35] in the form (*haykal*)[36] of the *tatanjayn*,[37] in order that the people of distinction[38] may not suppose that what God has determined in the point of the two *barzakhs*[39] is the allotment (*hukm*)[40] of the two gulfs (*al-khalíjayn*).[41] The All-Merciful created the point of syntax (*nuqtat al-nahw*)[42] from the world of effacement (*'álam al-mahw*) and God placed within it (*ahkam alláh fí nafsihá*) the allotments of demarcation (*al-tahdíd*)[43] according to the allotment[44] of the object of fancy from the point of the object of knowledge.[45] To God belongs the alteration (*al-badá'*)[46] of His judgement.[47] Everything has a fixed record (*kitáb mu'ajjal*)[48] such that no 'thing' *(al-shay')*[49] is able to change (*'alá al-sabqa*)[50] the judgement of God, its Lord. That judgement from God, the Truth, is undertaken (*maqdiyyan*) in the mode of creation according to the pure Truth.

When God created the centre[51] of syntax (*markaz al-nahw*) around[52] the secret of the line (*sirr al-satr*),[53] We revealed unto it: 'Do not approach the tree of origination (*shajarat al-bad'*), for, verily, it is forbidden unto you.'[54] Whereupon I apportioned him a precinct (*aqsamtuhu hazran*)[55] from the dust of the land of proximity that was nearby. And so he drew nigh unto (the tree) without permission. Therefore we decreed (*hakamná*) for him exile from the paradise of the gate and from that exalted precinct (*al-hazr al-mutasá'ida*). From his utmost extremities (*asfal a'dá'ihi*)[56] we had created the point of morphology (*nuqat al-sarf*) as his wife. Then God commanded her to go in exile with the descent (*habt*)[57] of the tablets. Thus was the judgement written in the Mother Book among the people of alteration (*ahl al-taghyír*)[58] in the line of demarcation. Until the present time, the two points [syntax and morphology] have wept in the land of the tablets. Behold! By the leave of God, their Lord, I forgave them for drawing nigh since they acknowledged [their] powerlessness at that gate. In truth, today I am a forgiver[59] for all the worlds in accordance with the permission of God.

O pure gate! Know that after the dawning of the sun from the dayspring of [divine] permission, which hath been realized (*haqqa*) in that gate, believing children should not take the paths of knowledge (*subul al-'ilm*) from the books of contradiction since their fathers have tasted[60] the seed (*habb*)[61] of the fruit from the tree of eternity. It is not befitting for the rains descending from the ocean of the *Muzn*[62] to partake of love (*al-hubb*) from the love of the calf (*hubb al-'ijl*)[63] since God desired, [in order] to purify the earth[64] for His Most Great Day, that creation should worship naught but Him who is the Truth, no other god is there but Him.[65] Write down for children the teachings of the Creator of humankind in a beautiful manner (*'alá turuq al-hisán*). [These teachings] from the dawning-place of exposition are within you at the manifestation of his awe-inspiring visage (*'alá zuhúr haybatihi*) unto all generated beings (*al-akwán*) and entities (*al-a'yán*).[66] [Do this] until they testify, after reaching the age of perfection, to the transcendence of the gate (*tanzíh al-báb*) above the limit of exposition (*hadd al-bayán*). God had created the two sciences [syntax and morphology] from the mist rising (*al-rashha al-murasshaha*) from the two seas. 'He hath loosed the two seas, meeting together. Between them is a barrier which they do not transgress.'[67]

O people of earth and heaven! Verily, God has not decreed nobility (*al-sharaf*) for humankind in (attainment of) this knowledge (*al-'ilm*) from these two bodies of water because they are a lot (*hazz*)[68] belonging to the people of the two gulfs.[69] Verily, nobility, in the sight of God, is knowledge of the All-Merciful and the *barzakh* standing (*al-qá'im*) between the two worlds. Therefore, at the equator prefer that which is standing (*fa-rghabú fí khatt al-istiwá' ilá al-qá'im*) between the two bodies of water.[70] The pearl of case endings (*lu'lu' al-i'ráb*)[71] is brought forth from one and the inflection[72] of coral from the other (*tasríf al-marján*).[73] The first one has an exact limit (*hadd ... muhkam*) from God; thing (*al-shay'*) does not know separation (*faslan*) save by certain knowledge of union (*illá 'an al-qat' bil-wasl*).[74] The second is a precise allotment (*hukm mutqan*) that does not know stillness (*al-sukún*) except by certain knowledge of stillness (*illá 'an al-qat' bil-sukún*).[75]

Remove the dictate of grammatical rules (*sabíl al-qawá'id*)[76] from the water of the elixir [that is] upon the verdant tablets (*al-alwáh al-múriqát*)[77] (that are) from the temples of unity (*hayákil al-tawhíd*)[78] [that are] from the shade of the world of 'Alí (*min zill al-'álam al-'alawí*).[79] [Do this] until those who possess understanding among the people of faith bear witness that 'what is there is not known save by what is here'.[80] Only write a letter over which you have recited the judgement of alteration (*hukm al-badá'*) and the word of consummation (*kalimat al-imdá'*) from the All-Merciful. 'Verily, We belong to God and unto Him do we return.'[81] Open the gate of the book to (*'alá*)[82] the 29 letters and cause the judgement of drawing nigh (*hukm al-qurb*) unto the beginning (*al-bad'*)[83] to flow forth from your pen unto all things (*'alá al-kull*) by means of that which God has inspired you from the tongue of the gate. Begin with the Remembrance on the basis of the Act (*ibda' bil-dhikr 'alá al-fi'l*)[84] because it[85] is the ink of the judgement (*midád al-hukm*), and complete its number by repetition (*'alá al-takrír*) in the Act of the Ancient One (*fi'l al-qadím*). Decree (*uhkum*) for the point of the *barzakh* the allotment of the two invisible (*al-ghaybayn*) [worlds] in the two visible (*al-shahádatayn*) [worlds].[86] Differentiate its [the point's] allotment at the meeting of the two junctions (*iltiqá' al-jam'ayn*)[87] and mention the drawing nigh of the occultation (*qurb al-ghayba*) to the visible (*al-shaháda*) [world] after you contemplate (*ba'da nazratika*) the numbers of the letters in [terms of] fewness and multiplicity (*bil-qilla wa al-kathra*).[88] Place (*uhkum*) the smallest [number] in the abyss of nearness (*lujjat al-qurb*) and write (*uktub*) for the largest [number] the point of remoteness. Conjugate (*isrif*) the verb (*al-fi'l*)[89] according to the inflection of the theophany (*sarf al-zuhúr*) and decline (*'iráb*) the noun (*al-ism*)[90] by means of the pure water (*bil-má' al-tuhúr*). Allot (*uhkum*) the letters by means of the connection (*bil-rabt*) from the world of the theophany (*'álam al-zuhúr*) to the mountain of Túr.[91] There, the *náqúr*[92] is sounded and all the letters cry out [to] whomsoever is upon Túr, 'The sun has risen and the day has shone forth[93] and the noon has waned and night has slipped away.[94] That which God ordained for us on that day is to stand before the gate. God is our Lord besides whom there is no other god. Let those who will, strive for the like of this.'[95]

Know, O one who is dependable in strength (*mu'tamad al-quwá*),⁹⁶ that the Name (*ism*)⁹⁷ is the outward sign of the thing *qua* 'thing' (*simat al-shay' kamá hiya bimá hiya*). It has several degrees (*marátib*), including: the mirrors (*al-maráyá*) that are its qualification (*na'tuhu*),⁹⁸ the expressions (*al-alfáz*) that are its limit (*hadduhu*), the figures (*al-ashkál*) that are its quality (*wasfuhu*)⁹⁹ and the inscribed forms (*al-suwar al-manqúsha*)¹⁰⁰ that are its orthographic representation (*rasmuhu*). For every book (*kitáb*) there is no end to them [the degrees] according to an all-encompassing judgement (*hukm al-kull*) from God. Truly, God has made expressions (*al-alfáz*) as bodies (*ajsád*) for the spirits (*al-arwáh*), which are meanings (*al-ma'áni*).¹⁰¹ Verily, God has, with His own hands, inscribed (*kataba*) an affinity (*nisba*)¹⁰² [for each other] between them. There is naught between them save that which is between the *káf* and *nún*.¹⁰³

As for the Act (*al-fi'l*), it is the motion of a thing (*harakat al-shay'*), and the ink of the Name (*al-ism*) and the Letter (*al-harf*) had been upon it. The root (*asl*) of the Act is a still creation (*khalq sákin*) that is not known through stillness (*lá yu'rafu bil-sukún*).¹⁰⁴ According to our school (*madhhabiná*)¹⁰⁵ which is the truth, it is a moving creation (*khalq mutaharrik*) that is not known through movement (*bil-taharruk*). Whosoever knows separation (*al-fasl*) from union (*al-wasl*) has attained the point of knowledge.¹⁰⁶

As for the Letter (*harf*), it is a meaning (*al-ma'ná*) that does not speak except by being connected (*lá yahkí illá 'an al-rabt*). Verily, when God desired to create the letters, He originated (*abda'*) a word with four letters. God has given each letter a name (*ism*). For the first [He gave the name] 'Act' (*fi'l*), for the second 'Name' (*ism*), for the third 'Letter' (*harf*) and the [fourth is called] 'a concealed secret' (*sirr mustasarr*)¹⁰⁷ sustaining them (*muqawwimuhá*). Behold! I will inform you of that letter which al-Sádiq, peace be upon him, alluded to in the hadith of the Name (*hadíth al-ism*).¹⁰⁸ Originating (*al-ibdá'*) has been suffused with the emanation (*fayd*) of that letter and none knows its subtle production but Him. Put your trust in God and say, 'There is no power or strength save by God'. Cause your pen to flow upon the point of the gate by means of the gate¹⁰⁹ of 'In the Name of God, the Merciful, the Compassionate. Praise be to God, Lord of the Worlds!'¹¹⁰

Bibliography

Afnan, Abu'l-Qasim. *'Ahd-i A'lá: Zindigani-yi Hadrat-i Báb* (The Bábí Dispensation: The Life of the Báb). Oxford: Oneworld, 2000.

Afnan, Muhammad. '*Tafsír bism alláh al-rahmán al-rahím.*' *Áhang-i Badí'*, nos. 5 and 6, 126 BE.

Ahsá'í, Shaykh Ahmad. *Jawámi' al-kalim*, vol. 2. Tabriz: Muhammad Taqi Nakjavani, 1276/1856.

— *Sharh al-fawá'id*. Tehran?: Muhammad Shafiq, 1272/1856.

— *Sharh al-Ziyára*, vol. 1. Beirut: Dár al-Mufíd, 1999.

Amanat, Abbas. *Resurrection and Renewal: The Making of the Bábí Movement in Iran, 1844–1850*. Ithaca, NY: Cornell University Press, 1989.

al-Amín, Muhsin. *A'yán al-shí'a*. Beirut: Matba'at al-Insáf, 1960–.

Ámulí, Haydar. *Jámi' al-asrár.* Ed. Henry Corbin. Tehran: Institut Franco-Iranien de Recherche, 1969.

The Báb ('Alí Muhammad). *Kitáb al-Fihrist.* f. 1a-6b, Islamic Manuscripts, Third Series, vol. 4, Department of Rare Books and Special Collections, Princeton University Library, f. 5b. The title of this work, '*fí al-nahw wa al-sarf*,' is found under the heading '*jadwal al-masá'il al-mukhtalifa wa tafsír*' ('Table/index of various questions and exegesis').

— *Persian Bayan.* Trans. Denis MacEoin. In MacEoin, *The Messiah of Shiraz.* Leiden: Brill, 2009, pp. 659–704.

— *Risála Dhahabiyya* II. Unpublished MS, n.d.; http://www.bayanic.com/showPict.php?id=zahab&ref=0&err=0&curr=0.

— *Sahifih-yi 'Adliyyih.* Tehran: 1950; reprinted, East Lansing, MI: H-Bahai, 1998.

— '*Surat al-Shams*', in *Qayyúm al-Asmá'.* Unpublished MS, n.d.; www..bayanic.com/showPict.php?id=ahsan&ref=0&err=0&curr=0.

The Báb. *Selections from the Writings of the Báb.* Trans. Habib Taherzadeh with the assistance of a Committee at the Bahá'í World Centre. Haifa: Bahá'í World Centre, 1976.

Bahá'u'lláh. *La'áli' al-hikma*, vol. 1. Rio de Janiero: Editora Bahá'í-Brasil, 1986.

Behmardi, Vahid. '*Muqaddimih-yi dar bárih-yi sabk va siyáq áthár mubárikih-yi hazrat rabb a'lá*', *Khushih-há'í az kharman-i adab va hunar*, vol. 6. St Gallen: Landegg, 1995, pp. 47–67.

al-Bursí, Rajab. *Masháriq anwár al-yaqín* (The Dawning-places of the Lights of Certainty). Qum: Intishárát al-maktaba al-haydariyya, 1416/1995.

Carter, M. G. 'Arabic Literature'. *Scholarly Editing: A Guide to Research.* Ed. D. C. Greetham. New York: The Modern Language Association of America, 1995.

Cole, Juan. 'The World as Text: Cosmologies of Shaykh Ahmad al-Ahsa'i'. *Studia Islamica*, no. 80, 1994.

Cook, David. *Contemporary Muslim Apocalyptic Literature.* Syracuse, NY: Syracuse University Press, 2005.

Encyclopaedia of Islam [*EI2*]. Leiden and London: Brill. 2nd ed. 1960.

Gulpáyigání, Mírzá Abú'l-Fadl. *Kitáb al-fará'id.* n.p., n.d. Digitally reproduced. East Lansing, MI: H-Bahai, 2006.

al-Hamawí, Yáqút. *Mu'jam al-buldán*, vol. 4. Beirut: Dár al-Kutub al-'Ilmiyya, 1990.

Hamid, Idris. *The Metaphysics and Cosmology of Shaykh 'Ahmad al-'Ahsá'í: Critical Edition, Translation, and Analysis of* Observations in Wisdom. Unpublished Ph.D. diss., State University of New York at Buffalo, 1998.

Hillenbrand, Robert. *Shahnama: The Visual Language of the Persian Book of Kings.* Burlington, VT and Aldershot UK: Ashgate Publishing, 2004.

al-Hurr al-'Ámilí, Muhammad. *Wasá'il al-shí'a*, vol. 2. Qum: Ál al-Bayt Institute, 1989.

Ibn 'Arabí. *al-Futúhát al-makkiyya.* Cairo: Dar al-Kutub al-'Arabiyya, 1911.

Ibn Bábawayh, Muhammas ibn 'Alí. *'Uyún akhbár al-Ridá*, 2 vols. in 1. Ed. al-Shaykh Husayn al-A'lamí. Beirut: Mu'assast al-A'lamí lil-Matbú'át, 1404/1983.]

Ibn Bábúya. *Man la yahduruhu al-faqíh*, vol. 1. Qum: Islamic Publications Institute, 1993.

Ibn Manzúr. *Lisán al-'arab*, 15 vols. Beirut: Dar Sadir, 1955–6.

Ibn Rashíq, al-Hasan. *al-'Umda*, vol. 1. Beirut: Dar al-Jil, 1981.

— *al-'Umdah fí sina'at al-shi'r wa-naqdih*. 2 vols. Cairo: Maktabat al-Khanjí, 2000.

Iranian National Bahá'í Archives (INBA); Iranian National Bahá'í Manuscript Collection (INBMC).

Kirmání, Karím Khán. *Izháq al-Bátil*, Kirman: Sa'ádah, 1351/1973.

al-Kulayní, Al-Shaykh. *al-Káfí*, vol. 1. Ed. 'Alí-Akbar al-Ghaffárí. Tehran: Dár al-Kutub al-Islámíya, 1363AH/1984–5.

Lájavardí, Sayyid Mahdí. *'Uyún akhbár al-Ridá*. 2 vols. Tehran: Intishárát Jahan, 1959.

Landes, Richard. 'Owls, Roosters and Apocalyptic Time: A Historical Method for Reading a Refractory Documentation.' *Union Seminary Quarterly Review*, vol. 49, nos. 1–4 (1995), pp. 49–69.

Lawson, Todd. 'Coincidentia Oppositorum in the Qayyum al-Asma: The Terms "Point" (*nuqta*), "Pole" (*qutb*), "Center" (*markaz*) and the *Khutbat al-Tatanjiyya*.' *Occasional Papers in Shaykhi, Babi, and Baha'i Studies*, vol. 5, no. 1 (January 2001), http://www2.h-net.msu.edu/~bahai/bhpapers/vol5/tatanj/tatanj.htm.

— 'Qur'án Commentary as Sacred Performance: The Báb's Tafsírs of Qur'án 103 and 108, the Declining Day and the Abundance,' in eds. Christoph Bürgel and Isabel Schayani, *Iran im 19. Jahrhundert und die Entstehung der Bahá'í-Religion*. Hildesheim: G. Olms Verlag, 1998, pp. 145–58.

— 'Reading Reading Itself: The Báb's "Sura of the Bees". A Commentary from the Sura of Joseph – Text, Translation and Commentary.' *Occasional Papers in Shaykhi, Babi, and Baha'i Studies*, vol. 1, no. 5, (November 1997). http://www.h-net.org/~bahai/bhpapers/vol1/nahl1.htm.

— translation of '*Risála fí al-Sulúk*' in 'The Báb's Epistle on the Spiritual Journey towards God', in ed. Moojan Momen, *The Bahá'í Faith and the World's Religions*. Oxford: George Ronald, 2003, pp. 231–47.

MacEoin, Denis. 'Early Shaykhí Reactions to the Bab and His Claims', in ed. Moojan Momen. *Studies in Bábí and Bahá'í History*, vol. 1. Los Angeles: Kalimát, 1982, pp. 1–47.

— *The Sources for Early Bábí Doctrine and History: A Survey*. Leiden: Brill, 1992.

Majlisí, Muhammad Báqir. *Bihár al-anwár*, vols. 24, 97. Qum: Dár al-Kutub al-Islámiyya, 1983.

Mázandarání, Asadu'lláh Fádil. *Amr va Khalq*. 4 vols. Tehran: Mu'assasih-yi Millí-yi Matbu'át-i Amrí, 111–31 BE/1954–75; and http://reference.bahai.org/fa/t/c/.

— *Asrár al-Áthár*, 5 vols. Tehran: Bahá'í Publishing Trust, 124–9 BE/1968–9.

— *Tarikh Zuhur al-Haqq*, vol. 3. Tehran: n.p. 1941?, at http://www2.h-net.msu.edu/~bahai/areprint/vol2/mazand/tzh3.

Momen, Moojan. 'Bahá'u'lláh's Tablet of the Uncompounded Reality (*Lawh Basít al-Haqíqa*)'. *Lights of Irfán*, vol. 11. Darmstadt: 'Asr-i-Jadíd, 2010, pp. 203–21; and http://bahai-library.org/provisionals/basit.html.

al-Munajjid, Saláh al-Dín. *Qawá'id tahqíq al-makhtútát*. Beirut: Dár al-Kitáb al-Jadíd, 1970.

al-Núrí, al-Mírzá. *Mustadrak al-wasá'il*, vol. 6. Beirut: Mu'assasat ál al-bayt 'alayhim al-salám li-ihyá' al-turáth, 1408AH/1988.

Rafati, Vahid. '*Marátib-i Sab'ih va hadíth-i mashiyyat.*' *Safínih-i 'irfán*, vol. 1. Darmstadt: 'Asr-i-Jadíd, 1998, pp. 53–98.

— '*Nigáhí bih chand zamínih az Tajallí-yi Adab-i Fársí dar Áthár-i Bahá'í*'. *Khúshih-há-iy az Kharman-i Adab va Hunar*, vol. 1. Weinacht, Switzerland: Landegg Academy, 1990, pp. 65–80.

al-Saffár, Abú Ja'far Muhammad. *Basá'ir al-Daraját*. Qum: Publications of Ayatollah Mar'ashi Library, 1984.

al-Tabarí, Muhammad Ibn Jarír. *Jámi' al-bayán 'an ta'wíl al-qur'án*. 30 vols. Egypt: Mustafá al-Bábí al-Halabí, 1954–68.

Notes

1. My thanks to Stephen Lambden for allowing me to reproduce my semi-critical edition of the Báb's 'Treatise on Grammar', which I prepared for his as yet unpublished journal *Syzygy*, found online at http://www.hurqalya.pwp.blueyonder.co.uk/.

    I have chosen to focus on Bahá'í apologetics surrounding the Báb's grammar since most of the critiques of his prose written by Muslim authors are directed against the Bahá'ís, who believe that both the Báb and Bahá'u'lláh were the recipients of post-Quranic revelation. But it is worth noting that the Báb's irregular Arabic was also a sore point for early Bábís. For example, Mullá Jawád Wilyání, an early Shaykhi convert to Bábism who soon defected, wrote a letter to Táhirih criticizing the Arabic prose of the Báb (see MacEoin 1982, p. 26).
2. For a recent iteration of this view, see Behmardi '*Muqaddimih-yi dar bárih-yi sabk*', pp. 51–2.
3. See Hillenbrand, *Shahnama*, pp. 28–9.
4. In his *Tafsír Surat Kawthar* the Báb writes: 'All of my verses you have seen have been corrupted by the malicious, and scribes were unable to copy some of them properly. As a consequence, the people say there are mistakes in them, and some say there is no cohesion. I seek refuge with God from their deeds and slander and from the verses that do not conform to the balanced way. Verily, I am quit of the polytheists.' *Amr va Khalq* 2:103. Thanks to Omid Ghaemmaghami for this reference.
5. Several of these errors are catalogued in Karím Khán Kirmání's *Izháq al-bátil*, one of the earliest systematic critiques of the Báb's revelatory writing (see note below).
6. A copy of this text in the Báb's own handwriting is found in Afnan, *'Ahd-i A'lá*, p. 183.
7. For example, when the Báb was forced, in Shiraz, to deny that he was the *báb* of the Hidden Imam, he defended himself by saying: 'If words stream from the pen, it hath been due to pure, innate nature (*mahd-i fitrat*) and is totally contrary to the rules of the people and is not a proof of any *amr*.' (INBA 91, pp. 169–70; see Amanat 1989, p. 255 for another translation.) Here, *amr* could be translated as 'Cause' or divine 'mandate'.
8. One might also read the Báb's extemporaneous prose in the context of apocalyptic writing. In this regard, David Cook has noted that contemporary Arab authors who write apocalyptic works frequently misspell words and make grammatical mistakes. Drawing on the work of Richard Landes, he observes: 'Such defects arise not only from their sense of urgency but from their fatalistic view of their readers: those who were prepared to be convinced will be convinced; those who resist or oppose the apocalyptic view will see the truth soon enough, when the end of the world occurs before their eyes' (Cook 2005, p. 5). An earlier discussion of the Báb's writing as a

type of performance is Lawson, 'Qur'án Commentary as Sacred Performance'. See Landes, 'On Owls, Roosters and Apocalyptic Time'.
9. For examples of grammatical irregularities in the Qur'an, see Gulpáyigání 2006, pp. 469–77 containing a transcription of a 19th-century Arab Christian's critique.
10. 'Two' and 'magicians' are in the nominative case but 'two' should be in the subjunctive.
11. *Sahifih-yi 'Adliyyih*, p. 12. My thanks to Omid Ghaemmaghami for this reference.
12. See Afnan, *'Ahd-i A'lá*, p. 449.
13. All words occurring in the Qur'an.
14. *Risála Dhahabiyya*, pp. 42–3 (unpublished ms., n.d., accessed at http://www.bayanic.com/showPict.php?id=zahab&ref=0&err=0&curr=0).
15. Idris Hamid's 'The Metaphysics and Cosmology of Shaykh Ahmad al-'Ahsá'í' is the only work in a western language that attempts to make sense of the grammatical component of Shaykh Ahmad's metaphysical language (see ch. 2). It is an invaluable resource for students of Shaykh Ahmad's highly elusive metaphysical writings and for deciphering the Báb's treatises on cosmology and language, since he borrows heavily from Shaykh Ahmad.
16. Bahá'ís may want to preserve every revision made by the Báb and Bahá'u'lláh since each new redaction is believed to be a brand new revelation from God. For example, a critical edition of the Súrih-yi Haykal would have three versions of the text corresponding to the original text written in Edirne (Adrianople) and the two redactions made by Bahá'u'lláh in 'Akká. The critical apparatus for each version would include variants found in manuscripts that are derived from that version.
17. These and other concise guidelines for editing Arabic manuscripts are found in Saláh al-Dín al-Munajjid 1970, pp. 2–30.
18. For example, Moojan Momen used a corrupt manuscript when translating a portion of the Báb's *al-Sahífa al-dhahabiyya* in the introduction to his translation of Bahá'u'lláh's tablet on Uncompounded Reality (Momen 2010). Momen translates one portion as 'without the existence of anything having form and shape' (*shay'un bi-mithl ma inna-hu kana shayyár*), although he notes that this is a tenuous translation because the text is not clear. Another version of this portion is found in Behmardi, '*Muqaddimih-yi dar bárih-yi sabk*', p. 57. It seems to be drawn from a better manuscript since there is a clear connection between this sentence and the following sentence: *bi-lá wujúdi shay'in bi-mithli má anna-hu kana hayyan* ('without the existence of anything in the same manner that He is Living.') Thus the Báb was not being cryptic at all. Rather Momen's manuscript preserved a corrupt text.
19. A letter that precedes our text in INBMC 67 is dated Rajab 1264 (p. 121) and one several pages after is dated Rajab 17, [12]64, so this manuscript of the Risála was transcribed between 3 June 1848 and 19 July 1848, which would make it a much later copy than the 4011 manuscript.
20. MacEoin 1992, pp. 35, 73. Although MacEoin briefly mentions the text on p. 73 and provides a sample of its opening line, he omits it from his index of manuscripts.
21. The Báb, *Kitáb al-Fihrist*, f. 5b. The title of this work, '*fí al-nahw wa al-sarf*', is found under the heading '*jadwal al-masá'il al-mukhtalifa wa tafsír*' ('Table/index of various questions and exegesis').
22. The treatise is also known as *Risála fí nuqtat 'ilm al-nahw* and *Risála fí al-nahw*.
23. *Al-nahw* is roughly the equivalent of the English category of 'syntax' and *al-sarf* is roughly equivalent to 'morphology'. To designate grammar as a whole, Arab grammarians use the word *al-nahw* or the phrase *al-nahw wa al-sarf*.
24. See, for example, Bahá'u'lláh's letter to one of his chief scribes, Zayn al-Muqarribín, in which he explains some of his reasons for violating grammatical norms in Arabic (the letter is reproduced in Mázandarání's *Asrár al-Áthár* in the entry under 'Zayn al-Muqarribín').

25. To my knowledge, the first sustained, written critique of the Báb's grammar did not appear until 12 Rajab 1261 (17 July 1845) when Hájjí Muhammad Karím Khán finished writing his *Izháq al-bátil*. In the section on 'Examples of Some of the Simple-Minded Drivel of the Suspicious Báb' (*fí dhikri ba'di khuráfáti al-báb al-murtáb*, pp. 80–103), Kirmání criticizes the grammar and content of an early letter sent to him by the Báb and chapters of the Qayyúm al-Asmá'. His criticisms on both counts are illuminating since he was a well-educated man steeped in the intricacies of both Arabic grammar and Shaykhi terminology. With regard to the former, he was well positioned to pick out a number of grammatical and stylistic irregularities in the Báb's writings that might normally escape the attention of less capable readers (such as myself). Even though his aim is polemical (to prove that the Báb is not eloquent (*fasíh*), as the latter had claimed), his observations are helpful in understanding what was so striking about the Báb's prose to an educated audience. Even more valuable are his criticisms of the Báb's claims to divine authority in the Qayyúm al-Asmá'. Kirmání was one of a handful of people who knew enough of Shaykh Ahmad and Sayyid Kázim's terminology to be able to decipher the Báb's language in that book and he makes the important point that the Báb was claiming multiple stations at the same time. To prove his point, he goes verse by verse in several chapters and 'decodes' the Báb's cryptic claims. The chapter is an invaluable source for understanding how the Báb's early works were received by the religious elite and I hope to write a more detailed article on the subject in the future.

26. Hamid renders *al-fi'l*, 'the Acting' and its five degrees as gerunds to indicate that they are not substantives but processes (Hamid 1998, pp. 176–84). For example, the first degree of Acting, *al-mashí'a*, is generally rendered 'the Will' but in the metaphysics of Shaykh Ahmad, Hamid contends, it is better rendered as 'Willing' because it is not an entity but a process. It is not clear to me, however, that the Imams necessarily had this distinction in mind. Therefore, I will keep with the standard rendering of these terms but urge the reader to be mindful of Shaykh Ahmad's distinction. See the gloss under *aqdá* for a fuller discussion of the stages of the divine Acting.

27. *Al-insán* is a notoriously difficult word to translate in Bábí/Bahá'í scripture. It literally means 'the man' or 'the human being'. Thus, the phrase '*alá al-insán* would be more literally translated as 'unto the human being'. Sometimes, however, *al-insán* seems to be used in a generic sense to refer to all human beings, like the word *al-nás*. At other times it seems be a reference to the Perfect Man (*al-insán al-kámil*), a concept developed by Ibn 'Arabí. I have translated it in the generic sense since 1) there is no obvious reason why it should be rendered in the latter technical sense and 2) the Báb might have chosen to use *al-nás* (humanity) instead but he seems to want to preserve the rhyme with *al-bayán* at the end of the sentence.

28. The 'point' (*nuqta*) is a dot that is placed under or above a letter to differentiate it from another letter with a similar shape. Early Muslim philologists devised this system of pointing to differentiate similarly shaped letters in the Qur'an, early copies of which were not pointed. For example, only the memory of the oral recitation of the Qur'an could help an early Muslim reciter determine what phoneme a particular symbol signified in an early copy. By adding a point above or below the letter, or adding no point at all, the reader would know that the letter was, for example a 'j' sound, 'kh' sound or the hard 'h' sound, usually transliterated as 'h' with a dot under it.

For the Báb, the 'point' signified both a written dot and the highest ontological reality of absolute oneness. Both concepts are joined in a hadith attributed to 'Alí: 'All that is in the world is in the Qur'an, and all that is in the Qur'an is condensed in the Fátiha of the Book, and all that is in the Fátiha is in the *basmala*, and all that is in the *basmala* is in the (letter) *bá'* and I am the point beneath the *bá"* (cited by Todd Lawson in 'Reading Reading Itself'). The Fátiha is the first sura of the Qur'an and the *basmala* is its first line: *bismi'lláh al-rahmán al-rahím* ('In the Name of God, the

Merciful, the Compassionate'). The first letter of the first line is the letter *bá'*. The Báb often refers to himself as the *nuqtat al-bá'*, 'the Point of the B' (see his Qayyúm al-Asmá' in the 'Surat al-Shams' and *passim*). This is not only an allusion to this hadith but also a reference to himself as the author of the Bayán, the primary Bábí scripture. In this sense he also refers to Muhammad as the *nuqtat al-fá'*, 'the Point of the F' (the Fur'qán, i.e. the Qur'an), to Jesus as the *nuqtat al-alif*, 'the Point of the A' (the Injíl or Gospel) and to Moses as the *nuqtat al-tá'*, 'the Point of the Letter T' (the Torah) (see Mázandaráni, vol. 5, '*Nuqtih*']. In both senses the word *nuqta* might be better rendered as 'epitome'.

One final note on the tradition attributed to 'Alí. I have not been able to find the full text of this tradition in Shi'i literature as it is cited by Lawson. Haydar Ámulí (*fl.* 14th cent. AD), a transmitter of a number of hadith attributed to 'Alí that are not found in the canonical collections of Shi'i traditions, only relates the 'I am the Point beneath the *bá"* portion in his *Jámi' al-asrár*, pp. 411, 563, 695, 699–700 (thanks to Todd Lawson for this reference). I have found something similar to what is quoted by Lawson in the *Mashárìq anwár al-yaqín* (The Dawning-places of the Lights of Certainty) by Rajab al-Bursí (*fl.* 14th cent. AD) and perhaps it is the source of the tradition as it appears in the Báb's writings (al-Bursí was also the Báb's source for the *al-Khutba al-tatanjiyya* – see the entry on this sermon below). First, al-Bursí attributes the following statement to 'Alí: 'I am the point that is beneath the supine *bá'* (*al-bá' al-mabsúta*)' (al-Bursí 1995, p. 21). Concerning the 'supine *bá'*,' al-Bursí says it is the 'first thing revealed to the Messenger of God and the first page of scripture (*sahífa*) (belonging) to Adam, Noah, and Abraham and its [the scripture's] secret (*sirr*)' (ibid. p. 20). Elsewhere al-Bursí further elaborates on this 'secret':

> The secret (*sirr*) of God is deposited in His books. The secret of the books is in the Qur'an because it is comprehensive and indomitable and within it is the explanation of all things. The secret of the Qur'an is in the disconnected letters at the beginning of the suras. The knowledge of letters ('*ilm al-hurúf*) is in an *alif* in a *lám*, which is the curved *alif* that is curved into the letter *lám* which contains the secret of the exoteric (*al-záhir*) and the esoteric (*al-bátin*). The knowledge of the *lám* is an *alif* in the *alif*, and the knowledge of the *alif* is in the point (*al-nuqta*), and the knowledge of the point is in the root [or original] knowledge (*al-ma'rifa al-asaliyya*), and the secret of the Qur'an is in the Fátiha, and the secret of the Fátiha is in the opening (*miftáhihá*, or 'key'), which is *bismi'lláh*, and the secret of the *basmala* is in the *bá'*, and the secret of the *bá'* is in the point' (ibid. p. 23).

29. *Al-mutaharrika* means moving or starting to move. Used in a philosophical sense, it refers to the motion (*haraka*) of a created thing and is contrasted with *sukún* ('rest' or 'stillness'). In grammar, it means 'vocalized' or 'vowelled'. When Muslims set about writing down the Qur'an they found that the existing orthography was only capable of expressing consonants and long vowels. Short vowels and consonants would be understood but there was no way to represent them on the page. Thus the word *mutaharrik* would have been written *mthrk*, i.e. without vowel marks. In order to insure that a word would not be misread (there were a number of different readings of the Qur'an owing to the absence of short vowels), Muslim philologists adopted a system of small markings that denoted the short 'a', 'i' and 'u'. They also created a mark to show when a consonant was doubled. For example, *mthrk* could then be rendered *mutaharrik*.

Returning to the translation, the phrase *al-nuqta al-munfasila al-mutaharrika* could also be rendered as 'the separated, vocalized point'. A translator would usually render the term as 'moving' or 'starting motion' and I have not departed from this convention. But the reader should be aware that in these first few lines the Báb is already beginning to play on the grammatical meanings of his metaphysical terminology.

30. *Al-bayán* is another key term in the works of the Báb. Bahá'í exegetes generally see it as an allusion to a verse in the Qur'an (Q 75:17–19) in which the *bayán* ('clarification, explanation') is supposed to follow the *qur'án* (lit. 'recitation'). Thus many Bahá'í authors contend that the Báb's central book, the *Bayán*, fulfils this prophecy (see, for example, Behmardi, '*Muqaddimih-yi dar bárih-yi sabk*', pp. 49–50). While it is probable that the Báb saw his writings as a fulfilment of an eschatological prophecy, he may have also used it sometimes in its technical sense developed by Shaykh Ahmad. As Idris Hamid notes, the term *al-bayán* had a very particular meaning in the writings of the Shaykh, who viewed the 'science of declaration' ('*ilm al-bayán*) as an integral part of his experiential Wisdom metaphysics (Hamid 1998, pp. 540–1).
31. The reader may find my rendering of the terms *aqdá* (a verbal neologism coined by the Báb from the more standard verb *qadá*, 'to decree', for the purpose of rhyme) and *amdá* as 'undertook' and 'consummated' to be awkward. I agree. However, the Báb uses these terms in a very technical sense and I want to capture something of that in English as opposed to just rendering the terms as synonyms. *Al-qadá'* ('undertaking') and *al-imdá'* ('consummating'), which are verbal nouns derived from the same root as their verbs, are two of the five degrees of the Act (*al-fʻil*) in the world. The first degree is the Will (*al-mashí'a*). According to a tradition of the sixth Imam, Ja'far al-Sádiq, 'God created the Will by itself (*bi-nafsihá*), then things (*al-ashyá'*) were created by the Will' (*al-Káfí* 1985, p. 110). It is contemplation of this self-generating capacity of the upper-most stage of the Act that preoccupied Shaykh Ahmad's intellectual life and was the cornerstone of his metaphysical system. The second degree is Desire (*al-iráda*), the third is Determination (*al-qadar*), the fourth is Undertaking (*al-qadá'*) and the fifth is Consummation (*al-imdá'*). According to Shaykh Ahmad in his *al-Fawá'id*, the first four degrees 'constitute the Dawn of Pre-eternity (*subh azal*)' and are the 'pillars' (*al-arkán*) of the Act, while the degree of Consummation is the 'disclosure' of these higher degrees (see Hamid 1998, p. 294 [trans. of the Fourth Observation]). Elsewhere the number of stages in the Act is referred to as seven, based on traditions from the Imams al-Sádiq and Músá Kázim. The first four stages are the same but the last stage, Consummating, has been replaced with *al-idhn* ('permission'), *al-kitáb* ('book' or 'record') and *al-ajal* ('term [of duration]'). Curiously, Shaykh Ahmad and the Báb reverse the last two degrees although I cannot find a hadith with this variation. For a discussion of the use of the 'seven degrees' (*marátib sab'a*) in Bahá'í scripture, see Rafati, '*Marátib-i Sab'ih va hadíth-i mashiyyat*', vol. 1, pp. 53–81.
32. 'Joining' or 'uniting' (*wasl*) and 'separation' or 'division' (*fasl*) are recurrent themes in this treatise and are paralleled with stillness (*sukún*) and motion (*haraka*) later on in this text. Perhaps the Báb has in mind a hadith attributed to Ja'far al-Sádiq: 'Whosoever knows separation (*al-fasl*) and union (*al-wasl*) and motion (*al-haraka*) and stillness (*al-sukún*) has attained steadfastness (*al-qarár*) in (the profession of God's) unity (*al-tawhíd*)' (Ámulí 1969, p. 364).
33. In grammar, *sakkana* (the verb from which *al-musakkina* is derived) means to make a consonant vowel-less. The written symbol for the absence of a vowel is a *sukún* (ú), which literally means 'silence', 'state of rest', It is not surprising that the Báb is using it to parallel the 'moving' point, since it is also a reference to the philosophical notion of 'stillness' (*sukún*) as opposed to motion (*haraka*).
34. Mention of the 'two bodies of water' (*al-bahrán*) occurs frequently in the Qur'an. In 35:12 we find that they are different in quality. One is 'fresh' ('*adhb*), 'sweet' (*furát*), and 'easy to drink' or 'palatable' (*sá'igh*). The other is 'salty' (*milh*) and 'bitter' (*ujáj*). Yet both are beneficial since they provide sustenance, supply 'ornaments' (*hilya*) that can be worn and serve as a medium for the travel of ships. Presumably 'the two bodies of water' in this context are 1) a river whose water is drinkable, and 2) an ocean, whose water is too salty to drink. In other contexts, the 'two bodies of water' might

be better translated as 'the two seas'. For example, in 18:60 Moses tells a companion: 'I will continue until I reach the junction (*majma'*) of the two seas (*al-bahrayn*) or I will spend years [trying].' This episode is not the one in which Moses crosses the Red Sea with the Israelites but a journey on which he meets a mysterious guide (Muslim exegetes say it is with the mystical Khidr).

What is important for the Báb's treatise is the place at which the two bodies of water meet (*majma' al-bahrayn*). The great polymath al-Tabarí explains that *majma'* is a verbal noun signifying 'joining', so the phrase could also be rendered 'until I reach the joining of the two bodies of water'. He also notes that there is a variety of opinion about which two bodies of water are being referred to. Early commentators like the Successor (a Muslim who lived immediately after Muhammad's death) Qatáda (d. *c.* 117 AH/735 CE) said that it was the meeting of the Persian Sea (*bahr al-fáris*) and the Mediterranean (*bahr al-rúm*, lit. the Roman Sea). This would be the Suez isthmus. Another early exegete, Mujáhid (d. 100 AH/718 CE–104 AH/722 CE), confirms this interpretation and states that one of them (the Persian Sea) is in the East (*qibal al-mashriq*) and the other (the Mediterranean) is in the West (*qibal al-maghrib*). Another early interpreter, Muhammad b. Ka'b (d. *c.* 118 AH/736 CE) says that the joining place of the two bodies of water is Tangiers (Tanja) on the Straits of Gibraltar on the northern coast of Morocco. In this case, the 'two bodies of water' would be the Mediterranean and the Atlantic (see al-Tabarí 1954, pp. 271–5). Finally, the next verses, 18:60–3, indicate that the *majma'* is a piece of land, as Moses and his companion lose their fish upon reaching the *majma'* when they climb a rock (*al-sakhra*).

In 25:53 the two bodies of water are again differentiated from one another as in 35:12: one is fresh and sweet, the other is salty and bitter. In this verse we are also told that God loosed the two bodies of water (*maraja al-bahrayn*) so that they flow into one another but they will not mix because He has placed a 'barrier' (*barzakh*, seemingly a synonym for *hájiz* in verse 27:61) and a 'inviolable obstruction' (*hijran mahjúran*) between them. According to al-Tabarí, the verb *maraja* ('release', 'let loose') implies mixing. Following this definition of the verb, he lists the interpretations of several early Muslims who contended that the barrier is not one of land but one of nature, preventing the sweet water from mixing with the brine. If the barrier was made of land, they explain, then the two bodies of water could not have flowed into one another as the verb implies. Alternatively, a few exegetes maintained that the barrier could be made of land separating one body of water from another but they do not attempt to explain how they could have flowed into each other if there were a physical barrier of land between them. Other interpreters pointed out that this latter position is untenable, since several rivers in the region obviously flow into oceans. Another early interpretation is allegorical, casting the *barzakh* as the respite or time (*al-ajal*) in which the soul waits between this world and the next (al-Tabarí 1955, vol. 19, pp. 23–5).

In verses 55:19–20 we are again informed that the two bodies of water have been loosed (*maraja al-bahráyn*) and that they meet together (*yaltaqiyán*). Further, it is again reinforced that there is a barrier (*barzakh*) between them that they do not transgress (*lá yabghiyán*). At this point, al-Tabarí notes that the exegetes differ over the location of the two bodies of water. Some say one is in the sky (*fí al-samá'*) and one is on the earth, while others maintain that they are the Persian Sea and the Mediterranean, as we saw earlier (ibid. vol. 27, p. 128). In verse 55:22 we learn that pearls (*al-lu'lu'*) and corals (*al-marján*) are extracted from them. Tabarí states that pearls and corals are only extracted from the sea shells (*asdáf*) of the ocean on earth from the raindrops falling from the sky (al-Tabarí is referring to a common belief at the time about how pearls were produced. See 'Lu'lu'" *EI2*). He concludes, therefore, that one body of water is on earth and the other is in the sky (ibid. vol. 27, pp. 128–9).

Of course the Shi'i Imams interpreted many of the verses as allusions to the family of the Prophet. In reference to the last mentioned verse, Ja'far al-Sádiq reportedly stated that the two oceans that were joined are 'Alí and his wife Fátima, who do not oppress each other (*yabdhí*). The coral and pearls that issued forth from them are their sons Hasan and Husayn (Majlisí 1983, vol. 24, p. 97). In another tradition attributed to the Prophet, 'Alí is called the 'ocean of knowledge' (*bahr al-'ilm*) and Fátima is called the 'ocean of prophethood' (*bahr al-nubuwwa*) that have been 'joined' (*yattasaláni*) (ibid. vol. 24, p. 99). As for the meaning of *barzakh*, Ja'far is reported to have said that it is the grave in which the dead person resides between the time of his death and the day of Resurrection (Kulayní 1985, vol. 3, p. 243). The notion of the *barzakh* as a type of purgatory is reinforced by its definition as a 'matter between two matters' (*amr bayn amrayn*) (Majlisí 1983, vol. 6, p. 214, citing the *Tafsír* of al-Qummí). This interpretation probably arises from the Quranic depiction of the ungodly when they have died, whereon they beg God to let them return to the world and work good deeds. However, a barrier (*barzakh*) prevents them from doing so until the day of Resurrection (Q 23:100).

In the writings of Shaykh Ahmad there are two *barzakhs*, or 'interworlds' (as per Hamid's translation). The first is the Imaginal World between the Sensible World and the Intelligible World. The second interworld is Delimited Existence that separates the Intelligible World from Absolute Existence, which is the highest degree and the realm of Acting (Hamid 1998, p. 404).

35. See Q 55:19 and above.
36. Like *al-insán*, another difficult term to translate in Bábí/Bahá'í scripture. It literally means 'form' or 'temple'. In the writings of Shaykh Ahmad the term usually means the outer human form of those who possess higher levels of spiritual perception, such as Messengers and the Imams (see his Seventh Observation in the *al-Fawá'id*, p. 309 of Hamid's translation). Here the 'form of the two Tatanj' is probably an allusion to the station of the Imam 'Alí (see below).
37. This is an allusion to the *al-Khutba al-tatanjiyya*, 'The Tatanjí Sermon' (also spelled *Tatanj* or *Tutunj*), attributed to 'Alí. Its origins are obscure but it has strong Ismá'ílí elements. A 12th-century Shi'i scholar, Ibn Shahrashub, was the first person to mention the sermon and Rajab al-Bursí (see note above on *nuqta*) was the first person (that we know of) to write it down (see his Rajab al-Bursí 1995). Owing to the absence of any chain of transmission and al-Bursí's extremist views regarding the Imams, the *khutba* was not recorded in any of the canonical collections of Shi'i hadith. However, the sermon was very important for Shaykhi imamology. Sayyid Kázim wrote a long commentary on it and its theophanic language has had a strong influence on the Báb's writings (the Báb even composed a supercommentary on a line in Sayyid Kázim's commentary). He glosses *tatanj* as 'gulf' in his commentary on the sermon. For more information on the history of the Tatanjí Sermon and its significance in the Báb's writings, see Lawson 2001.

The meaning of *al-tatanjayn* is as obscure as the origin of the text. The title comes from the word *tatanj*, which is used throughout the text. The most significant statement is made by 'Alí near the beginning, 'I am the one who stands upon the two Tatanjs' (*aná al-wáqifu 'alá al-tatanjayn*). I have been unable to find the term in any standard medieval Arabic dictionaries. Two later commentators assert that it means 'gulf' (*khalíj*) (see Lawson 2001). While later authors may have understood it in this way, the etymological similarities of this word with the word *tanja* (the Arabic word for the town of Tangiers in Morocco) suggests something different. As noted above, one of the commentators on verse 18:60 (Muhammad b. Ka'b) asserts that the *majma' al-bahrayn* (the place of the joining of the two oceans) is Tanja, on the very tip of the Moroccan side of the Straits of Gibraltar that are the gateway between the Mediterranean Sea and the Atlantic Ocean and mark the western edge of the medieval Islamic world. Shi'i authors were also familiar with this interpretation (see, for example, Majlisí 1983, vol. 13, p. 282). So perhaps 'Alí is being depicted as standing at Tanja.

But why are their two Tanjas named in the sermon? Perhaps the Spanish tip of the straights is also being called Tanja, a mirror image of the Moroccan town. Thus 'Alí is straddling the Straits of Gibraltar. Or it might be purely stylistic. The dual form sometimes occurs in the Qur'an instead of the singular if the rhyme scheme at the end of a verse calls for it. For example, 'two paradises' are mentioned in 55:46 in order to keep with the rhyme scheme of the preceding verses. In reference to the 'Tatanjí Sermon', the word *Tatanj* may be in the dual form to rhyme with the following sentence 'I am gazing towards the two Easts (*al-mashriqayn* – also 'two dawning-places [of the sun]') and the two Wests (*al-maghribayn* – also 'two setting-places [of the sun]).' Interestingly, these phrases immediately precede 55:19, which I commented on above (see *al-bahrayn*), and it may be that the 'two Easts' and the 'two Wests' are just meant to be 'East and West' but are put in the dual form for the sake of the Quranic rhyme scheme.

If, however, one were to insist that two Tatanj are being referred to in the *khutba*, we do not necessarily have to abandon the theory that 'Tatanj' in this text derives from the Arabic word for Tangiers. In the *Mu'jam al-Buldán* of the medieval Muslim geographer Yáqút al-Hamawí (d. 1229 CE), we find mention of another Tanj on the opposite end of the Muslim world:

> **Tanj** . . . does not (derive from) an Arabic root. It is a village in Khurásán close to Marv.

> **Tanja** . . . is a city in the fourth clime. Its longitude is 80 degrees from the West and its latitude is 35 ½ degrees from the South. It is a town on the coast of the Western Ocean [the Atlantic] opposite of Algeciras . . . It is in the land of the Berbers (Yáqút al-Hamawí 1990, vol. 4, p. 49).

From Yáqút we learn that there were two towns at the polar opposite ends of the Muslim domains. Tanja lies at the very western edge of the land of the Maghrib, 'the setting sun', and Tanj is located at the eastern edge of the land of Khurásán, 'the rising sun'. Thus 'Alí's statement, 'I am standing upon the two Tatanj', could have also meant that he was straddling the two poles of the Muslim lands.

Regardless of what the passage originally meant in the mind of the author, Shaykh Ahmad, Sayyid Kázim and the Báb prize it for its statement of polarity, with the Imam 'Alí centred between two opposites. As Lawson observes in his article, these authors see the Imam as the point at which all opposites arise and are ultimately resolved. To the believer who has accepted the authority of the Imam, the latter represents a new paradise on earth since he can explain the inner mysteries of the Qur'an. To the person who has denied the authority of the Imam, the latter represents God's judgement and wrath towards his wayward servant. In short, the Imam does not embody these contradictions in his own person but comes to symbolize them based on the person's choice to obey or disobey his spiritual authority. The duality represented by the two Tatanj in the sermon is very important in Shaykhi cosmology and imamology and perhaps even more so for the Báb, who claimed many of the spiritual stations delineated by 'Alí in the text.

38. *Ahl al-a'yán* could also be rendered as 'the people of entities', which would give this phrase a much more philosophical shade since *al-a'yán* refers to a 'concrete entity' as opposed to *al-akwán*, which is 'generated beings'. This pair appears later in the treatise but I can see no obvious reason why *a'yán* should be translated according to its more technical sense here. Generally, *al-a'yán* refers to the prominent members of

a community, as in the well-known biographical dictionary of Shi'i scholars, *A'yán al-shí'a*.

39. See note above on *al-bahrayn*.
40. It is sometimes difficult to translate the term *hukm* in the Báb's writings owing to its multifarious uses. Its primary meaning is a 'judgement', usually from God. But the Báb often speaks of the *hukm* of something other than God, as in the statement here: 'the *hukm* of the two gulfs'. Rendering this phrase as 'the judgement of the two gulfs' does not make sense in English and does nothing to clear up the ambiguity of the term in the original text. To make a distinction between a *hukm* from God and a *hukm* that belongs to something other than God, I have translated the former as 'judgement' or 'decree' and the latter as 'allotment' or 'state'. God makes a judgement regarding a particular thing and it attaches to that thing as its allotment or its designated role. This latter meaning is also the translation of *hukm* in its grammatical senses. Two grammatical definitions of the word are 1) 'the proper function which the word performs at its *martaba* [degree] in which it is placed, its activity' and 2) 'the proper function *to be performed* by the *martaba* in which it is placed'. For example, when we combine the specific activities (*ahkám*, pl. of *hukm*) of *law* (= if) and *lá* (= not) they have a new activity (*hukm*) independent of their constituent parts (*law lá* = if not). For more examples of the grammatical aspects of the word *hukm*, see 'Hukm', *EI2*.
41. The meaning of this final clause is unclear to me but the Báb seems to be saying that the 'point of the two *barzakhs*' does not have the same status as 'the two gulfs'. Again, the Báb often uses the term 'point' (*nuqta*) rather loosely to mean 'epitome' (see above note on *nuqta*).
42. The specific meaning of the term *al-nahw* is 'syntax' but, when used alone, can also designate 'grammar' as a whole. In this case, however, the Báb is using it in its specific sense since he mentions its usual counterpart, *sarf* (morphology), a few lines down.
43. Limits (*hudúd*) and demarcation (*al-tahdíd*) are the properties of created things. Perhaps *al-tahdíd* here is also an allusion to a statement attributed to Imam al-Ridá: 'His ultimate reality (*kunh*) is the separation between Him and His creation; His jealousy (*ghuyúruhu*) is the demarcation (*tahdíd*) of that which is besides Him' (cited in Shaykh Ahmad's *al-Fawá'id*, Hamid trans. p. 344). This tradition is found in *'Uyún al-akhbár*, vol. 1, p. 149.
44. Perhaps 'principle' or 'rule' would also work here.
45. The Báb seems to be alluding to the *Hadíth al-Haqíqa* by 'Alí, related by his companion of 23 years, Kumayl. One day, Kumayl asked, 'What is reality?' ('*má al-haqíqa*'). 'Alí responded with a cryptic explanation that Kumayl asked him to further elucidate, which 'Alí then followed with another cryptic explanation and so forth. This hadith is prominent in the Báb's writings – he wrote a treatise on it in the first year of his ministry (*Fihrist* f. 5b) – and he alludes to it often (See Lawson's translation of the Báb's *Risála fí al-Sulúk* for another early allusion, Lawson 1998, vol. 2, no. 1). Here the reference is to one line of the hadith which states that 'reality' is 'the effacing of the objects of fancy and the clarifying of the objects of knowledge' (*mahw al-mawhúm wa sahw al-ma'lúm*). This hadith is also central in the writings of Shaykh Ahmad, who explains this line with the following in his *al-Fawá'id*: 'Every time a servant reaches a station wherein the Compeller self-manifests to him, this effacing and clearing occur to him. So there, through effacing and clearing, he has cognisance of his Lord because through effacing and clearing, he knows his soul' (Hamid trans., p. 318). The 'hadíth al-haqíqa' does not appear in the canonical collections of Shi'i hadith but is found in several 14th-century works, including Haydar Ámalí's *Jámi'al-asrár*.
46. A distinctly Shi'i doctrine which holds that God is able to decree something and then later rescind it if he so wishes. Shaykh Ahmad wrote a great deal on the subject of

al-badá' and God's knowledge (see Hamid 1998, p. 413, n. 123). It was also a subject of one of the Báb's early treatises 'Alteration and the Preserved Tablet' (*al-badá' wa al-lawh al-mahfuz*). This text is listed in the *Kitáb al-fihrist* (Princeton MS, f. 5b) – making it a first-year text – and several copies exist.

47. Alternatively, 'The alteration of its allotment belongs to God.'
48. *Ajal* and *kitáb* are two of the three categories of essence (*máhiyya*) in the writings of Shaykh Ahmad (*idhn* is the third). As noted above (see gloss on *aqdá*), these three categories are taken from a hadith attributed to the sixth Imam. The phrase *kitáb mu'ajjal* is from Q 3:145: 'A soul cannot die, save by God's permission (*idhn*), a fixed record (*kitában mu'ajjalan*).'
49. In the works of Shaykh Ahmad the term 'thing' (*al-shay'*) applies to any 'composite or concrescence of essence and existence', including humans (Hamid 1998, p. 550). I have not seen evidence that the Báb's notion of 'thing' contradicts that of the Shaykh.
50. Literally, 'to slip', as in a pen slipping in the hand of a scribe.
51. *Markaz* is another term that occurs frequently in the writings of the Báb and is often a synonym for *qutb* (pole) and *nuqta* (point). See Lawson 2001.
52. *Min hawl* or *hawl* frequently occurs in the Báb's writings. The former occurs in Q 39:75: 'And you will see angels surrounding (*háffín min hawl*) the Throne singing the praises of their Lord.' The latter occurs in Q 19:68: 'Now, by thy Lord, We shall surely muster them, and the Satans, then We shall parade them about Gehenna (*hawl jahannam*) hobbling on their knees' (Arberry trans.). In both places it has the sense of surrounding something.
53. To my knowledge, this term does not occur in the works of Shaykh Ahmad or Sayyid Kázim. It does, however, occur frequently in the early writings of the Báb, particularly in relation to the four-fold secret found in several Imami hadiths. Concerning the station of the Imams, Imam Ja'far reportedly said, 'Our command (*amr*) is the secret (*sirr*), the secret of the secret (*sirr al-sirr*), the secret of that which is concealed (*sirr al-mustasarr*), and a secret veiled by the secret (*sirr al-muqanna' bil-sirr*)' (al-Saffár al-Qummí 1984, p. 29). Shaykh Ahmad also wrote a detailed chapter on the four-fold secret in the *Sharh al-ziyára*, relating each one to a different station of the Imams' reality (see Ahsá'í, *Sharh al-ziyára* 1999, vol. 1, pp. 42–50).

Allusions to the four-fold secret hadiths are scattered throughout the works of the Báb. In his *Tafsír al-basmala* (*Interpretation of the Opening Line of the Qur'an*), he writes: 'Verily God hath made four stations (*maqámát*) for His manifestation unto His creation by means of His creating. [These four stations] are alluded to and mentioned cryptically in the words of the family of God, peace be upon them, as secrets: the secret (*as-sirr*), the secret of the secret (*sirr as-sirr*), the secret of that which is concealed (*sirr al-mustassar*), and the secret veiled by the secret (*al-sirr al-muqanna' bil-sirr*)' (Mázandaráni, *Asrár al-áthár*, 'Sirr'). For more on the four-fold secret, see the gloss of *sirr mustasarr* near the end of the treatise.

As for the 'secret of the line', the Báb often couples it with the four-fold secret. For example, in chapter nine of the Qayyúm al-Asmá', the Báb writes: 'He is God! He has desired an esoteric interpretation of the concealed place of the secret (*mustasarr al-sirr*), upon the secret of the line, upon the Point of the *Bá'*.' Perhaps in the mind of the Báb, the 'secret of the line' was the opening line of the Qur'an, as this example suggests. Or perhaps it is a more general reference to the ability to read concealed divine knowledge, as we find in Ibn 'Arabí's *al-Futuhát al-makkiyya*. In the chapter on 'Knowledge of the Spirit from whom I Took what He Revealed in Detail and Set Down in This Book', near the beginning of his *magnum opus*, he talks about an encounter with an enigmatic youth (*fatá*) at the Ka'ba who is 'neither living nor dead' and who explains to Ibn 'Arabí certain secrets about existence. Towards the end of the section Ibn 'Arabí says that the youth instructed him to lift his (the youth's) veil and read/recite (like the angel Gabriel tells Muhammad to recite) his lines (*sutúr*). He then instructs Ibn 'Arabí to write down the things he had shared with him so that others might benefit from them. Ibn 'Arabí says, 'The first line (*satr*) that I read and the first secret (*sirr*) of that line (*satr*) which I learned is that which I now mention in this second chapter.' Finally, references to the 'secret of the line' also carried over into Bahá'u'lláh's writings (see, for example, a short letter in *La'álí' al-hikma*, vol. 1, p. 24).

54. A paraphrase of God's admonition to Adam and Eve. Cf. Q 2:35, 7:19.
55. *Aqsama* is a fourth form intransitive verb that means 'to swear an oath'. However, the Báb seems to be using the verb in its second form, transitive sense, which means to 'divide, set aside'. As for *hazran*, I am inclined to read it adverbially but the Báb uses it as a noun a few lines down. However, the noun means 'a ban, forbiddance', which does not make sense in this context or in the second instance. The Báb's intended meaning seems to be closer to a noun from the same root, *hazíra*, which means 'a precinct, enclosure'. It makes more sense to read it with this meaning in mind since grammar is being prohibited from drawing close to, but still allowed to dwell near, the 'tree of origination'. Therefore, I have translated *hazr* as 'precinct'. This reading also fits one common usage of the term *hazíra*: *hazírat al-quds*, which means the 'precinct of holiness' or 'paradise' (*janna*). See *Lisán al-'arab* under 'h-z-r'.

Of course, the reading preserved in INBA 4011, *khatran* ('danger, peril'), could be correct, but it does not fit very well with the rest of the sentence. Hopefully this problem will be cleared up once more manuscript copies are available.

56. Ja'far al-Sádiq was reportedly asked about verse 25:54 in the Qur'an: 'It is He who hath has created a man from water . . .' Ja'far explains that 'God created Adam from the sweet-tasting water and created his wife from his root (*sinkhihi*). Thereupon he fashioned her from his utmost extremities (*asfal a'dá'ihi*) . . .' (Majlisí 1983, vol. 57, p. 277).
57. *Habt* is a noun meaning 'lowering, decrease'. Here the word is an allusion to Q 2:36, 2:38 and 7:24, where God commands Adam, Eve and Satan to 'fall down' (*ihbitú*) upon the earth (i.e. cease to dwell in Paradise) owing to their transgressions.
58. I have not seen this phrase used by the Báb before. *Al-taghyír* is a verbal noun derived from the verb *ghayyara* (to change, alter). This verb occurs several times in the Qur'an with different associations. For example, in Q 13:11 change is positively associated with humanity's free will: 'God changes not what is in a people, until they change what is in themselves. [But] when God desires to evil for people, there is no turning it back' (slightly modified Arberry trans.). In Q 4:119 change is negatively associated with Satan's corruption of human nature: 'I will lead them astray, and fill them with fancies . . . I will command them and they will alter (*fala-yughayyirunna*) God's creation (*khalq alláh*).' Given the context, perhaps the Báb has this latter verse in mind. Or perhaps he is alluding to those philosophers who contended that the essence of God changed when He created the world (i.e. he was not a Creator and then he was).
59. Cf. Q 71:10.
60. As it appears in the two manuscripts I have consulted, this phrase is grammatically incorrect and is therefore difficult to decipher. From the context it seems that the intended verb is *dháqú*, meaning 'they tasted'. However, in the two manuscripts the middle long vowel has dropped out, indicating the imperative form of the verb. But an imperative cannot follow the particle *qad* and it does not fit the context of the sentence. Further, *abá'ahum* is in the accusative, which would make it the object of the verb and render the sentence rather nonsensical ('they tasted their fathers'). Therefore I have read the phrase as *qad dháqú abá'uhum* ('their fathers have tasted').
61. I have read this as *habb* (seed) because of the context but it could just as well be *hubb* (love). In the next line there is some blurring between the two and I have switched to *hubb* because of the Quranic allusion.

62. The word *al-muzn* occurs only once in the Qur'an in the course of a monologue by God directed at His creation in Q 56:57–74. God chastises his creatures for not knowing who created them and failing to recognize the source of their sustenance. In 56:68–70, God asks, 'Do you see the water that you drink? Do you think that you sent it down from the cloud (*al-muzn*) or that We are the one who sends (it) down?' In Imami hadith *al-muzn* was held to be the name of a tree in Paradise. For example, in one tradition attributed to Ja'far al-Sádiq he says: 'Verily, in Paradise there is a tree named *al-muzn*. If God desires to create a believer, he takes (*aqtara*) a single drop from it. Neither herbs nor fruit can partake of it. [Only] a believer or an unbeliever can eat of it, but God, exalted and glorified is He, will draw out a believer from his loins (*sulbihi*)' (Kulayní 1985, vol. 2, p. 14). Another tradition from Ja'far relates that angels used the water of the *muzn* to cleanse the body of a martyr between heaven and earth who had not been washed properly (Ibn Bábúya 1993, vol. 1, p. 159). In a tradition from 'Alí there is also the following: 'Verily, the rain (*al-matar*) from which animals are provided for (comes) from beneath the Throne (*al-'arsh*). Then the Messenger of God asked for rain the first time and he stood until his head and his beard were wet. Then he said, "Verily, water is recently (placed) (*qaríba 'ahdin*) at the Throne. If God, blessed and exalted is He, wants to make rain, He sends it down from this (water) to the ocean (then) to heaven [*samá'* – also sky] after heaven until it reaches a place called *muzn*. Thereupon God, blessed and exalted is He, reveals to (*yuhí . . . ilá*) the wind (*al-ríh*). Then it blows the cloud (*al-saháb*) until it reaches a place. Then it [the rain] descends from the *muzn* to the cloud. Therefore, every drop upon the earth is put in its place by an angel and no drop falls on another drop"' (al-Núrí 1988, vol. 6, p. 191) The *muzn* also plays an important role in the writings of Shaykh Ahmad (see the relevant section in Cole 1994).
63. In Q 2:93, Moses' disobedient followers are said to have been made to 'drink (*ushribú*) the calf (*al-'ijl*) into their hearts on account of their unbelief'. Early commentators were split over meaning of this verse. Some said that what Moses' disobedient followers drank into their hearts was the love (*hubb*) of the calf but it is only implied in the verse (al-Tabarí 1954, vol. 1, pp. 422–3). The Báb seems to agree with this reading, which is also found in the Shi'i *tafsír* literature (for example, see Majlisí 1983, vol. 22, p. 498). Others contended that Moses' followers were made to drink of the water that held small bits of the calf accumulated when Moses destroyed it (al-Tabarí 1954, vol. 1, p. 423).
64. Cf. 8:11 and Majlisí 1983, section on '*Tathír al-ard*', vol. 77, pp. 147–59.
65. Cf. 12:40, 17:23.
66. For the distinction between *al-a'yán* and *al-akwán*, see note on *al-a'yán* above.
67. Q 55:19–20. See note on *al-bahrayn*.
68. *Hadhdh* is used in the Qur'an in a variety of senses. First, it is used in its general sense as 'part' of a whole, such as in Q 5:13–14 and in a legal sense, as in a 'share' or 'portion' given to heirs (see Q 4:11, 176). It is also someone's good fortune (see Q 28:79 and 41:35). Finally, it is people's portion in the next world based on their belief or unbelief (Q 3:176). Given the context, the Báb is probably alluding to verses Q 28:78–9, in which the Pharaoh's wealthy minister Qarún (the biblical Korah), is chastised by his people. They counsel him not to rejoice in his wealth, since true wealth comes from God in the form of a home in the next world. Qarún retorts that he attained his wealth by means of 'a particular knowledge' (*'ilmin*) and he walks with pride among the people because of it, making them envious of his 'great fortune' (*hadhdhin 'azímin*). But the people who had knowledge (*al-'ilm*, which is apparently contrasted with its indefinite counterpart that Qarún possessed) remind him that true wealth is garnered by those who believe and do good works. Thereupon God causes the earth to swallow up Qarún and his home. To account for his wealth, as well as the

enigmatic phrase *'alá 'ilmin 'indí* ('on account of a particular knowledge I possess') in 28:78, Muslim authors often state that Qarún was a master of alchemical wisdom that had been passed down from Moses through Aaron (see 'Karún', *EI2*). As in the passages from the Qur'an, the Báb seems to be saying that the particular science of grammar is of a second order compared to the first-order knowledge of the hereafter. See the following few lines.

69. As in the beginning of this text, the Báb places the status of the two gulfs (*al-khalíjayn*) at a level lower than the *barzakh*.
70. Here the Báb seems to make the location of the 'two bodies of water' explicit: the water north of the equator, all the way to the north pole, and the water south of the equator, all the way to the south pole. As we saw earlier, however, early exegetes also thought the 'two bodies of water' could refer to the water that is on the earth (one body of water) and the water that is in the sky (another body of water). In this case, that which stands (*al-qá'im*) between the two bodies of water (i.e. between earth and heaven) is either an isthmus or barrier (*barzakh*) or the person of 'Alí (as in the Tatanjí sermon). The meaning of the Báb's allusion is further complicated by the fact that the circle of the zodiac is equivalent to the circle of the 'equator' (*khatt al-istiwá'*) (see 'Istiwá', 'Khatt', *EI2*). Allusions such as this will be more easy to decipher once more research has been done on the terrestrial and celestial topography of Shaykh Ahmad, Sayyid Kázim and the Báb.
71. *Al-'iráb* are the case endings of a word that indicate its grammatical function in the sentence (this should be familiar to those with a knowledge of German or Greek). Unlike English, which relies more on syntax to convey meaning, proper declension is essential for comprehension of the meaning of an Arabic sentence. The Báb often puts the wrong case ending on a word, particularly for sound masculine plurals (masculine words that are made plural by adding *úna* to the end), which makes it difficult to understand his intended meaning. There are several possible reasons for this (see the first part of this article). For examples of this phenomenon in the present text, see the Báb's conjugation of the verb *dháqa* and his declension of the word *ábá'* earlier in the treatise. The former seems to resemble a violation of Arabic verb conjugation in verse 63:10 of the Qur'an (the dropping of a middle letter of a root), while the latter is another example of the irregular use of case endings.
72. *Tasríf* is a verbal noun that means 'to inflect' a word or 'to conjugate' a verb depending on its object. For the sake of simplicity, I have chosen one of these translations. Both operations are part of the part of Arabic grammar called *sarf* (morphology). *Tasríf* is also a technical term denoting a theurgic act (my thanks to Vahid Brown for this latter observation). As with the dual meaning of many other grammatical terms in this text, the Báb is probably playing with both senses of the word.
73. An allusion to Q 55:22.
74. This passage is particularly difficult to render because of the ambiguous meaning of the word *al-qat'*. Second, it is unclear whether this is an independent clause with a dependent clause that modifies 'an exact limit' or two independent clauses. Both are plausible since there is no *wa* or other connecting word to indicate a new sentence but I am reading it as two independent clauses. As for the word *al-qat'*, its root has the general meaning of 'cutting' and 'severing' and I am tempted to read it this way because of the context of 'separation' (*fasl*) and 'union' (*wasl*) (see the gloss above on *al-muttasila*). The 'f' and the 'w' can look similar in Arabic script ('A thing does not know separation except by severance from union'). As it is written, I suppose the sentence could also be rendered, 'A thing does not know separation except from severance by means of union.' However, the phrase *al-qat' bi* almost always means 'certain knowledge of something', which is a synonym of *al-yaqín*, 'certainty', and often contrasted with *al-zann*, 'probable doubt', and *al-shakk*, 'doubt'. All of the instances of

this phrase that I have been able to find in the writings of the Báb or Shaykh Ahmad indicate its standard use as 'certain knowledge of (s.th.)'. It remains a puzzle for the time being.

75. This final phrase is a surprise, since we would expect to see the contrasting condition of 'motion' (*al-haraka*), similar to the contrasting pairs of 'separation' and 'union' in the preceding phrase. Since there is a major discrepancy between my two manuscripts here (see the critical edition), I am hopeful that comparison with other manuscripts will clear up this problem.

76. *Al-qawá'id* generally means rules or standards. When used with regard to language, it means the rules governing writing; in other words, grammar.

77. Perhaps an allusion to the Emerald Tablet, an alchemical tract attributed to Hermes Trismegistus, often equated by Muslims with the Quranic Idrís.

78. This phrase is often used in Shaykh Ahmad's writings to refer to the Messengers of God and the Shi'i Imams. See note above on *haykal*.

79. This could also be rendered as 'from the shade of the celestial world' but I have opted for 'the world of 'Alí' owing to the Báb's reference to the 'temples of unity', which often connotes the Shi'i Imams (see above).

80. This is a paraphrase of a statement by Imam al-Ridá' during his debate with a Sabian philosopher in the presence of the 'Abbasid Caliph, al-Ma'mún. In the course of explaining the relationship between God and His creation, al-Ridá' states: 'Those who possess understanding (*dhawú al-albáb*) know that seeking information (*al-istidlál* – also 'evidence') of what is there cannot be saved by what is here' (see Majlisí 1983, vol. 10, p. 316). Shaykh Ahmad drew heavily on the text of this debate (for example, see his paraphrase of this passage in the Thirteenth Observation of his *al-Fawá'id*), as did the Báb (he quotes another passage from this debate below).

81. Q 2:156.

82. In this and the following passages the Báb's use of the preposition *'alá* is somewhat vague. I have tried to translate it according to my sense of the context and its usual meaning. Further exploration of the Báb's metaphysical terminology and gemantria should illumine some of the more obscure references in this part of the text.

83. The language of this and the preceding sentences reminds the reader of the Báb's earlier allegory of syntax and morphology being exiled from Paradise.

84. *Al-dhikr* ('the remembrance') is a word that the Báb often uses to refer to the Imams and to himself. The imperative phrase *ibda' bil-dhikr 'alá al-fi'l* is difficult to render because of the prepositional phrase *'alá al-fi'l*. If the Báb had written the clause without the definite article before *dhikr* and the preposition *'alá* (*ibda' bi-dhikr al-fi'l*), we could easily read it as 'Begin with mention of the Acting'.

85. It is unclear if the pronoun refers to 'the Remembrance' or 'the Acting'.

86. By itself, *al-shahádatayn* would mean the two *shahádas* or testimonies recited by Muslims at the call to prayer: 'I bear witness that there is no god but God. I bear witness that Muhammad is the Messenger of God.' For the Twelver Shi'a in Iran, a third testimony is often added: 'I bear witness that 'Alí is the friend/saint/guardian of God (*walí alláh*). However, when contrasted with *al-ghayb* ('invisible' or 'unseen'), it has the meaning of 'visible'. For example, in the Qur'an God is repeatedly referred to as 'He who knows the invisible and the visible (*'álim al-ghayb wa al-shaháda*)' (for example, see Q 6:73; 9:94, 105; 13:9). The Qur'an also asserts that knowledge of the *ghayb* only belongs to God: 'He knows the *ghayb* and does not manifest (*yuzhir*) His *ghayb* unto anyone' (Q 72:26). In medieval Islam the term *ghayb* was associated variously with God's hidden decree, the suprarational worlds of *jabarút*, *malakút* and *lahút* penetrated by gnosis (as per Ibn 'Arabí), and the realm of occult knowledge, like magic (see 'al-Ghayb', *EI2*). For Shi'as, the Imams were held to have access to the knowledge of the *ghayb* and for Twelver Shi'as the term is also closely connected with the Twelfth

Imam who disappeared at some point and is waiting in occultation (*al-ghayba*) to return one day and fill the world with justice. In the metaphysical world of Shaykh Ahmad, there is a bleeding together of these two terms since he held that the spirit of the Twelfth Imam is occulted in the *ghayb* (dwelling in a region that he variously equates with the interworld (*barzakh*), the world of similitudes (*'álam al-mithál*), and *Hurqalyá*) and the Perfect Shi'a can commune with him to attain esoteric knowledge. As the foregoing indicates, Shaykh Ahmad's conception of the *ghayb* incorporated much of Ibn 'Arabí's terminology and also aspects of the occult. In the writings of the Báb this terminology is also used to describe the *ghayb* and the connotations of the term also overlap with *al-ghayba*, as seen a few lines below in this text.

87. Cf. Q 18:60 and note above on *al-bahrayn*.
88. *Al-qilla* (fewness) and *al-kathra* (plurality) are terms used to describe the quantity of a created thing. They are also grammatical terms: *jam' al-qilla* ('the plural of paucity') is used for things numbering between three and ten and *jam' al-kathra* ('the plural of multitude') is for things numbering more than this. Here the Báb seems to be alluding to gemantria or the 'science of letters' (*'ilm al-hurúf*) in which the esoteric meaning of scripture is discerned by complex calculations involving the numerical equivalents of letters in a word or words. The Báb wrote a long treatise on the subject that has yet to be translated or studied in depth.
89. Here, as elsewhere, the Báb is playing with the grammatical meanings of his metaphysical terminology. I have translated *al-fi'l* as 'the Act' throughout this text but here the Báb is clearly bringing out its grammatical denotation as 'verb'. However, the reader should keep in mind that the Báb is still primarily talking about metaphysical matters.
90. The fourth form verb *a'raba* also has the meanings of 'to Arabize' or 'to make manifest' and *al-ism* also means 'the name', so this phrase could also be rendered as 'Manifest the name with the pure water'.
91. The Quranic name for Mount Sinai.
92. A type of wind instrument. Cf. Q 74:8.
93. Cf. Q 92:2.
94. Cf. Q 74:33.
95. Cf. Q 37:61.
96. Cf. Q 53:5.
97. Also 'noun'. See the relevant section in the introduction.
98. In Arabic grammar, the *na't* is 'used to designate a qualifying adjective and its function as an epithet' ['Na't', *EI2*]. The term is usually synonymous with *wasf* (see below).
99. In Arabic grammar, *wasf* is also a subdivision of the *ism* and would be translated as 'adjective'.
100. Shaykh Ahmad equates the 'loftiest book' (*al-kitáb al-a'lá*) with the 'inscribed forms in the exalted realms, which are the loftiest (regions) of Paradise (*al-suwar al-manqúsha fí 'illíyín wa 'illíyún a'lá al-janna*)'. He also equates the 'inscribed forms' with the 'lowest book' (*al-kitáb al-asfal*) and they are written on the *sijjín*, 'which is a rock beneath the earth' (see Q 83:7–9; Shaykh Ahmad 1858, p. 150). According to the Qur'an, both realms (the most exalted Paradise and the lowest Hell) have their own 'inscribed book' (*kitáb marqúm*) (Q 83:9, 20).
101. *Lafz* (linguistic expression) and *ma'ná* (intended meaning) are classic pairs in Arabic grammar and Muslim thinkers quickly realized that a particular *lafz* could have a variety of *ma'ání* (pl. of *ma'ná*). We have already seen an example of this in the expressions *ism* and *fi'l*, whose denotation differ depending on the context. *Ma'ná* also has its philosophical counterpart in medieval Muslim discussions of language and abstractions (see 'Ma'ná', *EI2*).

The comparison of the *lafz* to the body and the *ma'ná* to the spirit was probably quite common, since the soul was thought to give life to the body and the body indicated the existence of the soul. I have been able to find one such equivalence by the North African belle-lettreist Ibn Rashíq (d. 456 AH or 463 AH/1063–4 AD or 1070–1 AD) in his *al-'Umda* in the chapter on '*al-lafz wa al-ma'ná*'. There he writes, 'Expression (*al-lafz*) is a body (*jism*) and its spirit (*rúhuhu*) is meaning (*al-ma'ná*) and meaning is connected with expression like the connection of the spirit with the body. The spirit is weakened when the body is weak and strong when it is strong. If the meaning is sound and the expression is weak, then it diminishes poetry and it is faulty, just as occurs to bodies on account of lameness, paralysis, blindness and so forth without the spirit leaving. Likewise, if the meaning is weak and some of it is defective, then the expression is better off, like that which occurs to bodies when the spirits are ill [i.e. the expressions still appear sound even though the meaning is defective]' (Ibn Rashíq 1981, p. 124).

102. A *nisba* is also an adjective derived from a noun that indicates affiliation with a person, place or thing, like the word 'Bábí' (one who follows the Báb).

103. The Arabic imperative *kun* ('be!') comes from the root k-w-n, which means 'to be', Since the middle letter, called a *wáw* (the long 'ú' sound), is considered a 'weak' long vowel, it is dropped in the imperative form and replaced with a short vowel (the short 'u' sound). This imperative often appears in the Qur'an as an expression of God's unbounded creative ability – God says 'be and it is' (*kun fa-yakún*). Since there is nothing separating the letter *káf* from the letter *nún*, the Báb is saying that meaning and expression are inextricably bound, like matter and form coming together as a 'thing' (*shay'*).

Concerning what lies between the two letters, Shaykh Ahmad writes:

> By the letter *káf* He alludes to the first innovating (*al-iktirá'*), that is the willing (*al-mashiyya*), which is the *káf* that circles itself (*al-káf al-mustadíra 'alá nafsihá*), because it is the source of being. By the letter *nún* He alludes to the First inventing (*al-ibdá'*), that is, the desiring (*al-iráda*), because it is the source of entity. Between these two letters is a letter dropped because it is phonetically weak. In order to allude to what is meant by that letter, it is outwardly dropped yet subsists inwardly. It is the *water* from which everything was made alive; it is existence; it is the signifying by an expression [of its signification]; it is the water from the clouds; it comprises the smoke particles which obtain their illumination from the fire, sustained by the thick oil that lies close to the smoke particles. That dropped letter is *wáw*, the original [verb], before dropping the weak letter, was *kún*. It comprises the *six days* within which each thing was created (Gulpáyigání 2006). See Hamid 1998, pp. 297–8 for translation.

104. This is the second time that the Báb is paraphrasing a passage that occurs in al-Ridá''s debate with the Sabian philosopher (referred to above). The Sabian asks al-Ridá' to explain God's 'originating' (*al-ibdá'*): 'Is it something created (*khalq*) or not (*ghayr khalq*)?' Al-Ridá' answers that it is 'a still creation that is not perceived through stillness (*khalq sákin lá yudrak bil-sukún*). It only becomes a creation because it is an originated thing (*shay' muhdath*) and God is the One Who originated it (*ahdathahu*). Therefore, it became His creation. There is only God, powerful and glorified is He, and His creation and there is no third thing (*thálith*) between the two and no third thing other than them' (Majlisí 1983, vol. 10, p. 316). Shaykh Ahmad also quotes this tradition in his *al-Fawá'id* and applies it to the first 'originating' (*ibdá'*), which is equated with the Will (*al-mashí'a*), and to the first 'inventing' (*ikhtirá'*), which is equated with Desire (*al-iráda*). The Báb also paraphrases this statement in the letter to 'Isfahání' (cited earlier): 'Verily, the root of the Act (*asl al-fi'l*) is the manifestation of the name

of that which is hidden (*mazhar ism al-maknún*), which is a still creation that is not known through stillness . . .' (Ra'fatí, '*Nigáhí*', p. 66).

105. I am not sure if the Báb intends Imami Shi'ism by this term, Shaykh Ahmad's teachings more specifically or his own school of thought.

106. This seems to be a paraphrase of the tradition attributed to Ja'far quoted earlier (see *al-muttasila*).

107. As noted above, the *sirr mustasarr* or *sirr al-mustasarr* is one of the four-fold secrets mentioned by Ja'far al-Sádiq in two different hadith found in the *Basá'ir al-Daraját* (author 1984, pp. 28–9). In Shaykh Ahmad's *Sharh al-ziyára*, he treats the two terms differently. He equates the first, the *sirr mustassar* ('a concealed secret'), with the station of the Imams or the imamate (*maqám al-imám* or *maqáq al-imáma*), which he contends is the fourth station of the Imams (*al-maqám al-rábi'*). On the other hand, he equates the *sirr al-mustassar* ('the secret of the concealed place') with the station of exposition (*maqám al-bayán*), which is the first station (*Sharh al-ziyára*, pp. 42–3). A detailed examination of Shaykh Ahmad's treatment of this subject is beyond the scope of this gloss but I have appended the two traditions from Ja'far below and given a table of some of the equivalencies that Shaykh Ahmad sets out in the *Sharh al-ziyára* (pp. 42–50):

> 1) . . . Abú 'Abd Alláh [Ja'far] said, 'Verily, our command (*amr*) is the truth and the truth of the truth; and it is the exoteric and the esoteric of the esoteric; and it is the secret, and the secret of the secret, and the secret of the concealed place, and the secret veiled by the secret.'
>
> 2) . . . Abú 'Abd Alláh said, 'Verily, our command is a secret in a secret, and a concealed secret, and a secret that is only known as a secret, and a secret upon a secret and a secret veiled by a secret.'

As I have already noted in my explanation of the 'secret of the line' (*sirr al-satr*), the Báb alludes to the four-fold secret frequently in his writings and connects the *sirr al-mustasarr* with the point of the letter *bá'* in the Qayyúm al-Asmá'. The Báb also mentions the four-fold secret in his *Tafsír al-basmala*, an early exegesis of the meaning of the opening line of the Qur'an (it was written between 1260 and 1262 AH according to the Báb. See a reprint of his second index of his writings in *Zuhúr al-haqq*, vol. 3, p. 290).

Regarding the *al-sirr al-mustasarr bil-sirr* (the secret concealed by the secret), he equates it with 'the green pearl' (*al-durra al-khadrá'*) and Determining (*qadar*), the third level of Acting (Afnan 126 BE, p. 124).

108. This hadith is recorded in *al-Káfí* (vol. 1, p. 112) and translated below:

> Abu 'Abd Alláh (Ja'far al-Sádiq) said: 'Verily, God, exalted and glorified is He, created a name with letters that are not voiced, and with a pronunciation that is not uttered, and with individuality that is not corporeal, and with likeness that cannot be described, and with colour that has no colour. Diameters (*al-aqtár*) are shut out from it, the borders [or limits] are banished from it [and] the sense perception of everyone [capable of] conceiving is veiled from it. It is something hidden that is not veiled. He made it a word completed with the coming together of four parts. There is not one [letter] from it [the word] [that comes] before the other. He made three names to appear from it, owing to the need of created things for them, and concealed one of them, which is the hidden, treasured name. The outer form of these names which have been manifested is 'Allah, Blessed and Exalted'. And He, praised is He, made four pillars subservient to each of these names. Therefore, there are twelve pillars.

Then for each pillar He created 30 names, which are acts related to them [lists 35 names with one repeat].

These names and the names that [make up] the Most Beautiful Names comprise 360 names and are related to these three names. These three names are pillars and He concealed the single, hidden, treasured name by these three names, even as He, exalted is He, says: 'Say: Call upon Allah or call upon the Merciful. By whatsoever you call Him, His are the Most Beautiful Names' (Q 17:110).

A certain Shaykh 'Alí b. Shaykh Sálih asked Shaykh Ahmad to explain this tradition and the latter wrote a detailed treatise in response. At the beginning of the treatise, Shaykh Ahmad acknowledges that the meaning of this tradition is very difficult to understand since it 'is composed of an exposition on the separation of existence into classes (al-ajnás) and parts (al-fusúl) and division [into] derivatives and roots' (Ahmad 1856, vol. 2, p. 311). He then proceeds to give a concise description of his cosmology as it relates to this tradition. Finally, he closes with the assertion that 'I have mentioned what none of the other interpreters of this noble hadith have mentioned and from the riddle of its secrets (mu'ammá asrárihi) I have laid bare that which a subtle mind can barely stumble upon . . .' (p. 313). Here is a translation of his summative paragraph at the end of the treatise:

> The name that is mentioned is the totality of Absolute Existence (al-wujúd al-mutlaq), which is the World of the Command ('álam al-amr), and Delimited Existence (al-wujúd al-muqayyad), which is the World of Creation ('álam al-khalq). It is upon four pillars that are successive in manifestation and some precede others in the essence [but outwardly exist at the same time]. The first [pillar] is that which is concealed and treasured, which is the Willing (al-mashiyya). The three [pillars] that are manifest, which are the World of Creation, are the World of Jabarút, the World of Malakút and the World of Mulk. Each one of these three [pillars] has four pillars: a pillar of creation (khalq) and existentiation (íjád), a pillar of life, a pillar of sustenance (rizq) and a pillar of death. Each pillar is composed of nine celestial spheres and an earth and every one of these ten [spheres] is set made to revolve upon three cycles (dawra): a cycle in its mineral [existence], a cycle in its plant [existence] and a cycle in its animal [existence]. In every 30 is an action (fi'lan) associated with it [the pillar] and especially applicable to it, which is one of the particular (al-juz'iyya) names of God. Verily these three all-encompassing (al-kulliyya) names are the pillars for Delimited Existence, the beginning of which is mind (al-'aql) and the end of which is dust. Verily He, exalted is He, has concealed the hidden name on account of the sufficiency of the manifestation of its effects on the [other] three since creation does not need to increase from it [i.e. creation has all it needs to exist from the appearance of the three manifest names]. Beneath these three [names] are all of the remaining names, just as they [the three names] are beneath the concealed, treasured name (p. 313).

According to Shaykh Ahmad, the three manifest names are Alláh, Tabáraka ('Blessed is He') and Ta'álá ('Exalted is He'). He also notes that in another version of this hadith the word al-'Alíy ('Exalted') is substituted for Ta'álá, and al-'Azím is substituted for Tabáraka (p. 312). Finally, he explains that one name is hidden by the manifestation of the other three because the hidden name would conceal the other three if it manifested itself. In other words, they can only appear if it remains hidden 'because if the One Who Wills appears, the Will (al-mashiyya) disappears' (p. 313).

This hadith plays a prominent role in some of the later writings of the Báb, including his Tafsír wa al-'asr and his treatise on Nubuwwa khássa.

109. *Al-báb bil-báb* is a constant refrain in the Báb's Qayyúm al-Asmá' (it appears, for

example, in the first sura). Other translators might put a full stop between this phrase and the following verse but I would point out that the phrase runs into the following Quranic verse without a conjunction between them, giving me the sense that the Báb wanted his readers to connect the two. Further, the Báb often ended his letters with *al-hamdu li-lláhi rabbi al-'álamína* ('Praise be to God, the Lord of the worlds!') but I have never seen an instance in which he ends with the *basmala,* which is traditionally used to begin a letter (as the Báb has done at the opening of this treatise). Therefore I am inclined to think that the phrase is connected with the verse that follows it and I have tried to sketch out some of the reasons why the Báb might have done so in the following note.

110. Q 1:1–2. By the 'gate' (*al-báb*) of the phrase 'In the Name of God, the Merciful, the Compassionate', the Báb is probably alluding to the letter *bá'* (the first Arabic letter of the phrase) and tying together four different groups of traditions. The first three groups deal with the authority and knowledge of the Imams. One group is the fourfold secret traditions of al-Sádiq in which he equates the 'command' or 'mandate' (*amr*) of the Imams with various kinds of secrets. As I have already observed, one of these secrets (the *mustasarr al-sirr*) is linked by the Báb in the Qayyúm al-Asmá' with a group of traditions by 'Alí in which he declares that he is the 'point beneath the *bá''* (see the gloss of *sirr al-satr* above). 'Alí is also alluded to when the Báb describes the opening of a line of the Qur'an as a 'gate' (*báb*), reminiscent of a tradition attributed to Muhammad in which he calls himself the city of knowledge (*madínat al-'ilm*) and names 'Alí as its 'gate' (*báb*) (al-Hurr al-'Ámilí 1989, vol. 2, p. 34). Given these allusions and the Báb's reference to the *basmala,* he is also probably expecting his readers to remember a tradition by al-Sádiq that he often quotes in which the Imam explains the meaning of the first three letters of the opening line of the Qur'an that the Báb has just referred to: 'The (letter) *bá'* is the glory of God (*bahá' alláh*), the (letter) *sín* is the radiance of God (*saná' alláh*), and the (letter) *mím* is the majesty of God (*majd alláh*)' (Kulayní 1985, vol. 1, p. 114). According to other transmitters, the *mím* is also equated with the 'sovereignty of God' (*mulk alláh*).

6

Secrets Concealed by Secrets: *Taqiyya* as Arcanization in the Autobibliographies of the Báb[1]

J. Vahid Brown

While much of the sustained research into the writings of the Báb in modern scholarship has focused on his earliest writings,[2] the works written between 1844 and 1846 continue to present some of the most serious challenges to analysis and understanding. Apart from the general problems facing a reader of the Báb's famously obscure works, the Báb's earliest writings are rendered particularly difficult by an ever-shifting authorial voice. One must constantly ask in reading these early texts, *who* is the author, *who* is addressing us from the page? The obvious answer, of course, is the Báb, Sayyid 'Alí Muhammad. That this answer does not resolve our problem can best be indicated by an example. The following two passages are both drawn from the Báb's writings from this earliest period:

> Verily, We have bestowed revelation upon you [the Báb] just as We bestowed revelation upon Muhammad and the Messengers before him, with clear signs, that perchance you might be a Proof unto God for the people after the [four] gates . . . O people of the earth! Stray not from the bounds of the word of the Remembrance, and speak not concerning Him save by the truth, for the Remembrance has not revealed His verses but by the truth (Qayyúm al-Asmá', sura 61, pp. 244f., in MS dated 1323; provisional translation[3]).

> I have not claimed a single word of revelation. They say, 'He has laid claim to spiritual authority and its trappings.' May God kill them for that in which they lie! I have neither made claims to nor spoken a word with regard to anything other than servitude . . . The Remnant of God, the Lord of the Age, has, after the four gates, no designated gate and no specific deputy . . . Verily, revelation from Thy presence, the like of which was sent down upon Muhammad, was closed and ended with Him (Du'á-yi alif, in Mazandaráni, *Asrár al-Áthár*, vol. 1, pp. 179–82; provisional translation).

These excerpts are both from the pen of the Báb, though ironically neither is in the authorial voice of 'the Báb'. The first is from the Qayyúm al-Asmá', written in 1844, and the authorial voice is that of God. The second is from the Du'á-yi alif, written in 1845, and is in the voice of a pious Shi'i sayyid of Shiraz. The problem that these two texts exemplify is an acute one – the problem of *taqiyya*.[4]

In its most well-known sense, *taqiyya* means the dissimulation of belief for reasons of self-preservation but it has in Shi'ism a much broader range of meaning. From the many injunctions to practise *taqiyya* found in the recorded sayings of the Imams, it becomes clear that *taqiyya* was not simply a negative obligation not to put oneself in harm's way but was also a positive duty to conceal secrets. Regarding the nature of these secrets, one scholar of Shi'ism put it this way:

> In the corpus of the Imams, certain subjects appear to constitute the main objects of taqiyya: information relating to the 'Qur'an of the imams', the [pious hatred] toward the Companions of the Prophet and in particular toward the first three caliphs, or the identity of the Qa'im . . . (Amir-Moezzi 1994, p. 129).

Two of the three primary objects of *taqiyya* given in this list have to do with Shi'i messianism – the Qur'an of the Imams and the identity of the Qá'im. *Taqiyya*, then, was a Shi'i religious obligation, concerned with the concealment of secrets and, more importantly, such secrets were often of an eschatological nature.[5]

It is important to understand *taqiyya* in this wider sense and not just as dissimulation or self-preserving denial, especially in considering the writings of the Báb. When understood as a technique of arcanization, as concealment of secrets, we are able to discern *taqiyya* in the early writings of the Báb as operating at a variety of levels and layers. It is not simply that these earliest writings present two stark extremes of declaration and denial of messianism, as in the passages from the Qayyúm al-Asmá' and the Du'á-yi alif cited above. Rather, there exists in these earliest works a range of revelation and concealment, a spectrum that extends from the open directness of the Qayyúm al-Asmá' to the opaque covering of the Du'á-yi alif and includes in between a variety of shades of coding, allusiveness and encryption of the messianic secret. And what is perhaps most important for our present-day attempts to understand these texts, this spectrum of *taqiyya* is not solely involved in claims or denials of a messianic station but rather extends to the Báb's communication of personal belief and statements of doctrine. For example, the Báb in some texts expresses views of the Imams that he apparently contradicts in other works or states belief in certain orthodox Usúlí–Shi'i tenets that he elsewhere completely rejects.[6] It is thus imperative that we make some attempt to crack the Báb's *taqiyya* code, to read between the lines of his esoteric writing, if we are to have any hope of success in understanding what the Báb thought – what, in other words, Bábí doctrine really was.

The three autobibliographical works that I will discuss here – the Khutba al-Jidda, the Kitáb al-Fihrist and the Khutba dhikriyya – are indices of this spectrum and provide a window into the chronology of the Báb's practice of *taqiyya* during this period. I refer to the three texts in question as 'autobibliographies' for the simple reason that they all share the characteristic of including lists by the Báb of works he had previously written. Autobibliography is a well-established genre in Islamic letters and has traditionally been employed for a variety of reasons. In the Báb's milieu of 19th-century Shi'ism, autobibliographies were generally written by established scholars and are perhaps best understood as having the combined function of a curriculum vitae and a course syllabus: they indicated the areas of learning that a given scholar had covered or specialized in and, to use the language of the modern academy, provided students with a list of courses in which they could seek a degree.

While one might be tempted to understand the Báb's autobibliographical works against this scholastic background, there are a number of factors that would point to the inadequacy of such a view. For one thing, Shi'i scholars were not generally in the habit of describing their own works as divine revelations. As with the Báb's Qur'an commentaries, the Báb's autobibliographies are radically different from previous works in the genre in that they are bound up with his claims to be the Shi'i messiah. When there is light to be shed on these works from the Shi'i textual tradition, it is to be found not in the curriculum vitae of hadith scholars but rather in the apocalyptic imagery, the culturally-shared body of images and ideas associated with the coming of the Promised One. As I go through the three texts, I will highlight the Báb's utilization of this 'imagery of the end' in signalling – sometimes directly, sometimes obliquely – his messianic authorial voice.

The earliest of the three works is the Khutba al-Jidda, written during the Báb's return journey from his pilgrimage during the late winter or early spring of 1845. The Báb was in Jidda for only a few days, from 24 February to 4 March, at which point he sailed from Jidda for Bushihr. We know these precise dates because they are given by the Báb himself in the Khutba al-Jidda. Further, since the last date he gives there is 4 March (24th of Safar), this provides a *terminus post quem* for the Khutba itself. It seems most likely that it was written aboard ship soon after sailing from Jidda, though Abu'l-Qasim Afnan has noted that in one extant manuscript of the Khutba al-Jidda, the scribe headed it 'Khutba fí jidda, written in Bushihr by His Holiness the Báb' (Afnan, *'Ahd-i A'lá*, p. 474, n. 18). It is indeed possible that the Khutba al-Jidda was written in Bushihr – i.e. in mid-May or late June of 1845 – although the *terminus ante quem* for composition is 21 June 1845, the date of composition of the Kitáb al-Fihrist, since the Khutba al-Jidda is listed in the Kitáb al-Fihrist.[7]

The Khutba al-Jidda is a short work, just 13 pages long in the manuscript collection INBA 91.[8] It begins with a page and a half of cosmogonic narrative – a style of exordium common to many of the works of the Báb during this period – describing the creation of the cosmos and its metaphysical structure in terms of a set of quaternities standard to Shaykhism and ubiquitous in the Báb's writings throughout his ministry. The Báb then launches into a brief polemic against Ishráqí philosophical theology, mentioning by name one of the works of Mullá Sadrá Shírází and stating that the Ishráqís have gone astray in their particular views on the quaternality of being and the status of the names and attributes of God. The Báb then extends his critique to include those ulama who have taken a favourable view of Ishráqí thought. There follows a brief transition to the next major section of the text – a detailed recounting of his pilgrimage journey – and here the Báb shifts to a more directly messianic register. Thus, for example, he writes:

This is the light that hath borne the letter *há'* through the land of the innermost heart and hath gone forth from the bounds of the letter *wáw* through the pen of God's Remembrance, to whom hath been revealed verses in the language of God, the Speaker, as divine proofs, that all people might realize the forbiddenness of their drink and recognize the true meaning ordained in this pearl-white water (INBA 91, p. 65; provisional translation).[9]

The Báb then describes his pilgrimage journey, the messianic overtones continuing strongly throughout this section of the Khutba. The action in this section is ascribed to God rather than to the Báb. Thus this portion of the Khutba begins, 'Praise be to God . . . who hath dispatched the Word of His servant from the land of his birth' (provisional translation). The text continues in this vein for another four and a half pages, naming the points on the Báb's journey to and from Mecca and providing the dates of each stage of the journey in extremely indirect language. Towards the end of this itinerary, the Báb writes:

> So praised be God, the One, the Self-Subsisting, the Single, the Worshipped, who hath spoken in praise of His Remembrance and the days of His journey and hath made mention of the path of His ascent in visitation of the manifestations of His power, Muhammad and His family, that all might learn the meaning of destiny and the secret thereof through the knowledge of the days of His ascent and from the knowledge of the days of His journey might proceed to the inner meaning of the Throne and the Footstool, and make that holiest of journeys into the concourse of Names and Attributes, until all people might enter the blessed House of God by the exalted verses sent down in this pearl-white tablet and prostrate themselves at the place of prostration as they did the first time . . . So praised be He who hath ordained in the path of these journeys what He had ordained for all of the Gates aforetime (INBA 91, pp. 68f.; provisional translation).

This passage clearly states, among other things, that the Khutba al-Jidda is a work of divine revelation (*tanzíl*), that contemplation of the Báb's doings can provide the reader with various forms of cosmological gnosis and that the Báb himself is in some way equivalent to the Gates of the Hidden Imam.

The remainder of the Khutba is devoted to a listing of the works of the Báb that were stolen from him during his journey from Mecca to Medina. More than a dozen individual works appear to be listed but there is some ambiguity here, since some of what he writes may not be in regard to individual works but rather meant to characterize his writings in general. A number of specific works are named, however, and most of these were listed again in the Báb's Kitáb al-Fihrist, written less than four months later. The first item listed – if indeed it is an item *per se* – is rather representative of the list as a whole. The Báb writes:

> Among that which was stolen are verses regarding the inner mysteries of the writing that hath been inscribed by the hand of the Remembrance in red ink upon eleven pearl-white leaves, gilded with liquid gold and lined about in red, concerning the knowledge of two parts of the hidden secret manifest through the greatest secret,

the true meaning of the inner mysteries of the Qur'an [*bátin al-Qur'án*]. These verses are such as no one aforetime has touched upon, nor shall any hereafter encompass them in knowledge (Kitáb al-Fihrist; provisional translation).

One of the most interesting features of this list is that the Báb describes almost every item on the list as being concerned with the *bátin al-Qur'án*, the esoteric meaning of the Qur'an, or even of the *bátin al-ta'wíl*, the inner meaning of the esoteric interpretation of the Qur'an. His language of 'secrets' and 'concealed secrets' makes constant allusion to a saying ascribed to the sixth Imam, Ja'far al-Sádiq, which says, in a form quoted by the Báb in his first commentary on the letter *há'*: 'Our Cause is a secret, a secret concealed by a secret, a secret veiled within a secret, a secret that cannot be known save by means of a secret' (cited by the Báb in INBA 67, p. 23; provisional translation).[10]

If we return to our original problem, the problem of *taqiyya*, we might ask how much does this Khutba reveal and how much does it conceal? This text is a far cry from the 'verily, verily, I am God' of the Báb's latest works but, on the other hand, there is nothing here in the way of outright dissimulation. The Báb openly describes his works as revelation and compares himself to the Gates of the Imam but the real messianic punch of this Khutba is communicated only between the lines, in an esoteric manner, and is necessarily selective in the readership to whom it will reveal its secret. That ideal readership is the Shaykhi community, in whose language the Báb expresses himself throughout this text and in terms of whose apocalyptic imagery the Báb encodes his messianic declaration.

As noted above, the Báb opens this work with a cosmogonic narrative that is markedly Shaykhi in its terminology and symbolism, discussing cosmic reality in terms of a symbolic system of quaternities that was first codified, as it were, in the writings of Shaykh Ahmad al-Ahsá'í. It then proceeds to a polemic against Ishráqí philosophy, mentioning by name the *Kitáb al-Mashá'ir* by Mullá Sadrá, a book against which Shaykh Ahmad penned a gigantic, refutation-style 'commentary'. At the end of that polemic, after remarking that most of the ulama have sided with the Ishráqís, the Báb mentions that this state of affairs had continued up until his own time, when suddenly there had dawned the twin lights of the luminescent sun and moon – a reference to the first two leaders of the Shaykhiyya, Shaykh Ahmad and Sayyid Kázim al-Rashtí. The Báb then writes:

> People of late carried out a campaign of lies against those two luminaries in contradiction to what is encompassed in the knowledge of the Creator, just as the people of old had calumniated against the Friends of God [the Imams], without certain knowledge and having no clear book. Thus it went until the letter *káf* returned (*raja'a*) to the place [of the appearance] of the Cause, in the region of God's command, and the cycles of time came full circle to the Day of God, in a new and wondrous mode, and the lights that had been an inaccessible mystery dawned forth with knowledge of the divine cloud of unknowing, and the Siniatic Tree was made to speak forth upon the ocean of praise, and the word of glorification was made manifest upon the crimson earth (INBA 91, pp. 64f.; provisional translation).

One would have to have been an avid reader of Sayyid Kazim to be able to decode this messianic declaration, for in writing here of the return of the Arabic letter *káf*, the Báb is alluding to a prophecy made in Kázim's *Sharh al-Qasída* that the name of the Qá'im will be numerically equal to double the value of the letter *káf* when pronounced. The abjad value of the pronounced *kaf* – or *kaf, alif, fa* – is 101, so the doubled value is 202. The abjad value of 'Alí Muhammad is 202. The Báb also refers to himself elsewhere as *'this letter, káf'* and Táhirih Qurrat al-'Ayn would later point out that this specific prophecy of Sayyid Kázim was fulfilled by the Báb (see Rafati, *Development*, pp. 181f.; and Mazandarani, *Ta'ríkh-i zuhúr al-haqq*, vol. 3, pp. 402 and 509).

The list of the stolen works at the end of the Khutba al-Jidda provides a similar instance of this encoding of the Báb's messianic declaration in language that would likely only be decipherable by Shaykhi initiates. In terms very similar to earlier Isma'ilism, the Shaykhis had developed an elaborate theory of the cycles of spiritual history that centred on a notion of a dialectic between the *záhir* and the *bátin*, the manifest and the hidden. According to this cyclical theory, Muhammad and the Qur'an initiated a cycle of the *záhir*, the outward, and so during Muhammad's prophetic cycle the *záhir* of the Qur'an was in force. According to all of the Shaykhi writers, including the anti-Bábí Karím Khán Kirmání, the cycle of the *bátin* began in the year 1200 and would witness the coming of the Qá'im, who would initiate a spiritual cycle under the sign of the *bátin al-Qur'án*.[11] As noted above, the Báb refers to nearly all of the works in the list given at the end of the Khutba al-Jidda as being verses of the *bátin al-Qur'án*. Also, he begins the recounting of his pilgrimage itinerary by dating it as 'the year after the year 1200', without further specifying the date. Taken together with the earlier reference to the cycles of time having come full circle, and in the hands of an attentive Shaykhi reader, these references to the revelation of the *bátin al-Qur'án* in the 13th Islamic century would signal the Báb's claims to be the Messiah. The Báb, then, has hidden the secret in plain sight, visible only to those who know what they are looking at.

I move now to the Kitáb al-Fihrist, a work clearly dated to the 15th of Jumadá al-thání 1261, or 21 June 1845. This work is extremely valuable in that it provides lengthy lists of works that the Báb had produced up to that time, including dozens of books, commentaries, letters, *khutbas* and prayers. Like the Khutba al-Jidda, it also encodes the Báb's messianic claims, though the Báb in this text approaches the balancing act of revelation and concealment with altogether different methods. It is not markedly Shaykhi in its language or symbolism but appears to assume a wider audience. It evokes the Qur'an at the beginning by opening with a series of disconnected Arabic letters. The Báb had earlier affixed disconnected letters to the suras of the Qayyúm al-Asmá' and the Kitáb al-rúh, the two most explicitly messianic texts written by the Báb during the earliest period of his ministry.

In contrast to the Khutba al-Jidda, in which the Báb describes his works as verses sent down by God, at the beginning of the Kitáb al-Fihrist the Báb states that it was sent down from the *Baqiyyat Alláh*, the Remnant of God, a title given to the Hidden Imam. The Báb states that he is himself a servant of the Remnant of God and he then goes on to testify to his belief in Muhammad, the twelve Imams, Fatima and the four Gates of the Twelfth Imam. He then proceeds for several pages to describe his writings as verses sent down to him from the Remnant of God, refers to himself consistently as a servant of God and of the Remnant of God, though all the while indicating that his own works technically constitute revelation, writing, for example, that 'the reading of these verses in these, the days of God, is more excellent than all the deeds recorded in the Book of God' (provisional translation). He states that his revealed works will endure until the day of Resurrection, which to a Shaykhi audience meant until the arising of the Qá'im. In any case, the whole of this introduction serves to simultaneously reveal and conceal the Báb's claims. He clearly is claiming to be capable of producing inspired verses but by saying that these verses are sent down from the Hidden Imam he is distancing himself from any identification with that messianic figure, even implying that he is waiting, just like all other orthodox Shi'a, the Messiah's *future* appearance. At this point in the text the Báb takes a most fascinating approach to concealing his revealed secret. He cites a handful of lengthy traditions, all of which, in one way or another, indicate the possibility for post-Quranic revelation. I provide below a translation of this lengthy section of the Kitáb al-Fihrist:

> Verily, all that has been revealed by the hand of the Remembrance will remain in force until the Day of Resurrection, and the decree of God will suffer no alteration – unto Him do all return! Say: I, verily, have laid claim to no Cause other than that whose reality has been revealed in the tradition (*al-hadíth*). Would that you might read these traditions, that haply you would be of those who have attained certitude in the verses of God!
>
> God said (exalted be He), in a sacred tradition: My servant ceases not from drawing nigh unto me through supererogatory acts of worship until I love him, and when I love Him I become the ear with which he hears, the vision by which he sees, the tongue wherewith he speaks, and the hand by which he strikes. If he beseeches Me, I will answer his prayer, and if he asks of Me, I will grant him his request. Even if he holds his peace, I will then take the initiative [and answer his unspoken prayer].
>
> He [an Imam] (upon him be peace) said: One who loves us and only grows in his love for us, who devotes himself to our knowledge and asks about certain matters from us and not from others – the heart of such a one we inspire with the answers to those matters about which he asked.
>
> In al-Káfí[12] [it is related that] a Christian monk asked about certain things from Músá ibn Ja'far (upon him and his father be peace), saying: 'Teach me about the eight letters that were revealed, four of which were made known on earth and four of which remained in heaven. To whom were these latter four revealed, and who will interpret their meaning?' Músá replied, 'The one about whom you ask is none other than he who will arise from among us (*qá'imuná*). God will reveal these unto him and he will interpret their meaning. God will reveal to him what has not been revealed to any of the truthful ones, the messengers, nor the rightly-guided.' Then the monk said, 'Teach me about two of the four letters that were made known in this world. What are they?' Músá replied, 'I will tell you about all four of them. The first of them is "there is no god but God, His unity eternally without peer". The second of them is "Muhammad is the Righteous Messenger of God (the blessings of God

and His peace be upon him and his family)". The third is "We are the People of the Household". The fourth is "Our partisans (*shí'a*) are from Us, and We are from the Messenger of God (the blessings of God be upon him and his family), and the Messenger of God (blessings) is from God (but by way of intermediate causes)".'[13]

In al-Káfí [it is related] from Abí 'Abd Alláh (upon whom be peace), who said: Verily, God, exalted and glorified is He, created a name with letters that are unutterable, with a pronunciation that cannot be voiced, with an individuality that is not corporeal, of a likeness that cannot be described, and with colour that has no hue. It transcends measurement and delimitation, and is veiled from the senses of all possessors of sense. It is hidden without being concealed. He made it to be a word perfected by the joining of four parts, yet not one letter thereof comes before any of the others. He manifested from it three names, since creation depended on these latter names. He veiled one of them, and that is the hidden, treasured name. The outer form of these names that have been manifested is 'God', 'Blessed' and 'Exalted'. And He, praised be He, gave to the service of each of these names four pillars, making twelve pillars in all. Then for each pillar He created thirty names, names which are related to them.

The Merciful, the Compassionate, the King, the Holy One, the Creator, the Fashioner, the Former, the Living, the Self-Subsisting, Whom neither weariness nor sleep overtake, the Knower, the All-Informed, the Hearing, the Perceiving, the Wise, the Almighty, the All-Compelling, the Most Great, the Exalted, the Mighty, the All-Powerful, the Omnipotent . . . [lists 35 names in all, with one repeat]. These names and the names that [make up] the Most Beautiful Names comprise three hundred and sixty names and are related to these three names. These three names are pillars and He concealed the single, hidden, treasured name by these three names, even as He, exalted is He, says: 'Say: Call upon God or call upon the Merciful. By whatsoever name you call Him, His are the Most Beautiful Names' (Q 17:110).

Those who claim, however, to have met the Proof of God, such as they are none but liars! Say: this, My Path, is the like of what has been set forth in the above traditions, and my inner heart lied not about what it saw . . . (cf. Q 53:12).[14]

The Báb prefaces this brief compilation, as you can see, by saying that he has claimed no Cause other than in accordance with these traditions. The first two traditions describe modes of extra-Quranic revelation or inspiration, the third alludes to secrets that the Qá'im will reveal and the last describes the hidden name of God, the revelation of which is frequently associated in Shi'i apocalyptic literature with the messiah. Nowhere in this text, then, does the Báb state that he is the Qá'im but he leaves wide open for the reader the option of drawing that conclusion. Once again, he has hidden the messianic secret in plain sight.

The last text to be considered, written in 1846, is the Báb's *Khutba dhikriyya*, the title of which has been the source of considerable confusion among western scholars, although there is no space here to go into these perplexities.[15] The Báb begins the work with a very brief cosmogonic exordium and then proceeds to a lengthy creedal statement. He first affirms the unity and absolute unknowability of God and then goes through a series of doxological statements, testifying to his belief in Muhammad, the Imams, Fatima and so forth. The Báb refers to the coming of the Qá'im in the future tense, certainly giving no indication here of his identification with that figure. He states that he believes in the standard dogmas of the Shi'i faith in a perfectly orthodox manner – 'just as the people have believed concerning it' (provisional translation), as he says. We know from other works of the Báb that he did *not*, in fact, believe in these dogmas 'just as the people did', and much of the first *wáhid* of the Persian Bayán is devoted to spelling out the Báb's radical interpretations of things like resurrection and so forth.

In contrast with the Khutba al-Jidda and the Kitáb al-Fihrist, there is really nothing in the way of a direct indication of the Báb's claims in this text. The only hint of these claims is given in the list of works at the end and here again the Báb draws from the symbolism of the apocalyptic imagery to communicate this allusion. The Báb writes:

> I testify that everything set forth in this book is the truth, by the grace of God, the Exalted, though many of mankind are of the ungrateful. Indeed, there is delineated in this book all that went forth from my hands from the year 1260 unto the middle of the [first?] month of the year 1262. These consist of four perfect books and ten masterful epistles, each one of which is a sufficient proof for leading all who dwell in the heavens and on earth unto a station of servitude. Thus I now mention their names by the names of the members of the Family of God, who are their revealers, that these texts may be canonical within the realm of exposition and honoured with divine titles in the domain of conclusive proof.[16]

Following this, the Báb lists 14 works – the number of the Shi'i Holy Family – and renames each work after a member of this Family. That the purpose of this list is primarily symbolic is indicated towards the end. The eleventh, twelfth and thirteenth works do not correspond to any actual works of the Báb and serve here to fill out the list and underscore the repetition of the sacred number 14.

In comparison with the other two texts that I have discussed, the Khutba dhikriyya is the most obvious in its practice of *taqiyya*. It conceals much more than it reveals but it *does* reveal something. For one thing, like the Kitáb al-Fihrist, it serves as an index to *other* works of the Báb, works in which he is quite explicit about his claims. But more importantly there is the symbolic nature of the list itself and the renaming of his works here as the 'Alid Book, the *suhuf* (scrolls) of the Imams and so forth. One of the central elements of Shi'i apocalypticism is the belief that the Hidden Imam is in possession of secret books and *suhuf*. According to these traditions, Muhammad was given *suhuf* containing the true revelations that had been sent down to all of the previous prophets and he passed these on to the succession of the Imams. Among them was the Sahifat Adam, the Suhuf Ibráhím wa Músá, etc. There is also the Kitáb 'Alí, said to contain a detailed list of all possible rulings of Islamic law, which when revealed would obviate the need for all disputation and legal interpretation in determining the rules of the sharia. Descriptions of these messianic *kutub* and *suhuf* are scattered across dozens of traditions and in many of them number symbolism has a prominent role.[17] That the Báb considered his own writings in relation to these hidden books is made plain by more or less direct references to them in the Qayyúm al-Asmá'.[18] Beliefs regarding these books were even drawn upon by Bahá'u'lláh in communicating his own messianic claims, inasmuch as the Hidden Words were originally given out as the Suhuf Fatima, one of the hidden books in the possession of the Hidden Imam.

In looking at these three works of the Báb, we have seen that the practice of *taqiyya* in this early period meant more than simply directly denying messianic claims and was more often a technique of esoteric communication. Given the right readership, with initiation or familiarity with the right body of apocalyptic lore, the Báb was able in these works to simultaneously reveal and conceal his messianic claims, to set forth, in the words of Ja'far al-Sádiq, 'a secret concealed by a secret, a secret veiled within a secret, a secret that cannot be known save by means of a secret.'

A Provisional Translation of the Khutba Dhikriyya

Khutba Dhikriyya.[19]

The sixth epistle[20] of sermons,[21] consisting of 14 sermons: first sermon.

I have revealed this sermon regarding all that hath been inscribed in this book,[22] that all might thereby be of those who bear witness.

In the Name of God, the Compassionate, the Merciful!

Praise be to God who hath created the water by the mystery of construction (*sirr al-inshá'*), hath established the throne upon the water[23] by the modality of execution (*al-imdá'*), hath sent down the verses from the world of the divine cloud by the flowing of decree (*al-qadá'*), hath set forth what He determined on Mount Sinai by the power of praise and accomplished in glory (*bahá'*) whatsoever He determined by the deliquescence (*dhawaban*[24]) of necessity.[25] So glorified and exalted be He who hath sent forth the messengers – givers of glad-tidings and warners – that none may worship aught but Him. He hath given into their hands a rank of His own power such as all else but He must fail to attain, that they might establish the truth through His words and frustrate falsehood by His verses, that haply these verses might be a proof leading unto a station of wisdom for any who take cognisance thereof, and thus may all be of those who submit unto Him.

So glorified and exalted be He, who hath made between Himself and His messengers a rank of glory in utterance – the supreme grace in the world of creation – and hath honoured thereby some of the messengers above others, as hath been sent down in the revelation[26] by the decree of God, the All-Glorious. Indeed, God hath not spoken to mankind except by prophetic inspiration (*wahî*), or from beyond a veil or by sending inspired messengers by His permission and according to His will. Verily, He is exalted, wise. He hath established in His utterance a mode of power the like of which He hath not granted unto the utterance of His servants.

Verily, He is living, almighty, and sends down unto whomsoever He wills whatsoever He wills of His verses. Glorified and exalted be He above what is attributed to Him.

I testify unto God in this book according to what God hath testified of Himself, by Himself, without any need of the testimony of the foremost in knowledge among His servants, that verily there is no God save Him, who hath existed from everlasting without the mention of any thing and is now the Existing One as He hath ever been, with nothing with Him. Immeasurably exalted is His Essence above the depiction of the realm of construction and its inhabitants. Supremely magnified is His Self above the description of the realm of origination (*ibdá'*) and whatever is like unto it, glorified be He!

The realm of origination is cut off from His existential reality, as is the realm of fashioning (*ikhtirá'*) from His inner identity. Whoever says, 'He is He' hath truly lost Him, for none may find Him other than He Himself, and He hath no attribute other than His Essence, no name other than His glory(*bahá'*). And whoever declares His unity hath indeed denied Him, for nothing recognizes Him and no servant comprehends Him. The world of names is cut off from the world of the divine cloud by [the interposition of] His realm of omnipotence, and the world of attributes is inaccessibly removed from the imaginal world (*'álam al-mithál*) by [the interposition of] His sovereign Kingdom.[27] He hath from time immemorial been the Lord, with none as objects of His Lordship, the Knower without objects of knowledge, the Almighty without objects of His might, the Creator without any creatures, and He is now as He hath ever been.[28] There is for Him no name, no description, no depiction and no designation. All things are entirely cut off from His Essence, as are all entirely severed from His existential reality. He cannot be mentioned in terms of separation, nor can He be spoken of in terms of union. Whoever says 'He is the True One' depends in this matter [of so designating Him] upon the creation. And whoever says 'He is the Just', nevertheless fails to give His justice any description, glorified and exalted be He. The act of origination[29] hath been brought into being by means of the act of construction itself, without a touch of the fire of God's Essence. The Will was fashioned by the act of origination, without any division of God's own Self. Verily, the originated is barred from recognizing the act of origination, while the fashioned realm is severed from His love by its mere fashioned station. Glorified and exalted be He, for whom no praise can be mentioned – not by negation, nor assertion, nor praise, nor signs, nor glory, nor indications, nor by mention of [the letter] *há'*, nor by flight from *wáw*, nor arising between the two affairs, nor by the letter *lá'*.[30] Glorified and exalted be He above what is attributed to Him.

I testify unto Muhammad (blessings . . .) according to what God Himself hath testified concerning Him, wherein none have knowledge save Him. He hath fashioned Him for the magnification of His Essence, hath chosen Him for the holiness of His honour, and hath made Him, among His people, unique in beauty, that He be established upon the station of 'no vision taketh in Him, but He taketh in all vision. He is the Subtile, the All-Perceiving'. I testify that Muhammad ibn 'Abd Alláh is His messenger, who hath transmitted that which He bore of God's cause and held fast with His own hands to carrying out the Divine Decree, glorified and exalted be He. God hath warned you all lest anyone speak concerning Him other than what

God hath Himself determined for Him. Glorified and exalted be He above what is associated with Him.

I testify that the vicegerents of Muhammad – the blessings of God be upon Him and His family – are 12 souls [inscribed] in the Book of God on that day when no letter save them had been created, just as God hath testified of them in the grandeur of His omnipotent realm, the holiness of the world of His divinity, the magnificence of the expanse of His majesty and the loftiness of the kingdom of His everlasting bounty, of which none has knowledge save Him. I bear witness that they have transmitted what they bore from the bequest of the messenger of God – the blessings of God be upon Him and His family – and that they are truly the triumphant, with whom it shall be well. I testify that He who will arise from among them[31] – the salutations of God be upon Him – is alive, that by Him God hath raised up all things, that to Him God will extend all things and that by Him He will unite all things. I testify that His return is the truth, as is the return of all [of the vicegerents]. Verily, God will give new life to the earth by His manifestation, and He will utterly confound the works of those who join partners with God.

I testify that Fatima, the daughter of the messenger of God – the blessings of God be upon Him and His family – is a blessed leaf from the snow-white tree of 'No god is there but God', glorified and exalted be He above what is associated with Him.

I testify unto the truth of all things unto which God hath testified in His hidden knowledge, and in the same manner do I testify unto the falsity of falsehood. Verily, I am a servant of God, a believer in Him, His verses and His book, the Discrimination[32] – the like of which there hath never been – and in the love of all that which is most beloved of Him and the rejection of all that which is most despised by Him. Sufficient as a witness is God, the Exalted. I testify unto [the reality of] death, and of the questioning [in the grave], and of the resurrection, and of the reckoning, and of the raising of the bodies of the dead, and unto whatever God hath established, beyond these, in His knowledge, just as the people have believed concerning it.

I testify that everything set forth in this book is the truth, by the grace of God, the Exalted, though many of mankind are of the ungrateful. Indeed, there is delineated in this book all that went forth from My hands from the year 1260 unto the middle of the [first?] month of the year 1262. These consist of four perfect books and ten masterful epistles, each one of which is a sufficient proof for leading all who dwell in the heavens and on earth unto a station of servitude. Thus I now mention their names by the names of the members of the Family of God, who are their revealers, that these texts may be canonical within the realm of exposition and honoured with divine titles in the domain of conclusive proof.

First is the Ahmadian Book, in elucidation of the first thirtieth of the Qur'án and in commentary on the Sura of Praise.[33]

Second is the 'Alawian Book, divided into seven hundred perfect suras, each of which is of seven verses.[34]

Third is the Hasanian Book, divided into 50 books of irresistible verses.

Fourth is the Husaynian Book, in elucidation of the Sura of Joseph – upon whom be peace – arranged in 111 suras of 42 verses, each one of which is a sufficient proof unto whomsoever is on the earth and whatsoever is beneath the throne, should it not suffer any alteration. Sufficient is God as a witness.[35]

Fifth is the Fátimid Epistle, comprising 14 chapters on the acts [of worship related to] the 12 months in the Book of God.[36]

Sixth is the 'Alawian Epistle, comprising 14 prayers in answer to 92 questions, composed during the month of fasting, after my return from the pilgrimage.

Seventh is the Báqirian Epistle, comprising 14 chapters in commentary on the letters of the *basmala*.[37]

Eighth is the Ja'farian Epistle, comprising 14 chapters in elucidation of [Ja'far's] prayer – upon him be peace – for the days of the Occultation.[38]

Ninth is the Músawian Epistle, comprising 14 chapters in answer to two souls from among the servants of God, provided [in answer to them] in the land of the Two Holy Sanctuaries.[39]

Tenth is the Ridáwian Epistle, comprising 14 chapters concerning the recitation of 14 sermons – which are the very height of eloquence – from the tree of the laudation, 'No god is there save Him, the All-Glorious, the Beneficent.'[40]

Eleventh is the Jawádian Epistle, comprising 14 chapters in answer to 14 questions concerning the realm of Divinity [*láhút*].

Twelfth is the Hádian Epistle, comprising 14 chapters in answer to 14 questions concerning the Dominion of Power [*jabarút*].

Thirteenth is the 'Askarian Epistle, comprising 14 chapters in answer to 14 questions concerning the Kingdom [*malakút*].

Fourteenth is the Hujjatian Epistle, comprising 14 holy prayers which were revealed at the beginning of this Cause and are related to the Imam of Justice.[41]

All 14 of these holy texts are present in this book, along with – at the end of the text – that illustrious epistle regarding the 14 books of the Imams.[42] All of these are inscribed in this book. Regarding that which went forth from My hand and was stolen while [I was] on the path of pilgrimage, a detailed account thereof hath been made in the Ridáwian Epistle. It is incumbent upon whomsoever may find any of those [stolen texts] to carefully preserve them. Happy is he who preserves all that hath been sent down from My presence in exquisite tablets with the finest of handwriting. And [I testify] by Him who hath honoured me with His verses that a single letter thereof is more glorious in My sight than the kingdoms of this world and the next – may God forgive me for such a comparison.

And glorified be God, Lord of the worlds, above what they attribute to Him. And peace be upon His messengers, and praise be to God, the Lord of all the worlds.

Bibliography

Afnan, Abu'l-Qasim. *'Ahd-i A'lá: Zindigani-yi Hadrat-i Báb* (The Bábí Dispensation: The Life of the Báb). Oxford: Oneworld, 2000.

Amanat, Abbas. *Resurrection and Renewal: The Making of the Bábí Movement in Iran, 1844-1850*. Ithaca, NY: Cornell University Press, 1989.

Amir-Moezzi, Mohammad Ali. *The Divine Guide in Early Shi'ism: Sources of Esotericism in Islam*. Trans. David Streight. Albany, NY: SUNY Press, 1994.

Báb, Sayyid 'Alí Muhammad Shírází. *Qayyúm al-Asmá': Tafsír Súrat Yúsuf.* MS dated 1 Muharram, 1323 AH/8 March, 1905 CE.

— INBA 64. *Majmú'ih-yi Áthár-i Hadrat-i A'lá, 64.* MS collection photoreproduced by the National Spiritual Assembly of the Bahá'ís of Iran, Tehran, 133 BE/1976 CE.

— INBA 67. *Majmú'ih-yi Áthár-i Hadrat-i A'lá, 67.* MS collection photoreproduced by the National Spiritual Assembly of the Bahá'ís of Iran, Tehran, 133 BE/1976 CE.

— INBA 91. *Majmú'ih-yi Áthár-i Hadrat-i A'lá, 91.* MS collection photoreproduced by the National Spiritual Assembly of the Bahá'ís of Iran, Tehran, 133 BE/1976 CE.

The Báb. *Selections from the Writings of the Báb.* Trans. Habib Taherzadeh with the assistance of a Committee at the Bahá'í World Centre. Haifa: Bahá'í World Centre, 1976.

Browne, E.G. and Reynold A. Nicholson. *A Descriptive Catalogue of the Oriental MSS belonging to the late E.G. Browne.* Cambridge: Cambridge University Press, 1932.

Ekbal, Kamran. '*Taqiyya* und *kitmán* in den Bábí und Bahá'í Religionen', in Stefan Wild and Hartmut Schild (eds.). *Akten des 27. Deutschen Orientalistentages (Bonn – 28. September bis 2. Oktober 1998). Norm und Abweichung.* Würzburg: Ergon Verlag, 2001, pp. 363–72.

Eschraghi, Armin. *Frühe Shaikhi- und Bábí-Theologie: die Darlegung der Beweise für Muhammads besonderes Prophetentum: (ar-Risála fi itbat an-Nubúwa al-hassa): Einleitung, Edition und Erläuterungen.* Leiden: Brill, 2004.

Iranian National Bahá'í Archives (INBA).

Kohlberg, Etan. 'Authoritative Scriptures in Early Imami Shi'ism', in E. Patlagean and A. Le Boulluec (eds.). *Les retours aux Écritures: fondamentalismes présents et passés.* Louvain-Paris: Peeters, 1993, pp. 295–311.

— 'Taqiyya in Shi'i Theology and Religion', in Hans G. Kippenberg and Guy G. Stroumsa (eds.). *Secrecy and Concealment: Studies in the History of Mediterranean and Near Eastern Religions.* New York: E.J. Brill, 1995, pp. 345–60.

Lawson, B. Todd. *The Qur'an Commentary of Sayyid 'Alí Muhammad, the Báb.* Unpublished Ph.D. diss., McGill University, 1987. http://bahai-library.com/index.php5?file=lawson_quran_commentary_bab (accessed 21 October 2007).

MacEoin, Denis. *From Shaykhism to Bábísm: A Study in Charismatic Renewal in Shi'ite Islam.* Unpublished Ph.D. diss., University of Cambridge, 1979.

— *The Sources for Early Bábí Doctrine and History: A Survey.* Leiden: E.J. Brill, 1992.

Manuchehri, Sepehr. 'The Practice of Taqiyyah (Dissimulation) in the Babi and Bahai Religions'. 'Research Notes in Shaykhi, Babi and Baha'i Studies', vol. 3, no. 3 (September 1999), H-Bahai Digital Publications Series. http://h-net.org/~bahai/notes/vol3/taqiya.htm (accessed 21 October 2007).

Mázandarání, Asadu'lláh Fádil. *Asrár al-Áthár,* 5 vols. Tehran, 1968–9.

— *Ta'ríkh-i Zuhúr al-Haqq,* vol. 3. Tehran, 1941.

Rafati, Vahid. *The Development of Shaykhi Thought in Shi'í Islam.* Unpublished Ph.D. diss., University of California, Los Angeles, 1979.

Notes

1. An earlier version of this paper was presented at an 'Irfán Colloquium in Flint, Michigan in October 2004 and was subsequently printed in the proceedings volume *Lights of 'Irfan*, vol. 6, ed. Iraj Ayman. Evanston, IL: Haj Mehdi Memorial Fund, 2005, pp. 47–68. I wish to take this opportunity to thank Dr Ayman for making my participation at that gathering possible.
2. For instance, the three major dissertations on the Báb's writings – by MacEoin, Lawson and Eschraghi – all focus on the Báb's early writings.
3. All translations are my own and are provisional unless otherwise noted.
4. On *taqiyya* in the Bábí and Bahá'í religions, see Eqbal, '*Taqiyya* und *kitman*'; Manuchehri, 'Practice of Taqiyya'; and Eschraghi, *Frühe Shaikhi*, index s.v. *taqíya*. Eschraghi's work is particularly relevant to my argument here, as he discusses *taqiyya* in the Báb's writings in the context of secrets (*asrár*) and allusions (*ishárát*) and not simply as defensive dissimulation.
5. An excellent overview of *taqiyya* in Shi'ism can be found in Etan Kohlberg's 'Taqiyya in Shi'i Theology and Religion'.
6. For example, in his Sahífa-yi 'Adliyya, written in Shiraz after his pilgrimage, the Báb condemns as heresy the belief that the Imams were cosmogonic powers (pp. 20–2), whereas in many other works the Báb affirms this very principle in the strongest possible terms, as in INBA 67, pp. 102f., where he identifies the essence of 'Alí with the essence of God (*dhát alláh*) in the station of origination (*maqám al-ibdá'*), the Báb's term for the primordial cosmogonic process. In the same Sahífa-yi 'Adliyya the Báb writes that 'anyone who says that anything other than God was the creator of the existing things is an infidel' (provisional translation), whereas his writings teem with cosmogonic forces and personae, including himself, as per his statement, 'I am the Primal Point from which have been generated all created things' (*Selections*, p. 12; INBA 64, p. 109).
7. I am sceptical of a later, Bushihr dating of the Khutba al-Jidda because of the absence of any mention of the length of the journey by ship, the length of stay at port in Bushihr or of disembarking at Bushihr, whereas throughout the Khutba al-Jidda the Báb goes into minute detail into all of the earlier stages of his pilgrimage journey. If he had already arrived at Bushihr when composing it, why give so much chronological detail about his trip and yet leave off the details regarding these final legs of the journey? Fortunately, Dr Stephen Lambden is currently working on this text, so I will leave the resolution of these thorny matters to his able hands. For now, see Dr Lambden's introduction and partial translation of the Khutba online at: http://www.hurqalya.pwp.blueyonder.co.uk/03-THE%20BAB/KHUTBAS%20BAB/KHUTBA%20JIDDAH-TEXT%20AND%20TRANS.htm (accessed 12 February 2007).
8. INBA stands for Iranian National Bahá'í Archives and refers to a series of just over a hundred book-length collections of manuscripts that were photoreproduced and distributed in an extremely limited fashion during the latter half of the 20th century, partly to avoid the irrevocable loss of this material at the hands of Iranian authorities committed to the complete destruction of the Bahá'í community. Some authors (e.g. MacEoin, Lambden) refer to these volumes with the acronym INBMC and reserve INBA as an acronym preceding individually numbered manuscripts once housed in the archives of the National Spiritual Assembly of Iran, a discrete collection which no longer exists owing to the dismantling of Bahá'í institutions and the execution of the entire membership of the National Spiritual Assembly following the Islamic Revolution of 1979.
9. The symbolism in this passage is bound up with the Báb's quaternities: the letter *há'*, the innermost heart, verses and the colour white are the highest terms in their respective quaternities and all are related to divinity.

10. *amruná huwa al-sirr wa mustasirr bil-sirr wa-sirr muqanna' bil-sirr wa-sirr la yufídahu ila 'l-sirr*. This tradition is often quoted by Shaykh Ahmad and frequently alluded to by the Báb. There are several variants of this tradition; see, for example, those given in Amir-Moezzi, *Divine Guide*, p. 231, n. 687.
11. See MacEoin, *From Shaykhism*, p. 213.
12. The famous early collection of Imami traditions, *Usúl al-Káfí*, compiled by Muhammad b. Ya'qúb al-Kulayni (d. *c.* 940 CE).
13. The quaternity implied here – of divinity, prophecy, imamate and party of believers – is a commonplace in the Báb's writings. Indeed, many of his quaternities come from early Imami traditions, many of which are studied in Amir-Moezzi, *Divine Guide*, *passim*. I hope to publish in the future a primer to the quaternities used in the writings of the Báb.
14. Provisional translation, in *Lights of 'Irfán'*, no. 6, pp. 54–6. For the texts of the Kitáb al-Fihrist, a number of manuscripts were consulted, though my translation of these passages is based primarily upon the Princeton MS (Bábí Collection of William McElwee Miller, vol. 4, ff. 1a–6a).
15. For a summary of the issue up to the period of MacEoin's bibliographic labours, see Appendix Four in his *Sources*, p. 207. MacEoin's conclusions there are incorrect; the text in fact is the *Khutba dhikriyya* and has no relationship whatsoever with the *Risála-yi dhahabiyya*, other than the fact that Nicolas mistakenly referred to this text by that name. I provide a full translation of this Khutba as an appendix to this article, below.
16. Provisional translation, in *Lights of 'Irfán'*, no. 6, p. 57. Translated from a typewritten copy of a single manuscript, with handwritten corrections by Nader Saiedi, whom I thank here for kindly sharing the typescript and his corrections with me. A lengthy portion of the Khutba is also printed in A.-Q. Afnan, *'Ahd-i A'lá*, p. 473, n. 2.
17. On these *suhuf*, see Kohlberg, 'Authoritative Scriptures', pp. 299ff.
18. MacEoin writes: 'The Qayyúm al-Asmá' may be said to combine something of the character of the tawqi'at written by the hidden Imam through his intermediaries, the four abwáb, of the various books reputed to be in possession of the Imams – the Mushaf of Fatima, Al-sahifa, Al-jami'a, Al-jabr, the complete Qur'an, and the previous scriptures – and of the Qur'an itself' (MacEoin, *From Shaykhism*, p. 159).
19. See Browne, *Descriptive Catalogue*, p. 68, where he calls this the *Sahifa-yi-ridáwiyya*. For a full discussion of the various confusions regarding this tablet and its title see MacEoin, *Sources*, p. 207. I do not agree with MacEoin that this work should be titled 'Risála-yi dhahabiyya' but this issue cannot be dealt with here. See also A. Q. Afnan, *'Ahd-i 'Alá*, pp. 437f.
20. Here and throughout this text 'epistle' translates *sahífa*.
21. 'Sermon' renders *khutba*.
22. Here and throughout this text the Báb refers to the Sahífa al-Ridáwiyyih as *dhalik al-kitáb* or, literally, 'that book'. Since this text is itself one of the sections of that Sahífa, this phrase will be rendered here as 'this book'.
23. Cf. Qur'an 11:7: 'And it is He Who hath created the heavens and the earth in six days, and His throne was upon the waters.' In the Báb's Ziyára jámi'a kabíra, He says of the Imams: 'I swear by my father and mother, and by whatsoever is in the knowledge of my Lord, that the heavens were raised not by pillars but by your name[s]; that the Throne was set upon the waters by your command (*istaqara al-'arsha 'ala l-má' bi-amrikum*); and that *káf* was joined to *nún* for the mention of your afflictions' (INBA 50, pp. 55f.)
24. This term appears to belong to the nomenclature of alchemy. For example, Shaykh Ahmad al-Ahsá'í uses the term in this sense in *Jawámi' al-Kilam*, vol. 2, p. 258.
25. Compare this passage with the Tafsír súrat al-hamd, INBA 69, p. 123. 'No thing will

ever know Him and no thing will ever be united with Him inasmuch as the mention of the thing (*dhikr al-shay'*) is made to exist (*kuwwina*) by means of the Will (*mashiyya*), and the mention of existence (*dhikr al-kawn*) is made to have an essence (*dhuwwita*) by means of Purpose (*iráda*), and the mention of the essence (*dhikr al-dhát*) is delimited (*huddida*) by means of Determination (*qadar*), and the mode of Determination is realized (*huqqiqa*) by means of Decree (*qadá'*), and the alteration (*badá'*) of the Decree is fixed (*yuthbat*) after the [stage of] Execution (*imda'*). Therefore, the station of the secret of construction (*sirr al-inshá'*) and the exaltation of its status in itself is by means of the manifestation of Mt. Sinai in the crimson pillar.'

Also relevant to this passage is the Báb's letter in answer to questions about alteration of the divine will (*badá'*) and the Preserved Tablet (*lawh al-mahfuz*) in INBA 67, pp. 172–6.

26. i.e. the Qur'an.
27. There appears to be a hierarchy implied in this sentence: the '*álam al-'amá* is above *jabarút*, while the '*álam al-amthál* is above *malakút*. I have inserted the clarifying phrases in brackets in line with this reading of the passage.
28. Here the previous sentence is repeated, with *al-ká'in* replacing *rabb*: 'He is the Existent with none as objects of His Lordship, the Knower without objects of knowledge, the Almighty without objects of His might, the Creator without any creatures.' This would appear to be a scribal error.
29. Alternatively, the world of origination; only the word *al-ibdá'* is used but this is often used by the Báb as a designation for a level of a distinctive four-fold cosmological hierarchy. Likewise, the term is used by the Báb to designate the first of four levels of creative *activity* that are proper to the generation of four different levels of cosmic reality.
30. The allusions here are many and baroque but on one level these references to letters can be understood to imply that God is exalted above being truly qualified by affirmation (*huwa*, written in Arabic with the letters *ha'* and *wáw*) nor by negation (*la*, 'no').
31. The Qá'im, the awaited Twelfth Imam.
32. *al-Furqán*, a synonym for the Qur'an.
33. This is the Báb's Tafsír súrat al-baqara.
34. This refers to the Kitáb al-rúh.
35. This refers to the Qayyúm al-Asmá'.
36. This refers to the Sahífa a'mál al-saná.
37. This refers to the Tafsír al-basmala.
38. This refers to the Sharh du'á al-ghayba.
39. The Sahífa bayn al-haramayn is most likely intended here.
40. On the basis of the statement later in this Khutba to the effect that the Ridáwian Epistle (Sahífa ridáwiyya) contains details about the works which were stolen from the Báb during his pilgrimage, MacEoin was of the opinion that this is none other than the Kitáb al-fihrist. If that were the sole criterion, however, it is equally likely that this refers to the Khutba al-jidda. Neither of these works is divided into 14 sections.
41. The Sahífa makhzúna is probably intended here.
42. The text here has *awliyá il-'ibád*, which could be translated 'the Guardians of the worshippers'.

7

The Súrat adh-Dhikr of the Qayyúm al-Asmá' (chapter 108):
A Provisional Translation and Commentary

Moojan Momen

This paper is an initial attempt to understand a sura (chapter) of the Qayyúm al-Asmá'.[1] The text of the Qayyúm al-Asmá' is very abstruse in places and the present paper can be regarded only as a preliminary and provisional attempt to capture some of its meaning. It will be many years, perhaps many generations, before all of these meanings are successfully unravelled, if indeed that is possible.

The story of the Qayyúm al-Asmá' is well known and does not require repetition here. Nabíl records that the Báb wrote the first sura of the book, the Súrat al-Mulk, on the night of the declaration of his mission to Mullá Husayn Bushrú'í (Nabíl 1962, p. 61). However, as will become evident, the sura being considered here, the 108th of the book, gives rise to the question of whether all of the book was written by the Báb before his pilgrimage to Mecca in 1844 or whether some of it may not have been written in 1845 after his return, or at any rate after the end of the pilgrimage rites, which he completed on 24 December 1844.

The 108th sura of the Qayyúm al-Asmá', which is given the title Súrat adh-Dhikr (Sura of the Remembrance), occurs towards the end of the book. The Qayyúm al-Asmá' is in form a commentary on the Quranic Sura of Joseph (sura 12). Each sura of the Qayyúm al-Asmá' is a commentary on a verse of the Quranic sura. Thus the 108th sura of the Qayyúm al-Asmá' is a commentary on the 108th verse of the Quranic Sura of Joseph, which is cited at the opening of the sura (see below).

The Súrat adh-Dhikr is written, as is the rest of the book, in the literary style known as *saj'*, which is usually translated as 'rhyming prose'. This translation does not fully reflect this literary form, as some may imagine that it means that there is rhyme but no rhythm in the verses. In fact, both rhyme and rhythm are present. The only reason that it is not possible to call it poetry, in the classical literary meaning of this word, is the fact that the rhyme and rhythm do not follow any uniform or regular pattern and there are short passages of prose linking parts of the text. The text contains much alliteration. See, for example, the words *sirr*, *mastúr* and *satr* as they occur in verses 4, 15 and 21 (transliteration provided in the translation below).

Indeed, as suggested below in the commentary on verse 40, this text may have been intended as much for recitation as study, in that several elements of it are clearly intended to be heard rather than read. It is thus a performative text as much as a cognitive one; it is meant to be experienced as much as understood.

As with other suras of the Qayyúm al-Asmá', this sura can be divided into verses because each unit ends in the rhyme -á. The final word is usually in the form of the accusative indefinite ending -an, which is pronounced -á when it is placed at the end of a sentence or clause. All suras of the Qayyúm al-Asmá' have 42 verses in them, 42 being the number equivalent to balá (Yea, verily!), which is the response to the Quranic covenantal question: 'Am I not your Lord?' (Q 7:172).[2] The whole book is thus a symbolic affirmation of the eternal divine covenant.

The Súrat adh-Dhikr can be divided into three sections with axial verses marking the transition point between each section. Not only do these three sections differ in content and tone but there is even a change of voice.

Section 1

This section runs from verse 1 to verse 11. The first verse of the sura is a citing of the 108th verse of the Quranic Sura of Joseph, the verse on which this sura is a commentary. As with much of the rest of the Qayyúm al-Asmá', the text of this sura contains only faint echoes of the Quranic verse, its supposed subject.

The second verse begins with the disconnected Arabic letters *'Ayn Lám Yá*. This is an echo of many Quranic suras which also start with disconnected letters but this set of three letters is not Quranic.

Having exalted God in the second verse, the third verse declares that God has sent down (*anzala*) the mysteries upon his servant in the lines of the tablets. Although it is not explicitly stated here, but is elsewhere in the book, this implies the revelation of divine verses – something that Muslims consider occurs only when holy books such as the Qur'an are being revealed. This point is repeated, this time explicitly at the beginning of verse 5, where the word used, *awhá*, is derived from *wahy*, which in the Qur'an is almost exclusively specific to the revelation of divine verses. Thus the Báb, while outwardly stating that this book was given to him by the Hidden Imam, is in fact implicitly claiming that the book is divine revelation, a point that was very clear to the Sunni and Shi'i ulama who tried the Letter of the Living Mullá 'Alí Bastámí in Baghdad in January 1845 on the basis of the text of the Qayyúm al-Asmá' (Momen 1982).

The phrase 'around the fire' (*hawl an-nár*) occurs in verse 5 for the first time in this sura and recurs frequently (vv. 6, 16, 17, 21, 25, 26, 31, 36 and 38) in this sura and in the text of the book as a whole. While in many places in the writings of the Báb the word 'fire' is an allusion to hellfire, this is clearly not the correct interpretation here. The most obvious allusion is to the fire of the Sinaitic experience of Moses and in particular the words that were heard by Moses as he approached the fire: 'Blessed are they who are in the fire and those who are around it' ('*man fí 'n-nár wa man hawlahá*', Q 27:8). References to Sinai and Sinaitic imagery abound in this sura, as they do throughout the book (see also vv. 19 and 24).

Verses 8, 9 and 10 are perhaps the most interesting of this sura from the historical viewpoint. They refer to the Báb's pilgrimage to Mecca (*hajj*), his circumambulation of the Ka'ba (seven circumambulations are performed), his journey to Mount Arafat on 9 Dhu'l-Hijja and then proceeding to Mash'ar or Muzdalifa on the eve of that day and performing a final circumambulation some day after 10 Dhu'l-Hijja – all essential parts of the *hajj* ritual. The fact that the Báb writes about this event and what he found there as having already occurred means that this sura, at least, was probably written after the Báb had concluded his pilgrimage to Mecca. This, of course, is contrary to the accepted view that the book was completed prior to the Báb's departure for pilgrimage. We know that some, perhaps all, of the Letters of the Living as they dispersed from Shiraz had copies of the Qayyúm al-Asmá' with them, therefore we know that copies of it were being distributed before the Báb's departure. The question is whether these were copies of the whole book or copies of only part of it. Did the Báb write part of the Qayyúm al-Asmá' before leaving for pilgrimage – the Letters of the Living taking with them copies of this part – and then complete the book as we know it today after his pilgrimage? Fádil Mázandaráni cites a tablet of the Báb in which he states that he completed the book in 40 days (Mázandaráni n.d., p. 285) but this does not necessarily mean 40 consecutive days.

Unfortunately, no copies of the Qayyúm al-Asmá' as carried by the Letters of the Living in 1844 are known to have to have survived (although it is not impossible that somewhere in Baghdad or Kirman or elsewhere there is such a manuscript). We do have evidence, however, of the content of the copies of the Qayyúm al-Asmá' the Letters of the Living carried with them because it was cited in two documents. The first is the fatwa given by Shi'i and Sunni ulama against the Letter of Living Mullá 'Alí Bastámí in January 1845. In the fatwa document, 17 extracts from the Qayyúm al-Asmá' carried by Mullá 'Ali are cited as evidence. The highest numbered sura of these extracts is sura 65 (see Momen 1982). Our second source of information about the copies of the Qayyúm al-Asmá' carried by the Letters of the Living is from the writings of the Shaykhi leader Hájjí Mírzá Muhammad Karím Khán Kirmání. The Letter of the Living Quddús came to Kirman and interacted with the Shaykhi leader there. He was followed by Mullá Sádiq Muqaddas Khurásání and another Letter of the Living, Mullá Yúsuf Ardabílí. From one of these, probably the first, Karím Khán obtained a copy of the Qayyúm al-Asmá' from which he quoted in his refutation of the Báb, *Izháq al-Bátil*, which was completed on 12 Rajab 1261/17 July 1845. Quddús left the company of the Báb immediately after they set foot ashore in Bushihr following their pilgrimage journey. If the Báb had completed the Qayyúm al-Asmá' before this time, then it is possible that Karím Khán was given a copy of the entire text. But if the Báb completed the Qayyúm al-Asmá' after his return to Iran, then Quddús probably had with him only the same Qayyúm al-Asmá' that the other Letters of the Living had taken with them. In any case, the evidence from Izháq al-Bátil is virtually identical to that from the Mullá 'Alí Bastámí fatwa document. The last sura of the Qayyúm al-Asmá' that is cited in this book is sura 62^3 (Kirmání 1973, pp. 97–8).

Assuming that the Báb wrote the Qayyúm al-Asmá' in sequence, it seems likely that he stopped writing it at some point between sura 65 and sura 108 before he went on pilgrimage and that it was this incomplete Qayyúm al-Asmá' that the Letters of the Living took with them when they dispersed from Shiraz in 1844. The Báb then completed the 111 suras of the Qayyúm al-Asmá' after his pilgrimage.

Section 2

Verse 13 forms what can be called an axial point in the sura in that the tone and voice change at this point. In the first section the Báb refers to himself in the first person and writes about the book itself and about his pilgrimage. In the second section he writes mainly about himself but in the third person. In verse 13 the Báb exhorts his readers to listen to his call. From this point onwards the whole of this section is a series of statements referring back to the Báb and to his call. Most of the verses in this section start '*Inna hadhá lahuwa*' (literally, 'Verily, this person, he is . . .'). The rhythm of the sura also changes here.

In verse 13 the Báb refers to himself as the tree (*ash-shajara*), a term which he frequently uses in referring to himself,[4] and in verse 14 he refers to himself as the path (*sirát*), another term that he uses many times in relation to himself (see Persian Bayán 2:12; Momen 1987, p. 333). This verse states that the Báb is himself the straight path mentioned in the opening sura of the Qur'an (1:6) to which Muslims ask to be guided when they use this sura as part of their daily prayers. The word *al-'amá*, which occurs in verse 13 and frequently thereafter in this sura and throughout the book, is a reference to the Primordial Cloud which, according to a Tradition related of the Prophet Muhammad, was where God was before he created the Creation. The word is derived from the root meaning 'blindness' or 'being in the dark' and refers to the concept of God being wrapped in a mist, enshrouded in darkness. In the present translation this has mostly been rendered as 'the Unseen'.[5]

Al-Yamaní, mentioned in verse 18, is an eschatalogical figure in Islam who is expected to return at the same time as the Mahdi. The '70' in this verse and the 'two' in the previous verse make 72, the number of companions of the Imam Husayn at Karbala, who are also expected to return with the Imam Husayn when he returns at the time of the Mahdi.

Verses 20 to 36 continue this theme of the Báb describing himself in the third person in mystical terms, many of which are highly abstruse. Verse 20 contains allusions to Muhammad (*al-abtahí*), the Imam 'Alí (*'Alawî*) and Fatima (*Fátimí*). Mount Qáf (verse 22) is the name of a mystical mountain that encircles the earth. Although originating in Zoroastrianism, it became for Sufis the symbol of the goal which they sought, the true home of the soul, the nesting place of the immortal phoenix. There is also a Quranic sura of this name. The adjectives Ahmadí 'Arabí in verse 29 refer to the Prophet Muhammad while the perceptive Arabic Guardian (*al-walí al-alma'í al-'Arabî*) in verse 31 would probably be a reference to the Imam 'Alí. Buráq (verse 36) was the steed of Muhammad during his mystical night ascent (*mi'ráj*).

Section 3

The opening words of verse 37 differ from the opening words of the preceding verses, thus interrupting the rhythm and flow of the text and signalling the start of the third and last section of this sura. Verse 37 introduces the image of a bird flying through the air, which then becomes the central theme of this section. This mystic bird is, of course, the Báb himself and the reader is invited to learn about the pathway of servitude from this bird.

Verse 38 is a key verse. Not only does the Báb identify himself with Bahá' in this verse but the verse contains several allusions back to the heretofore neglected Qur'an 8:108, which is, of course, the supposed subject of commentary for this sura. The literary technique in this verse is very typical of the Báb, who weaves in among the words of Qur'an 12:108 his own words so as to transform the plain cloth of the Quranic verse into a rich mystical fabric. 'His awaited remnant' (*baqiyyatihi 'l-muntazar*) is a reference to the awaited Twelfth Imam, one of whose titles was the Baqiyyatu'lláh (the Remnant of God).

Verse 39 is an important verse in that it introduces and, I propose, explains the following verse. Verse 40 is very long and the outward meaning of it is not at all clear. It consists of a series of 11 short statements each beginning 'To me, to me', most of which are followed by a number of words in the dual form. As distinct from English, which has only singular and plural forms of a noun, Arabic has three: singular, dual and plural. The dual form is created by adding the ending '*-ayn*' to the singular form of the word. In the fifth and sixth lines of the verse, however, the words following 'To me, to me' are in the *nisba* form, ending in '*-í*'.

In considering what this verse could mean, it seems possible that verse 39, which introduces verse 40, might be taken literally when it states that the following verse is the song of the bird; in other words, that verse 40 might actually be an onomatopoeic rendering, imitating the warbling of a bird. Other than this, it is difficult to understand the import of this verse. A transliteration of the first four lines is:

Illayya illaya hukm al-má'Ayn
wa illaya illaya hukm al-hawá'Ayn fi'l-ardayn
wa illaya illaya arba' al-harfayn fi'l-ismayn
wa illaya illaya arba' al-hawá'Ayn fi's-satrayn min sirrayn

The following two verses round off the sura with a number of formulaic statements, indicating the author's submission to God and the inability of words to convey the whole truth. Other allusions in the text are suggested in the endnotes.

***

The manuscripts used for this translation have been the following three and an attempt has been made to create a critical text (see notes of variants in the endnotes):

Manuscript A: Photocopy of manuscript completed 1 Muharram 1323 (8 March 1905) written in a neat *naskh* script, 17 lines per page; given to the author by Mr Abul-Qasim Afnan, ff. 430–4.

Manuscript B: Photocopy of manuscript completed on 1 Rabí' II 1309 (4 November 1891) in *nasta'líq* handwriting of Husayn Írání (i.e. Mírzá Áqá Khán Kirmání) in Istanbul and sent to E. G. Browne by Shaykh Ahmad Rúhí. 22 lines per page, MSS F11 (9) in Browne collection, University Library, University of Cambridge, ff. 192–3 (see Browne 1892, pp. 261–8).

Manuscript H: Photocopy of manuscript completed 28 Jamádí I 1261 (4 June 1845) written in a neat *naskh* hand by Muhammad Mahdí ibn Karbalá'í Sháh Karam for Mullá Husayn Bushrú'í and sent by him through Mírzá Habíbu'lláh Cháhí to 'Sarkár Amír' (possibly the Amir of Qá'inát). Entered Iranian National Bahá'í Archives, Rabí' al-Awwal 1298, INBA 3, ff. 382–6.

Provisional translation

In the Name of God, the Merciful the Compassionate

1. 'Say this is my way (*sabílí*). I summon unto God with clarity (*'ala basírah*), I and those who follow me. Praise be to God, I am not one of the idolators' (Q 12:108).

2. 'Ayn Lám Yá. He is God, there is no God but Him, the Lord of the Throne and of Heaven. And He is God who is exalted, mighty.

3. He is the one who sent down (*anzala*) upon His servant, in truth, the mysteries from the tablets[6] in lines (*astur*), in order that he may teach the scholars that He is,[7] according to this mighty word, detached from the world, in truth and through the truth.

4. O People of the Unseen! Listen to my call from this illumined moon that did not desire that its orb should eclipse the countenance of this Youth who is of both the East and the West, whom you will find in every tablet as a concealed secret recorded upon a line, written in red, which has, in truth, been hidden (*fi kulli l-alwáh sirran mustasirran 'ala as-satr musattaran 'ala 's-satr al-muhammir qad kána bi'l-haqq mastúran*).[8]

5. Say: God has revealed (*awhá*) to me: I am God, there is no god but Me, the worshipped. I did not create among the Gates the like of this Remembrance. The most great Word is as this Remembrance[9] and all come to him in the tablet of the inmost heart (*fu'ád*), as instructed[10] from around the fire.

6. O people of the earth! The point (*al-nuqtah*) has reached the region (*al-mantaqah*). So listen to my call from that Arabian, Muhammadan, 'Alawí youth, whom you will find in all tablets, a most mighty secret witnessed around the fire.

7. O believers! Verily, God has enjoined upon you after the book, the writing of it with the best handwriting in gold ink. So thank God your Lord for the creation of the heavens and the earth and what is between them and prostrate before God who has created them in order that you may worship Him[11] in truth. And He is God who sees what you do.

8. O Consolation of the Eye! Say: When I set out for the [Sacred] House [i.e. Mecca or the Ka'ba], I found the Ka'ba[12] itself raised up upon four-fold legs [A 430] in the presence of the Gate.

9. And when I set off to perform the circumambulation (*at-tawwáf*) [B 193] of the House I found the obligations in the Mother Book to be seven, in very truth.

10. And when I wanted to perform the recitation upon the earth, I found the Mash'ar and the Arafat were both in distress[13] around the Báb.

11. O Concourse of Lights! By God, the True One! Verily the most great word of God is, in truth, the hidden truth. And He is God who is the mighty, the Ancient of Days.

12. Verily the inner truth of this chapter is difficult and mighty. Even were the oceans of the heavens and the earth to be joined together as ink and all things for pens [cf. Q 18:109, 31:27], they would not be sufficient or able [to write it] except for an unconnected Alif (*alif ghayr ma'túfah*), just as the Command, in truth, now exists thus in the form of heaven or the shape of the earth and was [previously] with God the Lord of the heavens.

13. O people from the Temple of Divine Unity who are attracted (*ahl al-jadhb min haykal at-tawhíd*)! Listen to my call from this yellowed leaf (*al-waraqa al-musaffirah*) sprouting in red oil (*bi 'd-dahn al-muhammir*) from the tree (*ash-shajara*) moving in the atmosphere[14] of the Unseen (*al-'amá'*). This[15] [tree] is that of which God did not decree anything on earth as its root and it is, by the command of God, planted in the air (*hawá'*) of the Unseen (*al-'amá'*) by the hands of the Remembrance.

14. Verily, this pathway (*sirát*) of your Lord has been set straight (*mustaqíman*) in the Mother Book.

15. And verily, this is the secret (*as-sirr*) in the hiding place (*mustasarr*) of the veils (*as-satr*), written (*mastúran*) on the line (*satr*) above the Unseen (*al-'amá'*) and above the heavens.

16. Verily this is the Arabic form (*ash-shikl*) of the two which was, in truth and upon the truth, witnessed around the fire[16] [H 224].

17. And it is the truth, the form of al-Yamaní mentioned in the 70, the two paths,[17] in truth, around the fire.

18. In order that the believer may be mentioned in that Book in the name of truth, upon the truth.

19. Verily, this is the light upon the [Sinaitic] Mountain and it is shining (*al-mutajallí*) from the [Divine] Names on the concourse of the Manifestation (*zuhúr*). And He is the True One and only He knows what He is about. And He is God who is the Exalted,[18] the Ancient of Days.

20. Verily, this [A 422] is the True One in the Meccan (*al-abtahí*) cadence. And he is

the secret shining (*al-mutajallí*) from the 'Alawí body (*al-jism*). And he is the light stored in the form of a dove in the Fátimí heart (*kabad*). Exalted is God, his Creator, Exalted and Great, above what the wrong-doers assert of Him.

21. Verily, this is the secret (*as-sirr*) [B 193] veiled (*mastúran*) within the secrets (*al-asrár*) which are around the fire.[19]

22. Verily, this is the light which was hidden and stored among the lights in the midst of the mountains (*al-jibál*) on the right hand of the Throne behind the Qáf.

23. Verily, these are the coverings of Manifestation (*qumus az-zuhúr*) and the secret of the depths (*sirr al-butún*) which are inscribed around the secret in the books of heaven.[20]

24. Verily, this is the tree of the inner heart (*shajarat al-fu'ád*) which is witnessed for God, the True One, upon Mount Sinai.

25. Verily, these are the leaves (pages) of holiness which have been written around the fire upon the thrones of the spheres (*fí surur al-aflák*) from the attributes (*siffát*).

26. Verily, this is the Truth which hath been decreed in the Mother Book around the fire.

27. Verily, this is the Point in the beginning which hath appeared, lauded in truth, in the centre of the seal (*al-khatm*) by the permission of God, the Ancient of Days.

28. Verily, this is the secret in praise of the book upon the Thrones[21] of Grandeur which are equal with regard to fire and water.

29. Verily, this part (*qiddah*) of the secret, the secret of the Arabian Ahmad [the Prophet Muhammad], is the centre of the Throne in the Unseen (*al-'amá*) upon the water which was, in truth, prostrating before and beloved of God, the Ancient of Days.

23. Verily, this is the secret inscribed upon the heart of the Prophet, which was hidden in the exalted truth.

31. Verily, this is the hidden unknown which was written around the fire in the breast of the perceptive Arabic guardian (*walí*).

32. Verily, this is the glorious pearl that was kept safe, through God the praiseworthy One, in the shell of the Friend (*al-khalíl*, Abraham) in the ocean of the Unseen (*al-'amá*) that is around [the Garden of] Eden.

33. Verily, this is the one who flees from every refuge, in truth, and He is God who is, in truth, a witness against you.

34. Verily, thou art in truth and through the truth, giving praise to God in holiness[22] in the pillar of the praise of God (*rukn at-tasbíh*) [A 423].

35. Verily, this is, in truth, the Maghribí sheen (*at-talq al-maghribí*) upon[23] the 'Alawí[24] hair (*ash-sha'r al-'alawí*) for the shaving of the head (*li'l-sahq*) after the untying (*ba'd al-hall*) [of the locks],[25] which is concealed in the point of the fire.

36. Verily, this is Buráq in the Concourse on High; the other Buráqs (*al-burqá*) do not resemble him or anything like him, for he is the lofty similitude (*al-mathal al-a'lá*) which was seen around the fire in every Mystic Cloud (*al-'amá'*) [B 194].[26]

37. O people of Paradise! Learn the pathway[27] of servitude from this bird skimming[28] through the atmosphere of the Unseen (*al-'amá'*) and plunging into the ocean of red musk, and annihilate yourselves in this white fire through God the True One. You have been able to settle in the East and the West[29] by the permission of God, the King of earth and heaven. He is, in truth, the All-Knowing. He is God, who is powerful over all things.

38. O Consolation of the Eye! Say: I am Bahá' and this is the pathway of God [cf. Q 12:108]. I summon unto God [Q 12:108] alone and to His awaited remnant (*ilá baqiyyatihi 'l-muntazar*). And I am looking, in truth, upon the East and the West (*al-mashriqayn*) with discernment (*'alá basíra* [cf. Q 8:108]). Verily, I and whoever follows me [Q 8:108], we are questioned, in truth and upon the truth, around the fire.

39. O people of [H 225] the Lights! Listen to my call from this bird that is singing, raised in the atmosphere of heaven in accordance with the melody (*'ala 'l-lahn*) of David the prophet.

40. To me, to me is the judgement of the two waters (*al-má'Ayn*).

And to me, to me is the judgement of the two airs (*al-hawá'Ayn*) in the two worlds.
And to me, to me are four of the two letters in the two names.
And to me, to me are four of the two airs in the two lines from the two secrets.
And to me, to me is the bearer of the Throne of seven and one (*sab'í wáhidí* or *wa ahadí*).
And to me, to me are the eight heavens,[30] narrated and concealed.
And to me, to me is the judgement of the two first lights upon the two mountains.
And to me, to me is the judgement of the two shining lights (*al-nayyirayn*, sun and moon) on the two last lines from those two inner depths (*al-batnayn*).
And to me, to me is the judgement of the two heavens concerning the eight of the Báb, in this Báb[31] there are two Bábs.
And to me, to me is the judgement of the two earths concerning the seven of the Báb by the two letters.
And to me, to me is the command and the judgement and there is no God but Him, our Lord alone. He has no partner and He is God the Exalted, the Great [A 424].

41. O Consolation of the Eyes! Say: all that God has caused to flow from my pen in this Book is only by the permission of God, the True One, and the book has only borne[32] in this chapter but a letter of the chapter which is witnessed around the water.

42. And praised be to God, the True One, except for whom there is no God. And He is God who is powerful over all things. And He is God who is independent of the worlds.

Bibliography

Browne, E. G. 'Some Remarks on the Bâbî Texts Edited by Baron Victor Rosen in Vols. I and VI of the "Collections Scientifiques de l'Institut des Langues Orientales de Saint Petersbourg"'. *Journal of the Royal Asiatic Society*, vol. 24 (1892), pp. 259–332.

Iranian National Bahá'í Archives (INBA).

Kirmání, Karím Khán. *Izháq al-Bátil*, Kirman: Sa'ádah, 1351/1973, pp. 97–8.

Lambden, Stephen. 'Some Notes on the Use of the Term *'amá* in Bábí-Bahá'í Scripture'. *Bahá'í Studies Bulletin*, vol. 3, no. 2 (September 1984), pp. 42–114.

Lawson, B. Todd. *The Qur'an Commentary of Sayyid 'Alí Muhammad, the Báb*. Unpublished Ph.D. diss., McGill University, 1987. http://bahai-library.com/index.php5?file=lawson_quran_commentary_bab (accessed 21 October 2007).

Mazandarani, Fadil. *Tarikh Zuhur al-Haqq*, vol. 3 (n.p., n.d.).

Momen, Moojan (ed.). 'Summary of the Persian Bayan', in *Selections from the Writings of E. G. Browne on the Bábí and Bahá'í Religions*. Oxford: George Ronald, 1987.

— 'The Trial of Mullá 'Alí Bastámí: A combined Sunní-Shí'í fatwá against the Báb'. *Iran*, vol. 20 (1982), pp. 113–43.

Nabíl-i-A'zam. *The Dawn-Breakers: Nabíl's Narrative of the Early Days of the Bahá'í Revelation*. Wilmette, IL: Bahá'í Publishing Trust, 1970.

Notes

1. I am grateful to Todd Lawson for suggesting to me the translation of this sura and encouraging me to persevere in the task.
2. In Todd Lawson's Ph.D. thesis *The Qur'an Commentary of Sayyid 'Alí Muhammad, the Báb*, this observation is attributed to Dr Muhammad Afnan and there is the following additional comment: 'The work has elsewhere been described as containing forty verses per *súra* [Browne,'Some Remarks on the Bâbî Texts', pp. 261–2], representing the *abjad* value of the quranic *lí* 'to me' or 'before me' . . . The prepositional phrase is an explicit allusion to the dream of Joseph: *Father, I saw eleven stars, and the sun and the moon: I saw them bowing down before me (lí)* [Q 12:4]. Browne notes, however, that several chapters of the British Library MS (probably Or. 3539; another MS of the work there is Or. 6681) are described in the MS itself as having 42 verses (as is one chapter of F11). In both cases, however, the number of verses is taken to be symbolic of either the acceptance or assertion of spiritual authority (Browne, 'Remarks', p. 262).'
3. Kirmání, *Izháq al-Bátil*, pp. 97–8.
4. For example, this term occurs frequently in the Persian Bayán; see 2:1, 2: 2, 2:11, 2:12,

etc. See 'Summary of the Persian Bayán' in Momen, *Selections from the Writings of E.G. Browne*, pp. 327, 333, 334; Bahá'u'lláh, of course, continued this metaphor when he referred to himself as the Ancient Root from which the Aghsán (branches) spread forth. Interestingly, this image of a tree, the roots of which are in heaven and whose branches stretch towards earth, occurs in the Hindu scriptures (Bhagavad Gita 15:1–2).

5.. For a fuller discussion of this term, see Lambden, 'Some Notes on the Use of the Term *'amá'*.

6. *Al-alwáh*. B has *al-arwáh*.

7. H omits the words *al-'alimún bi-annahu*.

8. This and the previous verse are repeated almost exactly in sura 111, the last sura of the Qayyúm al-Asmá', vv. 25–6.

9. B and H have *kalimat al-akbar hadhá dhikran*; A has *kalimat al-akbar hadhá dhikr allah* (the most great word is this Remembrance of God).

10. A has *ma'múran*; B has *ma'múran* (populated); H has *ma'húdan* (authorized, commissioned, enjoined).

11. B and H have *iyyáhu*; A has *iyyáná* (us).

12. A and B have *as-sakína* (tranquillity of the presence of God, a word that has powerful connotations in Jewish and Islamic mysticism); H has *al-ka'ba*. I have chosen to use Ka'ba because these three verses, 9–11, have a parallelism of structure all related to the *hajj*.

13. B has *baliyyatan* (in distress); A has *malínatan* (gently, softly); H has no word here.

14. B and H have *jaw* (atmosphere, air), A has *huww* (black or dark red, plural).

15. B and H have *hadhihi*, which appears more correct; A has *hadha*.

16. A and B have *bi'l-haqq hawl an-nár 'ala al-haqq*; H has *bi'l-haqq 'ala al-haqq hawl an-nár*.

17. A has *sirátan*.

18. A and H have *'aliyan* (the Exalted); B has *ghaniyan* (the Rich, the Self-Sufficient).

19. A and B have *hawl an-nár*; H has *hawl al-má'* (around the water).

20. *Fi'l-kutub as-samá'* might also be translated as 'in the exalted books'. The translation in the text is not grammatically correct; the translation given in this note is not correct lexically.

21. A has *saráyir* (thrones); B and H have *sará'ir* (secrets).

22. A and B have *bi'l-quds*; H has *fi'l-quds*.

23. A and B have *wa 'ala ash-sha'r*; H has just *'ala ash-sha'r*.

24. B and H have *al-'Alawí*; A has *al-'Arabí*.

25. *Sahq*, the shaving of the head, is in mystical terminology, a reference to the shedding of worldly attachment and becoming selfless.

26. H has *fi hall al-'amá*; A and B have *fi kull al-'amá*. The coming together of the words *mathal* and *nár* in this sentence alludes to the Light Verse of the Qur'an (24:35). Even the name Buráq here may be feeding into this allusion to the Light Verse since it is derived from *barq*, referring to the first flash of light that dawns upon the horizon.

27. A and H have *sabíl*; B has *subul*.

28. H has *at-tayr al-mudaff*; A and B have *at-tayr al-muwarraq* (leafy bird!).

29. H has *al-gharb*; A and B have *al-ghurbá*.

30. B and H have *al-jannát*; A has *al-jaththát* (bodies).

31. This phrase *fi hadha 'l-báb* is omitted in B.

32. H has *ma hamala*; A and B have *ma hamaltu* (I have not borne).

8

The Surát al-'Abd of the Qayyúm al-Asmá' (chapter 109): A Provisional Translation and Commentary

Todd Lawson

Introduction

The *Súrat al-'Abd*, the Sura (or Chapter) of the Servant, is the 109th sura of the Báb's Qayyúm al-Asmá' (The Transcendent Source and Sustainer of the Divine Names[1]); the work is also known as the *Tafsír súrat Yúsuf* or the *Commentary on the Sura of Joseph* and *Ahsan al-Qasas* (*The Fairest of Stories*). Beginning on the night of his meeting with Mullá Husayn Bushrú'í, 22 May 1844, this commentary was revealed by the Báb in the form of the long-awaited true Qur'an that had been (according to the beliefs and lore of the Shi'a) expected to be restored to its rightful place in the community at the time of the return of the Hidden Imam, the Qá'im, on the Day of Resurrection (*yawm al-qiyáma*). The Hidden Imám, Muhammad ibn Hasan al-'Askari, had been in occultation since 873 CE. Together with the true Qur'an, in his care and protection since his disappearance from public ken, he would appear wearing the robe of Joseph and carrying the staff of Moses. There is no space here (nor is it relevant) to delve into the historical accuracy of these beliefs. It is important, however, to recognize that they were (and are) widespread amongst the followers of *Ithná 'asharí* or Twelver Shi'ism. Thus the Qayyúm al-Asmá' is a messianic or chiliastic text and its 'publication' or appearance (cf. *khurúj, zuhúr*) is every bit as charged with the considerable charisma of 'expectation-to-be-fulfilled' as is the actual appearance of the Hidden Imam. After all, the return of the true Qur'an to replace the current corrupted version would be a logical and important step in the unfolding of the specifically Shi'i religious apocalyptic drama and vision: 'To fill the earth with justice as it is now filled with injustice.'

As emblems and proofs of the arrival of the Day of Resurrection, the return of the Hidden Imam and the revelation of the heretofore hidden true Qur'an together form an evidentiary miracle quite unparalleled, each being the credential of the other and representing a kind of sub-messianic theme of their own, related to the seminal Day of the Covenant first mentioned in the Qur'an (Q 7:172) and subsequently contemplated as the *par excellence* scenario and dramatization of the birth and genesis of spiritual authority (*waláya*) in Shi'i Islam, a myth, it has been suggested, which accounts for the birth of consciousness itself.² The primordial day is explicitly and unmistakably identified by the Báb in a work he composed prior to the Qayyúm al-Asmá', with the actual historical day Ghadír al-Khumm, which took place 18 Dhu'l-Hijja 10 AH (= 16 March 632 CE) as the Prophet Muhammad was returning to Medina from the Farewell Pilgrimage and he and his large entourage rested at the pond (*ghadír*) of Khumm, half-way between Mecca and Medina. Here he publicly announced that he would soon die and that when this happened the community should turn to 'Alí as their leader (*mawlá*). Here also the Prophet enjoined unwavering belief in two things after him: 1) the Book of God and 2) his descendants, the Holy Family. For the Twelver Shi'a this means 'Alí, the Prophet's son-in-law, cousin and half-brother, his wife Fatima (the Prophet's daughter) and their descendants. Both sources of authority and guidance are referred to in the tradition as 'the Two Formidable Ones', 'the Two Weighty Ones' or even 'the Two Decisive (and Infallible Sources of Guidance)' (*al-thaqalayn*). Their reappearance after such prolonged and epic absence are thus seen by the Shi'a as not only a promise fulfilled but an umbilical reconnection with the original Day of the Covenant – whose earthly dramatization, imitation or recital (cf. *hikáya*) was mentioned above – a connection which serves to merge the spiritual power of that primordial event with the messianic consummation of history and time: each is identified with the other. For this reading it is not accidental that the Day of Resurrection is explicitly mentioned in the verse that recounts the primordial covenant. This provides essential background for understanding why the verses of the Qayyúm al-Asmá' have been precisely established at 42³ because this is the spiritual or *abjad* value of the word *balá* (Yea verily!) which was the first part of the response uttered by the assembled, universal humanity in the original answer to the divine 'originating' question asked on the primordial Day of the Covenant: *Am I not your Lord?* (Q. 7:172).⁴ For convenience, we reproduce here a translation of this pivotal verse:

> When your Lord took out the offspring from the loins of the Children of Adam and made them bear witness about themselves, He said, 'Am I not your Lord?' and they replied, 'Yes, we bear witness.' So you cannot say on the Day of Resurrection, 'We were not aware of this.'⁵

The revelation, composition and promulgation of the Qayyúm al-Asmá' deserves first to be seen as a spiritual re-enactment of both the primordial Day of the Covenant and the earthly reiteration of those originating spiritual energies at Ghadír al-Khumm, spiritual energies that, according to the Shi'i tradition, had for their object the making absolutely clear the line of succession from the Prophet and the identification of the locus of all authority (*waláya*) on earth, namely the designation of 'Alí ibn Abí Tálib as the first Imam and bearer of this authority after the passing of Muhammad. The guiding purpose and defining message of the Qayyúm al-Asmá' is the invocation, evocation and identification of the very same authority with the purpose of its author, the Báb. Such a powerful and compelling message is achieved through the efficacy of typological figuration. In literary terms, this is the metaphorical representation of the key features and persons of Islamic history in the new garment woven by the Báb with this text. These events are frequently of a metahistorical nature and therefore deemed utterly present (even if invisible) and true and vital in the cultural *imaginaire*: the long-awaited 'True Qur'an' with its rightful guardian, the Hidden Imam. At this stage in our research it is quite impossible to offer a positive opinion about the literal similarity between the Qayyúm al-Asmá' and the textual evidence for what in fact may prove to be a legendary book whose importance was and is more in its continued absence and hiddenness than in its actual appearance. The interested reader is directed to some pertinent bibliography.[6] Such typological iteration or figuration may also be considered a performance of a sacred script, existing from a time that precedes time itself and is therefore beyond the scrutiny and analysis of earthly historians.

This particular sura was chosen for translation out of a number of other possibilities because of several factors. First of all, it is part of a pair of suras (108 and 109) whose relationship to each other is clearly indicated by their titles (Súrat al-Dhikr and Súrat al-'Abd) that are in fact titles of authority or prophethood, the analogue to what would eventually come to be known as the quality of being a divine manifestation.[7] *Dhikr* means remembrance and it is one of the more common titles assumed by the Báb throughout this work and elsewhere in his writings.[8] It applies to his spiritual authority and simultaneously applies to spiritual authority (*waláya*) in general. Indeed, all prophets and messengers and the Imams of the Shi'a are rightfully recognized by such a term. It is also important to add that the other infallible source of spiritual authority, the Qur'an itself, is also recognized by the same word. Thus a chapter going by this name can be reasonably expected to speak directly to the nature of spiritual authority as manifested or personified in a particular instance. In this instance, of course, the spiritual authority being described and taught is the one obtaining – again in umbilical fashion – between the Hidden Imam and 'Alí Muhammad Shírází, in whose very name the spiritual authority of both Muhammad, the 'Seal of the Prophets' and 'Alí, his appointed guardian (*walí*) is invoked. It is, of course, not only invoked but in the exquisite atmosphere of revelation these names are felt to be personified anew in the person of the Báb. As if to substantiate and emphasize this, the Báb employs the unique trope of using the familiar device of Quranic disconnected letters to spell, rather surprisingly, an actual word, which is in fact (and even more remarkably) his name.[9] The disconnected letters that head the *Súrat al-Dhikr* are *'ayn, lám, yá'*, which together spell the sacred name 'Alí. The 'disconnected' letters heading the *Súrat al-'Abd* are *mím, há', mím, dál*, which together spell the sacred name Muhammad. Both unmistakably indicate the author of the text at hand, 'Alí Muhammad Shírází, the Báb, while simultaneously invoking and evoking the spiritual authority of the original bearers of these names, first the Prophet and his appointee, the first Imam, but then also several of the actual subsequent Imams as well. It should be remembered, also, that such names in Islamic culture are significant because their actual semantic values are not lost sight of in the way names in other cultures are rarely noticed for the literal meaning of the word. When we hear the name 'Robert' we are not immediately reminded of its meaning 'bright fame'. When we encounter the name 'Jesus', derived from the Hebrew Joshua meaning 'the Lord is salvation', we are not mindful of this etymology, even though we may acknowledge some portentous or spiritual power in the name. Generally, such power sensed is by association with the life and ministry of Jesus and not derived from the meaning of the word 'Jesus/Joshua'. The words *'alí* and *muhammad* do have specific meanings, which are very much in operation when used as names and especially in the instance of the spiritual leaders of Islam. *Muhammad* is based on the Arabic triliteral root *há', mím, dál* which denotes the idea and action of 'praise'. Thus the name may be roughly translated as 'praiseworthy'. *'Alí* is based on the Arabic triliteral root *'ayn, lám, yá'* and denotes loftiness and sublimity. Thus the name may be roughly translated as 'exalted'. Quite apart from their function as designating the two most important figures in the history and teachings of (Shi'i) Islam, these two names are widely used throughout Islamic culture as preferred names for male children. In the Islamic cultural context of naming, as is the case with so many other cultures, names are chosen for their spiritual value, the way in which they represent, encourage and cultivate selected and esteemed virtues for the one so named. It is as if individual words have effective energies of their own and may be set to work upon both their bearer and the world with which the one so named comes into contact. Naming is a serious matter. In the case of these two names, another factor must be taken into consideration. Each may, to some degree, be thought of as being applicable also to God. This is most clear in the case of 'Alí, which is used as a divine epithet numerous times in the Qur'an.[10] Indeed, the Shi'a have long held that the frequent mention of this word as a divine attribute was a clear indication of the truth of 'Alí's Imamate. While the other name, Muhammad, is not used in the same way in the Qur'an, its meaning indicates that it could logically be applied to God as 'One worthy of praise'.[11] Thus in both instances a blurring of the identities of the manifestation and the godhead occurs. This blurring of the line of distinction is intentional since it bespeaks a central principle of the faith and practice at hand: God is utterly and infinitely unknowable in Essence; however, certain extraordinary beings appear from time to time in order to teach humanity the truth about God, the world and the role of the human race. These emissaries are called divine manifestations, or more to the point, 'special places' where – or channels through which – divinity is caused to appear by means of its own self-manifestation (cf. *tajallí*), viz. *mazáhir iláhí'*. They represent for their respective time and place both all that can be known of the divine and a reminder that God is ultimately unknowable. As representatives of all that can be known of the divine, they are functionally identical with 'God'. In respect of their role as reminders of the unknowableness of God, they are utterly dependant upon and eternally other than God.

This discussion of personal names and divine attributes is offered to help set the stage for an aspect of the Báb's writings that is extremely difficult to translate, yet may be reasonably assumed to stand for the great appeal his writings had for his followers from the time of revelation. This feature would be called 'punning' if there was not such a danger thereby of misrepresenting the work at hand as something less than utterly and absolutely serious and non-negotiable. Word play as such is a prime feature of language and its growth and use in literature, whether poetry or prose.[12] This is true in English and it is true to an almost unimaginable degree in Arabic and Persian, the languages of the author of this work. Word play – pointing out and exploiting for artistic and rhetorical effect the similarities of different words and their oppositions, appositions and resonances – is a delight and proof of the profound and durable relation between language, meaning and truth. The degree to which both Arabic and Persian thus express and generate meaning and poetic effect is a source of cultural pride in each instance.

In a sense, the form and contents of the Qayyúm al-Asmá' may, in fact, be considered an extended instance of 'revelational' paronomasia. As pointed out in earlier scholarship, much of it consists of lengthy and copious direct quotations from the Qur'an in which this or that key word or key phrase has been altered, sometimes slightly and sometimes more profoundly, in order to focus the lens of *waláya* more closely and precisely on the historical circumstances, the life and ministry of the Báb. Thus in a grand gesture of deadly serious punning, an indelible and unchangeable identification is made between the meaning of two events, in the same way that homophony draws attention to the identity of two otherwise distinct words. But in the present case, there is no 'otherwise distinct' in operation unless one focuses to a distorting and irrelevant degree upon what must be considered in the context of absolute truth (*al-haqq al-mutlaq*) respective (and superficial) cultural and biographical contexts of, on the one hand, Muhammad ibn 'Abd Alláh of Mecca (b. *c.* 570 CE, d. 632 CE), and Sayyid 'Alí Muhammad of Shiraz (b. 1819 CE, d. 1850 CE). The Qayyúm al-Asmá' insists in numerous passages that it is bringing the same truth originally revealed to Muhammad, a truth uncorrupted by the evil designs of enemies or accidental lapses of scribes (*tahríf*).

The following attempt at translation will allow the reader to experience firsthand, as it were, just how often the specific paronomastic device centred on the word 'Alí is used. Here it must be remembered that in order to read this text it is never a case of either/or with regard to the 'true intention' of such references. The name 'Alí, even when in the form of the divine attribute *al-'Alí*, simultaneously points to 1) the historical figure of the first Imam, and perhaps even more importantly, 2) the universal charismatic authority (*waláya*) which he inherited from the Prophet; 3) the process of such inheritance or transmission, thus implicating and involving (or causing to be present, conjuring) each of the subsequent Imams of the Shi'a; 4) God himself both in his unknowable, apophatic aspect, mentioned above, and the process of self-manifestation by means of which the cosmos and all that is in it came to be; and 5) this as a direct counterpart or subsidiary side effect of self-manifestation (*tajallí*); and 6) the Báb himself. All is to be understood simultaneously. It is thought that humans are capable of this. This rule applies to each and every one of the divine attributes encountered in the text but it is with *al-'Alí* that it becomes most obvious.

An attempt is made also in the following translation to indicate the degree and frequency with which the Qur'an figures in the actual text. To do this, the somewhat cumbersome expediency of typography is employed. Here, all identified Quranic quotations and words – what might best be thought of as moments of sacred meaning and melody – appear in small capitals. This is not the best method but it is the only one I can think of which clearly shows the presence of the Qur'an and the bold innovation the composition of the Qayyúm al-Asmá' actually represents. What might be thought by the sceptical or ungenerous as a heretical or worse appropriation of scripture, reveals itself in the eventual performance of the revelation to have been another compelling feature of the appeal of the young Messiah. Those who recognized the use of the Qur'an would easily have been deeply impressed by the extent to which this young layman had internalized and indeed become one with the sacred word, to a degree that in his first great proclamatory gesture the actual distinction between 'his' words and the words of the Qur'an is so blurred as to be nearly impossible to draw a distinct line between them. This, as we know, was an extremely compelling aspect of the new revelation and one which is impossible to experience unless the trouble is taken to attempt to distinguish between the Quranic material and the rest of the composition.[13]

As important as it obviously is, the Qur'an is not the only 'source' (to use a very unsatisfactory term) found to play such a formative and definitive role in the composition of the Qayyúm al-Asmá'. The other major formative element is, as might be expected, the *hadíth*. The so-called 'second scripture' of Islam plays an extensive role in the composition of this work. It is not as easy to track the use of *hadíth* (*akhbár*) because of the nature and history of the genre. There are of course well-known 'orthodox' compilations of this material in both Sunni and Shi'i Islam. But there are also other collections that are not always readily available and even some that may have never been committed to writing in the first place. Thus while many references to or 'occurrences' of *hadíth* are identifiable, many remain elusive and untraceable. These *hadíth* come largely from the Shi'i collections but some come also to Shi'ism from the Islamic mystical tradition. One of the great influences here is the magnum opus of Ibn al-'Arabí (d. 1240) entitled *The Meccan Revelations* (*al-Futúhát al-Makkiyya*). Such sometimes opaque and puzzling references as, for example, the Earth of Saffron (*ard al-za'farán*) or the Red Sandhill (*kathíb al-ahmar*), owe their currency to this work, even if the immediate audience of the Báb's theophanic performance was largely inimical to the great mystic and had no idea that he was being quoted in the service of the new revelation. By the time of the Báb many such references, tropes and topoi had been thoroughly domesticated to Shi'ism through the work of such scholars as Haytham al-Bahrání (d. 1280 CE), Haydar Ámulí (d. after 1385 CE), Rajab al-Bursí (d. 1411 CE) and Ibn Abí Jumhúr al-Ahsá'í (d. 1499 CE).

There is no space here to pursue at any adequate length the study of the *hadíth* quoted or referred to by the Báb in this commentary. But it is important to draw attention to one particular *hadíth* that has had an enduring formative influence on the distinctive expressive style of both the Bábí revelation and the subsequent Bahá'í revelation. This is the remarkable (and depending upon one's religious temperament, celebrated or reviled), *Hadíth Khutbat al-tutunjiyya*. Henry Corbin first brought it to the attention of western scholarship in the 1960s but by that time it had long been recognized as a key component of an esoteric or at least elitist stream of Shi'ism. Since then it, along with a number of similar texts, has been studied by a number of scholars, both western and eastern.[1]

The reader of translations of the Qayyúm al-Asmá' should know that the basic attitude of the text, the voice of the commentary and the structure of its theophanic claims echo the form and contents of this sermon. The sura translated here was chosen also because it is a particularly clear illustration of the impact of the *Khutbat al-tutunjiyya* on the mind of the Báb and his audience. It had been the object of a lengthy commentary by Sayyid Kázim Rashtí (d. 1844 CE), and the Báb himself would later compose an explanation of one of the statements of his 'beloved teacher' found in that commentary. But its presence is already quite palpable in the earlier commentary by the Báb, the *Tafsír súrat al-Baqara*. Thus the *Khutbat al-tutunjiyya* exercised a strong hold on the collective consciousness and imagination of the immediate milieu out of which the Báb's message arose. It becomes important, therefore, in light of the advice of the Guardian of the Bahá'í Faith quoted in the introduction to this collection of essays, to become aware of the basic outline and contents of this central – if extra-Quranic – source and its influence on the language of the new revelation.

The fascination with this text may be partly understood by referring to its main topic: the role and nature of the bearer of divine authority (*waláya*). The main text of the sermon is a lengthy catalogue of divine epithets and sometimes otherwise obscure Quranic and other references in which their proper intention is clarified. Without exception, each and every noun or symbol of divinity is identified with the person of 'Alí, by 'Alí himself, as a result of a powerful vision he experienced between Kufa and Medina, between two gulfs (*tatanjayn, tutunjayn*), and as a result of which the nature and mystery of divine transcendence is expressed in such a way that 'none can bear its divine power'. A brief extract may be helpful.

> I understood the wonders of God's creation, wonders that only God Himself understood.
>
> And I knew all that had been and all that would be. And all that occurred on the Day of the pre-Primordial Covenant that preceded the First Adam.
>
> It was unveiled to me and I understood. My Lord taught me and I knew. And if it were not that I feared for you I would disclose everything destined to happen to you between now and the DAY OF RESURRECTION.
>
> . . .
>
> I am the master (*sáhib*) of the first creation before Noah.
>
> And if you knew what wondrous things occurred between the time of Adam and Noah and the nations that passed away you would understood more fully the Quranic word: HOW VILE THEIR DEEDS WERE (Q 5:79)!
>
> And I am the master of the prior FLOOD (*túfán*, Q 7:133) and I am the master of the second FLOOD (Q 29:14), and I am the master of the FLOOD OF 'ARAM (Q 34:16), I am the master of the hidden SECRETS (Q *passim*), I am the master of 'AD and THE GARDENS (Q *passim*), I am the master of THAMÚD (*Q passim*) and all the DIVINE SIGNS (*al-áyát*, Q *passim*), I am their destroyer and I cause them to tremble, I am their authority and I am their annihilator.
>
> . . .

I am the one who causes them to die and I am the one who causes them to live.

I am THE FIRST, I am THE LAST, I am the OUTWARD, I am the INWARD (cf. Q 57:3).

Thus the Imam 'Alí addresses his faithful followers in the *Khutbat al-tutunjiyya*. We have translated here just a very small series of excerpts to demonstrate the closeness between that sermon and this revolutionary work by the Báb. In the former, 'Alí's words accomplish two primary objectives. First they explain heretofore obscure or controversial references in the Qur'an; frequently these are of the interesting category *hapax legomenon*, a word or phrase that occurs only once in the Qur'an and thus may be especially difficult to define or understand because of such limited usage. An example of this in the above excerpt is THE FLOOD OF 'ARAM. This refers to a legendary deluge which was visited upon a certain region as divine punishment. The details are a matter of debate, though most Qur'an commentators incline towards the view that it is a reference to the breaking of the Ma'rib dam, not long before the coming of the Prophet. Nonetheless, the exact meaning of the phrase is elusive. By instructing his followers that it was actually 'Alí himself who was the 'master' of that great event, great progress is made in neutralizing a source of uncertainty in the sacred Book by giving assurance that whatever else is not known about the event, it is known that the one who was responsible for it is their own leader. This means that if his followers wished to know more specific details about the famous yet obscure Quranic pronouncement, they have but to ask. This leads to the second objective accomplished in this sermon and those like it, namely that by his words, which are a distinctive appropriation of the sacred scripture, sometimes paraphrased with his own 'original' formulations, he has claimed unique and comprehensive religious authority of the type frequently, if not usually, ascribed to God alone.

There can be no doubt that the Qayyúm al-Asmá' accomplishes these same two objectives. But this is not the only basis upon which the comparison and genetic relationship is posited. The deft and compelling intermixing of the Báb's words with the words of the Qur'an is obvious and we have mentioned above the central place the *Khutbat al-tutunjiya* occupied in the religious culture of both the Báb and his immediate audience. There is more, namely the prevailing atmosphere of the text: it is an atmosphere generated by the certitude or certainty of its verses, a certainty and absoluteness that can be found only in the Qur'an itself and the functioning of what may be called the prophetic or apocalyptic imagination which illumines each word. It is audacious. It is artistic. It is creative. Each of these observations may be made with regard to its contents or meaning. The form of both the *Khutbat al tutunjiyya* and the Qayyúm al-Asmá' also share much in common with the way in which the Arabic language is used, or better, orchestrated. It is not possible at this time to delve deeply into this aspect of the two compositions but it is important to point out that the structure of the Arabic language together with its distinctive genius for generating meaning is intimately bound up with the relationship between sound and sense in which the two frequently change places with regard to priority and semiotic circumstance. The sound and the music of the composition is that without which any meaning cannot be compelling. Thus there is a great deal of rhyme of all kinds (internal, end-stop, enjambed, slant and so on) as well as assonance, consonance and all the usual 'devices' at play in a poetic composition, whether written or oral. In addition, there are many features of classical oral composition present in both works. It is, after all, cast in rhymed prose (*saj'*) from beginning to end, an ancient and venerable emblem of supernatural communication that came to be identified with the Qur'an alone after the profound and transformative spiritual experience of Muhammad and his 'translation' of that experience into the words and message of the holy Qur'an. This is a topic whose full discussion must be postponed for a later time.

The arrogation to himself by the author of absolute authority is accomplished in the *Khutbat al-Tutunjiyya* in a rather straightforward, literal manner. The Báb is also straightforward and literal with regard to the claims being put forth, but not always. The authority that may be thought to flow through the composition and find its rightful bearer in the author is negotiated and evoked in a number of different ways. In the first place, and in the very first sura, the remarkable *Súrat al-mulk*, written in the presence of Mullá Husayn on that fateful night in Shiraz, the Báb employs what might appear to the uninitiated as the pious fiction of a constructed pedigree for his composition. A consideration of the opening chain of authority by means of which the Báb tells us that this Book was conveyed to him shows that it has much in common with a familiar feature of the genre of literature commonly referred to as apocalyptic. There can be no discussion of the inadequate and badly conceived topic of the 'historical accuracy' of the claim by the Báb that this Book was conveyed to him directly by the Hidden Imam. Or, furthermore, that the Hidden Imam received it from his father who received it from his father and so on up the chain of transmission until it stops with the first Imam himself. This important passage runs as follows:

> God decreed that THIS IS THE BOOK in explanation of the FAIREST OF STORIES come forth from its place of hiding (*yakhraja*) with Muhammad ibn al-Hasan ibn 'Alí ibn Muhammad ibn 'Alí ibn Músá ibn Ja'far ibn Muhammad ibn 'Alí ibn al-Husayn ibn 'Alí ibn Abí Tálib to HIS SERVANT that it be the CONCLUSIVE PROOF OF GOD in the possession of the REMEMBRANCE unto ALL THE WORLDS (QA I.9).

One of the things to observe about this statement is that it is cast in the form of a *hadíth*. Without digressing further, suffice it here to say that such a form is intended to evoke authority. In this instance, the authority could not be more intense since the names mentioned are the names of all the 12 Imams except one. This together with the reference to Quranic emblems of authority such as the significant quotation from Q 2:2: THIS IS THE BOOK, in the Shi'i tradition is understood to refer to both the book and its bearer simultaneously despite, or perhaps because of, the inherent grammatical ambiguity.[15] Another such emblem is the epithet PROOF OF GOD which in the construction of this particular verse is a direct reference in partial paraphrase of Qur'an 6:149: SAY: [KNOW,] THEN, THAT THE FINAL EVIDENCE [OF ALL TRUTH] RESTS WITH GOD ALONE; AND HAD HE SO WILLED, HE WOULD HAVE GUIDED YOU ALL ARIGHT. Authority, then, is largely evoked through the employment of Quranic words and phrases but also by reference to the sacred history of suffering and messianic expectation distinctive to the Shi'i tradition. The use of the phrase HIS SERVANT is also fraught with typological meaning inasmuch as no reader or listener could hear it without also thinking of the Prophet Muhammad for whom the phrase is a frequent Quranic epithet.[16] So, while the sceptic or uninitiated might cavil that the Báb has artificially structured his composition to exploit the expectations and presuppositions of his audience, it is more the case that the Báb actually experienced and felt the mysterious unity of time and history in the spiritual and apocalyptic energies of which he saw himself the centre. Corbin is helpful here, and while his main subject is Islamic philosophy, what he says pertains also to the general intellectual culture of Islam and especially Shi'i Islam.

> Because it has not had to confront the problems raised by what we call the 'historical consciousness', philosophical thought in Islam moves in two counter yet complementary directions: issuing from the Origin *(mabda')*, and returning *(ma'ad)* to the Origin, issue and return both taking place in a *vertical* dimension. Forms are thought of as being in space rather than in time. Our thinkers perceive the world not as 'evolving' in a horizontal and rectilinear direction, but as ascending: the past is not behind us but 'beneath our feet'. From this axis stem the *meanings* of the divine Revelations, each of these meanings corresponding to a spiritual hierarchy, to a level of the universe that issues from the threshold of metahistory. Thought can move freely, unhindered by the prohibitions of a dogmatic authority. On the other hand, it must confront the *shari'ah*, should the *shari'ah* at any time repudiate the *haqiqah*. The repudiation of these ascending perspectives is characteristic of the literalists of legalistic religion, the doctors of the Law.[17]

This insight is invaluable for not only helping us understand the transcendent logic of the Báb's writings but also the transcendent logic of the historical events associated with his Revelation.

This introduction to the inadequate attempt at the translation of one of the suras of this remarkable 'book' has already gone on too long. But before ending it is important to return to the last statement above about the history of the Shi'a as an underlying emblem of authority in this work, a feature that, in the nature of chronology, could not really have been at work in the earlier *Khutbat al-tutunjiyya*. This history is chiefly characterized by expectation of the return of the Hidden Imam and all of those emblems of authority associated with him, including the true Qur'an.[18] This return is the symmetrical and spiritual counterpart, as mentioned above, to the Day of the Covenant and may therefore be considered identical with it. A number of characteristic verbs are associated with this event, having to do with 'advent', 'appearance', 'emergence' [from hiding], 'unveiling', 'revelation', 'apocalypse' (which means 'unveiling'), 'return' and so on. In the above verse from QA I.2 the verb translated as 'come forth from hiding' is one of these venerable verbal icons of return and victory: *kh-r-j,* upon which the messianically charged idea of *khurúj* 'advent' or 'rising' or even 'rebellion' is constructed. Like other similar words, such as *zuhúr, kashf, ma'ád, raj'a* and so on, it is impossible to encounter its sound in the context of the Shi'i religious tradition without automatically thinking of the glad day when the Master of Time (*sáhib al-zamán*), the Lord of the Resurrection (*qá'im al-qiyáma*) who is also, in the distinctive logic of this metahistorical world view, the Resurrection itself,[19] would return to fill the earth with justice as it is now filled with injustice. Its use here indicates the time has come.

Reference was made above to the greater Islamic mystical tradition and its presence in this work. All writers on the Bábí movement have largely ignored this important topic, yet it is one of the most important. The intertwined relationship between Shi'ism as such and mysticism or Sufism is an acknowledged, if imperfectly understood, fact. It is logical, therefore, to accept that the same relationship may be descried in the writings of not only the Báb but Bahá'u'lláh as well. Perhaps one day we will all overcome our strange allergy to Sufism and celebrate properly the way in which this perhaps most distinctive and most universal dimension of Islam has been given new life and energy in the Báb's writings, not to mention the writings of his successor (which are, in fact, more closely wedded to that tradition). That this is the case is nowhere more plangent than in one of the more characteristic features of the Qayyúm al-Asmá'. This feature, which occurs in a number of closely related variants, is the refrain constructed around the central notion of the divine reality or truth, *al-Haqq*. This word, one of the favourites of the Sufi tradition because of its conceptual translucence, is used to designate the highest reaches of what we normally call 'God'. It is a word redolent of numerous connotations which may be thought harmonized in its invocation. The familiar Sufi usage is in greeting or salutation (*Yá Haqq*) or in exclamatory expressions of assent to truth, sometimes spontaneous, sometimes not. It is, of course, Quranic and this is whence its real power derives.[20] But it became an emblem of Sufism and to some degree philosophy because of the purity of its abstraction of the idea of absolute reality and truth beyond the ken and limitation of this sub-lunar realm. In the Qayyúm al-Asmá' – from the very first verse – we encounter the word literally thousands of times, and frequently in a sonorous, somewhat hypnotic refrain such as in these two verses (13 and 14) from the first chapter of the Qayyúm al-Asmá', the *Súrat al-mulk*:

> *wa man yakfaru bi'l-islám lan yaqbalu Alláh min a'málihi fí yawm al-qiyáma min ba'd al-shay'* **'alá al-haqq bi'l-haqq shay'an**
> *wa haqqun 'alá Alláh an yuharriqahu bi-nár Alláh al-badí' bi-hukm al-kitáb min hukm al-báb* **'alá al-haqq bi'l-haqq mahtúman**

A provisional rendering of such an integral and expressive yet imminently untranslatable phrase may vary slightly in what follows depending upon context, but the basic translation is: 'By *the* Truth, in *the* Truth' where the italics here are meant to indicate the qualifiers 'one and only utter and absolute, namely God himself in his overwhelmingly remote and overwhelmingly intimate modes'. The music of the refrain, as mentioned, may bring to mind the rhythmic hymnic quality of prayers and phrases associated with Sufi gatherings known, incidentally, as sessions of remembrance or *dhikr* (Persian *zekr*). The various ways in which this basic phrase occurs throughout the text is a subject of study by itself. We mention it only briefly here to give the reader some idea of the pervasive musicality of the original, a musicality in which the illusions of time and space are simultaneously dissolved and made urgent.

THE SURA OF THE SERVANT

IN THE NAME OF GOD THE MERCIFUL THE COMPASSIONATE[21]

NOR DID WE SEND BEFORE THEE [AS MESSENGERS] ANY BUT MEN WHOM WE DID INSPIRE — [MEN] LIVING IN HUMAN HABITATIONS. DO THEY NOT TRAVEL THROUGH THE EARTH, AND SEE WHAT WAS THE END OF THOSE BEFORE THEM? BUT THE HOME OF THE HEREAFTER IS BEST, FOR THOSE WHO DO RIGHT. WILL YE NOT THEN UNDERSTAND?[22]

Verse 1

Mím Há Mím Dál

Verse 2

O People of the THRONE![23] Listen to the CALL[24] of your Lord, THE MERCIFUL,[25] He who THERE IS NO GOD EXCEPT HIM (*huwa*),[26] from the tongue of the REMEMBRANCE,[27] this YOUTH (*al-fatá*),[28] son of the Sublime (*al-'alí*), the 'Arab[29] to whom [God has] in the MOTHER BOOK[30] testified.[31]

Verse 3

Then LISTEN[32] to WHAT IS BEING REVEALED TO YOU FROM YOUR LORD:[33] VERILY VERILY I AM GOD[34] of WHOM THERE IS NO GOD BUT HIM.[35] NOTHING IS LIKE UNTO HIM[36] while He is God, Lofty (*'aliyan*) Great (*kabíran*).[37]

Verse 4

O People of the Earth! HEARKEN[38] to the CALL[39] of the BIRDS[40] upon the TREES[41] leafy and perfumed[42] with the CAMPHOR[43] of Manifestation (*káfúr al-zuhúr*) describing this YOUNG MAN (*ghulám*)[44] descended from the Arabs, from MUHAMMAD,[45] from 'Alí, from Fatima, from Mekka, from Medina, from Bathá',[46] from 'Iráq with what the MERCIFUL[47] HAS MANIFESTED (*tajallá*)[48] upon their leaves, namely that he is THE SUBLIME (*al-'aliy*)[49] and he is God, MIGHTY,[50] PRAISED.[51]

Verse 5

This YOUTH[52] most white[53] in colour and most beautiful of eye (*ad'aj fí al-'ayn*),[54] even of eyebrow, limbs well formed like gold freshly cast from the two springs, soft of shoulder like pure malleable silver in two cups, sublimely awesome in appearance, like the awe-inspiring appearances of the Elders,[55] and outspreading his MERCY[56] as the two Husayns spread mercy over the land, the centre of the sky (i.e. the sun) has not seen the like of the justice of the two justices, and in grace like the two Lights (*nayyirayn*)[57] joined in the two names[58] from the most lofty of the two beloveds and the ISTHMUS[59] between the two causes in the SECRET[60] of al-Tatanjayn, the abider (*al-wáqif*) like the upright *alif* (*al-alif al-qá'im*)[61] between the two scrolls at the centre of the two worlds, THE JUDGE,⁶² BY THE PERMISSION OF GOD⁶³ in the two later births (*nash'átayn*) the SECRET⁶⁴ of the two 'Alawís and the splendour⁶⁵ of the two Fátimís and an ancient fruit⁶⁶ from the BLESSED TREE⁶⁷ encrimsoned by the FIRE⁶⁸ of the Two Clouds and a group of those of the sacred veils pulsating with the shimmering light,⁶⁹ the abider around the FIRE⁷⁰ in the TWO SEAS⁷¹ the glory of heaven unto the causes of the two earths⁷² and a handful of the clay of the earth over the people of the two, these two GARDENS⁷³ of DARK GREEN FOLIAGE⁷⁴ over the point of the TWO WESTS⁷⁵ and those SECRET⁷⁶ two names in the creation of the TWO EASTS⁷⁷ born in the two Harams and the one looking towards the two Qiblas beyond the two Ka'bas, the one who prays over the THRONE⁷⁸ of the splendiferous (*'arsh al-jalíl*) twice a possessor of the two causes and the Pure Water in the two gulfs (*khalíjayn*), the speaker in the two stations and the knower of the two Imams, the Bá' that circulates in the water of the two groups of letters (*hurúfayn*) and the Point Abiding (*al-nuqta al-wáqifa*) over the DOOR⁷⁹ of the Two Alifs revolving around God in the two cycles and the one made to speak on the authority of God in the two cycles (*kawrayn*), the SERVANT OF GOD⁸⁰ and the REMEMBRANCE⁸¹ of His PROOF⁸² This YOUNG MAN CALLED, because his grandfather is ABRAHAM, THE SPIRIT⁸³ in the forerunners and he is the Gate, after the two later gates. and PRAISE BE TO GOD THE OF ALL THE WORLDS.⁸⁴ And he is God, indeed the one who comprehends everything concerning ALL OF THE WORLDS.⁸

VERSE 6

This same YOUTH⁸⁶ WHO IS CALLED⁸⁷ by the People of the Cloud⁸⁸ the MYSTIC SECRET⁸⁹ (*sirr ladunní*)

and by the People of the VEIL,⁹⁰ the Flashing Mysterious SYMBOL⁹¹ (*ramz lum'í*)

and by the People of the PAVILION (*surádiq*),⁹² the WESTERN Divine Attribute (*wasf maghribí*)⁹³

and by the People of the THRONE,⁹⁴ the Divine EASTERN Name (*ism mashriqí*)⁹⁵

and by the People of the FOOTSTOOL,⁹⁶ the Exalted/'Alid Image (*rasm 'alawí*)

and by the People of the EMPYREAN,⁹⁷ an Arab TRUTH⁹⁸

and by the People of the GARDENS,⁹⁹ a Fatimid SPIRIT¹⁰⁰

and by the People of the EARTH,¹⁰¹ a SERVANT¹⁰² of the KINGDOM¹⁰³

and by the People of the Water, the FISH¹⁰⁴ of Timelessness (*hút sarmadí*)

While he remains in the atmosphere of the EMPYREAN¹⁰⁵ the SINGLE¹⁰⁶ who is LUMINOUS¹⁰⁷ even as he is in the presence of multitudinous SIMILITUDES,¹⁰⁸ solar

And he is LIGHTNING¹⁰⁹ WESTERN¹¹⁰ and THUNDER¹¹¹ EASTERN¹¹²

And he is the SECRET¹¹³ in the Syrian GOSPEL¹¹⁴

And he is the SECRET¹¹⁵ in the Rabbinic TORAH¹¹⁶

And he is the SECRET¹¹⁷ enwrapped in a SECRET¹¹⁸ in the Ahmadí FURQÁN¹¹⁹

So praised be God,¹²⁰ the Ancient Originator, He of whom THERE IS NO GOD EXCEPT HIM (*huwa*), none comprehends His CREATION (*san'*)¹²¹ in its subtlety except whom He wills; and He is God, Lofty (*'alí*), Praised.¹²²

Verse 7

PRAISED BE TO GOD[123] who bestowed, for the SOLACE OF MY EYES[124] this small AHMAD,[125] and we verily exalted him to God in truth, according to a single letter from the knowledge of the Book.[126] And indeed, the rule in this matter is according to the knowledge of the TABLET[127] directly from God, the Truth, decreed irrevocably.[128]

Verse 8

O Qurrat al-'Ayn![129] Endure the decree of thy Lord[130] that is in you, VERILY GOD DOTH, in truth, WHATSOEVER HE WILLETH[131] and He is the ALL-WISE[132] in JUSTICE[133] and He is God, thy MASTER[134] who in His decision (*hukm*) is praised (*mahmud*).[135]

Verse 9

Indeed, you have obeyed the CAUSE/COMMAND of God,[136] the Truth, through God and verily you have been accepted, through God my Lord, He of whom [it is the case that] THERE IS NO GOD EXCEPT HIM (*huwa*)[137] and I desire only what God desires, my Lord[138] in the Truth, and He is God, a Witness to ALL CREATED THINGS.[139]

Verse 10

Our Lord! Forgive ME AND MY PARENTS[140] and whoever loves the REMEMBRANCE OF GOD[141] the Most Great in truth sincerely, BELIEVING MEN OR BELIEVING WOMEN.[142] Thou art verily the Lord of GRACE[143] and Bounty (*fadl* and *júd*). And verily Thou art in Truth Powerful over ALL CREATED THINGS.[144]

Verse 11

Verily WE HAVE TAKEN A COVENANT ON THE MOST GREAT THRONE,[145] a law of love, over the truth[146] through the truth,[147] for OUR SERVANT.[148] Verily God, HIS ANGELS,[149] His FRIENDS (*awliyá'*), follow this law in all matters over the point of the Fire[150] according to what God decreed[151] in the BOOK[152] and He decreed the DIVINE PERMISSION. Verily, they are concerning His truth, according to the Truth[153] through the Truth,[154] witnesses (*shahídan*) to this.[155]

Verse 12

And verily We did generously bestow (*faddala*) Our remembrance[156] OVER THE TWO WORLDS,[157] as God had indeed imposed upon Himself AND HE IS THE ONE,[158] THE SINGLE, THE ETERNALLY BESOUGHT,[159] He whom there is no god except Him (*huwa*),[160] and He is God, witness over and against all created things.[161]

Verse 13

O Qurrat al-'Ayn![162] Do not be saddened by the words of the polytheists[163] WHAT

AILETH this 'Ajami Youth (*al-fatá*)![164] The truth? THAT HE EATS FOOD AND WALKS IN THE MARKETS!![165] and associates with men in speech WHILE MANKIND ACQUAINT ONE ANOTHER[166] with the Word of Truth, upon the Truth[167] in the Mighty Word upon a WEIGHTY truth, only slightly.[168]

Verse 14

And this is THE WORD WHICH WENT BEFORE[169] to Muhammad, the Messenger of God,[170] AND YOU NEVER WILL FIND IN OUR SUNNA from before, neither from after, upon the truth[171] through the truth[172] to the smallest degree CHANGE.[173]

Verse 15

O People of the Earth! Give thanks to God,[174] for verily WE HAVE SAVED YOU[175] from the ulama who follow mere conjecture (*zann*)[176] and have brought to you from the RIGHT SLOPE OF TÚR,[177] this adorable Arab Youth,[178] who is [the one for whom] God appointed the kingdoms of heaven and earth[179] TO BE IN HIS GRASP,[180] [AS] IN A HANDFUL OF DUST[181] upon the earth, through the truth[182] upon the truth[183] ENFOLDED.[184]

Verse 16

O People of the Cloud![185] Listen to my call[186] from my REMEMBRANCE[187] on the authority of the point of the Fire:[188] this is God, of Whom there is no god but Him (*huwa*).[189] So worship him according to the upright Alif around the Gate.[190] Verily he is the OUTSPREAD[191] PATH[192] in truth in the presence of God THE TRUTH.[193]

Verse 17

O Qurrat al-'Ayn![194] Announce upon TÚR[195] the secret[196] of the Light:[197] VERILY VERILY I AM THE SERVANT[198] through the truth in the centre of manifestational advent from the rising of the light [of] there is no god but Him (*huwa*)[199] and He is God, Knowing, Wise.[200]

Verse 18

O People of the Cloud! Know that this is an Arab Youth[201] who speaks the Truth[202] in the centre of the Water[203] from the centre of the Fire:[204] there is no god except Him (*huwa*) the Mighty[205] and He is God,[206] Mighty,[207] Ancient.

Verse 19

Indeed! this is the one, the Light[208] in the Fire[209] on behalf of the water:[210] THERE IS NO GOD EXCEPT HIM[211] and he is God, Knower, Wise.[212]

Verse 20

AND WHEN[213] he ASCENDED[214] through the air of the HEAVEN[215] of the THRONE[216] speaking on the authority of the secret[217] of the Dust,[218] the mighty mystery of God[219] to the CONCOURSE of the air[220] of the exalted Cloud,[221] and He is God, over all created things a Witness.[222]

Verse 21

AND WHEN he sat upon the Dust[223] speaking on the authority of the veiled secret,[224] like a Fish stranded flailing out of water UPON THE DUST,[225] as if he were killed upon the earth by the sword of the servants[226] according to the truth[227] through the truth,[228] Unique.

Verse 22

And it is as if I see him with his blood covering him for the sake of the secret[229] enwrapped in a secret between the scrolls in the SACRED MOUNT[230] of manifestation when those veiled from the meeting with the Beloved saw him[231] with the Beloved they accounted him, according to mere CONJECTURE[232] like motionless ice in the heart of the most great frozen mountain; and when those for whom the veils of attributes had been torn asunder saw him they testified before God the Truth that WE INDEED KNEW NOT A SINGLE THING concerning his truth.[233] How long will he be until this was cast down slain upon the earth? How long will this be forbidden to be upon the Throne?[234] So, praised be to God[235] the Lofty (*al-'alī*)[236] that this is him, the very secret[237] completely purged from the description of the attributes, firmly established by God the greatest. God is Greater in magnifying [him], lofty (*'aliyan*).[238]

Verse 23

None knows how to remember Him except Him and He is God, MIGHTY, WISE.[239]

Verse 24

This YOUTH[240] made of the essence of CLAY[241] was designated AT THE TIME OF THE RISING of the Muhammadan[242] SUN. He verily is in THE MOTHER BOOK,[243] in the secret[244] of the Light,[245] an easterner upon the point of the Fire.[246]

Verse 25

And this YOUTH[247] is at once made of salt[248] and of the Most Great Heaven.[249] The Persians say of him 'this is a Shirazi angel'[250] and nothing was, in truth,[251] or will be except that it is written in the MOTHER BOOK[252] He is indeed the FRUIT[253] of the Arabs and the most noble of the noble ones on the authority of those who are expert in Arabic,[254] decreed [written][255] as such in the precincts of the fire.[256]

Verse 26

He is THE LIGHT[257] in TÚR[258] and the TÚR[259] in the rising of the Manifestation which, by the permission of God,[260] the Lofty (*al-'alí*),[261] has been hidden[262] in the point of happiness (*al-surúr*) upon the mountain[263] of the snow of manifestation.

Verse 27

This is an Arab, a YOUNG MAN[264] in form (*khalq*) and Persian in reality, in the presence of the Lord. And the form that has, around the Fire[265] on the authority of the secret[266] of the Dust[267] in the point of the attributes, been testified to.[268]

Verse 28

O Concourse of Lights![269] Listen to my call from this gilt white Leaf. VERILY, VERILY, I AM GOD![270] NO GOD IS THERE EXCEPT ME.[271] Say: 'Only those believe in our signs who, when they are reminded of them fall down prostrate' to God, the Truth 'and hymn the praise of their Lord and they are not scornful'[272] of the Truth and He is God, their Master, the Truth[273] and He is a Witness over all created things.[274]

Verse 29

O Qurrat al-'Ayn![275] Speak by the Permission of God[276] in the melody of the two beloveds and say: 'VERILY VERILY I AM THE TRUTH[277] in the two lights in the two vicinities. AND VERILY VERILY I AM the one who speaks on the authority of God in the two Mounts (*al-túrayn*)[278] AND VERILY VERILY I AM the revealer (*al-munzil*) by God these two Furqáns[279] to the two beloveds in the two names, this one to the beloved Muhammad,[280] the greater of years by two years and the other to the beloved Muhammad,[281] the younger in years by two years. These two Furqáns[282] are from the Lord of the worlds[283] to the People of al-Tutunjayn – the People OF THE TWO EASTS[284] AND THE TWO WESTS.[285] Indeed, God is verily a witness[286] of the worlds.'

Verse 30

O People of the Earth! God does testify to the Truth[287] and likewise His angels[288] and the Believers,[289] the righteous martyrs[290] in the name of justice, that this remembrance[291] is the servant of God[292] and Our word[293] by the Truth *('alá al-haqq)*.[294] Indeed, God has sent down[295] the verses upon the awaited Proof[296] and verily I, by the permission of God,[297] have sent them down with the angels[298] of the Cloud to the heart of my Most Great Remembrance,[299] that mankind might surely believe in God and in His Words and that they might surely help[300] the remembrance[301] in my Most Great Cause.[302] And verily God is over all created things a witness.[303]

Verse 31

O Qurrat al-'Ayn![304] ESTABLISH THE PRAYER[305] through the Truth[306] in an even script[307]

AT THE TIME OF THE SETTING OF THE SUN (*dulúk al-shams*)[308] by the permission of God[309] in the zone of Bahá and remember God your LORD UNTIL THE DARK OF NIGHT[310] according to the rule of the Book about the secret[311] of the Gate[312] who is the true intention.

Verse 32

And BLESS[313] the rising OF THE WHITE IN THE BLACK HORIZON.[314] And verily this is the Book of the Dawn[315] that has been witnessed[316] in the MOTHER BOOK.[317]

Verse 33

So ARISE IN THE NIGHT[318] for the ANCIENT REMEMBRANCE,[319] your Lord of WHOM THERE IS NO GOD EXCEPT HIM (*huwa*).[320] Then thou art, through the Truth, THE STATION OF PRAISE[321] in the MOTHER BOOK,[322] and thou art indeed upon the Truth[323] by the Truth[324] with God the one intended.

Verse 34

And say: Lord, cause me to enter[325] into the deeps of creational wonder[326] in the station of thy love[327] and FORGIVE WHOEVER ENTERS THIS GATE[328] through the Truth[329] for the affairs of the CAUSE[330] by thy attribute and give me from Thy presence a SUSTAINING POWER[331] upon the CAUSE.[332] Verily, thou art indeed powerful over all created things.[333]

Verse 35

O Qurrat al-'Ayn![334] Say: VERILY, I AM NAUGHT BUT[335] the sign of the divine Essence[336] in the deeps of the Exclusive Unity[337] and *shirk*[338] at the time of the rejection[339] of the Most Great Word,[340] he whom God has made to be with me upon the truth[341] by the truth[342] prevailing over the earth, immovable.[343]

Verse 36

O People of the Cloud! LISTEN[344] to my call from the LAMP in this whitened LAMP, this is the GLASS in this reddened GLASS who was spoken to (*mantúqan*) in truth by the sea of the earth of saffron[345] in the HOUSE OF THE GATE.[346]

Verse 37

VERILY VERILY I AM GOD,[347] HE WHOM THERE IS NO GOD EXCEPT HIM.[348] INDEED, I HAVE ESTABLISHED THE HEAVENS AND THE EARTH around this Word[349] through a single letter LIKE IT. So obey My Word. FOR VERILY VERILY I AM THE TRUTH. There is no god except I, the Exalted (*al-'alí*)[350] who am by God the comprehender of all the worlds.[351]

Verse 38

AND LISTEN[352] to this Most Mighty INTERPRETATION (*ta'wíl*)[353] from the TONGUE[354] of this man made great, he whom I have brought up in My presence. NO HUMAN desire TOUCHED HIM[355] in Reality. Verily, he is the Truth[356] upon the Truth.[357] And his significance, by the law of FIRE,[358] HAS BEEN FULLY RECORDED IN THE MOTHER BOOK.[359]

Verse 39

And Say, by the Truth, WE HAVE SENT BEFORE YOU NO MEN [as messengers] EXCEPT WE INSPIRED THEM be ye THE PEOPLE of that blessed TOWNSHIP,[360] and conceal yourselves IN THE EARTH of the heart (*fu'ád*) in order to help him. Know that for those who deny him (*mushrikín bihi*),[361] they will suffer the dire punishment of the Hereafter[362] over the Fire[363] in the Fire,[364] and this has been written[365] with Fire.[366]

Verse 40

And He is God, over all created things a Witness.[367]

Verse 41

And verily, God is Comprehender of all the worlds.[368]

Verse 42

And verily thou art, through God, SELF SUFFICIENT, able to dispense with ALL THE WORLDS.[369]

BIBLIOGRAPHY

Abdel Haleem, M. A. S. *The Qur'an (A New Translation)*. Oxford: Oxford University Press, 2004.

Amir-Moezzi, Mohammad Ali. '*Aspects de l'imámologie duodécimaine I: Remarques sur la divinité de l'Imám*'. Studia Iranica, vol. 25, no. 2 (1996), pp. 193–216.

Bahá'u'lláh. *Kitáb-i-Íqán, the Book of Certitude*. Trans. Shoghi Effendi. Wilmette, IL: Bahá'í Publishing Trust, 2nd ed. 1974.

Bausani, Alessandro. *Persia Religiosa: Da Zaratustra a Bahá'u'lláh*, Milan: Il Saggiatore, 1959 (J. M. Marchesi translation: *Religion in Iran: From Zoroaster to Baha'ullah*, New York: Bibliotheca Persica Press, 2000).

Browne Collection. Cambridge University Library, Browne Or. Ms. F11.

Corbin, Henry. *History of Islamic Philosophy*. Trans. Liadain Sherrard, et al. London, New York: Kegan Paul International in association with Islamic Publications for the Institute of Ismaili Studies (London), 1993.

Encyclopaedia of Islam [EI2]. Leidon and London: Brill, 2nd ed. 1960.

Ghaemmaghami, Omid. 'And the Earth will Shine with the Light of its Lord (Qur'an 39:69): Qa'im and Qiyama in Twelver Shi'i Islam'. Forthcoming.

Ibn al-'Arabí, Muhyi al-Dín. *al-Futuhát al-makkiyya*. 9 vols. Beirut: Dár al-Kutub al-'Ilmíyah, 1999.

Kohlberg, Etan and Mohammad Ali Amir-Moezzi. *Revelation and Falsification: The* Kitáb al-qirá'át *of Ahmad b. Muhammad al-Sayyárí (Critical edition with an introduction and notes)*. Leiden, Boston: Brill, 2009.

Lambden, Stephen. '*Rashh-i 'Amá*' 'Sprinkling of the Cloud of Unknowing'. Bahá'í Studies Bulletin, vol. 3, no. 2 (September 1984). http://bahai-library.com/provisionals/rashh.ama.lambden.html.

Lawson, Todd. 'A 14th Century Islamic Gnostic, Rajab Bursí and His *Mashátiq al-anwár*'. *Ishraq: Islamic philosophy yearbook, No. 1 (2010)*. Moscow: Languages of Slavonic Cultures, 2010, pp. 422–38 (slightly revised reprint of earlier 1992 version).

— 'Duality, Opposition and Typology in the Qur'an: The Apocalyptic Substrate', *Journal of Qur'anic Studies* X.2 (2008): 23–49.

— 'Seeing Double: The Covenant and the Tablet of Ahmad'. Bahá'í Studies, vol. 1. Ed. Moojan Momen, *The Bahá'í Faith and the World's Religions*. Oxford: George Ronald, 2003 [2004], pp. 39–87.

— 'The Terms Remembrance (*Dhikr*) and Gate (*Báb*) in the Báb's Commentary on the Sura of Joseph', in Moojan Momen, *Studies in Honor of the Late Hasan M. Balyuzi*. Los Angeles: Kalimát Press, 1989, pp. 1–63.

Momen, Moojan. 'The Trial of Mullá 'Alí Bastámí: A combined Sunní-Shí'í fatwá against the Báb'. *Iran*, vol. 20 (1982), pp. 113–43.

Rafati, Vahid. *The Development of Shaykhi Thought in Shi'i Islam*. Unpublished Ph.D. diss., University of California, Los Angeles, 1979.

Ricoeur, Paul. 'Creativity in Language: Word, Polysemy, Metaphor'. *Philosophy Today*, vol. 17, no. 2 (Summer 1973), pp. 97–128.

Rippin, Andrew. 'The Poetics of Qur'anic Punning'. *Bulletin of the School of Oriental and African Studies*, vol. 57, no. 1 (1994), pp. 193–207.

von Rosen, Baron Viktor. *Collections scientifiques de l'Institut des Langues orientales de St. Petersbourg*. v.1: *Manuscrits arabes* (1877), pp. 186–91.

Welch, A.T. 'al-Kur'án, d. the mysterious letters' and accompanying bibliographical references, *EI2*.

NOTES

1. '*Colui che s'erge sugli Attributi*' (Bausani, *Persia Religiosa*, p. 460). = 'He who rises up on the attributes.' (J. M. Marchesi translation: *Religion in Iran*, p. 381.)
2. Lawson, 'Duality, Opposition and Typology in the Qur'an'. *Journal of Qur'anic Studies*, vol. 10, no. 2 (2008), pp. 23–49.
3. In the manuscript designated *QA*, the oldest extant transcription. Other manuscripts offer different versifications, sometimes centring on the number 40. Such discrepancies are of course interesting but must await another occasion for detailed discussion.
4. The complete response is *Yea verily, we do bear witness [that you are our Lord]: balá shahidná*. In the context of the distinctive motif of martyrdom in Shi'ism, its strong

presence in the writings of the Báb and the actual history of the Báb's short-lived religion, it is important to note the semantic charge of the second word *shahidná*. The word indicates both 'bear witness' and 'to be a martyr'. For more on the covenant as it relates specifically to the Bábí and Bahá'í contexts see Lawson, 'Seeing Double', in Momen, *The Bahá'í Faith and the World's Religions*, pp. 39–87.

5. Abdel Haleem, *Qur'an*.
6. See the extensive bibliography in Kohlberg and Amir-Moezzi, *Revelation and Falsification*.
7. See above in this volume the chapter on the Súrat al-Dhikr by Moojan Momen.
8. Lawson, 'The Terms Remembrance (*Dhikr*) and Gate (*Báb*) in the Báb's Commentary on the Sura of Joseph', in Momen, *Studies in Honor of the Late Hasan M. Balyuzi*, pp. 1–63.
9. The disconnected letters of the Qur'an have puzzled readers of the Book from the very beginning. One thing about which there was no mystery, however, was, whatever they might stand for, whatever might be their deeper import, much of their significance attached to the fact that they did not spell anything but were rather seen as initials or perhaps even sacred acronyms. The exegetical literature on them is vast and rich (see Welch, 'al-Kur'án, d. the mysterious letters' and accompanying bibliographical references, *EI2*). In a gesture that may in fact be interpreted as somewhat ironic, the Báb makes bold here to actually employ the device of disconnected letters to spell his own name: 'Alí for sura 108, and Muhammad, for sura 109. The poetic tension of such a gesture resides in the trope of 'clarity from obscurity' or 'truth in chaos' tradition, so familiar to the audience to whom this composition was addressed.
10. The root, '-L-Y occurs (apart from the preposition *'alá* 'upon, over, against', innumerable times, *passim*) a total of 72 times in various nominal and verbal forms. As a name of God, it occurs in the company of three other divine names in Q 2:255; 42:4, *al-'aliy al-'azím* – the Lofty the Mighty; Q 22:62; 31:30; 34:23; 40:12 *al-'aliy al-kabír* – the Lofty the Great; Q 42:51; 43:4 *'aliy hakím* – Lofty, Wise.
11. The name occurs precisely four times in the Qur'an and in each case it is an unambiguous reference to the Prophet: Q 3:144; 33:40; 47:2; 48:29.
12. See Ricoeur, 'Creativity in Language' in *Philosophy Today,* vol. 17, no. 2 (Summer 1973), pp. 97–128. For a useful discussion of 'punning' in the Qur'an itself, see Rippin, 'The Poetics of Qur'anic Punning', in *Bulletin of the School of Oriental and African Studies*, vol. 57, no. 1 (1994), pp. 193–207.
13. Táhirih, herself obviously so moved by this simultaneously new and ancient book, actually translated it into Persian for use in her preaching in Kirmánsháh. See also, Momen, 'The Trial', for evidence that it was not only his followers who were impressed by his 'appropriation' of the Qur'an.
14. Rafati, 'The Development of Shaykhí Thought in Shí'í Islam', p. 133; Lawson, 'A 14th Century Islamic Gnostic', pp. 422–38; Amir-Moezzi, 'Aspects de l'imámologie duodécimaine I', pp. 193–216; among others. See the chapter in this volume by Khazeh Fananapazir for a translation of a similar sermon transmitted and preserved in the Shi'i tradition through the hadith genre. Readers familiar with Bahá'í sacred writings will immediately recognize the style.
15. The Arabic, *dhálika al-kitáb*, is more naturally translated as 'that is the book' or 'that book'.
16. Q 17:1; 18:1; 25:1; 39:36; 53:10; 57:9. By comparison, the name Muhammad occurs in the Qur'an only four times: Q 3:144; 33:40; 47:2; 48:29.
17. Corbin, *History of Islamic Philosophy*, pp. 4–5.
18. Note the pertinent statement in Bahá'u'lláh, *Book of Certitude*, p. 4:

> Consider the past. How many, both high and low, have, at all times, yearningly awaited the advent of the Manifestations of God in the sanctified persons of His

chosen Ones. How often have they expected His coming, how frequently have they prayed that the breeze of divine mercy might blow, and the promised Beauty step forth from behind the veil of concealment, and be made manifest to all the world. And whensoever the portals of grace did open, and the clouds of divine bounty did rain upon mankind, and the light of the Unseen did shine above the horizon of celestial might, they all denied Him, and turned away from His face – the face of God Himself. Refer ye, to verify this truth, to that which hath been recorded in every sacred Book.

19. See Ghaemmaghami, 'And the Earth will Shine with the Light of its Lord', forthcoming.
20. It occurs in the Qur'an 227 times.
21. Q 1:1. This is the standard Quranic *basmala* which opens every sura of the Qur'an except one.
22. Q 12:109. Translated by Yusuf 'Ali.
23. Q 27:2 and *passim*.
24. Cf. Q 19:3.
25. Q 20:90.
26. Q 2:163 and *passim*.
27. Q 15:9 and *passim*.
28. Cf. Q 21:60.
29. A pun, as mentioned in the introduction above. The reference is simultaneous to both 'Alí, the first Imam and God.
30. Q 3:7; 13:39; 43:4.
31. Cf. Q 17:78.
32. Q 20:13.
33. Q 33:2.
34. Q 28:30: *inní aná 'lláh* is frequent in the Qayyúm al-Asmá'. It suggests that the Báb is claiming revelation by equating his rank to that of Moses. See Lawson, *The Qur'an Commentary of Sayyid 'Alí Muhammad, the Báb.*
35. Q 2:163 and *passim*.
36. Q 42:11; *hadíth* ascribed to Ja'far al-Sádiq: 'Jábir hath said that Abú-Ja'far – peace be upon him – spoke to him as follows: "O Jábir! Give heed unto the Bayán (Exposition) and the Ma'ání (Significances)." He – peace be upon him – added: "As to the Bayán, it consisteth in thy recognition of God – glorified be He – as the ONE WHO HATH NO EQUAL [*laysa ka-mithlihi shay'* Q 42:11], and in thy adoration of Him, and in thy refusal to join partners with Him. As to the Ma'ání, We are its meaning, and its side, and its hand, and its tongue, and its cause, and its command, and its knowledge, and its right. If We wish for something, it is God Who wisheth it, and He desireth that which We desire."' Bahá'u'lláh, *Epistle to the Son of the Wolf*, trans. Shoghi Effendi, p. 113.
37. Q 4:34.
38. Q 2:93 and *passim*.
39. Cf. Q 19:3.
40. Cf. Q 27:16 and *passim*.
41. Cf. Q 7:19; 24:35; 28:30.
42. Cf. Q 6:59; 7:22; 20:12.
43. Cf. Q 76:5.
44. Q 12:19.
45. Q 3:144; 33:40; 47:2; 48:29.
46. Name of the 'hollow' or centre of Mecca, where the Ka'ba is located.
47. Q 1:1 and *passim*.
48. Q 7:143.
49. Q 2:255 and *passim*.
50. Q 48:19.

51. Q 4:131.
52. Cf. Q 21:60.
53. For this and other references to colours in this sura, see the chapter by Vahid Rafati in this volume on colours in the writings of the Báb.
54. Thanks to W. McCants, verbal communication, 'Irfán Colloquium, Louhelen, September 2003, for shedding light on this phrase.
55. Cf. Q 8:38 and *passim*.
56. Q 2:64 and *passim*.
57. Cf. Bahá'u'lláh about Shaykh Ahmad and Siyyid Kazim: 'Likewise, there appeared on earth Aḥmad and Káẓim, those twin resplendent lights (*núrayn nayyirayn*) – may God sanctify their resting-place!' *Kitáb-i-Íqán*, p. 65; and about the King and Beloved of the martyrs: 'The twin shining lights (*núrayn nayyirayn*), Ḥasan and Ḥusayn (The King of Martyrs and the Beloved of Martyrs) offered up spontaneously their lives in that city [Isfahan].' *Epistle to the Son of the Wolf*, p. 72.
58. 'Alí and Muhammad (see introduction).
59. Q 23:100; 25:53; 55:20.
60. Q 20:7; 25:6.
61. On this sermon and its significance in the works of Shaykh Ahmad, Siyyid Káẓim and the Báb, see the introduction to this chapter. Its influence reaches its highest intensity in this verse, a verse which alone, or together with the following one, being the subject of a lengthy detailed analysis, demonstrates the remarkable manner in which the Báb combines the imagery, vocabulary voice and mood of the Qur'an and the Sermon of the two Gulfs. Such a study would shed much light on the expressive 'style' of the Bábí revelation. See also Lawson, 'Coincidentia Oppositorum in the Qayyum al-Asmá', *Occasional Papers in Shaykhi, Babi, and Baha'i Studies*, vol. 5, no. 1 (January 2001); Lawson, '*The Dawning Places of the Lights of Certainty in the Divine Secrets Connected with the Commander of the Faithful* by Rajab Bursi (d. 1411)'. *The Heritage of Sufism*, vol. 2, pp. 261–76.
62. Cf. Q 7:87 and *passim*.
63. Q 2:97 and *passim*.
64. Q 20:7, 25:6.
65. Q 27:60.
66. Q 2:25. As pointed out in a footnote in *Selections from the Writings of the Báb* (p. 3), 'Shoghi Effendi, in his writings, refers to the Báb as the 'Thamarih' (fruit) of the Tree of God's successive Revelations. (See Shoghi Effendi's letter to the Bahá'ís of the East dated Naw-Rúz 110, p. 5).' Elsewhere in the Qayyúm al-Asmá', the Báb is addressed as the cherished Fruit: 'O Thou cherished Fruit of the heart! Give ear to the melodies of this mystic Bird warbling in the loftiest heights of heaven. The Lord hath, in truth, inspired Me to proclaim: Verily, verily, I am God, He besides Whom there is none other God. He is the Almighty, the All-Wise.' The Báb, *Selections*, p. 67.
67. Cf. Q 24:35.
68. Cf. Q 27:8; 2:24 and *passim*.
69. *qiddatun min qiddati al-hujub al-mutala'li'ayn bi'l-khafaqayn*
70. Cf. Q 27:8, 2:24 and *passim*.
71. Q 55:19. According to a famous *hadíth* ascribed to Ja'far al-Sádiq, the two seas are 'Alí and Fatima.
72. *sharaf al-samá' ilá 'ilal al-ardayn*
73. Q 55:54.
74. Q 55:64.
75. Q 55:17.
76. Q 20:7, 25:6.
77. Q 55:17.

78. Q 27:2 and *passim*.
79. Cf. Q 2:58 and *passim*.
80. Q 19:30, 72:19.
81. Cf. Q 12:104 and *passim*.
82. Cf. Q 6:149.
83. Cf. Q 21:60.
84. Q 1:2.
85. Cf. Q 4:108, 126.
86. Cf. Q 21:60.
87. Q 21:60.
88. See the *hadíth* of the Prophet. See the masterful article on the word in Lambden, '*Rashh-i 'Amá*' 'Sprinkling of the Cloud of Unknowing', *Bahá'í Studies Bulletin*, vol. 3, no. 2 (September 1984). http://bahai-library.com/provisionals/rashh.ama.lambden.html.
89. Cf. Q 18:76; 20:7; 25:6.
90. Cf. Q 17:45; 42:51.
91. Cf. Q 3:41.
92. Cf. Q 18:29. See also the tradition attributed to Imam al-Báqir stating that out of the entire world, God chose Mecca, and within Mecca, He choose Bakka, and within Bakka, He chose a *surádiq* made of light surrounded by pearls and rubies, and placed four supports in the middle of the *surádiq*, etc. Cited in al-Tabrisí (d. 1902), *Mustadrak al-wasá'il*, vol. 9, pp. 335–6. He takes the *hadíth* from Muhammad bin Mas'úd al-'Ayyáshí (d. *c.* 932), *Tafsír al-Ayyáshí*, vol. 1, pp. 39–40.
93. Cf. Q 24:35; 55:17.
94. Cf. Q 27:26.
95. Cf. Q 24:35; 55:17.
96. Cf. Q 2:255.
97. Q 2:19 and *passim*.
98. Cf. Q 3:86 and *passim*.
99. Cf. Q 2:82 and *passim*.
100. Cf. Q 97:4 and *passim*.
101. Q 2:22 and *passim*.
102. Q 43:59 and *passim*.
103. Cf. Q 6:75 and *passim*.
104. Cf. The story of Moses, the mysterious stranger and the equally mysterious fish: Q 18:61; 18:63; Cf. the story of Jonah and the whale, also *al-hút*: Q 37:142; 68:48.
105. Q 16:79.
106. Q 12:39 and *passim*.
107. Cf. Q 24:35 and *passim*.
108. Q 13:17 and *passim*.
109. Cf. Q 13:12.
110. Cf. Q 24:35.
111. Cf. Q 13:13.
112. Cf. Q 24:35.
113. Q 20:7; 25:6.
114. Q 3:3 and *passim*.
115. Q 20:7; 25:6.
116. Q 3:3 and *passim*.
117. Q 20:7; 25:6.
118. Q 20:7; 25:6. Cf. 'Similarly, repeated use of such terms as *sirr mustasirr* (*passim*) is meant to allude to the corresponding Shaykhí theology' (Lawson, *The Qur'an Commentary of Sayyid 'Alí Muhammad, the Báb*, pp. 115–45). See two Traditions ascribed to Imam Ja'far al-Sádiq. The Traditions are cited by Shaykh Ahmad in his

Shar' al-Ziyára and discussed and translated by Lawson in his thesis (ibid. p. 117). The earliest extant *hadíth* collection that contains these Traditions is Muhammad b. al-Hasan al-Saffár al-Qummí (d. 903), *Basá'ir al-darájat*, pp. 48–9.
119. Q 25:1.
120. Q 37:159 and *passim*.
121. Cf. Q 27:88.
122. Q 4:131.
123. Q 1:2 and *passim*.
124. Cf. Q 25:74.
125. Q 61:6.
126. Q 13:43. Reference to the Báb's son who died in infancy.
127. Cf. Q 85:22.
128. Q 19:21.
129. Cf. Q 25:74.
130. Cf. Q 68:48.
131. Cf. Q 22:18.
132. Q 2:32 and *passim*.
133. Cf. Q 4:58.
134. Cf. Q 8:40 and *passim*.
135. Q 17:79. Rosen offers a slight variant for this verse: *wa huwa alláh mawlá(y)k al-qadím*. von Rosen, *Collections scientifiques de l'Institut des Langues orientales de St. Petersbourg*, v. 1: Manuscrits arabes (1877), pp. 186–91.
136. Q 4:47 and *passim*.
137. Q 2:163 and *passim*.
138. Cf. Q 6:80.
139. Cf. Q 4:33; 33:55 and *passim*.
140. Q 14:41.
141. Q 5:91 and *passim*.
142. Q 9:72 and *passim*.
143. Q 2:105 and *passim*.
144. Q 33:27; 48:21. Cf. Q 2:20 and *passim*.
145. Cf. Q 9:129; 23:86; 27:26.
146. Q 27:79.
147. Cf. Q 2:71 and *passim*.
148. Q 2:23 and *passim*.
149. Q 33:56.
150. Cf. Q 27:8; 2:24 and *passim*.
151. Q 33:36. Cf. Q 8:42, 44.
152. Q 2:159 and *passim*.
153. Q 27:79.
154. Cf. Q 2:71 and *passim*.
155. Cf. Q 4:33 and *passim*.
156. Q 18:28; 53:29.
157. Or 'all the worlds'. Cf. Q 2:251.
158. Q 12:39 and *passim*.
159. Q 112:2.
160. Q 2:163 and *passim*.
161. Cf. Q 4:33 and *passim*.
162. Cf. Q 25:74.
163. Q 2:105 and *passim*.
164. Cf. Q 21:60.
165. Q 25:7.

166. Cf. Q 49:13; 10:45.
167. Q 27:79.
168. Q 2:41 and *passim*.
169. Q 10:19 and *passim*.
170. Q 48:29.
171. Q 27:79.
172. Cf. Q 2:71 and *passim*.
173. Cf. Q 17:77; 35:43.
174. Q 2:172.
175. Q 2:50; 7:141; 20:80.
176. Q 53:28 and *passim*.
177. Q 19:52 and *passim*.
178. Cf. Q 21:60.
179. Q 7:185.
180. Q 39:67.
181. Q 3:59 and *passim*.
182. Cf. Q 2:71 and *passim*.
183. Q 27:79.
184. Cf. Q 39:67. Cf. also the opening of the Sermon of the Two Gulfs for a similar image.
185. al-'amá.'This word carries with it extensive symbolic and mystical meaning. In the famous hadith, the Prophet Muhammad designates it as the "place" where God "was" before creation.' See the masterful article on the word in Lambden, 'Rashh-i 'Amá' 'Sprinkling of the Cloud of Unknowing', *Bahá'í Studies Bulletin*, vol. 3, no. 2 (September 1984). http://bahai-library.com/provisionals/rashh.ama.lambden.html.
186. Cf. Q 19:3.
187. Q 15:9 and *passim*.
188. Cf. Q 27:8; 2:24 and *passim*.
189. Q 2:163 and *passim*.
190. Q 2:58; 4:154; 5:23; 7:161; 9:25.
191. Q 74:12. Cf. Q 56:30.
192. Q 1:6 and *passim*.
193. Cf. Q 2:71 and *passim*.
194. Cf. Q 25:74.
195. Q 2:63 and *passim*.
196. Q 20:7; 25:6.
197. Q 2:257; 24:35 and *passim*.
198. Cf. Q 2:23 and appropriation of the theophanic energy in *inni ána alláh* at Q 28:30 and the slight variation at Q 20:14 mentioned above. Such usage, suffice it to say for the moment, alludes to the profound mystery of manifestation in powerfully effective and daring appropriation of Quranic phrases.
199. Q 2:163 and *passim*.
200. Q 4:11 and *passim*.
201. Q 21:60.
202. Q 23:62.
203. Q 2:74 and *passim*.
204. Cf. Q 27:8; 2:24 and *passim*.
205. Q 3:6, 3:18.
206. Q 6:3 and *passim*.
207. Q 4:56 and *passim*.
208. Q 2:257; 24:35 and *passim*.
209. Cf. Q 27:8; 2:24 and *passim*.
210. Q 2:74 and *passim*.

211. Q 2:163 and *passim*.
212. Q 4:11 and *passim*.
213. *wa idha passim*
214. Cf. Q 70:4 and *passim*.
215. Q 16:79.
216. Q 7:54 and *passim*.
217. Q 20:7; 25:6.
218. Q 3:59 and *passim*.
219. Q 20:7; 25:6.
220. Cf. 'The Concourse on High' (*al-mala' al-a'lá*) mentioned in Q 37:8; 38:69.
221. Q 69:33.
222. Cf. Q 4:33 and *passim*.
223. Q 3:59 and *passim*. This is a possible reference to the story of how 'Alí got the nickname 'Abu Turáb' ('Dusty'). See Kohlberg, 'Abu Turab', *Bulletin of the School of Oriental and African Studies*, vol. 41 (1978), pp. 347–52.
224. Q 20:7; 25:6.
225. Cf. Q 4:43; 5:6; 18:8; 18:40.
226. Cf. Q 2:207 and *passim*.
227. Q 27:79.
228. Cf. Q 2:71 and *passim*.
229. Q 20:7; 25:6.
230. Q 19:52 and *passim*.
231. Cf. Q 6:31 and *passim*.
232. Q 53:28 and *passim*.
233. Cf. Q 10:36; 53:28.
234. Q 27:2 and *passim*.
235. Q 21:22 and *passim*.
236. Q 2:255 and *passim*.
237. Q 20:7; 25:6.
238. Cf. Q 4:34.
239. Q 4:56.
240. Q 21:60.
241. Q 3:49; 5:110; 28:38.
242. Cf. Q 3:144; 33:40; 47:2; 48:29.
243. Q 3:7; 13:39; 43:4.
244. Q 20:7, 25:6.
245. Q 2:257; 24:35 and *passim*.
246. Cf. Q 27:8; 2:24 and *passim*.
247. Q 21:60.
248. Cf. Q 25:53; 35:12.
249. Q 2:19 and *passim*.
250. Cf. Q 12:31.
251. Cf. Q 2:71 and *passim*.
252. Q 3:7; 13:39; 43:4.
253. Cf. Q 2:25.
254. *'an al-fi'a al-fusahá'*; n.b. Rosen *al-ghammat al-fusahá'*.
255. Cf. Q 3:157.
256. Cf. Q 27:8; 2:24 and *passim*.
257. Q 2:257; 24:35 and *passim*.
258. Q 19:52 and *passim*.
259. Q 19:52 and *passim*.
260. Q 2:97 and *passim*.

261. Q 2:255 and *passim*.
262. Q 17:45.
263. Q 59:21.
264. Cf. Q 12:19 and *passim*.
265. Cf. Q 27:8; 2:24 and *passim*.
266. Q 20:7; 25:6.
267. Q 3:59 and *passim*.
268. Cf. Q 17:78; 85:3.
269. Cf. Q 24:35.
270. Q 28:30. Cf. Q 20:14.
271. Q 16:2; 20:14; 21:25.
272. Q 32:15. Pickthall translation.
273. Cf. Q 10:30.
274. Q 4:33; 33:55.
275. Cf. Q 25:74.
276. Q 2:97 and *passim*.
277. Q 2:26 and *passim*.
278. Cf. Q 19:52 and *passim*.
279. Cf. Q 2:53 and *passim*.
280. Q 3:144; 33:40; 47:2; 48:29.
281. Q 3:144; 33:40; 47:2; 48:29.
282. Cf. Q 2:53 and *passim*.
283. Q 1:2 and *passim*.
284. Q 43:38; 55:17.
285. Q 55:17.
286. Q 4:33; 33:55.
287. Cf. Q 43:86.
288. Q 4:136; 33:43, 56.
289. Q 2:285 and *passim*.
290. Q 5:8.
291. Q 3:58 and *passim*.
292. Q 19:30; 72:19.
293. Q 37:171. Cf. Q 9:40.
294. Q 27:79.
295. Q 2:174 and *passim*.
296. Cf. Q 6:149.
297. Q 2:97 and *passim*.
298. Cf. Q 4:166.
299. Q 3:58 and *passim*.
300. Cf. Q 22:60.
301. Q 3:58 and *passim*.
302. Cf. Q 20:90 and *passim*.
303. Q 4:33; 33:55.
304. Cf. Q 25:74.
305. Q 20:14 and *passim*.
306. Cf. Q 2:71 and *passim*.
307. *khatt min al-istawá*: in plain script?
308. Q 17:78.
309. Q 2:97 and *passim*.
310. Q 17:78.
311. Q 20:7; 25:6.
312. Q 2:58; 4:154; 5:23; 7:161; 9:25.

313. Cf. Q 33:56.
314. Cf. Q 53:7; 81:23; 41:53.
315. Q 89:1; 97:5. Cf. Q 17:78.
316. Cf. Q 17:78.
317. Q 3:7; 13:39; 43:4.
318. Cf. Q 17:79.
319. Q 3:58 and *passim*.
320. Cf. Q 6:106 and *passim*.
321. Cf. Q 17:79.
322. Q 3:7; 13:39; 43:4.
323. Q 27:79.
324. Cf. Q 2:71 and *passim*.
325. Q 17:80.
326. Q 27:44. *lujjat min al-bad'*
327. Cf. Q 20:39.
328. Q 2:58; 4:154; 5:23; 7:161; 9:25.
329. Cf. Q 2:71 and *passim*.
330. Cf. Q 2:210 and *passim*.
331. Cf. Q 17:80.
332. Cf. Q 2:210 and *passim*.
333. Q 33:27; 48:21.
334. Cf. Q 25:74.
335. Cf. Q 46:9.
336. *áyat al-húwíya*
337. Q 27:44. *al-lujja al-ahadíya*
338. Q 31:13. Cf. Q *passim*.
339. Cf. Q 6:35.
340. Cf. Q 3:39 and *passim*.
341. Q 27:79.
342. Cf. Q 2:71 and *passim*.
343. Q 14:26.
344. Q 2:93 and *passim*.
345. *ard al-za'farán*. A spiritual realm referred to by, for example, Ibn al-'Arabí (d. 1240) in his major work, the *Kitáb al-futúhát al-Makkiyya* on which see Corbin, *Spiritual Body and Celestial Earth*, p. 140.
346. QA: *al-bayt al-báb*; R & F11: *bayt báb*; cf. Q 2:58; 4:154; 5:23; 7:161; 9:25.
347. Q 28:30.
348. Q 59:22, 23 and *passim*.
349. Cf. Q 3:39 and *passim*.
350. Q 16:2; 20:14; 21:25. QA: *lá iláha illá aná al-'aliy*; R: *lá iláha illá huwa aná al-'aliy*; F11: *lá iláha illá huwa al-'aliy*.
351. Cf. Q 4:108, 126.
352. Q 7:204; 22:73.
353. Cf. Q 3:7; 12:6 and *passim*.
354. Cf. Q 20:27.
355. Cf. Q 3:47; 3:174; 19:20; 24:35.
356. Q 2:91 and *passim*.
357. Q 27:79.
358. Cf. Q 27:8; 2:24 and *passim*.
359. Q 3:7; 13:39; 43:4.
360. Cf. Q 12:109.
361. Cf. Q 9:7 and *passim*.

362. Q 11:103 and *passim*.
363. Cf. Q 27:8; 2:24 and *passim*.
364. Cf. Q 27:8; 2:24 and *passim*.
365. Cf. Q 7:157.
366. Cf. Q 27:8; 2:24 and *passim*.
367. Q 4:33; 33:55.
368. Cf. Q 4:108, 126.
369. Cf. Q 3:97; 29:6.

9

The *Khutba al-Jidda* (The Literary Sermon at Jeddah) of the Báb

Text and Translation from INBA vol. 91:60–73
with reference to other selected sources

Stephen Lambden

The Arabic text

As yet there is no assured critical edition of the *Khutba al-Jidda*. Original manuscripts are uncommon and difficult to obtain. Three such manuscript texts of the *Khutba al-Jidda* are currently known to exist: 1) INBA 5006C, pp. 332–3; 2) INBA 3036C, pp. 494–6; and 3) the manuscript behind INBA 91, pp. 60–73. The Arabic text of the *Khutba al-Jidda* translated below is based on the latter largely legible Arabic manuscript currently in private hands (photocopy in my possession). It was this manuscript containing the full text of the *Khutba al-Jidda* that was photocopied in the mid-1970s and included in the privately published (in bound photocopied form) Manuscript Collection of the Iran National Bahá'í Archives (INBA), volume 91, pp. 60–73. A typed electronic version was sent to the present writer more than a decade ago from the Bahá'í World Centre in Haifa, Israel. The Arabic text of the *Khutba al-Jidda* set out below occasionally incorporates good corrective readings found in a number of printed citations (based on undisclosed manuscripts) of the *Khutba al-Jidda* contained in a few modern Bahá'í publications, including (see bibliography for details):

- *Taqwím-i Táríkh-i Amr* (1970), an annotated Bábí–Bahá'í chronology with a very brief citation (p. 24) from the Khutba al-Jidda by the late 'Abd al-Hamid Ishraq Khavari (d. 1971).

- *Muhádirát* (Khavari 1987, see vol. 2, pp. 729–31).

- *Hadrat-i Nuqtáyi úlá* of Muhammad 'Ali- Faydi (pp. 142–5).

- *'Ahd-i A'lá* of Abu'l-Qasim Afnán (pp. 86–7).

The several significant variant citations of the *Khutba al-Jidda* printed in 'Abu'l-Qasim Afnán's *'Ahd-i A'lá* and a few other printed Bahá'í books cannot be fully dealt with here. Though the text behind the INBA 91 manuscript and (the mostly brief) printed citations of the *Khutba al-Jidda* have obvious copyists' errors and occasional textual difficulties, it remains possible to generate a reasonably sound semi-critical text with a fairly small percentage of uncertain readings. It is clear that quite a few of the variant readings in the aforementioned sources result from copyist lapses and/or varied attempts to read a difficult, unpointed original manuscript(s). Other errors seem to have resulted from a failure to recognize the Quranic basis of certain Arabic phrases in the *Khutba al-Jidda* or to correctly pick up on the vocabulary and style of the Báb. The unavailability of most of the extant manuscripts has prevented anything like a fully critical edition being set forth or translated. I am confident, however, that both the text and the still admittedly speculative and inadequate translation set out below are not too far from being reliable.[1]

The *Khutba al-Jidda* (The Literary Sermon at Jeddah) of the Báb[2]

I

Verse 1

In the name of God, the Merciful, the Compassionate.

Praised be to God! who raised up the Celestial Throne (*al-'arsh*) upon the watery expanse (*al-má'*) and the atmosphere (*al-hawá'*) above the surface (*wajh*) of the watery expanse (*al-má'*). And he separated between these two through the word 'benefits' (*alá'*). Then he divided the firmaments from the sphere of the theophanic cloud (*'álam al-'amá'*). Betwixt these twain a division (*hifzan*) suggestive of the (Arabic) letter *'ha'* (*al-há'*). And from this atmosphere (*al-hawá'*) there emerged the sinaitic tree (*shajarat al-si-ná'*), its subtle graciousness overshadowing the ocean of laudation (*bahr al-thaná'*) nigh the watchtower of the light of radiant glory (*li-matla' núr al-bahá'*) above the crimson thrones (*sará'ir al-hamrá'*). This that all might hearken through the dawning-place of the snow-white script (*khatt al-baydá*) at the black horizon (*'ufq al-sawdá'*) unto the call of the crimson leaves (*waraqát al-hamrá'*) upon the green tree (*al-shajarat al-khudrá'*), [saying] 'God, there is no God except him, the Lord of the celestial throne (*al-'arsh*) and of the heavenly realm (*al-samá'*)'.

II

Verses 1–8

The divine theophany and the tripartite reality of the Báb

So be assured of that divine artistry (*sana'*) which is expressive of his wisdom (*hikmat*), the fullness of the divine handiwork evident in all things (*kull shay'*).

This to the end that every tongue might assuredly acknowledge the purpose of his power (*qudrat*) actualized through the theophanic manifestation (*zuhúr*) of his self-revelation (*tajiliyyat*) within the blessed tree upon Mount Sinai (*túr al-síná'*) disclosing thereby but a token of the crimson pillar (*rukn al-hamrá'*), 'God, no God is there save him'. And he caused to be made manifest through his power what is evident in the essential realities of all existing things (*dhawát al-mawju-dát*) at the midmost heart of preexistence (*min buhbúhiyyat al-qidam*) according to the deep gnosis of that essential reality (*ma'rifat al-dhát*) which is expressive of the divine Essence by virtue of the essential detachedness [from the divine Essence] of the divine names and attributes (*'an al-asmá' wa'l-sifát*).³ This to the end that the realities of the inmost hearts might diligently persevere with their coming to realize the intention of the providential purpose of the divine Will (*ni'at al-mashiyyat*) expressed by virtue of the logos-word of creative genesis, 'God, there is no God save him' (*lá iláha illá huwa*).

And he did subsequently stipulate, on account of the realization of the foreordained scheme (*al-muqaddar*), the knowledge of the ocean of the divine foreordination (*al-muqaddar*) through the surging waves of triplicity (*tamtám al-tathlíth*) expressive of the multiplicity of the waves upon the oceanic expanse of the crucifix (*abhár al-salíb*). This did cause the Christians to unhesitatingly perceive the upright letter '*alif*' (*alif al-qá'im*) positioned betwixt two streams (*al-nahrayn*) on account of his [the Báb's] likeness being even as twofold images (*al-mithlayn*) in the form characterized by dual [alphabetical] counterparts (*shakl fí'l-ukhtayn*). And this was such that they might assuredly come to realization respecting the dawning-place of the breezes of the sinaitic morn [the Báb] which are expressive of the [truth of the] multiplicity of the waves in the watery expanse (*al-má'*). Persons would thus assuredly come to glorify God, the Lord of the cosmic ocean, despite the issue of the multiple waves of the brackish abyss (*al-lujjat al-ujáj*) which lie beyond the snow-white logos-word (*kalimát al-baydá'*), situated within the hollow depth of the seventh sea (*qa'r yamm al-sábi'*) which emerges from the green ocean. God, no God is there except him.

III

Verses 1–4

Renewed creation, the covenant and the eschatological theophany

Then came to pass, subsequent to the decree of the divine destiny (*hukm al-qadar*), the sea of the divine foreordainment (*al-qidá'*) through the 'letter' [locus] of the creative genesis (*bi'l-harf al-badá'*). This such that the inmost hearts of all existing things might of a certainty be made to sparkle brilliantly through the watery expanse (*al-má'*) which sprinkles forth from this fiercely billowing, yet brackish sea (*al-bahr al-mawwáj al-ujáj*). This indeed that all existing microcosmic entities of the world of creation (*kull dharrát al-khalq*) might rise ascendant nigh the glorious transfiguration of that crimson light (*'ind tajallí núr al-hamrá'*) which is expressive of the justice of God and his wisdom. Wherefore shall there assuredly be a speaking forth

through proximity to the glorious transfiguration of the snow-white light; a primordial declaration (*kalimát al-dharr*) distinct from that of the microcosmic entities (*al-dharr*), namely, 'God, no God is there save him. So glorified be God, the Creator, the Wondrous, the Separate, the Living, the Self-Subsisting, the Preexistent.'

IV

Verses 1–4

The folly of the Ishráqí philosophers, followers of Shiháb al-Dín Suhrawardí (d. 587 AH/1191 CE)

It was the case that the Ishráqí sages (*hukamá' al-tashríq*) described the depth of the fourfold [world of nature] (*al-tarbí'*) subsequent to the divine foreordainment (*al-qidá'*) of [the authority of] the divine Will (*al-mashiyya*) through the decree of the threefold reality (*hukm al-tathlíth*) and its counterpart [= the Báb]. They [the Ishráqí sages] thus speculated regarding the principle of materiality (*al-turáb*) which [they regarded] as something other than what God destined for hellfire (*al-nár*). They supposed that the realities of the divine attributes (*haqá'iq al-sifát*) are other than the knowledge [sanctioned] in the Book (*al-kitáb*). And they [further vainly] supposed that they are ones well-situated on the path of God and persons who have attained a great restraint. And upon this rock-strewn [Ishráqí] path and tortuous road these [Ishráqí] sages (*hukamá'*) went astray, being ones fit for hellfire according to the dictates of fate (*hukm al-qadr*) and according to an extent predestined.

So they [the Ishráqí philosophers] ultimately attained a position contrary to the decree of God (*hukm Alláh*) in the realm of things veiled away (*ard al-mustatir*). They taught that they stood upright in the shadow of the sun and the moon. Nay, on the contrary! for thy Lord testifies to the fact that they are indeed wayward and are to be numbered among such dubious sophists (*al-mushubbahún*) as are reckoned among the untruthful.

V

Verses 1–10

Sound theology and waywardness of the followers of Mullá Sadrá (d. 1050 AH/1640 CE)

Say: God, the Lord of Creation is the supreme Creator (*abda'*) of everything (*fí kull shay'*), one beyond anthropomorphism (*hadd al-tashbiyya*) and utterly abstracted from fragmentation (*al-taqtí'*), perchance some soul might calumniate in the presence of the countenance of God (*tilqa' wajh Alláh*) through an [inappropriate] expression of union [with him] (*al-wasl*). He hath ever been one known on account of [his] justice (*bi'l-'adl*) as is evident in the loci of the Cause (*mawáqi' al-amr*) on the level of the divine bounty (*al-fadl*). This although the sight of the Sadriyyín [followers of Mullá Sadrá', d. 1050 AH/1640 CE] hath been blinded to the gnosis of the Lord (*ma'rifat al-rabb*). They scattered abroad the scriptural tablets (*al-alwáh*) that were sent down in the Qur'an and failed to progress with the assistance of the custodians of the truth (*ahl al-haqq*). They [acquired naught but] what they had themselves written in their tablets (*alwáh*) such as the [Kitáb al-] Masháʻir ('[Book of] Metaphysical Penetrations') and its like, involving an augmentation of intricacies (*daqá'iq zakwán*)],[4] issues complex (*ajrad*) and impenetrable (*khushn*).

Yet glorified be God! It is as if they fail to register the [clear] guidance of the Qur'an (*hukm al-Qur'án*) and proved unable to comprehend the dictates of the custodians of clear exposition (*ahl al-tibyán*). They make judgements respecting the gnosis (*ma'rifat*) of their Lord that are even as a judgement regarding the [existence of] water in trees (*al-má' fi'l-ashjár*)! So exalted be God above what is a calumny respecting the beneficent power of his Word (*al-muhsin fí kalámihi*) and with respect to his not encompassing every minutiae within the knowledge of God! They even strike a similitude about the divine Essence (*al-dhát*) [to the effect that] there is a negation of the All-Glorious [Godhead] (*kánafy al-abhá*) within the 'waves' (*al-amwáj*) [of the ocean of existence] or [an analogy] of 'water' (*al-má'*) subsumed nigh the alluring effect of 'ice' (*ta'áyn al-thalj*) on account of their similarity. God and the angels observe these philosophers (*al-hukamá'*) who have anthropomorphized themselves as signs of the Creator (*áyát al-khalq*) in the gnosis of the divine Essence (*bíma'rifat al-dhát*). And they [furthermore] subsume within themselves the [authority of] the Imams for they make decrees contrary to the decree of God in the Qur'an.

VI

Verses 1–18

The twin exponents of Shiʻi Islamic wisdom, Shaykh Ahmad al-Ahsáʼí (d. 1241 AH/1826 CE) and Sayyid Kázim Rashtí (d. 1259 AH/1843 CE)

Verses 1–12

Since they were unaware of the decree issued by the people of clear exposition (*ahl al-bayán*) many of the [Shiʻi] ulama (divines) imitated them [the Mullá Sadrá philosophers] in their pursuit of good deeds (*bi'l-ihsán*). This until the day dawned forth in splendour (*diyá'*) and the 'sun' and the 'moon' shed illumination on account of the verdict of recreation (*hukm al-inshá'*). [It was then that] These twain [= Shaykh Ahmad and Sayyid Kázim] expounded for thee [the truth respecting] the [Shiʻi] family of God (*Ál Alláh*) established in the gnosis of the regeneration (*ma'rifat al-ibdá'*) and discoursing at the very pinnacle of abstraction (*sadd al-inqitá'*), [in ways] all but beyond impenetrability (*qata' al-imtiná'*)!

And these twain [Shaykh Ahmad and Sayyid Kázim] acquired the persona of their [the Shiʻi family of God's] gnosis (*haykal al-ma'rifatihá*) as accords with whatsoever God had willed respecting their twofold reality (*haqq*). And these twain [Shaykh Ahmad and Sayyid Kázim] did write with their two hands something of the import of the Qur'an [in the form of] scriptural tablets (*alwáh*), such as the tablet setting forth the *fawá'id* (observations) (*lawh fi'l-fawá'id*) and the *lawámi'* (brilliances) among their writings (*lawámi' áthárihi*). This such that the inmost hearts of the people might be established through the deep observations implicit in their verses (*min fawá'id al-áyátihi*) and the radiance of the realities of the brilliances implicit in their writings (*min lawá'mi' áthárihi*).

And persons did follow these two in line with the dictates of destiny (*hukm al-qadr*), the people of innermost mystery (*ahl al-mustansir*) who thereby returned unto their pristine, God-bestowed human condition (*fitrat Alláh*) as stipulated in the Qur'an, on the level of that which is foreordained (*fi sha'n al-muqaddar*). So all such persons acquired for themselves their [foreordained] destiny (*nasíb*) as accords with the decree implicit in the Book.

And these latter-day persons (*al-ákhirún*) did bear the calumny (*bi'l-iftirá'*) surrounding these twain [Shaykh Ahmad and Sayyid Kázim] as accords with that destiny which was other than something encompassed by the knowledge that concerns what is preordained (*'ilm al-wádi'*). This was after the likeness of such as did slacken, bereft of knowledge, before the chosen ones of God (*awliyá' Alláh*). They failed to [pay due attention to] a manifest book (*kitáb mubín*) such that the letter *'kaf'* in the locus of the [real] cause (*al-káf fi mahall al-amr*) returned unto the sphere of his decree (*mintaqat hukm*) and the cycle of cycles (*dawr al-adwár*) [was initiated] with the onset of the day of God (*líyawm Alláh*) in a manner revolutionary (*fi sha'n badí'*).

This when the lights (*al-anwár*) did configure according to a transcendent mystery (*sirr maní'*) for these lights (*al-anwár*) dawned forth through the knowledge of the realm of the divine cloud (*min 'ilm al-'amá'*). Then [also] did the sinatic tree (*shajarat al-síná'*) cry out in the ocean of laudation (*bahr al-thaná'*) when there was made manifest the word of glorification (*kalimát al-tasbíh*) in the crimson land (*ard al-hamrá'*).

Verses 13–18

Wherefore, O people of the inmost heart (*ahl al-fú'ád*), did the tree of creative potency (*shajarat al-sáni'*) dawn forth with the ascendant, deeply secreted mysteries (*al-mustansirrát taláyi'*) along with the brilliant sun and the irrefutable name (*al-ism al-qáti'*), this light (*al-núr*) which beareth the letter *'há"* (*harf al-há'*) in the land of the inmost heart (*ard al-fú'ád*). There emerged from the boundary of the letter *'wáw'* (*hadd al-wáw*) through the pen flowing with ink (*qalam al-midád*), the *Dhikr-Alláh* (Remembrance of God) who was in receipt of revealed verses in the language of God (*lisán Alláh*), one crying out with proofs to the end that all humanity might know the locale of their [destined] drinking-place (*hadd al-mashrab*) and the decree respecting this snow-white watery expanse (*al-má' al-baydá'*). And this to the end that all tainted with the sin of the most depraved utterance (*kalimát al-suflá*) might bear whatsoever hath been decreed [for them] in a tablet which expresses something even more contemptible (*lawh aw adná'*).

Thus was it that God did send down the verses of the sinaitic mount (*áyát al-túr*) from the most transcendent abode (*mustaqarr al-a'lá*) to the end that all might be cognisant of his Cause (*al-amr*) and expound its branches (*mufári'*), that all might hear and appreciate the words of Paradise (*kalimát al-quds*) in the Tablet of Holiness (*Lawh al-Quds*) and the verses which descend from [the realm of] the dusky zones of the divine cloud (*mukfahirrát al-'amá'*) in the very shadow of Paradise.

This that all the luminaries (*al-anwár*) might bestow life through the water of life (*má' al-hayawán*) which cometh from the crashing crests of the surging waves that are of the watery expanse of camphor (*má' al-káfúr*) as accords with the decree of the Book. This took place that he might unveil all mysteries through the crimson watery expanse (*má' al-hamrá'*) from this snow-white ocean (*al-bahr al-baydá'*), the watery expanse that is purified on account of the decree of God through the word of the Book.

VII

Verses 1–15

The pilgrimage journey and the Islamic pilgrimage of the Báb

Verses 1–4

So unto God be the praise, the grandeur and the laudation for there are none that encompass his knowledge save whomsoever[5] he wills. He, verily, [of whom it is rightly said that] no God is there except him. God, no God is there except him, the Living, the Elevated. God, no God is there except him, the Independent, the Bountiful.

The word of His servant [= the Báb] was transported (cf. Q 17:1) from the land of his birth (Shiraz) in the year 1260 of the sacred Hijra reckoning, on the sixth day of the third decad[6] [= the 26th] of the month preceding the month which is the sacred month of God (*al-shahr Alláh al-harám*) in which he sent down the Qur'an [= 26th Sha'bán which precedes the month of Ramadán = 10 September 1844] for thereon he enabled him [the Báb] to attain unto the shore of the ocean (*jazírat al-bahr*) [= Bushihr] on the day which is the sixth of the sacred month, the month of Ramadán[7] [= 19 September 1844] on which he instituted that destiny (*al-qadr*) as accords with the decree of God (*hukm Alláh*) enacted on that night (*layla*) which is better than 1000 months apart therefrom (cf. the *laylat al-qadr* in Q 97:1ff.).

Verses 5–8

So he indeed raised him [= the Báb] up through his bounty upon an oppressive ship (*fulk al-musakhir*) [sailing] upon the water on the day which was the ninth day of the second decad [= 19th] of the sacred month, the month of God on which he instituted fasting (*al-siyám*) [= 19th Ramadán = 2 October 1844]. And he [the Báb] attained unto the mother of cities [= Mecca] (*umm al-qurá*), the sacred house of God (*bayt Alláh al-harám*) on the first day of the sacred month of the month of God [= 1st Dhu'l-Hijjah = 12 December 1844] which is the month wherein he instituted the decree of pilgrimage (*al-hajj*) for the people of Islam and completed it with hastening to and fro between Safá and Marwa and what he decreed regarding circumambulation and rising up. And he also decreed [the completion of the events with] the ceremonial sacrifices (*manásik*) consonant with the *'umra* (the sacred visitation) and the *hajj* (pilgrimage) on the third day of the second decad [= the 13th] of the selfsame sacred month which precedes the month of God [= the 13th Dhu'l-Hijjah = 24 December 1844].[8]

Then he enabled him to advance unto the land of his beloved one (*habíb*) [= Medina], Muhammad, the Messenger of God (*rasu-l Alláh*), may the blessings of God be upon him and his family, the seal of the prophets (*khátam al-nabiyyín*), from the onset of this day which is the seventh day of the year 1261 of the sacred Hijra calendar, on the sacred month [= 7th Muharram = 16 January 1845], the month of God whereon was killed [the one who embodied] the glorification of God [*tasbíh* = *subhán-Alláh*', 'glorified be God'] and the hallowing testimony [*tahlíl* = *lá iláh ilá Alláh*, 'there is no God but God'], through the killing of [the embodiment of] the very word of the magnification of God [*kalimát al-takbír* = *Alláh akbar*, 'God is greatest'] and of the laudation of God [*tamhíd* = *al-hamd lílláh*, 'praise be God'], namely, the forefather (*'abí*) of the servant of God (*'Abd-Alláh*) [= the Bab], the [third Imam]) Husayn [martyred 'Áshúrá' = the 10th Muharram 61AH/680 CE], upon him be peace!

Verses 9–15

So unto God belongs the destiny and the grandeur for he protected him [the Báb] in the sacred sanctuary (Mecca–Medina region) for 27 days between the two stupendous months [= from 7th Muharram until 4th Safar = 27 days]. And unto him be the glory and the grandeur at the onset of the departure (from Medina) on the fourth day of the last month after the sacred month of God [= Safar after Muharram = 4th Safar = 12 February 1845] from amongst his chosen ones (*awliyá'*) [in Mecca–Medina] [proceeding] unto the rest of the created realm (*kull al-khalq*) through the fulfilment of the stipulation of the sacrificial killing after dawn time (*kalimát al-qat' ba'd al-fajr*), in line with the knowledge of the family of God (*ma'rifat Ál Alláh*) (may the peace of God be upon them), with the completion [of pilgrimage through] the hindering [of Satan] (*muhtahá al-man'*). And to him [God] belongeth the glory and the beauty.[9]

From the day of the departure (from Mecca–Medina) until the day of the arrival in the land of Jeddah, may the blessings of God be upon its indescribable and innumerable inhabitants, there transpired 12 days on the road [4th Safar + 12 = 16th Safar = 24 February]. This after the manner of the decree of departure (*al-nuzúl*) from the glorious sanctuary [Mecca] (*haram al-jalíl*) unto the fount of Salsabíl (*'ayn al-salsabíl*) [= Zamzam]. Then there came about the decree of the book (*hukm al-kitáb*) regarding halting in the land of Eve (*bi'l-wuqúf fí ard al-hawá'*) [= Jeddah] for a period amounting to three days [16th + 3 = 19th Safar = 27 February 1845].

So glorified be God and praised be to God who gave permission unto his servant on the fourth day of the third decad[10] [= the 24th] of the month which follows the sacred month [= 24th Safar after Muharram = 4 March 1845] for the embarkation upon the ship of oppression (*al-fulk al-musakhir*), upon the water, upon an ark (*safínat*) on which he commenced the journey on the day of his departure unto the sacred house of God [in Shiraz] *(bayt Alláh al-harám)*.

VIII

Verses 1–23

Divine foreordainment and the episode of the theft

Verses 1–7

So unto God be that praise which is scintillating (*sha'sha'aniyya an*), glittering (*mutaláma' an*) and sanctifying (*mutaqaddas an*) by virtue of the very sanctity of God himself (*bítaqdís Alláh*) and of his bounty which passeth beyond all created things. And unto him be the praise and the grandeur like that lauded by his people, a praise which giveth bounty unto all things like unto the bounty of God (*fadl Alláh*) vouchsafed unto his own logos-self (*línafsihi*). He, verily, [of whom it is rightly said that] no God is there except him. There is nothing like unto him for he is one elevated and mighty.

So glorified be God, the One, the Self-Subsisting, the Unique, the One Served, who cried out through his remembrance on the day of the embarkation marked by a laudation of his logos-self and a remembrance of the pathway of his journey in visitation unto his house (*ziyárat baytihi*) and unto the manifestations of his power, Muhammad and his family, [who constitute] the treasury of the divine grandeur (*ma'dan al-'azimat*) a quintessence of his Cause (*muntahá amrihi*) and of his bounty. This for the instruction of every soul towards an awareness of the days of his journey as accords with the decree of foreordained destiny (*hukm al-qadr*) and its mystery. This in order that every possessor of spirit [may be aware that] the days of his journey are consonant with the decree of the divine throne and of the celestial chair (*hukm al-'arsh wa kursí*), as well as the motion of the spheres (*al-aflák*) within the concourse of the divine names and attributes. This such that all might enter the sacred house of God (*bayt Alláh al-harám*) through the mighty verses revealed within these snow-white scriptural tablets (*al-alwáh al-baydá'*), that they might assuredly fall prostrate in the mosque just as they did aforetime and thereby wreak an utter destruction (*líyutabbirú*) upon that which is upstanding (*má 'alaw tatbi-r an*) [see Q 17:7b].

Verses 8–13

So glorified be he who made decree respecting the path of his [pilgrimage] journey just as he had decreed for all of the gates (*al-abwáb*) of the past. And he saw in the path of God all of the suffering caused by the people of infidelity and blasphemy for such is the practice of God. Relative to the past I did not find any change in the practice of God [see Q 48:23] nor any modification respecting the condition of anything.

And there was not found any change relative to the decree of God even respecting a single letter until there occurred the theft of the thief in the land of the two shrines (*al-haramayn*) [the region of Mecca and Medina] at the [third] halting place (*fí manzal al-thálith*) [thus removing] all that God wrote along the path. This [theft] took place on the first night of [the second decad] [= the 11th] in [the year] 1261 [AH] of the second month after the month of the *hajj* [pilgrimage = *Dhu-'l-Hijja*, thus the 11th Safar [1261 AH] = 19 February 1845] for such was [in accordance with] the decree issued from primordial times (*sunnat al-awwalín*). And I did not find any change relative to any aspect of the way of God (*lísha'n Alláh*) regarding anything decreed by God.

Verses 14–23

This although, O people of the concourse (*al-mala'*)! Fate itself acted in accordance with the decree about the [stolen] verses (*al-áyát*) for the thief stole outside of any clear knowledge (*'ilm mubín*) [of the divine plan]. Among them [the stolen writings] were verses expressive of the inner dimension of the foundational alphabetical script (*bátin al-satr*) which was scribed by the hand of the remembrance (*yad al-dhikr*) in crimson ink upon eleven snow-white leaves. They were gilded with liquid gold and inscribed round about in crimson script expressive of dual dimensions of the secreted mystery which is veiled up within the greatest mystery in accordance with the inner dimension of the Qur'an (*bátin al-Qur'án*). From the outset [this material was of such sacredness that] no one aforetime had even touched it [cf. Q 56:79, etc.], nor shall anyone in later times ever encompass its knowledge. Such was revealed in a scriptural tablet from heaven containing deeply secreted verses (*áyát mustasirrát*) and established expositions from God, the Lord of the heavens and of the divine throne, over all the worlds.

Wherefore indeed is it that whoso finds a portion thereof shall fail to unravel even a letter thereof in reciting its wisdom, save, that is, with the permission of he who revealed it unto him. Such is in accordance with the stipulation of the Qur'an for they are the supreme treasuries (*khazá'in al-kubrá*) in that 'the inmost heart (*al-fú'ád*) lieth not about what it [he] sees' [Q 53:11]. So do you suppose that they see this after the manner of his [visionary] seeing? For there was indeed revealed therein [the inmost heart] the wisdom of thy Lord in the 'garden of the abode' (*jannat al-ma'wá*) [Q 53:15] pertaining to that which was decreed in the divine throne (*'arsh*) or [as a result of] our [visionary] insight! And whoso lieth about our most elevated verses, we shall decree for him [on] the day of Resurrection (*yawm al-qiyáma*) [a place] within our nethermost, blazing hellfire of Jahím.

IX

Verses 1–25

The revealed writings of the Báb and the Episode of the Theft

Verses 1–5

Then fear ye God, O people of ecstasy (*ahl al-wijdán*)! for these [revelations] were sent down in [the manner of the disclosures] of the custodians of the Exposition (*rijál al-bayán*). And God is not restrained by the ways of all the worlds. This is indeed the book which hath differentiated in line with the decree of the inner dimension of the tablet [of destiny] (*hukm bátin al-lawh*) as revealed from one Mighty and Wise.

And there was furthermore, a [stolen] book [of the Báb] which was distinguished after the fashion of the 'throne verse' (*áyat al-kursí*) [= Q 2:255] in accordance with the decree of thy Lord, into two hundred suras, every one of which hath been allocated 12 verses among the verses of the inner dimension of the Qur'an. It is a guidance and a mercy from before us unto the people who bear witness, for this is something revealed on our part in line with wisdom.

Verses 6–7

And there was, furthermore, a [stolen] Book [of the Báb] in four hundred verses, as accords with the decree of thy Lord, within 40 well-established suras (*súrat muhkamát*), and [commenting upon] the [poetical] data which the spirit (*al-rúh*) sent down upon the heart of [Sayyid] al-Himyarí (*qalb al-himyarí*) [d. c. 173 AH/789 CE] [containing] deeply secreted, incomparable verses the like of even a letter of which no eye shall ever see for it was revealed from the realms of the veiled secret (*sará'ir sirr al-muqanna'*). Thus hath it been characterized by mystery sublime (*sirr al-mujallil*) [inscribed] in the primordial script (*bi'l-satr al-awwál*), in the threefold state (*bi'l-hall al-thálith*) as regulated through the fourfold talisman (*tilasim al-rábi'*) and revealed through us for such people as do hearken.

Verses 8–13

And there was, furthermore, a [stolen] book [of the Báb] concerning the niche (*al-mishkat*) aside from the lamp (*al-misbáh*), yet both from the lamp which is the lamp and in the lamp of the glass (*al-zujája*) of the glass then [again] the glass within the glass which are the [four] gates (*al-abwáb*) above that which shines forth from the dawn of eternity (*subh al-azal*). At every orient-dawn (*al-mashriq*) there were indeed established therefrom radiant leaves (*waraqát*) ignited through the blessed tree (*shajarat al-mubáraka*) neither eastern nor western, but with verses (*áyát*) expressive of the mysteries of the divine Realm (*asrár al-láhút*) and expressive of the clear expositions of the Book of thy Lord about the dictates of the Kingdom (*ahkám al-mulk*) and of the empyrean heaven (*al-jabarút*). They were sacred, radiant scriptural tablets (*alwáh*) from the sinaitic tree (*shajarat al-síná'*) upon the mount (*al-túr*) that were revealed through the decree of radiant glory (*bahá'*). God, no God is there save him. It was indeed a book from before us, powerful and guarded. And that which was sent down therein expressed the parameters of the inner dimensions of the Qur'an, a guidance and a glad-tiding for such people as are believers. So whomsoever is ignited through the light of the decree which was revealed therein is certainly among the rightly guided.

Verse 14

And there was, furthermore, a [stolen] book [of the Báb] about the dictates of the Qur'an (*hukm al-Qur'án*), about the second portion of the sura [the Súrat al-Baqara,

Q 2] covering what God revealed therein unto its conclusion, verses which came from God including expositions of the inner dimension of the *ta'wíl* [inner sense], a revelation on our part for the people given to contemplation.

Verse 15

And there was, furthermore, a [stolen] book [of the Báb] which was set forth through mine own self whilst upon the ocean, in a *sahífa* (scroll) about *du'á'* (supplication) in 15 sections (*abwáb*) consonant with the command. It was revealed in seven dialects of literary style (*alsun al-sab'at fi'l-inshá'*) after the likeness of purified verses replete with allusions revealed by us for the people given to prostration.

Verses 16–17

Then, furthermore, was a [stolen] *sahífa* (scroll) [of the Báb] written on the path of the *hajj* (pilgrimage) something decreed by he who intended [to visit] the family of the sanctuary of God (*haram Alláh*) with justice (*'adl*) according to the mode which has not been encompassed by the heart of any human being aforetime nor sent down through the instrumentality of a servant (*'abd*) [of God]. It was in 14 assured sections all containing expository verses from God for the people of contemplation.

Verses 18–19

Then, furthermore, were [stolen] 17 mighty sermons (*khutab*) cried out from the hallmark of the judgement assured within Mount Sinai (*al-túr al-síná'*). God, no God is there except him. They were delivered such that nobody was capable of producing the likeness of but a letter thereof even among the pure-blooded Arabs (*a'ráb al-'urabá'*), or, indeed, any soul among the most noble of eloquent ones (*al-fusahá'*).

Verse 20

Then, furthermore, among the [stolen materials] were assured letters (*kitáb muhkamat*), 12 [of them] after the manner of the verses of the Qur'an. It was, in truth, sent down unto the Persian and Arab ulama (*'ulamá' al-a'jamín wa'l-'arabín*), verses of clear exposition from God unto the people given to intellectual activity.

Verse 21

Then praise be unto God who is informed of the truth of his verses and the destiny that was sent down for his gate (*al-báb*). So by the Lord of the house (*rabb al-bayt*) whom no God is there except him. There is nothing in either the heavens or upon the earth that can evaluate [the veracity of] even a letter thereof, for it is a revelation from a manifest Imam. None can estimate the truth of these verses except him for he, verily, is one gentle and wise.

X
The final address and benediction

Verses 1–7

Wherefore, O thou concourse! The stealing of [revealed] materials from God took place within the domain of justice (*mulk al-'adl*), the land of the sanctuary of God (*haram Alláh*) [Mecca]. There was nothing about it in line with justice for it consisted of the treasures of the inhabitants of the heavens and of the earth. And God is witness to [the truth of] that which I relate, for God, in this respect, is sufficient [witness] along with whomsoever recites the decrees of the Qur'an in an informed manner. And if God thy Lord should will it he would assuredly, in very truth, bring his verses to light for he, verily, no God is there except him. And he is one hearing, knowing. So praised be unto God, Lord of the heavens and of the earth above that which they suppose. And peace be upon the Messengers and praised be to God, the Lord of all the worlds.

Bibliography

Afnan, Abu'l-Qasim. *'Ahd-i A'lá: Zindigani-yi Hadrat-i Báb* (The Bábí Dispensation: The Life of the Báb). Oxford: Oneworld, 2000.

Faydí. *Hadrat-i Nuqtáyi úlá*. Tehran: Mu'assasah-i Millí-yi Matbú'át-i Amrí, 1352 SH/1973, rep. Hofheim-Langenhain: Bahá'í-Verlag, 144 BE/1987.

Iranian National Bahá'í Archives (INBA).

Ishraq Khavari, 'Abd al-Hamid. *Muhádirát* (rep. 2 vols. Hofheim-Langenhain: Bahá'í-Verlag 143 BE/1987, see vol. 2, pp. 729–31.

— *Taqwím-i Tárikh-i Amr hava-yi waqá'i'-i Muhammih-i qarn-i awwal-i Badi'*. Tehran: Mu'assasah-i Millí-yi Matbú'át-i Amrí, 126 BE/1970.

Nabíl-i-A'zam. *The Dawn-Breakers: Nabíl's Narrative of the Early Days of the Bahá'í Revelation*. Wilmette, IL: Bahá'í Publishing Trust, 1970.

Notes

1. In due course a full commentary on the *Khutba al-Jidda* with detailed textual notes will be posted onto my personal website: http://www.hurqalya.pwp.blueyonder.co.uk
2. The sub-heads below are not in the original text.
3. The manuscript reading is uncertain here (INBA 91, p. 61, line 8) where we read *min buhbúyati al-qidam*. I have translated as if this is a slight spelling error or misreading of *min buhbúhiyyat al-qidam* 'at the midmost heart of preexistence'.
4. The text and translation of *daqá'iq zakwán* as 'an augmentation of intricacies' is uncertain. *Zakwán* appears not to exist! I have translated it as if it is derived from the root Z-K-W = 'to grow, increase, augment'.
5. Read here *man* not *má*.
6. Add the missing (cf. INBA manuscript, p. 66, line 2) *al-sittín* (= sixty) in the spelling of the year, from Ishraq Khavari 1987, vol. 2, p. 729; Faydí 1987, p. 143 and Afnán 2000, p. 86.

7. The phrase *shahr al-ramadán* 'month of Ramadan' is most probably a scribal gloss or addition as it does not occur in the Ishraq-Khavari 1987, vol. 2, p. 730 or Faydí 1987, p. 143, though it is present in Afnán 2000, p. 86.
8. '... the *'umra* (the lesser pilgrimage) and the *hajj* (= pilgrimage) itself on the third day of the second decad (= the 13th) of the selfsame sacred month which precedes the month of God (= the 13th Dhu'l-Hijjah = 24 December 1844).' The Arabic word meaning 'second' (= *al-tháni*) in 'second decad' [*al-*]*'ushr al-tháni* is actually 'third' in the manuscript behind INBA 91, p. 66, line 12. The undoubtedly correct reading 'second decad', however, is found in Ishraq-Khavari 1987, p. 730; Faydí 1987, p. 144 (line 6) and Afnán 2000, p. 86.
9. The translation of *al-man' muntahá* (mss. p. 67, line 9) as 'with the completion [of pilgrimage] through the hindering [of Satan] (*muhtahá al-man'*)' makes sense as indicating one of the final (*muntahá*) acts of pilgrimage through the 'warding off' or 'hindering' (*man'*) of Satan with the ritual stoning of the three pillars. An alternative reading at this point of *muntahá al-miná*, meaning 'through the completion [of pilgrimage] at Miná [about four miles from Mecca] (*muntahá al-miná*)', suggests itself, and though this has no support in the manuscript (or printed text citations) I have consulted, it would make very good sense in the light of the final pilgrimage rituals (animal sacrifice) associated with Miná which is visited towards the end of the Muslim pilgrimage. These two aforementioned readings could easily result from an unpointed Arabic text in the Báb's cursive hand. Worth noting is that Bábí tradition registered in Nabíl-i Zarandí's *Dawn-Breakers* 1970, pp. 132–3 (here Miná is spelled colloquially as Muná) makes specific mention of the Báb's performing Islamic ritual sacrifice at Miná during the latter days of his pilgrimage (as the Khutba al-Jidda here implies).
10. Here in INBA 91, p. 68, line 1; as well as Faydí 1987, p. 145 and Ishraq Khavari 1987, p. 731, the phrase *al-'ushr al-thálith* ('the third decad') should read [*al-*]*'ushr al-tháni* 'the second decad' (as in Afnán 2000, p. 86) and has been emended accordingly.

10

Muhammad Shah Qájár in Four Early Writings of the Báb

Sholeh A. Quinn*

Department of History, University of California, Merced

During his brief messianic career, Sayyid 'Alí Muhammad Shírází, the Báb (1819–50), addressed the reigning Qájár king, Muhammad Shah (1808–48/r. 1834–48), several times. That a religious claimant to the 'office' of Hidden Imam would address the king of his country not just once or twice but several times during his ministry, and that at least one if not more of these communications were considered sufficiently important for the king allegedly to pen a reply, should merit the attention of historians. Nevertheless, very little scholarship has been devoted to examining this correspondence. The purpose of this paper is to analyse the first four available early communications of the Báb to Muhammad Shah, focusing on the theme of kingship in them. As the Báb was writing to a king, one of the most important themes in his letters is kingship. The Báb's attitudes towards and understanding of kingship informed his expectations of Muhammad Shah specifically and of kings in general. Although the nature of his relationship with the king changed owing to the changing historical circumstances in which he found himself, the Báb continued to communicate with the king over time and express his opinions to him.

Pre-19th-century Islamicate kingship

The history of the Middle East generally and Iran specifically has a rich tradition of kingship, stretching far back into the pre-Islamic period. So that we may better understand the nature of the Báb's statements regarding kingship, in particular that of Muhammad Shah, a brief overview of the history of kingship in the Islamic world, with particular emphasis on Iran, is apposite.

Iran had experienced a long history of kingship by the time Islamic rule established itself in the country and put an end to the Sasanian dynasty. Successive Islamic dynasties that ruled over Iran, beginning with the Umayyads and the

---

* I would like to thank Dr. Stephen N. Lambden for his invaluable assistance throughout the preparation of this paper.

'Abbasids, led to the articulation of new forms of authority and political legitimacy. Whereas kings had ruled as the *sháhansháh*, or king of kings, the caliphs based their legitimacy on their claim of succession to the Prophet Muhammad. When the 'Abbasids came to power they transferred the capital of the empire from Damascus to Baghdad, resulting in a strong Sasanian influence on their style of rulership. Indeed, 'Abbasid caliphs lived in palaces and held ceremonies similar to those of Persian kings. For example, it is interesting to note that the 'Abbasid caliphs wore a crown known as the 'crown of the caliph' (*táj al-khalífa*) and indeed were the first Islamic dynasty to have done so (see *EI2*,'tádj'). It may be the case that in thus imitating this Persian tradition the 'Abbasids were distinguishing themselves from the earlier Umayyad dynasty and, at the same time, bolstering their legitimacy by invoking something much earlier and perhaps more 'powerful' in the history of the region.

We must look to the later 'Abbasid period, however, when the entire Middle East witnessed a long period of political fragmentation and decentralization, for movements in which Persian kingship was revived. Between the years 950 and 1258, as 'Abbasid rule diminished and gradually became restricted to the city of Baghdad, leaders who carved out territory for themselves and their descendants came to rule Iran, while at the same time acknowledging the religious authority of the caliph in Baghdad. These individuals claimed political authority for themselves, however, and legitimized their rule by, for example, attaching old pre-Islamic titles such as Áqásísháhansháh to their names and forging genealogies showing descent from Iran's pre-Islamic kings.

In 1258 Hulagu Khan, grandson of Genghis Khan (Chingiz Khan), invaded the Middle East, sacked the city of Baghdad, which had long been a centre of culture and learning, and brought an end to the 'Abbasid caliphate. The Mongols brought with them their own notions of kingship, based on nomadic principles of authority. The absence of the caliph meant that post-caliphal rulers had to work out other ways to legitimize their rule, often by combining pre-Islamic and/or Perso-Turko-Mongol forms of kingship (see Woods 1999, p. 4).

When the Safavid dynasty came to power in the 16th century, new ideas of political legitimacy and kingship emerged, which blended with older theories and currents. Shah Ismá'íl, founder of the Safavid dynasty, initially presented himself in his poetry as a virtually divine messianic figure, but after he crowned himself king in 1501 he established Twelver Shi'ism as the official state religion. As time passed, the Safavids tried to distance themselves from their *ghuluww* past and, gradually, a class of Shi'i religious clerics became increasingly powerful and challenged the ways in which Safavid kings were legitimizing their rule. By the time Shah 'Abbás (r. 995–1038 AH/1587–1629 CE) came to power, Safavid kingship rested on three main pillars: the Safavid ruler as head (shaykh) of the Safaviyya Sufi order which brought the Safavids to power; the Safavid ruler as descendant of Músá al-Kázim, the seventh Imam of the Twelver Shi'a and therefore ruler in the name of the Hidden Imam; and the Safavid ruler as the shadow of God on earth in line with pre-Islamic Iranian notions of kingship.

Qájár kingship

In the late 18th to 19th centuries the Qájár dynasty ruled Iran. The Qájárs were one of the original Turkic Qizilbásh tribes forming the confederation that had put the Safavid Shah Ismá'íl in power some three hundred years earlier. The Qájárs rose to power in the wake of political fragmentation and decentralized rule in Iran following the fall of the Safavids. In his biography of Násir al-Dín Shah (r. 1848–96), Muhammad Shah's son, Abbas Amanat characterizes the legitimacy of Qájár kings as having four major dimensions: 1) the pre-Islamic Persian dimension, 2) the Islamic/Shi'i dimension, 3) the nomadic concept of power and leadership and 4) the western/European model of government (Amanat 1997, p. 7). At least three of these dimensions or motives/motifs are present in the communications between the Báb and Muhammad Shah.

Muhammad Shah and the correspondence of the Báb

The Qájár monarch who had the most interaction with the Báb was Muhammad Shah and that interaction was in the form of written communications. Muhammad Shah came to power in 1834. He grew up being tutored by a Ni'matu'lláhí Sufi dervish, Hájjí Mírzá Áqásí (d.1264 AH/1848 CE), resulting in the king's largely mystical religious persuasion. He was the third ruler of the Qájár dynasty, succeeding his grandfather Fath 'Alí Shah (r. 1212–50 AH/1797–1834 CE). Muhammad Shah had received practical experience in kingship by serving as governor of Azerbaijan before becoming king. Upon succeeding to the throne Muhammad Shah placed his teacher Hájjí Mírzá Áqásí in an important ministerial position. He faced many challenges during his rule, both internal, in the form of tribal and religious uprisings, and external, in the form of Russian and British influence in the country.[1]

The Báb wrote to Muhammad Shah throughout his lifetime, beginning with statements that he made to him in one of his earliest works, the Qayyúm al-Asmá'. The Báb wrote other letters to the king while travelling through Bushihr, Kulayn, Siyáh Dahán, Mákú and Chihríq.[2]

Muhammad Shah and dominion (*mulk*) in the Qayyúm al-Asmá'

The Qayyúm al-Asmá', the first major post-declaration work of the Báb, appears to be the earliest instance in which the Báb directly addresses Muhammad Shah. The passages concerning the king can be found primarily in the Súrat al-Mulk (the Sura of the Dominion/Authority), the title of the first chapter of this lengthy text. Although the Qayyúm al-Asmá' has not been published or fully translated into English, Stephen Lambden has electronically published a partial translation and commentary on several chapters, including the Súrat al-Mulk.[3]

The most significant word in the Súrat al-Mulk is, not surprisingly, *mulk* (dominion). It appears in the body of the chapter at least nine times. In more general statements in the chapter, the Báb explains the term in connection with those who possess it. *Mulk*, he says, belongs to God (QA 1:22) and it is also invested in the 'Remembrance' (the Báb) (QA 1:28), whose *mulk* is elevated 'in the Garden of

Eternity (*jannat al-khuld*) which We bestow upon such as We desire among Our servants' (QA 1:33).[4] In contrast, the *mulk* that belongs to kings is vain because 'God hath set aside earthly possessions for such as have denied Him' (QA 1:32).

The Báb's comments regarding *mulk* help to explain the context of his statements in this chapter to kings in general and to Muhammad Shah. These are outlined most specifically in Qayyúm al-Asmá' 1: 22–9, which forms a discrete portion of the chapter, with a distinct beginning, middle and end. This section opens with a general address not directed specifically to this particular king but to kings and the sons of kings in general. Here, the Báb states that kingly dominion actually belongs to God and that kings should set it aside:

> O concourse of kings and the sons of kings (*ya ma'shar al-mulúk wa abná' al-mulúk*)! Lay aside, one and all [in truth, as befits the Truth] your dominion which belongeth unto God (*mulk Alláh*) . . . (The Báb 1976, p. 41).

In subsequent verses the Báb specifically addresses Muhammad Shah, referring to him as the 'king of Islám' and asking for his assistance. He makes promises to the king regarding the positive outcomes that would result from his compliance and at the same time warns him of the consequences of disobedience. Muhammad Shah's destiny is quite exalted, the Báb claims, if he comes to his assistance:

> O king of Islám [lit. 'king of the Muslims', *malik al-muslimín*]! Aid thou, with the truth, after having aided the Book, Him Who is Our Most Great Remembrance (*dhikriná al-akbar*), for God hath, in very truth, destined for thee, and for such as circle round thee, on the Day of Judgement [Resurrection] (*yawm al-qiyáma*), a responsible position in His Path. I swear by God, O [Muhammad] Sháh! [lit. O thou king!] If thou showest enmity unto Him Who is His Remembrance (*dhikr*), God will, on the Day of Resurrection, condemn thee, before the kings, unto hell-fire, and thou shalt not, in very truth, find on that Day any helper except God, the Exalted (ibid. pp. 41–2).

The Báb's commands to the king are not at all vague; on the contrary, he lays out quite explicitly what he expects from Muhammad Shah in terms of assistance. Specifically, he wants the king to help him by waging a holy war, or jihad, against various regions, starting with Iraq and continuing to other countries. Muhammad Shah should do this because, the Báb says, the king has been 'mercifully invested' with sovereignty and complying with the Báb's request will reward him in the next world:

> Purge thou, O [Muhammad] Sháh, the Sacred Land (*al-ard al-muqaddas*) from such as have repudiated the Book (*ahl al-radd*), ere the day whereon the Remembrance of God (*al-dhikr*) cometh, terribly and of a sudden, with His potent Cause (*al-amr al-qawiyy*), by the leave of God, the Most High (ibid. p. 42).[5]

The Báb then broadens his request to the king, requesting that he subdue 'the countries':

God, verily, hath prescribed to thee [Muhammad Shah] to submit unto Him Who is His Remembrance (*al-dhikr*), and unto His Cause (*al-amr*), and to subdue (*taskhar*), with the truth and by His leave, the countries (*bilád*), for in this world thou hast been mercifully invested with sovereignty (*al-mulk*), and wilt, in the next, dwell, nigh unto the Seat of Holiness, with the inmates of the Paradise of His good-pleasure (*jannat al-ridwán* [lit. Garden of Ridván]) . . . (ibid.).

The Báb ends his address to Muhammad Shah by reminding him of his own limited sovereignty, stating that he will eventually die and that true sovereignty rests in the hands of the 'Remembrance':

Let not thy sovereignty (*al-mulk*) deceive thee, O [Muhammad] Sháh, for 'every soul shall taste of death' [Q 3:182], and this, in very truth, hath been written down as a decree of God . . .
Be thou content with the commandment of God, the True One, inasmuch as sovereignty (*al-mulk*), as recorded in the Mother Book (*umm al-kitáb*) by the hand of God is surely invested in Him Who is His Remembrance (*al-dhikr*) . . . (ibid. pp. 41–2).[6]

The section concludes with a final emphatic call to kings in general, the same kings and sons of kings whom the Báb addressed at the beginning of the section. This passage can be read with Qayyúm al-Asmá' 1:20 as the end of a complete sentence or phrase. In this final portion the Báb specifies what it means for kings to lay aside their sovereignty (*mulk*):

And [O kings!] give aid towards victory before God through thy very own selves and thy swords (*bi-anfusikum wa asyáfikum*) in the shade of the Most Great Remembrance (*al-dhikr al-akbar*) for the sake of this pure Religion (*al-din al-khalis*) which is, in very truth, mighty.

Sovereignty, then, as the Báb expresses it in this section of the Qayyúm al-Asmá', is a highly complex issue. First and foremost, according to the Báb, sovereignty belongs to God, and kings should lay aside their own sovereignty because, apparently, the eschaton has arrived. If kings have any interest in preserving their sovereignty or *mulk* in the next world, which appears to be the only place where they can enjoy any dominion whatsoever, then they must come to the assistance of the Báb in this world, aiding him to spread his religion by means of their selves and their swords. In addition to waging war on behalf of the Báb, he also calls on kings to perform a second major task: that of distributing his writings to Turkey, India and everywhere else:

O concourse of kings (*ya ma'shar al-muluk*)! Deliver with truth and in all haste the verses sent down by Us, to the peoples of Turkey and of India and beyond them, with power and with truth, to lands in both the East and the West (QA 1: 34–5).

In the Qayyúm al-Asmá' these two tasks – waging war (jihad) and distributing his writings – are connected and it is incumbent upon the king to do both.

Many of the ideas that the Báb articulates in this section of the Qayyúm al-Asmá' openly conflict with notions of kingship that were established in the Safavid period (1501–1722) and evolved during the Qájár era. For example, the second Safavid 'pillar of legitimacy' – the notion that the Safavid kings could rule in the name of the Hidden or occulted Imam – was based on an 'invented' genealogy, replicated in every official and unofficial Safavid history, showing them as lineal descendants of Músá al-Kázim, the seventh Imam of the Twelver Shi'a (see Quinn 2000, pp. 83–6). In this way the Safavids could claim that, based on this genealogy, they had the authority to rule in the name of the Hidden Imam. By the Qájár period, however, this model of kingship and authority had evolved into a situation where two rival loci and foci of authority, the king and the clergy, were making similar legitimizing claims. In the Qayyúm al-Asmá' the Báb asserts his own legitimacy and, at the same time, theoretically diminishes the first locus of authority, the king, by stating that he, the Báb, possessed true sovereignty. Significantly, the second chapter of the Qayyúm al-Asmá' is called the Súrat al-'Ulamá' and here, in the same way that he downplays kingly authority in the Qayyúm al-Asmá', the Báb lessens clerical authority, forbidding the ulama to engage in various forms of legal opinions and interpretations that traditionally formed part of their jurisdiction. These include engaging in personal legal opinions (*ra'y*), considered (and 'mere' as the polar opposite of *yaqín*) opinion (*zann*) and independent judgement (*ijtihád*) (QA 2:13–17, see provisional translation).

The Báb's comments regarding sovereignty in the Qayyúm al-Asmá' also address another of the dimensions of sovereignty outlined above: the pre-Islamic Iranian dimension of Qájár kingship.[7] This pillar of legitimacy is characterized by a number of elements, one of the most central having to do with the so-called 'circle of justice', a notion that was elaborated in the medieval Islamic period. In a recent article, Linda Darling succinctly summarizes this circle of justice by quoting the 9th century Sunni Muslim theologian and belles-lettreist/*adíb* and political theoretician Ibn Qutaybá's (d. 276 AH/889 CE) *'Uyún al-akhbár*:

> There can be no government without men,
> No men without money,
> No money without cultivation [or, prosperity],
> And no cultivation [or, prosperity] without justice and good administration (Darling 2002, p. 1).

Countless treatises have been written elaborating this theme, which form a genre of advice literature called 'Mirrors for Princes'. These texts often appear in the form of a wise man or sage giving advice to a king. Some of this advice, such as that which appears in Kaykavus's *Qábúsnámah*, is quite practical, covering diverse topics like how to play backgammon, how to eat properly and the importance of showing gratitude to one's parents (Kaykavus ibn Iskandar 1951). Other advice is more abstract, as seen in Nizam al-Mulk's *Siyásatnámah*, a treatise that outlines the rules for kingly conduct, explaining how the king should treat ambassadors, make kingly appointments and engage in other official kingly activities (Nizam al-Mulk 1978). In this model, responsibility for maintaining the circle of justice begins with the king. The Báb, however, in the Qayyúm al-Asmá' inserts into the circle of justice the sovereignty of God as mediated through him, the Báb. As representative of the Hidden Imam, he ultimately possesses true sovereignty. Thus the king's sovereignty does not depend on maintaining an army but, in this instance, using that army to come to the Báb's assistance. Otherwise, his sovereignty is subject to removal, at best.

Evidence from the Báb himself suggests that Muhammad Shah never received or read the Qayyúm al-Asmá'. In 1844 Mullá Husayn Bushrú'í, the Báb's first major disciple who, according to Nabíl's history, was present in his home when he revealed the Qayyúm al-Asmá', went to Tehran (Nabíl-i-A'zam 1932. p. 55).

During that trip Mullá Husayn apparently attempted to present the king with a copy of the Qayyúm al-Asmá' and a letter that the Báb had written to the king; but the Báb states in a later communication, to be discussed below, that he knew the letters had been intercepted and did not reach the king (see MacEoin 1982, p. 105).[8] We do know, however, that ultimately he did not comply with the Báb's requests: he did not wage a holy war on behalf of the Báb, nor did he disseminate his writings or give up his dominion.[9]

The letter from Bushihr

The Báb repeats some of the same themes of the Qayyúm al-Asmá' in an undated letter he wrote to Muhammad Shah some time during his stay in Bushihr after his return from pilgrimage in June 1845 (Afnan 2000, pp. 102–3).[10] The Báb places great significance in this letter on the importance and truth of his verses and Muhammad Shah's role in disseminating them. Although his request to Muhammad Shah to help spread his writings appears in the Qayyúm al-Asmá', the emphasis on this is even greater in the Bushihr letter. Here he asks the king to read/recite his writings and recognize their truth and importance. One of the earliest commands to the king in the letter is for him to read the Báb's writings: 'So recite, O thou king (*malik*) the Book [Epistle] of thy Lord to the end that thou mayest be numbered among such as have attained.' The Báb combines this emphasis on his verses with his earlier command to Muhammad Shah in the Qayyúm al-Asmá' to assist the Báb in order to make his religion victorious. In this letter, however, rather than asking him to accomplish this with his sword *and* spreading his writings, the Báb only states that the king must disseminate his writings, and in that way, the religion would succeed:

> God who is thy Lord hath willed that the Ottomans (*al-rúm*) come to faith through the veracity of his verses along with most of the peoples of the earth. Render victorious the Religion of God (*dín Alláh*) that the Day of Resurrection (*yawm al-qiyáma*) be realized through such as are inclined towards victory.[11]

The Báb gives very explicit instructions to the king as to how he should help him. Specifically, the king is to have copied out what the Báb had written to him in golden ink and a beautiful cursive Arabic (*naskh*) script, send it to the Ottoman sultan and then to all the other kings, so that the Báb would know who accepted his message and who did not:

We indeed sent down a Book . . . unto thee [Muhammad Sháh] to the end that thou command that there be written the like of what We sent down therein in golden ink (*al-midád al-dhahab*) in a noble, *naskh* script (*khatt, naskh karím*). Then shall thou dispatch this Book [Epistle] of thy Lord unto the Ottoman Sovereign (*malik al-rúm*) [i.e. Sultan 'Ard al-Majíd] then unto all the [other] kings (*mulúk*). This to the end that We might know which faction (*tá'ifa*) among them hath been just with respect to the command of God and which faction (*tá'ifa*) among them hath been untruthful. Wherefore shall We judge among them with justice.

Historical context may help explain this shift of emphasis away from waging war solely to spreading the word. Although it has not yet been possible to date this letter precisely, we know that the Báb arrived in Bushihr sometime in June 1845 (see Amanat 1989, p. 243). In his letter he states that he has returned from his pilgrimage to Arabia and has also heard of the troubles that Mullá 'Alí Bastámí faced in Iraq.[12] He tells the king to seek out Bastámí because he is 'elevated and mighty'. At least five months prior to writing this letter, partly due to Bastámí's imprisonment, the Báb had cancelled the gathering that his followers expected to take place in Karbala, where he would disclose something of his messianic role and – in accordance with the predictions in Shi'i hadith literature of eschatological holy war – embark on a universal jihad. Furthermore, on 10 Muharram[13] 1261/20 January 1845, the Báb had sent a letter to Mullá Husayn Bushrú'í. In this letter the Báb redirects his followers in the 'Atabát to leave that region and go to Shiraz (Amanat 1989, p. 251). Shiraz specifically and Iran in general, then, became the new focus of the Báb and his followers, and this new emphasis is reflected in the Báb's statements about kingship in the Bushihr letter.

Iran and kingship in the Bushihr letter

In the very first section of the letter the Báb states that he does not desire worldly dominion or other-worldly kingly power, nor does he desire clerical power:

> The [personified] Word of God (*kalimát Alláh*) does not desire worldly dominion (*mulk al-dunyá*) nor [that of] the world to come [Hereafter] (*al-akhira*); neither the decree of religious judgement (*fatwá*) after the fashion of the clerics (ulama) of the True God (*haqq*) (provisional translation).

However, at the same time he reminds Muhammad Sháh that true power rests with 'my Master' (*mawla*), a reference to the Hidden Imam:

> Know ye that every king (*malik*) is in the hands of my Master (*mawlá*) [the Hidden Imam]. This even as the likeness of the seal (*khátam*) in thine own hands which He imprints even as He wills after the manner that He wills.

Here he reminds his audience that it is the Hidden Imam who legitimizes kings and kingship. Furthermore, the Báb compares the relationship between the Imam and the king to the king and his seal, which has long been in Islamic history a symbol of royal authority and power.¹⁴ Towards the end of the letter he tells Muhammad Shah that he wants to establish the throne of God in his dominion, meaning that divine authority should come to regulate and exercise control over his kingdom: 'We desire the [establishment of the] Throne of God (*'arsh Alláh*) [justice] in thy dominion (*mulk*) [Persia].' This letter, then, like the communication to Mullá Husayn Bushrú'í, reflects the real life circumstances in which the Báb found himself. The jihad was cancelled and problems in the 'Atabat had forced the Bábís to regroup in Iran, the location where the Báb states the throne of God should now be established.

Justice in the Bushihr letter

Another significant theme in this letter is justice, a very important concept for the Báb, as it is for Islam in general and Shi'ism in particular. For example, he states that his words are the words of justice:

> O thou king [Muhammad Shah]! Follow the decree (*hukm*) of thy Lord then bear thou witness unto His verses [which constitute] the Word of Justice (*kalimát al-'adl*)' (provisional translation).

The Báb himself is just: 'Know O thou king! that I am a non-Arab [Persian] youth (*fata 'ajami*) from the party of justice (*ta'ifat al-'adl*), an unlettered merchant (*al-tujjar ummi*).' Here, by emphasizing the notion of justice and by stating that both he and his revelations, or writings, were 'just', the Báb seems to imply that Muhammad Shah himself would or could come to faith himself because he was a just king. Later in the letter he advises Muhammad Shah to act in accordance with justice:

> Rise ye up over the dominion (*al-mulk*) with justice (*bi'l-'adl*) as accords with the Providence/Rule of thy Lord (*hukm rabbika*) expressed in the Book (*al-kitáb*).

In summary, the ideas in the Bushihr letter continue some of the themes expressed in the Súrat al-Mulk. At the same time, the Báb modifies the earlier request for the king to participate in holy war, owing to changing historical circumstances. Nevertheless, he continues to exhort the king to disseminate his writings and draws the king's attention to Iran. He appears still to have faith in the king's sense of justice and reminds him of his ancient kingly duty to be just.

After writing to Muhammad Shah from Bushihr, the Báb went to Shiraz and then to Isfahan. In Isfahan he revealed some important scriptural writings and spent several months as a guest in a private residence of the governor of Isfahan, Manúchihr Khan, the Mu'tamid al-Dawla. Ultimately, after the death of Manuchihr Khan, and the instalment of his nephew, Gurgin, Muhammad Shah ordered that he leave Isfahan and go to Tehran, which he did, under escort, in February-March 1847. The Báb had wanted to meet the king but owing to the intervention of Hájjí Mírzá Áqásí, the above-mentioned Ni'matu'lláhí Sufi prime minister, this did not take place. Instead, the Báb received notification from the king that he was being sent to

Mákú, where the king would meet him. Two versions of the king's letter to the Báb exist. One is quoted in 'Abdu'l-Bahá's *Traveler's Narrative* and another in *Nabíl's Narrative*, and both are reproduced in Hasan Balyuzi's *The Báb* (see Balyuzi 1973, pp. 122–3).[15] The texts of those letters, written in April 1847, are as follows:

A Traveler's Narrative:

> Since the royal train is on the verge of departure from Tihrán, to meet in a befitting manner is impossible. Do you go to Mákú and there abide and rest for a while, engaged in praying for our victorious state; and we have arranged that under all circumstances they shall show you attention and respect. When we return from travel we will summon you specially ('Abdu'l-Bahá 1980, p. 12).

Dawn-breakers (Nabíl's Narrative):

> Much as we desire to meet you, we find ourselves unable, in view of our immediate departure from our capital, to receive you befittingly in Tihrán. We have signified our desire that you be conducted to Máh-Kú, and have issued the necessary instructions to 'Alí Khán, the warden of the castle, to treat you with respect and consideration. It is our hope and intention to summon you to this place upon our return to the seat of our government, at which time we shall definitely pronounce our judgement. We trust that we have caused you no disappointment, and that you will at no time hesitate to inform us in case any grievances befall you. We fain would hope that you will continue to pray for our well-being and for the prosperity of our realm (Nabíl-i-A'zam 1932, pp. 230–1).

Siyáh Dahán

As the Báb was escorted towards Mákú he stopped in the village of Siyáh Dahán two days after he passed through Qazvin. While in Siyáh Dahán he again wrote to Muhammad Shah. Unlike his earlier communications, this letter is primarily in Persian, with Qur'an and hadith citations in Arabic (Afnan 2000, p. 250). The letter consists mainly of the Báb's reprimand of Muhammad Shah for ordering him to Mákú, stating that this kind of command (*hukm*) was completely inappropriate and unfair. He again invokes notions of Persian kingship, stating:

> If I am a believer, and that I am, may God and his friends be witness . . . such treatment is not fair, and if I am an infidel, and that I swear to the sacred divine essence and the high status of the Prophet of the House of Innocence I am not – and be it known that under the shadow of that imperial bounty (*dar zill-i 'inayat-i shahanshahi*) in every [part of this] land, there are many infidels – still such a verdict is [still] unjust . . . (Amanat 1989, p. 372; Afnan 2000, p. 262.)

In this passage, the Báb again invokes notions of ancient Persian kingship. His use of the word *sháhansháh* is evocative of the Sasanian *sháhansháh* or king of kings, who was considered the 'shadow of God on earth'. The king's responsibility, the

Báb seems to say, is to protect everyone in his land and to treat them all with justice. Unlike in the earlier letters, however, the Báb does not call on the king to assist him in becoming victorious. Rather, he invokes the king's sense of justice by objecting to the order sending him to Mákú. This shift in focus continues in the Báb's next letter to Muhammad Shah, which he wrote from the fortress in Mákú.

The Báb's letter from Mákú

By the time the Báb wrote to Muhammad Shah from the fortress in Mákú, probably in 1848, his relationship with the king and the nature of his comments had changed considerably. The letter is remarkable for several reasons. One of its most striking features is the amount of detail that the Báb provides in it regarding his personal situation. The letter is in Persian and Arabic; whenever the Báb writes of his own life experiences he does so in Persian, and whenever he speaks of religious, abstract or non-personal themes, he writes in Arabic. In making reference to his earlier communications with Muhammad Shah, he acknowledges that his first communication, presumably his letter and the Qayyúm al-Asmá' sent via Mullá Husayn, never reached the king:

> In that same year [year 60] I dispatched a messenger and a book unto thee, that thou mightest act towards the Cause of Him Who is the Testimony of God as befitteth the station of thy sovereignty. But inasmuch as dark, dreadful and dire calamity had been irrevocably ordained by the Will of God, the book was not submitted to thy presence, through the intervention of such as regard themselves the well-wishers of the government (The Báb 1976, p. 13; Afnan 2000, p. 301).

He then says that because four years have passed since he wrote that letter, he thought he should let the king know what had happened to him since. The Báb spells out in great detail the circumstances of his imprisonment. He complains about his treatment in Shiraz by the governor (Husayn Khan) and indicates that if the king knew about this, he would mete out 'retributive justice' to him. Furthermore, he says, owing to the governor's behaviour, the king's court would be 'until the Day of Resurrection, the object of the wrath of God' (ibid.).

The Báb continues by describing how the 'vicious' Gurgín (Mírzá Gurgín Khan, Manuchihr Khán's nephew) had sent him 'away from Isfáhán with an escort of five guards on a journey which lasted seven days, without providing the barest necessities for My travel (Alas! Alas! for the things which have touched Me!), until eventually Your Majesty's order came, instructing Me to proceed to Mákú' (The Báb 1976, p. 14; Afnan 2000, p. 301). He then describes his situation in Mákú:

> I swear by the Most Great Lord! Were thou to be told in what place I dwell, the first person to have mercy on Me would be thyself. In the heart of a mountain is a fortress [Mákú] . . . the inmates of which are confined to two guards and four dogs. Picture, then, My plight . . . (ibid.).

At the time he was imprisoned in Mákú the Báb's attitude towards Muhammad Shah seems to be one of still giving the king the benefit of the doubt, yet at the same time warning him to some degree of the consequences of his actions. Realizing that his earlier letter or letters had been intercepted, he writes to inform the king of his predicament and to let him know that an injustice has taken place. The letter, and the nature of the Báb's appeals in it, so different from his initial requests and commands, reflects the changing human circumstances in which he found himself. As in the Siyáh Dahán letter, the Báb does not appeal to the king to help him in waging a universal jihad against the Ottomans and others, nor does he ask the king to help him by engaging in diplomatic correspondence and spreading his writings. In fact, he does not directly call on the king to take any specific action. However, certain indirect statements in this letter could be interpreted as warnings or statements suggesting what might happen to Muhammad Shah as a result of his actions thus far:

> Whatever reacheth Me is ordained to reach Me; and that which hath come unto Me, to him who giveth will it revert. By the One in Whose hand is My soul, he hath cast no one but himself into prison . . . Woe betide him from whose hands floweth evil, and blessed the man from whose hands floweth good (The Báb 1976, p. 15; Afnan 2000, p. 301).

Later in the letter the Báb comments on sovereignty, telling the king that if he were aware of what the Báb knew, he would give up his sovereignty:

> Were thou to know that which I know, thou wouldst forgo the sovereignty (*saltanat*) of this world and of the next, that thou mightest attain My good-pleasure, through thine obedience unto the True One . . . (The Báb 1976, p. 16; Afnan 2000, p. 302).

The Báb does not, however, ask or demand that the king give up his sovereignty, as he did in the Qayyúm al-Asmá'. Here, the choices remain with the king.

The Mákú letter was written before the Báb's imprisonment in Chihríq and marks the end of the first phase of his communications with the king. During his approximately two-year imprisonment in the fortress of Chihríq (April 1848 – July 1850), the Báb's situation deteriorated significantly. Despite the severe difficulties he faced, this was an extremely prolific period for the Báb. It was during this time that he sent the first of the Chihríq letters to Muhammad Shah and Hájjí Mírzá Áqásí. These communications are known as the sermons of wrath (*khutab-i qahri-yyah*) (Amanat 1989, p. 381). Although he continues to give Muhammad Shah more opportunities to come to faith, even at this late stage, he seems to assume that neither the king nor his minister will change their ways (see The Báb 1976, pp. 11–28). Muhammad Shah died on 6 Shawwál 1264/4 September 1848, two months after the Báb arrived in Chihríq and almost two years before the Báb's execution.

Conclusion

In the Báb's earliest correspondence with Muhammad Shah, he continually called on the king to come to his assistance. The exact nature of the assistance required changed over time, as the Báb's circumstances changed and became increasingly precarious. Thus at first the Báb asked Muhammad Shah to wage a universal jihad and spread his writings. By the time the Báb reached Bushihr, he no longer requested the king to fight on his behalf but renewed the request to spread his writings. After the order arrived banishing the Báb to Mákú, he called on the king to consider the injustice that he showed towards the Báb. In Mákú, however, he stopped making demands on the king and instead recounted for the monarch the suffering that he experienced and indirectly warned the king of the consequences of his actions. Throughout the correspondence, however, the Báb never stopped appealing to notions of justice, which he connected to kingship by invoking traditional concepts.

Bibliography

'Abdu'l-Bahá. *A Traveler's Narrative*. Wilmette, IL: Bahá'í Publishing Trust, 1980.

Afnan, Abu'l-Qasim. *'Ahd-i A'lá: Zindigani-yi Hadrat-i Báb* (The Bábí Dispensation: The Life of the Báb). Oxford: Oneworld, 2000.

Amanat, Abbas. *Pivot of the Universe* Berkeley: University of California Press, 1997.

— *Resurrection and Renewal: The Making of the Bábí Movement in Iran, 1844–1850*. Ithaca, NY: Cornell University Press, 1989.

The Báb. *Selections from the Writings of the Báb*. Trans. Habib Taherzadeh with the assistance of a Committee at the Bahá'í World Centre. Haifa: Bahá'í World Centre, 1976.

Balyuzi, H. M. *The Báb: The Herald of the Day of Days*. Oxford: George Ronald, 1973.

Cole, Juan R. *Modernity and the Millennium*. New York: Columbia University Press, 1998.

Darling, Linda T. '"Do Justice, Do Justice, for that is Paradise": Middle Eastern Advice for Indian Muslim Rulers'. *Comparative Studies of South Asia, Africa and the Middle East*, vol. 22, no. 1 (2002).

Encyclopaedia of Islam [EI2]. Leiden and London: Brill. 2nd ed. 1960.

Iranian National Bahá'í Archives (INBA).

Kaykavus ibn Iskandar. *Qabusnamah*. Trans. Reuben Levy as *A Mirror for Princes: The Qabusnama*. London: Cresset Press, 1951.

Lambden, Stephen. 'The Messianic Roots of Babi-Baha'i Globalism', in Margie Warburg, et. al (eds.). *Baha'i and Globalisation*. Aarhus, Denmark: Aarhus University Press, 2005.

— http://www.hurqalya.pwp.blueyonder.co.uk/03-THE%20BAB/QAYYUM%20AL-ASMA'/Q-ASMA.001.htm (accessed 15 April 2008)

— http://www.hurqalya.pwp.blueyonder.co.uk/03-THE%20BAB/post%201844/MUHAMMAD%20SHAH-BUSHIRE.htm (accessed 15 April 2008)

Lawson, B. Todd. 'Interpretation as Revelation: The Qur'an Commentary of Sayyid 'Alí Muhammad Shírází, the Báb', in ed. A. Rippin, *Approaches to the History of the Interpretation of the Qur'an*. Oxford: Oxford University Press, 1988.

— *The Qur'an Commentary of Sayyid 'Alí Muhammad, the Báb*. Unpublished Ph.D. diss., McGill University, 1987. http://bahai-library.com/index.php5?file=lawson_quran_commentary_bab (accessed 21 October 2007).

— 'The Terms Remembrance (*Dhikr*) and Gate (*Báb*) in the Báb's Commentary on the Sura of Joseph', in Moojan Momen. *Studies in Honor of the Late Hasan M. Balyuzi*. Los Angeles: Kalimát Press, 1989, pp. 1–63.

MacEoin, Denis. 'The Babi Concept of Holy War'. *Religion*, vol. 12 (1982), pp. 93–129.

— *The Sources for Early Babi Doctrine and History: A Survey*. Leiden: E.J. Brill, 1992.

Nabíl-i-A'zam. *The Dawn-Breakers: Nabíl's Narrative of the Early Days of the Bahá'í Revelation*. Wilmette, IL: Bahá'í Publishing Trust, 1970.

Nizam al-Mulk. *The Book of Government, or Rules for Kings*. London: Routledge & Kegan Paul, 1978.

Quinn, Sholeh A. *Historical Writing during the Reign of Shah 'Abbas: Ideology, Imitation and Legitimacy in Safavid Chronicles*. Salt Lake City: University of Utah Press, 2000.

Rassekh, Shapour. '*Payámhá-yi hazrat-i nuqtah'-i awlá bih hukkám-i zamán*', in *Safinah-i Irfan*, vol. 8 (2005), pp. 88–104.

Woods, John E. *The Aqquyunlu*. Salt Lake City: University of Utah Press, rev. and exp. 1999.

Notes

1. For more details, see *EI2*, 'Muhammad Shah', from which this brief sketch was drawn.
2. In addition to these known letters, there is some correspondence whose existence appears uncertain, as 'Abdul-Bahá explains in his *Traveler's Narrative*. After describing a letter of the Báb to Muhammad Shah, written when the Báb was at the end of a two-week stay in Kulayn and on his way to Mákú, 'Abdul Bahá suggests that there may have been several more that were intercepted by Hájjí Mírzá Áqásí: 'Besides this the followers of the Báb recount certain messages conveyed [from Him] by the instrumentality of Muhammad Big (amongst which was a promise to heal the foot of the late king, but on condition of an interview, and the suppression of the tyranny of the majority), and the prime minister's prevention of the conveyance of these letters to the Royal Presence. For he himself laid claim to be a spiritual guide and was prepared to perform the functions of religious directorship. But others deny these accounts ('Abdu'l-Bahá 1980, p. 12). For a study of some of the Báb's writings to Muhammad Shah and other leaders, see Rassekh 2005, pp. 88–104.
3. All the provisional translations in this essay are by Stephen Lambden and can be found at: http://www.hurqalya.pwp.blueyonder.co.uk. For this translation see http://www.hurqalya.pwp.blueyonder.co.uk/03-THE%20BAB/QAYYUM%20AL-ASMA'/Q-ASMA.001.htm (accessed 15 April 2008). For scholarship on the Qayyúm al-Asmá', see Lawson 1988, pp. 223–53; Lawson 1987.
4. The Báb refers to himself in this chapter as 'the Remembrance' (*dhikr*). For more information on this, see Lawson 1989, pp. 1–63.
5. The 'sacred land' (*al-ard al-muqaddas*) the Báb refers to here must be the 'Atabat region. Although the official translation of this passage includes a parenthetical gloss equating the 'sacred land' with Tehran, other evidence from the Báb's writings, including elsewhere in the Qayyúm al-Asmá' itself, suggest that he actually means the Iraqi 'Atabat. See, for example, Qayyúm al-Asmá', sura 17: 'O peoples of the earth! Inflict not upon the Most Great Remembrance what the Umayyads cruelly inflicted upon Husayn in the Holy Land. By the righteousness of God, the True One, He is indeed the Eternal Truth, and unto Him God, verily, is a witness' (The Báb 1976, p. 69).

6. See Lawson 1989 for more information on the Báb as *al-dhikr* or 'the Remembrance'.
7. Some of the issues I am going to discuss next have been addressed by Juan Cole in his analysis of Bahá'u'lláh's Tablets to the Kings and other works but here I will be examining them in a Bábí context. See, for example, Cole 1998, pp. 52–68.
8. According to MacEoin a copy of this letter exists in the INBA (Iranian National Bahá'í Archives) collections 4011C, 332–6 and 5006C, 367–9. See MacEoin 1992, pp. 58 and 192. The INBA collections containing this first letter of the Báb were unavailable to me. Regretfully, Rassekh does not make use of MacEoin's valuable study, resulting in inaccuracies in his study regarding the number of letters that the Báb wrote to Muhammad Shah.
9. It is unclear the degree to which the Báb expected him to do so. In the Qayyúm al-Asmá', the Báb makes claims in line with various expectations found in the massive heritage of Shi'i Muslim messianic traditions. Numerous Imami messianic hadith informed the religiosity of the Báb's first followers. These individuals were Twelver Shi'as who had certain expectations of the Qa'im, such as his waging of a universal jihad. See MacEoin 1982, pp. 93–129; Amanat 1989, pp. 33–69; Lambden 2005, pp. 17–34.
10. For a recent English translation by Stephen Lambden, see http://www.hurqalya.pwp.blueyonder.co.uk/03-THE%20BAB/post%201844/MUHAMMAD%20SHAH-BUSHIRE.htm.
11. See also the following passage: 'Yea indeed! the thing most beloved is that thou should render victorious the *Dhikr-Alláh* (Remembrance of God) to the end that both the Easts of the earth and the Wests thereof might come to faith through the verses of thy Lord (*áyát rabbika*) and they be numbered among the rightly guided.'
12. 'We have heard of the day when the Messenger [of the Bâb = Mullá 'Alí Bastámí] was imprisoned in Baghdad.'
13. 10 Muharram corresponds with the day of 'Áshúrá, the anniversary of the martyrdom of the Imam Husayn in Karbala. See *EI2*, 'Muharram'.
14. For more on the royal seal, see *EI2*, 'Khátam/Khátim'.
15. Further research, necessitating examination of the Persian original of Nabíl's history, is needed in order to understand the relationship between these two versions of the letter.

11

A Youth of Medium Height: The Báb's Encounter with the Hidden Imam in *Tafsír Súrat al-Kawthar*

Omid Ghaemmaghami[1]

Deep within the heart of the Báb's voluminous commentary (*tafsír*) on the Qur'an's Súrat al-Kawthar[2] the reader comes across the remarkable story of an encounter he had during his pilgrimage to Mecca over a year earlier: while completing the *tawáf* – the ritual of encircling the Ka'ba which serves as the central rite of the Islamic pilgrimage – his eyes fell upon a mysterious youth (*shább*) who may have been the hidden Qá'im. This account was adduced in the work of a prominent ayatollah in an attempt to disparage the Báb and repudiate his claim to be the long-awaited Shi'i deliverer. In the following pages, I will offer a provisional translation and gloss on the complete account. By situating the episode within the context of Shi'i messianic texts, I will advance the thesis that in this account the Báb is utilizing a stock of conventions, images and tropes that were common devices in the *zeitgeist* dominating the religious milieu of 19th-century Persia to implicitly affirm his own claim to be the Qá'im – the eagerly awaited Twelfth Imam – while simultaneously ensconcing the same claim in a manner that is characteristic of the early years of his ministry. A close reading of the Báb's account not only suggests that it is in concert with other statements made by the Báb about his station in the same *tafsír* but it also corresponds to the dialectic between concealment and disclosure that runs throughout his earliest writings.

The Tafsír Súrat al-Kawthar

A comprehensive study of the Báb's unconventional two thousand verse commentary on the shortest sura of the Qur'an remains a desideratum.[3] For our purposes, a review of some of the basic facts must suffice. We know that the *tafsír* was composed in Shiraz in the early summer of 1846 in response to a request by Siyyid Yahyá Dárábí – later surnamed Vahíd Akbar (d. 1850) – an erudite Shi'i scholar who had been sent by Muhammad Shah (d. 1848) to conduct an inquiry into the

Báb's claims.[4] Denis MacEoin has styled the commentary 'the most important work' authored by the Báb during the period of his residency in Shiraz following his return from pilgrimage and prior to his move to Isfahan (MacEoin 1992, p. 71). That the *tafsír* is atypical in the genre of Qur'an commentaries no one would deny but it is difficult not to be surprised by MacEoin's dismissive appraisal of most of its contents: 'Interesting as it undoubtedly is in places, and highly regarded as it was by early Babis, this work is, for the most part, almost unreadable, consisting of highly abstract and insubstantial speculation on the words and even letters of the sura on which it is supposed to be a "commentary"' (MacEoin 2009, pp. 188–9). Since MacEoin has not offered any concrete examples, one does not know how to respond to the second part of his statement. Todd Lawson's assessment, on the other hand, is both measured and nuanced: 'As for the content of the *Tafsír Súrat al-Kawthar,* it will be found to contain many terms and ideas which although unfamiliar to modern Western readers, were common coin in the milieu where it was first read' (Lawson 1987, p. 60).

Lawson's view is corroborated by the fact that the *tafsír* played an important role in the early propagation efforts of Bábís to teach their new faith among the Shi'i inhabitants of Iran and Iraq. According to an eyewitness of the early Bábí mission, in the course of her debates with ulama in Kúfa and Karbala, Tahirih eloquently invoked verses from the Báb's commentary on súrat al-kawthar' (*kitáb sharh al-kawthar*) causing the religious leaders to complain to the government which in turn led to her exile to Baghdad.[5] The same source informs us that the *tafsír* was also used in efforts to spread the Báb's message in Kirmánsháh where it was translated into Persian.[6]

The Báb's encounter with the Hidden Imam

The Báb's account of his meeting with the Hidden Imam is found midway through the *tafsír*. As far as I am aware only two Bahá'í scholars have taken note of this account in their writings. Fádil Mázandarání cites the passage in full in his encyclopedia of terms and locutions in the Bahá'í writings with small differences in the way the account is cited in INBA 53 (Mázandarání 124–9 BE, vol. 4, pp. 525–6 'Qá'im'). Although he does not discuss this passage, Mázandarání does state two pages earlier that the first three years of the Báb's ministry was 'the period of gatehood' (*dawrih-yi bábiyyat*) when, owing to the requirements of the time, the Báb had not yet publicly divulged that he was the Qá'im (Mázandarání 124–9 BE, vol. 4, p. 523).The account is also referred to by Nosratollah Mohammadhosseini in his extensive tome on the Báb where it is erroneously identified as a Shi'i hadith found in the works of the late-Safavid Traditionist Muhammad Báqir Majlisí (d. 1699).[7] This is not a difficult mistake to make considering that the account is nestled among numerous hadiths. However, no such hadith is found in any of Majlisí's works – or any other work for that matter – and a close reading of the text confirms that it is in fact the Báb who is speaking in the first person.

Between Fádil Mázandarání and Mohammadhosseini, the account was also cited by Ayatollah Ibráhim Amíní (b. 1925)[8] in his apologetic/polemical work *Dádgustar-i Jahán*.[9] This book presents the traditional Shi'i doctrines vis-à-vis the

Twelfth Imam, his putative occultation, the signs of his return, etc. First published in 1968, at least three other editions have been produced and the book itself has been reprinted more than 30 times, a testimony, perhaps, to its popularity in Iran. Translations into Arabic and Urdu have also been published.[10] According to the Iran Book News Agency (IBNA), Amíní's monograph is 'the most comprehensive book' written in the field of the Twelfth Imam and was recognized in 1999 by Iran's Ministry of Culture and Islamic Guidance as the best book written in Arabic or Persian on the figure of the Shi'i saviour.[11] In 1996 Professor Abdulaziz Sachedina[12] translated the monograph into English under the title *al-Imam al-Mahdi: The Just Leader of Humanity*. This translation has itself been reprinted numerous times – most recently by the prolific Qum-based publisher Ansariyan Publications – and found its way to the Internet. Currently one can find copies or links to it on hundreds of web sites, including a number of anti-Bahá'í sites.[13]

The last part of the final chapter of Amíní's book, in essence its crest and climax, is a polemical attack on the Báb.[14] Here Amíní seeks to discount the Báb as essentially a very confused young man who was in reality a pseudo-Qá'im. What is clear is that Amíní has attempted to read parts of the Báb's *Tafsír Súrat al-Kawthar*. In this section of his book Amíní translates selections from the Báb's *tafsír* from Arabic into Persian. In his translation Sachedina has translated these selections from Persian into English without consulting any of the original Arabic manuscripts of the *tafsír*. Citing the Báb's encounter with a 'young man in the sacred mosque of Mecca whom he thought to be the Hidden Imam' (Amíní 2004, p. 344), Amíní contends that this is clear proof that the Báb did not in fact harbour any claims to be the awaited Twelfth Imam. After all, how could the Báb have been the Twelfth Imam when he is claiming to have seen him? Since Sachedina's translation is for the most part an accurate rendition of Amíní's text, I will quote from it here:

> In another place in the same book [i.e. the Tafsír Súrat al-Kawthar] he writes about his own experience of having seen the twelfth Imam in Mecca: 'One day I was busy praying in the holy mosque of Mecca, on the side of the Yamani pillar [of the Ka'ba]. I noticed a well built and good looking young man who was deeply involved in performing the circumambulation (*tawáf*). He had a white turban on his head and a woollen cloak on his shoulder. He was with the merchants' group from Fars. There was no more than a few steps of distance between us. All of a sudden a thought came to my mind that he could be the Master of the Command (*sáhib al-amr*). But I was embarrassed to go closer to him. When I finished my prayers I did not find him. Nevertheless, I am not so sure that he was the Master of the Command' (ibid. p. 342[15]).

Amíní does not provide any details about the manuscript of the *tafsír* he has consulted. Furthermore, his use of quotation marks gives the false impression that he is directly quoting from the *tafsír* when, in fact, the *tafsír* was written by the Báb in Arabic and he is 'translating' this passage into Persian. More importantly, there are numerous problems with Amíní's Persian translation. To highlight these, I will begin by providing here a new translation of this section of the *tafsír* for ease of comparison with Amíní's translation above.

> One day, while I was inside the Sacred Mosque, standing near the House, next to the Yemeni pillar, in the late afternoon, I saw a youth of medium height – shining, radiant, bursting with light. His face was as luminous as the moon and he was seated on the ground as the people circumambulated the House. He sat in front of the Yemeni pillar in a humble self-effacing manner, his eyes fixed on the House, oblivious of everyone. I saw no one around him. He wore a white turban, similar to the turbans worn by the merchants of Fárs, and a wool cloak, the kind worn by the most eminent merchants, yet he commanded reverence and respect and was marked by majesty and radiance. When I looked at him – between us was a distance of only a few feet, I don't recall the precise distance – my heart was deeply moved. However, I was embarrassed to approach his holy presence and immersed myself in prayer. I said to myself: 'If he is truly my heart's desire, then he will ask me to attain his presence and will ease the yearning in my heart and subdue my fears.' I prayed more fervently, but when I had finished, I looked and he was no longer in the place where he had been sitting. I walked all around the Sacred Mosque, but could not find him [anywhere]. What occurred left a strong impression on my heart. Throughout my time in Mecca, day and night, I searched everywhere to see him again, but God did not permit it. I am not saying that I really did see him because I do not know what God wanted from that (experience). Perhaps he was not outwardly the desired one. But when I saw (him), it occurred to me to mention that honour to you as a token of my love for his Cause. Truly, if a servant attains the station of recognizing him, there is no doubt that he will recognize him . . .[16]

I now move to offer a gloss of the three sections of this account.

Section 1

> *One day, while I was inside the Sacred Mosque,[17] standing (qá'iman) near the House,[18] next to the Yemeni pillar,[19] in the late afternoon (waqt al-'asr), I saw a youth (shábban) of medium height[20] – shining, radiant, bursting with light. His face was as luminous as the moon[21] and he was seated on the ground as the people circumambulated the House.*

In Shi'i parlance mention of a radiant youth at the Ka'ba would have instantly been read by a learned scholar such as Vahíd as a metonymy for the Twelfth Imam. In the compilations of hadith about this figure, hadith after hadith ascribed to the Imams predicts that the Qá'im will emerge as a youth at the time of his appearance.[22] In a long Tradition ascribed to the sixth Imam, Ja'far Sádiq (d. 765) and narrated on the authority of his close disciple Mufaddal bin 'Umar (d. late 7th century),[23] we are told that when the Imam manifests himself and appears at the Ka'ba, 'No one will recognize him [because] he will appear as a youth (*yazhar wa-huwa shább*)'.[24] Another hadith recounts the same Imam as having said, 'The Lord of this cause is the youngest of us in age and the most beautiful of us in appearance (*sáhib hádhá al-amr asgharuná sinnan wa-ajmaluná shakhsan*).' When asked about the time the Imam would appear, Sádiq responded allusively: 'When travellers set out to pay homage to the lad (*idhá sárat al-rukbán bi-bay'at al-ghulám*).'[25]

Elsewhere, the Qá'im's age is hinted at: 'The Lord of [this] cause is not older than forty . . . he will manifest himself in the form of a youth (*yazhar fí súrat shább*)' (Túsí 1425 AH/2004–5 CE, p. 419, n. 396). When one of his disciples asked Sádiq whether he was the Lord of the Age, the Imam was stunned: 'Me? Your Master (*inní la-sáhibukum*)?!?' Pulling his wrinkled skin, he proclaimed: 'I have grown old whereas your Master will [appear] in the prime of his youth (*aná shaykh kabír wa-sáhibukum shább hadath*).[26] A similar hadith is ascribed to Ja'far's father, Imam Muhammad Báqir (d. *c.* 735). When pressed by one of his disciples to reveal whether or not he was the promised Qá'im, Báqir at last answered: 'How could I be him when I have already reached fifty-four years of age?! The Lord [of the Age] is much younger than I and much lighter on the saddle of a mount.'[27] Commenting on this hadith, the Shi'i scholar 'Alí al-Há'irí (d. 1915) remarks: 'People will see (the Qá'im) as a youth (*shább*) with perfect strength and without evincing any of the signs of advanced age.'[28] According to a separate hadith attributed to Imam Husayn, 'When the Qá'im rises, the people will reject him because he will return as a youth in his best years (*law qad qáma al-qá'im la-ankarahu al-nás li-annahu yarji'a ilayhim shábban muwaffaqan*). No one will remain believing in him except those with whom God has kept a covenant since [creating] the first atoms.'[29] A different hadith states that the Qá'im 'will appear in the form of a rightly guided youth (*shább muwaffaq*), a young man thirty-two years old' (al-Nu'mání 1422 AH/2001–2 CE, p. 195, n. 44). Elsewhere Imam Husayn laments that 'among the greatest tests [that will face the Shi'a] is that their Master will appear to them as a youth [when] they expect that he will be an elder (*shaykh*)'.[30] And a Tradition ascribed to Muhammad Báqir, we read: 'They asked the Commander of the Faithful, 'Alí – peace be upon him – about the attributes of the Mahdí. 'Alí responded: "He is a youth of medium height with a beautiful countenance, elegant hair – the hair on his head flows down over his shoulders. The light of his face covers the blackness of his beard and hair."'[31] The youth (*ghulám*) is also listed as one of the epithets of the Twelfth Imam.[32] Moreover, the beauty of the expected Imam is emphasized in numerous hadiths. One tradition ascribed to the Prophet states: 'The Mahdi will be one of my descendants. His face will be like a brilliant star (*wajhuhu ka-al-kawkab al-durrí*). His skin colour will be like the colour of the Arabs; his body like the body of the Israelites. He will fill the earth with justice just as it will have been full of tyranny. The people of the heavens (*ahl al-samá'*) and the birds in the air will be pleased by his rule. He will rule for twenty years.'[33] These hadiths and reports far from exhaust the theme in Shi'i sources.

In the over 1,100 years that the Twelfth Imam has been in occultation, there have been numerous believers – particularly from the ranks of the ulama – who have claimed to have met him, whether in dreams and visions or in a wakeful state. In these accounts the Hidden Imam is often an Arab descendant of Imam 'Alí from the *hijáz*.[34] In account after account he is described as being a comely, courtly youth marked by overwhelming, if not ineffable, beauty. Radiance, youth and refinement are among the first attributes ascribed to the Imam in these accounts. A typical narrative describes the Imam as a youth with 'a broad forehead, white complexion, brilliant eyes, wide palms, bent knees, a birthmark on his right cheek, and a part of his hair in locks'.[35] In another account that dates back to the 10th century CE, the believer meeting the youthful Imam in a tent 'bursting with light' outside of Mecca recounts:

> I entered into his presence, may the blessings of God be upon him, and found him sitting on a rug with brown and red-coloured spots, reclining on a pillow. We greeted each other. I looked at him closely and saw a face as luminous as the moon. He was strong yet refined and mild-tempered, not too tall and not too short. He was of medium build and possessed a broad forehead, beautifully arched eyebrows, deep-black and large eyes, an aquiline nose, and two smooth cheeks with a birthmark on the right. My mind was lost in his features as I looked upon him.[36]

In many of the earliest accounts the Imam is encountered in the vicinity of the Ka'ba. In one such report from the first century of the occultation, the believer narrating the experience recounts:

> As I was circumambulating the Ka'ba and had completed the sixth encirclement and was about to begin the seventh, my eyes suddenly fell upon a group sitting to the right of the Ka'ba. A most comely, sweet-smelling, awe-inspiring youth (*shább*) reverently approached them and began speaking to them. I have never [listened to] words more beautiful than his, nor [heard] a tongue sweeter than his nor [seen] sitting more exquisite than the manner of his sitting.[37]

It is also worth noting that in a version of the famous hadith known as the hadith of the vision, Muhammad declared that during his ascent into the heavens, he saw God in the most beautiful of forms: a youth in his best years (*shább muwaffaq*).[38]

Turning to the Báb's writings, we find that youth and beauty are very significant self-describing motifs. The Báb refers to himself as the 'the Persian Youth' and 'the Arabian Youth' in numerous places.[39] He is repeatedly portrayed as being 'comely'[40] and having been fashioned by God 'in a most comely form' (*bi-ahsan súra*).[41] In one of his works he is proclaimed as 'the Garden of Repose, the loftiest Point of adoration, the Tree beyond which there is no passing, the blessed Lote-Tree, the Most Mighty Sign, the most beauteous Countenance (*tal'at al-'uzmá*) and the most comely Face (*wajhat al-husná*)' (The Báb 1976, p. 155).

Expressions of praise of the Báb's youth and beauty appear to have been important themes for his earliest followers as well. Regarding the attention the Báb's beauty and mansuetude received, A.L.M. Nicolas writes: 'He was already predisposed to meditation and inclined to be silent, while his fine face, the radiance of his glance as well as his modest and contemplative mien drew, even at that early date, the attention of his fellow-citizens' (Nicolas 1908, pp. 188–9, cited in Nabíl 1970, p. 77). Mullá Husayn's first description upon seeing the Báb on the eve of his declaration outside the gates of Shiraz was 'a Youth of radiant countenance' (Nabíl 1970, p. 52). And in a letter to her fellow believers in Isfahan, Táhirih reminded them that 'Tablets have been revealed from the heaven of divine decree in description of the comely Arabian Youth (*fatá al-'arabí al-malíh*) mounted on the most noble of steeds' (cited in Mázandarání 1944, vol. 3, p. 364).[42]

In the opening lines of the account of his experience in Mecca, the Báb states that he saw the youth in the late afternoon (*al-'asr*). This could be read as a specific reference to the time of the afternoon prayer recited between noon and sunset or as a general reference to the time of day. In Shi'i sources the period of *'asr*, in particular on Mondays and Thursdays, is reserved for the Hidden Imam. It is said that this is the time when the works and deeds of the believers are presented to the Imam.[43] It *al-'Asr* also the name of the one of the suras of the Qur'án.[44] In a hadith ascribed to the sixth Imam, *al-'asr* is interpreted as being 'the advent [or coming forth] of the Qá'im'.[45] al-'Asr also denotes a period or space of time and can be translated as 'the age' or 'the era'.[46] In Shi'i sources three of the Imam's most popular titles are *Imam al-'Asr* (the Imam of the Age), *Sáhib al-'Asr* (the Lord of the Age) and *Walí al-'Asr* (the Guardian of the Age).

Furthermore, the Báb indicates that the radiant young man he saw was seated on the ground (*al-turáb*) while pilgrims circumambulated the shrine. This may be a veiled reference to a famous sobriquet of 'Alí, the first, and in a sense archetype, of the twelve Shi'i Imams: Abú Turáb (lit. father of ground). According to Shi'i sources, this title was given to 'Alí by the Prophet Muhammad upon finding 'Alí lying on the ground next to the Ka'ba, his body covered with dirt. The Prophet gently woke him, began to wipe the dirt off his back and affectionately called him Abú Turáb. Shi'i sources maintain that the sobriquet was one of the most favourite nicknames of the Prophet for 'Alí and that the latter 'would become overjoyed when called by it' (Majlisí 1983, vol. 35, p. 66). It is bears noting here that Abú Turáb is also one of the epithets of the Twelfth Imam in Shi'i sources.[47]

The image of the youthful Imam sitting calm and composed on the ground while around him swelling phalanxes of pilgrims are circumambulating could also be read as a proleptic reference to a passage found in the Persian Bayán, the most significant of the Báb's later works. In the second *báb* of the eighth *váhid* of that work, the Báb states that when a Manifestation of God appears the certitude of his believers must be so strong that if 100,000 people are circumambulating the Ka'ba and he commands them to stop circumambulating (*lá tatúfú*), they must immediately obey. Otherwise, all their deeds and acts of worship will become void and empty (*bátil*) (The Báb, *Persian Bayán*, p. 275).

Section 2

> *He sat opposite the Yemeni pillar in a humble self-effacing manner, his eyes fixed on the House, oblivious of everyone. I saw no one around him. He wore a white turban,[48] similar to the turbans worn by the merchants of Fárs, and a wool cloak, the kind worn by the most eminent merchants, yet he commanded reverence and respect and was marked by majesty and radiance.*

First, it is worth noting the colour of the turban on the youth's head. Although the colour green is often associated with the descendants of the Prophet, according to a number of Shi'i Traditions, the colour worn most often by the supporters of 'Alí was white. Numerous Traditions indicate that the Imams wore white garments and white turbans. According to one such hadith, the eighth Imam, 'Alí Ridá' (d. 818) wore a white cotton turban (*'imáma baydá min qutun*) during the *'íd* prayers after agreeing to become the caliph Ma'mún's (d. 833) successor.[49]

The key sentence in this section of the account – if not the most crucial sentence in the entire account – is the Báb's description of the youth as a merchant from the Persian province of Fárs. It is important to note that the great Andalusian mystic Ibn al-'Arabí (d. 1240) is said to have expected the Mahdí to be a Persian: '... he is the "Lord of the Two Dominions" (*sahib hukmayn*). He is of a foreign people (*al-'ajam* [also meaning Persian]), not an Arab. His complexion is of a fair, ruddy hue, his hair reddish, and he is rather tall than short. He is like the radiant full-moon (*al-badr al-azhar*).'[50] However, I know of no account in Shi'i sources where the Hidden Imam is described as being a merchant, to say nothing of him being a Persian from Fárs.[51] The Báb, born and raised in the province of Fárs and a merchant for most of his youth, was of course both. This sentence is the clearest proof that the youth the Báb is describing in none other than his own self.

Vahíd must certainly have been apprised of the Báb's profession prior to his interviews. The Báb's occupation was alluded to in his earliest works and was known by his followers. In a letter to Mullá Husayn, Táhirih describes him as the Youth (*al-fatá*) who 'has appeared dressed in the garment of [those engaged in] trade' (*fí libs al-tajára mashhúdan*) (Mázandarání 1944, vol. 3, p. 338). This passage may be a direct reference to the above account in the Tafsír Súrat al-Kawthar, especially in light of the fact that Táhirih is said to have recited this work during her debates with religious scholars.

In the introduction of the *tafsír* the Báb describes himself to Vahíd as 'a Persian youth (*fatá 'ajamí*)'.[52] Statements praising the province of Fárs as the Báb's homeland and the place where his revelation began are scattered throughout his writings. In the Qayyúm al-Asmá' the Báb addresses the inhabitants of Fárs: 'O People of Fárs! Is not this inestimable honour from the Supreme Remembrance sufficient for you: God has chosen you for this Most Great Word [i.e. the Báb]!'[53] Fárs (*madínih-yi fá'*) is further extolled as the place of revelation (*mahall-i zuhúr*) in the Persian Bayán, where the Báb commands that all (*kull nufús*) must prostrate themselves before entering it.[54]

Section 3

> *When I looked at him – between us was a distance of only a few feet, I don't recall the precise distance – my heart was deeply moved. However, I was embarrassed (Cf. Q 33:53) to approach his holy presence and immersed myself in prayer. I said to myself: 'If he is truly my heart's desire, then he will invite me to attain his presence and will ease the yearning in my heart and subdue my fears.' I prayed more fervently, but when I had finished, I looked and he was no longer in the place where he had been sitting. I walked all around the Sacred Mosque, but could not find him [anywhere]. What occurred left a strong impression on my heart. Throughout my time in Mecca, day and night, I searched everywhere to see him again, but God did not permit it. I am not saying that I really did see him because I do not know what God wanted from that [experience]. Perhaps he was not outwardly the desired one. But when I saw [him], it occurred to me to mention that honour to you as a token*

of my love for his Cause. Truly, if a servant attains the station of recognizing him, there is no doubt that he will recognize him . . .'[55]

The Báb's hesitation about whether the youth was in fact the promised Imam and his inability to find him after opening his eyes are again refigurations of traditional topoi found in accounts describing *tête-à-têtes* with the Imam. That during the season of pilgrimage the Qá'im 'is at Mecca, unrecognized, scrutinizing the hearts of the believers' is a prominent theme in early Shi'i sources (MacDonald and Hodgson, 'Ghayba', *EI2*, vol. 2, pp. 1025–6). I will cite just one of many typical accounts, this one found in Kulayní's (d. 940) hadith compendium *al-Káfí*:

> I was performing the pilgrimage with one of my companions. We came to the halting station at the plain of 'Arafát (*al-mawqif*). Suddenly, [we saw] a youth sitting down (*shább qá'id*) wearing a cloth around his waist and over one of his shoulders . . . He did not show any of the signs of travel. A mendicant came to us but we shooed him away. He then went to the youth and begged him [for money]. [The youth] picked up something from the ground and gave it to him. The beggar prayed for him, praying fervently and for a long time. The youth then stood up (*qáma*) and disappeared (*ghába 'anná*).

The narrator and his companion immediately approached the mendicant and asked what the youth had given him. The beggar showed them a piece of gold which they estimated to be 20 *mithqáls*[56] in weight. Only then do the two realize that the youth they had seen was the Hidden Imam. Frantically, they begin searching for him but are unable to find him anywhere. The Imam has vanished. They ask whether anyone knows anything about the young man. They learn only that he is 'a youth and a descendant of Imam 'Alí (*shább 'alawí*) who performs the pilgrimage on foot every year'.[57]

Henry Corbin captures well the spirit and tenor of the phenomenon of encounters with the Imam when he observes that,

> These manifestations, however, never occur except at the initiative of the Imam; and if he appears most often in the guise of a young man of supernatural beauty, almost always, subject to exception, the person granted the privilege of this vision is only conscious afterward, later, of whom he has seen. A strict incognito covers these manifestations . . . (Corbin 1995, p. 23).

The practice of *taqiyya* – a characteristic feature of the Báb in this phase of his short ministry – is a palpable component of this pericope.[58] In fact, if there were one passage that best captures the sense of secrecy and the dialectic between an open disclosure of his claim to be the Qá'im and a desire to conceal that notion, it may be this passage from the Tafsír Súrat al-Kawthar.

Other verses in the *tafsír* – which Amini had conveniently chosen to neglect – leave no doubt that its author is laying claim to a sublime rank and station. In the introduction to the *tafsír* the Báb repeatedly states that this work has been 'revealed' to him (INBA, vol. 53, p. 182). The Báb declares: 'Verily, the Burning Bush hath been planted in My chest! How then can you hear the Verses of God and yet fail to understand?' (INBA, vol. 53, p. 192). Again speaking of himself in the third person, the Báb states that 'God has chosen a servant from among the Persians to preserve the religion of His Messenger and Friends (*Alláh qad ikhtára li-hifz dín rasúlihi wa-awliyá'ihi 'abdan min al-a'jamíyín)*'. Moreover, '[God] has bestowed on Him what no one in all the worlds has ever brought' (INBA, vol. 53, p. 184). In introducing the section of the *tafsír* in which we find this narrative, the Báb states that, unlike the ulama, he has not had access to the books of hadith and has not studied the Traditions (*akhbár*) of the Prophet and the Imams, owing to the fact that he has been a youth and a merchant (*li-anní kuntu fatáan tájiran*) (INBA, vol. 53, p. 276). Elsewhere, he presents an ultimatum to the ulama: 'Verily, the One proclaiming this Cause is of the people [who reside] on Mount Qáf. He has commanded the ulama to (either) answer Him or render themselves slanderers and disbelievers in God' (INBA, vol. 53, p. 187).[59] In connection with this, the Báb also proclaims openly to Vahíd that the hour (*al-sá'a*) of the Resurrection has come.

Finally, what are we to make of the Báb's sense of embarrassment to approach the youth? This may again be an example of *taqiyya*. It may also reflect a feeling of extreme meekness and humility on the part of the Báb towards his own self. Similar to, for example, Bahá'u'lláh's Fire Tablet, it may be possible to read this account as another brilliant example of dialogue between the human nature and the divine spirit that animate and co-subsist in the Manifestation of God. In such dialogues the human and divine natures of the Manifestation are not divided. Rather, it can be said that human nature chooses to express its utter lowliness before the Manifestation's divine nature. 'Abdu'l-Bahá's interpretation of a hadith ascribed to the seventh Imam, Músá Kázim (d. 799), may be apropos in this context. According to this hadith, God has promised to reveal four concealed letters to the Qá'im.[60] Commenting on this tradition, 'Abdu'l-Bahá states that the four letters which the Báb divulged were in fact four stages or stations (*marátib-i arba'ih*) that he progressively revealed and passed through during his six-year ministry. These were 1) the stage of servitude (*rutbih-yi 'ubúdiyyat*) which, according to 'Abdu'l-Bahá, the Promised One manifested in the beginning (*dar avval*) of his ministry; 2) the stage of the Imamate manifested by his declaring 'I am the Qá'im whose appearance you have been promised'; 3) the stage of prophethood (*nubuvvat*) where he declared that the Manifestations of God have no beginning or end; and finally 4) the stage where he declared the words 'Verily, I am God'. 'Abdu'l-Bahá concludes his commentary by citing Q 53:3–4: 'Nor does he speak of his own desire. It is nothing but revelation revealed to him' ('Abdu'l-Bahá, *Muntakhabát* online, vol. 6, p. 366 (no. 503)). If the youth in the Báb's account is in fact his divine nature, it is possible to understand the Báb's reticence as an expression of the utter servitude of his human nature to his divine nature, God, represented on earth by his Manifestation, i.e. the Báb himself.

Conclusion

In these tentative notes to the Báb's account of his encounter with the Hidden Imam I have attempted to follow the trajectory charted by Todd Lawson in exploring questions of audience and milieu in reading the early writings of the Báb. The Tafsír

Súrat al-Kawthar may contain more Traditions – many of which relate to the Qá'im – than any of the Báb's other works. Considering the fact that his interlocutor was a learned Shi'i scholar who by some accounts had memorized 30,000 hadiths, is it any wonder that the Báb would choose to speak to him in a 'language' he had mastered by invoking the theme of encounters with the Imam? In an exquisite performance of storytelling the Báb is able to carefully present himself as the promised Imam. In the process, the Traditions and narratives accentuating the physical beauty and youth of the Qá'im come to represent a typological prerepresentation or prefiguration – the type – of which the Báb's encounter with the Qá'im, i.e. with himself, provides the corresponding realization or recapitulation – the antitype. Judging from Vahíd's writings and actions after leaving Shiraz, there is little doubt he did not discern who the mysterious youth in the Báb's account was. The account is thus another stunning portrait of the abiding Quranic template: 'We have never sent a Messenger save with the tongue of his own people, that he might make everything clear to them' (Q 14:4).

Bibliography

'Abdu'l-Bahá. *Memorials of the Faithful*. Wilmette, IL: Bahá'í Publishing Trust, 1971.

— *Muntakhabátí az Makátíb-i Hadrat-i 'Abdu'l-Bahá*, vol. 6. http://reference.bahai.org/download/swa6-fa-pdf.zip.

— *A Traveler's Narrative*. Wilmette, IL: Bahá'í Publishing Trust, 1980.

Afnan, Abu'l-Qasim. *'Ahd-i A'lá: Zindigání-yi Hadrat-i Báb* (The Bábí Dispensation: The Life of the Báb). Oxford: Oneworld, 2000.

Afnán, Mírzá Habíbu'lláh. *The Genesis of the Bábí-Bahá'í Faiths in Shíráz and Fárs*. Trans. Ahang Rabbani. Leiden: Brill, 2008.

Afnan, Muhammad. *Maráhil-i Da'vat-i Hadrat-i Nuqtih-yi Úlá*. n.p.: Mu'assasih-yi Millí-yi Matbú'át-i Amrí, 132 BE/1976.

— 'Sha'n-i tafsír dar áthár-i hadrat-i nuqtih-yi úlá', *Khúshihháyí az kharman-i adab va hunar*, vol. 6. Weinacht, Switzerland: Society for Persian Letters and Arts, Landegg Academy, 152 BE/1995, pp. 94–119.

Ál Muhammad, A. H. *al-Dalíl wa-al-irshád fí liqá' rabb al-'ibád*. Beirut: n.p., 1966.

Amini, Ibrahim. *Dádgustar-i jahán*. n.p.: Intishárát-i Shafaq, 1368/1989.

— *al-Imam al-Mahdi: The Just Leader of Humanity*. Trans. Abdulaziz Sachedina. Qum: Ansariyan Publications, 2004.

— *Munqidh al-bashariyya*. Trans. Sayyid 'Alí Háshimí. Beirut: Dár al-Hádí, 1413/1993.

Amir-Moezzi, Mohammad Ali. 'Aspects de la Figure du Sauveur dans l'Eschtologie Chiite Duodécimaine'. *Messianismes*. Ed. Jean-Christophe Attias, et al. Geneva: Labor et Fides, 2000, pp. 213–28.

Áyát-i Bayyinát: Tablets Revealed by Bahá'u'lláh and 'Abdu'l-Bahá in Honour of Samandar, Nabíl ibn-i-Nabíl, and Their Families. Dundas, Canada: Association for Bahá'í Studies in Persian, 156 BE/1999.

The Báb. *The Persian Bayán*. http://www.h-net.org/~bahai/areprint/bab/G-L/I/inba62/INBA62.pdf.

— *Selections from the Writings of the Báb*. Trans. Habib Taherzadeh with the assistance of a Committee at the Bahá'í World Centre. Haifa: Bahá'í World Centre, 1976.

— *Sharh súrat yúsuf*. Princeton. NJ: Princeton University Library. Uncatalogued Bábí Manuscript no. 269.

— *Tafsír Surat al-Kawthar*. INBA vol. 53. http://www.h-net.org/~bahai/areprint/bab/G-L/I/inba53/INBA53.pdf.

al-Baghdádí, Muhammad Mustafá. *al-Risálah al-Amriyyah*. Appended to Ahmad Sohráb. *al-Risálah al-Tis'a 'Ashariyya*. Cairo: Matba'at al-Sa'ádah, 1338/1919.

Bahá'u'lláh. *Kitáb-i-Íqán*. Hofheim: Lahjnah-yi Millí-yi Nashr-i Áthár-i Bahá'í bih Zabán-i Fársí va 'Arabí, 155 BE/1998.

al-Bahrání, Háshim. *Madínat al-ma'ájiz*. Qum: Mu'assasat al-Ma'árif al-Islámiyya, 1416/1995.

Balyuzi, H.M. *Khadijih Bagum: The Wife of the Báb*. Oxford: George Ronald, 1981.

'Bár-i dígar bá "dádgustar-i jahán".' http://www.ibna.ir/vdci.wavct1au5bc2t.html (accessed 18 June 2009).

Bausani, Alessandro. *Religion in Iran: From Zoroaster to Bahá'u'lláh*. Trans. J.M. Marchesi. New York: Bibliotheca Persica Press, 2000.

Behmardi, Vahid. '*Muqaddamih'í dar bárih-yi sabk va siyáq-i áthár-i mubárakih-yi hadrat-i rabb-i a'lá rúh má sawáhu fadáhu*'. *Khúshihháyí az kharman-i adab va hunar*, vol. 6. Weinacht, Switzerland: Landegg Academy, 152 BE/1995, pp. 47–67.

Browne, E. G. 'A Catalogue and Description of 27 Bábí Manuscripts'. *Journal of the Royal Asiatic Society*, vol. 24, 1892.

Corbin, Henry. *En Islam Iranien: Aspects Spirituels Et Philosophiques*, 4 vols. Paris: Gallimard, 1972.

— *Inside Iranian Islam: Spiritual and Philosophical Aspects*. Trans. Hugo M. Van Woerkom. 2003. http://www.scribd.com/doc/9664772/Henry-Corbins-In-Iranian-Islam-Vol2 (accessed 1 February 2009).

— 'Mundus Imaginalis, or the Imaginary and the Imaginal', in *Swedenborg and Esoteric Islam*. Trans. Leonard Fox. West Chester: Swedenborg Foundation, 1995, pp. 1–33.

— 'Visionary Dream in Islamic Spirituality', in *The Dream and Human Society*. Eds. G.E. von Gurnebaum and Roger Caillois. Berkeley: University of California Press, 1966, pp. 381–408.

Elmore, Gerald T. *Islamic Sainthood in the Fullness of Time: Ibn al-'Arabi's Book of the Fabulous Gryphon*. Leiden: Brill, 1999.

Encyclopaedia of Islam [*EI2*]. Leiden and London: Brill. 2nd ed. 1960.

van Ess, Josef. *The Youthful God*. Tempe, AZ: Dept. of Religious Studies, Arizona State University, 1988.

Faydí, Muhammad-'Alí. *Hadrat-i-Nuqtay-i Úlá*. Hofheim-Langenhain: Bahá'í-Verlag, 150 BE/1994.

— *Nayríz Mushgbíz*. n.p.: n.p., n.d.

Ghaemmaghami, Omid. *Numinous Vision, Messianic Encounters: Typological Represent-*

ations in a Version of the Prophet's hadíth al-ru'ya and in Visions and Dreams of the Hidden Imam. Forthcoming.

Gulpáyigání, Mírzá Abú al-Fadl and Mírzá Siyyid Mihdí Gulpáyigání. *Kashf al-Ghitá'*. http://www.h-net.org/~bahai/areprint/kashf/kag.htm.

al-Há'irí, al-Hájj al-Shaykh 'Alí al-Yazdí. *Ilzám al-násib fí ithbát al-hujja al-ghá'ib*. 2 vols. Beirut: Mu'assasat al-A'lamí lil-Matbú'át, 1977.

al-Hillí, al-Hasan b. Sulaymán. *Mukhtasar basá'ir al-daraját*. Najaf: Manshúrát al-Matba'a al-Haydariyya, 1370/1950.

Horovitz, J. and L. Gardet. 'Kawthar', *EI2*, vol. 4, pp. 805–6.

Ibn al-'Arabí. *The Meccan Revelations*, vol. 2. Ed. Michael Chodkiewicz. Trans. Cyrille Chodkiewicz and Denis Gril. New York: Pir Press, 2004.

Iranian National Bahá'í Archives (INBA).

al-Isfahání, Mírzá Muhammad Taqí. *Mikyál al-makárim*. Beirut: Mu'assasat al-A'lamí lil-Matbú'át, 1421/2001.

Ishráq Khávarí, 'Abd al-Hamíd (ed.). *Má'idih-yi Ásimání*, 9 vols. http://reference.bahai.org/fa/.

— *Qámús-i Íqán*, vols. 1, 4. n.p.: Mu'assasih-yi Millí-yi Matbú'át-i Amrí, 128 BE/1972.

al-Jazá'irí, al-Sayyid Ni'mat Alláh. *Kitáb riyád al-abrár fí manáqib al-a'imma al-athár*, vol. 3 (*Ahwál al-Imám al-Mahdí*). Beirut: Mu'assasat al-Táríkh al-'Arabí lil-Tibá'a wa-al-Nashr wa-al-Tawzí', 1427/2006-7.

al-Kulayní, al-Shaykh. *al-Káfí*, vol. 1. Ed. 'Alí-Akbar al-Ghaffárí. Tehran: Dár al-Kutub al-Islámiyya, 1363/1984–5.

Lambden, Stephen. 'Commentary Upon the *Rashh-i 'Amá*'. http://www.hurqalya.pwp.blueyonder.co.uk/BAHA%27-ALLAH/rashh-i%20%60ama%27/RASHH1YES-COMM.htm.

— 'Moses/Sinai Motifs', in ed. Moojan Momen. *Studies in Honor of the Late Hasan M. Balyuzi*. Los Angeles: Kalimát Press, 1989.

— 'The Tafsír Surat al-Kawthar of Sayyid 'Alí Muhammad, the Báb'. http://www.hurqalya.pwp.blueyonder.co.uk/03-THE%20BAB/post%201844/TAFSIR%20SURAT%20AL-KAWTHAR%20-%20THE%20BAB.htm (accessed 12 July 2009).

Lane, *Arabic-English Lexicon*, Book 1.

Lawson, B. Todd. 'The Dangers of Reading: Inlibration, Communion and Transference in the Qur'an Commentary of the Báb', in ed. Moojan Momen. *Scripture and Revelation*, Oxford: George Ronald, 1997, pp. 171–215.

— 'Qur'an Commentary as Sacred Performance', in eds. Johann Christoph Buergel and Isabel Schayani. *Iran im 19. Jahrhundert und die Entstehung der Baha'i Religion*. Hildesheim: Georg Olms, 1998, pp. 145–58.

— *The Qur'an Commentary of Sayyid 'Alí Muhammad, the Báb*. Unpublished Ph.D. diss., McGill University, 1987.

— 'Reading Reading Itself: The Báb's "Sura of the Bees". A Commentary from the Sura of Joseph – Text, Translation and Commentary.' *Occasional Papers in Shaykhi, Babi, and*

Baha'i Studies, vol. 1. no. 5 (November 1997). http://www.h-net.org/~bahai/bhpapers/vol1/nahl1.htm.

MacDonald, D.B. and M.G.S. Hodgson. 'Ghayba', *EI2*, vol. 2, pp. 1025–6.

MacEoin, Denis. *The Messiah of Shiraz*. Leiden: Brill, 2009.

— *The Sources for Early Bábí Doctrine and History: A Survey*. Leiden: Brill, 1992.

Má'idiy-i-Ásmání, vol. 2. Compiled by 'Abdu'l-Hamid-i-Ishráq Khávarí. New Delhi: Bahá'í Publishing Trust, 1984.

al-Majlisí, Muhammad Báqir. *Bihár al-Anwár*. 110 vols. Beirut: Mu'assasat al-Wafá', 1403/1983.

— 'Sharh hadíth: inna Muhammadan ra'á rabbahu fí surat al-shább al-muwaffaq.' *Majmú'ah-yi rasá'il dar sharh-i ahádíthí az káfí*, vol. 2. Eds. Áshtiyání, Mahdí Sulaymán and Muhammad Husayn Diráyatí. Qum: Dár al-Hadíth, 1387SH/2008–9, pp. 639–43.

Mázandarání, Asadu'lláh Fádil. *Asrár al-Áthár*, 5 vols. Tehran: Bahá'í Publishing Trust, 124–9 BE/1968–73.

— *Tárikh-i Zuhúr al-Haqq*, vol. 2. http://www.h-net.org/~bahai/arabic/vol4/2tzh/2tzh.htm.

vol. 3. Hofheim: Bahá'í-Verlag, 2008.

— *Tárikh-i Zuhúr al-Haqq*, vol. 3. Tehran: n.p., 1944.

Modarressi, Hossein. *Crisis and Consolidation in the Formative Period of Shi'ite Islam: Abu Ja'far Ibn Qiba al-Razi and His Contribution to Imamite Shi'ite Thought*. Princeton, NJ: Darwin Press, 1993.

— *Tradition and Survival: A Bibliographical Survey of Early Shí'ite Literature*. Oxford: Oneworld, 2003.

Mohammadhosseini, Nosratollah. *Hadrat-i Báb*. Dundas, ON: Institute for Bahá'í Studies in Persian, 152 BE/1995.

— *Hadrat-i Táhirih*. Dundas, ON: Institute for Bahá'í Studies in Persian, 2000.

Momen, Moojan. 'Dárábí Sayyed Yahyá'. *Encyclopaedia Iranica Online*, 1996. www.iranica.com.

Nabíl-i-A'zam. *The Dawn-Breakers: Nabíl's Narrative of the Early Days of the Bahá'í Revelation*. Wilmette, IL: Bahá'í Publishing Trust, 1970.

Nicolas, A.L.M. *Siyyid Ali-Muhammad dit le Bab*. Paris: Librairie Critique, 1908.

al-Nu'mání, Abú Zaynab. *al-Ghayba*. Qum: Anwár al-Hudá, 1422/2001–2.

al-Núrí, al-Mírzá. *Mustadrak al-wasá'il*, vols. 3 and 8. Beirut: Mu'assasat ál al-bayt 'alayhim al-salám li-ihyá' al-turáth, 1408/1988.

— *Najm al-tháqib*[sic]. Tehran: Intishárát-i Masjid-i Muqaddas-i Jamkarán, 1410/1989–90.

Périgold, Emily McBride. *Translation of French Foot-Notes of the Dawn-Breakers*. Wilmette, IL: Bahá'í Publishing Trust, 1970.

Quinn, Sholeh. 'Some Preliminary Comments on the Historiography of Sayyid Yahyá Dárábí's Conversion'. Paper presented at the 'Irfán Colloquium, London, July 2001.

al-Qummí, 'Alí bin Ibráhím. *Tafsír al-Qummí*, 2 vols. Najaf: Matba'at al-Najaf, 1386/1966–7.

Rabbani, Ahang. *The Bábis of Nayriz: History and Documents.* Self-published by the author, 2006. http://ahang.rabbani.googlepages.com/nayriz (accessed 16 June 2008).

— 'The Family of Vahid Darabi'. *Research Notes in Shaykhi, Bábi and Baha'i Studies*, vol. 7, no. 1 (April 2004). http://www.h-net.org/~bahai/notes/vol7/darabi.htm#_ftn2 (accessed 16 June 2008).

al-Ráwandí, Qutb al-Din. *al-Khará'ij wa-al-jará'ih*, vol. 2. Ed. Sayyid Muhammad Báqir al-Muwahhid al-Abtahí. Qum: Mu'assasat al-Imám al-Mahdí, 1409/1988.

Sachedina, Abdulaziz Abdulhussein. *Islamic Messianism: The Idea of the Mahdi in Twelver Shi'ism.* Albany: SUNY Press, 1981.

al-Sadúq, al-Shaykh Abú Ja'far Muhammad b. 'Alí b. al-Husayn b. Bábúya al-Qummí. *Kamál al-dín wa-tamám al-ni'ma.* Ed. 'Alí Akbar al-Ghaffárí. Qum: Mu'assasat al-Nashr al-Islámí al-Tábi'a li-Jamá'at al-Mudurrisayn, 1363/1984.

— *'Uyún akhbár al-Ridá'*, vol. 1. Ed. al-Shaykh Husayn al-A'lamí. Beirut: Mu'assasat al-A'lamí lil-Matbú'át, 1404/1983.

Shoghi Effendi. *God Passes By.* Wilmette, IL: Bahá'í Publishing Trust, rev. ed. 1995.

Sohrab, Ahmad. *al-Risálah al-Tis'a 'Ashariyya.* Cairo: Matba'at al-Sa'ádah, 1338/1919.

Streck, M. and A. Miguel, 'Káf', *EI2*, vol. 4, p. 400.

al-Tabarí, Ibn Jarír. *Jámi' al-bayán*, vol. 27. Beirut: Dár al-Fikr lil-Tibá'a wa-al-Nashr wa-al-Tawzí', 1415/1995.

al-Tabarí al-Saghír, Abú Ja'far Muhammad b. Jarír b. Rustam. *Dalá'il al-imáma.* Qum: Mu'assasat al-Ba'tha, 1413/1992–3.

Taherzadeh, Adib. *The Revelation of Bahá'u'lláh*, vol. 1. Oxford: George Ronald, 1974.

al-Túsí, al-Shaykh Muhammad b. al-Hasan. *Kitáb al-ghayba.* Qum: Mu'assasat al-Ma'árif al-Islámiyya, 1425/2004–5.

Wensinck, A.J. 'Masdjid al-Harám', *EI2*, vol. 6, pp. 708–9.

al-Zubaydí, al-Shaykh Májid. *Qisas al-Imám al-Mahdí.* Beirut: Manshúrát al-Fajr, 1427/2006.

Notes

1. I would like to record my thanks to Dr Todd Lawson for his help in studying the account of the Báb's encounter in Tafsír Súrat al-Kawthar. My appreciation as well to Dr Muhammad Afnan, Dr Stephen Lambden, Dr Mina Yazdani and Dr Khazeh Fananapazir for their insights into different aspects of this article. An earlier version of this chapter was presented at the Association for Bahá'í Studies-North America Annual Conference in Toronto, August 2007.
2. Súrat al-Kawthar is the 108th sura of the Qur'an and consists of only three verses. Bahá'u'lláh states that the sura was revealed to the Prophet Muhammad to console him after the premature death of his sons and the derision he was forced to endure at the hands of his enemies. (Tablet cited in *Áyát-i Bayyinát*, p. 147.) On the meaning of *kawthar* (usually translated as 'the abundance'), see Horovitz and Gardet, 'Kawthar', *EI2*, vol. 4, pp. 805–6. 'Abdu'l-Bahá states that *kawthar* is derived from *kathrat* (Arabic, lit. to be numerous, multitude) and means abundance or intensification (*izdiyád*). He adds, 'Today, the divine *kawthar* is the sweet savours of holiness which quicken the souls of men.' (Tablet cited in Ishráq-Khávarí (ed.), *Má'idih-yi Asimání*,

vol. 2, p. 95.) See also Lambden's discussion of the word in Bahá'u'lláh's earliest known work, *Rashh-i 'Amá*, in Lambden, 'Commentary Upon the *Rashh-i 'Amá*". Available online at: http://www.hurqalya.pwp.blueyonder.co.uk/BAHA%27-ALLAH/ rashh-i%20%60ama%27/RASHH1YES-COMM.htm.

3. Edward Browne introduced the Tafsír Súrat al-Kawthar and cited a few short selections in his 'A Catalogue and Description of 27 Bábí Manuscripts', *Journal of the Royal Asiatic Society* 24 (1892), pp. 643–7. Passages from the *tafsír* are also cited by Mázandaráni in *Táríkh-i Zuhúr al-Haqq*, vol. 2, pp. 107–9; Faydi, *Nayríz Mushgbíz*, pp. 13–14; and by Afnan in his excellent study '*Maráhil-i Da'vat-i Hadrat-i Nuqtih-yi Úlá*', pp. 5–18. Todd Lawson has translated some difficult passages and discussed several significant points in *The Qur'an Commentary of Sayyid 'Alí Muhammad, the Báb*, pp. 58–63; and 'Qur'an Commentary as Sacred Performance', pp. 145–9, 153–8. See also Mohammadhosseini, *Hadrat-i Báb*, pp. 768–73; MacEoin, *The Sources for Early Babi Doctrine and History*, p. 71; MacEoin, *Messiah of Shiraz*, pp. 165, 188, 194, 201, 223, 235–6, 246, 279, 601, 641–2; Ishráq Khávarí, *Qámús-i Íqán*, vol. 1, pp. 206–7; Behmardi, '*Muqaddamih-'í dar bárih-yi sabk va siyáq-i áthár-i mubárakih-yi hadrat-i rabb-i a'lá rúh má sawáhu fadáhu*', vol. 6, pp. 54, 57; Afnan, '*Sha'n-i tafsír dar áthár-i hadrat-i nuqtih-yi úlá*', vol. 6, p. 99. See also Afnan, *'Ahd-i A'lá: Zindigání-yi Hadrat-i Báb*, pp. 164, 455, n. 3. In this work Mr Afnan indicates that several pages of the Tafsír Súrat al-Kawthar in the handwriting of the Báb are available at the Bahá'í World Centre; *idem*, p. 475, n. 21. A sample page is presented on p. 466 of the same work. See also Lambden, 'Moses/Sinai Motifs', pp. 104–5, pp. 168–9, n. 113; *idem*, 'The Tafsír Súrat al-Kawthar of Sayyid 'Alí Muhammad, the Báb', available online at: http://www.hurqalya.pwp.blueyonder.co.uk/03-THE%20BAB/post%201844/ TAFSIR%20SURAT%20AL-KAWTHAR%20-%20THE%20BAB.htm.

4. See Momen, 'Dârâbî Sayyed Yahyâ', *Encyclopaedia Iranica Online*, 1996, available at www.iranica.com. Bahá'u'lláh would later refer to Vahíd as the 'unique and peerless figure of his age', *Kitáb-i-Íqán*, p. 223. He has been described by Shoghi Effendi as 'the most preeminent figure to enlist under the banner of the [Báb's] Faith . . .' *God Passes By*, p. 50. By far the most comprehensive source on his biography in English is Rabbani, *The Babis of Nayriz*, available online at: http://ahang.rabbani.googlepages.com/nayriz (accessed 1 June 2008). This work incorporates the author's previous study, Rabbani, 'The Family of Vahid Darabi', *Research Notes in Shaykhi, Babi and Baha'i Studies*, vol. 7, p. 1, available online at: http://www.h-net.org/~bahai/notes/vol7/darabi.htm#_ftn2 (accessed 16 June 2008). See also, Ishráq Khávarí, *Qámús-i Íqán*, vol. 4, pp. 1830–40; Fadil-i-Mazandarani, *Táríkh-i Zuhúr al-Haqq*, vol. 2, pp. 87–90, vol. 3, s.v. index 'Yahyá Dárábí'; Muhammad-'Alí Faydi, *Hadrat-i-Nuqtay-i Úlá*, pp. 267–70; and Taherzadeh, *Revelation of Bahá'u'lláh*, vol. 1, pp. 325–31. Mohammadhosseini summarizes the details of Vahíd's encounter with the Báb (as found mainly in *A Traveler's Narrative* and *The Dawn-Breakers*) in his *Hadrat-i Báb*, pp. 257–61. See also Gulpáyigání, *Kashf al-Ghitá'*, pp. 81–2. Sholeh Quinn has compared some of the earlier accounts of his conversion experience with later sources in her article 'Some Preliminary Comments on the Historiography of Sayyid Yahyá Dárábí's Conversion' (my thanks to Dr Quinn for sharing a copy of her paper with me). One intriguing account of Vahíd's arrival and subsequent conversion not discussed by Quinn is that of Mírzá Habíbu'lláh Afnán, recently translated by Rabbani, *The Genesis of the Bábí-Bahá'í Faiths in Shíráz and Fárs*, pp. 38–40. Of even greater significance are the writings of Vahíd himself, including a treatise he wrote soon after his conversion. Many of his available writings were translated by Rabbani, *The Babis of Nayriz: History and Documents*, pp. 382–95, and must be consulted in any future attempt at a historiography of his initial encounters with the Báb and the writing of the Tafsír Súrat al-Kawthar.

5. Baghdádí, *al-Risálah al-Amriyyah*, appended to Sohrab, *al-Risálah al-Tis'a 'Ashariyya*,

p. 108. On the author, one of the 19 Apostles of Bahá'u'lláh, see 'Abdu'l-Bahá, *Memorials of the Faithful*, pp. 131–4. MacEoin also makes a reference to this in *The Messiah of Shiraz*, p. 214.
6. Baghdádí, *al-Risálah al-Amriyyah*, p. 112. The Persian translation of the Tafsír Súrat al-Kawthar, like Táhirih's Persian translation of the Qayyúm al-Asmá', does not appear to have survived. See MacEoin, *Sources*, p. 71.
7. Mohammadhosseini, *Hadrat-i Báb*, pp. 771, 773 (note 8). Mohammadhosseini does not appear to have known of Fádil Mázandarání's earlier reference to the account.
8. As of June 2009 Ayatollah Amíní was the Deputy Chairman of the Council of Experts (the body that elects Iran's Supreme Leader, *maqám-i mu'azzam-i rabharí*). He is a well-known scholar and respected author and teacher at the Shi'i seminary in Qum.
9. Amíní, *Dádgustar-i jahán*.
10. The Arabic translation is titled *Munqidh al-Bashariyya* and the Urdu translation is titled *Áftáb-i 'Adálat*.
11. '*Bár-i dígar bá "Dádgustar-i jahán"*'.
12. Abdulaziz Sachedina is Frances Myers Ball Professor of Religious Studies at the University of Virginia and one of the leading authorities on Twelver Shi'ism in North America.
13. For example, the English translation is the only book on the Twelfth Imam featured on the popular Shi'i website Shiasite.net. See http://www.islam-guidance.com/en/index.php?option=com_content&view=category&id=282&Itemid=392.
14. The work is markedly different from other anti-Bábí/anti-Bahá'í polemics that have been written in recent years in that political accusations are entirely absent. Here we find no accusations of the Báb being an agent of the Russian government or at the centre of a nefarious anti-Iranian conspiracy. In fact, the substance of Amíní's polemic closely resembles anti-Bábí and anti-Bahá'í works written in the first century of the Bahá'í Faith.
15. The original Persian can be found in Amini, *Dádgustar-i Jahán*, p. 334.
16. INBA 53: 297–8. All references to INBA 53 are from the Báb's Tafsír Súrat al-Kawthar. http://www.h-net.org/~bahai/areprint/Báb/G-L/I/inba53/inba53.htm.
17. al-Masjid al-Harám (lit. the Sacred Mosque) is the name of the mosque and sanctuary in Mecca that contains the Ka'ba. See Wensinck, 'Masdjid al-Harám', *EI2*, vol. 6, pp. 708–9. References to it in the Qur'an include 2:144, 149–50.
18. The Ka'ba.
19. This is one of the four pillars of the Ka'ba. As the name suggests, it is the pillar that faces the direction of Yemen.
20. Cf. Nabíl, *Dawn-Breakers*, pp. 25, 38, 57.
21. Mázandarání has 'like a luminous sun' (*mithl shams munír*). (Mázandarání 124–9 BE, vol. 4, pp. 525.) Cf. the description of the Báb's wife upon seeing Him engaged in devotions on the roof of their house prior to his declaration: 'And His face was luminous; rays of light radiated from it' (Balyuzi, *Khadíjih Bagum*, p. 11).
22. See Amir-Moezzi, 'Aspects de la Figure du Sauveur dans l'Eschtologie Chiite Duodécimaine', p. 218.
23. One of Ja'far Sádiq's foremost disciples on whose authority a number of mainly esoteric Traditions are narrated. Regarding him see Sachedina, *Islamic Messianism*, p. 215, n. 27. On the works that are attributed to him, see Modarressi, *Tradition and Survival*, pp. 333–7, n. 146. See also *idem*, *Crisis and Consolidation* s.v. index 'Mufaddal b. 'Umar al-Ju'fí'.
24. al-Majlisí, *Bihár al-anwár*. vol. 53, pp. 6–7. al-Majlisí's source for this hadith is al-Hasan bin Sulaymám al-Hillí (d. early 9th/15th century). See al-Hillí, *Mukhtasar basá'ir al-daraját*, p. 182. See also al-Jazá'irí, *Kitáb riyád al-abrár fí manáqib al-a'imma al-athár*, vol. 3 (*Ahwál al-imám al-mahdí*), p. 216; al-Há'irí, *Ilzám al-násib*. vol. 2, p. 223.

Cf. Sachedina, p. 161. It is interesting that in every version of this Tradition – with the exception of al-Jazá'irí's, Mufaddal asks Imam Ja'far a follow-up question: 'My Master, will he [really] return as a youth or will he appear as an old man (*ya'úd shábban aw yazhar fí shayba*)?' Ja'far responds by affirming that the Qá'im will manifest himself in whatever form God has willed (*bi-ayy súra shá'a*). Mufaddal's question demonstrates his expectation that the Imam will appear as a white-haired (*shayba*) old man and his surprise to learn from Ja'far that the Qá'im will emerge as a youth.

25. al-Majlisí, *Bihár al-anwár*, vol. 51, pp. 38–9, n. 15; cf. al-Nu'mání, *Kitáb al-ghayba*, p. 190, n. 35, which has a slightly different version of the first part of this Tradition: 'The Lord of this Cause is the youngest of us in age and the most obscure of us in appearance (*sáhib hádhá al-amr asgharuná sinnan wa-akhmaluná shakhsan*).'
26. al-Majlisí, *Bihár al-anwár*, vol. 52, p. 280.
27. al-Kulayní, *al-Káfí*, vol. 1, p. 536, n. 1. Also cited in al-Majlisí, *Bihár al-anwár*, vol. 51, pp. 140–1, n. 14.
28. al-Há'irí, *Ilzám al-násib*, vol. 2, p. 252.
29. al-Nu'mání, *Kitáb al-ghayba*, p. 194, n. 43. Cf. al-Majlisí, *Bihár al-anwár*, vol. 52, p. 287, n. 23, where the Tradition begins with *law kharaja* in place of *law qad qáma*. I have translated the uncommon expression *shább muwaffaq* as 'rightly guided youth'. The same expression has been translated by Josef van Ess as 'youth in his best years', while noting that it lacks 'lexicographical parallels' (Josef van Ess, 'The Youthful God', p. 18, n. 82). According to *Táj al-'arús*, another meaning for *muwaffaq* is 'rightly guided' (*rashíd*). al-Majlisí postulates it is someone who is in the middle years of his youth (al-Majlisí, *Bihár al-anwár*, vol. 52, p. 287).
30. al-Nu'mání, *Kitáb al-ghayba*, pp. 194–5, n. 43. This hadith is cited by 'Abdu'l-Bahá in a very important tablet published in *Muntakhabátí az Makátíb-i Hadrat-i 'Abdu'l-Bahá*, vol. 6, pp. 196–203, n. 282.
31. al-Majlisí, *Bihár al-anwár*, vol. 51, p. 36, n. 6. Cf. a similar Tradition cited in ibid. p. 44, n. 33. Mention should also be made here of Shaykh Ahmad (d. 1826) who stated in a short autobiographical account that the first intimations of unveiling came to him in a dream in which he saw 'a young man, holding a book, who taught the visionary *ta'wîl* (a spiritual exegesis) of two Quranic verses (87:2–3) ([Glorify the name of your Lord, the Most Exalted], he who created and shaped, he who ordained then granted guidance), condensing elevated philosophic teachings' (Corbin, 'Visionary Dream in Islamic Spirituality', p. 402). See also Corbin, *En Islam Iranien*, vol. 4, p. 218.
32. Núrí, *Najm al-tháqib*, pp. 60–1.
33. al-Tabarí al-Saghír, *Dalá'il al-imáma*, p. 441.
34. See for example, al-Há'irí al-Yazdí, *Ilzám al-násib*, vol. 2, p. 28. One exception in this regard is an undated account that describes the Imam dressed as a Persian seminary student with a white turban (!) ' *'alayhi 'ammáma baydá*". Earlier in the same account the Imam is seen with the customary green turban, a sign of his noble lineage. The account is narrated by 'Alí al-Rashtí, one of the students of Murtadá al-Ansárí (d. 1864). See al-Zubaydí, *Qisas al-Imám al-Mahdí*, pp. 271–2.
35. *Bihár al-anwár*, vol. 52, p. 25, n. 17. Originally cited in al-Sadúq, *Kamál al-dín*, p. 407, n. 2.
36. al-Sadúq, *Kamál al-dín*, pp. 468–9. The Báb cites this account in the Tafsír Súrat al-Kawthar, introducing it with the following words: 'The third matter concerns the authority of those who have been honoured with [gazing on] the countenance of the Qá'im during [the period of] his lesser occultation. God [alone] knows their number. I myself will mention one of them in order that it may serve as a remembrance for every longing heart and [a source] of honour for those who enjoy near access to God. Praised be unto God, the Lord of all the worlds' (INBA, vol. 53, p. 303).
37. al-Majlisí, *Bihár al-anwár*, vol. 52, p. 1, n. 1. Originally cited in al-Sadúq, *Kamál al-dín*,

pp. 444–5, n. 18, which has *nutqihi* instead of *mantiqihi*; also cited in al-Túsí's *Kitáb al-ghayba*, p. 253, n. 223. See also Sachedina, *Islamic Messianism*, p. 75. Cf. Ibn 'Arabí's (d. 1240) encounter with a mysterious youth (*fatá*) at the Ka'ba whom he described in his *magnum opus* as being 'of a spiritual essence', endowed 'with lordly attributes', who spoke only in silence (*al-mutakallim al-sámit*). It is this youth that serves as Ibn 'Arabí's inspiration for the composition of his work by telling him: 'O you who search for the path that leads to the secret, Turn back: for the entire secret is within you' (Ibn al-'Arabí, *The Meccan Revelations*, vol. 2, pp. 20–1, 24). Cf. a tale from the Safavid period of the Archangel Gabriel's encounter with a majestic youth, presumed to be 'Alí, on the shores of the Sea of Reality, who proclaims that he is the Mystery of God and initiates Gabriel into the knowledge of 700,000 sciences (Bausani, *Religion in Iran: From Zoroaster to Bahá'u'lláh*, pp. 308–9); and the earliest initiatory dream of Shaykh Ahmad al-Ahsá'í (d. 1826) when he encountered a mysterious youth who taught him the esoteric interpretation of Qur'án 87:2–3 (Corbin, 'Visionary Dream in Islamic Spirituality', p. 402).

38. See Ghaemmaghami, *Numinous Vision, Messianic Encounters: Typological Representations in a Version of the Prophet's hadíth al-ru'yá and in Visions and Dreams of the Hidden Imam*, Forthcoming. The Arab Bahá'í apologist Ál Muhammad interprets the youth that the Prophet saw as a proleptic reference to the appearance of the Báb as a youth (Ál Muhammad, *al-Dalíl wa-al-Irshád*, pp. 124–5). For a Shi'i commentary on this hadith by the prominent Safavid scholar Muhammad Báqir al-Majlisí (d. 1699), see al-Majlisí,'*Sharh Hadíth: Inna Muhammadan Ra'á Rabbahu fí Surat al-Shább al-Muwaffaq*'.

39. See for instance, passages translated from the Qayyúm al-Asmá' in *Selections from the Writings of the Báb*, pp. 50, 54; the Báb's letter to Muhammad Shah discussed in the article by Sholeh Quinn in this volume; and the Súrat al-'Abd of the Qayyúm al-Asmá' translated by Todd Lawson in this volume.

40. See for example, Lawson, 'Reading Reading Itself'. Lawson's gloss of this verse is highly instructive:

> This is a kind of enjambment with verse 21 [of the Sura of the Bees]: *aniqan* rhyming with the above *'amiqan* 'profound' (cf. also line 1 of the *Khutbat al-tatanjiya*). In a hadith of the Prophet, he is quoted as referring to the Qur'an in the following words: 'Its literal meaning (*zahir*) is beautiful (*aniq*) and its hidden meaning (*batin*) is profound (*'amiq*).' Here, then, is yet another example of that apparently inexhaustible and quintessentially Shi'i motif of the Imam as the embodied Qur'an and the Qur'an as the inlibrated Imam. This verse may also be read as a parenthesis, *mashhudan* 'witnessed' (same root as martyr) referring to the *sirr hádhá 'l-Báb* 'the mystery of this Gate' in the above verse. This is an allusion to the proverbial physical beauty of Joseph, which the Báb is said to have shared. The Prophet said: 'God created beauty (*husn*) in a hundred parts and gave Joseph ninety-nine.' It should be noted that in this context physical beauty is a reflection of moral beauty, most dramatically represented in the case of Joseph in the Quranic episode in which he resists (with the assistance of God) the wiles of the Egyptian woman and as a result of which moral athleticism he is unjustly imprisoned.

41. The Báb, *Selections*, p. 173. The phrase *ahsan súra* is not found in the Qur'an but is encountered in a famous hadith ascribed to the Prophet and known as the hadith al-ru'ya (the hadith of the vision):

> The Messenger of God said: I saw my Lord in the most beautiful of forms (*ra'aytu rabbí fí ahsan súra*). He said to me, 'O Muhammad! Do you know what the Concourse on High are disputing about?' I answered, 'I do not know Lord.' And so he put His Hand between my shoulders, and I felt its coolness between my breasts,

and I learned about all that is in heaven and on earth (al-Tabarí 1415/1995, vol. 27, p. 64, n. 2513).

42. See also Nabíl-i-A'zam, *Dawn-Breakers*, p. 512, n. 1.
43. The various hadiths on this theme are presented and discussed by al-Núrí, in *al-Najm al-tháqib*, pp. 643–6.
44. God swears by *al-'asr* (translated as the age or the declining day/afternoon) in the short Meccan sura of the same name, Súrat al-'Asr (Q 103:1). The Báb revealed a commentary on this sura as well. For a discussion, see Lawson, 'The Dangers of Reading', pp. 171–215, esp. pp. 180ff.
45. al-Sadúq, *Kamál al-dín*, p. 656. The full translation of the hadith is provided by Lawson, 'Qur'an Commentary as Sacred Performance', pp. 150–1, n. 17.
46. On the semantic field of *'asr*, see Lane, *Arabic-English Lexicon*, Book 1, p. 2062.
47. Núrí, *Najm al-tháqib*, p. 45. Núrí comments that Abú Turáb means the Lord of the Earth (*sáhib-i khák*). He refers to the famous hadith that identifies the Twelfth Imam as the Lord of the earth referred to in Q 39:69 (For the hadith, see al-Qummí, *Tafsir al-Qummí*, vol. 2, p. 253). See also al-Há'irí, *Ilzám al-násib*, vol. 1, p. 426. al-Há'irí comments that Abú Turáb is one of the Twelfth Imam's titles 'because he is the [divine] educator of the world (*murabbí al-ard*)'.
48. Cf. 'On the eve of the Báb's arrival at Káshán, Hájí Mírzá Jání, surnamed Parpá, a noted resident of that city, dreamed that he was standing at a late hour in the afternoon at the gate of 'Attár, one of the gates of the city, when his eyes suddenly beheld the Báb on horseback wearing, *instead of His customary turban, the kuláh usually worn by the merchants of Persia*. Before Him, as well as behind Him, marched a number of horsemen into whose custody he seemed to have been delivered. As they approached the gate, the Báb saluted him and said: "Hájí Mírzá Jání, We are to be your Guest for three nights. Prepare yourself to receive Us"' (Nabíl, *Dawn-Breakers*, p. 217; emphasis mine).
49. al-Kulayní, *al-Káfí*, vol. 1, p. 489. Also cited in al-Sadúq, '*Uyún akhbár al-Ridá*', vol. 1, p. 162. The Tradition suggests that it was also the custom of the Prophet and 'Alí to wear white turbans.
50. Elmore (trans.), *Islamic Sainthood in the Fullness of Time*, p. 522.
51. However, there are hadiths that suggest that he will appear from the east (of Arabia), that his followers will be Persian, and that his message will be difficult for the Arabs to bear.
52. INBA, vol. 53, p. 184. Cf. vol 53, pp. 194, 195.
53. The Báb, *Sharh súrat yúsuf*, Uncatalogued Bábí Manuscript no. 269, folio 42.
54. The Báb, *The Persian Bayán*, p. 260. Elsewhere, the Báb refers to Fárs as the Abode of Knowledge (*dár al-'ilm*). See *The Persian Bayán*, p. 305. Cf. 'In the country of Fars, there is a Mosque in the centre of which rises a structure similar to the Ka'bih, (Masjid-i-Jum'ih). It was built only as a sign indicating the Manifestation of the Will of God through the erection of the house in that land. (Allusion to the new Mecca, i.e. the house of the Báb in Shíráz.) Blessed be he who worships God in that land; truly we, too, worshipped God there, and prayed for him who had erected that building' ('Le Bayán Persan', vol. 2, p. 151, translation of Nabíl, *Dawn-Breakers*, p. 4 in Périgord, *Translation of the French Footnotes of the Dawn-Breakers*, p. 1).
55. INBA 53: 297–8. All references to INBA 53 are from the Báb's Tafsír Súrat al-Kawthar.
56. One *mithqál* is equivalent to approximately 4.8 grams.
57. al-Kulayní, *al-Káfí*, vol. 1, p. 332, n. 15. Also cited in al-Bahrání (d. 1695), *Madinat al-ma'ájiz*, vol. 8, p. 71, n. 2684; al-Núrí, *Mustadrak al-wasá'il*, vol. 3, p. 241, n. 3482; vol. 8, p. 49, n. 9046; al-Há'irí al-Yazdí, *Ilzám al-násib*, vol. 1, p. 340 (account 14).
58. On *taqiyya* in the Báb's early writings as a mechanism for guarding the secret of his message, see J. Vahid Brown's article in the present volume.

59. Borrowed from pre-Islamic Iranian traditions, Mount Qáf is the name given in some Muslim cosmological texts to a mountain range that surrounds the earth and marks the end of the world. According to certain descriptions, the mountain is made of green emerald. In Faríd al-Dín 'Attár (d. 1221), *Mantiq al-tayr*, Mount Qáf is the home of the mythical king of the birds, the Símurgh. See Streck and Miguel, 'Káf', *EI2*, vol. 4, p. 400. In one of Shaháb al-Dín al-Suhrawardí's (d. 1187) initiatory tales, Mount Qáf is the home and origin of another youth of unsurpassed beauty who initiates the wayfarer to his true identity:

> At the beginning of the tale that Sohravardí entitled 'The Crimson Archangel', the captive, who has just escaped the surveillance of his jailers, that is, has temporarily left the world of sensory experience, finds himself in the desert in the presence of a being whom he asks, since he sees in him all the charms of adolescence, 'O Youth! Where do you come from?' He receives this reply: 'What? I am the first-born of the children of the Creator . . . and you call me a youth . . . I come from beyond the mountain of Qáf . . . It is there that you were yourself at the beginning, and it is there that you will return when you are finally rid of your bonds' (Corbin 1995, p. 3. Cf. Corbin 2003, pp. 139–40).

60. In this tradition, Músá al-Kázim initiates a Christian monk in the knowledge of four concealed letters. al-Kázim then adverts to four other unnamed letters that have not been revealed. When asked who will interpret these, the Imam responds, 'That will be our Qá'im (*dhálika qá'imuná*). God will reveal [them] to him and he will elucidate them (*fa-yunzil Alláh 'alayhi fa-yufassiruhá*). He will reveal to him what has never been revealed to the righteous, the Messengers, and the rightly guided (*wa-yunzil 'alayhi má lam yunzil 'alá al-siddiqín wa-al-rusul wa-al-muhtadín*)' (al-Kulayní, *al-Káfí*, vol. 1, p. 483. Also cited in al-Bahrání, *Madinat al-ma'ájiz*, vol. 6, p. 309, n. 2024; al-Majlisí, *Bihár al-anwár*, vol. 48, p. 95; al-Isfahání, *Mikyál al-makárim*, vol. 1, p. 86). This intriguing hadith suggests not only that the Qá'im will receive the revelation of previously unrevealed knowledge but that his station may in some respects be epistemologically higher than even the Messengers of the past since this knowledge has not been revealed to any of them. This Tradition is similar to a hadith attributed to Ja'far al-Sádiq: 'Knowledge is twenty-seven letters. All that the Messengers have brought is two letters thereof (*fa-jamí' má já'at bihi al-rusul harfán*). Until this day humanity has not known more than these two letters. But when our Qá'im appears, he will cause the remaining twenty-five letters to be made manifest and will spread them among the people (*fa-baththahá fí al-nás*). He will adjoin the two [previous] letters to them so that he may propagate them [together] as twenty-seven letters' (al-Majlisí, *Bihár al-anwár*, vol. 52, p. 336, n. 73). al-Majlisí identifies his source for this hadith as Qutb al-Din al-Ráwandí's (d. 1177) *al-Khará'ij wa-al-jará'ih* but in this work the Tradition is worded slightly differently: 'Knowledge is [composed of] twenty-seven parts (*juz'án*). All that the Messengers have brought is two parts thereof. Until this day, humanity has not known more than these two parts. But when our Qá'im appears, he will cause the remaining twenty-five parts to be made manifest and will spread them among the people. He will add the two parts to [the twenty-five parts] and propagate them [together] as twenty-seven parts' (al-Ráwandí 1988, vol. 2, p. 842, n. 59). The hadith is also referred to by Bahá'u'lláh in *Kitáb-i-Íqán* (Persian edition), pp. 161–2. Cf. Fadl Alláh Astarábádí (d. 1398), the founder of Hurúfism, who declared that the four letters were the four additional letters found in the Persian version of the Arabic language which he had been invested with (Muhammad having been given only twenty-eight).

12

Phenomenology of Occultation and Prayer in the Báb's *Sahífiy-i Ja'faríyyih*

Nader Saiedi

Although Sahífiy-i Ja'faríyyih is frequently mentioned as one of the writings of the Báb, its conceptual framework is rarely, if ever, subject to scholarly analysis. Instead, when this work of the Báb is approached it is normally defined in terms of a chaotic list of fragmented issues that are addressed in the text. However, the overall logic, harmony or unity of the work is never investigated. In fact it appears that the readers of Sahífiy-i Ja'faríyyih assume that there is no overall logical order and conceptual unity present in the text. This assumption, however, is mistaken. In fact, one of the most amazing points about this text of the Báb is the incredible conceptual unity and harmony of the entire work. No issue discussed in the text is random, fragmented or accidental. All issues are interconnected in the context of a harmonious totality that defines the structure of the text. What I just mentioned about Sahífiy-i Ja'faríyyih is in reality applicable to all the writings of the Báb. Existing scholarship on the writings of the Báb usually misses the creative unity in his writings. I will not address other works of the Báb in this article but will treat Sahífiy-i Ja'faríyyih as an example of this phenomenon.

Before discussing the conceptual framework and message of Sahífiy-i Ja'faríyyih, it is necessary to give basic information about the text and clear out some common mistakes in the literature.

Three titles of the text and the date of its revelation

This text of the Báb is called by different names. Its given title is Sharh-i-Du'á'-i-Ghaybat or Commentary on the Occultation Prayer. The entire text is an interpretation of a prayer that is attributed to Imam Sádiq, which is expected to be read by the believers during the time of the occultation of the Hidden Imam. The prayer is short and consists of three statements. The Báb's Commentary on the Occultation Prayer consists of 14 chapters but only chapters 11, 12 and 13 are devoted to a direct interpretation of each one of the three parts of the prayer. The reader who neglects the holistic conceptual framework of the tablet may be puzzled by this sequence. Why does it deal with its object of commentary only in those three chapters? What is the relation between all the other issues discussed in the first ten chapters and those three chapters?

The other name of the text is Sahífiy-i Ja'faríyyih. In his work Khutbiy-i-Dhikríyyih (Recounting/Remembering Epistle), revealed on 15 Muharram 1262 (13 January 1846), the Báb presents a list of his works up to the day of the writing of that text. The Báb lists 14 works written during the years 1260 to 1262, comprising four major books (*kitáb*) and ten shorter ones, or epistles (*sahífih*). He implies that these 14 texts are written by the 14 sacred figures of Shi'i Islam (the Prophet Muhammad, his daughter Fátimih, and the 12 Imams). Khutbiy-i-Dhikríyyih (together with his earlier work Kitábu'l-Fihrist) is crucial for identifying the date of the writing of various early works of the Báb. The Báb first lists his four books and then his ten epistles. The fourth epistle is the Sahífiy-i Ja'faríyyih, the Epistle of Imam Ja'far-i-Sádiq, the sixth Imam. The Báb explains that this text is a commentary on the occultation prayer that is to be recited during the days of the occultation of the Twelfth Imam. He mentions that it consists of 14 chapters: 'Eighth is the Sahífiy-Ja'faríyyih which consisteth of 14 chapters on the interpretation of his prayer concerning the days of occultation (The Báb, Khutbiy-i-Dhikríyyih, quoted in Mázandarání 1944, vol. 3, p. 290). The fact that the Báb identifies the commentary on the prayer revealed by the sixth Imam as the epistle of that same Imam points to a subtle mystical point that is present in much of his early writings: the interpreting text is the same as the interpreted text and the Báb is the same as the author of the prayer. This is a reference to the station of the heart, a transcendental epistemological perspective which goes beyond the apparent pluralities and focuses on the identical truth of all beings.

The other title of the text is the Tafsír-i-Há' or Commentary on the Letter *Há'*. This title is normally associated with two other works of the Báb. Denis MacEoin calls them Tafsír al-Há' I and Tafsír al-Há' II (MacEoin 1992, p. 72). Although these two texts are explicitly defined as interpretations of the letter *há'* (the second is in fact the interpretation of the Mystery of the Letter *Há'*), the same Persian or Arabic term is used for denoting Sahífiy-i Ja'faríyyih. This designation is made by Bahá'u'lláh, who quotes from Sahífiy-i Ja'faríyyih in his Kitáb-i-Íqán. This is what Bahá'u'lláh writes:

> Likewise, in His interpretation of the letter 'Há', He craved martyrdom, saying: 'Methinks I heard a Voice calling in my inmost being: "Do thou sacrifice the thing which Thou lovest most in the path of God, even as Husayn, peace be upon him, hath offered up his life for My sake." And were I not regardful of this inevitable mystery, by Him, Who hath my being between His hands even if all the kings of the earth were to be leagued together they would be powerless to take from me a single letter, how much less can these servants who are worthy of no attention, and who verily are of the outcast . . . That all may know the degree of My patience, My resignation, and self-sacrifice in the path of God' (Bahá'u'lláh 1989, pp. 231–2).

It is a most interesting question why Bahá'u'lláh calls this text of the Báb The Interpretation of the Letter *Há'*. We will see that Bahá'u'lláh's description is related to the hidden essence of the text. However, there are many misunderstandings with regard to Sahífiy-i Ja'faríyyih. One of these confusions is present in the work of the great scholar Ishraq Khavari. In his *Qámús-i Íqán*, volume one, under the title Tafsír al-Ha' (in reference to the statement of Bahá'u'lláh quoted above), Ishraq Khavari describes the content of the text and quotes several pages from different chapters of Sahífiy-i Ja'faríyyih. He explains that this work of the Báb is called Interpretation of the Letter *Há'* because it is a response to a letter written by a questioner whose letter began with the words *'Hádhá Kitábí . . .'* (This is my letter . . .). Since the first word of this letter was the letter *há'*, therefore the Báb wrote this text as an interpretation of the letter *há'*. Ishraq Khavari adds that this point is mentioned in the text of the Báb itself (Ishraq Khavari 1972, vol. 1, pp. 439–44). However, nowhere in this text of the Báb is such a point mentioned. It seems that Ishraq Khavari has confused this text of the Báb with another of his works called by the same name, Commentary on the Letter *Há'* (what MacEoin calls Tafsír al-Há' I). But Ishraq Khavari's description is not even entirely correct in terms of that work. In that work the Báb explains that since the questioner begins his letter with the words *Huva'l-'Azíz* (He is the sovereign), therefore the Báb answers all the questions of the questioner by interpreting the first alphabetical letter in his missive (The Báb, Commentary on the Letter *Há'*, INBA 86, pp. 109–10). It is clear that Ishraq Khavari is referring to this text of the Báb, yet he has substituted the words *'Hádhá Kitábí'* for the words *'Huva'l-'Azíz'*. In any case these are two different works of the Báb but both are interpretations of the letter *há'*.

Other confusions in regard to Sahífiy-i Ja'faríyyih can be found in the works of Denis MacEoin. In discussing the Báb's Lawh-i Hurúfát (Tablet of Letters) or Kitáb al-Hayákil, MacEoin refers to a tablet of Bahá'u'lláh in which the Tablet of Hurúfát is called by the name Ja'faríyyih. Then MacEoin, referring to the other work of the Báb, Sahífiy-i Ja'faríyyih, writes:

> The *Sahífa-yi Ja'fariyyah* mentioned (and treated as a different work to the *Lawh-i huráfát*) by Shoghi Effendi in his rather spurious list of the Báb's 'best-known works' is not, as might at first sight appear, this same work under yet another title, but the treatise of that name already discussed in chapter two. How this piece comes to be regarded as one of the Báb's best-known works must remain a mystery (MacEoin 1992, pp. 89–90).

However, these statements need to be reexamined. First, it is not Risáliy-i Ja'faríyyih that is mentioned by Bahá'u'lláh in reference to Kitáb-i-Hayákil or the Book of 19 Temples (the Tablet of Letters), but Risáliy-i Jafríyyih, namely the Book of Numerology. The fact that the Tablet of 19 Temples discusses numerological constructions is well known but this same fact is also explicitly mentioned several times in the tablet itself.[1] Second, MacEoin criticizes Shoghi Effendi for considering Sahífiy-i Ja'faríyyih one of the well-known works of the Báb. But the reason why Shoghi Effendi has identified it as one of the Báb's best-known works is not a mystery. First, a number of pages of this particular tablet were translated, discussed and published in Nicolas's introduction to his French translation of the Persian Bayán (Nicolas 1908, pp. 17–25). This becomes even more relevant when we see that Shoghi Effendi quotes in *The Dawn-Breakers*, whose appendix lists the names of the best-known works of the Báb, passages from Nicolas's French translation of that same text. Yet another reason for the assertion of Shoghi Effendi is, as we saw before, the reference of Bahá'u'lláh to this same Sahífiy-i Ja'faríyyih in his Book of Certitude when he quotes a well-known statement from that text.

A more direct discussion of Sahífiy-i Ja'faríyyih is found on pages 66 and 67 of MacEoin's *The Sources for Early Bábi Doctrine and History*. According to MacEoin, Sahífiy-i Ja'faríyyih was revealed during Muharram of the year 1261, while he was in Arabia. He argues that 'several passages are stated in the text to have been composed on various days in the month of Muharram, the year being given as 1261' (MacEoin 1992, p. 67). Yet MacEoin recognizes it as a problem that several parts of the text, including the very first chapter, explicitly discuss events that took place after the Báb's return to Shiraz. However, all these confusions are due to a simple error on the part of MacEoin. The date of the revelation of Sahífiy-i Ja'faríyyih is Muharram 1262, not 1261. The reason MacEoin has assumed that the text is written in 1261 is a number of references to Muharram 61 and Muharram 1261 in the Báb's work. Yet those passages deal with very different questions. The reference to Muharram 61 is not a reference to the date of the revelation of the text but is rather a reference to the date of the martyrdom of Imam Husayn. Reference to the year 1261 is in the context of the discussion of the return of Husayn as the Báb, arguing that the spiritual martyrdom of the Báb *after* the year 1261 is the return of the physical martyrdom of Husayn. Thus the Báb says that after the completion of 12 centuries and the termination of the age of the outward meanings, it is in the year *after* the year 1261 – that is, in 1262 – that the tenth of Muharram, the time of the revelation of that passage, becomes also a Friday, a return of the martyrdom of Husayn in Muharram 61.

This is what the Báb says:

Verily the martyrdom of Husayn occurred not in this world save for the manifestation of the guardianship of the family of God, the certitude of their Shi'i followers regarding the pure truth of the Imams, and the enduring of the religion of Muhammad until the day when there is a blast on the trumpet and this mighty Cause. Thus it is necessary, according to divine wisdom, that Husayn's martyrdom would take place in the year 61 AH on Friday the tenth of the month of Muharram for many reasons . . .

Thus according to that subtle and snow-white cord it is necessary that the bearer of that Most Great Name, one of the Shi'i of the Imams, should be afflicted with their affliction within a year that is similar to the year of the martyrdom of Husayn in 61. Thus the 10th of Muharram, the day of the martyrdom of Husayn, became in this year [1262], after that year [1261], a Friday, that those endued with understanding may recognize that verily that which is there will not be known except through that which is here.

The secret of this matter is this: Verily after the completion of the letters 'There is none other God save God' in the perfect year which is 1200, and *after* the year 61, corresponding to the martyrdom of Husayn, it is necessary that the bearer of that Most Great Name of God would be wronged in this life by the oppression of the unjust . . .

> Thus bear thou witness that *at this moment, alone by myself in this house, my abode*, I speak in the station of the inward of the inward of that which was spoken by the prince of martyrs in this same day in the station of inward of the outward . . . Thus in regard to afflictions, I am inwardly as Husayn was outwardly. This is out of the covenant God made with me that my situation should resemble that of Husayn (The Báb, Sahífiy-i Ja'faríyyih, INBA 60, pp. 116–17; emphasis mine).

Thus as the Báb is sitting alone in his house in Shiraz, under house arrest, his heart is being martyred, just as the body of Husayn was martyred on that same day, the tenth of Muharram. The physical martyrdom of Husayn took place in the year 61. Thus when the 'age of outward' is ended and the 'age of the heart' begins, the martyrdom of the Báb as the return of the martyrdom of Husayn takes place *after* the year 1261. In 1262 the tenth of Muharram also happened to be a Friday, just as the tenth of Muharram of 61 was a Friday.

This is why MacEoin's other assertion that in Sahífiy-i-Ja'faríyyih the Báb refers to a dream he had on 12 Muharram 1261 is equally incorrect. That dream took place on the eve of the second of Muharram (and not 12) of the year 1262.

The Báb refers to Sahífiy-i Ja'faríyyih as one of his texts in his work Khutbiy-i Dhikríyyih. We know the exact date of the revelation of the latter text because it is referred to in the text itself: 15 Muharram 1262 (13 January 1846). Sahífiy-i Ja'faríyyih was revealed in the few days prior to the revelation of Khutbiy-i Dhikríyyih, during the first two weeks of the month of Muharram 1262. Likewise, in his Epistle of Justice, revealed in early 1262, the Báb refers the readers to his discussion of the question of resurrection in Sahífiy-i Ja'faríyyih (The Báb, The Epistle of Justice, p. 34). It is also necessary to note that in Sahífiy-i Ja'faríyyih the Báb affirms that he has revealed four books and ten epistles, a fact that shows that this text was revealed just before the revelation of Khutbiy-i Dhikríyyih, which lists those same 14 texts (The Báb, Sahífiy-i Ja'faríyyih, INBA 60, p. 119). Finally it is noteworthy that the text of Sahífiy-i Ja'faríyyih *begins* with a prayer in which the Báb complains of his house arrest in Shiraz and then recounts the story of his afflictions after his return from the trip to Arabia (ibid. pp. 59–60). None of these could have happened in Muharram of 1261 when the Báb was still in Arabia. There is absolutely no reason to assume that any part of the text was written in Muharram 1261. The entire text was revealed in the first two weeks within the month of Muharram 1262.

Aside from these confusions, it is a lack of attention to the overall conceptual framework of the text and the creative interpretation of occultation and prayer offered by the Báb that is missing in existing descriptions of the text. In what follows I try to address the central theme of the text.

The real meaning of occultation and prayer

Both Nicolas and MacEoin find Sahífiy-i Ja'faríyyih of primary interest in relation to the early claims of the Báb, his apparent negation of any station for himself in some of his earlier writings and his reference to his expressing the 'word of negation after that of affirmation' for the sake of wisdom (ibid. p. 60). Yet neither of these authors has noted the immense insights that are provided within that text in relation to this same question. In this short paper I will not address that specific question. Yet the Báb's interpretation of the twin concepts of the occultation of the Imam and prayer during the times of occultation is one of the ways that Sahífiy-i Ja'faríyyih clarifies the nature of the Báb's early claims, his use of wisdom and his true station.

The entire text, as we shall see, is an interpretation of the occultation prayer. It is evident that this issue is directly related to the apparent claim of the Báb in his early writings that he is the gate to the Hidden Imam during the latter's occultation. Thus the interpretation of the meaning of occultation and prayer, intended for realizing the advent of the Imam, is directly relevant for understanding the meaning of his own words regarding his true claims. In chapter 2 the Báb addresses the addressee of the tablet and mentions that he has read the book Sanábarq written by Mullá Ja'far Kashfí, the father of Siyyid Yahyá Dárabí, surnamed Vahíd. He refers to the interpretation offered by Mullá Ja'far concerning the 'prayer that hath dawned from the holy direction' and his discussion of the station of the Imams. I believe that it is likely that the prayer interpreted in Sanábarq is the same occultation prayer that is revealed by the sixth Imam (whose name is the same as that of Mullá Ja'far). It is probable that the questioner asked the Báb about this prayer and Mullá Ja'far's interpretation and had asked the Báb to interpret the prayer as well as to clarify his own station. However, I have not yet found a copy of Sanábarq and cannot be certain of this possibility. The Báb argues that what the author of Sanábarq has said with regard to the station of the Imams is simply inadequate to describe their lofty station and that all his descriptions are merely descriptions of the author's own self. Yet the Báb praises the attempt by Mullá Ja'far. The next chapter is an introduction to the interpretation of the occultation prayer, discussing the idea of prayer as *asking* a favour from God.

It is in chapter 4 that the Báb undertakes the discussion of the occultation prayer. He affirms that this prayer is found in Kitáb-i Káfí and quotes the tradition. According to this tradition Imam Ja'far speaks about the Hidden Imam who will undergo occultation. The Báb then reveals a prayer that is supposed to be read by the believers during the time of the occultation of the awaited Imam. The prayer has three parts and is as follows:

> O my God! Make known to me thy self, for shouldst thou enable me not to recognize thy self, I would not be able to recognize thy Prophet.
>
> O my God! Make known to me thine Apostle, for shouldst Thou enable me not to recognize thine Apostle, I would not be able to recognize thy testimony.
>
> O my God! Make known to me thy testimony, for shouldst thou enable me not to recognize thy testimony I would stray from my religion.

It is necessary to mention that in the last chapter of the text, the Báb himself adds a fourth part to the above prayer and argues that the previous parts would not be acceptable without it. This fourth part affirms the station of gatehood. This is the fourth part:

> O my God! Make known to me the gate to thy testimony, for shouldst thou enable

me not to recognize the gate to thy testimony I would stray from my religion (ibid. p. 148).

Although it is only in chapters 11, 12 and 13 that the three parts of the prayer are directly interpreted, all the chapters following chapter 4 are systematic discourses on the interpretation of the prayer. Before discussing how this is the case we need to investigate the essence of such interpretation that is already offered in chapter 4.

In dealing with the prayer, the Báb engages in a radical reinterpretation of the concept of occultation and prayer. Thus the occultation of the Hidden Imam refers not to a specific historical event, rather it is an existential description of the human situation. Similarly, the prayer that is to be read during the time of occultation is a description of the universal dynamics of the process of a spiritual journey. The Báb explains that in his primordial act of creation God has created humans perfect and self-sufficient. This perfection is the result of the fact that God has enshrined the sign of his own revelation within the heart of humans. This sign of divinity is nothing other than human 'existence' (*vujúd*), which is the direction of divine revelation in the created world. In addition to this existence, humans possess a specific 'essence', quidity, or determination (*máhíyyat*). This unity of essence and existence defines the station of perfect servitude, where one's essence is annihilated and only the direction of the divine sign within one's heart is manifest. Thus in their original station, humans are defined by the direction of divinity within their own being and nothing is seen in them except the revelation of God and his attributes. In such a situation humans are not alienated from their true reality and origin, which is the sign of divinity enshrined within their hearts. According to the Báb in this primordial situation humans transcend any dependence on others and have no need to ask from anyone anything. In this station of divinity 'prayer', namely calling unto one other than oneself, is meaningless and unnecessary. Prayer pertains to the situation of remoteness, imperfection and need. Yet in the original situation, where it is the divinity of humans that is sovereign, none of these categories are allowed. Thus in this primordial station of the human situation asking questions or calling to anyone is absolutely forbidden. In fact, asking for anything is an unforgivable sin. That is why chapter 3 of the text, which is an introductory preparation for an interpretation of the occultation prayer, is entirely devoted to an analysis of such a sin. The same point is again emphasized in chapter 4 in the context of a substantive interpretation of the prayer. In chapter 3, discussing the issue of asking questions in general, the Báb writes:

> Chapter 3 on a divine and sublime introduction: Verily I seek in this chapter to discuss the principles of all knowledge . . . The path to God through knowledge of his eternity is barred, and he, in his truth, is not known by anyone save himself. Thus it is mentioned in the tradition that verily all sins committed by the faithful may be forgiven by God except the sin of asking, which shall never be forgiven. For God, glorified be he, hath made the faithful a partner with his own self, as in his words: 'Glory is for God and for his Apostle and for the faithful' (ibid. p. 66; the verse quoted is Q 63:8).

In chapter 3 the Báb emphasizes that for the people of inner truth there is no interest in any question that concerns anything other than the essence of God and such questioning is an unforgivable transgression since there is no path to such knowledge. Furthermore, since the essence of God is inaccessible, any such question would be directed to the created realm. But no such dependence and debasement is allowed. But in chapter 4 the Báb discusses the same point in a more specific way. He tells us that because humans in their primordial station of existence are created partners with God there can be no question and no calling (prayer) addressed to either God or any created being. He writes:

> Chapter 4 on the description of the Prayer for the Days of Occultation: I now seek to interpret the prayer that Imam Sádiq commanded to be recited during the days of occultation . . .
> O thou who gazest on the effects of glory! Know thou first of the truth, that verily God, glorified be he, hath not created anything save he hath made it with utmost perfection according to his power. Had it been otherwise, his artifact would not have been perfect and thus would not have been worthy of attribution by God to himself. When thou recognizest this reality and beholdest its mystery by thy truth, thou wouldst recognize that verily in the primordial station of its existence no being is in need of anything, that it then may supplicate unto God its Lord for its sake. Nay rather, God hath created all beings as it behoveth his glory (ibid. pp. 68–70).

Thus at this stage there can be no 'prayer' since there is no 'absence' and no 'occultation'. Yet the concept of prayer becomes possible and a duty when there is alienation of one's true reality. This means that the truth of one's being, the direction of divinity, is forgotten and one is revolving around one's own essence or specific determination. In this situation one needs to return to one's original true existence and thus needs to call to God, to engage in prayer and supplication and beseech the Lord for attainment of the truth of one's self. At this time, therefore, reciting prayer becomes a duty of human beings. Thus in chapter 4 the Báb explains:

> But when one turneth away from one's true station, in such manner that one falsifieth one's identity and suffereth dependence on all things, God then enjoineth upon him the duty of prayer for the sake of his emancipation. Thus it is revealed in his book: 'but those who are too proud for my worship shall soon enter hell abased' (Q 40:60). And it is forbidden unto him in this station to ask from anyone save God (The Báb, Sahífiy-i Ja'faríyyih, INBA 60, p. 70).

Thus the concept of prayer – calling and making a request – becomes meaningful within the existential station of self-alienation and enslavement to one's particularistic self or essence. In this station of occultation of the Imam it is necessary to engage in a relation of request addressed to a being other than one's self. But this other must only be God and such asking should only be directed to the Lord. Thus recitation of the occultation prayer becomes a duty of the faithful in the days of occultation. It is clear that occultation or absence of the Imam is in fact the state of forgetfulness of one's original truth, the alienation from one's true self, which is nothing other than one's existence. This true self is the state of the divinity of human beings, the sign of divinity that is enshrined within their hearts. Thus the Báb is speaking of the dialectics of self-consciousness that has to be attained after one's alienation from one's true self and station. The truth of one's being is ultimately a spiritual reality, the revelation of God within one's being. But it is the fall from this state of perfection and unity that separates humans from all others and imprisons them within the realm of pluralities and phenomenal selves. It is thus necessary that such state of unconsciousness and unfreedom be overcome through a spiritual journey which attempts to realize one's true reality. Prayer to God becomes the dynamics of such journey.

The verse of the Qur'an that is quoted by the Báb in the above passage follows the divine command for prayer: 'And thy Lord sayest: "Call on me; I will answer your prayer."' The real meaning of hell and paradise is also obvious from this same Quranic verse. First God commands humans to pray to him and then he says that those who are too proud to worship him will enter hell abased. One can see that in the interpretation of the Báb, hell is the station of self-alienation and non-recognition of one's true reality while heaven is the realization of one's true self. This point is emphasized in various writings of the Báb, both earlier and later.

The Báb explains why calling to any one save God is forbidden. In chapter 4 he again refers to the Islamic tradition which states that all sins may be forgiven except asking, since according to the Qur'an, glory belongs to God, his Apostle and the believers (Q 63:8). Then he writes:

> Verily the faithful is far more exalted than can be described and he is far more glorious than to have to beg and ask, and it is not worthy of his station to be debased and humiliated. Nay rather, he hath ever been and will continue forever to be glorious by virtue of the glory of God. Therefore what sin could be more grievous for him than asking, and what transgression could exceed that debasement? He who beholdeth the mystery of the highest end will indeed cast into oblivion his existence by virtue of such asking . . . Verily among the humans, with all their poverty and weakness, should one's slave asketh anyone other than his master for anything, this, in the sight of people, would hurt his honour and bring shame to him. Then how much more disgraceful such asking would be for God, glorified be he, with his absolute might, wealth, glory and generosity! (The Báb, Sahífiy-i Ja'faríyyih, INBA 60, p. 71)

Thus prayer and asking is forbidden to be directed to anyone except God. The purpose of this prayer is to return man to his true reality, his existence, the direction of divine revelation within his heart. Asking anyone else results in the opposite, where one is further alienated from his existence and glory. The purpose of prayer, therefore, is to realize the true station of servitude when nothing is seen in oneself except the divinity of the Lord. This is the stage of true self-realization and self-consciousness. At this stage man is God, except that man is man and God is God. Such prayer, therefore, is qualitatively different from any other prayer. As we can see, already in chapter 4 the Báb is interpreting the idea of occultation of the Imam and the need for prayer at such time in terms of the dialectics of the arc of descent and the arc of ascent. It is the universal human condition that is symbolized by the twin concepts of the Imam's occultation and the duty to engage in prayer at such times. As we will see, the fundamental claim of the Báb is directly related to this inner meaning of occultation and prayer. He is the objective realization of such a stage of true servitude, the integration of servitude and divinity, the station of absolute and universal gatehood. Attaining true self-recognition is identical with recognition of the Báb. He is the fulfilment of all recognitions: the recognition of God and the recognition of the sign of divinity within one's heart. Although the station of the Báb can also be expressed in terms of the story of the occultation of the Hidden Imam, such description is only a token expression of his true station.

Yet one does not call on God to receive material possessions or various worldly favours. This prayer requires a particular mode of orientation of human being to God, which presupposes a specific gaze of unity. This is a prayer for recognition of one's true self, which is the recognition of God and his revelation. This principle defines the harmonious order of the text of the Báb.

The order of the text

Although the Báb identifies the essence of his interpretation of the occultation prayer in chapter 4, the entire text is the elaboration of such interpretation. Readers of Sahífiy-i Ja'faríyyih are usually bewildered by the fact that it is only in chapters 11, 12 and 13 that the Báb addresses the three parts of the prayer. In between chapter 4 and chapter 11 are six chapters in which apparently no direct discussion of the occultation prayer takes place. In addition, the reader is usually puzzled by the relationship of these discussions. The truth, however, is that all the chapters of the text are direct interpretations of the occultation prayer. Given the mystical interpretation that the Báb offers for the concepts of both occultation and prayer, it is evident that such prayer could not be a mere ritualistic attempt to influence divine Will for various utilitarian favours. This is a prayer in the station of the heart, with the gaze of unity, and aims to recognize God and his signs within. At the end of chapter 4, therefore, the Báb states that for such prayer and request to be granted it is necessary that the one who engages in such prayer recognize various spiritual principles, without which his prayer will not be granted. But if one fulfils all these conditions then God will definitely grant his prayer. The next six chapters are in fact a detailed discussion of these principles. Therefore, chapters 5 to 10 are devoted to the discussion of these prerequisites of the prayer. It is only after such a discussion that the Báb then directly discusses the content of the occultation prayer in the subsequent three chapters. The concluding chapter is a mirror expression of the previous ones. Thus chapter 14 is devoted to negation of the letters of negation, an affirmation of the fact that prayer and asking should only be directed to God and to none other than God. Thus at the end of chapter 4 the Báb writes:

> Know thou that it is incumbent upon one who engageth in prayer, first recognition of his Lord, then recognition of his attributes, then recognition of the names of his self, then of his object of search, then of his end . . . When thou hast attained these stations it is irrevocable that God shall grant thy prayer (ibid. pp. 71–2).

One reason for the bewilderment of the readers is that the apparent titles of chapters 5 and 6 do not relate to the first two preconditions that are listed in chapter 4. Yet chapters 5 and 6 are explicitly devoted to those two preconditions. Hence chapter 5 pertains to the question of recognition of God and his essence while chapter 6 is a discussion of God's attributes. Chapter 7 discusses God's names, chapter 8 the divine signs, chapter 9 one's true objects of desire, and chapter 10 one's true end and return. In this short paper I will not address the details of these chapters. But they are all an affirmation of the true meaning of both occultation and prayer as the binary oppositions of the human situation. For example, the entirety of chapter 9 is an affirmation of the fact that in the act of prayer the favour sought and the object desired are none other than the attainment of self-consciousness and regaining one's true reality, the mystical union with the sign of God within.

It is noteworthy that the essence of the interpretation of the concepts of occultation and prayer is also the essence of the following words of Bahá'u'lláh:

O SON OF BEING! With the hands of power I made thee and with the fingers of strength I created thee; and within thee have I placed the essence of My light. Be thou content with it and seek naught else, for My work is perfect and My command is binding. Question it not, nor have a doubt thereof.[2]

O SON OF SPIRIT! I created thee rich, why dost thou bring thyself down to poverty? Noble I made thee, wherewith dost thou abase thyself? Out of the essence of knowledge I gave thee being, why seekest thou enlightenment from anyone beside Me? Out of the clay of love I moulded thee, how dost thou busy thyself with another? Turn thy sight unto thyself, that thou mayest find Me standing within thee, mighty, powerful and self-subsisting.[3]

O SON OF MAN! Thou art My dominion and My dominion perisheth not; wherefore fearest thou thy perishing? Thou art My light and My light shall never be extinguished; why dost thou dread extinction? Thou art My glory and My glory fadeth not; thou art My robe and My robe shall never be outworn. Abide then in thy love for Me, that thou mayest find Me in the realm of glory.[4]

O SON OF UTTERANCE! Turn thy face unto Mine and renounce all save Me; for My sovereignty endureth and My dominion perisheth not. If thou seekest another than Me, yea, if thou searchest the universe for evermore, thy quest will be in vain.[5]

Sahífiy-i Ja'faríyyih as the interpretation of the letter *há'*

As we saw, Bahá'u'lláh calls Sahífiy-i Ja'faríyyih by the title The Interpretation of the letter *Há'*. It is time to see how this title relates to this work of the Báb.

In the beginning of this discussion I referred to a confusion in Ishraq Khavari's description of Sahífiy-i Ja'faríyyih. Since Bahá'u'lláh has called this text The Interpretation of the Letter *Há'*, Ishraq Khavari seems to have confused this work of the Báb with the other work that is called by that same Persian title. However, I will call the other tablet (called by MacEoin Tafsir al-Ha' I) by the name Commentary on the Letter *Há'*.

The reason the Báb engages in interpretation of the letter *há'* in the Commentary on the Letter *Há'* is directly relevant for understanding the fact that Sahífiy-i Ja'faríyyih is also an interpretation of the letter *há'*. The Commentary on the Letter Há, a work of about 45 pages revealed a few months after the revelation of Sahífiy-i Ja'faríyyih, is universally believed to have been written in honour of Siyyid Yahyá Dárábí, surnamed Vahíd. But this is certainly inaccurate. The addressee is Abu'l-Hasani'l-Husayní, a prominent notable of Shiraz. In his letter to the Báb, Husayní wrote: 'He is the sovereign. O my master! Favour me by lifting the veil from the countenance of the Cause, as you will.' The Báb grants his wish. He pierces the veils and reveals the truth through a medium of his choice. He finds the words of Husayní similar to the words of Kumayl, who asked for the unveiling of the truth. Thus the Báb begins his work by referring to Kumayl's tradition (The Báb, Commentary on the Letter *Há'*, INBA 86, p. 101). The Báb argues that one who has attained the vision of the heart can see the divine truth shining in all things. Then such a person can unveil the mystery of all reality through anything he chooses. As a demonstration of this fact, he chooses the first letter of the words of Husayní and shows that it, like everything else, contains the entire reflection of the truth. Husayní's letter began with the word 'He' (*Huva*), commencing with the Arabic letter *há'*. The rest of the work is an unveiling of truth through a discourse on the letter *há'* (ibid. pp. 109–10).

The reason that the Báb chooses to unveil the truth by interpreting the first letter of Husayní's missive is not random. He is affirming a profound spiritual truth through his choice. Referring to Kumayl's tradition, the Báb argues that the recognition of truth is the recognition of God. But recognition of God is impossible. He therefore discusses the transcendence of the divine Essence beyond any attribute, any association with any contingent being and any relation of causation. Thus the recognition of truth becomes the recognition not of the Essence of God but of the revelation of God within the world. The truth of all beings, including the truth of one's own true self, is none other than the divine revelation enshrined within. Thus true recognition of the countenance of the beloved is the same as the recognition of the sign of God within one's own being. The Báb wants Husayní to recognize that within his own being he can see the answer to his question. Therefore, even in the very first letter of the word uttered by Husayní the answer to all his questions is present. The Báb writes:

> Verily the mystery of truth that is mentioned in the sacred traditions, whose knowledge distinguishes the truly learned, is an originated and created sign. God hath shed upon it, and through it, the splendours of his revelation and hath ordained it to be a sign of his own self, that all that is possible to exist out of the grace of God may vibrate, by its aid, towards his recognition and attain, by its aid, unto his truth. It is an originated sign . . . the sign of thy truth, the truth of thy being . . . Verily the first letter of thy letter is the letter *há'* and I now refer unto its true meaning that which God hath ordained for me to reveal (ibid. pp. 108–9).

This same point, as we have seen, is the essence of the interpretation offered by the Báb in his Sahífíy-i Ja'faríyyih. The interpretation of the letter *há'* in the Commentary on the Letter *Há'* affirms the mystical nature of human reality. Similarly, according to Sahífíy-i Ja'faríyyih, humans are the sign of divinity and they contain within themselves the ultimate truth, namely the revelation of God within their hearts. A state of self-alienation results from forgetting this fundamental truth. The answer to all questions is already present within the reality of the questioner. Truth is the nearest thing to humans, though humans are not aware of it. This state of forgetfulness is the same as the state of occultation. The reality of the Hidden Imam is present but is unseen by the people. This Imam is the 'existence' of humans that is present in the heart of humans but is apparently absent owing to the forgetfulness of humans and their fall into the state of particularistic 'essence'. Discourse on the first letter of the word of the questioner is an affirmation of the truth of one's being and the presence of truth within one's own reality.

Just as the Commentary on the Letter *Há'* identifies the question with the answer, the Sahífíy-i Ja'faríyyih refers to the same situation within the realm of the heart. In the primordial station of one's existence there is no need for any questions. Here too the question is the same as the answer and the two are not yet differentiated. However, in a state of occultation and forgetfulness, questions appear to be different from their answers. Yet finding true answers, at this stage, requires asking God alone. Thus one has to engage in a spiritual process through the vision of the heart. In this situation one discovers the answer to all his questions within his own being. Here the question contains within itself the answer. Thus in chapter 3 the Báb writes:

> When thou attainest certitude that the way to recognition of the Essence of God is barred, tie then thy cord to God's good pleasure . . . and know of a certainty that the reality of divine good pleasure is thy love for thyself insofar as thyself is 'he is he', which is the sign of thy Lord within thee, and it is that around which revolve all divine names and attributes and all duties and laws. When thou attainest unto such a station, thou wouldst find all the divine descriptions as thy own self-description and thou wouldst understand the true mystery of the tradition 'Verily the faithful is above any description' . . . When one attaineth such a station one would know all things and would not need to ask any question from anyone save God (The Báb, Sahífíy-i Ja'faríyyih, INBA 60, pp. 67–8).

In addition to the common epistemological approach of the two texts, we can recognize various substantive commonalities between Sahífíy-i Ja'faríyyih and the Commentary on the Letter *Há'*. The Báb wrote the latter text in response to a enquirer who asked him to unveil both the truth of being and the truth of the station of the Báb himself. But the letter *há'* is an answer to both questions, or rather, is an affirmation of the identity of both answers. This is the essence and the heart of the Commentary on the Letter *Há'*. The letter *há'* is a reference to the word 'he' (*huva*, which consists of two letters *há'* and *váv*) and thus a reference to God. Analysis of the letter *há'* is an attempt to recognize the ultimate truth, that is, God. Thus interpretation of the letter *há'* is a discussion of the ways to recognize God – and this is precisely the topic of Sahífiy-i Ja'faríyyih. Remember that while this text is an analysis of the occultation prayer, the entire content of that prayer is a discourse on the recognition of God. As mentioned above, the prayer consists of three parts which speak of the recognition of God, recognition of the Apostle and recognition of testimony. This prayer, which begins 'O my God! Make known to me thy self, for shouldst Thou enable me not to recognize thy self, I would not be able to recognize Thy Prophet', is thus a direct discourse on God, the letter *há'*.

Thus both texts are discourses on recognition of ultimate truth, which is recognition of God. But both texts affirm that recognition of the essence of God is impossible. Thus recognition of God becomes recognition of divine revelation within the created world. This revelation becomes ultimately the unity of two realities. One is the true reality of one's own self, aspect of existence, the divine revelation within and the sign of divinity in one's heart. The other is the realization of the sovereign source of this sign, the realm of divine revelation, the Primal Will, the Manifestation of God, and the objective realization of divine Will. The latter, however, is best described as the letter *há'*. In interpreting the tradition of Kumayl, the Báb set out the two primordial meanings of truth: the truth of one's being, which is the divine sign within the human heart, and the truth of 'Alí, who is the one who was being asked about truth by Kumayl. One's true self is a reflection of the truth of 'Alí in one's heart. Thus self-recognition and recognition of 'Alí are identical. Both the Commentary on the Letter *Há'* and Sahífiy-i Ja'faríyyih affirm the same idea. Although both texts use a language of wisdom and allusion, both emphasize the indistinguishability of recognizing one's true self and recognizing the Báb. This is the heart of the interpretation of the letter *há'*.

The letter *há'* is numerically equal to five and is a reference to the word '*báb*' (which is also five). Thus the Báb as the Remembrance and the Word of God becomes the truth of all reality, the manifestation of divine unity and the fulfilment of the tradition of truth. In his Commentary on the Letter *Há'* the Báb explains that the letter *há'* refers to the word '*báb*'. The word '*báb*' is the 'lightest word', the Quranic 'good word' and the secret of divine unity:

> Verily the letter *há'* is the spirit of all the letters and the utmost remembrance of servitude for the Best Beloved . . . It is by virtue of this letter that the divine unity is affirmed and the realm of pluralities is negated. Verily, those endued with true understanding recognize the truth of all the worlds through the symbolism of this letter, for that which is there cannot be known except through that which is here.
>
> The letter *há'* is the number of that word which is the lightest word revealed by God in the Qur'an.
>
> That letter is identical with that word in all its outward manifestations and inward meanings . . . Verily that word is naught but the upright *alif* between the two *bá*s. That referreth unto the Cause of God between the twin names . . . Thus God hath not ordained for this word, unlike other words, any half, third or fourth, for it is the manifestation of the everlasting light and thus naught proceedeth from it (The Báb, Commentary on the Letter *Há'*, INBA 14, pp. 279–80).

In this passage, the Báb explains that the word *báb* represents the inner and outer truth of divine unity. The word consists of the most simple letters – an A between two Bs. The A, or upright *alif*, refers to the creative divine command, the divine Cause which is manifested through the twin names of 'Alí and Muhammad. The Arabic letter A is written as a vertical line, while B is written as a horizontal line. Since the Báb is the manifestation of divine unity, and since nothing else proceeds out of the divine Essence, the word '*báb*' also represents an indivisible unity.

It is important to note that various writings of the Báb, both earlier and later, offer complex interpretations of the word '*báb*'. In fact, according to his writings the entire spiritual reality is present within the mystery of this word, the mystery of the letter *há'*. Later writings of the Báb argue that the '*báb*' (equal to five) is the difference between light (*núr* = 256) and hellish fire (*nár* = 251). Thus the term '*báb*' indicates the concept of light since it is equivalent to the difference between fire and light. The Báb is the supreme standard of truth and the day of Resurrection. Throughout the writings of the Báb, the word '*báb*' represents an upright vertical line (the letter A) which unites two horizontal lines (two letter Bs). The Báb is the middle path that unites the two extreme opposites. The most important realization of this station is the unity of divinity and servitude in the being of the Báb. This is ultimately the reality of the point that is defined by the two stations of divinity and servitude, or divinity and prophethood. The name of the Báb, 'Alí Muhammad, is primarily a reference to this station of the Báb. Muhammad refers to the station of servitude of the point, whereas 'Alí, one of the names of God, symbolizes divinity of the point. Simultaneously 'Alí Muhammad represents the unity of prophethood and vicegerency. The Báb is the reality that unites in his being the two stations of servitude and divinity, as well as prophethood and vicegerency.

Yet the word '*báb*' also refers to the first three stages of divine creative action. Will (*mashíyyat*) is the first divine creative action, corresponding to the concept of existence. Determination (*irádih*) is the second station of divine creative action, corresponding to the essence of things. Destiny (*qadar*), the third stage of divine action, is the link and unity between the previous two. It corresponds to the linking of existence and essence. This unity is the very idea of justice, the middle path between absolute determinism and absolute freedom. These three stages are the conditions of the possibility of all reality. The Báb is the embodiment of these three stages.

In Sahífiy-i Ja'faríyyih the Báb discusses the letter *há'* in this way. As we have seen, *há'* refers simultaneously to the word *huva* (he) and to the Báb, while the word *huva* consists of two Arabic letters *há'* and *váv*. The first is equal to five and the second to six. Thus the word *huva* is equal to 11. An interesting point frequently emphasized by the Báb is the identification of this word with the name of the Báb, that is 'Alí. Numerically 'Alí is equal to 110, which is in reality a higher expression of 11. In this complex symbolic structure we can see the identity of the Báb=5=*há'*=*Huva*=11='Alí=110. Yet '*huva*', which is equal to 11, is also defined as the twin upright *alif*s (the first letter of the Arabic alphabet which is both equal to one and is written like the numeral 1). Thus *huva* is the twin *alif*s or 11, which is nothing but the truth of the letter *há'*.

The interpretation offered by the Báb of *huva* as the twin *alif*s is most fascinating. It refers to the unity of the two stations of divinity (higher) and servitude (lower). It simultaneously refers to the word *huva* and the word 'Alí, 11 and 110, the stations of the point and the vicegerency. Discussing the fifth of the five stations of divine action and revelation in the world, the Báb writes:

> The fifth station testifieth unto God in the mirror of the letter *há'*, and it is the word that consisteth of twin *alif*s, that is 11. It is by virtue of the first *alif* that it surgeth unto the supreme cloud of the Essence, the station of 'There is none other God than he (*huva*)', while through the other *alif* it falleth down unto the heaven of vicegerency, the station of 'he is the most great *'Alí*. (The Báb, Sahífiy-i-Ja'faríyyih, INBA 60, pp. 103–4).

It is crucial to note that the letter *há'* or *huva* is defined as a reference to the unity of both existence and essence. This theme is central to the Báb's interpretation of the concepts of occultation and prayer. The stage of perfect servitude is one in which the defining feature of being is negation of one's particularistic essence so that nothing except existence, the divine revelation within, is seen. This is both a moral and epistemological principle in the writings of the Báb. The essence of knowledge and morality is defined by the vision of the heart where the truth of one's reality is witnessed and nothing except the sign of divinity is mentioned. The essence of morality is defined as revolving around or circumambulating one's heart, one's existence, one's true existence. The essence of immorality is described as circling around one's particularistic essence, selfish desires and self-alienation. In Sahífiy-i Ja'faríyyih and other writings of the Báb both these points are emphatically emphasized. Hence in the first chapter of Sahífiy-i Ja'faríyyih the Báb writes: 'Thus beware, beware ... lest thou gaze upon thy essence (*máhíyyatika*), and take heed, take heed to focus thy gaze upon thy heart and its command' (ibid. p. 62). As we saw above, the station of occultation is the station of falling into the abyss of particularistic essence and forgetting one's existence, the true spiritual reality of human beings.

Given the identification of the letter *há'* with the word '*báb*', one can note a fundamental truth that is discussed in the Sahífiy-i Ja'faríyyih. Referring to those writings of the Báb in which he apparently denies having any specific station of gatehood, as the appointed gate to the Hidden Imam, the Báb affirms the Quranic point that although the enemies of God used their best tricks to plot against God, it is God who has the best tricks of all (Q 3:54). The trick used by the Báb is explained by him: what he denied in fact was the station of specific gatehood as the appointed gate to the Imam. The Báb explains that although his station is one of gatehood (he is the Báb), this is the station of absolute gatehood, the universal concept of the Báb, a station that is not limited to any particular specification. Rather, he is the Báb in the universal sense of the term. In chapter 1 of Sahífiy-i Ja'faríyyih he writes:

> Then thou (God) brought me in the utmost state of degradation to the place of the oppressors and revealed unto me the word of negation after that of affirmation ... But I verily intended not in that which I wrote except the specific station of appointed gatehood, yet gatehood is in reality an absolute word that falleth into limitation by such specification. By thy glory! They failed to plot against me. Nay, rather, I was the swiftest in such planning (The Báb, Sahífiy-i Ja'faríyyih, INBA 60, pp. 60–1).

One of the most perplexing issues to me in this regard is that Nicolas discusses Sahífiy-i Ja'faríyyih in his preface to the French translation of the Persian Bayán in order to prove that 'Abdu'l-Bahá's account of the Báb's announcement in the mosque of Vakíl in Shiraz is inaccurate. Nicolas quotes from *A Traveler's Narrative* and then argues that this description of the event does not fit with the words of the Báb himself who has explicitly mentioned in Sahífiy-i Ja'faríyyih that he has used the word of negation in relation to his claims (Nicolas 1908, pp. xvii–xxv). Yet when Nicolas quotes the above passage in Sahífiy-i Ja'faríyyih in which the Báb explains what he actually meant by the word of negation, he comes to the same conclusion that is offered in 'Abdu'l-Bahá's *Traveler's Narrative*. Nicolas argues that the Báb's account in Sahífiy-i Ja'faríyyih – that his denial of specific gatehood was in fact accurate since he was the manifestation of absolute gatehood – is compatible with his true claim because he was the Qá'im and a new prophet and not the specific gate to the Imam (ibid. p. xix). But this is exactly the point that is raised by 'Abdu'l-Bahá. He contends that the words of the Báb were perceived differently by the audience in the mosque, who assumed that he was denying being the gate to the Imam (and thus they became 'quiet and tranquil') from the spiritual elect, who concluded that the Báb claimed a higher station and a more exalted meaning of gatehood.[6] I should acknowledge that the hasty judgement of Nicolas may be a result of seeing Browne's translation and not the original. The original words of 'Abdu'l-Bahá clearly imply that the audience became silent and tranquil because they *assumed* that an actual recantation had taken place but Browne's translation does not convey this point clearly.

It is interesting that even when the Báb appears to be using a language of wisdom and denies specific claims for himself, he is in fact arguing that the truth of his station cannot be described by any linguistic category, including prophethood, vicegerency or appointed gatehood. Those categories can be equally attributed to him or denied with regard to his station. The truth of his station is in fact beyond any description but the closest is the perfect station of servitude to God, the station in which nothing except God can be seen. The point emphasized by the Báb in these discussions is this: regardless of the title and description of his claim, he represents the supreme divine testimony and therefore he should be obeyed even if he calls the day night and the night day. This is also applicable to the definition of his station: his possession of supreme testimony requires perfect obedience to his command whether he calls himself the supreme sign of God on earth or the most abased atom of existence. For example, in the second chapter of Sahífiy-i Ja'faríyyih the Báb refers to the doubts of the questioner concerning the truth of the Báb and then guides him on the path of truth. The Báb argues that the Cause of God is most manifest and there is no doubt about it. Then he asks the questioner to ponder the truth of the Báb. He argues that if you see that the Báb has appeared with an incontrovertible testimony and proof the like of which no one else can produce, then it is your duty to obey his words and not to ask why or wherefore:

> Behold the one who calleth thee unto God. Should he possess an incontrovertible testimony from his Lord in such manner that none is able to produce the like thereof, his cause would then be proven to be true and there would be no doubt

about it. Obey then his words and ask not why or wherefore . . . Shouldst thou acknowledge his testimony thou wouldst have no place to flee to save to obey him, even if he calleth night day, poison sugar, false true, and knowledge ignorance (The Báb, Sahífiy-i Ja'faríyyih, INBA 60, pp. 62–3).

One of the main discussions of the truth of the letter *há'* is undertaken in chapter 7 of Sahífiy-i Ja'faríyyih. As we have seen, the Báb argued that achieving true prayer presupposes six forms of recognition. The third requirement is recognition of the names of God, which is the topic of chapter 7. An adequate discussion of this chapter is not possible here.

The essence of the Báb's discourse is to define the Most Great Name of God, the true realization of such recognition. The Báb defines the Most Great Name of God as the letter *há'*, namely *huva*, as well as the name 'Alí (which is the name of the Báb and a reflection of *huva*) and the twin names 'Alí Muhammad (his own name). At the same time he identifies the Most Great Name of God with the station of the perfect Shi'a, the station of gatehood. Yet the Báb appears in the arc of ascent. Thus contrary to the station of the specific gate in the arc of descent, the Báb's station precedes that of other figures of the hierarchy of spiritual recognition, namely Muhammad and the Imams. Explaining the Most Great Name of God he writes:

> He who prayeth unto God by the mystery of the name Muhammad and 'Alí, God shall never reject his call, even if he is amongst those who join partners with God. For that is the Most Great Name of God – when they are joined together and not separately . . . Verily the first name that God hath assumed for himself is the name 'Alí, the Great . . . Thus is it manifest to one who knoweth how to think the grandeur of the name *huva*, after detaching oneself from *váv* and focusing one's gaze on the letter *alif* that is present within the letter *há'*. Its numerical value is 11, which correspondeth to the name 'Alí, that is 110 . . . Take heed, O thou who prayest, and cling thou unto that most mighty name and the most great attribute . . .
>
> But now I allude to the inward truth of this station by discussing a tradition and a related one that thou mayest attain certitude that, verily, the Most Great Name is outwardly present within the phrase 'O God! Bless Muhammad and the Family of Muhammad', and inwardly in the name of guardianship ('Alí) before prophethood (Muhammad), apparent in the station of the true Shi'a.

A most exciting aspect of this section is again affirmation of the two types of recognition: recognition of the Báb and recognition of the mystical truth enshrined within the hearts of humans. Thus recognition of the Báb and self-recognition are identical. This point is discussed in chapter 7 in an exciting interpretation of the phenomenology of the concept of the Most Great Name of God. Here the Báb argues that all names are names of God, and all names when mentioned at the station of the heart and stripped of all limitations and references to the particular essence of things, point to the unity and divinity of all things and are, therefore, the Most Great Name of God. Thus, although the objective realization of this approach is the manifest station of the Báb himself, this is identical with the truth of all beings. In other words, all things in their primordial station of existence are named the Most Great Name of God. It is only when they are alienated from their true reality and forget their existence, falling into the abyss of particularistic selves, that their names are no longer the Most Great Name of God. Thus recognition of the Báb, the letter *há'*, is the path to achieve the Most Great Name of God within one's reality as well. Hence the Báb writes: 'Belittle not any name in the contingent world, for verily all names of God are great, and when they are purified from reference to aught save God they become the Most Great (ibid. p. 92).

Yet there are other significant reasons why Sahífiy-i Ja'faríyyih is an interpretation of the letter *há'*. One of the most important of these is the centrality of the station of the Imam Husayn in this text. The Báb wrote his work sometime around the anniversary of the martyrdom of Imam Husayn on the tenth Muharram. Various chapters of the text identify the date as the second, fourth and tenth of Muharram. That is why the entire text is a discourse on the station of the Báb through a discussion and remembrance of the station of the Imam Husayn. Various chapters are devoted to discussing Husayn's martyrdom as well as the similarity of the present situation of the Báb to the day of his martyrdom. As we know, according to the Báb, Imam Husayn is the letter *há'* in the Islamic dispensation. He is the fifth sacred figure within the hierarchy of the 14 immaculate souls, listed after Muhammad, 'Alí, Fatima, Hasan and Husayn. In fact among the works of the Báb, Sahífiy-i Ja'faríyyih is most pronounced in the centrality of such discussion on the letter *há'*. It is also noteworthy that in the Book of Certitude, where Bahá'u'lláh quotes from Sahífiy-i Ja'faríyyih and describes the text as the Interpretation of the Letter *Há'*, he is quoting the statement of the Báb in which he directly identified his present situation with the martyrdom of Imám Husayn.

As noted above, a central message of Sahífiy-i Ja'faríyyih is the idea that the martyrdom of Imam Husayn took place in the age of appearance and outward meaning and thus his martyrdom was a physical one. With the inception of the new Cause, the arc of ascent, the age of inward meaning has commenced and therefore it is the divine decree that the martyrdom of the Báb is to take place in an inward sense on that very day, the tenth of Muharram. If the body of Husayn were subjected to 950 blows from the swords his enemies, the heart of the Báb is now torn into pieces by thousands of blows from the swords of accusations and denials. To respond to his enemies' letters of refutation, particularly those from people such as Javád-i-Baraghání, is the height of affliction and martyrdom.

It is in this same regard that the Báb speaks in Sahífiy-i Ja'faríyyih as Husayn spoke on the day of his martyrdom. The Báb, like Husayn, engages in a lengthy 'champion's call for battle'. Here, however, it is the revelation of the divine verses that is offered as the matchless and subduing force of the champion. I cannot, however, pursue this issue here, as it needs a whole paper on its own.

Finally, perhaps the most important way that Sahífiy-i Ja'faríyyih is both an interpretation of the letter *há'* and an affirmation of the truth of the Báb's station is the very interpretation of the occultation prayer offered by the Báb. Chapters 11, 12 and 13 are devoted to a discussion of each of the three parts of the prayer. Yet the essence of all these interpretations is one and the same: the prayer affirms that recognition of God and his sacred representatives is only possible through God's act of self-description and self-unveiling. It is God who has made himself known to humans, otherwise no human could ever recognize God. This, however, is the essence of the Báb's principle that the standard of recognition of God is solely what God has defined as his testimony; that is, that, ultimately, the very revelation of divine verses is the very act of divine self-description. Thus the essence of the occultation prayer is an affirmation of the absolute sovereignty of the truth of the Báb by virtue of his revelation of divine words, the like of which cannot be produced by anyone.

Sahífiy-i Ja'faríyyih is an extensive discussion of this same fact. It is a discourse on the letter *há'*, that is, a discourse on the recognition of God and his gate. Various chapters of the text elaborate this theme and it is this fact that is ultimately the answer to all accusations against and attacks on the Báb. Chapter 2 is the chapter on methodology. Here the Báb *counsels* the questioner to focus his gaze on the standard of truth and the incontrovertible testimony of his truth. Chapters 11 to 13 extend this principle. Those familiar with the writings of the Báb and Bahá'u'lláh know that this same principle is defined as the principle of the heart, the sanctuary of unity and the gaze of God. In other words, this is the same as the return to the truth of one's self and the true realization of prayer in order to overcome the alienation of separation and occultation.[7]

Bibliography

'Abdu'l-Bahá. *A Traveler's Narrative*. Wilmette, IL: Bahá'í Publishing Trust, 1980.

The Báb. Commentary on the Letter *Há'*. INBA 86.

— The Epistle of Justice: The Root Principles. np., n.d.

— Interpretation of the Letter *Há'*. INBA 86.

— Khutbiy-i Dhikríyyih, quoted in Mázandarání, *Táríkh-i Zuhúr al-Haqq*, vol. 3.

— Sahífiy-i Ja'faríyyih, INBA 60.

Bahá'u'lláh. INBA 35 and 76.

— *Kitáb-i-Íqán*. Wilmette, IL: Bahá'í Publishing Trust, 1989.

Iranian National Bahá'í Archives (INBA)

Ishráq Khávarí, 'Abd al-Hamíd (ed.). *Má'idih-yi Ásimání*, 9 vols. http://reference.bahai.org/fa/.

— *Qámús-i Íqán*, vols. 1, 4. n.p.: Mu'assasih-yi Millí-yi Matbú'át-i Amrí, 128 BE/1972.

MacEoin, Denis. *The Sources for Early Babi Doctrine and History: A Survey*. Leiden: Brill, 1992.

Mázandarání, Asadu'lláh Fádil. *Táríkh-i Zuhúr al-Haqq*, vol. 3. Tehran: n.p., 1944.

Mohammadhosseini, Nosratollah. *Hadrat-i Báb*. Dundas, ON: Institute for Bahá'í Studies in Persian, 152 BE/1995.

Nabíl-i-A'zam. *The Dawn-Breakers: Nabíl's Narrative of the Early Days of the Bahá'í Revelation*. Wilmette, IL: Bahá'í Publishing Trust, 1970.

Nicolas, A.L.M. *Siyyid Ali-Muhammad dit le Bab*. Paris: Librairie Critique, 1908.

Notes

1. The reason MacEoin has made such a mistake is the error in transcription of the tablet as printed in Ishraq Khavari 1950, vol. 7, p. 60. That it *is* a mistake, all the other copies of the tablet make clear; see, for example, Bahá'u'lláh INBA 35, p. 233, and INBA 76, p. 90. See also Mohammadhosseini 1995, pp. 952–3.
2. Bahá'u'lláh, *Hidden Words*, Arabic no. 12.
3. ibid. Arabic no. 13.
4. ibid. Arabic no. 14.
5. ibid. Arabic no. 15.
6. This is Browne's translation:

    One day they summoned Him to the mosque urging and constraining Him to recant, but He discoursed from the pulpit in such wise as to silence and subdue those present and to establish and strengthen His followers. It was then supposed that He claimed to be the medium of grace from His Highness the Lord of the Age (upon Him be peace); but afterwards it became known and evident that His meaning was the Gatehood [*Bábíyyat*] of another city and the mediumship of the graces of another Person Whose qualities and attributes were contained in His books and treatises ('Abdu'l-Bahá 1980, pp. 6–7).

7. Sahífiy-i Ja'faríyyih is truly filled with spiritual wonders and miracles. In this short article I have tried to outline the structure of the text. However, any detailed discussion of the issues raised in the text needs independent work.

13

The Báb's *Panj Sha'n* (Five Modes)[1]
John Walbridge

Among the last works of the Báb is a large book consisting of rhapsodies on various names of God rendered in the five literary styles into which he divided his writings and written in a strange style full of artificial constructions from Arabic roots. This work, the *Panj Sha'n*, or 'Five Modes', and similar works of the Báb like the *Kitábu'l-Asmá'*, are not always easily explicable to the contemporary mind. The following is a very preliminary examination of this unusual work. It is based on a quick examination of the work and not a full reading of it. I have used the Azalí edition published in Iran in the early 1960s. It should be noted that there is also a Persian *Panj Sha'n*, a much smaller book, that I have not seen.

Circumstances of its composition

We know exactly when the *Panj Sha'n* was written: 19 March to 4 April 1850. The day it was begun was both Naw-Rúz and 5 Jumádá al-Úlá, the first day of the seventh Bábí year and the sixth anniversary according to the lunar calendar of the Báb's declaration of his mission to Mullá Husayn. That day and on each of the following 16 days he wrote a passage in each of the five styles in commentary on a name of God. In the published Azalí edition, four parts are missing, corresponding to the eighth, thirteenth, fifteenth and sixteenth days, and the Azalí scribe apologizes that one or two other parts are taken from manuscripts of lesser authority. Some, though not all, of the parts are dedicated to individual believers.

We know these particulars not from the text itself but from a document published at the end of the Azalí edition. This is evidently the Báb's correspondence log for the period 19 March – 20 June 1850. It consists of entries separated by horizontal lines. Each entry gives the name of God for that day (of which more later), the number of the day in the Bábí month, the day of the week in the conventional Arabic name and the Bábí name, and notes about what the Báb wrote on each day and what was dispatched to believers. The whole is firmly dated by a heading giving the opening date in both the lunar and Bábí calendars. There are certain minor difficulties relating to the dating but nothing that casts doubt on the authenticity of the document.

The notes on the Báb's writings are divided into three columns. The first is headed 'that which was sent down from God most high' and contains a note of the general content of the Báb's writing that day. This gradually dwindles from a long paragraph on the first day to a few words or nothing later in the document. Beginning on the second day, the second column contains a brief statement about the amount and type of writing on that day. For example on day 2, on which the Báb revealed a chapter in each of the five styles on the theme 'God is unique', we read, 'In commentary on the name "unity" revealed in the five modes. That which flowed from the Pen of God was five sheets [or pages].' The third column, 'That which ascended unto God most high by the Primal Point', seems to be notes concerning outgoing correspondence, with addressees indicated by abbreviations and numbers indicating the number of sheets. In some cases the addressees can be identified but not always.

The contents of the book are clearly indicated by the entries for the month of Bahá, the first month of the Bábí year; and it was this that enabled the Azalí scribe to compile his edition and put the chapters in their proper order. After 17 Bahá there are no further entries indicating writing in this style, evidence that the book as we have it is largely complete.

The log continues for several more Bábí months. Many days are blank except for the name of God for that day and the dates. Other days record the writing of talismans, prayers and so on. Mid-May saw a burst of correspondence, ending abruptly on 14 May. This presumably marks the departure of Sayyáh, the last Bábí courier to leave Chihríq, who carried the Báb's remaining papers to Mullá 'Abdu'l-Karím Qazvíní. Though the latter part of the month saw considerable writing, it was mainly prayers and other such things not necessarily intended to be sent immediately to the believers. The last recorded revelation was 1 Núr/3 June. The last ten days bear the same name of God, 'God is most high' (*Alláh A'lá*). The log ends on Friday, 18 Núr/20 June 1850, apparently the day after the Báb reached Tabriz. Most likely Sayyid Husayn Yazdí carried the log with him to safety after the execution of the Báb. Presumably it then passed into Bahá'u'lláh's hands and was among the Bábí manuscripts kept by Azal.

The historical interest of this document is clear but its full use must await a more determined effort to decipher its cryptic notations.

The style and content of *Panj Sha'n*

The *Panj Sha'n*, as I have indicated, consists of 14 sets of passages in each of the five styles into which the Báb conventionally divided his Revelation:

- verses (*ayát*)
- prayers (*munáját*)
- sermons (*khutbih*)
- commentary (*tafsír*)
- Persian (*fársí*)

Each day of the month – and presumably year – was assigned a name of God. These are all in the elative and are repeated twice:

- *al-a'lah al-a'lah*
- *al-awhad al-awhad*
- *al-a'had al-a'had*
- *al-ahyá al-ahyá*

These are dedicated – sometimes – to particular believers, including Dayyán, Azal, Táhirih, Bahá'u'lláh and – forlornly – the Báb's beloved uncle Hájjí Mírzá Sayyid 'Alí, who had been killed a month earlier in Tehran and of whose death the Báb was never told. Others are more difficult to identify.

The book contains nothing that might reasonably be called an argument. Instead, names of God and invocations are endlessly repeated and varied, often in ways unsanctioned by Arabic usage. Syntax is nearly as inventive. Thus, for example, the first page has *Alláh* used as a superlative in the form *a'lah*, an infinitive *ilhán*, participles *mu'talih, mu'lah* and so on. Thus the content of the book is not in the form of an extended argument but in enraptured rhapsodies about particular themes. Thus the sermon on the first day rhapsodizes about the first day of Bahá – Naw-Rúz – as the 'day of God', the name given it by the Báb in the Bayán. In such respects it is similar to the *Kitábu'l-Asmá'*, written sometime earlier and also arranged on a calendrical basis.

Evaluation

The question now arises as to why the Báb might have wished to write such a strange book – and why many Bábís chose to copy it and the Azalís to publish it. As one of my Bahá'í teachers commented about the similar work, *Kitábu'l-Asmá'*, 'After a while a modern person gets bored, puts down the book and reads something else.' But I do not think that would be true of its intended readers.

In the Persian Bayán 8:14 the Báb commands his followers to recite seven hundred verses of the Bayán or to mention God (Alláh) seven hundred times every 24 hours.[2] 'Bayán' in the Báb's usage refers to his writings in general, not just to the Bayán proper. Each part of *Panj Sha'n* is about 30 pages long, roughly equalling the requisite seven hundred verses (a verse according to the Báb being 40 letters, or about a line). Now it also seems clear that the Báb envisioned the believer meditating on a different name of God each day. Lists are given in the *Kitábu'l-Asmá'* and in the correspondence log mentioned above (though the lists do not agree). Thus the believer, I infer, might fulfil his obligation by reciting one chapter of five parts from the *Panj Sha'n* each day.

The Báb's manipulation of Arabic morphology is certainly deliberate, as is the case in his other Arabic works. An exact knowledge of Arabic was the most prized possession of the Islamic scholar, for the Arabic of the Qur'án was, as the Qur'án itself testifies, a miracle sufficient to demonstrate the truth of Muhammad's prophethood. Thus when the Báb flouted the rules of Arabic morphology and syntax and proclaimed the resulting works to be scripture, he was proclaiming his own authority to abrogate the whole Islamic religious system. The ulama understood this perfectly well and thus were extremely anxious to dismiss the Báb's literary innovations as the result of his ignorance of Arabic, for to acknowledge his right to use Arabic in this way would have been to implicitly acknowledge the old and hitherto unmet challenge of the Qur'án: 'Then produce a sura like it, and call on whom you can, apart from God, if you speak truly' (Q 10:39). It was exactly the debate played out in the arts in modern Europe, with modernists asserting their freedom by breaking with traditional forms and styles and traditionalists condemning them for being supposedly unable to master the traditional forms.

With this the stylistic challenges of the book begin to make sense. The book is to be understood as a sort of Bábí breviary, a work of devotions, not of instruction. For this the Báb's style is appropriate. While the style in this work may be numbing in large doses, it is unquestionably hypnotic – or, if you like, 'liturgical' – in smaller amounts. Recited, the *Panj Sha'n* is thus akin to Sufi *dhikr*, in which the same evocative words are repeated ceaselessly, in this case with gradual variations. The utter freedom with which the Báb reinvents Arabic grammar is an open proclamation of his claim to prophethood. The aesthetic is thus rather modern in certain ways, with its contempt for convention and rigorous formal rules. Perhaps we should see *Panj Sha'n* as a minimalist work or a sort of devotional *Finnegan's Wake*. There can be no doubt of its ethereal beauty.

The Báb's Variations on the Name 'God' in Five Styles
(Provisional Translation)

In the Name of God, Very God, Very God!

I, I am God – No God is there but Me – Very God, Very God.
In God's Name, Very God, Very God.
God by God, Very God, Very God.
In God's Name, Godlike God, Godlike God.
God, no God is there but He, Very God, Very God.
God, no God is there but He, Godlike God, Godlike God.
God, no God is there but He, God as God in Godhead.
God, no God is there but He, God, attainèd Godhood.
God of the heavens, God of the earth, God of what is between, that Godhead is
    God's, is His,
and God is High God, God, Divine.
God of the heavens, God of the earth, God of what is between, that Godhead is
    God's, is His,
and God is Godhead, God as God, attainèd Godhood.
God, King of Kings divine, God of the heavens, God of the earth, God of the void
    between, that Godhead is God's, is His,
and God is God, God as God, attainèd Godhood.

Say, God is Very God above all that is made god –
Nothing in the heavens, nothing in the earth,
nothing in the void between
can hinder Him as Sovereign King.
He is High God, God, Divine.

Say, God is Very God above all that is made god –
Nothing in the heavens, nothing in the earth,
nothing in the void between
can hinder Him, Divine in the Divinity of His Godhead.
He is High God, God, Divine.

You are exalted, O God –
God of the heavens, God of the earth, God of the void between –
You bestow divinity on whom You choose and withdraw it from whom You choose,
Exalt whom You choose, bring low whom You choose.
You aid whom You choose, forsake whom You choose,
Glorify whom You choose, abase whom You choose,
Enrich whom You choose, ruin whom You choose.
In Your grasp is the kingdom of all things.
You create what You choose by Your command.
You are powerful over all things.
You are exalted, O God.
You are the God of Divinities.
You entrust the Command to whom You choose,
and withdraw it from whom You choose,
Exalt whom You choose, bring low whom You choose.
You aid whom You choose, forsake whom You choose,
Enrich whom You choose, ruin whom You choose.
Glorify whom You choose, abase whom You choose.
In Your grasp is the kingdom of all things.
You create what You choose by Your command.
You, You are High God, God, Divine.

Say, You, O God, You are Very God of Very Gods.
Let all worship You who dwell
in the heavens, in the earth, in the void between.
Let all bow down to You who dwell
in the Kingdom of the Cause and Creation and beyond.
It is You Who knows all things.
Say, You, O God, You arise as God
of the heavens and the earth and the void between.
Then plant the tree of affirmation
in all that You have created
or will create by Your command
until that day on which You manifest
the Manifestation of Your Self
that all may believe in Him
and be sure through Him
then bow down before His face.

Say, God is Very God above
all who have gods.
None in the heavens, none in the earth,
none in the void between,
can hinder Him in the Godlike Godhead
of His Divinity in Himself.
He it is Who is High God, God, Divine.
This is a Book from God
to Him Whom God shall make manifest,
testifying that there is no God but I,
God-in-Self, Divine.
I have made the beginning of each religion the word
'There is no God but God'
that perhaps those who were given the Book
may seek certainty in the Day of Your manifestation.
Such as these are the proofs of affirmation in the Book of God.
These are the firm.
But those who are veiled from You
at the moment of Your manifestation,
though they affirm the unity of God
in the number of 'All Things',
will find no profit in their affirmation
of the unity of God, their Lord.
Say unto all things, Fear Me, for I am God,
there is no God but Me!
None but I shall behold Me.
Whoso seeks to behold Me,
Let him behold Him Whom God shall manifest,
for He is the narrow and dangerous Bridge!
I, I am God. There is no God but Me!
No thing shall see Me.
He who desires to look upon Me,
let him look to Him Whom God shall make manifest,
for He is the narrow and dangerous Bridge!
I, I am God. There is no God but Me!
No being shall know Me.
He who desires to know Me,
let him come to know Him Whom God shall make manifest,
for He is the lofty and exalted Book!

Notes

1. First published in 'Research Notes in Shaykhi, Babi and Baha'i Studies', vol. 2, no. 3 (April 1998), H-Bahai Digital Publications Series. http://www.h-net.org/~bahai/notes/vol2/panjshn.htm (accessed 12 February 2007).
2. The Báb, *Bayán-i-Fársí*, Iranian National Bahá'í Archives (INBA) 24, p. 387.

14

Undermining the Foundations of Orthodoxy: Some Notes on the Báb's Sharia (Sacred Law)*

Armin Eschraghi

The movement founded by Sayyid 'Alí-Muhammad Shírází, known to history as the 'Báb', is essentially a religious one. Various scholars have presented many widely differing explanations of the aims and characteristics of his teachings. In addition to proposing absurd conspiracy theories that need not be discussed here (for a discussion of some of these theories see Momen 2004, pp. 27 *passim*), some researchers have suggested that the Bábí movement was interested merely in the reform of the Islamic Twelver Shi'i sect. Others have seen it as an essentially political and thus non- or, at most, pseudo-religious revolutionary movement, while yet others have characterized it as a particularly radical and militant offshoot from Twelver Shi'ism. There are several reasons why interpretations differ so widely and even contradict each other. The most important factor is a failure to consult primary sources, i.e. the writings of the Báb and those of his early disciples. Only in the past two decades has interest been rekindled and a number of well-researched articles on Bábí writings published. Yet the focus of these works has largely been limited to the Báb's early writings, that is those written before 1847–8.

During his solitary confinement in Mákú the Báb wrote the Persian Bayán in which, for the first time, he explicitly put forth his true claim, elaborated his metaphysical teachings and laid down a new set of rituals as well as rules governing the affairs of the community. In 1848 a number of his most prominent followers formally declared a break with Islam. From, at the latest, 1848 onwards Bábism can no longer be deemed a Shi'i sect or an Islamic reform movement. It rather becomes an independent faith, fulfilling all the criteria of a separate religion, i.e. a founder figure, new holy writings, a new set of metaphysical and theological teachings distinct from those of Islam, new ritual observances as well as prescriptions for human relations.

---

*The following is a revised and expanded extract from a Persian manuscript presented at the annual gathering of the Society of Persian Letters and Arts in Tambach (Ger-many) in August 2004. Parts of the Persian manuscript are published in *Khúshih-há-'í az Kharman-i Adab va Hunar*, vol. 15 (Darmstadt: 'Asr-i Jadíd, 162BE/2005) under the title *Mabání-i Andíshih-yi Tajaddud dar Áthár-i Hadrat-i A'lá*, pp. 26–57.

Bayánic law has hitherto remained largely unstudied and it contains many ordinances and prescriptions that seem somewhat strange and puzzling to the uninitiated modern reader. It is only through, at the very least, a basic understanding of the aims underlying the Báb's new sharia that the historical significance of Bábism and its relationship to its successor, the Bahá'í Faith, can be adequately understood. The following is an attempt to shed light on a few characteristics of Bayánic law and to investigate the reasons why the Báb laid down these ordinances. A glance at some of his theological teachings will provide the necessary background, so that the importance of Bayánic law and its 'revolutionary' character can be seen in the context of the general aims of the Báb.

Theological background of the new sharia

A common trait of most religious movements, conservative or modernist, is that they equally perceive of themselves as 'reformist'. Nevertheless, somewhat paradoxically, they at the same time present their activities as reviving the 'original spirit' of their religion and as an effort to go 'back to their roots'. A few Islamic movements serve as examples. Amongst the most conservative groups are the 'Wahhábiyyah' or more generally the 'Salafiyyah'. In their view, the age of the Prophet Muhammad was the 'Golden Age' of Islam. Thus they consequently try to re-animate the spirit of those days by adapting their clothing, beard, speech and behaviour to standards they believe were common 1400 years ago in the Hijáz. According to their belief, present-day society has deviated from those standards and needs to be brought back to the 'Straight Path'. Thus, to them, reform means that Islam is cleansed of all traditions, customs and beliefs that have been added to it over the centuries.

Another example is the concept of 'Viláyat-i Faqíh' (governance by the [supreme] jurisprudent), introduced into Twelver Shi'i Islam by a couple of theologians around Ayatollah Ruhollah Khomeini (d. 1989). Twelver Shi'ism was in its origins a quietist and apolitical movement, a fact that has its doctrinal roots in the absence of the Imam (see below). Thus the idea that a jurisprudent can be the only legitimate head of state is essentially a departure from the very core of centuries-old Shi'i theology.[1] Yet Khomeini claimed that his new doctrine represented the true and original spirit of Islam. In his book *Hukúmat-i Islámí* (*Islamic Government*), where, for the first time, Khomeini detailed his views concerning the illegitimacy of any secular government, he presented numerous verses from the Qur'an and oral traditions attributed to Muhammad and the Imams in an attempt to present his ideas as original Islamic doctrine.

Numerous modernist groups and thinkers have tried to introduce progressive ideas into Islam. However, they also try to portray these measures not as changes but rather as a return to the original spirit of Islam. 'Alí Sharí'atí, who has become somewhat of a symbol for a subsequent generation of – at least, Iranian – reformers, used to teach that 'Safavid Islam'[2] was a departure from the original 'Islam of 'Alí'. According to him, the spirit of the latter needed to be rekindled in order to constructively change Iranian society (see Rahnema 1998, pp. 300ff.).

From the most conservative to the most progressive movements, no religious reformer has, for different reasons, been able or willing to wholly sever ties with past doctrines, which would have been a precondition for introducing substantial changes.³ The reason lies at the core of traditional Islamic dogma, according to which history is a linear process, starting from creation, then passing through several stages of progressive development and finally culminating in the revelation of God's final messenger. His message is complete and after him there will be no more progress; rather, the world will end on Judgement Day.⁴ The core issue all original thinkers and modernists struggle with is that Islamic dogma does not allow for any substantial reform. It is noteworthy that *bid'ah* (innovation) is a *terminus technicus* for heresy and deemed one of the gravest sins. New ideas can rarely be justified without either a great deal of allegorical interpretation or by simply ignoring certain Quranic prescriptions. Conservatives thus see reformist approaches as heresy and deviation from the Straight Path, whereas unbiased observers realize the logical contradictions in the arguments. This weakens the reformer's position from the outset.

The Báb, much like other founders of world religions, did not bother filling 'old skins with new wine'. He not only abrogated Islamic law and many dogmas but also actually replaced them with a new set of doctrines. Further, the idea of steady and infinite progress and renewal is at the core of his religious doctrine. In the first years of his ministry, he did not formally announce a break with Islam. Rather, he outwardly upheld the standard of the Islamic sharia and seemingly denied any claim to a new revelation or to end the Islamic dispensation.⁵ However, even in his earliest works for the initiated reader it is obvious that the Báb was already well aware of – and frequently alluded to – his full claim, which he later publicly declared.⁶

Some of the Báb's earliest verses were an open provocation to the Shi'i clerics. One example was his stance on the complex rules of Arabic grammar. He not only wrote in a fashion that contradicted those rules, he even went so far as to call them 'satanic' (*al-qawá'id al-shaytániyyah*) (Qayyúm al-Asmá', sura 86) and claimed that through his intercession God had decided to free language from the rules and chains placed on its neck in the past (Risálah fí 'Ilm al-Nahw, vol. 67, p. 121; cf. Amanat 1989, pp. 269f.). In another early work, his Persian Scripture of Justice (Sahífih-yi 'Adliyyih), the Báb wrote:

> Just as the worlds have progressed (*taraqqí namúdih*) the [usages of] words and vowels have progressed. It is well nigh possible that a day will shine forth when the verses of God shall be recited devoid of such rules as are now common among the people (Sahífih-yi 'Adliyyih, p. 12).⁷

Here the Báb uses symbolic language to express an idea that is constantly alluded to throughout his earliest works, namely that soon fundamental and far-reaching, sometimes painful, changes will occur.⁸ It is particularly noteworthy that the term *bid'ah* and derivatives of it, such as *badí'* and *bid'* occur in virtually every sura of the Qayyúm al-Asmá' and the Kitáb al-Rúh, the two most voluminous early works of the Báb presently known to us (Eschraghi 2004, pp. 170f.).

The Báb's early writings are, by far, less orthodox than they appear to be at first sight. Unorthodox ideas, mainly of Shaykhi origin, recur in them, such as belief in the 'Fourth Support' (*al-rukn ar-Rábi'*, *al-harf ar-rábi'*)⁹ and specific instructions for visiting the shrines of the Imams.¹⁰

However, it is in the Persian Bayán that the Báb conclusively and unequivocally abrogates the Islamic sharia and replaces it with a new one. A first sign of this break with the past is already evident from the opening verse of the Persian Bayán: 'In the Name of God, the Most Inaccessible, the Most Holy.'[11] Here the Báb departs from the Islamic custom, observed throughout his earlier works, to start any piece of writing with the Quranic 'In the Name of God the Forgiver, the Merciful' (for the theological aspects of this new opening verse see Lambden 1997, p. 54).

The idea of the steady renewal of the world had already been expressed by Islamic philosophers such as Mullá Sadrá (d. 1640) in his doctrine of 'essential movement (*al-harakah al-jawhariyyah*)', as well as by mystics following the ideas of Ibn 'Arabí (d. 1240), such as Muhsin Fayd al-Káshání (d. 1680) and 'Abd al-Razzáq Fayyád al-Láhíjí (d. 1661). It had also found its way into the writings of the Shaykhiyyah. The Creator, thus, steadily re-creates Creation. The divine bounties (*fayd*) flow incessantly back and forth from their source. The world, although it appears static to the observer, is actually in a constant process of change. In his early writings, the Báb often alludes to this philosophical concept and confirms it (cf. Eschraghi 2004, p. 320). Since, according to him, the lower spheres of the world mirror the upper ones, in this material world there also needs to be constant change. In the Persian Bayán he further develops this idea and teaches the steady re-creation of the world each time God sends a new messenger.

> Let it not be hidden from the reader of these words that God made the creation of the Qur'an return (*'awd farmúd*) on the Day of Resurrection through the appearance of his own Self (*bi-zuhúr-i nafs-i ú*) on that Day. Then He created all things anew (*bid'an*), as if they had been created in that very moment (Persian Bayán 1:1).[12]

The world does not cease to progress and there will always be messengers – or rather, as they are called in Bábí scripture, Manifestations (*mazáhir*) – of God. It is man's duty to recognize these Manifestations and on the day of their appearance, God creates every creature anew according to its belief or disbelief.[13]

> How many believe in one Revelation and in another fall into the Fire! And how many have been inmates of hellfire in the previous Revelation and reached Paradise in the next! Should a soul be a non-believer in a thousand and thousand Revelations and then, in the one after these thousand and thousand Revelations become a believer, all his worlds (*'awálim*)[14] will be turned into belief. And – God forbid – in the opposite case, the opposite will happen (*agar bar 'aks, bar 'aks*) (Persian Bayán 3:15).

The Báb sees every revelation of God as a radical change and a process of renewal. Each appearance of a Manifestation is equal to a new creation and whatever existed before it becomes obsolete, as if it had not existed at all. Once a new revelation appears, clinging to the former, its rules and customs, is not acceptable in the sight of God.

> Whatever pleasure is imagined today is in this Paradise, whereas all pleasure has been severed from the former Paradise (ibid. 2:16).

If the root (*asl*) becomes obsolete, how then should its derivatives (*far'*) remain? Fear ye God, O Servants! (ibid. 5:15).

In the second quotation the words used by the Báb as well as the context of the passage have an obvious technical background. *Asl* (lit. root) is used to denote the fundamentals and basics of Islamic theology and law. The *furú'* (lit. branches) are detailed prescriptions derived from the fundamentals. The Báb is thus clearly referring to the fact that sacred Law is abrogated in its derivatives as well as in its essentials. He goes beyond a mere attempt at reinterpretation of core issues in order to derive a more timely understanding of Islam.

To the Báb every new revelation of God is like a knife cutting off all relations with the preceding one. The following passage impressively documents to what extent the Báb expected people to be detached from tradition:

. . . Should a hundred thousand souls gather to circumambulate the House [the Ka'ba.] and leave their homes for the day when permission for circumambulating is given, and should on that very day the Tree of Truth appear and command: 'Don't circumambulate!' – should they all immediately abide, they have reached [true] circumambulating. However, should they fail, all their deeds will become naught (ibid. 8:2).

The Báb does not exempt his own religion from this rule. His own faith is not perceived of as everlasting. Rather, 'the Bayán is the balance of God until the Day of Him Whom God shall make manifest' (ibid. 2:6). The religion of the Báb is thus only valid until a new revelation of God takes place. The concept of a chain of divine revelations is further expressed in a passage that explains how every religion has as its ultimate goal the preparation of its adherents for the coming of the next Manifestation. Towards the end of that passage, the Báb says:

. . . and all [previous] Revelations and this Revelation and the Revelation of Him Whom God shall make manifest were created for the Revelation of Him who shall come after Him Whom God shall make manifest (*ba'd man yuzhiruh Alláh*). And all these Revelations [were] for the coming of the One after the One after Him Whom God shall make manifest. And in this manner incessantly the Sun of Truth shines forth and sets, without beginning or end (ibid. 4:12).

A number of core Islamic beliefs are either abrogated or completely changed by the Báb. For example, he denies corporeal resurrection on Judgement Day, a logical consequence of the symbolic interpretation given of 'resurrection' (ibid. 2:11).

The meaning of 'Day of Resurrection' is the Day when the Tree of Truth appears. Not a single soul is perceived among the Shi'a that has understood the 'Day of Resurrection'. Rather, they have all clung unto a vain imagining that has no truth in the sight of God (ibid. 2:7).[15]

The Báb further abrogates the whole notion of an oral tradition supplementing the revealed scriptures of God. He strongly decries narrating miracles and accounts that have no basis in the revealed text. In fact he makes clinging to tradition responsible for unbelief at the time of the revelation of any Manifestation.

> Whoever seeks to prove the truth of the Point of the Bayán [i.e. the Báb] through anything but divine verses has veiled himself from the greatest proof and the noblest path . . . In the Qur'an nothing other than this proof has been revealed. Had they all understood this, it would have been easier for them, rather than to profess faith in God through matters they narrate themselves and for which there is no proof in the book of God (Persian Bayán 6:8).[16]

Finally a point of great theological importance is the Báb's endorsement of 'alteration of divine decree (*badá'*)'. A matter of dispute for centuries, several theories have been presented by Shi'i thinkers. Some have argued that God, once he has made a decision, cannot alter it at a later point in time (for a discussion of *badá'* in Shi'i history see the entry in Khurramsháhí et al. 1995 and also see Goldziher 2003). Thus all prophecies will have to come true in exactly the way they have been recorded. Others have allowed for *badá'* only under specific historical circumstances, such as the nomination of the seventh Imam.[17] The view endorsed by the Báb was that God's omnipotence does not allow for any limitation of his freedom to choose and decide whatever he wishes. Paraphrasing a canonical hadith (al-Qummí 1967, Báb al-Badá' 54:1, pp. 331f.) the Báb writes:

> God is not worshipped through anything [as he is] through [belief in] *badá'* because *badá'* is recognition of his power to do what He willeth. If one worships God through all imaginable means – should he acknowledge belief (*i'tiráf*) in *badá'* it is still a greater act of worship than everything else he has done (Persian Bayán 4:3).

The importance of *badá'* for the Báb's Revelation can hardly be overestimated. The concept played an important role in Shi'i eschatology and Shaykhi thought as well as in early Bábí apologetics (see Eschraghi 2004, pp. 101f., 158f., 214f., 329).[18] However, what it stresses more than anything else is the Báb's belief that each Manifestation is completely free in his decisions and not bound by men's expectations or even by earlier prophecies. Thus a total break with the past such as the Báb's annulment the Islamic sharia receives its theological justification.

The point made above is that the Báb did not perceive himself as a reformer in the classical sense, nor did he intend to merely revive or reinterpret Islam. He went much further than reform and created the theological fundamentals as well as a new religious paradigm. We shall now examine the concrete implications of this new paradigm by looking at some of the Báb's laws.

General characterization of Bayánic law

As has been noted above, Bayánic law includes prescriptions that seem foreign and sometimes obscure and harsh. One wonders, then, what might have been the Báb's motivation for abrogating Islamic law, only to replace it with an at times more modern and suitable, but sometimes even more severe and altogether virtually impracticable one. In reply to such a question, Shoghi Effendi has given the following explanations:

> The severe laws and injunctions revealed by the Báb can be properly appreciated and understood only when interpreted in the light of his own statements regarding the nature, purpose and character of his own Dispensation. As these statements clearly reveal, the Bábí Dispensation was essentially in the nature of a religious and indeed social revolution, and its duration had therefore to be short, but full of tragic events, of sweeping and drastic reforms. Those drastic measures enforced by the Báb and His followers were taken with the view of *undermining the very foundations* of Shí'ih orthodoxy, and thus *paving the way* for the coming of Bahá'u'lláh. To *assert the independence* of the new Dispensation, and to prepare also the ground for the approaching Revelation of Bahá'u'lláh, the Báb had therefore to reveal very severe laws, even though most of them were never enforced. But the mere fact that He revealed them was in itself a proof of the independent character of His Dispensation and was sufficient to create such widespread agitation, and excite such opposition on the part of the clergy that led them to cause His eventual martyrdom (Bahá'u'lláh 1992, n109 (emphasis added)).

> . . . this Book [the Bayán] . . . should be regarded primarily as a eulogy of the Promised One rather than a code of laws and ordinances designed to be a permanent guide to future generations . . . Designedly severe in the rules and regulations it imposed, revolutionizing in the principles it instilled, calculated to awaken from their age-long torpor the clergy and the people, and to administer a sudden and fatal blow to obsolete and corrupt institutions, it proclaimed, through its drastic provisions, the advent of the anticipated Day, the Day when 'the Summoner shall summon to a stern business', when He will 'demolish whatever hath been before Him, even as the Apostle of God demolished the ways of those that preceded Him' (Shoghi Effendi 1979, p. 25).

From these two quotations three main underlying goals of the Báb's code of laws are gathered. One is 'paving the way' for the next Manifestation. The second is to deal a 'blow to obsolete and corrupt' institutions of Shi'i orthodoxy. The third is to 'assert the independence' of his Revelation.

Preparing for the advent of the Promised One

That the main goal of the Báb was to prepare people for the coming of the next Manifestation is so obvious to even a cursory reader of the Bayán that it need not be explained in much detail here. E.G. Browne's testimony to this effect reads as follows:

> We cannot fail but to be struck by the fact that when the Báb was a prisoner and an exile at Mákú, probably well aware of what his ultimate fate would be, he showed far more anxiety about the reception which should be accorded to 'Him whom God shall manifest' than about himself . . . Almost every ordinance in the Beyán is

similarly designed to be a perpetual reminder of 'Him whom God shall manifest' (Browne in Momen 1987, p. 232).

The following quotations confirm Browne's impression that the focal point of the Bayán was indeed intended to be the Promised One and the ultimate goal of all prescriptions therein his recognition:

> The Bayán and all who believe in it circumambulate the word of 'Him Whom God shall make manifest', just as the Gospel and all who believe in it circumambulated the word of Muhammad the Apostle of God (Persian Bayán 3:3, cf. 5:8, 2:6, 2:17, 2:19). Take good heed of yourselves, for the sum total of the religion of God is but to help Him, rather than to observe, in the time of His appearance, such deeds as are prescribed in the Bayán. Should anyone, however, ere He manifesteth Himself, transgress the ordinances, were it to the extent of a grain of barley, he would have transgressed His command (The Báb 1976, p. 85).

Later Bábí apologetics and polemics claimed that the Báb fixed a time for the coming of the next Manifestation or at least implied that it would take 1500 to 2001 years. This is not the place to treat this subject here since it has already been discussed by others (Afnán 1997, pp. 1–37; Mu'ayyad 1992, pp. 94–102).[19] In short, such an argument has no basis whatsoever in his writings. The Báb, quite to the contrary, stressed repeatedly that the future Manifestation was free to appear at any time and place and under any condition. One of the many warnings directed by the Báb towards his followers is this:

> At all times, await the beginning of the Revelation (*awwal-i zuhúr*). Should you hesitate for less than a moment you will be counted among the 'new [converts]' in the sight of God. Just as you call today those non-Muslims who enter Islam (Persian Bayán 6:13).[20]

Even if there were statements by the Báb placing conditions on Him Whom God shall make manifest, they would have to be considered in light of the following quotation:

> Beware, beware lest, in the days of His Revelation, the Váhid of the Bayán [Letters of the Living] shut thee not out as by a veil from Him, inasmuch as this Váhid is but a creature in His sight. And beware, beware that the words sent down in the Bayán shut thee not out as by a veil from Him (quoted in Bahá'u'lláh 1988, p. 153).[21]

That the Báb was very anxious about the fate of the next Manifestation is more than obvious. We shall now look at some of the concrete measures the Báb took to 'pave the way'.

The independent character of the Bayánic sharia

Much has already been said above about the independent character of the Báb's religion. Laying down a new sharia was indeed a vital factor in proclaiming a new religious paradigm and in giving the adherents of the new faith a distinctive identity. Had the Báb simply abrogated the sharia and not revealed a new code of laws, the separation of Islam would not have been as clear. Bábís have argued that the Báb revealed laws for a future state of society, when the majority at least of Iran's population will have embraced his faith. Their main argument was that the Promised One could not come so shortly after the Báb, since the Bayánic sharia had not even been put into effect and it was thus too early for it to be abrogated. As has been noted above, there is no indication anywhere in the Báb's writings that the Promised One was to come only after victory of the Báb's faith or, for that matter, at any specific point of time.

Furthermore, reading the Persian Bayán might leave the reader puzzled as to how some of the more complex and sometimes obscure regulations were ever to be put into practice. It seems obvious that the Báb's sharia was essentially symbolic in character. Virtually every prescription and regulation is designed to be either a reminder of the advent of the Promised One or a means of paying tribute to him. It is hard to imagine that the Báb should have anticipated any state to actually put *all* his laws, especially the ritual observances, into practice.[22]

Rituals are a central part of any religion and play an important part for the identity of its adherents. The Báb gave various complex and detailed prescriptions as to how and when a certain number of verses should be either recited or written down. These are too many to summarize here (for a more detailed description of Bábí ritual see MacEoin 1994). Further, several rituals are to symbolize constant change and foster detachment on behalf of the believers. Among these are the ordinances to renew personal belongings every 19 years (Arabic Bayán 9:14) and to renew books every 66 or 202 years (Persian Bayán 7:1).[23] In addition, a new calendar was introduced (ibid. 5:3) according to which the new law of fasting (ibid. 8:18) had to be observed. Obligatory prayer (*salát*) was enjoined on the believers in the Bayán. However, the exact nature of this prayer remains unclear.[24] It was, in any case, different from the Islamic obligatory prayer and the *qiblih* was to be the Promised One (Persian Bayán 7:19). The call to prayer (*adhán*) had already been changed in the early period of the Báb's Revelation ('The Báb', in Afnan 2000, pp. 99–100).

Various burial rites are part of the Bayánic sharia, differing considerably from Islamic custom, not least in that coffins are mandatory (Persian Bayán 5:11, 12; 8:11; 9:9). Pilgrimage is another ritual that completely differs from Islam. It is to be made to the house of the Báb in Shiraz. Additionally, shrines for outstanding believers of the Báb's dispensation are to be erected and visited (ibid. 4:15–5:2 and elsewhere). New codes of laws governing marriage (ibid. 6:7) and divorce (ibid. 8:15) as well as inheritance (ibid. 8:2) have also been revealed in the Bayán. Even the traditional Islamic greeting is substituted with other formulas (ibid. 6:5). Therefore, all major parts of religious law have been altered or replaced by the Báb.[25]

Since the Báb's laws were designed to pave the way for the next Manifestation, some of them aimed to reshape the general state of society. Therefore, despite what has been said above about the general impracticability of some Bayánic laws, there are a number of regulations that could have had a deep impact on 19th-century Iranian society.[26]

Largely because of the dramatic unveiling and subsequent tragic fate of an early outstanding disciple of the Báb, Táhirih 'Qurratu'l-'Ayn', Bábism has often been characterized as strengthening the role of women, although there seems to be no clear provision in the Bayán that would in fact establish the kind of equality that is to be found later on in Bahá'í writings, nor does there seem to be much proof that Táhirih was motivated by a struggle for women's rights. But nevertheless a number of Bayánic ordinances indeed improve the situation of women in society.

Although there seems to be no unequivocal abrogation of the Islamic law of veiling,[27] there is a provision that allows Bábí men and women to look at each other and communicate in a befitting manner.

> Those who have been brought up in this community (*tá'ifih*), men and women, are allowed to look [at each other], speak and sit together (ibid. 8:9, cf. Persian Bayán 8:10).

That men and women are allowed to see each other could be understood as at least a partial abrogation of the law of veiling. Modern western readers might not appreciate the revolutionary potential of this permission. Suffice it to say that up to the present Bábís and Bahá'ís are accused of committing all kinds of immoral acts during their religious meetings just because women are allowed to participate.

The Bayání sharia relieves women from obligatory pilgrimage (*hajj*) (Persian Bayán 4:19). The fact that marriage is dependant on mutual consent is another strengthening of women's position in religious law (ibid. 6:7). When embarking on trips men should exhaust all possibilities to take their wives with them (Haykal al-Dín 6:16). Men who maltreat their wives and daughters are said to deviate from the path of truth:

> Conduct yourselves with your women in the most loving manner. Believing women are like the leaves of the heavenly camphor tree. Do not mistreat (*mayázár*) them even for a blink of an eye, because were you to do so, you shall be veiled from the command of God for that very blink of an eye (Sahífih-yi 'Adliyyih, p. 38).

The greatest means to achieve nearness of God is showing utmost love and kindness to one's wife and children (Persian Bayán 4:19).

Another interesting part of Bábí law has to do with education. Children are to be treated with utmost care and loving-kindness. Parents are obliged to treat their offspring well and to ensure their education at least until they are 11 years old. The Báb does not make a distinction between boys and girls in that regard.[28] The love parents display in regard to their children is considered as the greatest act of worship and tantamount to showing love for God (Persian Bayán 4:19). Children may never be left alone and should be encouraged with kind words (Haykal al-Dín 6:10).[29] On holy days they should be allowed to play (Persian Bayán 6:11). In school they must be placed on chairs (Haykal ad-Dín 6:10; cf. Persian Bayán 6:11). Teachers are not allowed to beat children before they reach the age of five. Even then, they may only be beaten five times slightly, not on the flesh but on the clothes. Should a teacher beat a child more than five times or on the flesh, he may not approach his wife for

19 days, or if he is unmarried, he will have to pay a fine, even if the transgression occurred unintentionally (Persian Bayán 11:6).

As a further measure to improve the general condition of the state and making information available to all inhabitants, the Báb makes it a duty for every ruler to establish a postal system. He further says that, although such a system already exists in Iran, it is insufficient because 'the weak ones (*mustad'afín*)' have no access to it (ibid. 4:16). In a similar vein, the Báb approves and highly praises the printing of books so that the verses of God may be spread and made accessible to all (ibid. 7:1).

A further Bayánic law is the general prohibition of tobacco and intoxicating substances (ibid. 9:7, 8). Even animal rights feature in the Bayán. Thus, animals are not to be mistreated, otherwise they will demand a punishment from God for their possessor. Should someone seek to enlarge his profit through unduly burdening his animals, he will not succeed in doing so and be subject to divine punishment (ibid. 6:16).

Laws in relation to Shi'i clerics

According to Shoghi Effendi, one of the Báb's major goals was provocation and thus causing changes in the general structure of society. The most effective and necessary means to do this was to shatter the power of the clergy. Although initially of a quietist sect, certain Shi'i clerics developed an elaborate theology to justify their craving for worldly power. By the time of the Qajar dynasty (18th/19th century AD) the influence of the clerics had reached a new height. It is beyond the scope of the present article to describe the complex relations between government, monarchy, clerics and the people, neither can the historical development of certain theological ideas prevalent in Qajar times be discussed here.[30] But a few points are particularly important for understanding the revolutionary character of the Báb's Revelation. Unlike their predecessors, the Safavid dynasty (1501–1722), the Qajar rulers did not lay claim to charismatic religious authority. This vacuum could now be completely filled by the Shi'i ulama, who had by now successfully developed and implemented the doctrine of general vicegerency (*al- niyábah al-'ámmah*), thus seizing complete authority in religious matters. In addition, most Qajar monarchs were quite pious and supported the clerics and the Usúlí establishment in many regards. In return, the ulama did not openly challenge the authority of the monarch and even safeguarded its religious legitimization.

The 'fifth (*khums*)' or 'share of the Imam (*sahm-i Imám*)' was to be submitted to them, as sole representatives of the Hidden Imam. In addition, they were in control of religious endowments (*awqáf*). A third source of income was their legal function, such as issuing and confirming contracts, marriage certificates, etc. The clerics thus possessed great spiritual authority as well as financial power and enjoyed the great respect of both the royal court as well as the ordinary believers, the vast majority of whom were illiterate.[31] Although there seems to have been no serious attempts to actually usurp state power, the ulama in Qajar times were very keen on and successful in steadily broadening the scope of their authority and in exercising influence in state affairs.[32] Some ulama were influential enough to issue verdicts and punish perpetrators according to the sharia, thus indirectly denying allegiance to the executive and judicative powers of the state, at least in religious matters.[33] In religious matters, Shi'i Islam had increasingly become a legalistic construct, obsessed with detailed and often absurd minutiae of ritual or even everyday behaviour.[34] The foundations for church-like hierarchical structures that characterize contemporary Iranian Shi'ism were laid during this period. Charismatic, spiritual and mystical tendencies were looked upon with great contempt and often severely attacked. Religion had thus become a body without spirit.[35]

The government was in many regards rather frail. The state was constantly weakened by challenges to its central authority such as local revolutions by militant separatist movements and unwillingness to pay taxes. The overt activities of colonial powers and a disastrous defeat in a war with Russia further weakened the monarchy's position. For obvious reasons, the ulama were highly sceptical towards any change in the structure of the Qajar state. Any reform, whether religious, economic or social, was perceived as a potential threat to their newly consolidated position and thus faced with their utmost enmity.[36]

The Báb identified the Muslim clerics as those who showed forth the greatest enmity towards his Revelation and the utmost zeal in fighting it. He made them responsible not only for denying the truth of his Revelation but also for leading astray the people and thus not fulfilling their self-assumed duty to enjoy the good and support believers in their search after truth:

> At the time of every revelation the people of that revelation were veiled by the learned (ulama) of that revelation (Persian Bayán 7:11).[37]

> Had they been content with their own veiled condition and had they not dealt unjustly with anyone and not issued commands contrary to what has been revealed in the Book of God, they would have had cast themselves into hellfire. But now, their own punishment as well as that of whoever imagines them to be the ulama of Islam – nay, rather [the punishment] of whoever failed or will fail to believe in the Revelation of God, will be upon them (ibid. 2:1).

A central quotation in challenging the authority of the ulama is the following:

> The ulama today, because of the utterance of one of the Imams – peace be upon them – who said: 'Turn towards those who transmit our hadith', believe themselves to be supreme judges (*hakam*) appointed by the Imam. Moreover, they attribute titles (*asmá'*) to themselves which are not suitable. If they spoke honestly, they would not have remained as veiled from him, who confers authority (*wiláyah* or *waláyah*) and prophethood through a single word. However, when they perceived that the Revelation of God was not in accordance with [safeguarding] their own station ... they even issued a verdict (*fatwá*) against God (ibid. 2:3).

In addition to what has been said above, two further important points of criticism can be deduced from the last passage. Serious doubt is cast on the ulama's justification for their religious authority and the high titles and functions they have claimed for themselves.[38] Further, they are so attached to those titles and to their power that

– should God himself want to take it away from them – they would fight him with every means at their disposal.

From the very beginning of his declaration the Báb embarked on a confrontational course with the ulama. His very claim as presented in his earliest writings, although clouded in symbolic language and often minimized by him, already had far-reaching implications for the ulama establishment.

As has been noted above, the Shi'i divines' claim to authority rested on belief that the Twelfth Imam had gone into occultation. That during the time of the 'Greater Occultation' nobody was able to contact the Imam had become a religious dogma. Owing to the absence of the Imam and the impossibility of turning to him directly, the clergy as a whole was to be regarded as his representatives and enjoyed certain prerogatives as well as responsibilities.[39] The Báb's claim to being a 'specific (kháss) representative' who speaks on behalf of and receives direct instructions from the Imam was thus tantamount to annulling the ulama's central basis of authority.[40] Apart from its spiritual dimension, such a claim had clear economic implications for the clerics since, as has been explained above, the fifth (al-khums), for example, was to be paid to the representative of the Imam.[41]

The Báb further criticized the clerics for their incompetence in uniting the Islamic community. In this day he was to be the only authoritative source of guidance, sent by God to unite the many sects of Shi'i Islam (cf. *Sahífih-yi 'Adliyyih*, pp .6, 7, 9, 13; *Tafsír Súrat al-Kawthar* (INBA 53), pp. 184, 244; *Tafsír Súrah wal-'Asr* (INBA 69), p. 26; *al-Risálah al-Dhahabiyyah* (INBA 86), p. 89; *Sharh Hadíth Abí Labíd* (E.G. Browne Collection F21), p. 20). One of the prerogatives reserved exclusively for the Imam himself was the right to declare offensive holy war (jihad) against the enemies of Islam. The Báb from his earliest Revelation claimed this right for himself when speaking of the 'Day of Permission' that was soon to come or had already arrived. In addition, the frequently occurring terms *nasr* and *nusrah* (rendering assistance) are loaded with eschatological as well as militant connotations.[42] In the *Kitáb al-Rúh*, an important and yet neglected voluminous early work, the Báb wrote in reference to Quranic verses:

> About what do they ask each other about the command of your Lord on the Day of Permission? Say: Verily, now permission has come from your Lord, God, but whom there is no other God. Give permission for waging war (*qitál*) and say: 'Whatever God willeth!' and 'There is no power save with God!' . . . And when the Remembrance gives permission for waging war they [the believers] long for God and fight before God in truth (*Kitáb al-Rúh*, sura 222).

As can be concluded from later developments, the Báb clearly did not intend for his followers to actually engage in militant activities. His ideal was that of suffering and martyrdom.[43] However, by invoking messianic sentiments and claiming authority over declaring jihad he uttered a strong provocation against the ulama.[44]

Frequent calls to *mubáhalah*[45] and declaring the ulama's incompetence to produce verses like his own were another challenge to their authority. According to the Báb, although the learned spent many years studying grammar and literature, they were still unable to write in equal fashion to him, who was utterly unlearned but inspired by God. Even more, their whole literary output was worth less than a single word uttered by him (see The Báb, *al-Risálah al-Dhahabiyyah* (INBA 86), p. 82; *Kitáb al-'Ulámá* (INBA 67), p. 209; *Fí Bayán al-I'tiqádát*, in Eschraghi 2004, Appendix I); Persian Bayán 2:1; *Tawqí' li-Muhammad Sháh* (INBA 64), pp. 114, 125. For additional references and discussion of the Báb's concept of *mubáhalah* see Eschraghi 2004, pp. 105f., 126, 138, 160n, 162, 277, 352).

At the core of the authority the ulama exercised over ordinary believers was the Friday prayer. At least once a week every Muslim should come to the mosque and pray under the guidance of the prayer leader (Imam Jum'ih). Afterwards he would listen to the sermon (*khutbah*) given by that leader. Thus the clerics established constant contact with the believers and made themselves a focal point of social life. Friday prayers have also in the course of history proved to be a powerful tool for influencing popular opinion.

Appointment of Friday prayer leaders is a prerogative of the Hidden Imam but for obvious pragmatic reasons this has been suspended. The Báb, in his earliest writings, declared all Friday prayers as unlawful if they were conducted by a leader not appointed by him (*Kitáb al-Rúh*, sura 206). Later he abrogated congregational obligatory prayers altogether (Persian Bayán 9:9).[46] Additionally, preaching from pulpits was prohibited (Persian Bayán 7:11). These three provisions strike at the very foundation of the ulama's role as intermediaries between man and God and remove a crucial basis of their social influence. In a similar vein, the forgiveness of sins is to be sought solely in private communion with God or his Manifestation. The Christian and partly Islamic practice of seeking absolution from divines as representatives of God is prohibited (ibid. 7:14). Thus yet another tool of exercising strong psychological power over people was removed.

A major part of the ulama's charismatic authority was rooted in their knowledge. The Shi'i community is generally divided into clerics and laymen, although the terms generally used are *mujtahid* and *muqallid*. Only a man who has passed through specific stages of learning and has proved to be familiar with certain parts of Islamic doctrine and law can become a *mujtahid*. That means he is allowed to pass authoritative verdicts and judge in religious matters. Permission to exercise *ijtihád* (*an ijázah*) is granted by one or more high-ranking clerics. On the other hand, ordinary believers are bound to *taqlíd* (imitation). They do not have the right to investigate matters independently and come to their own conclusions. For them following the guidance of a *mujtahid* in all religious matters is mandatory.[47] The Shaykhi leader Karím Khán Kirmání summarizes this attitude as follows:

> Whoever seeks guidance in matters of faith, this is with us. Let him come to us and receive [answers] because these matters are to be found with us, not with shopkeepers (*baqqál*) and bakers (*Risálih-yi Radd-i Báb-i Khusrán Ma'áb*, p. 27).

The ulama, in short, possessed a monopoly on knowledge.[48] They claimed to be the only ones to properly understand the Qur'an and exclusively able to interpret it adequately. They not only knew the complex rules and peculiarities of the Arabic language but were also initiated into the mysteries of theology, philosophy and the oral traditions of the Prophet and the Imams.

The Báb had already, in the earliest days of his dispensation, made *ijtihád* dependent on conformity with his own Revelation. Similarly, the ulama were prohibited to study books other than his own writings.

> And verily, God has forbidden you [to issue] unlawful verdicts and [to practise] *ijtihád* without pure knowledge of this book (Qayyúm al-Asmá', sura 2).

> O Concourse of the Learned! Ye have been forbidden after [the revelation of] this Book to teach anything other than it. Acquaint the people with the prescriptions (*ahkám*) of the Book and turn away from the obsolete (*bátil*) writings that are spread amongst you . . . (ibid. sura 27).

The scope of the latter early provision was later enhanced. Extensive study of grammar was prohibited, just as were engaging in fruitless and unnecessary theological, philosophical and legalistic discussions and penning treatises about these 'invented' matters. The only works to be studied and taught were those of the Báb and treatises inspired by his writings (Persian Bayán 4:10; cf. Qayyúm al-Asmá', sura 27).[49] All other books were to be 'wiped out (*mahw*)' (Persian Bayán 6:6).[50] The right to interpret the Word of God was reserved solely for the Manifestation (Persian Bayán 2:2). Therefore a number of the ulama's prerogatives and the fundamentals of their claim to supreme authority were annulled in the Revelation of the Báb.

A very powerful tool to destroy opponents was the practice of *takfír* (declaring someone as an infidel). The ulama not only used it against non-Muslims and secularists but also against adversaries in their own ranks, such as Ahmad al-Ahsá'í. Declaring a Muslim a non-believer is tantamount to issuing a death warrant because apostasy, according to the Islamic sharia, is a capital crime. The Báb unequivocally prohibited this practice for his own followers.

> They may not refute each other, since whoever enters the Bayán is a believer. Whatever stage (*maqám*) he might have reached, it is good (*khúb ast*). Should one of the [people of the] Bayán refute another of the [people of the] Bayán, he shall be obliged to pay 95 mithqáls of gold . . . The purpose of God in [prescribing] this provision is that none in the Bayán shall dare to refute anyone by calling [him a] non-believer (ibid. 5:14).

Likewise, death verdicts were generally forbidden in the Persian Bayán.

> In case there should arise differences in questions of the [religious] sciences, God has not given permission for anyone in the Bayán to issue a death warrant (*fatwá-yi qatl*) against anyone, at any time, under any circumstances and under any condition. Moreover, it is God who judges and commands. How does it behove you, O wayward people, to issue a death warrant against anyone? (ibid. 4:5).

Apart from *takfír*, one specific theme of Shi'i theology is the idea of ritual impurity (*najásah*). Probably inspired by Jewish or Hindu thought,[51] Shi'i clerics have developed a complex system defining the conditions for ritual purity (*taháráh*) and, should it be lost, what measures need to be taken to regain it. 'Non-believers', which usually means non-Muslims and sometimes even non-Twelver Shi'as, are generally deemed unclean. Touching them or touching an item that has been touched by them previously will necessarily lead to loss of ritual purity and make ritual ablutions mandatory. *Najásah* in Shi'i doctrine, it is important to note, has little or nothing to do with hygiene.

The Báb, quite to the contrary, explicitly allows for trading and establishing business contacts with people from outside his Faith (Persian Bayán 5:7). In the following passage he treats the subject of ritual impurity and names all things that can restore it:

> The purifying (*al-mutahhirát*) are of diverse kinds (*anwá'*): fire, air, water, dust, the Book of God, the Point [i.e. the Báb himself] and his writings, whatever the name of God has been called upon 66 times . . . whoever enters this Faith and is immediately purified as well as whatever belongs to him, further whatever is handed over by someone from outside this Faith to people of this Faith. Ending its connection with him [the former possessor] and establishing connection with them [the believers] purifies it (ibid. 15:14).

It is hard to imagine anything that would not fit into at least one of the categories above. Particularly interesting is that believers and the Word of God are called purifying. This renders practically the whole Shi'i concept of *najásah* obsolete. Whereas in their view a believer becomes impure by touching an impure person or item, in the Báb's teaching it is the other way around. It is thus virtually impossible to lose ritual purity as a Bábí. Also, the Báb redefines *najásah* in that he connects it with general provisions to observe hygiene. For example, water is called purifying, especially flowing water (ibid. 6:2). One cannot but gain the impression that the Báb here, with a certain amount of irony, abrogated a concept that had kept the minds of numerous authors busy for centuries.[52]

Conclusion

The Báb pursued three major goals in revealing his new code of laws. One was preparation for the advent of the Promised One. The second was to provoke the clerical establishment and shatter the foundations of their often-abused institutionalized authority. These provisions were the ones that led to the ulama's hostility and the Báb's subsequent martyrdom. The third aim was to prove the independence of his own religion in relation to its predecessor, namely Islam. In the Persian Bayán the Báb basically renewed all aspects of religious life, i.e. he taught a new theological doctrine, set forth ritual ordinances and even made suggestions for reforming the general state of society. Thus the Bábí religion fulfils all the criteria of a new and independent religion and differs in many central issues from mere reform movements.

Bibliography

'Abdu'l-Bahá. *Risálih-yi Síyásiyyih.* Darmstadt: 'Asr-i Jadíd, 2005.

— *The Secret of Divine Civilization.* Wilmette, IL: Bahá'í Publishing Trust, 1990.

Afnan, Abu'l-Qasim. *'Ahd-i A'lá: Zindigání-i Hadrat-i Báb* (The Bábí Dispensation: The Life of the Báb). Oxford: Oneworld, 2000.

Afnan, Muhammad. 'Áthár-i Manthúr-i Táhirih', in *Khúshih-há-'i az Kharman-i Adab va Hunar.* vol. 3. Darmstadt: Druckservice und Verlag Reyhani, 149 BE/1992, pp. 89–106.

— *Ayyám-i Butún,* in *Pazhúhish-Námih,* vol. 2, no.1. Dundas: Association for Bahá'í Studies in Persian, 1997.

Ahsá'í, Shaykh Ahmad. 'Hayát an-Nafs', in *Jawámi' al-Kalim,* vol. 1. Tabriz: n.p., 1273–6/1856–7–1860.

— *Rasá'il al-Hikmah.* Beirut: al-Dár al-'Álamiyyah, 1993.

— *Sharh al-Ziyárah,* vol. 1. Kirmán: Cháp-khánih-yi Sa'ádat, 1979.

Amanat, Abbas. *Resurrection and Renewal: The Making of the Bábí Movement in Iran, 1844–1850.* Ithaca, NY: Cornell University Press, 1989.

The Báb. 'Fí Bayán al-I'tiqádát', in Eschraghi, *Frühe Shaikhi- und Bábí-Theologie,* Appendix I.

— Haykal al-Dín. n.p.: n.p., n.d.

— al-Khasá'il al-Sab'ah, in A. Q. Afnán, *'Ahd-i A'lá.*

— Kitáb ar-Rúh (unpublished manuscript).

— Kitáb al-'Ulámá. INBA 67.

— Letter to 'Abd al-Kháliq Yazdí, in A. Q. Afnán, *'Ahd-i A'lá.*

— Persian Bayán. n.p.: n.p., n.d.

— Qayyúm al-Asmá'. Manuscript of 'Tafsír súrat Yúsuf'. Bahá'í World Centre Library, uncatalogued, 1261 AH.

— al-Risálah al-Dhahabiyyah. INBA 86.

— Risálah fí 'Ilm al-Nahw. INBA 67.

— Sahífih-yi 'Adliyyih. n.p.: n.p., n.d.

— *Selections from the Writings of the Báb.* Trans. Habib Taherzadeh with the assistance of a Committee at the Bahá'í World Centre. Haifa: Bahá'í World Centre, 1976.

— 'Sharh Hadíth Abí Labíd', in E. G. Browne Collection F21.

— 'Sharh Qawl al-Sayyid al-Rashtí fi al-I'ráb', in E. G. Browne Collection F21.

— Tafsír Súrat wal-'Asr. INBA 69.

— 'Tafsír Súrat al-Baqarah', translated in Lawson, *The Qur'an Commentary of Sayyid 'Alí Muhammad.*

— Tafsír Súrat al-Kawthar. INBA 53.

— Tawqí' li-Muhammad Sháh. INBA 64.

Bahá'u'lláh. *Epistle to the Son of the Wolf*. Wilmette, IL: Bahá'í Publishing Trust, 1988.

— *The Kitáb-i-Aqdas* (*The Most Holy Book*). Haifa: Bahá'í World Centre, 1992.

— *Tablets of Bahá'u'lláh revealed after the Kitáb-i-Aqdas*. Haifa: Bahá'í World Centre, 1978.

Behmardi, Vahid. '*Muqaddamih'í darbárih-yi sabk wa siyàq-i Áthár-i Hadrat-i Nuqtih-yi Úlá*', in *Khúshih-há-'í az Kharman-i Adab va Hunar*, vol. 6. Darmstadt: Reyhani, 152 BE/1995, pp. 47–67.

Browne, Edward Granville. 'Babis of Persia II', reprinted in Momen (ed.). *Selections from the Writings of E. G. Browne*.

Browne Collection F21.

The Encyclopaedia of Islam. Leiden: Brill, 2003, web CD ed.

Eschraghi, Armin. *Frühe Shaikhi- und Bábí-Theologie: die Darlegung der Beweise für Muhammads besonderes Prophetentum: (ar-Risāla fī Ithbat an-Nubūwa al-Khāssa)*: Einleitung, Edition und Erläuterungen. Leiden: Brill, 2004.

Goldziher, Ignaz and A.S. Tritton. 'Badá'', in *The Encyclopaedia of Islam*.

Gulpáyigání, Mírzá Abu'l-Fadl, and Mírzá Mihdí Gulpáyigání. *Kashf al-Ghitá 'an Hiyal al-A'dá'*. n.p.: n.p., n.d. http://www.h-net.org/~bahai/areprint/kashf/kag.htm.

Halm, Heinz. *Die Schi'a*. Darmstadt: Wissenschaftliche Buchgesellschaft, 1988.

Iranian National Bahá'í Archives (INBA).

Kadívar, Muhsin. *Nazariyyih-há-yi dowlat dar fiqh-i Shí'ih*. Tehran: Nashr-i Nay, 1998.

Khomeini, Ruhollah. *Hukúmat-i Islámí* (republished as *Viláyat-i Faqíh*). Tehran: n.p. 1361 AH/1942–3.

— *Kashf-i Asrár*. Tehran: Intishárát-i Dár al-Kitáb, 1941.

Khurramsháhí, et al. (eds.). *Dá'irat al-Ma'árif-i Tashayyu'*. Tehran: Nashr-i Sa'íd Mahabbatí, 1995.

Kirmání, Karím Khán-i. *Izháq al-Bátil*. Kirman: Matba'at al-Sa'ádah, 1351AS/1973.

— *Risálih-yi Radd-i Báb-i Khusrán Ma'áb* (manuscript).

al-Kulayní, Muhammad b. Ya'qúb. *al-Usúl min al-Káfí*, vol. 1. Tehran: Dár al-Kutub al-Islámiyyah, 1388 AH/1968–9.

Lambden, Stephen. 'The Background and Centrality of Apophatic Theology in Bábí–Bahá'í Scripture', in McLean (ed.). *Revisioning the Sacred*.

— 'The Sinaitic Mysteries: Notes on Moses/Sinai Motifs in Bábí and Bahá'í Scripture' in Momen (ed.), *Studies in the Bábí and Bahá'í Religions*.

Lawson, B. Todd. *The Qur'an Commentary of Sayyid 'Ali Muhammad, the Báb*. Unpublished Ph.D. diss., McGill University, 1987.

— 'The Terms Remembrance (*Dhikr*) and Gate (*Báb*) in the Báb's Commentary on the Sura of Joseph', in Momen, *Studies in Honor of the Late Hasan M. Balyuzi*.

MacEoin, Denis. *From Shaykhism to Babism: A Study of Charismatic Renewal in Shi'i Islam*. Ph.D. Diss. Cambridge University, 1979.

— *Rituals in Babism and Baha'ism*. London: I. B. Taurus, 1994.

Mahmúdí, A. *Mabání-i Istinbát-i Huqúq-i Islámí*. Tehran: Intishárát-i Dánishgáh-i Tihrán, 2003.

Mázandarání, Fádil. Táríkh-i Zuhúr al-Haqq, vol. 3. n.p.: n.p., n.d. http://www.h-net.org/~bahai/areprint/vol2/mazand/tzh3/tzh3.htm.

McCants, William F. 'A Grammar of the Divine', in the present volume.

McLean, J. A. (ed.). *Revisioning the Sacred: New Perspectives on a Bahá'í Theology*. Studies in the Bábí and Bahá'í Religions, vol. 8. Los Angeles: Kalimát Press, 1997.

Moayyad, Heshmat. 'Man Yuzhiruhu'lláh', in *Mahbúb-i 'Álam*. n.p.: 'Andalíb Editorial Board of the National Spiritual Assembly of the Bahá'ís of Canada, 1992–3, pp. 94–102.

Momen, Moojan. *Studies in Honor of the Late Hasan M. Balyuzi*. Los Angeles: Kalimát Press, 1989.

— 'Conspiracies and Forgeries: The Attack upon the Bahá'í Community in Iran', in *Persian Heritage*, vol. 9, no. 35 (Fall 2004).

— *An Introduction to Shi'i Islam*. London: Yale University Press, 1985.

— *Selections from the Writings of E. G. Browne on the Bábí and Bahá'í Religions*. Oxford: George Ronald, 1987.

— (ed.). *Studies in the Bábí and Bahá'í Religions*; *Studies in Honor of the Late Hasan M. Balyuzi*, vol. 5. Los Angeles: Kalimát Press, 1988.

— 'The Trial of Mullá 'Alí Bastámí: A Combined Sunní-Shí'í Fatwá against the Báb', in *Iran*, vol. 20 (1982).

Núrí, Shaykh Fadl Alláh. *Lawá'ih*. Homa Ridvání (ed.). Tehran: n.p., 1983.

al-Qummí, Abú Ja'far Muhammad b. 'Alí b. Bábawayh. *Kitáb al-Tawhíd*. Beirut: Mu'assasat al-A'lamí, 1967.

Rahnema, Ali. *An Islamic Utopian: A Political Biography of Ali Shari'ati*. New York, I. B. Tauris, 2000.

Shoghi Effendi. *God Passes By*. Wilmette, IL: Bahá'í Publishing Trust, rev. ed. 1979.

Notes

1. This criticism was levelled against him by several high-ranking Shi'i ulama before the Islamic revolution and in the early months after it, notably amongst the members of the 'Mahdaviyyat (Hujjatiyyih)' Society, also known as the 'Anti-Bahá'í Society'. Nevertheless, Khomeini managed to overcome all resistance. In more recent times several books have been written and published in Iran which demonstrate that Khomeini's idea was in many regards new to Shi'i Islam. See Kadívar, *Nazaríyyih-há-yi dawlat dar fiqh-i Shí'ih*.
2. The Safavid dynasty came to power in the 16th century and subsequently initiated a process of converting Iran's hitherto Sunni population to the Shi'i sect.
3. Throughout history some esoteric groups, such as the Nizárí Ismá'ílís, have abrogated the Islamic law. But their views were essentially eschatological in nature and not aimed at reforming human or state society in general. The final consequence of their ideas was complete anarchy.

4. The same, in theory, holds true for Jewish and Christian dogma.
5. The reasons for the Báb's denial of his claims are complex and will not be presented here. For a detailed discussion on the basis of the Báb's own writings see Eschraghi, *Frühe Shaikhi- und Bábí-Theologie*, pp. 134–76.
6. Stephen Lambden ('The Sinaitic Mysteries') and Todd Lawson ('The Terms Remembrance') have shown this conclusively on the basis of his earliest writings. See also Eschraghi, *Frühe Shaikhi- und Bábí-Theologie*, pp. 156–76. Further proof is in the 1845 verdict (*fatwá*) against Mullá 'Alí Bastámí, translated and analysed by Moojan Momen ('The Trial of Mullá 'Alí Bastámí'). In his article Momen also draws attention to a very early Shaykhi polemic: Karím Khán Kirmání's *Izháq al-bátil*. In that work the Shaykhi leader quotes extensively from the Qayyúm al-Asmá' and concludes that despite the outward claim of the – as yet unknown – author to be a mere representative of the Imam, he actually proclaims himself a prophet, abrogates Islamic law and even sees himself as God.
7. All translations are, unless otherwise noted, provisional and only intend to give the content of a passage, not necessarily to adequately display the beauty of language and other stylistic features. The Báb is here most probably alluding to certain Shaykhi expectations. Apparently, Sayyid Kázim taught that the Promised One held authority to abrogate the rules of grammar. See the Báb's early Sharh Qawl al-Sayyid ar-Rashtí fí al I'ráb, in Browne Collection F21, pp. 26–35. On folio-page 31 of that work the Báb states that the Imams are endowed with divine authority to change the rules of grammar in whichever way they deem befitting.
8. M. Afnan speaks of a 'spiritual revolution' (*inqiláb-i rúhání*) which was initiated by the Báb's Revelation and is clearly reflected in the grammatical peculiarities of his own writings as well as those of his disciples. See his article 'Áthár-i Manthúr-i Táhirih', pp. 91f. For the peculiarities of the Báb's style see: Behmardi, *Muqaddamih'í darbárih-yi sabk wa siyáq-i Áthár-i Hadrat-i Nuqtih-yi Úlá'*; and McCants, 'A Grammar of the Divine', in the present volume. It seems that Quddús took the break with Arabic grammar to the extreme. In a manuscript of unknown origin but attributed to him we find incomprehensible and completely ungrammatical verb-forms such as *y-q-sh-'-rr-t* and *y-k-f-h-rr-t*, among others.
9. It is generally believed that Ahsá'í and Rashtí were heavily engaged in raising messianic expectations and anticipated the advent of the Promised One. Although only a few traces of such ideas are found in their writings, there are strong indications that an oral tradition existed at least among some Shaykhi circles. For details see Eschraghi, *Frühe Shaikhi- und Bábí-Theologie*, pp. 89ff. Thus a representative of the Imam existed at all times and, contrary to mainstream Shi'i belief, could be contacted by the believers. He was referred to as the Fourth Support of religion, the other three being belief in God, the Prophet and the Imams. Some Shaykhi sects state that Karím Khán Kirmání was the first to introduce the idea of the Fourth Support, a representative of the Hidden Imam present at all times. However, the fact that the term and concept occurs in the Báb's earliest writings as well as in a number of epistles penned by early Shaykhi converts proves that at least at the time of Rashtí such belief must have existed. One example is a letter written by Táhirih to a Shaykhi adherent defending the Báb's claim: Mázandarání, *Táríkh-i Zuhúr al-Haqq*, vol. 3, pp. 484–501. See also the Báb's Tafsír Súrat al-Baqarah translated in Lawson, *The Qur'an Commentary of Sayyid 'Alí Muhammad*, pp. 49ff. and *passim*.
10. Although the general custom is to pray at the head of an Imam, Shaykhis pray at his feet. This, they think, is a sign of great veneration and reverence. Owing to this practice, Shaykhis have also been called 'Pusht-i Sarís' and their adversaries 'Bálá-Sarís'. The Báb, in his early writings, endorsed the Shaykhi practice in this regard and enjoined prayers at the feet of the Imams; see Kitáb al-Rúh (unpublished manuscript),

sura 247; Ziyárat al-Jámi'ah al-Kabírah (Iranian National Bahá'í Archives, vol. 50), p. 3; Sahífah bayn al-Haramayn (manuscript dated 1261), pp. 37f.
11. The Báb further explains his new 'basmala' in the Persian Bayán 3:6. See also ibid. 7:2 where yet another basmala is introduced.
12. In the Báb's writings 'resurrection' symbolizes the appearance of the next Manifestation of God.
13. In this context Shaykhi writings and the Báb often quote the Quranic (7:172) tale of a pre-existential covenant.
14. His unbelief in all the previous worlds is indicated. Since each revelation is like a new creation, it can be imagined as a whole new 'world'.
15. Throughout Islamic history several individuals have denied corporeal resurrection. However, they do not seem to have interpreted it in the way the Báb does, namely a new revelation of God. It is sometimes stated that the Shaykhiyyah had already taught a spiritual interpretation of resurrection. In fact, Ahsá'í was attacked by other clerics for his seemingly heterodox views about resurrection and the Prophet's night journey (see below, note 40). However, his writings do not reveal such a purely spiritual interpretation. His foremost disciple and successor Kázim al-Rashtí wrote a lengthy treatise in defence of his spiritual master's orthodoxy. An incomplete manuscript in Rashtí's own handwriting is held at the Kirmání-Shaykhi library (photocopy in possession of present writer). A complete edition of the text was recently published in Beirut. In this work Rashtí repeatedly and unequivocally declares that beyond any doubt the views of Ahsá'í were in complete accordance with orthodox and traditional Shi'i belief held unanimously by all theologians. Whoever spoke to the contrary was either an enemy of the Shaykh or unaware of his specific terminology. Ironically, Ahsá'í himself had in a commentary on Mullá Sadrá's *'Arshiyyah* accused the latter of denying corporeal resurrection (see also *Rasá'il al-Hikmah*, p. 228). Whatever the case, it is clear that Ahsá'í's rather complex views about several bodies of different grades of subtlety (see ibid. pp. 96ff.) bear no resemblance whatsoever to the Báb's interpretation of resurrection. It is noteworthy that the Báb, although in his early works extensively uses specific Shaykhi terminology, never seems to endorse Ahsá'í's view about resurrection. The quotation above shows that he did not believe any Shi'i Muslim had understood the truth of the matter. This seems to include Ahsá'í and Rashtí.
16. In the beginning of the same chapter, the Báb also says that no miracles other than the verses of God should be ascribed to him.
17. Initially the sixth Imam Ja'far al-Sádiq had nominated his son Ismá'íl as his successor. When Ismá'íl died before his father, another son, Músá al-Kázim, was declared his successor. Since Imams are generally thought to have been appointed by God himself before creation came into being, and are also perceived of as omniscient and free from error, the matter caused confusion among the believers.
18. The Báb's very claim was an example of *badá'* and a core issue of early Bábí (and Bahá'í) apologetics. Twelver Shi'a believe that the Twelfth Imam went into occultation in the year 260 AH (873–4 CE), his life being mysteriously prolonged by God until the day when he shall come forth again and destroy the non-believers. Practically speaking, the Báb could not be the Qá'im because he was born and raised in Shiraz in the 19th century and was not a thousand years old. The Báb himself explained this as *badá'*. Generally, all prophecies could be rendered as naught by God if he wished to do so. See Sharh Hadíth Abí Labíd (in Browne Collection F21), p. 14. It seems that Ahsá'í had already paved the way for this interpretation of the Qá'im's existence. According to him, the Promised One was currently in the world of archetypal forms (*al-suwar*), which means that he could appear practically in any body (cf. *Sharh al-Ziyárah*, vol. 1, p. 77). The Promised One to him was the 'repository of the secret of

badá" (ibid. p. 319). Ahsá'í was possibly himself inspired by hadith reports like the following: "Abú Ja'far said: . . . If we tell you about a matter and it happens as we said, say: "God speaks the truth (*sadaqa'Alláh*)". And if we tell you about a matter and it happens contrary to what we said, [still] say "God speaks the truth" and ye shall be rewarded twice.' A footnote says, 'Once for belief, once for accepting *badá"* (al-Kulayní, *al-Usúl min al-Káfí*, vol. 1, pp. 367ff.).

19. The Bábís derived that number from the Arabic word Mustagháth, which the Báb mentions in connection with the Promised One in a few instances. Cf. 3:15, 7:10. The numerical equivalent of this word is 2001. However this is a rather arbitrary interpretation of the Báb's statements, since he does not at all imply that this was to be the date for the Promised One's arrival. Rather, he made it abundantly clear that the Promised One's revelation was bound by no restriction whatsoever.
20. In Islam new converts from religious minorities were labeled 'new to Islam (*jadíd al-Islámí*)', thus ranking them somewhat lower than others who were already born into Islam or had a long family tradition in that faith.
21. The source for this quotation is a letter by the Báb, printed as an appendix to Gulpáyigání's *Kashf al-Ghitá' 'an Hiyal al-A'dá'*. Another manuscript can be found in Folder 21 of the E. G. Browne Collection. The English text reads Vahíd for Váhid, which has been corrected here.
22. Some Bahá'ís believe that the Báb intentionally designed his laws to be severe and virtually impracticable, so that Bábís would not cling to them and soon realize their symbolic character as well as the need for a new revelation.
23. These numbers equal the words Allah (66) and Rabb (202) or Muhammad-'Alí (202), the name of the Báb.
24. The same is true of Islam. Although the Qur'an enjoins obligatory prayer on the believers, detailed provisions are not found in it. Therefore, there are considerable differences between the prayer rites of diverse Islamic sects.
25. In addition to rituals, the Báb has laid down a number of further provisions such as a new currency. For details see Persian Bayán 5:19.
26. The following quotation of Bahá'u'lláh points at the reformist potential inherent in the Báb's Revelation: 'If these obstructing veils had not intervened Persia would, in some two years, have been subdued through the power of utterance, the position of both the government and the people would have been raised . . . Thus, once Persia had been rehabilitated, the sweet savours of the Word of God would have wafted over all countries, inasmuch as that which hath streamed forth from the Most Exalted Pen is conducive to the glory, the advancement and education of all the peoples and kindreds of the earth. Indeed it is the sovereign remedy for every disease, could they but comprehend and perceive it' (Kalimát-i Firdawsiyyih in Bahá'u'lláh, *Tablets*, p. 73 (6:43)). The word translated here as 'power of utterance' is 'Bayán' and thus probably refers to the Báb's dispensation, a fact that might not be gained from reading the English translation.
27. The only reference known to the present writer is found in the late Haykal al-Dín (8:7). There the Báb says that women should not be forced to hide their hair when saying their obligatory prayer.
28. In contrast, a passage from Shaykh Fadl Alláh Núrí, a conservative 19th-century cleric who strongly opposed the constitutional movement and was eventually executed, comes to mind. In present-day Iran he is revered by the government as a martyr and a 'forerunner'. In his *Lawá'ih* (p. 28) he writes about the constitutionalists: 'Now we have all seen with our own eyes that from the beginning of the establishment of this parliament a group of . . . unbelievers (*lá madhhab*), which were earlier known to have been Bábís . . . have come into motion . . . And a number of newspapers and pamphlets have appeared, most of them including insults against the great learned and

the laws of Islam. And [in which it is stated] that changes to this sharia must be made . . . such as allowing for intoxicants, spread of sexual immorality and establishing schools for women and girls . . .' That he should see the establishment of schools for girls as tantamount to spreading immorality is revealing.

29. Eleven was fixed as the age of maturity in the dispensation of the Báb.
30. For a detailed introduction to the general state of society during the time of the Báb's ministry see Amanat, *Resurrection and Renewal*, especially the first part (pp. 1–108). For general theological developments and the rise to power of the clergy referred to on the following pages, see Momen, *Introduction to Shi'i Islam*, especially pp. 130ff.; Halm, *Die Schi'a*, especially pp. 132ff.
31. An example that reveals the state of mind as well as the degree of veneration some Qajar monarchs entertained for high-ranking clerics can be seen in Fath-'Alí Sháh's behaviour towards and his letters to Shaykh Ahmad al-Ahsá'í. The monarch's main interest seems to have revolved around the 'quality of intercourse in the hereafter'. See Ahsá'í's response in *Rasá'il al-Hikmah*, pp. 91ff.
32. The example of the second Perso-Russian war shows how the ulama used their influence to virtually force the rather unwilling Iranian government into a disastrous war that led to great financial as well as territorial loss.
33. One example was Muhammad-Báqir Shaftí in Isfahan.
34. This attitude is reflected in Khomeini's statement in his early *Kashf-i Asrár*, p. 107. According to him, the Prophet Muhammad 'has brought several divine ordinances and heavenly commands for going to the toilet [sic!], for being alone with a woman and for giving milk to a child. There is no little or big matter that He has not given instructions for.'
35. To use 'Alí Sharí'atí's terminology alluded to earlier, the label 'Safavid Islam' would be used to describe this religious paradigm.
36. In *The Secret of Divine Civilization* and even more in his *Risálih-yi Síyásiyyih*, 'Abdu'l-Bahá determined the clerics' interference in politics to be responsible for the miserable state of affairs in Iran.
37. The term ulama, though literally meaning 'knowing' or 'learned', is more likely used here by the Báb as a *terminus technicus*, common amongst Muslims to describe the divines.
38. The hadith the Báb is alluding to is attributed to the Twelfth Imam and generally quoted by Shi'i clerics to support their claim to authority. See Mahmúdí, *Mabání-i Istinbát-i Huqúq-i Islámí*, p. 14n. The passage reads in full: 'Regarding matters that will happen (*al-hawádith al-wáqi'ah*) turn to those who transmit our hadith. For verily, they are my proof over you and I am the Proof of God over you.'
39. The various theological disputes that surround this view cannot be discussed here. That neither the ulama as a whole nor a certain group but rather their most noble (*afdal*) representative is to exercise supreme authority is in any case a late development. It forms the doctrinal foundation of the current Iranian state form. An interesting question is whether and to what extent Khomeini-ist doctrine was influenced by the Shaykhi teaching of the Fourth Support. A passage in Ahsá'í's *Hayát al-Nafs*, in *Jawámi'al-Kalim*, vol. 1, pt. 1, pp. 7f.) describing the qualities of the supreme representative bears great resemblance with Khomeini-ist doctrine. See also *Sharh az-Ziyárah*, vol. 1, p. 34.
40. It is most probably for this reason, rather than for his obscure speculations about resurrection and the Prophet's night journey (*al-isrá'*), that Shaykh Ahmad al-Ahsá'í was declared an infidel and his later adherents faced severe persecution on behalf of Usúlí clerics. Ahsá'í's (and later Rashtí's) claim was to be in regular contact with the Imams. Thus they were allegedly able to meet them in dreams and visions and to receive guidance from them whenever they wished. Ahsá'í showed open disregard for the mechanisms of Usúlí hierarchy. In his short autobiography he mentioned none of

the seven regular *ijázahs* he had received by prominent clerics but rather based his claim on a 'paper' signed by all 12 Imams and handed over to him in a dream. For details see Eschraghi, *Frühe Shaikhi- und Bábí-Theologie*, pp. 35–9; MacEoin, *From Shaykhism to Babism*, p. 56.

41. Apart from the fifth, the Báb later removed another lucrative source of income for many ulama: he prohibited selling stones, sand and other relics of holy places. Further, selling land around holy sites was not allowed. Persian Bayán 4:13, 17.
42. They echo the Imam Husayn's words shortly before his martyrdom: 'Is there no one who will assist me [in fighting the infidels]?'
43. The Báb called for jihad only at a time when chances were unrealistic. When his followers were assembled in Karbala to wage the apocalyptic battle between the forces of good and evil, he changed his initial plan to go there. The reason for this, as he says in several letters from that time, was that he did not want any bloodshed to occur. See for example his letter to 'Abd al-Kháliq Yazdí, in Afnán, *'Ahd-i A'lá*, p. 184. For a discussion of the Báb's attitude towards and specific understanding of jihad see Eschraghi, *Frühe Shaikhi- und Bábí-Theologie*, pp. 166–9.
44. The Kirmání Shaykhi leader Karím Khán, a contemporary and fierce enemy of the Báb, wrote in one of his several refutations: 'During the period of the Greater Occultation, according to the unanimous verdict of the learned, there is no jihad. And no learned has permission to draw a sword and fight jihad and gather forces . . . This is another proof of his [the Báb's] blasphemy (*kufr*)' (Karím Khán, *Risálih-yi Radd-i Báb-i Khusrán Ma'áb*, p. 28).
45. *Mubáhalah* serves to establish the truth of a claim in the presence of witnesses. Conditions can be miracles or plainly calling God's curse upon the opponent. Muhammad is said to have done this during his own time. The practice is also attested to in the Old Testament (I Kings 18:17ff.). In the Báb's writings *mubáhalah* is confined to producing verses, prayers and treatises.
46. An exception, also known to Bahá'ís, is the Prayer for the Dead.
47. Khomeini took this dogma to a further extreme when he declared it unlawful even to report crimes to secular state authorities. If someone reported a theft to the police of a non-Islamic state, then the thief found and the item returned, the item stolen was still unlawful to its original possessor simply because it was obtained through 'illegal' channels (*Hukúmat-i Islámí*, republished as *Viláyat-i Faqíh*, Tehran 1361AH/1942–3, p. 84).
48. The little education the average citizen would receive was equally controlled by the ulama since the only institutions for learning during that time were *madrasas*.
49. From the passages in question one can conclude that the Báb mainly targeted the kind of fruitless hairsplitting that was prevalent amongst the learned, such as whether *jinn* (spirits, ghosts, demons) were male or female and whether one could have sexual intercourse with them, or how Siamese twins were to observe the religious rituals and whether such rituals were binding on other planets. In addition, theological discussions that had preoccupied the minds of philosophers for centuries and sometimes even led to bloodshed were possibly among the subjects the Báb had in mind, such as whether God knows only essentials or particulars as well, whether the Word of God is created or eternal, etc. In any case, in issuing these general condemnations he uttered yet another strong provocation against the ulama.
50. Apparently, at a later stage even the books of Ahsá'í and Rashtí were included in this provision. That was when influential Shaykhi ulama proved to be among the fiercest enemies of the new Faith. Karím Khán Kirmání quotes a letter attributed to the Báb in which study of the *Sharh al-Qasídah* and other central Shaykhi works is prohibited. See *Risálih-yi Radd-i Báb-i Khusrán Ma'áb*, pp. 43–4. It is unclear whether the Báb actually called for the physical destruction of books or merely meant that they should

be deemed obsolete. In the Arabic Bayán (9:13), at any rate, he prohibited the physical destruction of any book whatsoever.
51. There is only one verse in the Qur'an (9:28) that calls 'idol-worshippers unclean (*najas*)' and demands that they be kept out of mosques. No trace of the detailed instructions for ritual purity later developed by Shi'i theologians can be found in the Qur'an.
52. Even today all higher ranking Shi'i ulama write a 'thesis', usually called 'Answers to Questions (*Tawḍíḥ al-Masá'il*)'. A major part of these is dedicated to laws of *najásah* and *taháraḥ*. Bahá'u'lláh at any rate has quite clearly abrogated the whole notion of ritual uncleanliness in verse 75 of his Most Holy Book.

15

Concealment and Burial of the Báb

Chapter Five of

A Prophet in the Modern Age

Biography of Siyyid 'Alí Muhammad, the Báb

by A.L.M. Nicolas

Translated and annotated by Peter Terry

Hence the Báb was much vexed in his prison, and he remained there for a relatively long time¹ because the document which we have just cited is dated 1264,² and the execution of the martyr did not take place until 27 Sha'bán of the year 1266.³

However the execution was preceded by a change of prison – he was made to leave Mákú for Chihríq.⁴ Mírzá Taqí Khán,⁵ the Amír Nizám⁶ who was then the prime minister, seeing that the Bábí revolution loomed larger and greater and appeared to be formidable, told himself that the best way to calm all these revolts would be to do away with the one whom he considered to be the leader behind these events, that is to say, the Báb himself. He referred the matter to the shah⁷ who felt obliged to remark that all these troubles were due to Hájí Mírzá Áqásí, the former Sadr A'zam⁸ of his father,⁹ who ordained the imprisonment of the Reformer at Mákú without having him come first to Tehran where he could have made him submit to an enquiry.¹⁰

Násiri'd-Dín Sháh remarked, 'Also the vulgar believed that in him there was a [divine] knowledge or some miracle. If he had been allowed to come to Tehran for a public discussion, it would quickly have been seen that there was nothing special about him.' These judicious reflections attracted a response worthy of admiration. 'The words of kings, are the kings of words,' observed the prime minister in a convincing tone, 'which does not detract', he added, 'from the fact that today there is no longer any other way than to kill him.' I do not know whether the conversation continued a long time in this vein.¹¹

Nevertheless, Sulaymán Khán-i-Afshar¹² was sent to Tabriz to proceed with the execution. When Sulaymán Khán arrived at his destination, Hamzih Mírzá Hishmat al-Dawlih,¹³ who was then the governor of Ádhirbáyján, decreed that the Báb be brought thence from Chihríq. At the same time his disciples were brought with him, those who followed him everywhere, that is Áqá Siyyid Husayn¹⁴ and Mullá Muhammad-i-Yazdí.¹⁵

The ulama were then invited to a great conference but they refused to come, declaring that the ideas of the accused were heretical and that by this very fact he merited death.[16] Hishmat al-Dawlih, seeing the disgust – I here translate a Muslim author – of the ulama, had the Báb arrive at night, when he was encountered, in a meeting prepared for this purpose, by Mírzá Hasan Khán Vazír-Nizám[17] and Hájí Mírzá 'Alí.[18] They interrogated him, asking for the explanation of a difficult hadith, and the Reformer – which is implausible – remained silent. So Hishmat al-Dawlih, taking the floor, asked him to compose verses on the subject of the crystal candlesticks.[19]

The Báb obeyed but his response was not recorded. Some moments later, when invited to repeat the same verses, he was unable to do so.[20]

From that point he was condemned and sentenced to death. However, it was wished that his execution be in public, for it was thought that if it took place secretly, nothing would stop the people from believing in his miraculous ascension to heaven. It was thus decided that the Báb would be marched through the streets of the town and executed in the great common,[21] which, strange as it may seem, in Tabriz is called the 'Plaza of the Sáhib al-Zamán'.

Thus the Siyyid was taken with Mullá Muhammad-'Alí Yazdí and Siyyid Husayn, and they were conducted to Hájí Mírzá Báqir,[22] the Imám Jum'ih of the town, to Mullá Muhammad Mámáqání[23] and to Áqá Siyyid 'Alí Zunúzí,[24] who delivered a fatwa decreeing the execution.

From there commenced a sorrowful march through the bazaars,[25] during which Áqá Siyyid Husayn – charged by his master with the execution of his last wishes – disavowed and renounced the Báb, and, upon an order from the tormenters, spit in his face. He accomplished the mission which was confided to him, and was, a little later, executed in Tehran.[26] Having arrived at the fatal Plaza, all efforts were made, in vain, to separate Mullá Muhammad-'Alí[27] from his convictions – his wife and his little children were brought, but he obstinately refused to listen to them, limiting himself to one last request – the favour of being killed before his master.

It was then that a strange event occurred, unique in the annals of humanity. The two companions, solidly attached to one another, were placed before the Christian regiment of the Bahadurans.[28] Upon a signal given by their chief, the soldiers fired. Afterwards Mullá Muhammad-'Alí, covered with wounds, dying, was seen to turn towards his master, his words terrifying the witnesses: 'Master,' he said, 'Master, are you content with me?' The bullets had cut the cords which held the Báb, who dropped to his feet, without a scratch. 'Ah! If at this moment he had exposed his chest,'[29] says the historian of the 'Kitáb al-Mutanabbi'ín',[30] 'and if he had cried, "O soldiers, O men, you are yourselves the witnesses of this miracle, that of 1000 bullets[31] not a single one could reach me and some even cut my bonds", all would have begun to howl and throw themselves at his feet. But,' continues our author, 'God wished to make known the truth; that is why he made him run away.'

Concerning these last words, I am not, and cannot be, of the same opinion as I'tidád al-Saltanih. Christians are convinced that if Jesus Christ had wished to descend living from the cross, he could have done so without difficulty – he died voluntarily because he had to die in order to fulfil the prophecies. It is the same for the Báb, say the Bábís, who also wished to give clear evidence in support of his words. He also died voluntarily because by his death he was to save humanity. Who will ever reveal to us the words the Báb might have pronounced in the midst of the nameless tumult that greeted his departure? Who will know what memories agitated his beautiful soul? Who will ever tell us the secret of his death?

Be that as it may, the soldiers took him again,[32] bound him once more to the infamous pole and this time Siyyid 'Alí Muhammad rendered his soul to God. It was on Monday the 27th of Sha'bán that this event took place.[33]

The Comte de Gobineau (Gobineau 1865), who in this agrees with the authors of the *Nasíkhu't-Taváríkh* (Sipihr 1965), the *Rawdat al-Safá-yi Násirí* (Hidáyat 1959–60) and the *Mir'at al-Buldan*,[34] in a word with all the official court historians, reports that after the execution the cadaver of the Báb was thrown into the town ditch and devoured by dogs. In reality, this was not so but we will see why this account was circulated – as much by the authorities of Tabriz who were not at all anxious to bring the reprimand of the government upon themselves through a complacency bought at high cost, as by the Bábís who desired in this way to influence the police investigations.

The irrefutable testimony of those who witnessed this drama and of its actors leaves me in no doubt that the body of Siyyid 'Alí Muhammad was received into pious hands and that finally, after vicissitudes which I will recount, it received a sepulchre worthy of him.

When the execution was accomplished, the troops retired, the crowd dispersed and the bodies were committed to the soldiers on guard. The Comte de Gobineau, along with other authors, would have it that the body was marched through the streets of the town for three days. Although this is, in general, denied by tradition, I accept it to be true because it is believable. In any case, night having come, the body was left where it was, alone and abandoned, or it was guarded by soldiers. In the first case it is totally impossible that the numerous Bábís to be found in the town would have hesitated a single instant to steal the body while nobody watched. They have demonstrated too many proofs of their courage, their conviction and their enthusiasm to admit, for even a second, that they would have abandoned to the public the body of him whom they considered their god and which, moreover, would have been so easy to recover. But if the official historians are right, and if on the third day the body was thrown into the town ditch to become the prey of stray animals, it is very clear that after this it was no longer guarded and the sectarians could easily have appropriated it. Finally, even if it were guarded at night, its removal would have been relatively easy. One has no doubt been able to perceive in the course of this story what Persian sentinels are made of: their function essentially consists in sleeping in front of the thing they have been charged with guarding.

If one considers that ringing and dramatic arguments leave very few people untouched in Persia, one can easily accept that the Bábís could find a way into the hearts of these badly paid poor devils. Finally, courage not being, especially in this circumstance, the dominant characteristic of the enemies of the Bábí Faith, if one allows that the guard was composed of perhaps two or three soldiers, they would very probably have fled after a first serious attack.

This is what the Bábís resolved to do. The leaders, gathered at the home of Sulaymán Khán of Sá'ín Qal'a[35] in order to decide what measures to take to remove the body of the martyr from the insults and brutalities of the infidels, decided to mobilize their men, to go in groups to the place where the Báb lay, to wage battle if necessary, and to carry off the precious relic no matter what the cost. Sulaymán Khán was a considerable man and head of a large family having ties of friendship with the Kalantar of Tabriz.[36] He prevailed upon his co-religionists for permission to warn this official of the decision that had been taken and to make known to him that it would be better for him to allow the removal of the body than to risk civil war breaking out in the town. The Kalantar, struck by the imminence of this peril and by the sum that was offered him, thanked Sulaymán Khán for his message, prayed him to advise his companions not to budge and to wait until he himself could ensure that the body of the Báb could be removed by his people. But the Bábís responded that they would not permit the assassins to sully the body of the august victim by touching it. The Kalantar thus consented that some Bábís go to the place of execution to remove the body and he sent some of his men with them to silence the soldiers on guard, who, receiving attractive payment, easily consented to keep quiet. Everyone being thus satisfied, it was arranged to say that the [body of the] Báb had been devoured by stray animals. This could easily be believed, for it was credible. Hence the plan offered the immense advantage of maintaining the peace in a generally turbulent city, enriching the actors in the comedy, freeing them of all responsibility and, on the other side, closing the eyes of the authorities. The two bodies were thus carried off; that of Muhammad-'Alí-i-Zanjání[37] was buried and that of the Báb shrouded in a box and hidden in a house.[38]

I must here open a parenthesis to report what was told me by Subh-i-Azal during my visit to Cyprus:[39]

> Before his death the Báb decreed in one of his verses that I entomb his body in a casket of diamonds, with God's permission, and bury him opposite Sháh 'Abdu'l-'Azím.[40] He described the location of the sepulchre in such fashion that I alone could understand what he meant.
>
> He died thus, as well as Muhammad-'Alí-i-Zanjání. The executioners threw the members of the two martyrs one over the other haphazardly in such fashion that it was impossible to differentiate them.
>
> I put both of them in a casket of crystal,[41] not being able to make one in diamonds, and buried it at the very place which the Prophet had indicated to me. The location of the sepulchre remained a secret for thirty years.[42] The Bahá'ís especially knew nothing of it but a traitor revealed it to them. These blasphemers disinterred the body and destroyed it. If they did not destroy it, and if they can show a new sepulchre which truly contains the casket of crystal and the body of the Prophet which they have stolen, we cannot bring ourselves to consider this new tomb as sacred as it is not the place indicated by the Báb.[43]

This version, which I reported to the Bahá'ís of Tehran, exasperated them and caused them to renew their anathemas against the recluse of Cyprus.

This is how things passed ... We have said that the body of the Báb was hidden in one of the houses of Tabriz. It was that of Sulaymán Khán himself.[44] He informed Bahá'u'lláh of what had happened and asked him for his instructions. Bahá', in conformity with the order he had received in the testament of the Báb,[45] entrusted the transport of this box to Jamál. It was carried to the Imám-Zádih Ma'súm,[46] which has since become the favoured cemetery of the Bábís, outside what is called the gate of Qazvín[47] – because it is there that the road from this town to the capital ends. It was placed in a niche that was then walled in with bricks.

Things remained this way for a long time, when, twenty-nine years ago, Mírzá Husayn 'Alí Bahá', being then at Adrianople,[48] gave the order to Hájí 'Alí-Akbar Shahmírzádí[49] and to Áqá Jamál[50] to remove the box from the place where it had been and to transport it elsewhere. They obeyed without understanding why they had been ordered to make this change; but they understood this instruction some time later when the Imám-Zádih, which was on the verge of collapse, was demolished and then rebuilt. Its demolition – if Bahá' had not taken this precaution – would have revealed the box and the precious relics would have fallen into profane hands.

I cede speech here to Hájí Mullá 'Alí-Akbar Shahmírzádí, who told me the whole story in this way:[51]

> After having received the order in question we went, Áqá Jamál and I, to find the box at the Imám-Zádih Ma'súm. We found it behind the wall of bricks, which we had to destroy, and we took it to Sháh 'Abdu'l-'Azím.[52] Night had come and we did not know what to do, finding nowhere we could safely place the box that had been entrusted to us. We crossed the village and came to the edge of Chishmih-'Alí,[53] passing in front of the Masjid-i-Máshá'u'lláh,[54] which was then half ruined and far from any habitation.
>
> We had found a favourable location so we stopped. We opened the box and found the body enwrapped in a shroud. We left it where it was and wrapped the whole body in a shroud of silk we had brought. In the course of doing this we found on his chest a bouquet of flowers that had been placed there and which were completely dried out. We took this bouquet and shared the flowers. Then we replaced the body in the box which we carried into the mosque, where we placed it standing up under a little arch. In the opening of the two arches we built a wall of the bricks we found lying on the ground; some plaster had been brought to us by one of our co-religionists.
>
> While we were thus occupied, we did not notice that we were being watched by farmers who had been intrigued by our entry into this solitary place.
>
> After finishing our work, we went to Quts-i-Hesar,[55] a village situated below the Sháh 'Abdu'l-'Azím, where we rested the whole day.
>
> The evening having fallen, we travelled with Jamál. Having arrived at Sháh 'Abdu'l-'Azím at the place where the two roads meet, the one going towards Chishmih-'Alí, the other towards Tehran, Jamál took the road to the town. I stopped him, saying it would be good if we returned to the Masjid-i-Masha'u'llah to see if we had left any obvious traces of us having been there and if our trust was really secure. As you will see, this was an inspiration from heaven.
>
> We set out on the road and Jamál, whose mount was less tired, or more robust, than mine, preceded me. I shouted to him that I would wait for him where I was. He then went on and I stayed alone. I waited a very long time, so long that I became uneasy and I hastened to rejoin my companion.

I found him swooning on the threshold of the mosque. I tried to revive him but he was so troubled, so upset, that he did not have the strength to respond to my questions about what had caused him to faint. So I entered the mosque, fearing that something bad had happened, and, as it was dark, I felt for the wall we had built. I could feel that it had been destroyed! Half crazy, I stretched out my arms before me and found the box but at the same time discovered that it had been broken. In despair, I pulled it towards me violently but, finding it very heavy, my hope was restored. Very soon I had the immense joy of confirming that the body was still there. Relieved, I reassured my companion and we consulted about what we could do.

We did not see any alternative other than to trust to Providence and try to take the box back into the town. So we put it on one of our donkeys and set out.

Arriving near the fortifications, we stopped, much perplexed. If we tried to take our burden through the gate, the customs men and soldiers would stop us to examine the contents and we be imprisoned and our box confiscated. To cross through the ditch and climb up the bank was difficult and dangerous. We were at the point of despair when the storm that had been threatening for a long time suddenly broke. The rain poured down and the crowd of pilgrims crushed themselves into the gateway. Profiting from the occasion, we mixed in with them and, holding our abá[56] over the box, in all the chaos we were able to pass through without being noticed.

We carried the box to one of our number, Áqá Mírzá Hasan Vazír,[57] the son-in-law of Siyyid 'Alí Majdu'l-Ashraf;[58] I installed myself in his house without revealing the secret to him.

I continued for fourteen months as the guardian of this trust. I do not know how our co-religionists were told of this temporary sepulchre but I soon received letters from every province about it, and from all points of the Empire Bábís came on pilgrimage. I had to tell all of these people that I did not know what this was all about, that everything that had been said was false, but the pilgrimages continued nevertheless.

From the beginning, alarmed by these comings and goings that might arouse the attention of the authorities, I referred to Bahá', informing him that some Isfáhánís intended to buy the land on which the house was built in order to construct a befitting tomb on it.

Finally, at the end of fourteen months, as I have already said, Hájí Sháh Muhammad, surnamed Amín, came from 'Akká.[59] He was the bearer of an order enjoining me to deliver the trust to him without questioning him about what he was going to do with it. I gave it to him without asking him for any explanation.

Hájí Sháh Muhammad, who was later killed at Tabriz in the insurrection of Shaykh 'Ubayd'u'lláh,[60] carried the body in great secrecy to an unknown place, probably the house of one of his co-religionists.

Thus did things continue. We were all ignorant of the place where the remains of our Prophet were to be found, when, seventeen years ago, Áqá Mírzá Asad'u'lláh Isfáhání[61] came from 'Akká to Jamál. He took charge of the trust but no one knew where he was going to take it and to whom he confided it. Finally, two years ago,[62] Asad'u'lláh returned and transported the relic to 'Akká. It is said that the final sepulchre is found at the foot of Mount Carmel.[63]

Hence, it was only long after his death that Siyyid 'Alí, the greatest figure of modern times, he who, for love of his fellow men, took part in the most terrifying adventure ever dreamt of with a courage all the more marvellous for being tranquil and unchanging, and who is without doubt a hero without equal, finally rests in eternal peace. May the earth be light upon him!

Bibliography

'Abdu'l-Bahá. *A Traveler's Narrative*. Wilmette, IL: Bahá'í Publishing Trust, 1980. (Originally published as *A Traveller's Narrative*. Trans. E.G. Browne. Cambridge: Cambridge University Press, 1891.)

Afnan, Abu'l-Qasim. *'Ahd-i A'lá: Zindigani-yi Hadrat-i Báb* (The Bábí Dispensation: The Life of the Báb). Oxford: Oneworld, 2000.

Amanat, Abbas. *Pivot of the Universe: Násir al-Dín Sháh Qájár and the Iranian Monarchy, 1831–1896*. Berkeley: University of California Press, 1997.

— *Resurrection and Renewal: The Making of the Bábí Movement in Iran, 1844-1850*. Ithaca, NY: Cornell University Press, 1989.

The Báb. *Muntakhabát-i áyát az ár-i Hadrat-i Nuqta-yi Úlá*. Tehran: Bahá'í Publishing Committee, 1978.

— *Selections from the Writings of the Báb*. Haifa: Bahá'í World Centre, 1976.

The Bahá'í World. vols. 1–12, 1925–54. rpt. Wilmette, IL: Bahá'í Publishing Trust, 1980.

Bahá'u'lláh. *Kitáb-i-Íqán*. Wilmette, IL: Bahá'í Publishing Trust, 1989.

Balyuzi, H.M. *The Báb: The Herald of the Day of Days*. Oxford: George Ronald, 1973.

— *Bahá'u'lláh: The King of Glory*. Oxford: George Ronald, 1980.

— *Eminent Bahá'ís in the Time of Bahá'u'lláh: With some Historical Background*. Oxford: George Ronald, 1985.

Bamdad, Mahdí. *Sharh-i Hal-i Rijal Írán dar Qarn-i 12, 13, 14 Hijra*, vol. 1. Tehran, 1968–74.

Curzon, Lord. *Persia and the Persian Question*, vol. 2, 16. Cited in Nabíl-i-A'zam, *Dawn-Breakers* 1970, p. 595, n. 2.

Faydí, Muhammad 'Alí, in *Hadrat-i Nuqtah-i-Úlá*. Tehran, 1973.

Frahvashtí, 'Alí. 'Á'ín-i Báb'. Cited in MacEoin, *Sources for Early Babi Doctrine and History*.

de Gobineau, Comte Joseph Arthur. *Religions et philosophies dans l'Asie Centrale*. Paris: Didier & Cie, 1865.

Gulpáyigání, Mírzá Abu'l-Fadl. *Kashf al-Ghitá' an Hiyal al-A'dá*. Cited in Nabíl-i-A'zam, *Dawn-Breakers*, p. 431, n. 3.

Hidáyat, Ridá Qulí Khán, Lálá-báshí. *Rawdat al-Safá-yi Násirí*, vol. 10. Tehran, 3rd ed. 1959–60.

Huart, Clement. *La Religion du Bab*. Paris, 1889. Cited in Nabíl-i-A'zam, *Dawn-Breakers*.

Iranian National Bahá'í Archives (INBA); Iranian National Manuscript collection (INBMC).

Ishráq Khávarí, 'Abdu'l-Ḥamíd, ed. *Má'idiy-i-Ásmání*. Cited in MacEoin, *Sources for Early Babi Doctrine and History*.

— *Rahíq-i Makhtúm*. 2 vols. Tehran: Bahá'í Publishing Trust 1973–4.

Kazemzadeh, Firuz and Kazem Kazemzadeh. 'The Báb: Accounts of His Martyrdom'. *World Order* (Fall 1973).

Khusraví, Muhammad 'Alí Malik. *Táríkh-i Shuhadá-yi Amr*, vol. 3. Tehran, 1973–4.

Kitáb-i-Nuqtatu'l-Káf. Leiden: Brill, 1910.

Latimer, George Orr. *The Light of the World*. Boston: George Orr Latimer (self-published), 1920.

MacEoin, Denis. *The Sources for Early Babi Doctrine and History: A Survey*. Leiden: E.J. Brill, 1992.

Mázandarání, Asadu'lláh Fáḍil. *Asrár al-Áthár*, 5 vols. Tehran: Bahá'í Publishing Trust, 124–9 BE/1968–73.

— *Tarikh Zuhur al-Haqq*, vol. 3. Tehran: n.p. 1941?, at http://www2.h-net.msu.edu/~bahai/areprint/vol2/mazand/tzh3.

Momen, Moojan. *The Bábí and Bahá'í Religions, 1844–1944. Some Contemporary Western Accounts*. Oxford: George Ronald, 1981.

Mubagajian, Atrpet Sargis. *Imámat: Strana Poklonnikov Imámov* (Persidskoe Dukhovenstvo) [Imámate: The Country of the Worshippers of the Imáms]. Alexandropol, 1909. http://bahai-library.org/books/biblio/history.html.

Muhammad Hasan Khán. *Mir'at al-Buldan*.

Mu'ín al-Saltana Tabrízí, Hájjí Muhammad Ibn 'Abdu'l-Báqí. *Táríkh-i Mu'ín al-Saltana*, Cited in Amanat, *Resurrection and Renewal*.

Nabíl-i-A'zam. *The Dawn-Breakers: Nabíl's Narrative of the Early Days of the Bahá'í Revelation*. Wilmette, IL: Bahá'í Publishing Trust, 1970.

Nicolas, A.L.M. *Le Beyan Persan*, vol. 1, 1911.

Ruhe, David S. *Robe of Light: The Persian Years of the Supreme Prophet, Bahá'u'lláh*. Oxford: George Ronald, 1997.

'Sharh-i Hal'. Tehran,1946. Cited in Amanat, *Resurrection and Renewal*.

Sheil, Lady. *Glimpses of Life and Manners in Persia*. Cited in Nabíl-i-A'zam, *Dawn-Breakers*, pp. 595–6, n. 2.

Shoghi Effendi. *God Passes By*. Wilmette, IL: Bahá'í Publishing Trust, rev. ed. 1995.

Sipihr, Mírzá Muḥammad Taqí, Lisán al-Mulk. M.B. Bihbudi, ed. *Násikhu't-Taváríkh: Qájáríyya*, 4 vols. Tehran,1965.

Taherzadeh, Adib. *The Revelation of Bahá'u'lláh*, vol. 1. Oxford: George Ronald, 1974.

— *The Revelation of Bahá'u'lláh*, vol. 2. Oxford: George Ronald, 1977.

— *The Revelation of Bahá'u'lláh*, vol. 3. Oxford: George Ronald, 1983.

— *The Revelation of Bahá'u'lláh*, vol. 4. Oxford: George Ronald, 1987.

Táríkh-i-Jadíd. Cambridge: Cambridge University Press, 1893.

The Universal House of Justice. Letter of an ad hoc Committee appointed by the Universal House of Justice to Robert Stauffer, 20 March 1983. http://bahai-library.org/wwwboard/messages00/584.html

Zaʻím al-Dawlih Mírzá Muhammad Mahdí ibn Muhammad Taqí. *Miftáh Báb al-Abwáb aw Táríkh al-Bábíya*. Cairo: Matbáʻát Majallát al-Manár 1903, pp. 233–5. Cited in Amanat 1989, p. 400, n. 107.

Notes

1. The Báb was imprisoned at Mákú for nine months (Nabíl-i-Aʻzam 1970, p. 259; ʻAbdu'l-Bahá 1980, p. 12; *Kitáb-i-Nuqtatu'l-Káf*, p. 129, cited in Amanat 1989, p. 374, n. 9), and he departed for Chihríq 20 days after Naw-Rúz (Nabíl-i-Aʻzam 1970, p. 259), the fourth Naw-Rúz after his declaration, corresponding to the hijra year 1264 (Nabíl-i-Aʻzam 1970, pp. 255–6). Since the eve of Naw-Rúz was on the thirteenth day of Rabíʻ al-Thání of that year (Nabíl-i-Aʻzam 1970, pp. 255–6), then the twentieth day after Naw-Rúz must have been on the fourth day of Jamádí al-Úlá 1264. Amanat 1989, p. 380, gives precisely this date, with its Gregorian equivalent of 10 April 1848. Another conversion of this date is 8 April 1848, based on these two date converters:
   http://www.rabiah.com/convert/
   http://www.ori.unizh.ch/hegira.html
   Nine months before this date would place the Báb's arrival at Mákú during the month of Shaʻbán 1263, corresponding to 15 July 1847 to 12 August 1847 (http://www.ori.unizh.ch/hegira.html) or to 14 July 1847 to 11 August 1847 (http://www.rabiah.com/convert/).
2. The Báb could have written this tablet to Muhammad Sháh from Mákú at any time during the last five months of 1263 and the first four months of 1264. Nicolas's dating of this tablet to 1264 is entirely probable, although not proved beyond reasonable doubt.
3. The date of the Báb's death is reported in Nabíl-i-Aʻzam 1970 (p. 517), ʻAbdu'l-Bahá 1980 (p. 27), and Avarih (vol. 1, p. 245; cited in Amanat 1989, p. 402, n. 114) as 28 Shaʻbán 1266. Nabíl-i-Aʻzam 1970 (p. 517), states that it took place at noon, while ʻAbdu'l-Bahá 1980 (p. 27), affirms that it occurred before noon. In his dispatch dated 22 July 1850 to Lord Palmerston, the British Foreign Secretary Lt.-Col. Sheil reported the martyrdom of the Báb but seems to have omitted the date of this event (F.O. 60/152; cited in Balyuzi 1973, pp. 202, 241). At the time of the execution of the Báb, R.W. Stevens, the British consul then serving in Tabriz, was absent from the city, having left his brother George Stevens in charge; George did not report this event to Lt.-Col. Sheil, who seems to have been informed through some other channel (Balyuzi 1973, p. 202).
   On 24 July R.W. Stevens returned to Tabriz and promptly filed a report of the execution to Sheil (F.O. 248/142; cited in Balyuzi 1973, pp. 202, 241; Amanat 1989, p. 402, n. 114). Amanat 1989 (p. 402, n. 114) notes that R.W. Stevens reported that the Báb's martyrdom took place on 27 Shaʻbán 1266/8 July 1850 but casts doubt on the British consul's positive knowledge of the event, inasmuch as he was not present in Tabriz at the time of its occurrence. Amanat 1989 (p. 402, n. 114) notes that Sipihr 1965 (vol. 3, p. 305, cited in Amanat 1989, p. 402, n. 114) also reports this event as occurring on 27 Shaʻbán 1266, but that this chronicler mistakenly identifies 27 Shaʻbán/8 July as a Monday, while Nabíl-i-Aʻzam 1970 (p. 517) correctly identifies 28 Shaʻbán/9 July as a Sunday, and he reasons that this makes the Bábí/Baháʼí dating more reliable than the Muslim account and the British diplomatic report. It might also be noted that Nabíl-i-Aʻzam 1970 (pp. 507–8) relates the testimony of the Báb's amanuensis, Siyyid Husayn Yazdí, with regard to the night just prior to

the Báb's martyrdom, and it seems entirely unlikely that so devoted a disciple could have mistaken the date of his master's martyrdom. Various eyewitness reports of the martyrdom of the Báb were collected and translated by Dr Firuz Kazemzadeh and his father Kazem Kazemzadeh and published as 'The Báb: Accounts of His Martyrdom', in *World Order* (Fall 1973, pp. 23–6).

4. The date of the Báb's departure from Máh-Kú for Chihríq has been cited in note 1 above as 4 Jamádi al-Úlá 1264/8 or 10 April 1848. Since Chihríq is approximately 80 miles southwest of Máh-Kú, it seems likely that the Báb would have arrived in Chihríq a few days later, at the latest about 9 Jamádi al-Úlá 1264/13 or 15 April 1848. MacEoin 1992 (p. 82) indicates that the Báb departed Máh-Kú on 9 April 1848 and arrived at Chihríq at the beginning of Jamádi al-Thání 1264/early May 1848. It is entirely improbable that this journey would have taken an entire month. Hájí Mírzá Áqásí ordered that Ridá-Qulí Khán-i-Afshár lead the escort of the Báb from Máh-Kú to Chihríq (Balyuzi 1973, p. 134). For information about Ridá-Qulí Khán-i-Afshár's father, Hájí Sulaymán Khán-i-Afshár, see note 12 below. Ridá-Qulí Khán was married, through the intervention of his father, to the daughter of Siyyid Kázim Rashtí (Balyuzi 1973, pp. 13–14). This chief of the Báb's escort was attracted to his charge during the journey from Máh-Kú to Chihríq (Mu'ín, pp. 169–72, cited in Amanat 1989, p. 367, n. 192) and subsequently became a zealous Bábí (Balyuzi 1973, pp. 134–5; Amanat 1989, p. 247, n. 250). Mu'ín (pp. 173–6, cited in Amanat 1989, p. 367, n. 194) also reports that Ridá-Qulí Khán was deprived of his family estate at Sá'ín Qal'a by his anti-Bábí father, and then poisoned by his son, motivated also by religious enmity.

The transfer of the Báb from Máh-Kú to Chihríq is reported by Nabíl-i-A'zam 1970 (p. 259) to have been motivated by Hájí Mírzá Áqásí's 'fear and resentment' at the influence exercised by the Báb over his jailer, 'Alí Khán of Máh-Kú. 'Abdu'l-Bahá 1980 (p. 13) reports that the Báb was moved because of the entreaties of the 'accomplished' Muslim clerics of Ádhirbáyján. Amanat 1989 (p. 378, n. 23) indicates that Prince Dolgorukov, the Russian minister in Tehran from 1845 to 1854 (MacEoin 1992, p. 170, n. 63), in a dispatch dated 4 February 1848 to the Foreign Minister of the Czar, reported that the Báb was transferred away from the Russian border, i.e. from Máh-Kú to Chihríq, during the previous year, in 1847. It seems likely that the Báb was not transferred until April 1848 but perhaps Prince Dolgorukov was informed of the decision to transfer the Báb prior to its taking effect. In any case, it appears from this dispatch that one of Hájí Mírzá Áqásí's motivations for effecting the removal of his prisoner from Máh-Kú to Chihríq may have been to calm the fears of the Czar's representative at court that the Báb's presence in that location might result in civil unrest and that its consequences could cross over the border into the Russian Empire. Chihríq was chosen for the Báb's imprisonment because the governor of the fortress and chief Khán (leader) in the region was Yahyá Khán Shakaki, a Naqshbandí Súfí, the brother of Muhammad Sháh's favourite wife and an ally of Hájí Mírzá Áqásí (Amanat 1989, p. 380, n. 33). Nabíl-i-A'zam 1970 (p. 301) and 'Abdu'l-Bahá 1980 (p. 13) call him simply 'Yahyá Khán the Kurd', and Nabíl-i-A'zam (p. 301) also reports that his sister was the mother of Náyibu's-Saltanih, one of the daughters of Muhammad Sháh – this would likewise identify his sister as one of Muhammad Sháh's wives. According to Nabíl-i-A'zam (p. 302), Yahyá Khán was transformed through his contact with the Báb, as were the Kurdish inhabitants of the village of Chihríq and those of Iskí-Shahr, an hour's distance from the fortress. Soon after the death of Muhammad Sháh, his Grand Vazír, Hájí Mírzá Áqásí, was deposed and Násiri'd-Dín Sháh appointed Mírzá Taqí Khán the new Grand Vazír. According to 'Abbás Mírzá Mulk Ara (in *Sharh-i Hal* 1946, p. 17, cited in Amanat 1989, p. 380, n. 33), shortly after Hájí Mírzá Áqásí's fall from power, Yahyá Khán was summoned to Tabriz and imprisoned there, apparently because of his relationship with the former Grand Vazír. This would indicate that

Yahyá Khán was not governor of Chihríq during the last period of the Báb's imprisonment in that fortress. The last reference to Yahyá Khán in Nabíl-i-A'zam (p. 322) is immediately upon the Báb's return to Chihríq after the trial in Tabriz, which probably occurred in August 1848, a month prior to Muhammad Sháh's passing and Hájí Mírzá Áqásí's disgrace. See the next paragraph for details. It should be noted that there is another Yahyá Khán in this story, an attendant of 'Abbás Mírzá Sháh and of his son Muhammad Sháh (Balyuzi 1973, p. 149). He was a resident of Tabriz and the father of Hájí Sulaymán Khán ('Abdu'l-Bahá 1980, p. 28; Balyuzi 1973, p. 149). Balyuzi reports (p. 149) that it was intended that Hájí Sulaymán Khán follow his father in service to the court but that instead he went to the 'Atabat, where he studied with Siyyid Kázim Rashtí. Subsequently he embraced the Cause of the Báb and visited his master at Chihríq (Balyuzi 1973, p. 149). Nabíl-i-A'zam (pp. 518–19) reports that Hájí Sulaymán Khán tried to effect the deliverance of the Báb but arrived in Tabriz on the second day after the Báb's execution. Nabíl-i-A'zam (p. 519) and 'Abdu'l-Bahá 1980 (p. 28) indicate that Hájí Sulaymán Khán was instrumental in the initial retrieval and safeguarding of the mortal remains of Anís and the Báb, and Nabíl-i-A'zam (pp. 519–20) indicates that Hájí Sulaymán Khán reported the details of this matter to Bahá'u'lláh in Tehran.

According to 'Abdu'l-Bahá 1980 (p. 14), the Muslim clerics of Tabriz wrote to the government in Tehran after the Báb had been in residence at Chihríq for three months. Three months after the Báb's arrival, which probably occurred about 9 Jamádi al-Úlá, would be 9 Sha'bán. Nabíl-i-A'zam 1970 (p. 301) reports that the Báb was brought to Tabriz towards the end of Sha'bán. Is there any conflict between these two dates? Not at all. 'Abdu'l-Bahá 1980 (p. 14) reports that subsequent to the appeal of the clerics of Tabriz to Tehran, Hájí Mírzá Áqásí ordered the Báb to be taken from Chihríq to Tabriz to be examined by the ulama. It would have taken some days for the message of the ulama to reach Tehran, for the edict of the Grand Vazír to reach Chihríq, and then for the Báb to be conducted via Urúmíyyih to Tabriz. The Báb's imprisonment at Chihríq, which began in early Jamádi al-Úlá 1264/April 1848, was interrupted by his journey to Tabriz in Sha'bán 1264/July 1848 (Amanat 1989, p. 387; Balyuzi 1973, p. 139). MacEoin 1992 (p. 82) dates this journey in Sha'bán 1264 but later in that month, in August 1848 (the only day of Sha'bán which fell in August is the 1st; cited in Nabíl-i-A'zam 1970 p. 301, n. 1), probably calculating the Báb's three months imprisonment at Chihríq from an arrival date of Jamádi al-Thání 1264/May 1848. Balyuzi 1973 (p. 147) dates the Báb's return to Chihríq in early August 1848, which must have corresponded to Ramadán 1264. Amanat 1989 (p. 394) indicates that the death of Muhammad Sháh took place less than two months after the Báb's trial in Tabriz. Balyuzi 1973 (p. 147) reports the date of Muhammad Sháh's death as 4 September 1848, while Amanat (p. 394) states only that the monarch died in September 1848. Hence it appears that scarcely a month separated the return of the Báb to Chihríq and the death of Muhammad Sháh.

Whatever the duration of this interval, Nabíl-i-A'zam 1970 (p. 323) reports that the Báb wrote the Khutbiy-i-Qahríyyih to Hájí Mírzá Áqásí immediately after his return to Chihríq; that Mullá Muhammad 'Alí-i-Zanjání, known as Hujjat (Proof), personally delivered that tablet to the Grand Vazír; and that Bahá'u'lláh recalled the circumstances of that delivery as they had been related to him by Hujjat himself, shortly after the fact. Hájí Mírzá Áqásí must have received this epistle shortly before the death of Muhammad Sháh and just prior to his own fall from power.

Kitáb-i-Nuqtatu'l-Káf (p. 132, cited in MacEoin 1992, p. 92, n. 70) included the Khutbiy-i-Qahríyyih among the letters written to Muhammad Sháh and Hájí Mírzá Áqásí during the Báb's imprisonment at Chihríq. Balyuzi 1973 (p. 147) states that Hájí Mírzá Áqásí had already fallen from power when Hujjat delivered the Báb's letter to him in Tehran. This is entirely unlikely, given Bahá'u'lláh's account of the meeting between Hujjat and the Grand Vazír.

MacEoin 1992 (p. 92, n. 73) notes that the Khutbiy-i-Qahríyyih can be dated from a reference in the text (INBMC 64, p. 140) to the 40 months that had transpired since the Báb had written to Hájí Mírzá Áqásí for the first time. MacEoin (p. 58) cites the first letter of the Báb to Hájí Mírzá Áqásí as having been written most likely in 1844 and affirms that two manuscripts of this letter have survived (p. 192). The Báb meticulously listed all of his writings from 1 Muharram 1260/22 January 1844 to 15 Muharram 1262/14 January 1846 in the Kitáb al-Fihrist (cited in MacEoin, pp. 50–2), and no mention is made therein of a letter to Hájí Mírzá Áqásí. However, the Báb wrote the Qayyúm al-Asmá' during this period, as is attested by the Kitáb al-Fihrist and other independent sources – Nabíl-i-A'zam 1970 (p. 61), *Táríkh-i-Jadíd* 1893 (p. 39), 'Abdu'l-Bahá 1980 (p. 4) – and copies of this work were conveyed by Mullá Husayn Bushrú'í to Muhammad Sháh and Hájí Mírzá Áqásí in 1260/1844 according to the Báb's tablet to Muhammad Sháh from Máh-Kú. Forty months prior to August 1848 would have fallen around April 1845, and certainly by that date Hájí Mírzá Áqásí would have received a copy of the Qayyúm al-Asmá'. It is also possible that the Kitáb al-Fihrist is not a complete record of the Báb's writings during this period and that he may have written a letter directly to the Grand Vazír subsequent to his pilgrimage, from Búshihr, in April 1845. Inasmuch as the Báb wrote the Khutbiy-i-Qahríyyih to Hájí Mírzá Áqásí in August 1848, he may have been referring to one of the *khutub* he wrote as he was returning to Shiraz after his pilgrimage, which are listed in the Kitáb al-Fihrist (MacEoin 1992, p. 51) and briefly described by MacEoin (p. 63). According to the Khutba al-Jidda (cited in MacEoin 1992, p. 48, n. 25), the Báb sailed for Iran after the completion of his pilgrimage on 4 March 1845, arriving at Búshihr about two and a half months later, circa 19 May 1845. During this voyage, the Báb's vessel would undoubtedly have put into port a number of times and it may well have docked at a port in southern Iran, such as Bandar Abbas, in the strait of Hormuz and opposite the modern kingdom of Oman, in April 1845, 40 weeks prior to the writing of the Khutbiy-i-Qahríyyih in August 1848. Indeed, Amanat 1989 (p. 241) states that the Báb's sea journey from Persia to Arabia took 71 days and that the boat stopped at Kangan, Muscat and Mocha on its way from Búshihr to Jidda. This period of time closely resembles the two and a half months which the Báb spent returning from Jidda to Bushihr. Inasmuch as we do not know of any epistle to Hájí Mírzá Áqásí which can be accurately dated to April 1845, it is difficult to follow MacEoin's reasoning that the date of the Khutbiy-i-Qahríyyih can be dated from a reference in the text.

When the Báb returned to Chihríq, he remained imprisoned at that location from Ramadán 1264/August 1848 until Rajab 1266/June 1850 (Kazem-Beg, vol. 7, p. 371 – cited in French in Nabíl-i-A'zam 1970, p. 302, n. 2; cited and translated into English in Momen 1981, p. 75; cited in Amanat 1989, p. 395, n. 90). Nabíl-i-A'zam (pp. 504, 506) and Gobineau 1865 (p. 213; cited in Nabíl-i-A'zam 1970, p. 504, n. 1) report that Mírzá Taqí Khán – see notes 5 and 13 below for details – ordered Navváb Hamzih Mírzá, the governor of Ádhirbáyján, to arrange the transfer of the Báb from Chihríq to Tabriz for a second time, without divulging the purpose of this journey.

Amanat 1989 (p. 395) alleges that the Báb was escorted by a detachment of Afshár horsemen from Sá'ín Qal'a. Inasmuch as this was the location of the family estate of Hájí Sulaymán Khán-i-Afshár, who was the Grand Vazír's special envoy charged with overseeing the Báb's execution (Amanat 1989, p. 399), it may be that Hájí Sulaymán Khán was the instigator of this initiative. On his way to Tabriz, the Báb stayed at Salmás (Mu'ín, p. 289, cited in Amanat 1989, p. 396, n. 91), where he was the guest, for the second time, of Mírzá Lutf 'Alí Salmásí, the former steward of Muhammad Sháh who was dismissed when he conveyed one of the Báb's letters to His Majesty

(Mu'ín, pp. 175, 223; cited in Amanat 1989, p. 384, n. 47). Amanat (p. 396) reports that the Báb reached Tabriz on 19 June 1850.

During the first three months of his imprisonment at Chihríq (Jamádi al-Úlá 1264/April 1848 – Sha'bán 1264/July 1848) and the 22 months that followed his return from Tabriz (Ramadán 1264/August 1848 – Rajab 1266/June 1850), the Báb received many visitors, attracted many new followers and friends, and wrote many letters and other works. His visitors included his uncle Hájí Mírzá Siyyid 'Alí [Khál-i-A'zam] (Amanat 1989, p. 384; Balyuzi 1973, p. 150); Hájí Sulaymán Khán (Balyuzi 1973, p. 149); Muhammad Taqí Hashtrudi (Mu'ín, pp. 255–8, cited in Amanat 1989, p. 384, n. 46); Mullá 'Abdu'l-Karím Ahmad Qazvíní Kátib (Mázandaráni, p. 370); Shaykh Mullá Mírzá 'Alí called 'Azím by the Báb (Nabíl-i-A'zam 1970, pp. 306–7); Mullá Báqir Tabrizí (Nabíl-i-A'zam, pp. 504–5; Balyuzi 1973, p. 151); Mullá Ádí Guzal Marághih'í, called Sayyáh (the traveller), the student of Mullá 'Alí Akbar Marághih'í (Nabíl-i-A'zam, pp. 431–3; Mu'ín, p. 186; Mázandaráni, p. 59; all cited in Amanat 1989, p. 383, n. 43) – about whom see more details in note 15 below; Mullá 'Alí of Kuhnih Sháhr (Mu'ín, pp. 176, 231, 240, 254; cited in Amanat 1989, p. 384, n. 45); Dakhil Maraghih'i (ibid.; Faydí, p. 280). The Russian agent M. Mochenin states in his memoirs, as reported in Kazem-Beg (vol. 7, p. 371; cited in Nabíl-i-A'zam 1970, p. 302, n. 2; Momen 1981, p. 75; Amanat 1989, p. 395, n. 90) that he heard the Báb preaching in Chihríq shortly before his transfer to Tabriz, in June 1850, and that the eager listeners were so numerous that the courtyard of the fortress was too small to accommodate all of them, such that the majority remained in the street. His new followers, who became converts during his imprisonment at Chihríq, included the Indian dervish whom the Báb named Qahru'lláh (Nabíl-i-A'zam 1970, pp. 305–6; *Kitáb-i-Nuqtatu'l-Káf*, pp. 212–14; Mu'ín, pp. 226–30; all cited in Amanat 1989, pp. 384–5); 'Mírzá Muhammad-'Alí and his brother Búyúk-Áqá, both siyyids of distinguished merit who had risen with fevered earnestness to proclaim their Faith to all sorts and conditions of people among their countrymen' (Nabíl-i-A'zam 1970, p. 303); and 'Mírzá Asadu'lláh, who was later surnamed Dayyán by the Báb' (ibid. pp. 303–5; Mázandaráni, p. 64, cited in Amanat 1989, p. 383, n. 42); and others (Amanat 1989, p. 384), described by Nabíl-i-A'zam (p. 303) as including 'a number among the most eminent of the siyyids, the 'ulamás, and the government officials of Khuy'. The Báb's writings while at Chihríq included the following:

> 1) While according to some scholars (Nabíl-i-A'zam 1970, p. 248; Shoghi Effendi 1995, pp. 24–5; MacEoin 1992, pp. 84, 85, 88), the Bayán-i-fársí was revealed at Máh-Kú, Balyuzi 1973 (p. 132) indicates only that the Bayán-i-fársí was begun at Máh-Kú, while Amanat 1989 (p. 374) states that the Báb compiled parts of the Bayán-i-fársí at Máh-Kú. It is then possible that this book was begun at Máh-Kú and completed at Chihríq.
>
> 2) The Bayán al-'Arabíyya was written in Máh-Kú (MacEoin 1992, p. 85), at Chihríq (Balyuzi 1973, p. 152), or at some time during these two imprisonments (Shoghi Effendi 1995, p. 25).
>
> 3) The Lawh-i-hurúfát (Nabíl-i-A'zam 1970, p. 304), which is also called the Kitáb-i hayákil-i-váhid by the Báb in Dalá'il-i-sab'ih (pp. 45–6, lithographed edition; cited in MacEoin 1992, p. 90, n. 59); called the Kitáb-i-hayákil (Book of Talismans) and the Kitáb-i-dar hayákil-i-váhid (a book concerning the temples [talismans] of unity) in Bahá'u'lláh's letter to Mírzá Ibráhím Shírází (INBA 3003C, p. 19; cited in MacEoin 1992, p. 89, n. 55); called Risála-yi Ja'fariyya in Bahá'u'lláh's letter to Mullá 'Alí Muhammad Siráj Isfáhání (Ishráq Khávarí, vol.

7, p. 60, cited in MacEoin 1992, p. 89, n. 56); and called Kitáb-i-haykal in another letter written by Bahá'u'lláh (Ishráqát, p. 47; cited in MacEoin 1992, p. 89, n. 58). This work is not to be confused with the Báb's Sahífa-yi Ja'fariyya (ibid. pp. 66–7, 90, 198); with Bahá'u'lláh's Súrah-yi haykal (ibid. p. 90, n. 61); or with Mírzá Yahya Subh-i-Azal's Kitáb-i hayákil (ibid.). Nor should it be confused with the *hayákil* written by the Báb. These are elsewhere described by MacEoin (p. 90, n. 61; pp. 99–101, 186).

4) The Haykal al-Dín is preserved in at least three manuscripts (MacEoin 1992, pp. 91, 186) and was lithographed along with the Bayán al-'Arabíyya (ibid. pp. 91, 254). MacEoin describes the Haykal al-Dín as bearing a close resemblance to the Bayán al-'Arabíyya and taking the form of eight chapters of Bábí laws, each denominated a váhid. In the lithographed version, two commentaries are appended, allegedly written by the Báb on 12 Sha'bán 1266/22–3 June 1850 (ibid. p. 91).

5) The Kitáb al-Asmá' is also known as the Tafsír al-asmá' and the Kitáb asmá'i kulli shay (MacEoin 1992, p. 91), and 'Chahár sha'n' (Frahvashtí, cited in MacEoin 1992, p. 91, n. 67; p. 251) was composed during the last days of the Báb at Chihríq according to Mázindaraní 1968–73 (vol. 1, p. 126). This book consists of 19 váhids, each of 19 *abwáb*, each *báb* containing four grades of writing (MacEoin 1992, p. 91). MacEoin (pp. 92, 188) refers to 26 manuscript copies of this work, many of which are defective.

6) The Kitáb-i panj sha'n, which is also entitled Shu'ún-i khamsa dar Bayán-i shu'un-i da'wat and the Kitáb al-Bayán fí'l-shu'ún al-khamsa, is found in 11 manuscripts (MacEoin 1992, pp. 189–90), and it was also lithographed but this version is missing five passages out of the total of 65 (MacEoin 1992, p. 93). According to MacEoin (p. 95), the last five passages, or last two sections in the particular manuscript of Panj Sha'n consulted by him (INBMC 64:60, pp. 85–9, 89–94; cited in MacEoin p. 90, n. 60) are more or less identical with the Lawh-i-hurúfát – see 1, above, for details.

7) Two tablets addressed to Muhammad Sháh, listed in MacEoin 1992 (p. 97, n. 94; p. 193) are published in Persian (*Muntakhabát-i áyát az ár-i Hadrat-i Nuqta-yi Úlá*, pp. 5–8; pp. 9–13 and Mázandaraní 1941, pp. 82–5) and in English translation (The Báb 1976, pp. 18–23, 24–8). Amanat 1989 (p. 381) maintains that during his first few months at Chihríq, the Báb wrote two letters to Muhammad Sháh which were the first of a series of Arabic letters known as his Khutab-i Qahríyyih. Afnan 2000 (p. 354) states that the Báb wrote to Muhammad Sháh from Chihríq (p. 460) and cites a portion of one such letter in Arabic (p. 354).

8) The Khutbiy-i-Qahríyyih, mentioned above and by MacEoin 1992 (p. 92), addressed to Hájí Mírzá Áqásí and apparently written immediately after the Báb's return to Chihríq from his trial in Tabriz, is found in two manuscripts (MacEoin 1992, p. 186), and may be one of the Khutab-i Qahríyyih (sermons of wrath) quoted by Mu'ín (pp. 151–60, cited in Amanat 1989, p. 383, n. 41) and Faydí 1973 (pp. 304–6; cited in Amanat 1989, p. 383, n. 41).

9) Amanat 1989 (p. 381) asserts that the Báb wrote two letters to Hájí Mírzá Áqásí during his first months at Chihríq which were the first of the Khutab-i Qahríyyih. The quotation he cites from Mázandaraní 1941 (p. 84; Amanat 1989, p. 381, n. 36) consists of a portion of one of the Báb's letters to Muhammad Sháh, according

to MacEoin 1992 (p. 97, n. 94; p. 193). Mázandaráni 1941 (pp. 85–9; cited in MacEoin, p. 92, n. 78) quotes a letter written to Hájí Mírzá Áqásí that is different from the Khutbiy-i-Qahríyyih.

10) Letters to his followers: i) Thirty-seven letters and other short pieces, in Browne Or. F. 25 (cited in MacEoin 1992, pp. 95, 208–9); ii) Six letters, in Browne Or. F. 21, numbers 9, 16, 18, 23, 24, 25 (cited in MacEoin, p. 95, n. 90); iii) Ten letters, in Mázandaráni 1941 (cited in MacEoin, pp. 95–6); iv) Nine letters, published in facsimiles in an Azalí compilation entitled '*Qismatí az alwáh-i khatt-i Nuqta-yi Úlá wa Áqá Siyyid Husayn-i Kátib*' (cited in MacEoin, p. 96); v) Three letters, in Za'ím al-Dawla 1903 (cited in MacEoin 1992, p. 97).

11) Letter to the ulama in every city of Iran, and the 'Atabat, referred to by Shoghi Effendi 1995 (p. 24) as probably having been written in Máh-Kú or Chihríq; which information MacEoin (p. 98) suggests is derived from Bahá'u'lláh 1989 (p. 178). Amanat quotes a letter written by the Báb in late 1849 to the ulama of Tabriz, reproduced in Mu'ín (pp. 263–4, cited in Amanat 1989, p. 394, n. 86, 87). Abu'l-Qasim Afnan says that the Báb wrote a letter to the ulama of Tabriz while incarcerated at Chihríq.

12) *Munáját* (prayers), *ziyáratnámas* (tablets of visitation), *hayákil* and *dawá'ir* (talismans in the shape of pentacles and circles) written at this time are described in MacEoin 1992 (pp. 99–101, 186, 195, 203, 210).

Nabíl-i-A'zam 1970 (p. 307) reports this testimony from Shaykh Hasan-i-Zunúzí, one of the transcribers of the writings of the Báb in Máh-Kú (ibid. p. 31), speaking of the last days of the Báb in Tabriz, shortly before his martyrdom:

> At about the same time that the Báb dismissed Azím from His presence, I was instructed by Him to collect all the available Tablets that He had revealed during His incarceration in the castles of Máh-Kú and Chihríq, and to deliver them into the hands of Siyyid Ibráhím-i-Khalíl, who was then living in Tabríz, and urge him to conceal and preserve them with the utmost care.

Given the sheer quantity of writings cited above, it is quite remarkable that so many of them survive to the present day. However, it seems that Siyyid Ibráhím was not altogether unsuccessful in discharging his sacred trust. Indeed, Nabíl-i-A'zam 1970 (p. 31), writing circa 1888 about the location of the Báb's nine commentaries on the Qur'án authored at Máh-Kú, states that their 'fate is unknown until now'.

5. Mírzá Taqí Khán, whose full name was Mírzá Taqí Khán Farahani (Amanat 1989, p. 451), was appointed Grand Vazír by Násiri'd-Dín Sháh (Nabíl-i-A'zam 1970, pp. 332, 500; 'Abdu'l-Bahá 1980, p. 20; Balyuzi 1973, p. 152). He was determined to uproot the Bábí movement as it seemed to represent a challenge to the absolute authority of the central government; nor did he hesitate to employ the most brutal measures in order to effect his purpose (Nabíl-i-A'zam 1970, pp. 500–4; 'Abdu'l-Bahá 1980, pp. 20–2; Gobineau 1865, pp. 211–13, cited in Nabíl-i-A'zam 1970, pp. 501–2, n. 2; Balyuzi 1973, pp. 148, 152; Amanat 1989, pp. 395–7). While Shoghi Effendi 1995 (p. 164) called Hájí Mírzá Áqásí the 'Antichrist of the Bábí Revelation', it is nevertheless incontestable that Mírzá Taqí Khán was singlehandedly responsible for effecting the martyrdom of the Báb and of hundreds, if not thousands, of his followers during his Grand Vazírship, from the autumn of 1264/1848 to the spring of 1268/1852, when he was assassinated by order of Násiri'd-Dín Sháh (Nabíl-i-A'zam 1970, p. 595; Curzon,

Persia and the Persian Question, vol. 2, p. 16, cited in Nabíl-i-A'zam 1970, p. 595, n. 2; Sheil, *Glimpses of Life and Manners in Persia*, pp. 251–2, cited in Nabíl-i-A'zam 1970, pp. 595–6, n. 2; Shoghi Effendi 1995, p. 82; Ruhe 1997, p. 129). Nabíl-i-A'zam 1970 (pp. 596, 598) recites a litany of 'deeds of blackest infamy' of the so-called 'Amír Kabír', which amply demonstrates that the Bábís could not but regard him as the most formidable of their many enemies. For information on Mírzá Taqí Khán, the reader is urged to consult Nabíl-i-A'zam 1970 (pp. 332, 443, 445–8, 450–2, 500–2, 504–6, 539, 546–7, 554–6, 558, 568, 595, 597, 598, 615); 'Abdu'l-Bahá 1980 (pp. 20–1, 25, 26, 28–30); Balyuzi 1973 (pp. 146, 148, 152, 184, 185, 203, 207, 209, 212); and Amanat 1989 (pp. 27, 29, 281, 329, 339n, 355, 363, 366, 388n, 393, 395–9, 405–6, 411). Amanat 1997 contains much more information about Mírzá Taqí Khán.

6. Mírzá Taqí Khán was also called Amír-Nizám (Nabíl-i-A'zam 1970, pp. 332, 500, 504, 506, 526, 539, 547, 595; 'Abdu'l-Bahá 1980, p. 20); Amír Kabír (Balyuzi 1973, p. 148; Amanat 1989, pp. 394–401); and Amír (Nabíl-i-A'zam 1970, p. 332; 'Abdu'l-Bahá 1980, p. 25).
7. Násiri'd-Dín Sháh assumed the throne on the demise of his father, Muhammad Sháh, on 4 September 1848, and hence he was the reigning sovereign at the time of the Báb's execution. Ruhe 1997 (p. 129) reports that Násiri'd-Dín Sháh was made monarch at 17 years of age, while Balyuzi 1973 (p. 140) and Amanat 1989 (p. 387) indicate that Násiri'd-Dín Mírzá was 17 during the first examination of the Báb at Tabriz, earlier that same year. Balyuzi 1973 (p. 140) indicates that Násiri'd-Dín Mírzá had been recently appointed governor of Ádhirbáyján, and Amanat 1989 (p. 387) indicates this appointment as dating from February 1848. As the trial took place in July 1848, and Muhammad Sháh died in September 1848, it seems that these reports are mutually compatible.

'Abdu'l-Bahá 1980 (p. 20) describes Násiri'd-Dín Sháh as being 'in the prime of youthful years'. In view of the various accounts of the machinations to which Hájí Mírzá Áqásí resorted in order to avoid a meeting between the Báb and Muhammad Sháh, it seems entirely realistic and justifiable that Násiri'd-Dín Sháh should have blamed the imprisonment of the Báb at Máh-Kú and the missed opportunity for an examination of the Báb's claims at Tehran on the former Grand Vazír. Nicolas appears to base his account here on Sipihr 1965 (vol. 3, p. 302, cited in Amanat 1989, p. 396, n. 93).
8. Sadr-A'zam is a title meaning 'prime minister; dignity of premier; chief seat' (Steingass, p. 788). Not only did Hájí Mírzá Áqásí serve as Grand Vazír to Muhammad Sháh, but according to Amanat 1989 (p. 79, n. 42), he may also have been the Sháh's Súfí *pir* (guide) in the Ni'matulláhí taríqah of which he, under the name Mullá 'Abbás Írávání, was incontestably an adherent. It should also be noted that Muhammad Sháh consistently showed respect and reverence for Sufis (Amanat 1989, p. 79, n. 43).
9. Násiri'd-Dín Sháh's father was Muhammad Sháh.
10. Hájí Mírzá Áqásí's rationale for circumventing such an enquiry in Tehran was afterwards explained by him to Prince Farhad Mírzá.
11. Nabíl-i-A'zam 1970 (pp. 501–2) and 'Abdu'l-Bahá 1980 (p. 25) indicate that Mírzá Taqí Khán, the Amír-A'zam and Grand Vazír, decided that the only way to extirpate the Bábí movement was to strike at its source and bring about the execution of the Báb. 'Abdu'l-Bahá 1980 (pp. 25, 30) states that he came to this decision without consulting Násiri'd-Dín Sháh or any of his fellow ministers of the court, whereas Nabíl-i-A'zam 1970 (pp. 502, 504) affirms that he summoned his counsellors and that only one of them, Mírzá Áqá Khán-i-Núrí, the Minister of War, dared to advise him against this course of action. Balyuzi 1973 (p. 152) seems to follow Nabíl-i-A'zam in his account of this decision, and Amanat 1989 (p. 396) cites Sipihr 1965 (vol. 3, pp. 302, 303) and Nabíl-i-A'zam 1970 (pp. 502, 504). Nabíl-i-A'zam 1970 (p. 615)

states that a rumour was spread among the Bábís to the effect that shortly before his own demise, Mírzá Taqí Khán was haunted by a vision of the Báb, whom he regretted having executed, and that he wished to effect the release of Siyyid Husayn-i-Yazdí, the Báb's amanuensis, and of Táhirih, as well as the abandonment of further persecution of the Bábís. Nabíl-i-A'zam 1970 (pp. 615–16) also reports that Mírzá Áqá Khán-i-Núrí, who assumed the position of Grand Vazír after the forced departure of Mírzá Taqí Khán – and whom he described (pp. 502, 504) as the only minister to advise against the execution of the Báb – was inclined to follow a policy of reconciliation with the Bábís during the first period of his administration, until the attempt, in 1852, on the life of Násiri'd-Dín Sháh. 'Abdu'l-Bahá 1980 (pp. 29–30) affirms that the attempt of one Bábí to assassinate the shah was not representative of the wishes of the Bábí community and was moreover due to the ignorance of that individual. Nor was it justified, for the decision to execute the Báb had been taken by Mírzá Taqí Khán alone and without the cognizance of the shah. It should be noted that Táríkh-i-Nabíl (Nabíl-i-A'zam 1970) was composed circa 1887–92, while 'Abdu'l-Bahá 1980 was published in Persian in 1890 and in English translation in 1891. Note also that Násiri'd-Dín Sháh did not die until 1896 (Shoghi Effendi 1995, p. 296; *Webster's Biographical Dictionary*, p. 1084). It seems likely that if the shah had been instrumental in the decision to execute the Báb, the Bahá'í reports to the contrary would have come to the attention of his government and that efforts would have been carried out to correct such a misapprehension.

This story recalls the Book of Esther, in which Haman, the chief minister of King Ahashverosh (Artaxerxes), conspires without the knowledge of His Majesty to bring about the genocide of the Jewish people resident in his realms. In that story, Mordechai advises Esther to inform the King of the impending doom of her entire people, and as a result of this action, the Jewish people are saved, Haman is condemned along with his treacherous associates and Mordechai is appointed chief minister in his place. In this 19th-century story, Mírzá Áqá Khán-i-Núrí (like Mordechai) advised Mírzá Taqí Khán (like Haman) not to carry out a death sentence but he did not go to the shah himself and so the sentence was carried out. Ultimately, though, Mírzá Áqá Khán-i-Núrí replaced Mírzá Taqí Khán as Grand Vazír, and, just like Haman, Mírzá Taqí Khán went to his death by order of his sovereign.

12. Sulaymán Khán-i-Afshár (Nabíl-i-A'zam 1970, pp. 391, 402, 428) is also called Sulaymán Khán (ibid. pp. 391), Hájí Sulaymán Khán-i-Afshár (Balyuzi 1973, p. 125), Sulaymán Khán-i-Afshár-i-Shahríyárí (Nabíl-i-A'zam 1970, p. 378), and Hájí Sulaymán Khán Afshár Sá'ín Qal'a Amír al-Umará' (Amanat 1989, pp. 247, 460). He was a son-in-law of Fath 'Alí Sháh, the King of Persia prior to Muhammad Sháh (Amanat 1989, p. 247) and a devoted follower of Siyyid Kázim Rashtí, who had promised that he would meet the Qá'im (Balyuzi 1973, p. 134). He was on such close terms with Siyyid Kázim Rashtí that he was able to effect the marriage of one of his master's daughters with his son, Ridá-Qulí Khán-i-Afshár (Balyuzi 1973, p. 134). After the passing of his master, this Shaykhi chose to follow Hájí Muhammad Karím Khán Kirmání instead of the Báb (Balyuzi 1973, p. 134; Amanat 1989, p. 367). Sulaymán Khán met the Báb while on pilgrimage (the Báb, in Mázandaráni 1941, p. 271, cited in Amanat 1989, p. 246, n. 240 and p. 247, n. 250; Balyuzi 1973, p. 134). The Báb addressed a letter to Sulaymán Khán, probably during his pilgrimage, listed in Kitáb al-Fihrist (MacEoin 1992, p. 51), and three manuscripts of letters addressed to Sulaymán Khán are extant (MacEoin 1992, pp. 191, 192). Nabíl-i-A'zam 1970 (p. 235; cited in Balyuzi 1973, pp. 124–5) reports that in the course of his journey from Kulayn to Tabriz, while in the village of Síyáh-Dihán, the Báb was visited by Mullá Iskandar, whom he commissioned to deliver a message to Hájí Sulaymán Khán-i-Afshár, then in Zanján and preparing to leave for Tehran:

He whose virtues the late siyyid unceasingly extolled, and to the approach of whose Revelation he continually alluded, is now revealed. I am that promised One. Arise and deliver Me from the hand of the oppressor.

Hájí Sulaymán Khán-i-Afshár ignored the message. Nabíl-i-A'zam 1970 (pp. 378, 391, 402, 428) and Sipihr 1965 (vol. 3, p. 244, cited in Amanat 1989, p. 367, n. 193) report in some detail the contribution made by Hájí Sulaymán Khán to the destruction of the Bábís at Shaykh Tabarsí. Amanat (p. 399) indicates that Hájí Sulaymán Khán was subsequently sent to Tabriz by Mírzá Taqí Khán as his 'special envoy and troubleshooter' to assist Mírzá Hasan Khán (Amanat 1989, p. 399), the Vazír Nizám (secretary of the army) of Ádhirbáyján, and the Amír Kabír's brother and confidant (Amanat 1989, p. 398), in effecting the execution of the Báb. Other details pertaining to Hájí Sulaymán Khán-i-Afshár can be found in Amanat (pp. 246n, 247, 367, 398n, 399). He must not be confused with Hájí Sulaymán Khán, the Bábí, from Tabriz (see note 35 below).

13. Hamzih Mírzá Hishmat al-Dawlih (Balyuzi 1973, pp. 152–3) was also called Navváb Hamzih Mírzá (Nabíl-i-A'zam 1970, p. 504), and identified as a prince of the Qájár family (ibid.; 'Abdu'l-Bahá 1980, p. 25; Amanat 1989, p. 398). Nabíl-i-A'zam 1970 (pp. 504, 506) indicates that Navváb Hamsih Mírzá appointed one of his trusted officers and a mounted escort to accompany the Báb from Chihríq to Tabriz. Nabíl-i-A'zam 1970 (p. 504) states that Mírzá Taqí Khán, the Grand Vazír, did not disclose the reason why the Báb was being transferred to Tabriz and that the governor of Ádhirbáyján assumed that no harm would come to the Báb. Once the Báb had been delivered to Tabriz and the order for his execution was conveyed to Navváb Hamzih Mírzá, he was unwilling to carry out this order (Nabíl-i-A'zam 1970, p. 506; 'Abdu'l-Bahá 1851, p. 25). Nabíl-i-A'zam 1970 (p. 506) reports him as having told the Vazír-Nizám, Mírzá Hasan Khán, the brother of the Grand Vazír:

> The Amír would do better to entrust me with services of greater merit than the one with which he has now commissioned me. The task I am called upon to perform is a task that only ignoble people would accept. I am neither Ibn-i-Zíyád nor Ibn-i-Sa'd that he should call upon me to slay an innocent descendant of the Prophet of God.

Shoghi Effendi noted (in Nabíl-i-A'zam 1970, p. 506, n. 2) that Ibn-i-Zíyád and Ibn-i-Sa'd were 'persecutors of the descendants of [the Prophet] Muhammad'.

The sentiments of Mírzá Taqí Khán, the Grand Vazír, are further attested to by Nabíl-i-A'zam 1970 (p. 504), citing a discussion prior to this event with court officials in Tehran. He protested:

> Such considerations are wholly irrelevant to the issue with which we are faced. The interests of the State are in jeopardy, and we can in no wise tolerate these periodic upheavals. Was not the Imám Husayn, in view of the paramount necessity for safeguarding the unity of the State, executed by those same persons who had seen him more than once receive marks of exceptional affection from Muhammad, his Grandfather? Did they not in such circumstances refuse to consider the rights which his lineage had conferred upon him?

It is quite extraordinary that Mírzá Taqí Khán should have sought to justify his actions towards the Báb and his followers by referring to the assassination of the Imam Husayn and the suppression of his followers by order of Mu'áwiya, whom Sunni and Shi'i Muslims alike consider a usurper of authority and a murderer of innocents. Nabíl-i-A'zam 1970 (p. 506) and 'Abdu'l-Bahá 1980 (pp. 25, 26) state that Hamzih Mírzá explained his reasons for not carrying out the order of execution; that the Vazír-Nizám conveyed this message to the Grand Vazír; and that Mírzá Taqí Khán sent a second order to his brother, directing him to carry out the sentence immediately.

When Hamzih Mírzá would not do so, feigning illness (Nabíl-i-A'zam 1970, p. 506), Mírzá Hasan Khán took matters into his own hands. For more information about Hamzih Mírzá, Amanat (p. 398, n. 101) recommends that the reader consult Bamdad 1968–74 (pp. 462–8).

14. Áqá Siyyid Husayn-i-Yazdí, also called 'Azíz, in this context probably meaning 'precious, dear' (Steingass, p. 848), and given this name by the Báb in the Qayyúm al-Asmá' (sura 79, last verse), according to MacEoin 1992 (p. 204). He served as the principal amanuensis of the Báb, accompanying him to Máh-Kú, Chihríq and Tabriz. According to Nabíl-i-A'zam 1970 (p. 80) and MacEoin (p. 204), Siyyid Husayn-i-Yazdí was chosen as one of the Letters of the Living by the Báb. Sources for his life include Ishráq Khávarí 1973–4, vol. 1, (pp. 757–60); Khusraví 1973–4; Mázandarání 1941 (pp. 459–60, 460–1). See notes 15 and 26 for more details of his life.

15. Nicolas calls this disciple of the Báb Mullá Muhammad Yazdí. There is one Bábí by this name, Mullá Muhammad Rawdih-i-Khán-i-Yazdí, who is listed among the Letters of the Living in Nabíl-i-A'zam 1970 (p. 80) and Balyuzi 1973 (p. 27). Amanat gives this individual's name as Mullá Muhammad Rawza [Rawdih] Khan Yazdí, and Zakir, and reconstructs some of his actions in relation to the Bábí Cause (pp. 176, 178–9, 286). It is fairly certain, however, that Mullá Muhammad Yazdí was not a constant companion of the Báb. There were two Yazdís who reportedly were companions of the Báb, and these were Siyyid Husayn-i-Yazdí and his brother Siyyid Hasan-i-Yazdí. Nicolas mentions the first of these and perhaps he simply got the name wrong for the second. Siyyid Husayn-i-Yazdí joined the Báb in Shiraz shortly before the Báb departed for Isfahan, and the Báb sent him on ahead to join his other disciples in that city (Nabíl-i-A'zam 1970, pp. 192–3). Whether or not his brother accompanied him either to Shiraz or Isfahan is not indicated. Two other disciples who had settled in Shiraz, Mullá 'Abdu'l-Karím and Shaykh Hasan-i-Zunúzí, were also sent by the Báb to Isfahan at that time (ibid. p. 192). In Isfahan the Báb instructed Mullá 'Abdu'l-Karím Qazvíní, Shaykh Hasan Zunúzí and Siyyid Husayn-i-Yazdí to transcribe his writings (Nabíl-i-A'zam 1970, p. 212). Towards the end of his stay in Isfahan, the Báb sent Mullá 'Abdu'l-Karím (Qazvíní) and Siyyid Husayn-i-Yazdí as emissaries to the other Bábís in that city to advise them to scatter throughout the region (Nabíl-i-A'zam 1970, p. 214). The Báb then instructed Siyyid Husayn-i-Yazdí to proceed to Kashán, where they met shortly after the Báb's arrival there, on his way to Máh-Kú (Nabíl-i-A'zam 1970, p. 219). Two days after the Báb arrived in Kulayn, he was joined by Siyyid Husayn-i-Yazdí, his brother Siyyid Hasan-i-Yazdí, Mullá 'Abdu'l-Karím (Qazvíní) and Shaykh Hasan-i-Zunúzí (Nabíl-i-A'zam 1970, p. 227). Nabíl-i-A'zam (p. 243) records a conversation between the Báb and Siyyid Husayn-i-Yazdí in Tabriz while on his way to Máh-Kú and it is apparent from the context of this conversation that at least this one of two brothers was in the immediate company of the Báb at that time. Siyyid Husayn reports the transition to Máh-Kú: '... orders were issued to transfer Him and me to the castle of Máh-Kú and to deliver us into the custody of 'Alí-Khán-i-Máh-Kú'í' (ibid.). Then Siyyid Husayn describes their residence in Máh-Kú:

> For the first two weeks, no one was permitted to visit the Báb. My brother and I alone were admitted to His presence. Siyyid Hasan would, every day, accompanied by one of the guards, descend to the town and purchase our daily necessities. Shaykh Hasan-i-Zunúzí, who had arrived at in Máh-Kú, spent the nights in a masjid outside the gate of the town. He acted as an intermediary between those of the followers of the Báb who occasionally visited Máh-Kú and Siyyid Hasan, my brother, who would in turn submit the petitions of the believers to their Master and would acquaint Shaykh Hasan with His reply (Nabíl-i-A'zam 1970, p. 245).

At one point the warden of the fortress in Máh-Kú, 'Alí Khán, dreamed a dream, and upon waking he permitted other Bábís to visit the Báb, but Nabíl-i-A'zam asserts (p. 257), 'Until that time no one of the disciples of the Báb but Siyyid Husayn-i-Yazdí and his brother had been allowed to spend the night within the castle.' From Máh-Kú the Báb went to Tabriz and was then sent to Chihríq. Nabíl-i-A'zam 1970 (pp. 302–3) writes that at Chihríq, 'To no one would Yahyá Khán refuse admittance to the castle. As Chihríq itself was unable to accommodate the increasing number of visitors who flocked to its gates, they were enabled to obtain the necessary lodgings in Iskí-Shahr, the old Chihríq, which was situated at an hour's distance from the castle.' Up until sometime in Dhu'l-Qa'dih 1265, the Báb was attended in Chihríq by Siyyid Hasan-i-Yazdí along with his brother, the Báb's amanuensis, Siyyid Husayn. Nabíl-i-A'zam 1970 (p. 431) informs us that the Báb sent out 'Mullá Ádí Guzal, one of the believers of Marághih, who for the last two months had been acting as His attendant instead of Siyyid Hasan, the brother of Siyyid Husayn-i-'Azíz', to make a pilgrimage to Shaykh Tabarsí on his behalf. Gulpáygání (p. 241, cited in Nabíl-i-A'zam 1970, p. 431, n. 3) identifies the full name of this Bábí as Mírzá 'Alíy-i-Sayyáh-i-Marághih'í. 'He had acted as a servant of the Báb in Máh-Kú, ranked among His leading companions, and subsequently embraced the Message of Bahá'u'lláh.' It appears, then, that Siyyid Hasan-i-Yazdí was no longer a companion of the Báb from Dhu'l-Qa'dih 1265, as there is no mention of him accompanying the Báb to Tabriz.

Finally, the Báb was summoned to Tabriz, where the officer who had escorted him, Navváb Hamzih Mírzá, 'instructed one of his friends to accommodate Him in his home and to treat Him with extreme deference' (Nabíl-i-A'zam 1970, p. 506). Mírzá Hasan Khán, the Vazír-Nizám and brother of the Grand Vazír, arrived shortly thereafter and ordered the transfer of the Báb 'and those in His company from the house in which He was staying to one of the rooms of the barracks' (Nabíl-i-A'zam 1970, pp. 506–7). 'Deprived of His turban and sash, the twin emblems of His noble lineage, the Báb, together with Siyyid Husayn, His amanuensis, was driven to yet another confinement . . .' (ibid. p. 507). He was engaged in a conversation with Siyyid Husayn in that very barracks when it was interrupted and he was taken to the place of execution. When the first volley failed to touch him, the Báb was found 'seated in the same room which He had occupied the night before, engaged in completing His interrupted conversation, with Siyyid Husayn' (Nabíl-i-A'zam 1970, p. 513). For the last time, the Báb and Siyyid Husayn were together in the flesh. Nabíl-i-A'zam reiterates that Siyyid Husayn-i-Yazdí was 'the Báb's amanuensis both in Máh-Kú and Chihríq' (p. 629) and reports his imprisonment in the Síyáh-Chál in Tehran (pp. 629–30) and that he was joined in that prison by his 'Comforter', Bahá'u'lláh, in whose company he 'was privileged to remain until the hour of his death' (p. 631), which took place, in 1852, at the hands of the executioner of Táhirih, 'Azíz Khán-i-Sardár.

It is evident from this survey of the companions of the Báb that Siyyid Husayn-i-Yazdí accompanied him virtually non-stop from his departure from Shiraz to the time of his death in Tabriz, and that Siyyid Hasan-i-Yazdí was also in his company for most of that period. There were other close companions of the Báb, including Mullá 'Abdu'l-Karím Qazvíní and Shaykh Hasan-i-Zunúzí, but none were as constantly in the company of the Báb as the two brothers from Yazd.

16. Neither Nabíl-i-A'zam 1970 nor 'Abdu'l-Bahá 1980 refer to a second gathering of the ulama of Tabriz and this seems to confirm Nicolas's allegation. Nabíl-i-A'zam (p. 509) reports that Mírzá Muhammad-'Alí (see note 15 above) was summoned before a group of mujtahidún, who unsuccessfully tried to persuade him to renounce his ties with the Báb. Nabíl-i-A'zam (p. 510) also states that the Báb was conducted first to the house of Mullá Muhammad Mámáqání, then to that of Mírzá Báqir and finally to that of Mullá Murtadá-Qulí, and that none of these three mujtahidún consented to

meet the Báb face to face, although all three handed death warrants to the government authorities who were charged with carrying out the execution. This version of the events of that morning is also found in Balyuzi 1973 (pp. 155–6). Amanat 1989 (p. 398) indicates that the ulama of Tabriz were reluctant to associate themselves with this execution. Mu'ín (pp. 303–4) refers to a threatening message allegedly sent to the ulama of Tabriz by the Vazír-Nizám, warning them of the Grand Vazír's wrath should they refuse to sign death warrants for the Báb (cited in Amanat 1989, p. 398, n. 102).

Mu'ín (p. 305, cited in ibid. p. 399, n. 104) indicates that Mullá Muhammad Mámáqání was reluctant to sign a death warrant. Muhammad Taqí, who was an eyewitness to his father's last meeting with the Báb, writes in his Risála (mentioned in Amanat 1989, p. 399, n. 105; p. 400, n. 106, 107) that Mullá Muhammad Mámáqání tried to persuade the Báb to renounce his claims but that the Báb firmly refused to do so (Za'ím al-Dawlih 1903, pp. 233–5 (cited in Amanat 1989, p. 400, n. 107)), on the authority of his grandfather, Mullá Muhammad Ja'far and his father, Mullá Muhammad Taqí, both of whom he alleges to have been present on this occasion, gives similar testimony to the Risála of Muhammad Taqí. 'Abdu'l-Bahá 1980 (p. 26) states that the *farrásh-báshí* (chief of police) delivered the Báb and Anís over to the chosen executioner, with the death warrants of Mullá Muhammad Mámáqání, Mullá Mírzá Báqir, Mullá Murtadá-Qulí and others. Nabíl-i-A'zam 1970 (p. 510) says the same but mentions only three death warrants. The actual content of these death warrants is described by Mu'ín (vol. 1, p. 241), two different versions, according to Amanat 1989 (p. 400, n. 108).

Amanat 1989 (p. 398, n. 101) indicates that inasmuch as he was unable to bring together the clergy, Hamzih Mírzá summoned a small gathering of state officials to examine the Báb. Present at this examination, besides Hamzih Mírzá, were Mírzá 'Alí Khán and Sulaymán Khán-i-Afshár (Amanat 1989, p. 398, n. 101). Nicolas, citing no source, includes the Vazír-Nizám, Mírzá Hasan Khán, in this meeting, and does not mention the presence of Hájí Sulaymán Khán.

17. Mírzá Hasan Khán Vazír-Nizám was the secretary of the army in Ádhirbáyján and the brother of Mírzá Taqí Khán, the Grand Vazír, also known as Amír Kabír. The fate of Mírzá Hasan Khán subsequent to the execution of the Báb is not mentioned in any of the sources consulted for this study.
18. Hájí Mírzá 'Alí is also called Mírzá 'Alí Khán Ansárí, the son of Mírzá Mas'ud, and is named as having carried out the examination of the Báb before the state officials (Amanat 1989, p. 398, n. 101). Nothing more is said about this individual in any of the sources.
19. According to Amanat 1989 (p. 398, n. 101 and references), there is disagreement among those present regarding the quality of the verses revealed by the Báb.
20. Here it is reported that the Báb cannot reveal the same verses twice on the subject of crystal candlesticks, while in chapter 4 of Nicolas's book the Báb is asked to reveal verses on the subject of his cane and then is told that his audience cannot understand his verses. In both cases it is clear that the examiners are toying with the Báb, not taking his claim to divine inspiration at all seriously, nor comparing his verses with the only other revealed verses in their possession, namely, those of the Qur'án. The Prophet Muhammad is not reported to have revealed the same verses a second time upon demand, nor is it alleged that all the verses of the Qur'án are readily understood by its readers. Indeed, the Qur'án in Surat al-'Imrán states, as a matter of principle (Q 3:7):

> He it is who has revealed the Book to you; some of its verses are unambiguous (*muhkamátun*), they are the basis of the Book, and others are figurative (*mutashábihátun*). So that those in whose hearts is perversity will follow that part of it

which is figurative, seeking to mislead others and to give it [their own] interpretation. However none knows its interpretation except God, and those who are firmly rooted in knowledge.

This theme is referred to with specific reference to this Quranic passage by the Báb in Dalá'il-i-sab'ih and by Bahá'u'lláh in the Kitáb-i-Íqán.

21. Nabíl-i-A'zam 1970 (p. 502) and 'Abdu'l-Bahá 1980 (p. 26) alike affirm that Mírzá Taqí Khán intended that the Báb be given a public execution. The specifics of the manner in which this execution would be carried out may have been left to Mírzá Hasan Khán and his associates.

22. Hájí Mírzá Báqir, also called Mírzá Báqir (Nabíl-i-A'zam 1970, p. 510), Mullá Mírzá Báqir ('Abdu'l-Bahá 1980, p. 26), and Mullá Muhammad Báqir the Imám Jum'ih (Amanat 1989, p. 398), was the son of Mírzá Ahmad (Nabíl-i-A'zam 1970, p. 510; Amanat 1989, p. 398), the Imám Jum'ih of Tabriz who participated in the first examination of the Báb ('Abdu'l-Bahá 1980, p. 14) and signed a death warrant for the Báb at that time (Nabíl-i-A'zam 1970, p. 510). Mírzá Ahmad had died in 1265/1849 (Amanat 1989, p. 398, n. 99 and references) and it is indicated that Hájí Mírzá Báqir was one of the ulama of Tabriz who were reluctant to involve themselves in the condemnation and execution of the Báb. Amanat (p. 399, n. 103) indicates that there is some disagreement among the sources (Nabíl-i-A'zam 1970, pp. 509–10; Sipihr 1965, vol. 3, p. 304; Mázandarání 1941, p. 9; Mu'ín, pp. 300–1) regarding the signatories of the fatwa calling for the execution of the Báb but all of these sources seem to indicate that Hájí Mírzá Báqir Imám Jum'ih was one of the signatories. Balyuzi 1973 (p. 155) likewise lists him as one of the three clergymen who signed the death warrant for the Báb: 1) Hájí Mírzá Báqir, the Imám Jum'ih of Tabriz, is not to be confused with 2) Hájí Siyyid Muhammad-Báqir-i-Rashtí, known as Harati (Nabíl-i-A'zam 1970, pp. 19, 97, 264), also called Mullá Muhammad Taqí Harati (Amanat 1989, pp. 61, 158n, 262, 264–6, 283–4); nor with 3) Mullá Muhammad Báqir-i-Tabrizí (Nabíl-i-A'zam 1970, pp. 50–5, 63, 69), also called Mullá Báqir-i-Tabrizí (Nabíl-i-A'zam 1970, pp. 368, 504–5), and named one of the Letters of the Living (Nabíl-i-A'zam 1970, pp. 80, 368, 504); nor with 4) Muhammad Báqir, the nephew of Mullá Husayn Bushrú'í and one of the Letters of the Living (Nabíl-i-A'zam 1970, p. 80), also called Mullá Báqir (Nabíl-i-A'zam 1970, pp. 287, 683); nor with 5) Mullá Báqir, the Imam of Chinár-Súkhtih (Nabíl-i-A'zam 1970, p. 476); nor, finally, with 6) Muhammad-Báqir, the son of Zaynu'l-'Abidín, the fifth Imam of the Ithná 'Asharí Shi'a ('Abdu'l-Bahá 1980, note O, pp. 296–8; cited in Nabíl-i-A'zam 1970, p. lii).

23. Mullá Muhammad Mámáqání, described by Nabíl-i-A'zam 1970 (p. 316) as a 'one-eyed and white-bearded renegade' and by 'Abdu'l-Bahá 1980 (p. 26) as a 'learned divine', was a Shaykhi mujtahid (Amanat 1989, p. 39, n. 18) and one of the students of Shaykh Ahmad Ahsá'í who were reportedly envious of the attention he paid to Siyyid Kázim Rashtí, his subsequent appointment as the leader of the Shaykhi school (Nabíl-i-A'zam 1970, p. 11). Mullá Muhammad Mámáqání was one of the claimants to the leadership of the Shaykhis after the passing of Siyyid Kázim Rashtí according to Nabíl-i-A'zam 1970 (p. 9; cited in Amanat 1989, p. 285, n. 207). Mu'ín (p. 299, cited in Amanat 1989, p. 285, n. 208) reports that Mullá Mámáqání tried to preserve Shaykhism as a sect with only minor differences from the Úsúlís and hence comfortably within the fold of Ithna 'Asharí Shi'i Islam. Mullá Muhammad Mámáqání was a participant in the Tabriz trial of the Báb (Nabíl-i-A'zam 1970, pp. 316–20; 'Abdu'l-Bahá 1980, p. 14; Balyuzi 1973, pp. 140–4) and his memories of the trial of the Báb were preserved by his son, Shaykh Muhammad Taqí Mámáqání in a Risálá which is cited in part in Murtadá Mudarrisí Chahárdihí, *Shaykígarí va Bábígarí az Nazhar-i Falsafa, Tárikh Ijtimá'* (pp. 308–15, cited in Amanat 1989, pp. 386–9). Mullá Muhammad Taqí Mámáqání claimed that the official report of this trial, penned

by Hájí Mírzá Mahmúd, the Nizámu'l-'Ulama', was replete was misrepresentations (Balyuzi 1973, p. 143), and he wrote a refutation of those points. Apparently, and perhaps in reaction to the widespread dissemination of the Shaykh's Risála', Mullá Hájí Mírzá Mahmúd tried to recall all copies of his tract and destroyed those he could retrieve (Balyuzi 1973, p. 143). Mámáqání claimed that his report was the most accurate and reliable (Amanat 1989, p. 389, n. 69), in comparison with the official chronicles of Mírzá Muhammad Taqí Sipihr, *Násikhu't-Tavárikh*, Ridá Qulí Khán Hidáyat, Lálá-báshí, *Rawdat al-Safá-yi Násirí*. A detailed comparison of the various accounts has not yet been effected. Mullá Muhammad Mámáqání was, according to various accounts, one of the mujtahids who wrote a fatwa condemning the Báb of heresy and sentencing him to death (Balyuzi 1973, p. 155); the most prominent of the three leading mujtahids who wrote that fatwa ('Abdu'l-Bahá 1980, p. 26; Amanat 1989, p. 399); and the first of the mujtahids to be approached for his fatwa by the farrásh-báshí on the day of ther Báb's execution (Nabíl-i-A'zam 1970, p. 510).

24. Siyyid 'Alí Zunúzí was a well-known mujtahid in Tabriz (Amanat 1989, p. 401), and Nicolas follows Sipihr 1965 (vol. 3, p. 304, cited in Amanat 1989, p. 399, n. 103) in numbering him among the mujtahidún who delivered a fatwa condemning the Báb to death. Amanat (p. 399, n. 103) calls this 'an obvious error'. His stepson was none other than Muhammad-'Alí (Nabíl-i-A'zam 1970, p. 507), also called Muhammad-'Alíy-i-Zunúzí (ibid. p. 306), Mírzá Muhammad-'Alíy-i-Zunúzí (ibid. p. 507), Áqá Muhammad-'Alí ('Abdu'l-Bahá 1980, p. 26), and Mírzá Muhammad-'Alí (Nabíl-i-A'zam 1970, pp. 508, 509, 512), and was surnamed Anís (ibid. p. 306). Very little is known about Anís except that his stepfather, Siyyid 'Alíy-i-Zunúzí (ibid. pp. 306, 509; cited in Balyuzi 1973, p. 153) locked him into his home, refusing to allow him to join the Báb at Chihríq (Nabíl-i-A'zam 1970, pp. 306–7; Balyuzi 1973, p. 153). It is also reported that the Báb assured Anís, in a vision which he related to Shaykh Hasan-i-Zunúzí, a relative and one of the amanuenses and companions of the Báb, that he would be granted the privilege of sharing his master's martyrdom (Nabíl-i-A'zam 1970, pp. 307–8; cited in Balyuzi 1973, pp. 153–4). There are reports in Nabíl-i-A'zam 1970 (p. 509), Balyuzi 1973 (p. 156) and Amanat 1989 (p. 401) to the effect that attempts were made to persuade Anís to retract his confession of faith in the Báb's claims but to no avail. Amanat 1989 (p. 401, n. 111) cites Avarih (vol. 1, p. 240) and Mázandaráni 1941 (pp. 31–7), both of which claim to be accounts of an exchange between Anís and a Shaykhí mulla seeking to elicit his return to Islam. Nabíl-i-A'zam 1970 (pp. 509–10) reports a brief exchange between Anís and Mullá Muhammad Mámáqání, among others, and it is worth noting that Mámáqání was regarded as perhaps the leading Shaykhi 'Alím in Tabriz.

25. The humiliating removal of the Báb's turban and sash, the twin emblems of the 'siyyid' (descendant of the Prophet Muhammad) is reported in Nabíl-i-A'zam 1970 (p. 507) and 'Abdu'l-Bahá 1980 (p. 26), as well as Balyuzi 1973 (p. 153) and Amanat 1989 (p. 402). He was conducted around the city and through the bazaar before being brought to the square for his execution in order to demonstrate the government's full control of the situation (Amanat 1989, p. 402). This whole scene evokes many similar images of the public humiliation – the parade through the city streets and the open air – of Jesus of Nazareth, as depicted in the Gospels.

26. Siyyid Husayn-i-Yazdí, the amanuensis of the Báb, held his last earthly conversation with his master in the prison cell adjoining the place of the Báb's martyrdom, between the firings of the two regiments (Nabíl-i-A'zam 1970, pp. 513–14; 'Abdu'l-Bahá, p. 27). He was the Báb's amanuensis in both Máh-Kú and Chihríq (Nabíl-i-A'zam 1970, p. 629) and was imprisoned with Bahá'u'lláh in the Síyáh-Chál (ibid. pp. 629–30) until his death in 1852 at the hand of Táhirih's executioner, 'Azíz Khán-i-Sardár. According to MacEoin 1992 (pp. 13, 84, 182), a manuscript copy of the Bayán-i-fársí in the hand of

Siyyid Husayn-i-Yazdí is preserved at the Bahá'í International Archives in Haifa. Also in the handwriting of this amanuensis are 27 folios of the Kitáb al-Asmá' in the same location (ibid. p. 188) and six examples of letters reproduced in facsimile in the Azalí compilation entitled *Qismatí az alwah-i-khatt-i-Nuqta-yi-Úlá wa Siyyid Husayn-i-Kátib* (ibid. pp. 204, 254). The authenticity (and authorship) of the letters in this collection has yet to be independently confirmed. There is another trace of his influence which has been discovered, and a very interesting one at that. E.G. Browne (in Appendix 2 to *Táríkh-i-Jadíd* 1893, pp. 395–6; cited in Nabíl-i-A'zam 1970, p. 518, n. 1) quoted Hájí Mírzá Jání Kashání to the effect that Siyyid Husayn-i-Yazdí, whom he calls Áqá Siyyid Muhammad-Husayn, gave some of the writings of the Báb to the Russian consul at Tabriz (presumably Anitchkov, according to Amanat 1989, p. 381, n. 35), who came to ask Siyyid Husayn about the Báb shortly after his martyrdom. Browne indicates that this story is confirmed by the testimony of Bernard Dorn ('Bulletin de l'Academie Imperiale des Sciences de St. Petersbourg', vol. 8, p. 248), who, in describing a manuscript of one of the Báb's works in the possession of the Academie, indicates that it was 'received directly from the Báb's own secretary, who, during his imprisonment at Tabriz, placed it in European hands'. Amanat 1989 (p. 381, n. 35) notes that this interview is also found in *Kitáb-i-Nuqtatu'l-Káf* (p. 267), and Momen 1981 (p. 48).

Inasmuch as Siyyid Husayn was imprisoned shortly after the Báb's execution, it appears that the government authorities were not convinced by Siyyid Husayn's feigned repudiation of the Báb just prior to his martyrdom, an act which had been enjoined upon him by the Báb himself according to Nabíl-i-A'zam 1970 (p. 508) and Mázandarání 1941 (p. 460, cited in Amanat 1989, p. 381, n. 35). Two years later, immediately following the attempt on the life of Násiri'd-Dín Sháh in 1852, Siyyid Husayn was imprisoned in the Síyáh-Chál with Bahá'u'lláh until his execution (Nabíl-i-A'zam 1970, pp. 629–31). Nabíl-i-A'zam (p. 631) indicates that Siyyid Husayn was comforted in his separation from the Báb by Bahá'u'lláh, 'One who alone could banish, by the light of His presence, the anguish that had settled upon his soul'. Whether this indicates that Siyyid Husayn recognized the prophetic station of Bahá'u'lláh is not evident from this passage.

27. The attempts to persuade Mírzá Muhammad-'Alí (Anís) from his Bábí convictions are described in note 24 above. No mention is made in any of the Persian sources, however, to the pleas of this young man's wife and children. However, given the young age at which Persians were customarily married at this time, it is not improbable that he was married and had little children.

28. Nabíl-i-A'zam 1970 (pp. 511–14) indicates that Sám Khán and his men were designated the first executioners of the Báb. 'Abdu'l-Bahá 1980 (pp. 26–7) indicates the same, identifying Sám Khán as a colonel and his men as the Christian regiment of Urúmíyyih. Mu'ín (p. 306, cited in Amanat 1989, p. 402, n. 117) states that Sám Khán, better known as Sám Khán Urus, was a convert to Islam. This is clearly not reflected in Nabíl-i-A'zam 1970 or 'Abdu'l-Bahá 1980. Perhaps he became a convert to Islam after the execution of the Báb? Hidáyat 1959–60 (vol. 10, pp. 210, 329, 416–22; cited in Amanat 1989, p. 402, n. 117) reported that the Bahaduran regiment participated in all the major campaigns of Muhammad Sháh's reign under Sám Khán's leadership. Za'ím al-Dawla 1903 (p. 238; cited in Amanat 1989, p. 402, n. 116) indicates there were three regiments present at the place of execution and that Áqá Ján Bag Khamsih, the leader of the Násirí regiment refused, so the Bahaduran regiment was chosen. He indicates that *Kitáb-i-Nuqtatu'l-Káf* (p. 249; cited in ibid.) seems to confirm this report. Nabíl-i-A'zam 1970 and 'Abdu'l-Bahá 1980 state that Sám Khán and his men were selected first. Nabíl-i-A'zam (p. 514) indicates that upon the failure of the Bahaduran regiment to injure, let alone kill the two condemned ones, Sám Khán was excused and Áqá Ján Khán-i-Khamsih, colonel of the bodyguard, known as the

Khamsih or Násirí regiment, carried out the execution. 'Abdu'l-Bahá 1980 (p. 27) indicates the same, naming the colonel of the bodyguard as Áqá Ján Big-i-Khamsih.

29. Amanat 1989 (p. 403) has translated this passage from Sipihr 1965 (vol. 3, p. 305, cited in ibid. n. 122) and it is reproduced here in full for the convenience of the reader (the words in brackets are supplied by Amanat in order to assist reading comprehension):

> [His] escape [to one of the rooms in the barracks] was a demonstration of the might of the [Islamic] sharí'a since at that time when the bullets hit the rope and he was set free, if he exposed his bosom and cried out: 'O ye the soldiers and the people, didst thou not see my miracle that of a thousand bullets not even one hit me but instead untied my bonds', then no one would have fired a shot at him any more and surely the men and women in the barracks would have assembled around him and a riot would have broken out. It was God's will that the truth should be distinguished from falsehood and doubt and uncertainty be removed from among the people.

30. The author of the *Kitáb al-Mutanabbi'ín* is 'Alí-Qulí Mírzá, I'tidád al-Saltanih. Not to be confused with Muhammad Hasan Khán, Saní'ud-Dawlih, I'timád al-Saltanih Marághiyí. See note 34 for details related to the latter author. MacEoin 1992 (p. 253) indicates that part of the *Kitáb al-Mutanabbi'ín* is incorporated in *Fitna-yi Báb* by 'Abdu'l-Husayn Navá'í, who also wrote an article entitled 'Siyyid 'Alí Muhammad Báb va Kitáb al-Mutanabbi'ín-i-I'tidád al-Saltanih' (*Yaghmá*, vol. 3).

31. Dr Firuz Kazemzadeh and his father Kazem Kazemzadeh compiled various eyewitness accounts of this event, some of them being translated for the first time from Persian and Russian, in Kazemzadeh 1973. According to Nabíl-i-A'zam 1970 (p. 513) and 'Abdu'l-Bahá 1980 (p. 27), Mírzá Muhammad-'Alí (Anís) was untouched by the shots fired by the Bahaduran regiment. This seems to be confirmed by Kazem-Beg (translated from the Russian of *Bab i babidy* by Kazem Kazemzadeh in Kazemzadeh 1973). Justin Sheil's Foreign Office report to Lord Palmerston, cited by Balyuzi 1973 (p. 202) and by Momen 1981 (p. 78) does not make any mention of Mírzá Muhammad-'Alí (Anís) in connection with the martyrdom of the Báb. Neither does Clement Huart, the French Orientalist, in *La Religion du Bab* (pp. 3–4; cited in Nabíl-i-A'zam 1970, p. 513, n. 1). Sipihr 1965 (p. 305, cited in Amanat 1989, p. 403, n. 120; and translated by Dr Firuz Kazemzadeh for Kazemzadeh 1973) reports that Anís was killed in the first attempt and this is repeated by Gobineau (translated by Kazem Kazemzadeh in ibid.) and Za'ím al-Dawlah 1903 (translated by Dr Firuz Kazemzadeh in ibid.). Owing to the similarity of their accounts, it seems that both Gobineau and Za'ím al-Dawla 1903 based their descriptions of this event on Sipihr, and hence should not be taken as independent sources. A conversation between George Latimer and 'Abdu'l-Bahá on 19 November 1919 seems to confirm Sipihr 1965 in this regard (Latimer 1920, p. 70):

> Mr Latimer: 'Was the Babi, Aga Mohammed Ali, who was martyred with the BAB, killed with the first volley or the second?'

> Abdul Baha: 'With the first one he was killed. He was mutilated. But the body of His Holiness the BAB was not hit by the first discharge.'

However, this conversation was not confirmed either in substance or wording by 'Abdu'l-Bahá and it is possible that Latimer or his translator may have misunderstood his meaning.

Kazem-Beg stated that after the first attempt, the 'Christian soldiers immediately ran and showed the people the ropes severed by bullets; the criminal was again tied; Áqá Muhammad-'Alí was shot first, then the Báb' (Kazem-Beg, in Kazemzadeh 1973). This seems to suggest that neither Áqá Muhammad-'Alí nor the Báb was struck by the first attempt, made by the Christian regiment, but that in the second attempt first Áqá Muhammad-'Alí was struck and then the Báb. Nabíl-i-A'zam 1970 (p. 512) and 'Abdu'l-Bahá 1980 (pp. 43–4) state that the regiment consisted of three files of soldiers, each of 250 soldiers (Nabíl-i-A'zam 1970), and that each file was ordered to fire a volley of shots in its turn. Perhaps the attempt by the Christian regiment, after firing three volleys, did not injure either Áqá Muhammad-'Alí or the Báb but severed the ropes that secured the Báb, resulting in his seemingly miraculous disappearance from the scene. Once the next regiment was summoned to make a second attempt at this public execution, perhaps Áqá Muhammad-'Alí was hit by the first file of soldiers and the Báb by the second or third, and hence after him. This might explain this difference among the various accounts.

While Nabíl-i-A'zam 1970 (p. 512) and Balyuzi 1973 (p. 157) report that the regiment consisted of 750 men and that they fired in three volleys, one row at a time, Amanat 1989 (p. 403) states only that there were three volleys. Hence, it seems that I'tidád, here reported by Nicolas to have cited one thousand shots, is exaggerating the number of bullets fired during the first attempt to execute the Báb and his companion.

32. While one source says the Báb 'ran away' and accuses him of cowardice, and Sipihr 1965 (cited in Amanat 1989), Gobineu (translated by Kazem Kazemzadeh in Kazemzadeh 1973) and Za'ím al-Dawla 1903 agree with this source, Nabíl-i-A'zam 1970 (p. 513) and 'Abdu'l-Bahá 1980 (p. 27) indicate that after his disappearance from the place of execution, the Báb was found in the cell he had occupied earlier and in the company of Siyyid Husayn-i-Yazdí. Nabíl-i-A'zam 1970 (pp. 513–14) reports that the farrásh-báshí who was in charge of finding the Báb and returning him to the place of execution was so shaken by these events that he resigned his post and left the scene; Nabíl-i-A'zam further indicates that the farrásh-báshí told this story to his neighbour, Mírzá Siyyid Muhsin, who was immediately converted to the Bábí Cause and who later showed Nabíl-i-Zarandí the exact location of the room where the Báb was found and the nail from which he was suspended during the execution. Amanat 1989 (p. 403, n. 121) cites a report – without identifying the source – that a Muslim army sergeant, Ghuj 'Alí Sultán, retrieved the Báb, struck him in the face and dragged him back to the firing squad. In Sipihr 1965 (cited in Amanat 1989), Quch-'Alí Sultán is described as 'having hit him several times on the back of his head, returned him to the place of execution'. The same account is found almost word for word in Za'ím al-Dawlah 1903. Gobineau (in Kazemzadeh 1973) states that once freed of his bonds by the first attempt on his life, the Bab 'fell on his feet, quickly rose and sought to flee; then, all of a sudden seeing a guardhouse, he ran into it . . . when the Báb had entered the guard-room, an infantry captain, or Sultán, by the name of Quch-'Alí came in after him and cut him down with his sabre. The Báb fell without saying a word; then the soldiers, seeing him in a pool of blood, approached and ended his life with their rifles at point-blank range.' It thus appears that Amanat could have derived his information from any one of these sources.

Nabíl-i-A'zam 1970 (p. 514) and 'Abdu'l-Bahá 1980 (p. 27) insist that the Muslim regiment led by Áqá Ján of Khamsih stepped in to carry out the death sentence against the Báb. Nabíl-i-A'zam (p. 525) seems to have kept track of this Muslim regiment: he indicates that during the year 1266/1850, one third of the regiment died in an earthquake and that three years later the remaining five hundred mutinied and were mercilessly shot by order of Mírzá Sádiq Khán-i-Núrí.

33. See note 3 above for a detailed consideration of the date of the Báb's execution.
34. *Mir'at al-Buldan*, a work in several volumes (Khazeh Fananapazir, email 14/1/02) was written by Muhammad Hasan Khán (Fananapazir; and J.R.I. Cole, email 14/1/02), known as I'timád al-Saltanih (Cole) and as Saní'ud-Dawlih, I'timád al-Saltanih Marághiyí (Fananapazir). Cole points out that the author died in 1896 and he refers to the publication of his history in Tehran by Nashr-i-Asfar, with the first

volume dated 1364/1985. Fananapazir points out that the author of this history was the son of Hájibu'd-Dawlih Hájí 'Alí Khán Marághiyí, 'a cruel persecutor of the Bábís' and that his son, 'the author, was fair in description of geography, etc. but not in matters related to the [Bábí] Cause'. MacEoin 1992 (p. 252) cites *Kitáb al-ma'áthir wa'l-áthár* (Tehran, 1306/1888–9) by the same author.

35. There are two individuals named Hájí Sulaymán Khán who were directly associated with the Bábís during this period. Ridá-Qulí Khán-i-Afshár converted to the Bábí Cause (Mu'ín, pp. 173–6, cited in Amanat 1989, p. 367, n. 194) and was apparently deprived of his family estate at Sá'ín Qal'a by his anti-Bábí father, Hájí Sulaymán Khán-i-Afshár (see note 4 above). On the other hand, there is another Hájí Sulaymán Khán, a fervent and active Bábí, who is referred to in the context of the safeguarding of the Báb's body, in Nabíl-i-A'zam 1970 (pp. 518–20) and 'Abdu'l-Bahá 1980 (p. 28). When the body was retrieved from the street, it was first brought, according to Afnan 2000 (p. 408), to the house of Mírzá Hasan Vazír, the son-in-law of Hájí Mírzá 'Alí Tafrishí (Faydí 1973, p. 357), known as Majd al-Ashráf. From there the body was transported to Tehran by Hájí Sulaymán Khán, according to various accounts.

In a conversation between George Latimer and 'Abdu'l-Bahá on 19 November 1919, we find the following report (Latimer 1920, p. 70):

> Then Mr Latimer asked about the taking of the body of the BAB to Teheran.
> Abdul Baha: 'It is just as it is written in the Traveller's Narrative. Read it in the Traveller's Narrative. It is the same. All the other accounts are without foundation. Suleyman Khan, the martyr, brought His Blessed Body to Teheran.'

Actually, *Traveller's Narrative*" (that is, 'Abdu'l-Bahá 1891) does not state that the body of the Báb was brought to Tehran by Sulaymán Khán. It only states ('Abdu'l-Bahá 1980, p. 28) that he retrieved the body of the Báb, placed it in a box and sent it away from Ádhirbáyján according to instructions from Tehran. Nabíl-i-A'zam 1970 (p. 519) tells a similar story, indicating that Sulaymán Khán had the Báb's body retrieved, placed in a box and transferred 'to a place of safety'. Nabíl-i-A'zam 1970 (p. 521) does not report who delivered the body of the Báb to Tehran but he does state that he was in Tehran at the time and that the remains were transferred by Áqáy-i-Kalím and Mírzá Ahmad 'from the Imám-Zádih-Hasan, where they were first taken, to a place the site of which remained unknown to anyone excepting themselves'. Balyuzi 1973 (pp. 159–60) seems to rely on Nabíl-i-A'zam 1970 and 'Abdu'l-Bahá 1891, and does not clarify this matter. It would seem that 'Abdu'l-Bahá's words, cited above, are the only definite account we have of who was responsible for transferring the body of the Báb from Tabriz to Tehran. Shoghi Effendi 1995 (pp. 273–4) states that, according to Bahá'u'lláh's instructions, the remains of the Báb were 'transported to Tihrán and placed in the shrine of Imám-Zádih Hasan. They were later removed to the residence of Hájí Sulaymán Khán himself in the Sar-Chashmih quarter of the city, and from his house were taken to the shrine of Imám-Zádih Ma'súm, where they remained concealed until the year 1284 AH (1867–1868) . . .' This would seem to explain Nabíl-i-A'zam's omission of the name of Hájí Sulaymán Khán with regard to the process of the actual transfer of the Báb's body from Tabriz to Tehran – it was intended that this process be secret so that enemies of the Bábís (and later of the Bahá'ís) would be incapable of seizing the sacred relic. Nabíl-i-A'zam 1970 (pp. 610–11, 613–19) makes copious reference to the martyrdom of Sulaymán Khán, and other sources cited by Amanat 1989 (p. 367, n. 189) include Sipihr 1965 (vol. 4, p. 42), Mázandarání 1941 (p. 26n), Browne in *Táríkh-i-Jadíd* 1893 (pp. 330–1), Momen 1981 (pp. 128–46), and *Vaqayi' Ittifaqiya* (no. 82). Sepehr Manuchehri has indicated that Mázandarání 1941 (vols. 3 and 4) contains much material on Hájí Mírzá Sulaymán Khán, the Bábí, and on the transfer of the Báb's remains from Tabriz to Haifa. According to Manuchehri,

Mázandarání 1941 categorically denies that the Bábís intended to 'wage battle if necessary' in order to retrieve the body of the Báb. Instead, the Bábís sent two or three persons who pretended to be 'mentally disturbed' to the vicinity of the site. They were instructed not to leave the site under any circumstances. Bábí women were directed to bring them food and water. They were to remain there and attempt to smuggle the body out at a suitable time.

36. Hájí Mihdí Khán, the Kalantar (mayor) of Tabriz, was a long-standing friend of Hájí Sulaymán Khán (Balyuzi 1973, p. 159). Nabíl-i-A'zam 1970 (p. 519) calls the Kalantar a dervish and a member of the Sufi community, while 'Abdu'l-Bahá 1980 (p. 28) states that he was 'of the mystic temperament and did not entertain aversion or dislike for any sect' – important indications, inasmuch as Hájí Mírzá Áqásí and Muhammad Sháh were also Sufis, if clearly of a different stripe. The Kalantar arranged for Hájí Alláh-Yár (Nabíl-i-A'zam 1970, p. 519; 'Abdu'l-Bahá 1980, p. 28), a private servant of the mayor ('Abdu'l-Bahá 1980, p. 28), known for his exploits (Balyuzi 1973, p. 159) to recover the bodies of Anís and the Báb. These were delivered to Hájí Sulaymán Khán on the second night after the Báb's death (Nabíl-i-A'zam 1970, pp. 518, 519; 'Abdu'l-Bahá 1980, p. 27), at midnight. Both Nabíl-i-A'zam (p. 518) and 'Abdu'l-Bahá (p. 27) report that an official of the Russian consulate sent an artist to draw a sketch of the two bodies as they lay at the edge of the moat before they were recovered by the Bábís. Nabíl-i-A'zam (p. 518) received his report from Hájí 'Alí-Askar, a relative of an official of the Russian consulate, who showed him that sketch 'on the very same day it was drawn'.

> It was such a faithful portrait of the Báb that I looked upon! No bullet had struck His forehead, His cheeks, or His lips. I gazed upon a smile which seemed to be still lingering upon His countenance. His body, however, had been severely mutilated. I could recognize the arms and head of His companion, who seemed to be holding Him in his embrace. As I gazed horror-struck upon that haunting picture, and saw how those noble traits had been disfigured, my heart sank within me.

This sketch was thought to be lost until the Armenian author Atrpet Sargis Mubagajian published numerous photographs of early Bábís and some allegedly of the Báb in the second half of his *Imámat* 1909, entitled 'Bábíty I Bekhaiti' (pp. 87–208). Denis MacEoin, who inspected this volume himself and who was familiar with authenticated pictures of the Báb, wrote in his bibliography of Bahá'í literature, in which we find Atrpet's work cited, that 'none of which [photographs] appear to be in the least authentic'. This assessment is confirmed by an Ad Hoc Committee appointed by the Universal House of Justice to look into this question, replying on 20 March 1983 to a letter of Robert Stauffer dated 9 February 1983 asking about these pictures:

> In an early sketch of Atrpet Sargis Mubagajian's sources of information for his book 'Bábízm i Bekhaizm', a report was found among the documents filed by Shoghi Effendi indicating that Mubagajian went to Tabriz to investigate the Bahá'í Faith. He, unfortunately, met with Jalil Mishkar Khú'í, a Covenant-breaker, and received his information from this man. What Mubagajian was told, particularly about the period after Bahá'u'lláh, was grossly incorrect. Jalil also sold Mubagajian other pictures and portraits which later appeared in the book. The report further states that the portraits identified as those of Bahá'u'lláh, the Báb and Táhirih are obviously forged. However, the drawing made of 'Abdu'l-Bahá in his youth bears, of course, a great resemblance to the original picture.

Ismael Velasco (email 16/1/02) reported that 'Bahiyyih Nakhjavani and Bill Collins have done some research into this at the [Bahá'í] World Centre. It seems the portrait [found in Artpet's book] that was purportedly drawn by an artist who had been brought by the Russian consul to the spot where the bodies [of the Báb and Anís] were thrown the day after the Báb's martyrdom may not be authentic. Bill Collins wrote:

> "I served at the Bahá'í World Centre Library for thirteen years, and on a number of occasions, I was presented with difficult problems of identification. One of these problems had to do with a supposed sketch of the Báb's body that appeared in a Russian article. We could find no historical evidence that this sketch was anything other than the author's imagination. Yet there were people who criticized the finding that this was almost certainly not drawn at the time the Báb's body was thrown by His enemies beside the moat in Tabriz."'

It appears then that the original sketch of the Báb after his martyrdom has not been found and that the pictures found in Artpet's book are forgeries.

37. Mullá Muhammad-'Alíy-i-Zanjání was named Hujjat-i-Zanjání by the Báb (Nabíl-i-A'zam 1970, pp. 178, 529, 683) and was also called simply Hujjat (Nabíl-i-A'zam 1970, pp. 531–80). Nicolas has confused him with Muhammad-'Alí Zunúzí of Tabriz, named Anís, who was the Báb's companion in death. Nicolas's source for this misinformation would appear to be Mírzá Yahyá, as he quotes him to this effect (cited in note 41 below). Nicolas claims that the body of the Báb's companion was buried while that of the Báb himself was shrouded in a box and hidden in a house. Nabíl-i-A'zam 1970 (p. 519) and 'Abdu'l-Bahá 1980 (p. 27) affirm that the bodies of both these martyrs, the Báb and Anís, were carried away by the Bábís, and Nabíl-i-A'zam (p. 519) indicates that both were laid in a single casket. This is confirmed by Shoghi Effendi 1995 (p. 273) and by Mírzá Yahyá as well (see note 41 below).

38. As has been indicated in note 35, other reports confirm Nicolas's statement that the body of the Báb was placed in a casket and hidden in a house.

39. Nicolas attests that he was in contact with Mírzá Yahyá Subh-i-Azal in Cyprus for two years, in 1894 and 1895 (Nicolas 1911, 'Introduction', p. i, n. 1). Inasmuch as Nicolas refers here to his visit to Cyprus, it would seem likely that he may have made two visits, one in 1894 and another in 1895. Mírzá Yahyá did not die until 1911, so it appears that Nicolas discontinued contact with him by choice rather than necessity.

40. Nabíl-i-A'zam 1970 (pp. 520–1) indicates that Bahá'u'lláh ordered the transfer of the Báb's body from Tabriz to Tehran, 'prompted by the wish the Báb Himself had expressed in the "Ziyárat-i-Sháh-'Abdu'l-'Azím", a Tablet He had revealed while in the neighbourhood of that shrine and which He delivered to a certain Mírzá Sulaymán-i-Khatíb, who was instructed by Him to proceed together with a number of believers to that spot and to chant it within its precincts.' Nabíl-i-A'zam 1970 (p. 521) quotes some of the words of the Báb with regard to this location:

> 'Well is it with you,' the Báb addressed the buried saint in words such as these, in the concluding passages of that Tablet, 'to have found your resting place in Rayy, under the shadow of My Beloved. Would that I might be entombed within the precincts of that holy ground!'

Lord Curzon (*Persia and the Persian Question*, pp. 345–7, cited in Nabíl-i-A'zam 1970, p. 521, n. 1) described this sanctuary, which is located about six miles southeast of Tehran.

41. As was affirmed in note 38, Nabíl-i-A'zam 1970 (p. 519) and Shoghi Effendi 1995 (p. 273) report that the two bodies, of the Báb and Anís, were placed together in a single casket. This is corroborated here by Mírzá Yahyá. It is entirely unlikely, however, that the Báb's body could have been buried in a crystal casket, inasmuch as this would be so heavy, so cumbersome and possibly so costly as to make the movement of such a relic extremely difficult. Hence this contention of Mírzá Yahyá is highly suspect. None of the extant letters of the Báb, including those that have been published by the Azalís (see MacEoin 1992, p. 96) confirm Mírzá Yahyá's claim that he was personally and

exclusively chosen by the Báb to carry out the burial of his master in a location which he alone could identify. This is also unlikely because, had he been the only person who could identify this location, the priceless remains of the Báb might easily have been lost forever, should Mírzá Yahyá have died prior to informing another of the secret location. Finally, Mírzá Yahyá, if he has been accurately quoted by Nicolas, wrongly identifies the martyred companion of the Báb as Muhammad-'Alíy-i-Zanjání, called Hujjat, rather than Mírzá Muhammad-'Alí, called Anís.

42. Afnan 2000 (p. 408) affirms that the body of the Báb was taken to the house of Mírzá Hasan Vazír, the son-in-law of Majd-i-Ashráf. Faydí 1973 (p. 357) indicates that the full name of Majd-i-Ashráf was Hájí Mírzá Siyyid 'Alí Tafrishí. Nabíl-i-A'zam 1970 (p. 521) states that the location of the Báb's body was a closely guarded secret, apparently known only to Bahá'u'lláh and to Áqáy-i-Kalím (Bahá'u'lláh's brother, also known as Mírzá Músá) and Mírzá Ahmad, who were charged with effecting its concealment by Bahá'u'lláh, and perhaps also by 'Abdu'l-Bahá. However, Nabíl-i-A'zam 1970 (p. 521) indicates that upon the departure of Bahá'u'lláh for Adrianople, Áqáy-i-Kalím was to inform Munír, one of his fellow disciples, of the location but that he was unable himself to find the site. Bahá'u'lláh left Constantinople for Adrianople on 1 December 1863 (Shoghi Effendi 1995, p. 161) and it seems likely that Áqáy-i-Kalím wrote to Munír by this time, if not earlier in the year. Ismael Velasco (email 14/1/02) indicated that Mírzá Músá, Áqáy-i-Kalím, was 'a leading disciple of Bahá'u'lláh' who acted 'as His shield until 'Abdu'l-Bahá grew up' and that he was present when Bahá'u'lláh 'received [a] copy of [the] Qayyúmu'l-Asmá' sent by Mullá Husayn'. For a description of this event, the reader may refer to Nabíl-i-A'zam 1970 (pp. 106–107). For more details regarding Mírzá Músá, Áqáy-i-Kalím, please see Nabíl-i-A'zam 1970 (pp. 183, 255, 286, 288, 397, 432, 441, 582); Balyuzi 1980 (pp. 13, 36, 62, 66–7, 102, 105, 107, 112, 121, 128–9, 137, 139, 141, 148–50, 153, 155, 181, 184, 199, 204–7, 219, 221, 225–7, 229–30, 236, 243, 246, 275, 277, 283, 288, 315, 319, 327, 330, 347–8, 363, 369; Balyuzi 1985 (pp. 261–2); Taherzadeh 1974 (pp. 15–16, 53, 67n, 131, 144, 205, 228, 247, 284, 316n); Taherzadeh 1977 (pp. 58, 67, 154, 160, 163–4, 200, 211, 247n, 332, 402, 405); Taherzadeh 1983 (pp. 23, 181, 225n, 361, 424–5; Taherzadeh 1987 (pp. 242, 420n, 438).

Nabíl-i-A'zam 1970 (pp. 521–2) indicates that the casket containing the bodies of the Báb and Anís was subsequently discovered by Jamál, an adherent of the Cause who had been informed of its location while Bahá'u'lláh was in Adrianople. Shoghi Effendi 1995 (pp. 273–4) states that in 1284 AH (1867–8) in Adrianople Bahá'u'lláh wrote a tablet to Mullá 'Alí-Akbar-i-Shahmírzádí, whom he had appointed a Hand of the Cause (Balyuzi 1973, p. 189n), and to Jamál-i-Burújirdí, ordering them to transfer the sacred remains to a new location. It appears that the Jamál in Nabíl-i-A'zam may be identical with Jamál-i-Burújirdí. This is confirmed by Adib Taherzadeh, who reports in *The Revelation of Bahá'u'lláh* (1977, vol. 2, pp. 402–3):

> At this juncture it is appropriate to mention that before going to Adrianople, Jamál-i-Burújirdí had rendered an important service to the Faith in Persia. He and Mullá 'Alí-Akbar-i-Shahmírzádí, known as Hájí Ákhúnd, whom Bahá'u'lláh later appointed a Hand of the Cause of God, had been instructed by Him in 1284 AH (1867–8) to transfer the remains of the Báb which were concealed within the Shrine of Imám-Zádih Ma'súm to another place of safety.

The story of this transfer as found in Shoghi Effendi 1995 (pp. 273–6) is virtually identical to that found in Nicolas, and both accounts seem to be based on the memoirs of Mullá 'Alí-Akbar-i-Shahmírzádí. Photographs of the shrine of Imám-Zádih Ma'súm are published in *Bahá'í World*, vol. 5, p. 544; and vol. 6, p. 65. Hence Mírzá Yahyá's contention, that the location of the bodies remained a secret for 30 years, when they were apparently concealed in 1850 and moved in 1867–8, is also highly suspect; furthermore, his claim that the Bahá'ís in particular knew nothing of the whereabouts of the precious trust is preposterous, inasmuch as Bahá'u'lláh called upon two Bahá'ís to move the remains when he foresaw that they could be endangered by being left in the shrine of Imám-Zádih Ma'súm. His statement that the Bahá'ís disinterred the body and destroyed it is unbelievable, when one considers that Bahá'ís universally regard the Báb as a Manifestation of God, greater in station to any previous prophet, and the first of the two Manifestations of a cycle of fulfilment destined to last half a million years. Indeed, the Bahá'ís have a higher regard for the Báb than did the Bábís, inasmuch as the writings of Bahá'u'lláh depict his prophetic standing in more superlative terms than those employed by the Báb himself.

43. Mírzá Yahyá allows that if the Bahá'ís did not destroy the body of the Báb, and if they possess this sacred relic, nevertheless the tomb they chose for it is not sacred as it is not placed in the location stipulated by the Báb. According to the verses of the tablet cited by Nabíl-i-A'zam 1970 (p. 521), the Báb wanted to be buried in Rayy, near the shrine of Sháh 'Abdu'l-'Azím and just outside of Tehran, because he wished to have a resting place 'under the shadow of My Beloved'. Given the many hints in his writings to the identity of 'Him whom God shall manifest', which Bahá'u'lláh claimed to fulfil, it seems reasonable to regard this tablet as an expression of the Báb's wish to be buried close to Bahá'u'lláh. 'Abdu'l-Bahá seems to have had the Báb's wishes in mind as well as those of Bahá'u'lláh when he ordered that the Báb's remains be transported from Tehran to 'Akká, where they arrived on 19 Ramadán 1316/31 January 1899 (Shoghi Effendi 1995, p. 274). Finally, in the Bayán-i-fársí the Báb stated that certain geographical locations and buildings are sacralized through their association with holy souls. The Manifestation of God is the 'divine presence' during his earthly sojourn, and after his passing, the places associated with him are holy to his followers. His house becomes the House of God, his city the City of God. The Báb made all his ordinances and teachings contingent upon their acceptance by 'Him Whom God shall manifest', and hence, if Bahá'u'lláh, the successful claimant to this title, decreed that the Báb's remains be located in a place different from the place ordained by the Báb himself, it would appear that this is entirely in harmony with the Báb's wishes.

Regarding Mírzá Yahyá's version of these events, Nicolas writes:

> I hesitated for a long time to write down these words of Subh-i-Azal in my story. Everything he says is contradictory and unbelievable, but I thought that impartiality made it a duty for me to report what I heard. I will limit myself to remarking that Subh-i-Azal does not explain how the body came to him, or where and how he procured the casket of crystal. The confused members of the two victims respond to nothing that history tells us. If the two sects differ in opinion as to the person of the successor of the Báb, at least they envelope the Báb himself with the same love and the same respect. To accuse one of them of having destroyed him seems to be a calumny of which Mírzá Yahyá repents, moreover immediately, as he adds as a corrective that it is possible that the body was not destroyed. That the Bahá'ís would have ignored the location of the sepulchre for thirty years is impossible, because at the start there were only Bábís. Finally, how could Azal have hidden this [location] from his brother Bahá' in whom he had the greatest confidence and whom he even accuses of having abused that confidence?

Nicolas's comments are telling, considering that he relied on Mírzá Yahyá and his followers for much of his information and many of his copies of the writings of the Báb.

44. Nicolas does not identify his source here. Nabíl-i-A'zam 1970 (p. 519) states that Hájí Sulaymán Khán transferred the remains of Anís and the Báb from the silk factory in Mílán 'to a place of safety'. 'Abdu'l-Bahá 1980 (p. 28) reports that the sacred

remains were placed in a box in the workshop of a Bábí of Mílán and that afterwards, in obedience to instructions from Tehran, they were sent away from Ádhirbáyján to a secret location. Inasmuch as Hájí Sulaymán Khán's father was a Tabrizí (Balyuzi 1973, p. 149), and 'one of the nobles of Ádhirbáyján' ('Abdu'l-Bahá 1980, p. 28), it is very likely that the family had a residence in Tabriz itself and that the bodies of the Báb and Anís were taken to that location subsequent to their consignment to a casket. Furthermore, it is recorded by Shoghi Effendi 1995 (p. 273) that the casket was concealed in the Tehran residence of Hájí Sulaymán Khán after it was removed from the shrine of Imám-Zádih Hasan and before it was taken to the shrine of Imám-Zádih Ma'súm.
45. Nabíl-i-A'zam 1970 (pp. 519–20) indicates that Hájí Sulaymán Khán reported the location of the casket and its sacred trust to Bahá'u'lláh who was then in Tehran. Nabíl-i-A'zam (pp. 520–1) also indicates that Bahá'u'lláh gave instructions for the transfer of the Báb's body in compliance with a formal statement of the wishes of the Báb himself regarding his burial that was in his possession.
46. Nicolas identifies the resting place of the casket, which Nabíl-i-A'zam 1970 and 'Abdu'l-Bahá 1980 refrained from doing, either because they were not informed of its whereabouts or, more likely, because they did not wish to endanger its continued existence by making its location public knowledge in an untimely fashion. When Nabíl-i-A'zam was compiling his history, circa 1887–92, and when 'Abdu'l-Bahá was seeing his history published, in 1890 and 1891, the body of the Báb had already been transferred to another safe house, as it had been imperiled by the renovations being made to the Imám-Zádih Ma'súm. However, the casket was still in the keeping of the Bahá'ís in the vicinity of Tehran and it may have seemed risky to them to openly discuss the present whereabouts of this sacred trust. In 1899 the sacred remains made their way to 'Akká and out of Persia altogether; hence, what would have constituted a risky and potentially disastrous disclosure in 1890 was an entirely appropriate statement of historical fact in 1905.
47. Qazvín is a city located around one hundred miles northwest of Tehran.
48. Shoghi Effendi 1995 (p. 274) gives the date of this ordinance of Bahá'u'lláh as 1284 AH (1867–8), which would have been 37 to 38 years prior to 1905, when Nicolas published *Seyyed Ali Mohammed dit le Báb*. Twenty-nine years prior to 1905 would have been the year 1876. Bahá'u'lláh left Adrianople – from where, according to both authors, he wrote a tablet ordering the transfer of the Báb's remains – on 22 Rabí' al-Thání 1285 AH (12 August 1868) according to Shoghi Effendi 1995 (p. 180). Therefore, it is plainly impossible that he could have sent this order 29 years before the publication of Nicolas's book, as he had left Adrianople eight or nine years prior to that time. Was Nicolas referring to an earlier date, perhaps the time when he met and talked with Hájí Mullá 'Alí-Akbar Shahmírzádí? If so, then this meeting must have taken place eight years before the publication of his book, in 1897. This is entirely possible. Another possibility is that Nicolas did not calculate this period of time accurately, and as we have witnessed repeatedly in the course of this biography, as a chronicler of events the calculation of time was not one of his strong points.
49. Hájí 'Alí-Akbar Shahmírzádí, also known as Hájí Ákhúnd, was appointed a Hand of the Cause of God by Bahá'u'lláh (Balyuzi 1973, p. 189). Biographical references to Shahmírzádí can be found in Balyuzi 1980 (pp. 399, 454); Balyuzi 1985 (pp. 105–6, 139, 175, 258, 261–3, 265–6); Taherzadeh 1977 (p. 402); Taherzadeh 1983 (pp. 85–6, 200, 425–7); Taherzadeh 1987 (pp. 14, 185, 255, 275, 277, 279, 292, 294–301, 306, 311–12, 315–26, 337–8, 348, 380–1, 436).
50. Jamál-i-Burújirdí is described by Nabíl-i-A'zam 1970 (p. 521) as 'an old adherent of the Faith' and it thus appears that he had been a Bábí for some time prior to the martyrdom of the Báb. Mázandarání 1941 (vols. 5 and 6) and the memoirs of Dr Afrukhtih

and Dr Mu'ayyad contain biographical information related to this learned man, this devoted teacher who travelled throughout Persia to promote the Cause of Bahá'u'lláh. It has been reported that Jamál-i-Burújirdí eventually became proud of his knowledge and his eloquence, and it is certain that after the passing of Bahá'u'lláh he refused to accept 'Abdu'l-Bahá, the eldest son of Bahá'u'lláh who had been appointed by him in the Kitáb-i-Aqdas and the Kitáb-i-'Ahdí to serve as the leader of the Bahá'í community. He demanded that 'Abdu'l-Bahá appoint him the head of the Bahá'í Faith in Iran, even as George I. Kheirallah demanded to be made head of the Faith in North America. When 'Abdu'l-Bahá refused to accede to this demand, Jamál-i-Burújirdí joined forces with Mírzá Muhammad 'Alí, 'Abdu'l-Bahá's rebellious half-brother, in making a sustained attack upon the leadership of the appointed heir of Bahá'u'lláh. He maintained his opposition to 'Abdu'l-Bahá until his death at a very advanced age.

51. This account is virtually identical to that found in Shoghi Effendi 1995 (p. 274), although it is told in greater detail by Nicolas.
52. Sháh 'Abdu'l-'Azím is the shrine to which the Báb apparently referred in his tablet and which Nabíl-i-A'zam 1970 (p. 519) indicates as the preferred resting-place of the Báb. Sepehr Manuchehri states that it is found in southern Tehran.
53. Chashmih-'Alí is translated as the 'Alí Springs by Balyuzi (p. 190). Sepehr Manuchehri reports (email 22/1/02) that

> Chishmih-'Alí is now a part of the Nadí-Abad district in southern Teheran. It was famous for its natural spring water system. The local carpet dealers and weavers believed the quality of water would enhance the colour richness of their carpets and hence it was a popular spot for washing carpets. During the reign of Fath-'Alí Shah, a portrait of the king was engraved on the rocks surrounding the spring water way. Hence the name 'Chishmih-'Alí'.

54. Masjid-i-Masha'u'lláh, the 'abandoned and dilapidated' mosque (Shoghi Effendi 1995, p. 274) 'used to be in Chishmih-'Alí and was destroyed [a] long time ago to make way for development' (Sepehr Manuchehri in an email 22/1/02).
55. Quts-i-Hesar, according to Sepehr Manuchehri, is located approximately five kilometres from the shrine of 'Abdu'l-'Azím in southern Tehran. This name was retained right up to the 1979 Islamic Revolution.
56. 'Abá' is the Persian and Arabic term that denotes the heavy cloak or robe which was the preferred garb of most middle and upper class Persian men in the 19th century.
57. Áqá Mírzá Hasan Vazír is called Mírzá Hasan-i-Vazír by Shoghi Effendi 1995 (p. 190). Balyuzi 1973 (p. 190n) indicates that Yunis Khán-i-Afrukhtih learned that the descendants of this believer had pieces of linen that had been soaked in the blood of the Báb; he persuaded them to donate these relics to the leadership of the Bahá'í Faith and they are now kept in the International Bahá'í Archives.
58. Siyyid 'Alí Majdu'l-Ashráf is referred to in note 35, as being the father-in-law of Mírzá Hasan Vazír. Faydí 1973 (p. 357) gives his full name as Hájí Mírzá Siyyid 'Alí Tafrishi. MacEoin 1992 (p. 19) identifies his name as Hájí Mírzá Siyyid 'Alí Tafarshí Majdu'l-Ashráf.
59. Shoghi Effendi 1995 (p. 274) indicates that Hájí Sháh Muhammad-i-Manshadí, surnamed Amínu'l-Bayán, was commissioned by Bahá'u'lláh to receive the sacred remains from Mullá 'Alí-Akbar Shahmírzádí, as is also stated by Nicolas. Sepehr Manuchehri has pointed out that many details are known regarding the life of this believer, including references to him in tablets written by Bahá'u'lláh and 'Abdu'l-Bahá; in Mázandarání 1941 (vols. 5 and 6); and in Hájí Muhammad Tahir Malmiri's *Táríkh-i-Yazdí*.
60. When Mullá 'Alí-Akbar Shahmírzádí told his story to Nicolas, he was not apprised of the place in which Hájí Sháh Muhammad-i-Manshadi concealed the casket but

Shoghi Effendi 1995 (p. 274) indicates that he buried it beneath the floor of the shrine of Imám-Zádih Zayd.

61. Mírzá Asadu'lláh-i-Isfáhání was informed by Bahá'u'lláh of the location of the trust and was instructed to transfer it elsewhere, which he did, first to his own home and later to other locations (Shoghi Effendi 1995, p. 274).

62. Nicolas indicates that Mírzá Asadu'lláh Isfáhání returned to Tehran from 'Akká to effect the transfer of the sacred relic to the Holy Land, and this is confirmed by Shoghi Effendi 1995 (p. 274). Nicolas quotes Mullá 'Alí-Akbar Shahmírzádí to the effect that this occurred 'two years ago', and as the year of this transfer is stated as 1899, this would date his telling of this story to the year 1901.

63. The present location of the remains of the Báb and his fellow martyr, Anís, is a tomb whose site was 'blessed and selected by Bahá'u'lláh' (Shoghi Effendi 1995, p. 267); the construction of which was supervised by 'Abdu'l-Bahá and completed on 28 Safar 1327 AH, 21 March 1909; the superstructure, ornamentation and adjacent gardens of which were carried out with infinite care by Shoghi Effendi; and the 19 terraces and stairway of which were completed in summer 2001 under the supervision and management of the Universal House of Justice. The architectural emblem of the World Order of Bahá'u'lláh is the shrine of the Báb on Mount Carmel, in Haifa, Israel.

16

Collusion and Re-creation: Dogen and the Báb as Interpreters of Scripture

Gary Fuhrman

The Bábí movement emerged from the Shi'i Islam of 19th-century Iran; the movement now known as Soto Zen originated with the work of Eihei Dogen in the context of 13th-century Japanese Buddhism. Obviously there are vast cultural and doctrinal differences between the respective roots of these movements, to the extent that any comparison between Dogen and the Báb might seem gratuitous. All the more interesting, then, are certain similarities in their style of delivery, especially as interpreters of scripture: for each of them embodies in his works a highly original, creative and challenging hermeneutic practice.

The Báb began his meteoric career with a series of Quranic commentaries, taking the *tafsír* genre to an entirely new level. His commentary on the Súrat Yúsuf in particular 'purports to be both a commentary on the Qur'an, and a new Qur'an' (Lawson 1987) and his other works of this kind reveal a similarly innovative spirit even while (or because) they are 'anchored' in the text of the Qur'an. Many were delivered as improvised performances (Lawson 1998), in which the host at a gathering of the learned would choose a specific sura, ask the Báb for a commentary on it and he would deliver it on the spot. He was equally at home addressing major theological questions (such as the nature of the Resurrection) or expounding the meaning of every letter in the text (in the case of a short sura). Whatever the immediate subject, he was adept at incorporating into his commentary allusions and quotations from elsewhere in the Qur'an, the hadith literature and earlier commentaries. The Báb's *tafsír* are totally permeated with Quranic language in a way that cannot be duplicated, or even suggested, by an exact repetition or recitation of the original text itself, for the strictly Quranic elements in the Báb's text are seamlessly interwoven with spontaneous and original expression. It is as if the skeleton of the Qur'an had been 'fleshed out' (or perhaps resurrected) by the Báb to form the inner framework of a new, whole and living body. (If that comparison seems impious, perhaps that helps to explain why orthodox Iranian Islam was so profoundly shocked by the advent of the Báb.) This peculiar quality of his works is visible (if only dimly), even to those of us unfamiliar with the Qur'an and its language, if we peruse a translation of the Báb's work which displays the direct quotations from the Qur'an in a different typeface (see, for instance, Lawson 1987).

Thus the form and style of the Báb's commentaries demonstrated his own total immersion in the sacred text and required of his audience an almost equal immersion if they were to recognize his references and grasp their significance. Such a performance reflected an ability to *identify* with the Prophet, or with the Qur'an itself as the divine Word. This was, in a sense, a natural extension of the ecstatic spirit in which a devout Muslim reads the Qur'an (Lawson 1997). The engine of this ecstasy is a dynamic tension between the transcendent, 'uncreated' nature of the Qur'an on the one hand, and on the other, the human creature's act of submission to (or immersion in) the text, as expressed by his present 'recital' or performance of it. The greater the gap between God and his servants, the more all-consuming is the experience of uttering God's word with one's own breath – which becomes in the act the Prophet's breath. Lawson (1997) compares this to the Christian communion in its spiritual significance; for devout Muslims God is 'inlibrated' in the Qur'an just as he is 'incarnated' in Christ for Christians. The Báb's innovation was to take this deeply personal practice to the ultimate degree: the source of his inspiration as interpreter of the Qur'an was identical to the source of the Qur'an itself and this identity itself emerged as his central theme. The Báb's audacity in turning his commentaries into 'a new Qur'an', and in publicly claiming prophetic status, clearly exceeded the limits of orthodox Islam and led directly to his martyrdom. However, his role in history is not the primary focus of the present inquiry; that role is rather part of the context in which we may understand his style of interpretation and compare it with Dogen's.

For Dogen the interpretive situation was entirely different. Chan/Zen Buddhists (i.e. Chinese and Japanese members of the tradition to which Dogen belonged) are not 'people of the Book'; indeed their endeavour is classically defined as a 'special transmission outside the scriptures' with 'no dependence upon words and letters'. This did not mean that followers of this path did not make use of traditionally recognized Buddhist scriptures; rather they used the *sutras* and other texts as means to the end of enlightenment. For instance, Bodhidharma, the semi-legendary figure who (according to Zen tradition) brought authentic Buddhism from India to China, 'used only one scripture in his Chinese teaching activity – the *Lankavatara-sutra*, which he judged to be appropriate to the current state of Chinese civilization' (Cleary 1988, p. x). In orthodox Islam no such judgement or instrumental usage could apply to the Qur'an but in Mahayana Buddhism there is no single text venerated as is the Qur'an in Islam. 'It was common practice for Chan teachers to draw expressions from any available source – Buddhist, Confucian, Taoist scriptures, folklore, popular song, secular poetry – and use them freely in their own way, without any necessary connection with the original context' (ibid. p. xxxvii). However, scriptural study was an integral part of monastic life in the community headed by Dogen and he often quoted or alluded to scripture in his '*dharma* talks' to the assembled group. Even more frequently, he referred to the classical 'cases' or *koans*, mostly anecdotes featuring brief dialogues involving one or more of the Zen masters or 'Buddha ancestors'. These are collected in standard texts such as the Hekiganroku (known in English as the Blue Cliff Record), Mumonkan (Gateless

Gate), and Shoyoroku (Book of Serenity). Dogen apparently played a major role in bringing these texts from China and promoting their study in Japan.

All of these collections feature several layers of commentary, some in verse and some in prose at various levels of formality. More generally, we can say that the tradition of scriptural commentary was just as lively in Dogen's Buddhist milieu as in the Báb's Islamic one. But in the Zen context, this commentary is aimed at provoking realization in the reader (or listener) of his own inherent Buddha-nature; this is very different from the aim of bringing the reader's understanding into closer accord with a transcendent text or of enhancing his reverent participation in a sacred recital of eternal verities. For one thing, some of the Zen comments sound strikingly irreverent to a western reader; one might say that in Zen, no text is sacred. A firm distinction between scripture and commentary has therefore little cogency in this Buddhist milieu. Dogen's way of carrying that tradition forward had the effect of further erasing the distinction between text and commentary – that is, between traditional scripture and present study of it. Given the context of Dogen's interpretive work, it could not compare in audacity with the Báb's act of composing a new Qur'an under cover of commentary on the original; but Dogen's style of tightly interweaving scriptural phrases with his own original expression strikingly resembles the Báb's. This is evident to any close reader of the essays collected in Dogen's Shobogenzo (Treasury of the True *Dharma* Eye) and perhaps even more so in the Eihei Koroku, which collects his later *dharma* talks and poems. Perhaps one example, chosen almost at random from the Eihei Koroku (I:36), will suffice to illustrate Dogen's highly compressed style:

> Having turned the ancient sutras in each inhale and exhale, Now manifesting the ancient buddhas in each bowel movement, In every place apparent, with every item precious, To express such a principle, how would you speak? (Leighton and Okamura 2004, p. 104).

In this brief talk, which illuminates Dogen's concept of 'continuous practice', the first line alludes to a scriptural anecdote which had already been related by Dogen in an earlier discourse. In Dogen's version of the story (ibid. pp. 91–2), the sage Prajnatara had been asked by the king why he did not follow the usual pious practice of reciting *sutras*.

> *Venerable Prajnatara said*: 'This humble person while exhaling does not follow the various conditions, while inhaling does not dwell in mental or physical realms. Continuously I recite a hundred, a thousand, ten thousand, a billion volumes of such a sutra, not only one or two volumes.'
>
> *Dogen said*: 'Thus have I heard, and faithfully receive and respectfully practice it.'

Dogen's short talk develops in an original way the theme alluded to in the first line and the audience is required to recognize the allusion in order to furnish Dogen's expression with an appropriate context. This leads up to a direct challenge to the reader/listener: 'How would you speak?' Such overt challenges are essential features of

Dogen's *Dharma* Hall discourses and of the Zen literature of Dogen's lineage generally. Students in this tradition are thus encouraged and exhorted to participate actively in the *dharma* dialogue rather than playing the spectator's or passive recipient's role. What is unusual in Dogen is the intimate interplay between this explicit demand to 'Speak!' on the one hand and, on the other, the demand for deep and penetrating study of scriptural texts. Direct exhortations to concentrated study of the classical 'case' or *sutra* are not quite as frequent in Dogen's talks as the cues for an immediate response but they are pervasively implicit in the very allusiveness of Dogen's talks and texts – and doubly so when he comments directly on scriptural texts. Reading and responding to Dogen's text requires of the reader an intense commitment to, and immersion in, the scriptures to which he alludes, just as the Báb's commentaries and other texts require immersion in the Qur'an coupled with an equally intense response to the Báb's own words. Indeed both Dogen and the Báb transcend 'allusion': their relationship with the scriptural text might better be described as 'collusion'.

In addition to this pervasive collusiveness, Dogen – like the Báb – went beyond his predecessors in explicitly reinterpreting classic texts. Again, we will limit ourselves here to a single example, this one concerning the all-important concept of Buddha-nature.

Dogen's analysis of Buddha-nature starts with his own unique interpretation of a passage taken from the Mahapari-nirvana sutra, which reads: 'All sentient beings possess Buddha-nature without exception.' However, the same Chinese sentence can also be read as Dogen read it, 'All existence [i.e. all sentient beings] is Buddha-nature', and thus have its meaning dramatically transformed. In his reading of this classic passage, which revealed his ingenuity and versatility in interpreting scriptural passages, Dogen modified the conceptions of Buddha-nature and sentient beings (Kim 1975, pp. 125–6, omitting Kim's interpolated transliterations of the Japanese text).

The significance of Dogen's modification is explored at length in Kim (1975) but here we will pass over these doctrinal questions in order to focus on Dogen's interpretive method in comparison with the Báb's. The latter likewise transformed the meaning of central Islamic concepts such as 'resurrection'. This is explicated in detail in *Selections* (The Báb 1976, pp. 106–8); briefly, the Báb's interpretation is 'that the "day of resurrection" for one religion is the advent of a new religion which it is destined to supplant. Thus the time of Jesus was the day of resurrection for the religion of Moses, the time of Muhammad was the day of resurrection for the religion of Jesus, and his own *zuhur* represents the day of resurrection for Islam' (Lawson 1987, p. 326).

This example can serve to illustrate a doctrinal difference between Dogen and the Báb which may almost obscure their similarities. Dogen in his writings never advances explicit claims to a specific rank or station. More generally, Dogen's thought was 'highly antagonistic to models of hierarchies, layers, levels, degrees, strata, etc.' (Kim 1975, p. 284). Perhaps even more germane in this context is Dogen's adherence to 'the basic Buddhist hermeneutical principle, first enunciated by the Buddha, that what is important is what is actually being taught, not who is saying it' (Cleary 1988, p. xxxviii). In the Islamic context as addressed and transformed by the Báb, this principle was reversed; or perhaps it would be more pertinent to say that its basic distinction is obliterated, for what is being taught *is* the identity of the author. In other words, the primary task of the reader was recognition of the Author and the primary function of the text was to serve as proof of the Author's station. According to the Báb, this proof was manifested not only by the quality of the text (which he apparently considered self-evident to any sincere reader) but also its 'performance' aspects, especially the speed and fluency with which it was revealed in 'real time'. For those not present at the performance itself, the sheer volume of revealed verses constituted a weighty proof:

> There is no doubt that the Almighty hath sent down these verses unto Him, even as He sent down unto the Apostle of God. Indeed no less than a hundred thousand verses similar to these have already been disseminated among the people, not to mention His Epistles, His Prayers or His learned and philosophical treatises. He revealeth no less than a thousand verses within the space of five hours. He reciteth verses at a speed consonant with the capacity of His amanuensis to set them down. Thus, it may well be considered that if from the inception of this Revelation until now He had been left unhindered, how vast then would have been the volume of writings disseminated from His pen (The Báb 1976, pp. 81–2).

Dogen's works, in contrast, are much more remarkable for their economy of expression than their volume. Indeed, the contrast between Dogen and the Báb in the several respects mentioned just above could hardly be greater. But large as these differences are, they are transcended by a common quality manifested in both. The 'collusive' nature of their work, as explained above, is one aspect of this quality. But perhaps the essence of it is the author's way of *challenging* the reader to exert a total interpretive effort and thus to participate in the re-creation of the 'sacred text' or 'special transmission'.

In their comments on scripture, both Dogen and the Báb were careful (and often vehement) about directing their listeners and readers away from certain interpretations and, more generally, warning them against complacency in their reading. The challenge implicit in these warnings is paired with a challenge to read the current text (i.e. that written by Dogen or the Báb) *as scripture*, i.e. to read with the highest degree of concentration. This would seem to preclude the reader setting himself up as a passive recipient of revelation; rather his role in reading and recognizing the transforming power of scripture is better described as that of co-creator or re-creator.

In the case of the Báb, his reader is clearly expected to 'see through' the text rather than merely indulge in reverence for it. In some cases this means 'seeing through' explicit statements to an underlying message implying the opposite of what was stated explicitly. For instance, the Tafsír Surát al-Kawthar says repeatedly and directly that its author does not claim divine inspiration or authority, yet the bulk of it (citing 'an enormous number of hadith' as well as quotations from the Qur'an) is clearly to be read as evidence for just such a claim (Lawson 1998, p. 147 and see Ghaemmaghami in this volume). Dogen likewise keeps the reader on his or her toes by articulating an (often traditional) principle or premise and then drawing wholly unconventional conclusions from it (or by doing the same in reverse order).

The pattern to which I am referring here can be taken as a running demonstration of an overarching hermeneutic principle: that every interpretation – that is, every reading – is a 're-creation' of meaning. In other words, it's the reader who commits the current act of meaning and this act does not differ in kind from the author's original act of creating or 'revealing' the text. One manifestation of this principle is the Báb's re-creation of 'a new Qur'an', coupled with his insistence on the reader's responsibility for recognizing it as such. 'Thus on the Day of Resurrection God will ask everyone of his understanding and not of his following in the footsteps of others' (The Báb 1976, p. 90; see also p. 33). Another manifestation of the principle is Dogen's constant challenging of the reader to the practice of personally and urgently grappling with a *koan* (regardless of its source) and thus 'actualizing the fundamental point' of it (Tanahashi 1985, p. 69). This practice, according to Dogen, *is* enlightenment.

This pattern is perhaps most clearly visible in the commentary genre, for the writer in that mode is simultaneously both reader and author. But it is also possible for other kinds of work to raise the level, as it were, of the reader's role, by implying or evoking his responsibility for the act of meaning. Eco (1979) refers to such a text as an 'open work'. In these terms we could say that part of Dogen's exceptional contribution to Buddhism was a renewed emphasis on the 'openness' of Buddhist scriptures; and the Báb's contribution was to 'open up' the Qur'an to an unprecedented degree. Each of them encouraged his reader 'to cooperate more actively in the realization of the text' (Eco 1979, p. 13). This does not mean that the reader can legitimately find any meaning he likes in an open work; on the contrary, the open text creates or defines its own 'Model Reader' (ibid. p. 10) and the challenge for the individual reader is to realize that role. An equivalent formulation for 'people of the Book' would be that the Qur'an creates the authentic Muslim and the Báb's 'new Qur'an' creates the Bábí. And indeed some formulations along these lines can be found in the writings of the Báb.

Summing up, then, it appears that despite their many differences, Dogen and the Báb were very much alike in challenging the reader to realize his vital role as the re-creator of meaning – a practice penetrating straight to the heart of the sacred.

Bibliography

The Báb. *Selections from the Writings of the Báb*. Trans. Habib Taherzadeh with the assistance of a Committee at the Baha'i World Centre. Haifa: Bahá'í World Centre, 1976.

Cleary, Thomas (trans/intr. 1988). *Book of Serenity: One Hundred Zen Dialogues*. Boston: Shambhala, 2005.

Eco, Umberto. *The Role of the Reader*. Bloomington: Indiana University Press, 1979.

Kim, Hee-Jin. *Eihei Dogen: Mystical Realist*. Boston: Wisdom, 1975/2004.

Lawson, B. Todd. 'The Dangers of Reading: Inlibration, Communion and Transference in the Qur'an Commentary of the Báb', in ed. Moojan Momen. *Scripture and Revelation*, Oxford: George Ronald, 1997, pp. 171–215.

— 'Qur'an Commentary as Sacred Performance', in eds. Johann Christoph Buergel and Isabel Schayani, *Iran im 19. Jahrhundert und die Entstehung der Baha'i Religion*. Hildesheim: Georg Olms, 1998, pp. 145–58.

— *The Qur'an Commentary of Sayyid 'Alí Muhammad, the Báb*. Unpublished Ph.D. diss., McGill University, 1987. http://bahai-library.com/index.php5?file=lawson_quran_commentary_bab (accessed 21 October 2007).

Leighton, Taguan Dan and Shohaku Okamura (trans./ed.). *Dogen's Extensive Record: A Translation of the Eihei Koroku*. Boston: Wisdom, 2004.

Tanahashi, Kazuaki (ed.). *Moon in a Dewdrop: Writings of Zen Master Dogen*. New York: North Point Press, 1985.

Biographical Notes

Muhammad Afnan

Muhammad Afnan was born in Yazd, Iran, in 1930. After obtaining a doctorate in veterinary bacteriology and infectious diseases from Tehran University, he taught at Tehran University for 20 years before taking early retirement. He left Iran in 1979 and later settled in Canada where he joined the Department of Infectious Diseases at McMaster University and aided in establishing the Persian Institute for Bahá'í Studies in Dundas, Ontario. From 1989 to 2002 he served in the Department for the Study of the Texts at the Bahá'í World Centre.

Vahid Brown

Vahid Brown is a Ph.D. candidate in the Department of Near Eastern Studies at Princeton University. He has written extensively on the Bábí and Bahá'í religions, medieval Islamicate intellectual history, and contemporary Islamist and jihadist movements.

Armin Eschraghi

Armin Eschraghi was born in Iran and raised in Germany. In 2004 he obtained a Ph.D. in Islamic Studies from Johann Wolfgang Goethe University (Frankfurt). His dissertation was published under the title *Frühe Shaikhi und Babi-Theologie: Die Beweise für Muhammads besonderes Prophetentum (ar-Risála fí ithbát an-nubúwa al-khássa)* (Brill, 2004). He has also written several articles on Bábí and Bahá'í scriptures in both Persian and German languages.

Khazeh Fananapazir

Khazeh Fananapazir was born in Iran to a Bahá'í family. He has a keen interest in promoting interfaith dialogue and understanding, owing this interest to his late father Mr Enaayatullah Fananapazir. Khazeh grew up in Africa and has tried to cultivate his love for Bahá'í studies since his youth. He is especially interest in issues such as 'the Seal of the Prophets' and Exclusivism.

Gary Fuhrman

Gary Fuhrman is a retired English teacher living on Manitoulin Island (Ontario), where he is engaged in an interdisciplinary study focusing from several perspectives on the semiotic process of reading scriptures of all kinds.

Omid Ghaemmaghami

Omid Ghaemmaghami is a Ph.D. candidate in Islamic Thought at the University of Toronto. He received his MA in Islamic and Near Eastern Studies from Washington University in St Louis in 2005 and previously served as sessional instructor of Modern Standard Arabic at the University of Toronto.

Stephen Lambden

Dr Stephen Lambden received his Ph.D. in Religious Studies from the University of Newcastle upon Tyne in 2002 where he submitted a thesis about the emergence of the Bábí-Bahá'í interpretation of the Bible. He has specialized in Abrahamic religious texts and Semitic languages (Hebrew, Arabic, etc.) and has lectured in Bábí-Bahá'í Studies at Newcastle University and elsewhere. His work exhibits a special interest in the Bible and the Qur'an and their relationship to Bábí and Bahá'í Arabic and Persian primary scriptural texts and doctrinal teachings. He is currently a Research Scholar at University of California, Merced. Among his many publications are contributions to *Encyclopaedia Iranica*, *Encyclopedia of Language and Linguistics*, *Studies in the Bábí and Bahá'í Religions* (Kalimát Press series), and several other journals and books. He contributed the 'Islam' chapter for the *Blackwell Companion to the Bible and Culture* (Oxford, 2006) and is currently planning to publish a renewed periodical entitled *Syzygy: A Journal of Bábí-Bahá'í Studies* (from 2012) with an emphasis on textual aspects of Bábí-Bahá'í primary scriptural writings. A portion of his previous and ongoing research is registered on his (temporary) personal website, http://www.hurqalya.pwp.blueyonder.co.uk/.

Todd Lawson

Todd Lawson is Associate Professor in the Department of Near and Middle Eastern Civilizations at the University of Toronto, where he teaches Islamic Thought. He holds an MA and a Ph.D. from McGill University. His first area of interest is Qur'an commentary: at the Institute of Islamic Studies at McGill, his two graduate theses treated problems in the interpretation of the Qur'an, and his doctoral research was on the Qur'an commentary of the Báb. Professor Lawson's edited volume *Reason and Inspiration in Islam*, a collection of articles by leaders in the field of Islamic intellectual history, appeared in 2005. His *The Crucifixion and the Qur'an: A Study in the History of Muslim Thought* was published by Oneworld early in 2009. His *Gnostic Apocalypse & Islam*, on the earliest writings of the Báb, will be published by Routledge in 2011. He has written articles on the Bahá'í Faith and related topics for the *Encyclopaedia Iranica*, *The Oxford Encyclopedia of the Islamic World* and the

Encyclopaedia of Islam. An invited lecturer and visiting scholar in leading universities around the globe – Australian National University, American University Beirut, the Sorbonne, Oxford University, the University of London, Université Marc Bloch (Strasbourg), the Center for Islamic Studies (Damascus) and the Institute of Ismaili Studies (London) – he was the first research director for the Association for Bahá'í Studies, 1986–8. He became a member of the Bahá'í Encyclopedia Editorial Board in 1989. He has been a member of the Baha'i community since 1968.

William McCants

Dr William McCants is Senior Adviser for Countering Violent Extremism at the US Department of State and adjunct faculty at Johns Hopkins University. In 2008 he founded www.Jihadica.com, which has been featured on the cover of *The New York Times* and rated one of the top one hundred most influential blogs on global politics. Dr McCants's book on ancient and Islamic myths of civilization's origins will be published by Princeton University Press in 2011.

Nosratollah Mohammadhosseini

Dr Nosratollah Mohammadhosseini was born in 1935 in Tehran, Iran. He received his BA in Persian literature and later studied law and received his LLB, LLM, and LLD from Tehran University. He moved to Canada in January 1981 and received his Master's in criminology from Simon Fraser University (Burnaby, British Columbia). Dr Mohammadhosseini has taught law and criminology at several universities and colleges in Iran and Canada. He is a well-known Bahá'í scholar, teacher, speaker and prolific author. In 1960s and 1970s his many articles on Bahá'í history and teachings appeared in the Persian language Bahá'í journal *Ahang-i-Badí'* published in Iran. In the 1980s and 1990s tens of his articles on Bahá'í topics were published by five Persian language international journals in the West. He has written several books in Persian. His major works are *Hadrat-i Báb* (Institute for Bahá'í Studies in Persian); *Hadrat-i Táhirih* (Institute for Bahá'í Studies in Persian); *Qámús-i-Kitáb-i-Aqdas* (Century Press). His other published books are *Yúsuf-i-Bahá*; *Dr Henry August Forel*; and the first volume of *The Bahá'í History of the City of Qum*. He is also a contributor to *Encyclopaedia Iranica* and the *Bahá'í Encyclopedia*.

Moojan Momen

Dr Moojan Momen was born in Iran but raised and educated in England, attending the University of Cambridge. He has a special interest in the study of the Bahá'í Faith and Shi'i Islam, from the viewpoint of both their history and their doctrines. In recent years his interests have extended to the study of the phenomenon of religion. His principal publications in these fields include: *An Introduction to Shi'i Islam* (Yale University Press, 1985); *The Bábí and Bahá'í Religions 1844–1944: Some Contemporary Western Accounts* (George Ronald, Oxford, 1982); *The Works of Shaykh Ahmad al-Ahsá'í: A Bibliography* (Bahá'í Studies Monograph, no. 1,

Newcastle, 1991); and *The Phenomenon of Religion* (Oneworld, Oxford, 1999, republished as *Understanding Religion*, 2008). He has contributed articles to encyclopaedias such as *Encyclopaedia Iranica* and *Encyclopedia of the Modern Islamic World* as well as papers to academic journals such as *International Journal of Middle East Studies*, *Past and Present*, *Iran*, *Iranian Studies*, *Journal of Genocide Research* and *Religion*.

Sholeh Quinn

Sholeh Quinn is Associate Professor of History at the University of California, Merced. She received her Ph.D. from the Department of Near Eastern Languages and Civilizations at the University of Chicago. Her research speciality is Safavid Iran and Persian historiography. She is co-editor, along with Judith Pfeiffer, of *History and Historiography of Post-Mongol Central Asia and the Middle East: Studies in Honor of John E. Woods* (Wiesbaden: Harrassowitz Verlag, 2006). She is currently working on a biography of Shah 'Abbas I.

Vahid Rafati

Vahid Rafati was born in Shiraz, Iran, in 1945. He received his first degree in literature from the University of Tehran. In 1972 he travelled to Lebanon to continue his education at the American University in Beirut before the Lebanese civil war forced him to move to the United States. He subsequently completed a doctorate in Islamic Studies at the University of California, Los Angeles. Since 1980 he has been serving at the Research Department of the Bahá'í World Centre. He is the author of numerous articles and books in Persian and English.

Nader Saiedi

Dr Nader Saiedi was born in Tehran, Iran. He holds a Master's degree in economics from Pahlavi University in Shiraz and a Ph.D. in sociology from the University of Wisconsin. He has taught at the University of Wisconsin, UCLA, University of Virginia and Vanderbilt University. He is currently a Professor of Sociology at Carleton College in Northfield, Minnesota. He is strongly interested in social theory and social philosophy. His publications include *The Birth of Social Theory* (University Press of America, 1993), *Mazharíyyat* (Institute for Bahá'í Studies in Persian, 1995), *Logos and Civilization* (University Press of Maryland, 2000) and *Gate of the Heart: Understanding the Writings of the Báb* (Wilfrid Laurier University Press, 2008).

Peter Terry

Peter Terry has translated the complete works of A.L.M. Nicolas on the Bábí religion, with copious annotations. He is the author of several academic papers on topics related to Hájjí Siyyid 'Alí Muhammad Shírází, the Báb, including 'The Language of the Báb', 'The Persian Bayán of the Báb' and 'The Seven Proofs of the

Báb'. He studied Judaism in Jerusalem, Islam at the University of Massachusetts at Amherst and the University of Chicago, and the Bábí and Bahá'í religions as an independent scholar on four continents.

John Walbridge

John Walbridge is Professor of Near Eastern Languages and Cultures at Indiana University, Bloomington, and specializes in Islamic philosophy. He has a BA in Near Eastern Languages and Cultures from Yale University, where he studied with Franz Rosenthal, and a Ph.D. in Near Eastern Languages from Harvard, where he studied with Muhsin Mahdi and Annemarie Schimmel. He was the general editor of the Bahá'í Encyclopedia Project for seven years and was an assistant editor at *Encyclopaedia Iranica* for two. He is the author, co-author or translator of nine books, including two on the Bábí and Bahá'í religions, *Sacred Acts, Sacred Space, Sacred Time* (George Ronald, 1996); and an online volume, *Essays and Notes on Bábí and Bahá'í History* (H-Bahai Digital Library, 2002). He has also written three books on the Illuminationist school of Islamic philosophy, and with Hossein Ziai edited and translated the key text of the school, Suhrawardi's *Philosophy of Illumination*. His most recent works are *Muslim Voices and Lives in the Contemporary World,* edited with Frances Trix and Linda S. Walbridge (Palgrave Macmillan, 2008) and *God and Logic in Islam: The Caliphate of Reason* (Cambridge University Press, 2011).

George Ronald Bahá'í Studies Series

Bahá'í Studies is a challenging series developed for students of the Bahá'í Faith and those teaching courses on the religion. Subjects to be covered by the series include the history and development of the religion, its sociology, theology and literature, as well as the religious, social and cultural contexts of its birth and growth.

Bahá'í Studies will be especially interesting to those with an academic interest in the Bahá'í Faith, those who wish to undertake a serious study of the religion and those who want to study it at a level deeper than is possible with introductory books. Libraries and academic institutions will find the series a particularly useful addition to their collections.

The Bahá'í Faith and the World's Religions
Papers presented at 'Irfán Colloquia
Moojan Momen (editor)

The God of Bahá'u'lláh
Moojan Momen

Seeing Double: The Covenant and the Tablet of Ahmad
Todd Lawson

The Sufi Stages of the Soul in Bahá'u'lláh's The Seven Valleys and The Four Valleys
Julio Savi

The Bahá'í Faith and Higher Biblical Criticism
Robert Stockman

African Traditional Religion: A Bahá'í View
Akwasi O. Osei

African Traditional Religion and the Bahá'í Faith
Enoch Tanyi

Monotheistic Religion in Africa: The Example of the Swazi People
Margaret and Crispin Pemberton-Pigott

The Bahá'í Approach to Other Religions: The Example of Buddhism
Moojan Momen

Common Teachings in Chinese Culture and the Bahá'í Faith: From Material Civilization to Spiritual Civilization
Albert K. Cheung

The New Age Phenomenon and the Bahá'í Faith
Zaid Lundberg

The Báb's Epistle on the Spiritual Journey towards God
Todd Lawson

Soft Cover
ISBN: 978–0–85398–465–8
288 pages
24.7 x 16.9 cm. (9.5 x 6.5 in.)

The Spirit of Agriculture
Paul Hanley (editor)

Introduction: Agriculture and Religion: A Necessary Unity Paul Hanley

Agriculture in the World's Religions: An Overview P. J. Stewart

This Vital and Important Matter: A Survey of the Bahá'í Writings on Agriculture Paul Hanley

The Involvement of the Central Figures of the Bahá'í Faith in Agriculture Iraj Poostchi

A Perspective on Food in the Bahá'í Faith Paul Fieldhouse

Rethinking the Management of Small Rural Businesses Michel P. Zahrai

Reinventing the Village Gary Reusche

The Genetic Modification of Crops: A Bahá'í Scientist's Perspective Paul Olson

Igi Oko: The Tree Farms at Sapoba, Nigeria circa 1927 Richard St Barbe Baker

Strengthening Local Economies and Community Identity: FUNDAEC's Experience Pascal Molineaux

Balancing Science with Inspiration: A Bahá'í Scientist's Struggle to Discover the Hidden Secrets of Restoring Corals and Fish to Degraded Coral Reefs Austin Bowden-Kerby

Gardens for Mongolia: Growing the Capacity of Mongolia's Families The Mongolian Development Centre

*An Investment for Well-being: Restoring the Agricultural Environment on Bolivia's Altiplano (*from *One Country)*

*A Tanzanian School Promotes Self-reliance (*from *One Country)*

Rural Education in Northern Honduras Ineke Gijsbers

Felin Gelli Rural Training Farm Ineke Gijsbers

EcoAg Service: Farm Apprenticeships for Youth Nancy E. McIntyre

The Garden Terraces of the Shrine of the Báb: An Interview with the Architect, Fariborz Sahba

Soft Cover
ISBN: 978-0-85398-501-3
240 pages
24.7 x 16.9 cm. (9.5 x 6.5 in.)

Psyche and Eros
Bahá'í Studies in a Spiritual Psychology
by Rhett Diessner

Preface

Introduction by Julio Savi

The Image of the Manifestation as the Ontological Basis for a Bahá'í Psychology: Oneness as Absolute Oneness and Oneness as Unity-in-Diversity

Action Research

Developmental Psychology Made New: Glimmerings from Spiritual Psychology

Western and Middle Eastern Developmental Stage Theories

Selflessness: Congruencies between the Cognitive-Developmental Research Programme and the Bahá'í Writings

Differentiating Spiritual Principles from Kohlbergian Moral Principles: A Bahá'í Interpretation

Beauty and Moral Education (with a Chinese Flavour)

The Psychology of Beauty as a Foundation for Moral Education

Differentiating Physical, Social and Spiritual Aspects of Emotions

The Psychology of Materialism and Moral Development: Overcoming the Root Cause of Racism and Nationalism

The Myth of Psyche and Eros: An Interpretation Based on Correlates in the Bahá'í Writings

Soft Cover
ISBN: 978-0-85398-512-9
224 pages
24.7 x 16.9 cm. (9.5 x 6.5 in.)

Towards the Summit of Reality
An Introduction to the Study of Bahá'u'lláh's Seven Valleys and Four Valleys
by Julio Savi

Notes on Sufism
>   *What is Sufism?*
>   *Sufi Doctrine*
>   *Initiation and Sufi Orders*
>   *The Mystic Way*

The Country of the Soul: Symbols, Allegories and Allusions in The Seven Valleys and The Four Valleys
>   *The Pilgrim*
>   *The Lover*
>   *The Ascetic*
>   *Stories and Legends*
>   *Language and Literary Style*

Sufi Concepts and Ciphers revised by Bahá'u'lláh
>   *God, Creation, the Worlds of God*
>   *The Manifestation of God*
>   *Man*
>   *The Spiritual Path*

Bahá'u'lláh's Mystical Path
>   *The Journey of the Seven Valleys*
>   *The Journey of the Four Valleys*

Conclusion
Appendices
Bibliography
Index of Persian and Arabic terms
General Index

Soft Cover
ISBN: 978–0–85398–522–8
592 pages
24.7 x 16.9 cm. (9.5 x 6.5 in.)

Unsheathing the Sword of Wisdom
Reflections on Human Rights and Terrorism
by Julio Savi

Terrorism: An Escalating Violence

Introducing Reason into History: Human Rights

The Bahá'í Faith and Human Rights: An Overview

The Bahá'í Faith and Human Rights: The Path towards Justice

The Bahá'í Faith and Human Rights: The Path towards Unity

The Sword of Wisdom: Creating a Universal Culture of Human Rights

The Sword of Wisdom: Promoting Development

The Sword of Wisdom: Eliminating Discrimination

The Sword of Wisdom: Changing the Present World Order

Conclusion

Appendixes
    The International Bill of Human Rights, and other universal instruments
    A Bahá'í Declaration of Human Obligations and Rights (1947)
    Human Rights are God-Given Rights: A Bahá'í Statement on Human Rights (1968)

Soft Cover
ISBN: 978–0–85398–554–9
224 pages
24.7 x 16.9 cm. (9.5 x 6.5 in.)

www.ingramcontent.com/pod-product-compliance
Lightning Source LLC
Chambersburg PA
CBHW081759300426
44116CB00014B/2175